PENGUIN BOOKS
AN AUTOBIOGRAPHY

Jawaharlal Nehru was born on 14 November 1889 at Allahabad and educated in England, at Harrow and Cambridge. In 1912, Nehru returned home to play a central role in India's struggle for freedom from British colonial rule, and then, as prime minister of independent India for seventeen years, went on to shape the nation's future as a modern, secular and democratic state. He died in office, on 27 May 1964. Visionary and idealist, scholar and statesman of international stature, Nehru was also an outstanding writer. His three most renowned books—*An Autobiography, Glimpses of World History* and *The Discovery of India*—have acquired the status of classics, and are all published by Penguin.

D1003586

JAWAHARLAL NEHRU

AN AUTOBIOGRAPHY

PENGUIN BOOKS

PENGUIN BOOKS
Published by the Penguin Group
Penguin Books India Pvt Ltd, 11 Community Centre, Panchsheel Park, New Delhi 110 017, India
Penguin Group (USA) Inc., 375 Hudson Street, New York, New York 10014, USA
Penguin Group (Canada), 10 Alcorn Avenue, Toronto, Ontario, Canada M4V 3B2 (a division of Pearson
Penguin Canada Inc.)
Penguin Books Ltd, 80 Strand, London WC2R 0RL, England
Penguin Ireland, 25 St Stephen's Green, Dublin 2, Ireland (a division of Penguin Books Ltd)
Penguin Group (Australia), 250 Camberwell Road, Camberwell, Victoria 3124, Australia (a division of
Pearson Australia Group Pty Ltd)
Penguin Group (NZ), cnr Airborne and Rosedale Roads, Albany, Auckland 1310, New Zealand (a division
of Pearson New Zealand Ltd)
Penguin Group (South Africa) (Pty) Ltd, 24 Sturdee Avenue, Rosebank, Johannesburg 2196, South Africa

Penguin Books Ltd, Registered Offices: 80 Strand, London WC2R 0RL, England

First published by John Lane, The Bodley Head Ltd, London 1936
First published in India by Jawaharlal Nehru Memorial Fund, Teen Murti House, New Delhi 1980
This edition first published by Penguin Books India 2004

Copyright © Sonia Gandhi 2004

For sale in the Indian Subcontinent only

Typeset in Bembo by Mantra Virtual Services, New Delhi
Printed at Chaman Offset Printers, New Delhi

To
KAMALA
who is no more

CONTENTS

FOREWORD TO THE 2004 EDITION

Jawaharlal Nehru's three classics—*Glimpses of World History, An Autobiography* and *The Discovery of India*—remain essential reading for anyone who wishes to understand the ideas and personalities that have shaped India through the ages, and moulded the character and special genius of her people.

The three books deal with different subjects, yet through them runs the common thread of Pandit Nehru's own vision and ideals—his passionate commitment to democracy and social justice, his intense aversion to authoritarianism and fundamentalism, and his exuberant celebration of India's pluralistic culture. All three books were written while he was in prison during the freedom movement, yet they are remarkable for their absence of bitterness. This was characteristic of Panditji's personality, as were the deep humanity and delightful joie de vivre which illuminate these pages.

Though written more than fifty years ago, these books address issues that remain vitally relevant today—the choice between non-violence and terrorism to attain political goals, the perilous politics of caste and religion, the struggle to conquer hunger, disease and ignorance, the importance of cultivating a 'scientific temper'. Through his views on these and other crucial questions emerges Panditji's noble vision for the India of the future—a vision that is enshrined in our Constitution, that laid the firm foundations on which we have built our democratic, secular polity, and that has made us what we are today.

Generations of readers have been moved and, indeed, enthralled by the three classics, which reflect the power and lucidity of Jawaharlal Nehru's mind, the eloquence of his language, and the radiance of his spirit. I hope they will continue to educate, inspire and guide us for generations to come.

New Delhi
27 May 2004

SONIA GANDHI

FOREWORD

My father's three books—*Glimpses of World History, An Autobiography* and *The Discovery of India*—have been my companions through life. It is difficult to be detached about them.

Indeed *Glimpses* was written for me. It remains the best introduction to the story of man for young and growing people in India and all over the world. The *Autobiography* has been acclaimed as not merely the quest of one individual for freedom, but as an insight into the making of the mind of new India. I had to correct the proofs of *Discovery* while my father was away, I think in Calcutta, and I was in Allahabad ill with mumps! The *Discovery* delves deep into the sources of India's national personality. Together, these books have moulded a whole generation of Indians and inspired persons from many other countries.

Books fascinated Jawaharlal Nehru. He sought out ideas. He was extraordinarily sensitive to literary beauty. In his writings he aimed at describing his motives and appraisals as meticulously as possible. The purpose was not self-justification or rationalization, but to show the rightness and inevitability of the actions and events in which he was a prime participant. He was a luminous man and his writings reflected the radiance of his spirit.

New Delhi   INDIRA GANDHI
4 November 1980

This book was written by me more than a quarter of a century ago. Much of it, therefore, perhaps deals with matters which are no longer of topical interest. But it may still be of general interest to many people in India because it deals with a period of our national struggle in which many of us were personally involved.

People are apt to forget the inner content of that struggle and how it helped in changing the face of India, especially the rural masses. It is out of that struggle that present-day India has arisen. The problems today are naturally different from those of a generation ago. But there is a connecting link and, in order to understand the India of today, we have to have some understanding of what preceded it and what gave rise to it.

Many of us were moulded by that struggle and are what we are today as a result of that struggle and the ideals and objectives that governed us then. This is past history now, but sometimes it is worthwhile knowing that past in order to know better the present. Essentially an autobiography is a personal document and therefore it reflects personal views and reactions. But the person who wrote it became merged, to a large extent, in the larger movement and therefore represents, in a large measure, the feelings of many others.

I trust that this book will revive something of the past in the minds of many of those of the newer generation who did not have personal experience of what it describes.

New Delhi   JAWAHARLAL NEHRU
20 February 1962

This book was written entirely in prison, except for the postscript and certain minor changes, from June 1934 to February 1935. The primary object in writing these pages was to occupy myself with a definite task, so necessary in the long solitudes of gaol life, as well as to review past events in India, with which I had been connected, to enable myself to think clearly about them. I began the task in a mood of self-questioning and, to a large extent, this persisted throughout. I was not writing deliberately for an audience, but if I thought of an audience, it was one of my own countrymen and countrywomen. For foreign readers I would have probably written differently, or with a different emphasis, stressing certain aspects which have been slurred over in the narrative and passing over lightly certain other aspects which I have treated at some length. Many of these latter aspects may not interest the non-Indian reader, and he may consider them unimportant or too obvious for discussion or debate; but I felt that in the India of today they had a certain importance. A number of references to our internal politics and personalities may also be of little interest to the outsider.

The reader will, I hope, remember that the book was written during a particularly distressful period of my existence. It bears obvious traces of this. If the writing had been done under more normal conditions, it would have been different and perhaps occasionally more restrained. Yet I have decided to leave it as it is, for it may have some interest for others in so far as it represents what I felt at the time of writing.

My attempt was to trace, as far as I could, my own mental development, and not to write a survey of recent Indian history. The fact that this account resembles superficially such a survey is apt to mislead the reader and lead him to attach a wider importance to it than it deserves. I must warn him, therefore, that this account is wholly one-sided and, inevitably, egotistical; many important happenings have been completely ignored and many important persons, who shaped events, have hardly been mentioned. In a real survey of past events this would have been inexcusable, but a personal account can claim this indulgence. Those who want to make a proper study of our recent past will have to go to other sources. It may be, however, that this and other personal narratives will help them to fill the gaps and to provide a background for the study of hard fact.

I have discussed frankly some of my colleagues with whom I have been privileged to work for many years and for whom I have the greatest regard and affection; I have also criticized groups and individuals, sometimes perhaps rather severely. The criticism does not take away from my respect for many of them. But I have felt that those who meddle in public affairs must be frank with each other and with the public they claim to serve. A superficial courtesy and an avoidance of embarrassing and sometimes distressing questions do not help in bringing about a true understanding of each other or of the problems that face us. Real co-operation must be based on an appreciation of differences as well as common points, and a facing of facts, however inconvenient they might be. I trust, however, that nothing that I have written bears a trace of malice or ill-will against any individual.

I have purposely avoided discussing the issues in India today, except vaguely and indirectly. I was not in a position to go into them with any thoroughness in prison, or even to decide in my own mind what should be done. Even after my release I did not think it worthwhile to add anything on this subject. It did not seem to fit in with what I had already written. And so this 'autobiographical narrative' remains a sketchy, personal, and incomplete account of the past, verging on the present, but cautiously avoiding contact with it.

Badenweiler   JAWAHARLAL NEHRU
2 January 1936

DESCENT FROM KASHMIR

It is a hard and nice subject for a man to write of himself: it grates his own heart to say anything of disparagement, and the reader's ears to hear anything of praise for him.

Abraham Cowley

An only son of prosperous parents is apt to be spoilt, especially so in India. And when that son happens to have been an only child for the first eleven years of his existence there is little hope for him to escape this spoiling. My two sisters are very much younger than I am, and between each two of us there is a long stretch of years. And so I grew up and spent my early years as a somewhat lonely child with no companions of my age. I did not even have the companionship of children at school for I was not sent to any kindergarten or primary school. Governesses or private tutors were supposed to be in charge of my education.

Our house itself was far from being a lonely place, for it sheltered a large family of cousins and near relations, after the manner of Hindu families. But all my cousins were much older than I was and were students at the high school or the university and considered me far too young for their work or their play. And so in the midst of that big family I felt rather lonely and was left a great deal to my own fancies and solitary games.

We were Kashmiris. Over 200 years ago, early in the eighteenth century, our ancestor came down from that mountain valley to seek fame and fortune in the rich plains below. Those were the days of the decline of the Moghal Empire after the death of Aurungzeb, and Farrukhsiar was the Emperor. Raj Kaul was the name of that ancestor of ours and he had gained eminence as a Sanskrit and Persian scholar in Kashmir. He attracted the notice of Farrukhsiar during the latter's visit to Kashmir, and, probably at the Emperor's instance, the family migrated to Delhi, the imperial capital, about the year 1716. A *jagir* with a house situated on the banks of a canal had been granted to Raj Kaul, and, from the fact of this residence, 'Nehru' (from *nahar*, a canal) came to be attached to his name. Kaul had been the family name; this changed to Kaul-Nehru; and, in later years, Kaul dropped out and we became simply Nehrus.

The family experienced many vicissitudes of fortune during the unsettled times that followed and the *jagir* dwindled and vanished away. My great grandfather, Lakshmi Narayan Nehru, became the first Vakil of the 'Sarkar Company' at the shadow court of the Emperor of Delhi. My grandfather, Ganga Dhar Nehru, was Kotwal of Delhi for some time before the great Revolt of 1857. He died at the early age of thirty-four in 1861.

The Revolt of 1857 put an end to our family's connection with Delhi, and all our old family papers and documents were destroyed in the course of it. The family, having lost nearly all it possessed, joined the numerous fugitives who were leaving the old imperial city and went to Agra. My father was not born then but my two uncles were already young men and possessed some knowledge of English. This knowledge saved the younger of the two uncles, as well as some other members of the family, from a sudden and ignominious end. He was journeying from Delhi with some family members, among whom was his young sister, a little girl who was very fair, as some Kashmiri children are. Some English soldiers met them on the way and they suspected this little aunt of mine to be an English girl and accused my uncle of kidnapping her. From an accusation, to summary justice and punishment, was usually a matter of minutes in those days, and my uncle and others of the family might well have found themselves hanging on the nearest tree. Fortunately for them, my uncle's knowledge of English delayed matters a little and then someone who knew him passed that way and rescued him and the others.

For some years the family lived in Agra, and it was in Agra on the sixth of May 1861 that my father was born.[1] But he was a posthumous child as my grandfather had died three months earlier. In a little painting that we have of my grandfather, he wears the Moghal court dress with a

---

[1]   A curious and interesting coincidence: The poet Rabindranath Tagore was also born on this very day, month and year.

curved sword in his hand, and might well be taken for a Moghal nobleman, although his features are distinctly Kashmiri.

The burden of the family then fell on my two uncles who were very much older than my father. The elder uncle, Bansi Dhar Nehru, soon after entered the judicial department of the British Government and, being appointed successively to various places, was partly cut off from the rest of the family. The younger uncle, Nand Lal Nehru, entered the service of an Indian State and was Diwan of Khetri State in Rajputana for ten years. Later he studied law and settled down as a practising lawyer in Agra.

My father lived with him and grew up under his sheltering care. The two were greatly attached to each other and their relation with each other was a strange mixture of the brotherly and the paternal and filial. My father, being the last comer, was of course my grandmother's favourite son, and she was an old lady with a tremendous will of her own who was not accustomed to be ignored. It is now nearly half a century since her death but she is still remembered amongst old Kashmiri ladies as a most dominating old woman and quite a terror if her will was flouted.

My uncle attached himself to the newly established High Court and when this court moved to Allahabad from Agra, the family moved with it. Since then Allahabad has been our home and it was there, many years later, that I was born. My uncle gradually developed an extensive practice and became one of the leaders of the High Court Bar. Meanwhile my father was going through school and college in Cawnpore and Allahabad. His early education was confined entirely to Persian and Arabic and he only began learning English in his early 'teens. But at that age he was considered to be a good Persian scholar, and knew some Arabic also, and because of this knowledge was treated with respect by much older people. But in spite of this early precocity his school and college career was chiefly notable for his numerous pranks and escapades. He was very far from being a model pupil and took more interest in games and novel adventures than in study. He was looked upon as one of the leaders of the rowdy element in the college. He was attracted to Western dress and other Western ways at a time when it was uncommon for Indians to take to them except in big cities like Calcutta and Bombay. Though he was a little wild in his behaviour, his English professors were fond of him and often got him out of a scrape. They liked his spirit and he was intelligent, and with an occasional spurt he managed to do fairly well even in class. In later years, long afterwards, he used to talk to us of one of these professors, Mr Harrison, the principal of the Muir Central College at Allahabad, with affection, and had carefully preserved a letter of his, dating from the old student days.

He got through his various university examinations without any special distinction, and then he appeared for his final, the B.A. He had not taken the trouble to work much for it and he was greatly dissatisfied with the way he had done the first paper. Not expecting to pass the examination, as he thought he had spoiled the first paper, he decided to boycott the rest of the examination and he spent his time instead at the Taj Mahal. (The university examinations were held then at Agra.) Subsequently his professor sent for him and was very angry with him for he said that he (my father) had done the first paper fairly well and he had been a fool for not appearing for the other papers. Anyhow this ended my father's university career. He never Graduated.

He was keen on getting on in life and establishing himself in a profession. Naturally he looked to the law as that was the only profession then, in India, which offered any opening for talent and prizes for the successful. He also had his brother's example before him. He appeared for the High Court Vakils' examination and not only passed it but topped the list and got a gold medal for it. He had found the subject after his own heart, or rather, he was intent on success in the profession of his choice.

He started practice in the district courts of Cawnpore and, being eager to succeed, worked hard at it and soon got on well. But his love for games and other amusements and diversions continued and still took up part of his time. In particular, he was keen on wrestling and *dangals*. Cawnpore was famous for these public wrestling matches in those days.

After serving his apprenticeship for three years at Cawnpore, father moved to Allahabad to work in the High Court. Not long after this his brother, Pandit Nand Lal, suddenly died. That was a terrible blow for my father; it was a personal loss of a dearly loved brother who had almost been a father to him, and the removal of the head and principal earning member of the family. Henceforward the burden of carrying on a large family mainly fell on his young shoulders.

He plunged into his work, bent on success, and for many months cut himself off from everything else. Nearly all of my uncle's briefs came to him, and as he happened to do well in them the professional success that he so ardently desired soon came his way and brought him both additional work and money. At an early age he had established himself as a successful lawyer and he paid the price for this by becoming more and more a slave to his jealous mistress—the law. He had no time for any other activity, public or private, and even his vacations and holidays were devoted to his legal practice. The National Congress was just then attracting the attention of the English-knowing middle classes and he visited some of its early sessions and gave it a theoretical allegiance. But in those days he took no great interest in its work. He was too busy with his profession. Besides, he felt unsure of his ground in politics and public affairs; he had paid no great attention to these subjects till then and knew little about them. He had no wish to join any movement or organization where he would have to play second fiddle. The aggressive spirit of his childhood and early youth had been outwardly curbed, but it had taken a new form, a new will to power. Directed to his profession it brought success and increased his pride and self-reliance. He loved a fight, a struggle against odds and yet, curiously, in those days he avoided the political field. It is true that there was little of fight then in the politics of the National Congress. However, the ground was unfamiliar, and his mind was full of the hard work that his profession involved. He had taken firm grip of the ladder of success and rung by rung he mounted higher, not by any one's favour, as he felt, not by any service of another, but by his own will and intellect.

He was, of course, a nationalist in a vague sense of the word, but he admired Englishmen and their ways. He had a feeling that his own countrymen had fallen low and almost deserved what they had got. And there was just a trace of contempt in his mind for the politicians who talked and talked without doing anything, though he had no idea at all as to what else they could do. Also there was the thought, born in the pride of his own success, that many—certainly not all—of those who took to politics had been failures in life.

An ever-increasing income brought many changes in our ways of living, for an increasing income meant increasing expenditure. The idea of hoarding money seemed to my father a slight on his own capacity to earn whenever he liked and as much as he desired. Full of the spirit of play and fond of good living in every way, he found no difficulty in spending what he earned. And gradually our ways became more and more Westernized.

Such was our home in the early days of my childhood.[2]

---

2. I was born in Allahabad on the 14th November 1889, or, according to the Samvat calendar, Margshirsh Badi 7, 1946.

CHILDHOOD

M y childhood was thus a sheltered and uneventful one. I listened to the grown-up talk of my cousins without always understanding all of it. Often this talk related to the overbearing character and insulting manners of the English people, as well as Eurasians, towards Indians, and how it was the duty of every Indian to stand up to this and not to tolerate it. Instances of conflicts between the rulers and the ruled were common and were fully discussed. It was a notorious fact that whenever an Englishman killed an Indian he was acquitted by a jury of his own countrymen. In railway trains compartments were reserved for Europeans and however crowded the train might be—and they used to be terribly crowded—no Indian was allowed to travel in them, even though they were empty. Even an unreserved compartment would be taken possession of by an Englishman and he would not allow any Indian to enter it. Benches and chairs were also reserved for Europeans in public parks and other places. I was filled with resentment against the alien rulers of my country who misbehaved in this manner, and whenever an Indian hit back I was glad. Not infrequently one of my cousins or one of their friends became personally involved in these individual encounters and then of course we all got very excited over it. One of the cousins was the strong man of the family and he loved to pick a quarrel with an Englishman, or more frequently with Eurasians, who, perhaps to show off their oneness with the ruling race, were often even more offensive than the English official or merchant. Such quarrels took place especially during railway journeys.

Much as I began to resent the presence and behaviour of the alien rulers, I had no feeling whatever, so far as I can remember, against individual Englishmen. I had had English governesses and occasionally I saw English friends of my father's visiting him. In my heart I rather admired the English.

In the evenings usually many friends came to visit father and he would relax after the tension of the day and the house would resound with his tremendous laughter. His laugh became famous in Allahabad. Sometimes I would peep at him and his friends from behind a curtain trying to make out what these great big people said to each other. If I was caught in the act I would be dragged out and, rather frightened, made to sit for a while on father's knee. Once I saw him drinking claret or some other red wine. Whisky I knew. I had often seen him and his friends drink it. But the new red stuff filled me with horror and I rushed to my mother to tell her that father was drinking blood.

I admired father tremendously. He seemed to me the embodiment of strength and courage and cleverness, far above all the other men I saw, and I treasured the hope that when I grew up I would be rather like him. But much as I admired him and loved him I feared him also. I had seen him losing his temper at servants and others and he seemed to me terrible then and I shivered with fright, mixed sometimes with resentment, at the treatment of a servant. His temper was indeed an awful thing and even in after years I do not think I ever came across anything to match it in its own line. But, fortunately, he had a strong sense of humour also and an iron will, and he could control himself as a rule. As he grew older this power of control grew and it was very rare for him to indulge in anything like his old temper.

One of my earliest recollections is of this temper, for I was the victim of it. I must have been about five or six then. I noticed one day two fountain-pens on his office table and I looked at them with greed. I argued with myself that father could not require both at the same time and so I helped myself to one of them. Later I found that a mighty search was being made for the lost pen and I grew frightened at what I had done, but I did not confess. The pen was discovered and my guilt proclaimed to the world. Father was very angry and he gave me a tremendous thrashing. Almost blind with pain and mortification at my disgrace I rushed to mother, and for several days various creams and ointments were applied to my aching and quivering little body.

I do not remember bearing any ill-will towards my father because of this punishment. I think I must have felt that it was a just punishment, though perhaps overdone. But though my admiration and affection for him remained as strong as ever, fear formed a part of them. Not so with my mother. I had no fear of her, for I knew that she would condone everything I did, and, because of her excessive and indiscriminating love for me, I tried to dominate over her a little. I saw much more of her than I did of father and she seemed nearer to me and I would confide in her when I would not dream of doing so to father. She was *petite* and short of stature and soon I was almost as tall as she was and felt more of an equal with her. I admired her beauty and loved her amazingly small and beautiful hands and feet. She belonged to a fresher stock from Kashmir and her people had only left the homeland two generations back.

Another of my early confidants was a munshi of my father's, Munshi Mubarak Ali. He came from a well-to-do family of Badaun. The Revolt of 1857 had ruined the family and the English troops had partly exterminated it. This affliction had made him gentle and forbearing with everybody, especially with children, and for me he was a sure haven of refuge whenever I was unhappy or in trouble. With his fine grey beard he seemed to my young eyes very ancient and full of old-time lore, and I used to snuggle up to him and listen, wide-eyed, by the hour to his innumerable stories—old tales from the *Arabian Nights* or other sources, or accounts of the happenings in 1857 and 1858. It was many years later, when I was grown up, that "Munshiji" died, and the memory of him still remains with me as a dear and precious possession.

There were other stories also that I listened to, stories from the old Hindu mythology, from the epics, the Ramayana and the Mahabharata, that my mother and aunt used to tell us. My aunt, the widow of Pandit Nand Lal, was learned in the old Indian books and had an inexhaustible supply of these tales, and my knowledge of Indian mythology and folklore became quite considerable.

Of religion I had very hazy notions. It seemed to be a woman's affair. Father and my older cousins treated the question humorously and refused to take it seriously. The women of the family indulged in various ceremonies and *pujas* from time to time and I rather enjoyed them, though I tried to imitate to some extent the casual attitude of the grown-up men of the family. Sometimes I accompanied my mother or aunt to the Ganges for a dip, sometimes we visited temples in Allahabad itself or in Benares or elsewhere, or went to see a *sanyasi* reputed to be very holy. But all this left little impression on my mind.

Then there were the great festival days—the *Holi*, when all over the city there was a spirit of revelry and we could squirt water at each other;

the *Divali,* the festival of light, when all the houses were lit up with thousands of dim lights in earthen cups; the *Janmashtami* to celebrate the birth in prison of Krishna at the midnight hour (but it was very difficult for us to keep awake till then); the *Dasehra* and *Ram Lila* when tableaux and processions re-enacted the old story of Ramachandra and his conquest of Lanka and vast crowds assembled to see them. All the children also went to see the Mohurrum processions with their silken *alums* and their sorrowful celebration of the tragic story of Hasan and Husain in distant Arabia. And on the two *Id* days Munshiji would dress up in his best attire and go to the big mosque for prayers, and I would go to his house and consume sweet vermicelli and other dainties. And then there were the smaller festivals of which there are many in the Hindu calendar, *Rakshabandhan, Bhayya duj,* etc.

Amongst us and the other Kashmiris there were also some special celebrations which were not observed by most of the other Hindus. Chief of these was the *Naoroz,* the New Year's Day according to the Samvat calendar. This was always a special day for us when all of us wore new clothes, and the young people of the house got small sums of money as tips.

But more than all these festivals I was interested in one annual event in which I played the central part—the celebration of the anniversary of my birth. This was a day of great excitement for me. Early in the morning I was weighed in a huge balance against some bagfuls of wheat and other articles which were then distributed to the poor; and then I arrayed myself in new clothes and received presents, and later in the day there was a party. I felt the hero of the occasion. My chief grievance was that my birthday came so rarely. Indeed I tried to start an agitation for more frequent birthdays. I did not realize then that a time would come when birthdays would become unpleasant reminders of advancing age.

Sometimes the whole family journeyed to a distant town to attend a marriage, either of a cousin of mine or of some more distant relation or friend. Those were exciting journeys for us, children, for all rules were relaxed during these marriage festivities and we had the free run of the place. Numerous families usually lived crowded together in the *shadi-khana,* the marriage house, where the party stayed, and there were many boys and girls and children. On these occasions I could not complain of loneliness and we had our heart's fill of play and mischief, with an occasional scolding from our elders.

Indian marriages, both among the rich and the poor, have had their full share of condemnation as wasteful and extravagant display. They deserve all this. Even apart from the waste, it is most painful to see the vulgar display which has no artistic or aesthetic value of any kind. (Needless to say there are exceptions.) For all this the really guilty people are the middle classes. The poor are also extravagant, even at the cost of burdensome debts, but it is the height of absurdity to say, as some people do, that their poverty is due to their social customs. It is often forgotten that the life of the poor is terribly dull and monotonous, and an occasional marriage celebration, bringing with it some feasting and singing, comes to them as an oasis in a desert of soulless toil, a refuge from domesticity and the prosaic business of life. Who would be cruel enough to deny this consolation to them, who have such few occasions for laughter? Stop waste by all means, lessen the extravagance (big and foolish words to use for the little show that the poor put up in their poverty!), but do not make their life more drab and cheerless than it is.

So also for the middle classes. Waste and extravagance apart these marriages are big social reunions where distant relations and old friends meet after long intervals. India is a big country and it is not easy for friends to meet, and for many to meet together at the same time is still more difficult. Hence the popularity of the marriage celebrations. The only rival to them, and it has already excelled them in many ways even as a social reunion, is the political gathering, the various conferences, or the Congress!

Kashmiris have had one advantage over many others in India, especially in the north. They have never had any *purdah*, or seclusion of women, among themselves. Finding this custom prevailing in the Indian plains, when they came down, they adopted it, but only partly and in so far as their relations with others and non-Kashmiris were concerned. That was considered then in northern India, where most of the Kashmiris stayed, an inevitable sign of social status. But among themselves they stuck to the free social life of men and women, and every Kashmiri had the free *entrée* into any Kashmiri house. In Kashmiri feasts and ceremonies men and women met together and sat together, though often the women would sit in one bunch. Boys and girls used to meet on a more or less equal footing. They did not, of course, have the freedom of the modern West.

So passed my early years. Sometimes, as was inevitable in a large family, there were family squabbles. When these happened to assume unusual proportions they reached my father's ears and he was angry and seemed to think that all such happenings were due to the folly of women. I did not understand what exactly had happened but I saw that something was very wrong as people seemed to speak in a peculiarly disagreeable way or to avoid each other. I felt very unhappy. Father's intervention, when it took place, shook us all up.

One little incident of those early days stands out in my memory. I must have been about seven or eight then. I used to go out every day for a ride accompanied by a *sawar* from a cavalry unit then stationed in Allahabad. One evening I had a fall and my pony—a pretty animal, partly Arab—returned home without me. Father was giving a tennis party. There was great consternation and all the members of the party, headed by father, formed a procession in all kinds of vehicles, and set out in search of me. They met me on the way and I was treated as if I had performed some heroic deed!

3

THEOSOPHY

When I was ten years old we changed over to a new and much bigger house which my father named 'Anand Bhawan'. This house had a big garden and a swimming pool and I was full of excitement at the fresh discoveries I was continually making. Additional buildings were put up and there was a great deal of digging and construction and I loved to watch the labourers at work.

There was a large swimming pool in the house and soon I learnt to swim and felt completely at home in and under the water. During the long and hot summer days I would go for a dip at all odd hours, many times a day. In the evening many friends of my father's came to the pool. It was a novelty, and the electric light that had been installed there and in the house was an innovation for Allahabad in those days. I enjoyed myself hugely during these bathing parties and an unfailing joy was to frighten, by pushing or pulling, those who did not know how to swim. I remember, particularly, Dr Tej Bahadur Sapru who was then a junior at the Allahabad Bar. He knew no swimming and had no intention of learning it. He would sit on the first step in fifteen inches of water, refusing absolutely to go forward even to the second step, and shouting loudly if anyone tried to move him. My father himself was no swimmer, but he could just manage to go the length of the pool with set teeth and violent and exhausting effort.

The Boer War was then going on and this interested me and all my sympathies were with the Boers. I began to read the newspapers to get news of the fighting.

A domestic event, however, just then absorbed my attention. This was the birth of a little sister. I had long nourished a secret grievance at not having any brothers or sisters when everybody else seemed to have them, and the prospect of having at last a baby brother or sister all to myself was exhilarating. Father was then in Europe. I remember waiting anxiously in the verandah for the event. One of the doctors came and told me of it and added, presumably as a joke, that I must be glad that it was not a boy who would have taken a share in my patrimony. I felt bitter and angry at the thought that any one should imagine that I could harbour such a vile notion.

Father's visits to Europe led to an internal storm in the Kashmiri Brahman community in India. He refused to perform any *prayashchit* or purification ceremony on his return. Some years previously another Kashmiri Brahman, Pandit Bishan Narayan Dar, who later became a President of the Congress, had gone to England to be called to the Bar. On his return the orthodox members of the community had refused to have anything to do with him and he was outcast, although he performed the *prayashchit* ceremony. This had resulted in the splitting up of the community into two more or less equal halves. Many Kashmiri young men went subsequently to Europe for their studies and on their return joined the reformist section, but only after a formal ceremony of purification. This ceremony itself was a bit of a farce and there was little of religion in it. It merely signified an outward conformity and a submission to the group will. Having done so, each person indulged in all manner of heterodox activities and mixed and fed with non-Brahmans and non-Hindus.

Father went a step further and refused to go through any ceremony or to submit in any way, even outwardly and formally, to a so-called purification. A great deal of heat was generated, chiefly because of father's aggressive and rather disdainful attitude, and ultimately a considerable number of Kashmiris joined father and so a third group was formed. Within a few years these groups gradually merged into one another as ideas changed and the old restrictions fell. Large numbers of Kashmiri young men and girls have visited Europe or America for their studies and no question has arisen of their performing any ceremonies on their return. Food restrictions have almost entirely gone, except in the case of a handful of orthodox people, chiefly old ladies, and inter-dining with non-Kashmiris, Muslims and non-Indians is common. *Purdah*, the seclusion of women, has disappeared among Kashmiris even as regards other communities. The last push to this was given by the political upheaval of 1930. Inter-marriage with other communities is still not popular, although (increasingly) instances occur. Both my sisters have married non-Kashmiris and a young member of our family has recently married a Hungarian girl. The objection to intermarriage with others is not based on religion; it is largely racial. There is a desire among many Kashmiris to preserve our group identity and our distinctive Aryan features, and a fear that we shall lose these in the sea of Indian and non-Indian humanity. We are small in numbers in this vast country.

Probably the first Kashmiri Brahman in modern times to visit Western countries was Mirza Mohan Lal 'Kashmerian' (as he called himself) about a hundred years ago. He was a bright and handsome young man, a student of the Mission College at Delhi, and he was chosen to accompany a British mission to Kabul as Persian interpreter. Later he travelled all over Central Asia and Persia and wherever he went he managed to take a new wife unto himself, usually marrying in the highest circles. He became a Muslim and in Persia married a girl of the royal family, hence his title of Mirza. He visited Europe also and was presented to the young Queen Victoria. He has written delightful memoirs and accounts of his travels.

When I was about eleven a new resident tutor, Ferdinand T. Brooks, came and took charge of me. He was partly Irish (on his father's side) and his mother had been a Frenchwoman or a Belgian. He was a keen theosophist who had been recommended to my father by Mrs Annie Besant. For nearly three years he was with me and in many ways he influenced me greatly. The only other tutor I had at the time was a dear old Pandit who was supposed to teach me Hindi and Sanskrit. After many years' effort the Pandit managed to teach me extraordinarily little, so little that I can only measure my pitiful knowledge of Sanskrit with the Latin I learnt subsequently at Harrow. The fault no doubt was mine. I am not good at languages, and grammar has had no attraction for me whatever.

F.T. Brooks developed in me a taste for reading and I read a great many English books, though rather aimlessly. I was well up in children's and boys' literature; the Lewis Carroll books were great favourites, and *The Jungle Books* and *Kim*. I was fascinated by Gustave Doré's illustrations to *Don Quixote*, and Fridtjof Nansen's *Farthest North* opened out a new realm of adventure to me. I remember reading many of the novels of Scott, Dickens and Thackeray, H.G. Wells's romances, Mark Twain, and the Sherlock Holmes stories. I was thrilled by the *Prisoner of Zenda,* and Jerome K. Jerome's *Three Men in a Boat* was for me the last word in humour. Another book stands out still in my memory; it was Du Maurier's

Trilby, also *Peter Ibbetson.* I also developed a liking for poetry, a liking which has to some extent endured and survived the many other changes to which I have been subject.

Brooks also initiated me into the mysteries of science. We rigged up a little laboratory and there I used to spend long and interesting hours working out experiments in elementary physics and chemistry.

Apart from my studies, F.T. Brooks brought a new influence to bear upon me which affected me powerfully for a while. This was Theosophy. He used to have weekly meetings of theosophists in his rooms and I attended them and gradually imbibed theosophical phraseology and ideas. There were metaphysical arguments, and discussions about reincarnation and the astral and other super-natural bodies, and auras, and the doctrine of *Karma,* and references not only to big books by Madame Blavatsky and other Theosophists but to the Hindu scriptures, the Buddhist *Dhammapada,* Pythagoras, Apollonius of Tyana, and various philosophers and mystics. I did not understand much that was said but it all sounded very mysterious and fascinating and I felt that here was the key to the secrets of the universe. For the first time I began to think, consciously and deliberately, of religion and other worlds. The Hindu religion especially went up in my estimation; not the ritual or ceremonial part, but its great books, the *Upanishads* and the *Bhagavad Gita.* I did not understand them, of course, but they seemed very wonderful. I dreamt of astral bodies and imagined myself flying vast distances. This dream of flying high up in the air (without any appliance) has indeed been a frequent one throughout my life; and sometimes it has been vivid and realistic and the countryside seemed to lie underneath me in a vast panorama. I do not know how the modern interpreters of dreams, Freud and others, would interpret this dream.

Mrs Annie Besant visited Allahabad in those days and delivered several addresses on theosophical subjects. I was deeply moved by her oratory and returned from her speeches dazed and as in a dream. I decided to join the Theosophical Society, although I was only thirteen then. When I went to ask father's permission he laughingly gave it; he did not seem to attach importance to the subject either way. I was a little hurt by his lack of feeling. Great as he was in many ways in my eyes, I felt that he was lacking in spirituality. As a matter of fact he was an old theosophist, having joined the Society in its early days when Madame Blavatsky was in India. Curiosity probably led him to it more than religion, and he soon dropped out of it, but some of his friends, who had joined with him, persevered and rose high in the spiritual hierarchy of the Society.

So I became a member of the Theosophical Society at thirteen and Mrs Besant herself performed the ceremony of initiation, which consisted of good advice and instruction in some mysterious signs, probably a relic of freemasonry. I was thrilled. I attended the Theosophical Convention at Benares and saw old Colonel Olcott with his fine beard.

It is difficult to realize what one looked like or felt like in one's boyhood, thirty years ago. But I have a fairly strong impression that during these theosophical days of mine I developed the flat and insipid look which sometimes denotes piety and which is (or was) often to be seen among theosophist men and women. I was smug, with a feeling of being one-of-the-elect, and altogether I must have been a thoroughly undesirable and unpleasant companion for any boy or girl of my age.

Soon after F.T. Brooks left me I lost touch with Theosophy, and in a remarkably short time (partly because I went to school in England) Theosophy left my life completely. But I have no doubt that those years with F.T. Brooks left a deep impress upon me and I feel that I owe a debt to him and to Theosophy. But I am afraid that theosophists have since then gone down in my estimation. Instead of the chosen ones they seem to be very ordinary folk, liking security better than risk, a soft job more than the martyr's lot. But, for Mrs Besant, I always had the warmest admiration.

The next important event that I remember affecting me was the Russo-Japanese War. Japanese victories stirred up my enthusiasm and I waited eagerly for the papers for fresh news daily. I invested in a large number of books on Japan and tried to read some of them. I felt rather lost in Japanese history, but I liked the knightly tales of old Japan and the pleasant prose of Lafcadio Hearn.

Nationalistic ideas filled my mind. I mused of Indian freedom and Asiatic freedom from the thraldom of Europe. I dreamt of brave deeds, of how, sword in hand, I would fight for India and help in freeing her.

I was fourteen. Changes were taking place in our house. My older cousins, having become professional men, were leaving the common home and setting up their own households separately. Fresh thoughts and vague fancies were floating in my mind and I began to take a little more interest in the opposite sex. I still preferred the company of boys and thought it a little beneath my dignity to mix with groups of girls. But sometimes at Kashmiri parties, where pretty girls were not lacking, or elsewhere, a glance or a touch would thrill me.

In May 1905, when I was fifteen, we set sail for England, father and mother, my baby sister and I, we all went together.

4

HARROW AND CAMBRIDGE

On a May day, towards the end of the month, we reached London, reading in the train from Dover of the great Japanese sea victory at Tsushima. I was in high good humour. The very next day happened to be Derby day and we went to see the race. I remember meeting, soon after our arrival in London, M.A. Ansari, who was then a smart and clever young man with a record of brilliant academical achievement behind him. He was a house surgeon at the time in a London hospital.

I was a little fortunate in finding a vacancy at Harrow for I was slightly above the usual age for entry, being fifteen. My family went to the Continent and after some months they returned to India.

Never before had I been left among strangers all by myself and I felt lonely and homesick, but not for long. I managed to fit in to some extent in the life at school and work and play kept me busy. I was never an exact fit. Always I had a feeling that I was not one of them, and the others must have felt the same way about me. I was left a little to myself. But on the whole I took my full share in the games, without in any way shining at them, and it was, I believe, recognized that I was no shirker.

I was put, to begin with, in a low form because of my small knowledge of Latin, but I was pushed higher up soon. In many subjects probably, and especially in general knowledge, I was in advance of those of my age. My interests were certainly wider, and I read both books and newspapers more than most of my fellow-students. I remember writing to my father how dull most of the English boys were as they could talk about nothing but their games. But there were exceptions, especially when I reached the upper forms.

I was greatly interested in the General Election, which took place, as far as I remember, at the end of 1905 and which ended in a great Liberal victory. Early in 1906 our form master asked us about the new Government and, much to his surprise, I was the only boy in his form who could give him much information on the subject, including almost a complete list of members of Campbell-Bannerman's Cabinet.

Apart from politics another subject that fascinated me was the early growth of aviation. Those were the days of the Wright Brothers and Santos Dumont (to be followed soon by Farman, Latham and Blériot), and I wrote to father from Harrow, in my enthusiasm, that soon I might be able to pay him a week-end visit in India by air.

There were four or five Indian boys at Harrow in my time. I seldom came across those at other houses, but in our own house—the Headmaster's—we had one of the sons of the Gaekwar of Baroda. He was much senior to me and was popular because of his cricket. He left soon after my arrival. Later came the eldest son of the Maharaja of Kapurthala, Paramjit Singh, now the Tikka Sahab. He was a complete misfit and was unhappy and could not mix at all with the other boys, who often made fun of him and his ways. This irritated him greatly and sometimes he used to tell them what he would do to them if they came to Kapurthala. Needless to say, this did not improve matters for him. He had previously spent some time in France and could speak French fluently but, oddly enough, such were the methods of teaching foreign languages in English public schools, that this hardly helped him in the French classes.

A curious incident took place once when, in the middle of the night, the house-master suddenly visited our rooms and made a thorough search all over the house. We learnt that Paramjit Singh had lost his beautiful gold-mounted cane. The search was not successful. Two or three days later the Eton and Harrow match took place at Lord's, and immediately afterwards the cane was discovered in the owner's room. Evidently some one had used it at Lord's and then returned it.

There were a few Jews in our house and in other houses. They got on fairly well but there was always a background of anti-Semitic feeling. They were the 'damned Jews', and soon, almost unconsciously, I began to think that it was the proper thing to have this feeling. I never really felt anti-Semitic in the least, and, in later years, I had many good friends among the Jews.

I got used to Harrow and liked the place, and yet somehow I began to feel that I was outgrowing it. The university attracted me. Right through the years 1906 and 1907 news from India had been agitating me. I got meagre enough accounts from the English papers; but even that little showed that big events were happening at home, in Bengal, Punjab and Maharashtra. There was Lala Lajpat Rai's and S. Ajit Singh's deportation, and Bengal seemed to be in an uproar, and Tilak's name was often flashed from Poona, and there was Swadeshi and boycott. All this stirred me tremendously; but there was not a soul in Harrow to whom I could talk about it. During the holidays I met some of my cousins or other Indian friends and then had a chance of relieving my mind.

A prize I got for good work at school was one of G.M. Trevelyan's Garibaldi books. This fascinated me and soon I obtained the other two volumes of the series and studied the whole Garibaldi story in them carefully. Visions of similar deeds in India came before me, of a gallant fight for freedom, and in my mind India and Italy got strangely mixed together. Harrow seemed a rather small and restricted place for these ideas and I wanted to go to the wider sphere of the university. So I induced father to agree to this and left Harrow after only two years' stay, which was much less than the usual period.

I was leaving Harrow because I wanted to do so myself and yet, I well remember, that when the time came to part I felt unhappy and tears came to my eyes. I had grown rather fond of the place and my departure for good put an end to one period in my life. And yet, I wonder, how far I was really sorry at leaving Harrow. Was it not partly a feeling that I ought to be unhappy because Harrow tradition and song demanded it? I was susceptible to these traditions for I had deliberately not resisted them so as to be in harmony with the place.

Cambridge, Trinity College, the beginning of October 1907, my age seventeen, or rather approaching eighteen. I felt elated at being an undergraduate with a great deal of freedom, compared to school, to do what I chose. I had got out of the shackles of boyhood and felt at last that I could claim to he a grown-up. With a self-conscious air I wandered about the big courts and narrow streets of Cambridge, delighted to meet a person I knew.

Three years I was at Cambridge, three quiet years with little of disturbance in them, moving slowly on like the sluggish Cam. They were pleasant years, with many friends and some work and some play and a gradual widening of the intellectual horizon. I took the Natural Sciences Tripos, my subjects being chemistry, geology and botany, but my interests were not confined to these. Many of the people I met at Cambridge or during the vacations in London or elsewhere talked learnedly about books and literature and history and politics and economics. I felt a little at sea at first in this semi-highbrow talk, but I read a few books and soon got the hang of it and could at least keep my end up and not betray too great an ignorance on any of the usual subjects. So we discussed Nietzsche (he was all the rage in Cambridge then) and Bernard Shaw's prefaces and the latest book by Lowes Dickinson. We considered ourselves very sophisticated and talked of sex and morality in a superior way, referring casually to Ivan Block, Havelock Ellis, Krafft-Ebing or Otto Weininger. We felt that we knew about as much of the theory of the subject as anyone who was not a specialist need know.

As a matter of fact, in spite of our brave talk, most of us were rather timid where sex was concerned. At any rate I was so, and my knowledge for many years, till after I had left Cambridge, remained confined to theory. Why this was so it is a little difficult to say. Most of us were strongly attracted by sex and I doubt if any of us attached any idea of sin to it. Certainly I did not; there was no religious inhibition. We talked of its being amoral, neither moral nor immoral. Yet in spite of all this a certain shyness kept me away, as well as a distaste for the usual methods adopted. For I was in those days definitely a shy lad, perhaps because of my lonely childhood.

My general attitude to life at the time was a vague kind of cyrenaicism, partly natural to youth, partly the influence of Oscar Wilde and Walter Pater. It is easy and gratifying to give a long Greek name to the desire for a soft life and pleasant experiences. But there was something more in it than that for I was not particularly attracted to a soft life. Not having the religious temper and disliking the repressions of religion, it was natural for me to seek some other standard. I was superficial and did not go deep down into anything. And so the aesthetic side of life appealed to me, and the idea of going through life worthily, not indulging it in the vulgar way, but still making the most of it and living a full and many-sided life attracted me. I enjoyed life and I refused to see why I should consider it a thing of sin. At the same time risk and adventure fascinated me; I was always, like my father, a bit of a gambler, at first with money and then for higher stakes, with the bigger issues of life. Indian politics in 1907 and 1908 were in a state of upheaval and I wanted to play a brave part in them, and this was not likely to lead to a soft life. All these mixed and sometimes conflicting desires led to a medley in my mind. Vague and confused it was but I did not worry, for the time for any decision was yet far distant. Meanwhile, life was pleasant, both physically and intellectually, fresh horizons were ever coming into sight, there was so much to be done, so much to be seen, so many fresh avenues to explore. And we would sit by the fireside in the long winter evenings and talk and discuss unhurriedly deep into the night till the dying fire drove us shivering to our beds. And sometimes, during our discussions, our voices would lose their even tenor and would grow loud and excited in heated argument. But it was all make-believe. We played with the problems of human life in a mock-serious way, for they had not become real problems for us yet, and we had not been caught in the coils of the world's affairs. It was the pre-war world of the early twentieth century. Soon this world was to die, yielding place to another, full of death and destruction and anguish and heart-sickness for the world's youth. But the veil of the future hid this and we saw around us an assured and advancing order of things and this was pleasant for those who could afford it.

I write of cyrenaicism and the like and of various ideas that influenced me then. But it would be wrong to imagine that I thought clearly on these subjects then or even that I thought it necessary to try to be clear and definite about them. They were just vague fancies that floated in my mind and in this process left their impress in a greater or less degree. I did not worry myself at all about these speculations. Work and games and amusements filled my life and the only thing that disturbed me sometimes was the political struggle in India. Among the books that influenced me politically at Cambridge was Meredith Townsend's *Asia and Europe*.

From 1907 onwards for several years India was seething with unrest and trouble. For the first time since the Revolt of 1857 India was showing fight and not submitting tamely to foreign rule. News of Tilak's activities and his conviction, of Aravindo Ghose and the way the masses of Bengal were taking the swadeshi and boycott pledge stirred all of us Indians in England. Almost without an exception we were Tilakites or Extremists, as the new party was called in India.

The Indians in Cambridge had a society called the "Majlis". We discussed political problems there often but in somewhat unreal debates. More effort was spent in copying Parliamentary and the University Union style and mannerisms than in grappling with the subject. Frequently I went to the Majlis but during my three years I hardly spoke there. I could not get over my shyness and diffidence. This same difficulty pursued me in my college debating society, "The Magpie and Stump," where there was a rule that a member not speaking for a whole term had to pay a fine. Often I paid the fine.

I remember Edwin Montagu, who later became Secretary of State for India, often visiting "The Magpie and Stump". He was an old Trinity man and was the Member of Parliament for Cambridge. It was from him that I first heard the modern definition of faith: to believe in something which your reason tells you cannot be true, for if your reason approved of it there could be no question of blind faith. I was influenced by my scientific studies in the university and had some of the assurance which science then possessed. For the science of the nineteenth and the early twentieth centuries, unlike that of today, was very sure of itself and the world.

In the Majlis and in private talks Indian students often used the most extreme language when discussing Indian politics. They even talked in terms of admiration of the acts of violence that were then beginning in Bengal. Later I was to find that these very persons were to become members of the Indian Civil Service, High Court judges, very staid and sober lawyers, and the like. Few of these parlour-firebrands took any effective part in Indian political movements subsequently.

Some of the noted Indian politicians of the day visited us at Cambridge. We respected them but there was also a trace of superiority in our attitude. We felt that ours was a wider culture and we could take a broader view of things. Among those who came to us were Bepin Chandra Pal, Lajpat Rai and G.K. Gokhale. We met Bepin Pal in one of our sitting-rooms. There were only a dozen of us present but he thundered at us as if he was addressing a mass meeting of 10,000. The volume of noise was so terrific that I could hardly follow what he was saying. Lalaji spoke to us in a more reasonable way and I was impressed by his talk. I wrote to father that I preferred Lalaji's address to Bepin Pal's and this pleased him for he had no liking in those days for the firebrands of Bengal. Gokhale addressed a public meeting in Cambridge and my chief recollection of this meeting is of a question that was put by A.M. Khwaja at the end of it. Khwaja got up from the body of the hall and put an interminable question, which went on and on, till most of us had forgotten how it began and what it was about.

Har Dayal had a great reputation among the Indians but he was at Oxford a little before my time at Cambridge. I met him once or twice in London during my Harrow days.

Among my contemporaries at Cambridge there were several who played a prominent part in Indian Congress politics in later years. J.M. Sen-Gupta left Cambridge soon after I went up. Saif-ud-Din Kitchlew, Syed Mahmud and Tasadduk Ahmad Sherwani were more or less my contemporaries. S.M. Sulaiman, who is now the Chief Justice of the Allahabad High Court, was also at Cambridge in my time. Other contemporaries have blossomed out as ministers and members of the Indian Civil Service.

In London we used to hear also of Shyamji Krishnavarma and his India House but I never met him or visited that house. Sometimes we saw his *Indian Sociologist*. Long afterwards, in 1926, I saw Shyamji in Geneva. His pockets still bulged with ancient copies of the *Indian Sociologist*, and he regarded almost every Indian who came near him as a spy sent by the British Government.

In London also there was the student centre opened by the India Office. This was universally regarded by Indians, with a great deal of justification, as a device to spy on Indian students. Many Indians, however, had to put up with it, whether they wanted to or not, as it became almost impossible to enter a university without its recommendation.

The political situation in India had drawn my father into more active politics and I was pleased at this although I did not agree with his politics. He had, naturally enough, joined the Moderates whom he knew and many of whom were his colleagues in his profession. He presided over a provincial conference in his province and took up a strong line against the Extremists of Bengal and Maharashtra. He also became president of the U.P. Provincial Congress Committee. He was present at Surat in 1907 when the Congress broke up in disorder and later emerged as a purely moderate group.

Soon after Surat, H.W. Nevinson stopped with him at Allahabad as his guest for a while and, in his book on India, he referred to father as being "moderate in everything except his generosity". This was a very wrong estimate, for father was never moderate in anything except his politics, and step by step his nature drove him from even that remnant of moderation. A man of strong feelings, strong passions, tremendous pride and great strength of will, he was very far from the moderate type. And yet in 1907 and 1908 and for some years afterwards, he was undoubtedly a moderate of Moderates and he was bitter against the Extremists, though I believe he admired Tilak.

Why was this so? It was natural for him with his grounding in law and constitutionalism to take a lawyer's and a constitutional view of politics. His clear thinking led him to see that hard and extreme words lead nowhere unless they are followed by action appropriate to the language. He saw no effective action in prospect. The swadeshi and boycott movements did not seem to him to carry matters far. And then the background of these movements was a religious nationalism which was alien to his nature. He did not look back to a revival in India of ancient times. He had no sympathy or understanding of them and utterly disliked many old social customs, caste and the like, which he considered reactionary. He looked to the West and felt greatly attracted by Western progress, and thought that this could come through an association with England.

Socially speaking, the revival of Indian nationalism in 1907 was definitely reactionary. Inevitably, a new nationalism in India, as elsewhere in the East, was a religious nationalism. The Moderates thus represented a more advanced social outlook but they were a mere handful on the top with no touch with the masses. They did not think much in terms of economics, except in terms of the new upper middle class which they partly represented and which wanted room for expansion. They advocated also petty social reforms to weaken caste and do away with old social customs which hindered growth.

Having cast his lot with the Moderates, father took an aggressive line. Most of the Extremists, apart from a few leaders in Bengal and Poona, were young men and it irritated him to find that these youngsters dared to go their own way. Impatient and intolerant of opposition, and not suffering people whom he considered fools, gladly, he pitched into them and hit out whenever he could. I remember, I think it was after I left Cambridge, reading an article of his which annoyed me greatly. I wrote him rather an impertinent letter in which I suggested that no doubt the British Government was greatly pleased with his political activities. This was just the kind of suggestion which would make him wild, and he was very angry. He almost thought of asking me to return from England immediately.

During my stay at Cambridge the question had arisen as to what career I should take up. For a little while the Indian Civil Service was contemplated; there was a glamour about it still in those days. But this idea was dropped as neither my father nor I were keen on it. The principal reason, I think, was that I was still under age for it, and if I was to appear for it I would have to stay three to four years more after taking my degree. I was twenty when I took my degree at Cambridge and the age-limit for the I.C.S. in those days was twenty-two to twenty-four. If successful an extra year had to be spent in England. My people were a little tired of my long stay in England and wanted me back soon. Another reason which weighed with father was that in case I was appointed to the I.C.S. I would be posted in various distant places far from home. Both father and mother wanted me near them after my long absence. So the die was cast in favour of the paternal profession, the Bar, and I joined the Inner Temple.

It is curious that in spite of my growing extremism in politics, I did not then view with any strong disfavour the idea of joining the I.C.S. and thus becoming a cog in the British Government's administrative machine in India. Such an idea in later years would have been repellent to me.

I left Cambridge after taking my degree in 1910. I was only moderately successful in my Science Tripos examination, obtaining second class honours. For the next two years I hovered about London. My law studies did not take up much time and I got through the Bar examinations, one after the other, with neither glory nor ignominy. For the rest I simply drifted, doing some general reading, vaguely attracted to the Fabians and socialistic ideas, and interested in the political movements of the day. Ireland and the woman suffrage movement interested me especially. I remember also how, during a visit to Ireland in the summer of 1910, the early beginnings of Sinn Fein had attracted me.

I came across some old Harrow friends and developed expensive habits in their company. Often I exceeded the handsome allowance that father made me and he was greatly worried on my account, fearing that I was rapidly going to the devil. But as a matter of fact I was not doing anything so notable. I was merely trying to ape to some extent the prosperous but somewhat empty-headed Englishman who is called a "man about town". This soft and pointless existence, needless to say, did not improve me in any way. My early enthusiasms began to tone down and the only thing that seemed to go up was my conceit.

During my vacations I had sometimes travelled on the Continent. In the summer of 1909 my father and I happened to be in Berlin when Count Zeppelin arrived flying in his new airship from Friederichshafen on Lake Constance. I believe that was his first long flight and the occasion was celebrated by a huge demonstration and a formal welcome by the Kaiser. A vast multitude, estimated at between one and two millions, gathered in the Tempelhof Field in Berlin, and the Zeppelin arrived to time and circled gracefully above us. The Hotel Adlon presented all its residents that day with a fine picture of Count Zeppelin, and I have still got that picture.

About two months later we saw in Paris the first aeroplane to fly all over the city and to circle round the Eiffel Tower. The aviator's name was, I think, Comte de Lambert. Eighteen years later I was again in Paris when Lindbergh came like a shining arrow from across the Atlantic.

I had a narrow escape once in Norway where I had gone on a pleasure cruise soon after taking my degree at Cambridge in 1910. We were tramping across the mountainous country. Hot and weary we reached our destination, a little hotel, and demanded baths. Such a thing had not been heard of there and there was no provision for it in the building. We were told however that we could wash ourselves in a neighbouring stream. So, armed with table napkins or perhaps small face towels, which the hotel generously gave, two of us, a young Englishman and I, went to this roaring torrent which was coming from a glacier nearby. I entered the water; it was not deep but it was freezing and the bottom was terribly slippery. I slipped and fell and the ice-cold water numbed me and made me lose all sensation or power of controlling my limbs. I could not regain my foothold and was swept rapidly along by the torrent. My companion, the Englishman, however, managed to get out and he ran along the side and ultimately, succeeding in catching my leg, dragged me out. Later we realized the danger we were in for about two or three hundred yards ahead of us this mountain torrent tumbled over an enormous precipice, forming a waterfall which was one of the sights of the place.

In the summer of 1912 I was called to the Bar, and in the autumn of that year I returned to India finally after a stay of over seven years in England. Twice, in between, I had gone home during my holidays. But now I returned for good, and I am afraid, as I landed at Bombay, I was a bit of a prig with little to commend me.

5

BACK HOME AND WAR-TIME POLITICS
IN INDIA

Towards the end of 1912 India was, politically, very dull. Tilak was in gaol, the Extremists had been sat upon and were lying low without any effective leadership, Bengal was quiet after the unsettling of the partition of the province, and the Moderates had been effectively "rallied" to the Minto–Morley scheme of councils. There was some interest in Indians overseas, especially in the condition of Indians in South Africa. The Congress was a moderate group, meeting annually, passing some feeble resolutions, and attracting little attention.

I visited, as a delegate, the Bankipore Congress during Christmas 1912. It was very much an English-knowing upper class affair where morning coats and well-pressed trousers were greatly in evidence. Essentially it was a social gathering with no political excitement or tension. Gokhale, fresh from South Africa, attended it and was the outstanding person of the session. High-strung, full of earnestness and a nervous energy, he seemed to be one of the few persons present who took politics and public affairs seriously and felt deeply about them. I was impressed by him.

A characteristic incident occurred when Gokhale was leaving Bankipore. He was a member of the Public Services Commission at the time and, as such, was entitled to a first class railway compartment to himself. He was not well and crowds and uncongenial company upset him. He liked to be left alone by himself and, after the strain of the Congress session, he was looking forward to a quiet journey by train. He got his compartment but the rest of the train was crowded with delegates returning to Calcutta. After a little while, Bhupendra Nath Basu, who later became a member of the India Council, came up to Gokhale and casually asked him if he could travel in his compartment. Mr Gokhale was a little taken aback as Mr Basu was an aggressive talker, but naturally he agreed. A few minutes later Mr Basu again came up to Gokhale and asked him if he would mind if a friend of his also travelled in the same compartment. Mr Gokhale again mildly agreed. A little before the train left, Mr Basu mentioned casually that both he and his friend would find it very uncomfortable to sleep in the upper berths, so would Gokhale mind occupying an upper berth so that the two lower berths might be taken by them? And that, I think, was the arrangement arrived at and poor Mr Gokhale had to climb up and spend a bad night.

I took to the law and joined the High Court. The work interested me to a certain extent. The early months after my return from Europe were pleasant. I was glad to be back home and to pick up old threads. But gradually the life I led, in common with most others of my kind, began to lose all its freshness and I felt that I was being engulfed in a dull routine of a pointless and futile existence. I suppose my mongrel, or at least mixed, education was responsible for this feeling of dissatisfaction with my surroundings. The habits and the ideas that had grown in me during my seven years in England did not fit in with things as I found them. Fortunately my home atmosphere was fairly congenial and that was some help, but it was not enough. For the rest there was the Bar Library and the club and the same people were to be found in both, discussing the same old topics, usually connected with the legal profession, over and over again. Decidedly the atmosphere was not intellectually stimulating and a sense of the utter insipidity of life grew upon me. There were not even worthwhile amusements or diversions.

G. Lowes Dickinson is reported by E.M. Forster, in his recent life of him, to have once said about India: "And *why* can't the races meet? Simply because the Indians *bore* the English. *That* is the simple adamantine fact." It is possible that most Englishmen feel that way and it is not surprising. To quote Forster again (from another book), every Englishman in India feels and behaves, and rightly, as if he was a member of an army of occupation, and it is quite impossible for natural and unrestrained relations between the two races to grow under these circumstances. The Englishman and the Indian are always posing to each other and naturally they feel uncomfortable in each other's company. Each bores the other and is glad to get away from him to breathe freely and move naturally again.

Usually the Englishman meets the same set of Indians, those connected with the official world, and he seldom reaches really interesting people, and if he reached them he would not easily draw them out. The British *régime* in India has pushed up into prominence, even socially, the official class, both British and Indian, and this class is most singularly dull and narrow-minded. Even a bright young Englishman on coming out to India will soon relapse into a kind of intellectual and cultural torpor and will get cut off from all live ideas and movements. After a day in office, dealing with the ever rotating and never-ending files, he will have some exercise and then go to his club to mix with his kind, drink whisky and read *Punch* and the illustrated weeklies from England. He hardly reads books and if he does he will probably go back to an old favourite. And for this gradual deterioration of mind he will blame India, curse the climate, and generally anathematize the tribe of agitators who add to his troubles, not realizing that the cause of intellectual and cultural decay lies in the hide-bound bureaucratic and despotic system of government which flourishes in India and of which he is a tiny part.

If that is the fate of the English official, in spite of his leaves and furloughs, the Indian official working with him or under him is not likely to fare better, for he tries to model himself on the English type. Few experiences are more dreary than sitting with high-placed officials, both English and Indian, in that seat of Empire, New Delhi, and listening to their unending talk about promotions, leave rules, furloughs, transfers, and little tit-bits of Service scandal.

This official and Service atmosphere invaded and set the tone for almost all Indian middle-class life, especially the English-knowing intelligentsia, except to some extent in cities like Calcutta and Bombay. Professional men, lawyers, doctors and others, succumbed to it, and even the academic halls of the semi-official universities were full of it. All these people lived in a world apart, cut off from the masses and even the lower middle class. Politics was confined to this upper strata. The nationalist movement in Bengal from 1906 onwards had for the first time shaken this up and infused a new life in the Bengal lower middle-class and to a small extent even the masses. This process was to grow rapidly in later years under Gandhiji's[1] leadership, but a nationalist struggle though life-giving is a narrow creed and absorbs too much energy and

---

1. I have referred to Mr Gandhi or Mahatma Gandhi as "Gandhiji" throughout these pages as he himself prefers this to the addition of 'Mahatma' to his name. But I have

attention to allow of other activities.

I felt, therefore, dissatisfied with life in those early years after my return from England. My profession did not fill me with a whole-hearted enthusiasm. Politics, which to me meant aggressive nationalist activity against foreign rule, offered no scope for this. I joined the Congress and took part in its occasional meetings. When a special occasion arose, like the agitation against the Fiji indenture system for Indian workers, or the South African Indian question, I threw myself into it with energy and worked hard. But these were only temporary occupations.

I indulged in some diversions like *shikar* but I had no special aptitude or inclination for it. I liked the outings and the jungle and cared little for the killing. Indeed my reputation was a singularly bloodless one, although I once succeeded, more or less by a fluke, in killing a bear in Kashmir. An incident with a little antelope damped even the little ardour that I possessed for shikar. This harmless little animal fell down at my feet, wounded to death, and looked up at me with its great big eyes full of tears. Those eyes have often haunted me since.

I was attracted in those early years to Mr Gokhale's Servants of India Society. I never thought of joining it, partly because its politics were too moderate for me, and partly because I had no intention then of giving up my profession. But I had a great admiration for the members of the society who had devoted themselves for a bare pittance to the country's service. Here at least, I thought, was straight and single-minded and continuous work even though this might not be on wholly right lines.

Mr Srinivas Sastri, however, gave me a great shock in a little matter quite unconnected with politics. He was addressing a students' meeting

---

seen some extraordinary explanations of this 'ji' in books and articles by English writers. Some have imagined that it is a term of endearment—Gandhiji meaning 'dear little Gandhi'! This is perfectly absurd and shows colossal ignorance of Indian life. 'Ji' is one of the commonest additions to a name in India, being applied indiscriminatingly to all kinds of people and to men, women, boys, girls and children. It conveys an idea of respect, something equivalent to Mr, Mrs, or Miss. Hindustani is rich in courtly phrases and prefixes and suffixes to names and honorific titles. 'Ji' is the simplest of these and the least formal of them, though perfectly correct. I learn from my brother-in-law, Ranjit S. Pandit, that this 'ji' has a long and honourable ancestry. It is derived from the Sanskrit Arya meaning a gentleman or noble-born (not the Nazi meaning of Aryan!). This arya became in Prakrit ajja and this led to the simple 'ji'.

in Allahabad and he told them to be respectful and obedient to their teachers and professors and to observe carefully all the rules and regulations laid down by constituted authority. All this goody-goody talk did not appeal to me much; it seemed very platitudinous and somewhat undesirable, with all its stress on authoritarianism. I thought that this was perhaps due to the semi-official atmosphere which was so prevalent in India, Mr Sastri went on and called upon the boys to report each other's sins of omission and commission immediately to the authorities. In other words they were to spy on each other and play the part of informers. These hard words were not used by Mr Sastri but their meaning seemed to me clear, and I listened aghast to this friendly counsel of a great leader. I had freshly returned from England and the lesson that had been most impressed upon my mind in school and college was never to betray a colleague. There was no greater sin against the canons of good form than to sneak and inform and thus get a companion into trouble. A sudden and complete reversal of this principle upset me and I felt that there was a great difference between Mr Sastri's morality and the morality that had been taught to me.

The World War absorbed our attention. It was far off and did not at first affect our lives much, and India never felt the full horror of it. Politics petered out and sank into insignificance. The Defence of India Act (the equivalent of the British D.O.R.A.) held the country in its grip. From the second year onwards news of conspiracies and shootings came to us, and of press-gang methods to enrol recruits in the Punjab.

There was little sympathy with the British in spite of loud professions of loyalty. Moderate and Extremist alike learnt with satisfaction of German victories. There was no love for Germany of course, only the desire to see our own rulers humbled. It was the weak and helpless man's idea of vicarious revenge. I suppose most of us viewed the struggle with mixed feelings. Of all the nations involved my sympathies were probably most with France. The ceaseless and unabashed propaganda on behalf of the Allies had some effect, although we tried to discount it greatly.

Gradually political life grew again. Lokamanya Tilak came out of prison and Home Rule Leagues were started by him and Mrs Besant. I joined both but I worked especially for Mrs Besant's League. Mrs Besant began to play an ever increasing part in the Indian political scene. The annual sessions of the Congress became a little more exciting and the

Muslim League began to march with the Congress. The atmosphere became electric and most of us young men felt exhilarated and expected big things in the near future. Mrs Besant's internment added greatly to the excitement of the intelligentsia and vitalized the Home Rule Movement all over the country. The Home Rule Leagues were attracting not only all the old Extremists who had been kept out of the Congress since 1907 but large numbers of newcomers from the middle classes. They did not touch the masses.

Mrs Besant's internment stirred even the older generation, including many of the Moderate leaders. Just before the internment I remember how moved we used to be by the eloquent speeches of Mr Srinivasa Sastri which we read in the papers. But just before or after the internment suddenly Mr Sastri became silent. He failed us completely when the time for action came and there was considerable disappointment and resentment at his silence when most of all a lead was needed. I am afraid that ever since then the conviction has grown upon me that Mr Sastri is not a man of action and a crisis does not suit his genius. Other Moderate leaders, however, went ahead, some to draw back later, some to remain in the new position. I remember that there was a great deal of discussion in those days about the new Indian Defence Force which the Government was organizing from the middle classes on the lines of the European defence forces in India. This Indian force was treated very differently from the European force in a variety of ways, and many of us felt that we should not co-operate with it till these humiliating distinctions were removed. After much discussion, however, we decided to co-operate in the U.P. as it was considered worthwhile for our young men to have military training even under these conditions. I sent my application to join the new force, and we formed a committee in Allahabad to push the scheme on. Just then came Mrs Besant's internment and in the excitement of the moment I managed to get the committee members— they included my father, Dr Tej Bahadur Sapru, Mr C.Y. Chintamani and other Moderate leaders—to agree to cancel our meeting and all other work in connection with the Defence Force as a protest against the Government's action. A public notice was issued immediately to this effect. I think some of the signatories regretted later this aggressive act in war-time.

Mrs Besant's internment also resulted in my father, and other Moderate leaders joining the Home Rule League. Some months later most of these Moderate members resigned from the League. My father remained in it and became the president of the Allahabad branch.

Gradually my father had been drifting away from the orthodox Moderate position. His nature rebelled against too much submission and appeal to an authority which ignored us and treated us disdainfully. But the old Extremist leaders did not attract him: their language and methods jarred upon him. The episode of Mrs Besant's internment and subsequent events influenced him considerably but still he hesitated before definitely committing himself to a forward line. Often he used to say in those days that moderate tactics were no good, but nothing effective could be done till some solution for the Hindu–Muslim question was found. If this was found then he promised to go ahead with the youngest of us. The adoption by the Congress at Lucknow in 1916 of the Joint Congress-League Scheme, which had been drawn up at a meeting of the All India Congress Committee in our house, pleased him greatly as it opened the way to a joint effort and he was prepared to go ahead then even at the cost of breaking with his old colleagues of the Moderate group. They pulled together till and during Edwin Montagu's visit to India as Secretary of State. Differences arose soon after the publication of the Montagu–Chelmsford Report, and the final break in the United Provinces came in the summer of 1918 at a special provincial conference held at Lucknow over which my father presided. The Moderates, expecting that this conference would adopt a strong line against the Montagu–Chelmsford proposals, boycotted the conference. Later they also boycotted the special session of the Congress held to consider these proposals. Since then they have been out of the Congress.

This Moderate practice of quietly dropping out and keeping away from the Congress sessions and other public gatherings and not even presenting their viewpoint and fighting for it, even though the majority might be against them, struck me as peculiarly undignified and unbecoming in public workers. I think that was the general sense of large numbers of people in the country and I am sure that the almost total collapse of the Moderates in Indian politics was partly due to this timid attitude. Mr Sastri was, I think, the only Moderate leader who attended some of the early sessions of the Congress, which had been boycotted by the Moderates as a group, and put forward his solitary viewpoint. He went up in public estimation because of it.

My own political and public activities in the early war years were modest and I kept away from addressing public gatherings. I was still diffident and terrified of public speaking. Partly also I felt that public speeches should not be in English and I doubted my capacity to speak at any length in Hindustani. I remember a little incident when I was induced to deliver my first public speech in Allahabad. Probably it was in 1915 but I am not clear about dates and am rather mixed up about the order of events. The occasion was a protest meeting against a new Act muzzling the press. I spoke briefly and in English. As soon as the meeting was over Dr Tej Bahadur Sapru, to my great embarrassment, embraced and kissed me in public on the dais. This was not because of what I had said or how I had said it. His effusive joy was caused by the mere fact that I had spoken in public and thus a new recruit had been obtained for public work, for this work consisted in those days practically of speaking only.

I remember that many of us young men in Allahabad then had a faint hope that perhaps Dr Sapru might take up a more advanced attitude in politics. Of all the Moderate groups in the city he seemed to be the most likely to do so because he was emotional and could occasionally be carried by enthusiasm. Compared to him my father seemed cold-bloodedness itself, though underneath this outer cover there was fire enough. But father's strength of will left us little hope and for a brief while we actually had greater expectations from Dr Sapru. Pandit Madan Mohan Malaviya, with his long record of public work, attracted us of course and we used to have long talks with him, pressing him to give a brave lead to the country.

At home, in those early years, political questions were not peaceful subjects for discussion, and references to them, which were frequent, immediately produced a tense atmosphere. Father had been closely watching my growing drift towards Extremism, my continual criticism of the politics of talk and my insistent demand for action. What action it should be was not clear, and sometimes father imagined that I was heading straight for the violent courses adopted by some of the young men of Bengal. This worried him very much. As a matter of fact I was not attracted that way, but the idea that we must not tamely submit to existing conditions and that something must be done began to obsess me more and more. Successful action, from the national point of view, did not seem to be at all easy, but I felt that both individual and national honour demanded a more aggressive and fighting attitude to foreign rule. Father himself was dissatisfied with the Moderate philosophy, and a mental conflict was going on inside him. He was too obstinate to change from one position to another until he was absolutely convinced that there was no other way. Each step forward meant for him a hard and bitter tussle in his mind, and when the step was taken after that struggle with part of himself, there was no going back. He had not taken it in a fit of enthusiasm but as a result of intellectual conviction, and then, having done so, all his pride prevented him from looking back.

The outward change in his politics came about the time of Mrs Besant's internment and from that time onwards step by step he went ahead, leaving his old Moderate colleagues far behind, till the tragic happenings in the Punjab in 1919 finally led him to cut adrift from his old life and his profession, and throw in his lot with the new movement started by Gandhiji.

But that was still to be, and from 1915 to 1917 he was still unsure of what to do, and the doubts in him, added to his worries about me, did not make him a peaceful talker on the public issues of the day. Often enough our talks ended abruptly by his losing his temper with us.

My first meeting with Gandhiji was about the time of the Lucknow Congress during Christmas 1916. All of us admired him for his heroic fight in South Africa, but he seemed very distant and different and unpolitical to many of us young men. He refused to take part in Congress or national politics then and confined himself to the South African Indian question. Soon afterwards his adventures and victory in Champaran, on behalf of the tenants of the planters, filled us with enthusiasm. We saw that he was prepared to apply his methods in India also and they promised success.

I remember being moved also, in those days after the Lucknow Congress, by a number of eloquent speeches delivered by Sarojini Naidu in Allahabad. It was all nationalism and patriotism and I was a pure nationalist, my vague socialist ideas of college days having sunk into the background. Roger Casement's wonderful speech at his trial in 1916 seemed to point out exactly how a member of a subject nation should feel. The Easter Week rising in Ireland by its very failure attracted, for was that not true courage which mocked at almost certain failure and proclaimed to the world that no physical might could crush the invincible spirit of a nation?

Such were my thoughts then, and yet fresh reading was again stirring the embers of socialistic ideas in my head. They were vague ideas, more humanitarian and Utopian than scientific. A favourite writer of mine during the war years and after was Bertrand Russell.

These thoughts and desires produced a growing conflict within me and a dissatisfaction with my profession of the law. I carried on with it because there was nothing else to be done, but I felt more and more that it was not possible to reconcile public work, especially of the aggressive type which appealed to me, with the lawyer's job. It was not a question of principle but of time and energy. Sir Rash Behary Ghosh, the eminent Calcutta lawyer, who for some unknown reason took a fancy to me, gave me a lot of good advice as to how to get on in the profession. He especially advised me to write a book on a legal subject of my choice, as he said that this was the best way for a junior to train himself. He offered to help me with ideas in the writing of it and to revise it. But all his well meant interest in my legal career was in vain, and few things could be more distasteful to me than to spend my time and energy in writing legal books.

Sir Rash Behary in his old age was extraordinarily irritable and short of temper and a terror for his juniors. I rather liked him, however, and his very failings and weaknesses were not wholly unattractive. Father and I were once his guests in Simla. It was in 1918, I think, just when the Montagu–Chelmsford report came out. He invited to dinner a few friends one evening and among them was old Mr Khaparde. After dinner Sir Rash Behary and Mr Khaparde became loud and aggressive in their arguments for they belonged to rival schools of politics, Sir Rash Behary being a confirmed Moderate and Mr Khaparde was then supposed to be a leading Tilakite, although in later years he became as mild as a dove and too moderate even for the Moderates. Mr Khaparde began criticizing Mr Gokhale (who had died some years previously), saying that he had been a British agent who had spied on him in London. This was too much for Sir Rash Behary and he shouted that Gokhale had been the best of men and a particular friend of his and that he would not permit anyone to say a word against him. Mr Khaparde then branched off to Mr Srinivas Sastri. Sir Rash Behary did not like this but he did not resent it quite so much. Apparently he was not such an admirer of Mr Sastri's as he had been of Gokhale's. Indeed he said that so long as Gokhale had been alive he had helped the Servants of India Society financially but since his death he had stopped his contribution. Mr Khaparde then, as a contrast, began praising Tilak. Here was a truly great man, he said, a wonderful person, a saint. "A saint!" retorted Sir Rash Behary, "I hate saints, I want to have nothing to do with them."

6

MY WEDDING AND AN ADVENTURE IN THE HIMALAYAS

M y marriage took place in 1916 in the city of Delhi. It was on the *Vasanta Panchami* day which heralds the coming of spring in India. That summer we spent some months in Kashmir. I left my family in the valley and, together with a cousin of mine, wandered for several weeks in the mountains and went up the Ladakh road.

This was my first experience of the narrow and lonely valleys, high up in the world, which lead to the Tibetan plateau. From the top of the Zoji-la pass we saw the rich verdant mountain sides below us on one side and the bare bleak rock on the other. We went up and up the narrow valley bottom flanked on each side by mountains, with the snow-covered tops gleaming on one side and little glaciers creeping down to meet us. The wind was cold and bitter but the sun was warm in the day time, and the air was so clear that often we were misled about the distance of objects, thinking them much nearer than they actually were. The loneliness grew; there were not even trees or vegetation to keep us company—only the bare rock and the snow and ice and, sometimes, very welcome flowers. Yet I found a strange satisfaction in these wild and desolate haunts of nature; I was full of energy and a feeling of exaltation.

I had an exciting experience during this visit. At one place on our march beyond the Zoji-la pass—I think it was called Matayan—we were told that the cave of Amaranath was only eight miles away. It was true that an enormous mountain all covered with ice and snow lay in between and had to be crossed, but what did that matter? Eight miles seemed so little. In our enthusiasm and inexperience we decided to make the attempt. So we left our camp (which was situated at about 11,500 feet altitude) and with a small party went up the mountain. We had a local shepherd for a guide.

We crossed and climbed several glaciers, roping ourselves up, and our troubles increased and breathing became a little difficult. Some of our porters, lightly laden as they were, began to bring up blood. It began to snow and the glaciers became terribly slippery; we were fagged out and every step meant a special effort But still we persisted in our foolhardy attempt. We had left our camp at four in the morning and after twelve hours' almost continuous climbing we were rewarded by the sight of a huge ice-field. This was a magnificent sight, surrounded as it was by snow-peaks, like a diadem or an amphitheatre of the gods. But fresh snow and mists soon hid the sight from us. I do not know what our altitude was but I think it must have been about 15,000 to 16,000 feet, as we were considerably higher than the cave of Amaranath. We had now to cross this ice-field, a distance probably of half a mile, and then go down on the other side to the cave. We thought that as the climbing was over, our principal difficulties had also been surmounted, and so, very tired but in good humour, we began this stage of the journey. It was a tricky business as there were many crevasses and the fresh snow often covered a dangerous spot. It was this fresh snow that almost proved to be my undoing, for I stepped upon it and it gave way and down I went a huge and yawning crevasse. It was a tremendous fissure and anything that went right down it could be assured of safe keeping and preservation for some geological ages. But the rope held and I clutched to the side of the crevasse and was pulled out. We were shaken up by this but still we persisted in going on. The crevasses, however, increased in number and width and we had no equipment or means of crossing some of them. And so at last we turned back, weary and disappointed, and the cave of Amaranath remained unvisited.

The higher valleys and mountains of Kashmir fascinated me so much that I resolved to come back again soon. I made many a plan and worked out many a tour, and one, the very thought of which filled me with delight, was a visit to Manasarovar, the wonder lake of Tibet, and snow-covered Kailas near by. That was eighteen years ago, and I am still as far as ever from Kailas and Manasarovar. I have not even been to visit Kashmir again, much as I have longed to, and ever more and more I have got entangled in the coils of politics and public affairs. Instead of going up mountains or crossing the seas I have to satisfy my wanderlust by coming to prison. But still I plan, for that is a joy that no one can deny even in prison, and besides what else can one do in prison? And I dream of the day when I shall wander about the Himalayas and cross them to reach that lake and mountain of my desire. But meanwhile the sands of life run on and youth passes into middle age and that will give place to something worse, and sometimes I think that I may grow too old to reach Kailas and Manasarovar. But the journey is always worth the making even though the end may not be in sight.

> Yea, in my mind these mountains rise,
> Their perils dyed with evening's rose;
> And still my ghost sits at my eyes
> And thirsts for their untroubled snows.[1]

---

1. Walter de la Mare.

7

THE COMING OF GANDHIJI:
SATYAGRAHA AND AMRITSAR

The end of the World War found India in a state of suppressed excitement. Industrialization had spread and the capitalist class had grown in wealth and power. This handful at the top had prospered and were greedy for more power and opportunity to invest their savings and add to their wealth. The great majority, however, were not so fortunate and looked forward to a lightening of the burdens that crushed them. Among the middle classes there was everywhere an expectation of great constitutional changes which would bring a large measure of self-rule and thus better their lot by opening out many fresh avenues of growth to them. Political agitation, peaceful and wholly constitutional as it was, seemed to be working itself to a head and people talked with assurance of self-determination and self-government. Some of this unrest was visible also among the masses, especially the peasantry. In the rural areas of the Punjab the forcible methods of recruitment were still bitterly remembered, and the fierce suppression of the 'Komagata Maru' people and others by conspiracy trials added to the widespread resentment. The soldiers back from active service on distant fronts were no longer the subservient robots that they used to be. They had grown mentally and there was much discontent among them.

Among the Muslims there was anger over the treatment of Turkey and the Khilafat question and an agitation was growing. The treaty with Turkey had not been signed yet, but the whole situation was ominous. So, while they agitated, they waited.

The dominant note all over India was one of waiting and expectation, full of hope and yet tinged with fear and anxiety. Then came the Rowlatt Bills with their drastic provisions for arrest and trial without any of the checks and formalities which the law is supposed to provide. A wave of anger greeted them all over India and even the Moderates joined in this and opposed the measures with all their might. Indeed there was universal opposition on the part of Indians of all shades of opinion. Still the Bills were pushed through by the officials and became law, the principal concession made being to limit them for three years.

It is instructive to look back after fifteen years to these Bills and the upheaval they caused. They were made into law and yet, so far as I know, they were never used even once during the three years of their life— three years which were not quiet years but were the most troubled years that India had known since the Revolt of 1857. Thus the British Government, in the teeth of unanimous public opinion, pushed through a law which they themselves never used afterwards, and thus invited an upheaval. One might almost think that the object of the measure was to bring trouble.

Another interesting fact is this. Today, fifteen years later, we have any number of laws on the statute book, functioning from day to day, which are far harsher than the Rowlatt Bills were. Compared to these new laws and ordinances, under which we now enjoy the blessings of British rule, the Rowlatt Bills might almost be considered a charter of liberty. There is this difference, of course: since 1919 we have had a large instalment of what is called self-government, known as the Montagu–Chelmsford scheme, and now we are told that we are on the verge of another big instalment. We progress.

Gandhiji had passed through a serious illness early in 1919. Almost from his sick bed he begged the Viceroy not to give his consent to the Rowlatt Bills. That appeal was ignored as others had been and then, almost against his will, Gandhiji took the leadership in his first all-India agitation. He started the Satyagraha Sabha, the members of which were pledged to disobey the Rowlatt Act, if it was applied to them, as well as other objectionable laws to be specified from time to time. In other words they were to court gaol openly and deliberately.

When I first read about this proposal in the newspapers my reaction was one of tremendous relief. Here at last was a way out of the tangle, a method of action which was straight and open and possibly effective. I was afire with enthusiasm and wanted to join the Satyagraha Sabha immediately. I hardly thought of the consequences—law-breaking, gaol-going, etc.—and if I thought of them I did not care. But suddenly my ardour was damped and I realized that all was not plain sailing. My father was dead against this new idea. He was not in the habit of being swept away by new proposals; he thought carefully of the consequences before be took any fresh step. And the more he thought of the Satyagraha Sabha and its programme, the less he liked it. What good would the gaol-going of a number of individuals do, what pressure could it bring on the Government? Apart from these general considerations, what really moved him was the personal issue. It seemed to him preposterous that I should go to prison. The trek to prison had not then begun and the idea was most repulsive. Father was intensely attached to his children. He was not showy in his affection, but behind his restraint there was a great love.

For many days there was this mental conflict, and because both of us felt that big issues were at stake involving a complete upsetting of our lives, we tried hard to be as considerate to each other as possible. I wanted to lessen his obvious suffering if I could, but I had no doubt in my mind that I had to go the way of Satyagraha. Both of us had a distressing time, and night after night I wandered about alone, tortured in mind and trying to grope my way out. Father—I discovered later—actually tried sleeping on the floor to find out what it was like, as he thought that this would be my lot in prison.

Gandhiji came to Allahabad at father's request and they had long talks at which I was not present. As a result Gandhiji advised me not to precipitate matters or to do anything which might upset father. I was not happy at this, but other events took place in India which changed the whole situation, and the Satyagraha Sabha stopped its activities.

Satyagraha Day—all-India *hartals* and complete suspension of business—firing by the police and military at Delhi and Amritsar, and the killing of many people—mob violence in Amritsar and Ahmedabad—the massacre of Jallianwala Bagh—the long horror and terrible indignity of martial law in the Punjab. The Punjab was isolated, cut off from the rest of India; a thick veil seemed to cover it and hide it from outside eyes. There was hardly any news, and people could not go there or come out from there.

Odd individuals, who managed to escape from that inferno, were so terror-struck that they could give no clear account. Helplessly and impotently, we, who were outside, waited for scraps of news and bitterness filled our hearts. Some of us wanted to go openly to the affected parts of the Punjab and defy the martial law regulations. But we were kept back, and meanwhile a big organization for relief and enquiry was set up on behalf of the Congress.

As soon as martial law was withdrawn from the principal areas and outsiders were allowed to come in, prominent Congressmen and others poured into the Punjab offering their services for relief or enquiry work. The relief work was largely directed by Pandit Madan Mohan Malaviya and Swami Shraddhananda; the enquiry part was mainly under the direction of my father and Mr C.R. Das, with Gandhiji taking a great deal of interest in it and often being consulted by the others. Deshbandhu Das especially took the Amritsar area under his charge and I was deputed to accompany him there and assist him in any way he desired. That was the first occasion I had of working with him and under him and I valued that experience very much and my admiration for him grew. Most of the evidence relating to Jallianwala Bagh and that terrible lane where human beings were made to crawl on their bellies, that subsequently appeared in the Congress Inquiry Report, was taken down in our presence. We paid numerous visits to the so-called Bagh itself and examined every bit of it carefully.

A suggestion has been made, I think by Mr Edward Thompson, that General Dyer was under the impression that there were other exits from the Bagh and it was because of this that he continued his firing for so long. Even if that was Dyer's impression, and there were in fact some exits, that would hardly lessen his responsibility. But it seems very strange that he should have such an impression. Any person, standing on the raised ground where he stood, could have a good view of the entire space and could see how shut in it was on all sides by houses several storeys high. Only on one side, for 100 feet or so, there was no house, but a low wall about five feet high. With a murderous fire mowing them down and unable to find a way out, thousands of people rushed to this wall and tried to climb over it. The fire was then directed, it appears (both from our evidence and the innumerable bullet-marks on the wall itself) towards this wall to prevent people from escaping over it. And when all was over, some of the biggest heaps of dead and wounded lay on either side of this wall.

Towards the end of that year (1919) I travelled from Amritsar to

Delhi by the night train. The compartment I entered was almost full and all the berths, except one upper one, were occupied by sleeping passengers. I took the vacant upper berth. In the morning I discovered that all my fellow-passengers were military officers. They conversed with each other in loud voices which I could not help overhearing. One of them was holding forth in an aggressive and triumphant tone and soon I discovered that he was Dyer, the hero of Jallianwala Bagh, and he was describing his Amritsar experiences. He pointed out how he had the whole town at his mercy and he had felt like reducing the rebellious city to a heap of ashes, but he took pity on it and refrained. He was evidently coming back from Lahore after giving his evidence before the Hunter Committee of Inquiry. I was greatly shocked to hear his conversation and to observe his callous manner. He descended at Delhi station in pyjamas with bright pink stripes, and a dressing-gown.

During the Punjab inquiry I saw a great deal of Gandhiji. Very often his proposals seemed novel to our committee and it did not approve of them. But almost always he argued his way to their acceptance and subsequent events showed the wisdom of his advice. Faith in his political insight grew in me.

The Punjab happenings and the inquiry into them had a profound effect on father. His whole legal and constitutional foundations were shaken by them and his mind was gradually prepared for that change which was to come a year later. He had already moved far from his old moderate position. Dissatisfied with the leading Moderate newspaper, the *Leader* of Allahabad, he had started another daily, the *Independent*, from Allahabad early in 1919. This paper met with great success, but from the very beginning it was handicapped by quite an amazing degree of incompetence in the running of it. Almost everybody connected with it—directors, editors, managerial staff—had their share of responsibility for this. I was one of the directors, without the least experience of the job, and the troubles and the squabbles of the paper became quite a nightmare to me. Both my father and I were, however, soon dragged away to the Punjab, and during our long absence the paper deteriorated greatly and became involved in financial difficulties. It never recovered from them, and, although it had bright patches in 1920 and 1921, it began to go to pieces as soon as we went to gaol. It expired finally early in 1923. This experience of newspaper proprietorship gave me a fright and ever since I have refused to assume responsibility as a director of any newspaper. Indeed I could not do so because of my preoccupations in prison and outside.

Father presided over the Amritsar Congress during Christmas 1919. He issued a moving appeal to the Moderate leaders or the Liberals, as they were now calling themselves, to join this session because of the new situation created by the horrors of martial law. "The lacerated heart of the Punjab" called to them, he wrote. Would they not answer that call? But they did not answer it in the way he wanted, and refused to join. Their eyes were on the new reforms that were coming as a result of the Montagu–Chelmsford recommendations. This refusal hurt father and widened the gulf between him and the Liberals.

The Amritsar Congress was the first Gandhi Congress. Lokamanya Tilak was also present and took a prominent part in the deliberations, but there could be no doubt about it that the majority of the delegates, and even more so the great crowds outside, looked to Gandhi for leadership. The slogan *Mahatma Gandhi ki jai* began to dominate the Indian political horizon. The Ali Brothers, recently discharged from internment, immediately joined the Congress, and the national movement began to take a new shape and develop a new orientation.

M. Mohammad Ali went off soon on a Khilafat deputation to Europe. In India the Khilafat Committee came more and more under Gandhiji's influence and began to flirt with his ideas of non-violent non-co-operation. I remember one of the earliest meetings of the Khilafat leaders and Moulvies and Ulemas in Delhi in January 1920. A Khilafat deputation was going to wait on the Viceroy, and Gandhiji was to join it. Before he reached Delhi, however, a draft of the proposed address was, according to custom, sent to the Viceroy. When Gandhiji arrived and read this draft, he strongly disapproved of it and even said that he could not be a party to the deputation, if this draft was not materially altered. His objection was that the draft was vague and wordy and there was no clear indication in it of the absolute minimum demands which the Muslims must have. He said that this was not fair to the Viceroy and the British Government, or to the people, or to themselves. They must not make exaggerated demands which they were not going to press, but should state the minimum clearly and without possibility of doubt, and stand by it to the death. If they were serious, this was the only right and honourable course to adopt.

This argument was a novel one in political or other circles in India. We were used to vague exaggerations and flowery language and always there was an idea of a bargain in our minds. Gandhiji, however, carried his point and he wrote to the Private Secretary of the Viceroy, pointing out the defects and vagueness of the draft address sent, and forwarding a few additional paragraphs to be added to it. These paragraphs gave the minimum demands. The Viceroy's reply was interesting. He refused to accept the new paragraphs and said that the previous draft was, in his opinion, quite proper. Gandhiji felt that this correspondence had made his own position and that of the Khilafat Committee clear, and so he joined the deputation after all.

It was obvious that the Government were not going to accept the demands of the Khilafat Committee and a struggle was therefore bound to come. There were long talks with the Moulvies and the Ulemas, and non-violence and non-co-operation were discussed, especially non-violence. Gandhiji told them that he was theirs to command, but on the definite understanding that they accepted non-violence with all its implications. There was to be no weakening on that, no temporizing, no mental reservations. It was not easy for the Moulvies to grasp this idea but they agreed, making it clear that they did so as a policy only and not as a creed, for their religion did not prohibit the use of violence in a righteous cause.

The political and the Khilafat movements developed side by side during that year 1920, both going in the same direction and eventually joining hands with the adoption by the Congress of Gandhiji's non-violent non-co-operation. The Khilafat Committee adopted this programme first, and August 1st was fixed for the commencement of the campaign.

Earlier in the year a Muslim meeting (I think it was the Council of the Muslim League) was held in Allahabad to consider this programme. The meeting took place in Syed Raza Ali's house. M. Mohammad Ali was still in Europe but M. Shaukat Ali was present. I remember that meeting because it thoroughly disappointed me. Shaukat Ali was, of course, full of enthusiasm but almost all the others looked thoroughly unhappy and uncomfortable. They did not have the courage to disagree and yet they obviously had no intention of doing anything rash. Were these the people to lead a revolutionary movement, I thought, and to challenge the British Empire? Gandhiji addressed them and after hearing him they looked even more frightened than before. He spoke well in his best dictatorial vein. He was humble but also clear-cut and hard as a diamond, pleasant and soft-spoken but inflexible and terribly earnest. His eyes were mild and deep, yet out of them blazed out a fierce energy and determination. This is going to be a great struggle, he said, with a very powerful adversary. If you want to take it up, you must be prepared to lose everything, and you must subject yourself to the strictest non-violence and discipline. When war is declared martial law prevails, and in our non-violent struggle there will also have to be dictatorship and martial law on our side, if we are to win. You have every right to kick me out, to demand my head, or to punish me whenever and howsoever you choose. But so long as you choose to keep me as your leader you must accept my conditions, you must accept dictatorship and the discipline of martial law. But that dictatorship will always be subject to your goodwill and to your acceptance and to your co-operation. The moment you have had enough of me, throw me out, trample upon me, and I shall not complain.

Something to this effect he said, and these military analogies and the unyielding earnestness of the man made the flesh of most of his hearers creep. But Shaukat Ali was there to keep the waverers up to the mark, and when the time for voting came the great majority of them quietly and shamefacedly voted for the proposition, that is for war!

As we were coming home from the meeting I asked Gandhiji if this was the way to start a great struggle. I had expected enthusiasm, spirited language and a flashing of eyes; instead we saw a very tame gathering of timid, middle-aged folk. And yet these people, such was the pressure of mass opinion, voted for the struggle. Of course, very few of these members of the Muslim League joined the struggle later. Many of them found a safe sanctuary in Government jobs. The Muslim League did not represent, then or later, any considerable section of Muslim opinion. It was the Khilafat Committee of 1920 that was a powerful and far more representative body, and it was this Committee that entered upon the struggle with enthusiasm.

The 1st of August had been fixed by Gandhiji for the inauguration of non-co-operation, although the Congress had not considered or accepted the proposal so far. On that day Lokamanya Tilak died in Bombay. That very morning Gandhiji had reached Bombay after a tour in Sindh. I was with him and we joined that mighty demonstration in which the whole of Bombay's million population seemed to have poured out to do reverence to the great leader whom they had loved so well.

8

I AM EXTERNED AND THE CONSEQUENCES THEREOF

M y politics had been those of my class, the bourgeoisie. Indeed all vocal politics then (and to a great extent even now) were those of the middle classes, and Moderate and Extremist alike represented them and, in different keys, sought their betterment. The Moderate represented especially the handful of the upper middle class who had on the whole prospered under British rule and wanted no sudden changes which might endanger their present position and interests. They had close relations with the British Government and the big landlord class. The Extremist represented also the lower ranks of the middle class. The industrial workers, their number swollen up by the war, were only locally organized in some places and had little influence. The peasantry were a blind, poverty-stricken, suffering mass, resigned to their miserable fate and sat upon and exploited by all who came in contact with them—the Government, landlords, money-lenders, petty officials, police, lawyers, priests.

A reader of the newspapers would hardly imagine that a vast peasantry and millions of workers existed in India or had any importance. The British-owned Anglo-Indian newspapers were full of the doings of high officials; English social life in the big cities and in the hill stations was described at great length with its parties, fancy-dress balls and amateur theatricals. Indian politics, from the Indian point of view, were almost completely ignored by them, even the Congress sessions being disposed of in a few lines on a back page. They were not considered news of any value except when some Indian, prominent or otherwise, slanged or criticized the Congress and its pretensions. Occasionally there was a brief reference to a strike, and the rural areas only came into prominence when there was a riot.

Indian newspapers tried to model themselves on the Anglo-Indian ones but gave much greater prominence to the nationalist movement. For the rest they were interested in the appointment of Indians to important or unimportant offices, their promotions and transfers—when there was always a party given to the outgoing officer at which "great enthusiasm prevailed". At the time of a fresh Government settlement of an agricultural area, which almost always resulted in an increase of Government revenue, there was an outcry because the landlord's pocket was affected. The poor tenant was nowhere in the picture. These newspapers were owned and controlled chiefly by the landlords and the industrialists. Such was that which was called the "nationalist" press.

One of the persistent demands of the Congress itself, during its early years, was a permanent settlement of the land in the non-settled areas, in order that the rights of the landlords might be protected. No mention was made of the tenant.

Conditions have changed greatly during the last twenty years because of the growth of the nationalist movement, and now even the British-owned newspapers have to give space to Indian political problems if they are to retain their Indian readers. But they do so in their own peculiar way. Indian newspapers have developed a slightly wider outlook and talk benevolently of the worker and the peasant, because that is the fashion, and there is a growing interest in industrial and rural problems among their readers. But essentially now, as before, they voice the interests of the Indian capitalist and landlord class which owns them. Many Indian princes have also taken to investing money in these newspapers and they see to it that they get their money's worth. Yet many of these newspapers are called "Congress" newspapers, although many of those who control them are not even members of the Congress. But the Congress is a popular word with the public and many an individual and a group exploit it to their advantage. Newspapers which are prepared to take up a more advanced position have, of course, always to live in fear of big fines or even of suppression under the stringent press laws and censorship.

In 1920 I was totally ignorant of labour conditions in factories or fields, and my political outlook was entirely bourgeois. I knew, of course, that there was terrible poverty and misery, and I felt that the first aim of a politically free India must be to tackle this problem of poverty. But political freedom, with the inevitable dominance of the middle class, seemed to me the obvious next step. I was paying a little more attention to the peasant problem since Gandhiji's agrarian movements in Champaran (Behar) and Kaira (Gujrat). But my mind was full of political developments in 1920 and of the coming of non-co-operation which was looming on the horizon.

Just then a new interest developed in my life which was to play an important part in later years. I was thrown, almost without any will of my own, into contact with the peasantry. This came about in a curious way.

My mother and Kamala (my wife) were both unwell, and early in May 1920 I took them up to Mussoorie. My father was busy then in a big raj case in which he was opposing Mr C.R. Das. We stopped at the Savoy Hotel in Mussoorie. At that time, peace negotiations were proceeding between the Afghan and British envoys (this was after the brief Afghan War in 1919 when Amanullah came to the throne) at Mussoorie, and the Afghan delegation were stopping at the Savoy Hotel. They kept to themselves, however, fed separately, and did not appear in the common rooms. I was not particularly interested in them, and for a whole month I did not see a single member of their delegation, and if I saw them I did not recognize them. Suddenly one evening I had a visit from the Superintendent of Police and he showed me a letter from the local Government asking him to get an undertaking from me that I would not have any dealings or contacts with the Afghan delegation. This struck me as extraordinary since I had not even seen them during a month's stay and there was little chance of my doing so. The Superintendent knew this, as he was closely watching the delegation, and there were literally crowds of secret service men about. But to give any undertaking went against the grain and I told him so. He asked me to see the District Magistrate, the Superintendent of the Dun, and I did so. As I persisted in my refusal to give an undertaking an order of externment was served on me, calling upon me to leave the district of Dehra Dun within twenty-four hours, which really meant within a few hours from Mussoorie. I did not like the idea of leaving my mother and wife, both of whom were ailing; and yet I did not think it right to break the order. There was no civil disobedience then. So I left Mussoorie.

My father had known Sir Harcourt Butler, who was then Governor of the United Provinces, fairly well, and he wrote to him a friendly letter saying that he was sure that he (Sir Harcourt) could not have issued such a stupid order; it must be some bright person in Simla who was responsible for it. Sir Harcourt replied that the order was quite a harmless one and Jawaharlal could easily have complied with it without any injury to his dignity. Father, in reply, disagreed with this and added that, although there was no intention of deliberately breaking the order, if my mother's or wife's health demanded it, I would certainly return to Mussoorie, order or no order. As it happened, my mother's condition took a turn for the worse, and both father and I immediately started for Mussoorie. Just before starting, we received a telegram rescinding the order.

When we reached Mussoorie the next morning the first person I noticed in the courtyard of the hotel was an Afghan who had my baby daughter in his arms! I learnt that he was a minister and a member of the Afghan delegation. It transpired that immediately after my externment the Afghans had read about it in the newspapers, and they were so much interested that the head of the delegation took to sending my mother a basket of fruit and flowers every day.

Father and I met one or two members of the delegation later and we were cordially invited to visit Afghanistan. Unhappily we were unable to take advantage of this offer, and I do not know if the invitation stands under the new dispensation in that country.

As a result of the externment order from Mussoorie I spent about two weeks in Allahabad, and it was during this period that I got entangled in the *Kisan* (peasant) movement. That entanglement grew in later years and influenced my mental outlook greatly. I have sometimes wondered what would have happened if I had not been externed and had not been in Allahabad just then with no other engagements. Very probably I would have been drawn to the *kisans* anyhow, sooner or later, but the manner of my going to them would have been different and the effect on me might also have been different.

Early in June 1920 (so far as I can remember) about two hundred *kisans* marched fifty miles from the interior of Partabgarh district to Allahabad city with the intention of drawing the attention of the prominent politicians there to their woebegone condition. They were led by a man named Ramachandra, who himself was not a local peasant.

I learnt that these *kisans* were squatting on the river bank, on one of the Jumna *ghats*, and, accompanied by some friends, went to see them. They told us of the crushing exactions of the taluqadars, of inhuman treatment, and that their condition had become wholly intolerable. They begged us to accompany them back to make inquiries as well as to protect them from the vengeance of the taluqadars who were angry at their having come to Allahabad on this mission. They would accept no denial and literally clung on to us. At last I promised to visit them two days or so later.

I went there with some colleagues and we spent three days in the villages far from the railway and even the *pucca* road. That visit was a revelation to me. We found the whole countryside afire with enthusiasm and full of a strange excitement. Enormous gatherings would take place at the briefest notice by word of mouth. One village would communicate with another, and the second with the third, and so on, and presently whole villages would empty out, and all over the fields there would be men and women and children on the march to the meeting-place. Or, more swiftly still, the cry of *Sita Ram*—Sita Ra-a-a-a-m—would fill the air, and travel far in all directions and be echoed back from other villages, and then people would come streaming out or even running as fast as they could. They were in miserable rags, men and women, but their faces were full of excitement and their eyes glistened and seemed to expect strange happenings which would, as if by a miracle, put an end to their long misery.

They showered their affection on us and looked on us with loving and hopeful eyes, as if we were the bearers of good tidings, the guides who were to lead them to the promised land. Looking at them and their misery and overflowing gratitude, I was filled with shame and sorrow, shame at my own easy-going and comfortable life and our petty politics of the city which ignored this vast multitude of semi-naked sons and daughters of India, sorrow at the degradation and overwhelming poverty of India. A new picture of India seemed to rise before me, naked, starving, crushed, and utterly miserable. And their faith in us, casual visitors from the distant city, embarrassed me and filled me with a new responsibility that frightened me.

I listened to their innumerable tales of sorrow, their crushing and ever-growing burden of rent, illegal exactions, ejectments from land and mud hut, beatings; surrounded on all sides by vultures who preyed on them—zamindar's agents, money-lenders, police; toiling all day to find that what they produced was not theirs and their reward was kicks and curses and a hungry stomach. Many of those who were present were landless people who had been ejected by the landlords, and had no land or hut to fall back upon. The land was rich but the burden on it was very heavy, the holdings were small and there were too many people after them. Taking advantage of this land hunger the landlords, unable under the law to enhance their rents beyond a certain percentage, charged huge illegal premiums. The tenant, knowing of no other alternative, borrowed money from the money-lender and paid the premium, and then, unable to pay his debt or even the rent, was ejected and lost all he had.

This process was an old one and the progressive pauperization of the peasantry had been going on for a long time. What had happened to bring matters to a head and rouse up the countryside? Economic conditions, of course, but these conditions were similar all over Oudh, while the agrarian upheaval of 1920 and 1921 was largely confined to three districts—Partabgarh, Rae Bareli and Fyzabad. This was partly due to the leadership of a remarkable person, Ramachandra, Baba Ramachandra as he was called.

Ramachandra was a man from Maharashtra in western India and he had been to Fiji as an indentured labourer. On his return he had gradually drifted to these districts of Oudh and wandered about reciting Tulsidas's *Ramayana* and listening to tenants' grievances. He had little education and to some extent he exploited the tenantry for his own benefit, but he showed remarkable powers of organization. He taught the peasants to meet frequently in *sabhas* (meetings) to discuss their own troubles and thus gave them a feeling of solidarity. Occasionally huge mass meetings were held and this produced a sense of power. *Sita-Ram* was an old and common cry but he gave it an almost warlike significance and made it a signal for emergencies as well as a bond between different villages. Fyzabad, Partabgarh and Rae Bareli are full of the old legends of Ramachandra and Sita—these districts formed part of the kingdom of Ayodhya—and the favourite book of the masses is Tulsidas's *Hindi Ramayana*. Many people knew hundreds of verses from this by heart. A recitation of this book and appropriate quotations from it was a favourite practice of Ramachandra. Having organized the peasantry to some extent he made all manner of promises to them, vague and nebulous but full of hope for them. He had no programme of any kind and when he had brought them to a pitch of excitement he tried to shift the responsibility to others. This led him to bring a number of peasants to Allahabad to interest people there in the movement.

Ramachandra continued to take a prominent part in the agrarian movement for another year and served two or three sentences in prison, but he turned out later to be a very irresponsible and unreliable person.

Oudh was a particularly good area for an agrarian agitation. It was. and is, the land of the taluqadars—the "Barons of Oudh" they call themselves—and the zamindari system at its worst flourished there. The exactions of the landlords were becoming unbearable and the number of landless labourers was growing. There was on the whole only one class of tenant and this helped united action.

India may be roughly divided into two parts—the zamindari area with its big landlords, and the area containing peasant proprietors, but there is a measure of overlapping. The three provinces of Bengal, Behar, and the United Provinces of Agra and Oudh, form the zamindari area. The peasant proprietors are comparatively better off, although even their condition is often pitiable. The mass of the peasantry in the Punjab or Gujrat (where there are peasant proprietors) is far better off than the tenants of the zamindari areas. In the greater part of these zamindari areas there were many kinds of tenancies—occupancy tenants, non-occupancy tenants, sub-tenancies, etc. The interests of various tenants often conflict against each other and this militates against joint action. In Oudh, however, there were no occupancy tenants or even life tenants in 1920. There were only short-term tenants who were continually being ejected in favour of some one who was willing to pay a higher premium. Because there was principally one class of tenant, it was easier to organize them for joint action.

In practice there was no guarantee in Oudh for even the short term of the contract. A landlord hardly ever gave a receipt for rent received, and he could always say that the rent had not been paid and eject the tenant, for whom it was impossible to prove the contrary. Besides the rent there were an extraordinary number of illegal exactions. In one *taluqa* I was told that there had been as many as fifty different kinds of such exactions. Probably this number was exaggerated but it is notorious how taluqadars often make their tenants pay for every special expenditure—a marriage in the family, cost of the son's education in foreign countries, a party to the Governor or other high official, a purchase of a car or an elephant. Indeed these exactions have got special names—*motrauna* (tax for purchase of motor), *hathauna* (tax for purchase of elephant), etc.

It was not surprising therefore that a big agrarian agitation should develop in Oudh. What was surprising to me then was that this should have developed quite spontaneously without any city help or intervention of politicians and the like. The agrarian movement was entirely separate from the Congress and it had nothing to do with the non-co-operation that was taking shape. Or perhaps it will be more correct to say that both these widespread and powerful movements were due to the same fundamental causes. The peasantry had of course taken part in the great hartals that Gandhiji had proclaimed in 1919 and later his name was becoming a charm for the man in the village.

What amazed me still more was our total ignorance in the cities of this great agrarian movement. No newspaper had contained a line about it; they were not interested in rural areas. I realized more than ever how cut off we were from our people and how we lived and worked and agitated in a little world apart from them.

9

WANDERINGS AMONG THE KISANS

I spent three days in the villages, came back to Allahabad, and then went again. During these brief visits we wandered about a great deal from village to village, feeding with the peasants, living with them in their mud huts, talking to them for long hours, and often addressing meetings, big and small. We had originally gone in a light car and the peasants were so keen that hundreds of them, working overnight, built temporary roads across the fields so that our car could go right into the interior. Often the car got stuck and was bodily lifted out by scores of willing hands. But we had to leave the car eventually and to do most of our journeying by foot. Everywhere we went we were accompanied by policemen, C.I.D. men, and a Deputy Collector from Lucknow. I am afraid we gave them a bad time with our continuous marching across fields and they were quite tired out and fed up with us and the *kisans*. The Deputy Collector was a somewhat effeminate youth from Lucknow and he had turned up in patent leather pumps! He begged us sometimes to restrain our ardour and I think he ultimately dropped out, being unable to keep up with us.

It was the hottest time of the year, June, just before the monsoon. The sun scorched and blinded. I was quite unused to going out in the sun and ever since my return from England I had gone to the hills for part of every summer. And now I was wandering about all day in the open sun with not even a sun-hat, my head being wrapped in a small towel. So full was I of other matters that I quite forgot about the heat and it was only on my return to Allahabad, when I noticed the rich tan I had developed, that I remembered what I had gone through. I was pleased with myself for I realized that I could stand the heat with the best of them and my fear of it was wholly unjustified. I have found that I can bear both extreme heat and great cold without much discomfort, and this has stood me in good stead in my work as well as in my periods in prison. This was no doubt due to my general physical fitness and my habit of taking exercise, a lesson I learnt from my father, who was a bit of an athlete and, almost to the end of his days, continued his daily exercise. His head became covered with silvery hair, his face was deeply furrowed and looked old and weary with thought, but the rest of his body, to within a year or two of his death, seemed to be twenty years younger.

Even before my visit to Partabgarh in June 1920, I had often passed through villages, stopped there and talked to the peasants. I had seen them in their scores of thousands on the banks of the Ganges during the big *melas* and we had taken our Home Rule propaganda to them. But somehow I had not fully realized what they were and what they meant to India. Like most of us, I took them for granted. This realization came to me during these Partabgarh visits and ever since then my mental picture of India always contains this naked, hungry mass. Perhaps there was some kind of electricity in the air, perhaps I was in a receptive frame of mind and the pictures I saw and the impressions I gathered were indelibly impressed on my mind.

These peasants took away the shyness from me and taught me to speak in public. Till then I hardly spoke at a public gathering; I was frightened at the prospect, especially if the speaking was to be done in Hindustani, as it almost always was. But I could not possibly avoid addressing these peasant gatherings, and how could I be shy of these poor unsophisticated people? I did not know the arts of oratory and so I spoke to them, man to man, and told them what I had in my mind and in my heart. Whether the gathering consisted of a few persons or of 10,000 or more I stuck to my conversational and rather personal method of speaking, and I found that, whatever might be lacking in it, I could at least go on. I was fluent enough. Perhaps many of them could not understand a great deal of what I said. My language or my thought was not simple enough for them. Many did not hear me when the gathering was very large for my voice did not carry far. But all this did not matter much to them when once they had given their confidence and faith to a person.

I went back to Mussoorie to my mother and wife but my mind was full of the *kisans* and I was eager to be back. As soon as I returned I resumed my visits to the villages and watched the agrarian movement grow in strength. The down-trodden *kisan* began to gain a new confidence in himself and walked straighter with head up. His fear of the landlords' agents and the police lessened, and when there was an ejectment from a holding no other *kisan* would make an offer for that land. Physical violence on the part of the zamindars' servants and illegal exactions became infrequent, and whenever an instance occurred, it was immediately reported and an attempt at an inquiry was held. This checked the zamindars' agents as well as the police. The taluqadars were frightened and were on the defensive and the provincial government promised an amendment of the Oudh Tenancy Law.

The taluqadars and the big zamindars, the lords of the land, the "natural leaders of the people", as they are proud of calling themselves, had been the spoilt children of the British Government, but that Government had succeeded, by the special education and upbringing it provided or failed to provide for them, in reducing them, as a class, to a state of complete intellectual impotence. They did nothing at all for their tenantry, such as landlords in other countries have to some little extent often done, and became complete parasites on the land and the people. Their chief activity lay in endeavouring to placate the local officials, without whose favour they could not exist for long, and demanding ceaselessly a protection of their special interests and privileges.

The word 'zamindar' is rather deceptive, and one is apt to think that all zamindars are big landlords. In the *ryotwari* provinces it means the peasant proprietor. Even in the typical zamindari provinces, it includes in its fold the relatively few big landlords, thousands of middle landowners, and hundreds of thousands of persons who live in extreme poverty and are no better than tenants. In the United Provinces, so far as I can remember, there are a million and a half persons classed as zamindars. Probably over 90 per cent of these are almost on the same level as the poorest tenants, and another 9 per cent are only moderately well off. The biggish landowners are not more than 5000 in the whole province, and of this number, about one-tenth might be considered the really big zamindars and taluqadars. In some instances the bigger tenants are better off than the destitute petty landowners. Both these poor landowners and the middle landlords, though often intellectually backward, are as a whole a fine body of men and women, and, with proper education and training, can be made into excellent citizens. They have taken a considerable part in the nationalist movement. Not so the taluqadars and the big zamindars, barring a few notable exceptions. They have not even the virtues of an aristocracy. As a class they are physically and intellectually degenerate and have outlived their day; they will continue only so long as an external power like the British Government props them up.

Right through the year 1921 I continued my visits to the rural areas, but my field of activity grew till it comprised the whole of the United Provinces. Non-co-operation had begun in earnest and its message had reached the remotest village. A host of Congress workers in each district went about the rural areas with the new message to which they often added, rather vaguely, a removal of *kisan* grievances. Swaraj was an all-embracing word to cover everything. Yet the two movements—non-co-operation and the agrarian—were quite separate, though they overlapped and influenced each other greatly in our province. As a result of Congress preaching, litigation went down with a rush and villages established their *panchayats* to deal with their disputes. Especially powerful was the influence of the Congress in favour of peace, for the new creed of non-violence was stressed wherever the Congress worker went. This may not have been fully appreciated or understood but it did prevent the peasantry from taking to violence.

This was no small result. Agrarian upheavals are notoriously violent, leading to *jacqueries*, and the peasants of part of Oudh in those days were desperate and at white heat. A spark would have lighted a flame. Yet they remained amazingly peaceful. The only instance of physical violence on a taluqadar that I remember was when a peasant went up to him as he was sitting in his own house, surrounded by his friends, and slapped him on the face on the ground that he was immoral and inconsiderate to his own wife!

There was violence of another kind later which led to conflicts with the Government. But this conflict was bound to come, for the Government could not tolerate this growing power of a united peasantry. The *kisans* took to travelling in railway trains in large numbers without tickets, especially when they had to attend their periodical big mass meetings which sometimes consisted of sixty or seventy thousand persons. It was difficult to move them and, unheard of thing, they openly defied the railway authorities, telling them that the old days were gone. At whose instigation they took to the free mass travelling I do not know.

We had not suggested it to them. We suddenly heard that they were doing it. Stricter railway control prevented this later.

In the autumn of 1920 (when I was away in Calcutta attending the special session of the Congress) a few *kisan* leaders were arrested for some petty offence. They were to be tried in Partabgarh town but on the day of the trial a huge concourse of peasants filled the court compound and lined the route to the gaol where the accused leaders were kept. The magistrate's nerve gave way and he postponed the trial to the next day. But the crowd grew and almost surrounded the gaol. The *kisans* can easily carry on for a few days on a handful of parched gram. Ultimately the *kisan* leaders were discharged, perhaps after a formal trial inside the gaol. I forget how this came about but for the *kisans* this was a great triumph and they began to think that they could always have their way by weight of numbers alone. To the Government this position was intolerable and soon after a similar occasion arose and this time it ended differently.

It was at the beginning of January 1921. I had just returned to Allahabad from the Nagpur Congress when I received a telegram from Rae Bareli asking me to go there immediately as trouble was expected. I left the next day. I discovered that some leading *kisans* had been arrested some days back and had been lodged in the local gaol. Remembering their success at Partabgarh and the tactics they had then adopted, the peasants marched to Rae Bareli town for a mass demonstration. But this time the Government was not going to permit it and additional police and military had been collected to stop the *kisans*. Just outside the town on the other side of a little river, the main body of the *kisans* was stopped. Many of them, however, streamed in from other directions. On arrival at the station I learnt of this situation and immediately I proceeded straight to the river where the military were said to face the peasants. On the way I received a hurriedly written note from the District Magistrate asking me to go back. I wrote my reply on the back of it enquiring under what law and what section he was asking me to go back and till I heard from him I proposed to go on. As I reached the river sounds of firing could be heard from the other side. I was stopped at the bridge by the military and as I waited there I was suddenly surrounded by large numbers of frightened *kisans* who had been hiding in the fields on this side of the river. So I held a meeting of about a couple of thousand peasants on the spot and tried to remove their fear and lessen their excitement. It was rather an unusual situation with firing going on on their brethren within a stone's throw across a little stream and the military in evidence everywhere. But the meeting was quite successful and took away the edge from the *kisans*' fear. The District Magistrate then returned from the firing line and, at his request, I accompanied him to his house. There he kept me, under some pretext or other, for over two hours, evidently wanting to keep me away from the *kisans* and my colleagues in the city.

We found later that many men had been killed in the firing. The *kisans* had refused to disperse or to go back but otherwise they had been perfectly peaceful. I am quite sure that if I or some one else they trusted had been there and had asked them to do so they would have dispersed. They refused to take their orders from men they did not trust. Some one actually suggested to the Magistrate to wait for me a little but he refused. He could not permit an agitator to succeed where he had failed. That is not the way of foreign governments depending on prestige.

Firing on *kisans* took place on two occasions in Rae Bareli district about that time and then began, what was much worse, a reign of terror for every prominent *kisan* worker or member of a *panchayat*. Government had decided to crush the movement. Hand-spinning on the *charkha* was then spreading among the peasantry at the instance of the Congress. A *charkha* therefore became the symbol of sedition and its owner got into trouble, the *charkha* itself being often burnt. Thus the Government tried to crush by hundreds of arrests and other methods both the agrarian and the Congress movements in the rural areas of Rae Bareli and Partabgarh. Most of the principal workers were common to the two movements.

A little later, in the year 1921, Fyzabad district had its dose of widespread repression. The trouble started there in a peculiar way. The peasants of some villages went and looted the property of a taluqadar. It transpired subsequently that they had been incited to do so by the servants of another zamindar who had some kind of feud with the taluqadar. The poor ignorant peasants were actually told that it was the wish of Mahatma Gandhi that they should loot and they willingly agreed to carry out this behest, shouting "Mahatma Gandhi ki jai" in the process.

I was very angry when I heard of this and within a day or two of the occurrence I was on the spot, somewhere near Akbarpur in Fyzabad district. On arrival I called a meeting for the same day and within a few hours five or six thousand persons had collected from numerous villages within a radius of ten miles. I spoke harshly to them for the shame they had brought on themselves and our cause and said that the guilty persons must confess publicly. (I was full in those days of what I conceived to be the spirit of Gandhiji's Satyagraha). I called upon those who had participated in the looting to raise their hands, and strange to say, there, in the presence of numerous police officials, about two dozen hands went up. That meant certain trouble for them.

When I spoke to many of them privately later and heard their artless story of how they had been misled, I felt very sorry for them and I began to regret having exposed these foolish and simple folk to long terms of imprisonment. But the people who suffered were not just two or three dozen. The chance was too good to be lost and full advantage was taken of the occasion to crush the agrarian movement in that district. Over a thousand arrests were made, and the district gaol was overcrowded, and the trial went on for the best part of a year. Many died in prison during the trial. Many others received long sentences and in later years, when I went to prison, I came across some of them, boys and young men, spending their youth in prison.

The Indian *kisans* have little staying power, little energy to resist for long. Famines and epidemics come and slay them in their millions. It was surprising that they had shown for a whole year great powers of resistance against the combined pressure of government and landlord. But they began to weary a little and the determined attack of the Government on their movement ultimately broke its spirit for the time being. But it continued still in a lower key. There were not such vast demonstrations as before, but most villages contained old workers who had not been terrorized and who carried on the work in a small way. All this, it must be remembered, was prior to the gaol-going which the Congress started at the end of 1921. Even in this the *kisans* took a considerable part, in spite of all they had suffered during the previous year.

Frightened by the agrarian movement, the Government had hurried on with tenancy legislation. This promised some improvement in the lot of the *kisan* but the measure was toned down when it was found that the movement was already under control. The principal change it affected was to give a life tenancy to the *kisan* in Oudh. This sounded attractive to him but, as he has found out subsequently, his lot is in no way better.

Agrarian troubles continued to crop up in Oudh but on a smaller scale. The world depression which began in 1929, however, again created a great crisis owing to the fall in prices.

10

NON-CO-OPERATION

I have dealt with the Oudh agrarian upheaval in some little detail because it lifted the veil and disclosed a fundamental aspect of the Indian problem to me to which nationalists had paid hardly any attention. Agrarian troubles are frequently taking place in various parts of India, symptoms of a deep-seated unrest, and the *kisan* agitation in certain parts of Oudh in 1920 and 1921 was but one of them, though it was, in its own way, a remarkable and a revealing one. In its origin it was entirely unconnected with politics or politicians, and right through its course the influence of outsiders and politicians was of the slightest. From an all-India point of view, however, it was a local affair and very little attention was paid to it. Even the newspapers of the United Provinces largely ignored it. For their editors and the majority of their town-dwelling readers, the doings of mobs of semi-naked peasants had no real political or other significance.

The Punjab and the Khilafat wrongs were the topics of the day, and non-co-operation, which was to attempt to bring about a righting of these wrongs, was the all-absorbing subject. The larger issue of national freedom or Swaraj was for the moment not stressed. Gandhiji disliked vague and big objectives, he always preferred concentrating on something specific and definite. Nevertheless, Swaraj was very much in the air and in people's thoughts, and frequent reference was made to it in innumerable gatherings and conferences.

In the autumn of 1920 a special session of the Congress met at Calcutta to consider what steps should be taken and, in particular, to decide about non-co-operation. Lala Lajpat Rai, freshly back from the United States after a long absence from home, was the President. He disliked the new-fangled proposal of non-co-operation and opposed it. He was usually considered an Extremist in Indian politics, but his general outlook was definitely constitutional and moderate. Force of circumstances and not choice or convictions had made him an ally of

Lokamanya Tilak and other Extremists in the early days of the century. But he had a social and economic outlook, strengthened by his long residence abroad, and this gave him a broader vision than that of most Indian leaders.

Wilfrid Scawen Blunt in his "Diaries" describes an interview he had (about 1909) with Gokhale and Lalaji. He is very hard on both, considering them far too cautious and afraid of facing realities. And yet Lalaji faced them far more than most Indian leaders. Blunt's impressions make us realize how low was the temper of our politics and our leaders at that time, and how an able and experienced foreigner was struck by them. But a decade had made a great difference to that temper.

Lala Lajpat Rai was not alone in his opposition; he had a great and impressive company with him. Indeed, almost the entire Old Guard of the Congress opposed Gandhiji's resolution of non-co-operation. Mr C.R. Das led the opposition, not because he disapproved of the spirit behind the resolution, for he was prepared to go as far or even farther, but chiefly because he objected to the boycott of the new legislatures.

Of the prominent leaders of the older generation my father was the only one to take his stand by Gandhiji at that time. It was no easy matter for him to do so. He sensed and was much influenced by the objections that had led most of his old colleagues to oppose. He hesitated, as they did, to take a novel step towards an unknown region, where it was hardly possible to keep one's old bearings. Yet he was inevitably drawn to some form of effective action, and the proposal did embody definite action, though not exactly on the lines of his thought. It took him a long time to make up his mind. He had long talks with Gandhiji and Mr C.R. Das. Mr Das and he were thrown a great deal together just then as they were both appearing, on opposite sides, in a big *mofussil* case. They looked at the problem from much the same point of view and there was very little difference between them even as regards the conclusion. Yet that little difference was just enough to keep them on either side of the main resolution at the Special Congress. Three months later they met again at the Nagpur Congress, and from then onwards they pulled together, ever coming nearer to each other.

I saw very little of father in those days before the Calcutta Special Congress. But whenever I met him, I noticed how he was continually grappling with this problem. Quite apart from the national aspect of the question there was the personal aspect. Non-co-operation meant his withdrawing from his legal practice; it meant a total break with his past life and a new fashioning of it—not an easy matter when one is on the eve of one's sixtieth birthday. It was a break from old political colleagues, from his profession, from the social life to which he had grown accustomed, and a giving up of many an expensive habit which he had grown into. For the financial aspect of the question was not an unimportant one, and it was obvious that he would have to reduce his standard of living if his income from his profession vanished.

But his reason, his strong sense of self-respect, and his pride, all led him step by step to throw in his lot wholeheartedly with the new movement. The accumulated anger with which a series of events, cluminating in the Punjab tragedy and its aftermath, filled him; the sense of utter wrong-doing and injustice, the bitterness of national humiliation, had to find some way out. But he was not to be swept away by a wave of enthusiasm. It was only when his reason, backed by the trained mind of a lawyer, had weighed all the pros and cons that he took the final decision and joined Gandhiji in his campaign.

He was attracted by Gandhiji as a man, and that no doubt was a factor which influenced him. Nothing could have made him a close associate of a person he disliked, for he was always strong in his likes and dislikes. But it was a strange combination—the saint, the stoic, the man of religion, one who went through life rejecting what it offers in the way of sensation and physical pleasure, and one who had been a bit of an epicure, who accepted life and welcomed and enjoyed its many sensations, and cared little for what may come in the hereafter. In the language of psychoanalysis it was a meeting of an introvert with an extrovert. Yet there were common bonds, common interests, which drew the two together and kept up, even when, in later years, their politics diverged, a close friendship between them.

Walter Pater, in one of his books, mentions how the saint and the epicure, starting from opposed points, travelling different paths, one with a religious temper, the other opposed to it, and yet both with an outlook which, in its stress and earnestness, is very unlike any lower development of temper, often understand each other better than either would understand the mere man of the world—and sometimes they actually touch.

This Special Session at Calcutta began the Gandhi era in Congress politics which has lasted since then, except for a period in the twenties when he kept in the background and allowed the Swaraj Party, under the leadership of Deshbandhu C.R. Das and my father, to fill the picture. The whole look of the Congress changed; European clothes vanished and soon only khadi was to be seen; a new class of delegate, chiefly drawn from the lower middle classes became the type of Congressman; the language used became increasingly Hindustani, or sometimes the language of the province where the session was held, as many of the delegates did not understand English, and there was also a growing prejudice against using a foreign language in our national work; and a new life and enthusiasm and earnestness became evident in Congress gatherings.

After the Congress was over Gandhiji paid a visit to the veteran editor of the *Amrit Bazaar Patrika,* Syt Motilal Ghose, who was lying on his death-bed. I accompanied him. Motilal Babu blessed Gandhiji and his movement, and he added that, as for himself, he was going away to other regions, and wherever these might be, he had one great satisfaction—he would be somewhere where the British Empire did not exist. At last he would be beyond the reach of this Empire!

On our way back from the Calcutta Special Congress I accompanied Gandhiji to Santiniketan on a visit to Rabindra Nath Tagore and his most lovable elder brother 'Boro Dada'. We spent some days there, and I remember C.F. Andrews giving me some books which interested and influenced me greatly. They dealt with the economic aspects of imperialism in Africa. One of these books—Morell's *Black Man's Burden*—moved me greatly.

About this time or a little later, C.F. Andrews wrote a pamphlet advocating independence for India. I think it was called *Independence— the Immediate Need*. This was a brilliant essay based on some of Seeley's writings on India, and it seemed to me not only to make out an unanswerable case for independence but also to mirror the inmost recesses of our hearts. The deep urge that moved us and our half-formed desires seemed to take clear shape in his simple and earnest language. There was no economic background or socialism in what he had written; it was nationalism pure and simple, the feeling of the humiliation of India and a fierce desire to be rid of it and to put an end to our continuing degradation. It was wonderful that C.F. Andrews, a foreigner and one belonging to the dominant race in India, should echo that cry of our inmost being. Non-co-operation was essentially, as Seeley had said long ago, "the notion that it was shameful to assist the foreigner in maintaining his domination". And Andrews had written that "the only way of self-recovery was through some vital upheaval from within. The explosive force needed for such an upheaval must be generated within the soul of India itself. It could not come through loans and gifts and grants and concessions and proclamations from without. It must come from within . . . Therefore, it was with the intense joy of mental and spiritual deliverance from an intolerable burden, that I watched the actual outbreak of such an inner explosive force, as that which actually occurred when Mahatma Gandhi spoke to the heart of India the *mantram*—'Be free! Be slaves no more!' and the heart of India responded. In a sudden movement her fetters began to be loosened, and the pathway of freedom was opened."

The next three months witnessed the advancing tide of non-co-operation all over the country. The appeal for a boycott of the elections to the new legislatures was remarkably successful. It did not and could not prevent everybody from going to these councils and thus keep the seats vacant. Even a handful of voters could elect or there might be an unopposed election. But the great majority of voters abstained from voting, and all who cared for the vehemently expressed sense of the country refrained from standing as candidates. Sir Valentine Chirol happened to be in Allahabad on the election day, and he made a round of the polling booths. He returned amazed at the efficiency of the boycott. At one rural polling station, about fifteen miles from Allahabad city, he found that not a single voter had appeared. He gives an account of his experiences in one of his books on India.

The wisdom of this boycott had been questioned by Mr C.R. Das and others at the Calcutta session, but they stood by the Congress decision. The elections being over, this point of difference was removed, and the next full session of the Congress at Nagpur in December 1920 saw a reunion of many of the old Congress leaders on the plank of non-co-operation. The very success of the movement had convinced many a doubter and waverer.

A few old leaders, however, dropped out of the Congress after Calcutta, and among these a popular and well-known figure was that of Mr M.A.

Jinnah. Sarojini Naidu had called him the "Ambassador of Hindu–Muslim
unity", and he had been largely responsible in the past for bringing the
Muslim League nearer to the Congress. But the new developments in
the Congress—non-co-operation and the new constitution which made
it more of a popular and mass organization—were thoroughly disapproved
of by him. He disagreed on political grounds, but it was not politics in
the main that kept him away. There were still many people in the Congress
who were politically even less advanced than he was. But temperamentally
he did not fit in at all with the new Congress. He felt completely out of
his element in the khadi-clad crowd demanding speeches in Hindustani.
The enthusiasm of the people outside struck him as mob-hysteria. There
was as much difference between him and the Indian masses as between
Savile Row and Bond Street and the Indian village with its mud-huts.
He suggested once privately that only matriculates should be taken into
the Congress. I do not know if he was serious in making this remarkable
suggestion, but it was in harmony with his general outlook. So he drifted
away from the Congress and became a rather solitary figure in Indian
politics. Later, unhappily, the old Ambassador of Unity associated himself
with the most reactionary elements in Muslim communalism.

The Moderates or Liberals had, of course, nothing to do with the
Congress. They not only kept away from it; they merged themselves in
the Government, became ministers and high officials under the new
scheme, and helped in fighting non-co-operation and the Congress.
They had obtained almost what they desired, some reforms had been
granted, and so there was no need for them to agitate. While the country
was seething with excitement and becoming more and more
revolutionary, they became frankly counter-revolutionary, a part of the
Government itself. They were completely cut off from the people and
developed a habit, which has persisted since, of looking at problems
from the official point of view. They ceased to be a party in any real
sense and became a small number of individuals dotted about in a few
big cities. Mr Srinivasa Sastri became an Imperial Envoy, visiting, at the
instance of the British Government, various British dominions as well
as the United States of America, and strongly criticizing the Congress
and his own countrymen for the struggle they were carrying on against
that Government.

And yet the Liberals were far from happy. It is not a pleasant experience to be cut off from one's own people, to sense hostility even though one may not see it or hear it. A mass upheaval is not kind to the non-conformists, though Gandhiji's repeated warnings made non-co-operation far milder and gentler to its opponents than it otherwise would have been. But even so, the very atmosphere stifled those who opposed the movement, just as it invigorated and filled with life and energy those who supported it. Mass upheavals and real revolutionary movements always have this double effect: they encourage and bring out the personality of those who constitute the masses or side with them, and at the same time they suppress psychologically and stifle those who differ from them.

This was the reason why some people complained that non-co-operation was intolerant and tended to introduce a dead uniformity of opinion and action. There was truth in this complaint, but the truth lay in this, that non-co-operation was a mass movement, and it was led by a man of commanding personality who inspired devotion in India's millions. A more vital truth, however, lay in its effect on the masses. There was a tremendous feeling of release there, a throwing-off of a great burden, a new sense of freedom. The fear that had crushed them retired into the background, and they straightened their backs and raised their heads. Even in remote bazaars the common folk talked of the Congress and Swaraj (for the Nagpur Congress had finally made Swaraj the goal), and what had happened in the Punjab, and the Khilafat—but the word 'Khilafat' bore a strange meaning in most of the rural areas. People thought it came from *khilaf*, an Urdu word meaning 'against' or 'opposed to', and so they took it to mean: opposed to Government! They discussed, of course, especially their own particular economic grievances. Innumerable meetings and conferences added greatly to their political education.

Many of us who worked for the Congress programme lived in a kind of intoxication during the year 1921. We were full of excitement and optimism and a buoyant enthusiasm. We sensed the happiness of a person crusading for a cause. We were not troubled with doubts or hesitation; our path seemed to lie clear in front of us and we marched ahead, lifted up by the enthusiasm of others, and helping to push on others. We worked hard, harder than we had ever done before, for we knew that the conflict with the Government would come soon, and we wanted to do as much as possible before we were removed.

Above all, we had a sense of freedom and a pride in that freedom. The old feeling of oppression and frustration was completely gone. There was no more whispering, no roundabout legal phraseology to avoid getting into trouble with the authorities. We said what we felt and shouted it out from the house-tops. What did we care for the consequences? Prison? We looked forward to it; that would help our cause still further. The innumerable spies and secret-service men who used to surround us and follow us about became rather pitiable individuals as there was nothing secret for them to discover. All our cards were always on the table.

We had not only a feeling of satisfaction, at doing effective political work which was changing the face of India before our eyes and, as we believed, bringing Indian freedom very near, but also an agreeable sense of moral superiority over our opponents, both in regard to our goal and our methods. We were proud of our leader and of the unique method he had evolved, and often we indulged in fits of self-righteousness. In the midst of strife, and while we ourselves encouraged that strife, we had a sense of inner peace.

As our morale grew, that of the Government went down. They did not understand what was happening; it seemed that the old world they knew in India was toppling down. There was a new aggressive spirit abroad and self-reliance and fearlessness, and the great prop of British rule in India—prestige—was visibly wilting. Repression in a small way only strengthened the movement, and the Government hesitated for long before it would take action against the big leaders. It did not know what the consequences might be. Was the Indian Army reliable? Would the police carry out orders? As Lord Reading, the Viceroy, said in December 1921, they were "puzzled and perplexed".

An interesting circular was sent confidentially by the U.P. Government to its district officers in the summer of 1921. This circular, which was published later in a newspaper, stated with sorrow that the "initiative" was always with the "enemy", meaning the Congress, and this was an unfortunate state of affairs. Various methods were then suggested to regain the initiative, among them being the starting of those ludicrous bodies, the "Aman Sabhas". It was believed that this particular method of combating non-co-operation was adopted at the suggestion of the Liberal Ministers.

The nerves of many a British official began to give way. The strain was great. There was this ever-growing opposition and spirit of defiance which overshadowed official India like a vast monsoon cloud, and yet because of its peaceful methods it offered no handle, no grip, no opportunity for forcible suppression. The average Englishman did not believe in the *bonafides* of non-violence; he thought that all this was camouflage, a cloak to cover some vast secret design which would burst out in violent upheaval one day. Nurtured from childhood in the wide-spread belief that the East is a mysterious place, and in its bazaars and narrow lanes secret conspiracies are being continually hatched, the Englishman can seldom think straight on matters relating to these lands of supposed mystery. He never makes an attempt to understand that somewhat obvious and very unmysterious person, the Easterner. He keeps well away from him, gets his ideas about him from tales abounding in spies and secret societies, and then allows his imagination to run riot. So it was in the Punjab early in April 1919 when a sudden fear overwhelmed the authorities and the English people generally, made them see danger everywhere, a widespread rising, a second mutiny with its frightful massacres, and, in a blind, instinctive attempt at self-preservation at any cost, led them to that frightfulness, of which Jallianwala and the Crawling Lane of Amritsar have become symbols and bywords.

The year 1921 was a year of great tension, and there was much to irritate and annoy and unnerve the official. What was actually happening was bad enough, but what was imagined was far worse. I remember an instance which illustrates this riot of the imagination. My sister Swarup's wedding, which was taking place at Allahabad, was fixed for the 10th May, 1921, the actual date having been calculated, as usual on such occasions, by a reference to the Samvat calendar, and an auspicious day chosen. Gandhiji and a number of leading Congressmen, including the Ali brothers, had been invited, and to suit their convenience, a meeting of the Congress Working Committee was fixed at Allahabad about that time. The local Congressmen wanted to profit by the presence of famous leaders from outside, and so they organized a district conference on a big scale, expecting a large number of peasants from the surrounding rural areas.

There was a great deal of bustle and excitement in Allahabad on account of these political gatherings. This had a remarkable effect on the nerves of some people. I learnt one day through a barrister friend that many English people were thoroughly upset and expected some sudden upheaval in the city. They distrusted their Indian servants, and carried about revolvers in their pockets. It was even said privately that the Allahabad Fort was kept in readiness for the English colony to retire there in case of need. I was much surprised and could not make out why any one should contemplate the possibility of a rising in the sleepy and peaceful city of Allahabad just when the very apostle of non-violence was going to visit us. Oh, it was said, 10th May (the day accidentally fixed for my sister's marriage) was the anniversary of the outbreak of the Mutiny at Meerut in 1857 and this was going to be celebrated!

Owing to the prominence given to the Khilafat movement in 1921 a large number of Moulvies and Muslim religious leaders took a prominent part in the political struggle. They gave a definite religious tinge to the movement, and Muslims generally were greatly influenced by it. Many a Westernized Muslim, who was not of a particularly religious turn of mind, began to grow a beard and otherwise conform to the tenets of Orthodoxy. The influence and prestige of the Moulvies, which had been gradually declining owing to new ideas and a progressive Westernization, began to grow again and dominate the Muslim community. The Ali brothers, themselves of a religious turn of mind, helped in this process, and so did Gandhiji, who paid the greatest regard to the Moulvies and the Maulanas.

Gandhiji, indeed, was continually laying stress on the religious and spiritual side of the movement. His religion was not dogmatic, but it did mean a definitely religious outlook on life, and the whole movement was strongly influenced by this and took on a revivalist character so far as the masses were concerned. The great majority of Congress workers naturally tried to model themselves after their leader and even repeated his language. And yet Gandhiji's leading colleagues in the Working Committee—my father, Deshbandhu Das, Lala Lajpat Rai, and others— were not men of religion in the ordinary sense of the word, and they considered political problems on the political plane only. In their public utterances they did not bring in religion. But whatever they said had far less influence than the force of their personal example—had they not given up a great deal that the world values and taken to simpler ways of living? This in itself was taken as a sign of religion and helped in spreading the atmosphere of revivalism.

I used to be troubled sometimes at the growth of this religious element in our politics, both on the Hindu and the Muslim side. I did not like it at all. Much that Moulvies and Maulanas and Swamis and the like said in their public addresses seemed to me most unfortunate. Their history and sociology and economics appeared to me all wrong, and the religious twist that was given to everything prevented all clear thinking. Even some of Gandhiji's phrases sometimes jarred upon me—thus his frequent reference to *Rama Raj* as a golden age which was to return. But I was powerless to intervene, and I consoled myself with the thought that Gandhiji used the words because they were well known and understood by the masses. He had an amazing knack of reaching the heart of the people.

But I did not worry myself much over these matters. I was too full of my work and the progress of our movement to care for such trifles, as I thought at the time they were. A vast movement had all sorts and kinds of people in it, and so long as our main direction was correct, a few eddies and backwaters did not matter. As for Gandhiji himself, he was a very difficult person to understand, sometimes his language was almost incomprehensible to an average modern. But we felt that we knew him quite well enough to realize that he was a great and unique man and a glorious leader, and having put our faith in him we gave him an almost blank cheque, for the time being at least. Often we discussed his fads and peculiarities among ourselves and said, half-humorously, that when Swaraj came these fads must not be encouraged.

Many of us, however, were too much under his influence in political and other matters to remain wholly immune even in the sphere of religion. Where a direct attack might not have succeeded, many an indirect approach went a long way to undermine the defences. The outward ways of religion did not appeal to me, and above all I disliked the exploitation of the people by the so-called men of religion, but still I toned down towards it. I came nearer to a religious frame of mind in 1921 than at any other time since my early boyhood. Even so I did not come very near.

What I admired was the moral and ethical side of our movement and of satyagraha. I did not give an absolute allegiance to the doctrine of non-violence or accept it for ever, but it attracted me more and more, and the belief grew upon me that, situated as we were in India and with our background and traditions, it was the right policy for us. The spiritualization of politics, using the word not in its narrow religious sense, seemed to me a fine idea. A worthy end should have worthy means leading up to it. That seemed not only a good ethical doctrine but sound, practical politics, for the means that are not good often defeat the end in view and raise new problems and difficulties. And then it seemed so unbecoming, so degrading to the self-respect of an individual or a nation to submit to such means, to go through the mire. How can one escape being sullied by it? How can we march ahead swiftly and with dignity if we stoop or crawl?

Such were my thoughts then. And the non-co-operation movement offered me what I wanted—the goal of national freedom and (as I thought) the ending of the exploitation of the underdog, and the means which satisfied my moral sense and gave me a sense of personal freedom. So great was this personal satisfaction that even a possibility of failure did not count for much, for such failure could only be temporary. I did not understand or feel drawn to the metaphysical part of the Bhagavad Gita, but I liked to read the verses—recited every evening in Gandhiji's ashram prayers—which say what a man should be like: Calm of purpose, serene and unmoved, doing his job and not caring overmuch for the result of his action. Not being very calm or detached myself, I suppose, this ideal appealed to me all the more.

11

NINETEEN TWENTY-ONE AND THE
FIRST IMPRISONMENT

Nineteen twenty-one was an extraordinary year for us. There was a strange mixture of nationalism and politics and religion and mysticism and fanaticism. Behind all this was agrarian trouble and, in the big cities, a rising working-class movement. Nationalism and a vague but intense country-wide idealism sought to bring together all these various, and sometimes mutually contradictory, discontents, and succeeded to a remarkable degree. And yet this nationalism itself was a composite force, and behind it could be distinguished a Hindu nationalism, a Muslim nationalism partly looking beyond the frontiers of India, and, what was more in consonance with the spirit of the times, an Indian nationalism. For the time being they overlapped and all pulled together. It was *Hindu-Musalman ki Jai* everywhere. It was remarkable how Gandhiji seemed to cast a spell on all classes and groups of people and drew them into one motley crowd struggling in one direction. He became, indeed (to use a phrase which has been applied to another leader), "a symbolic expression of the confused desires of the people".

Even more remarkable was the fact that these desires and passions were relatively free from hatred of the alien rulers against whom they were directed. Nationalism is essentially an anti-feeling, and it feeds and fattens on hatred and anger against other national groups, and especially against the foreign rulers of a subject country. There was certainly this hatred and anger in India in 1921 against the British but, in comparison with other countries similarly situated, it was extraordinarily little. Undoubtedly this was due to Gandhiji's insistence on the implications of non-violence. It was also due to the feeling of release and power that came to the whole country with the inauguration of the movement and the widespread belief in success in the near future. Why be angry and full of hate when we were doing so well and were likely to win through soon? We felt that we could afford to be generous.

We were not so generous in our hearts, though our actions were circumspect and proper, towards the handful of our own countrymen who took sides against us and opposed the national movement. It was not a question of hatred or anger, for they carried no weight whatever and we could ignore them. But deep within us was contempt for their weakness and opportunism and betrayal of national honour and self-respect.

So we went on, vaguely but intensely, the exhilaration of action holding us in its grip. But about our goal there was an entire absence of clear thinking. It seems surprising now, how completely we ignored the theoretical aspects, the philosophy of our movement as well as the definite objective that we should have. Of course we all grew eloquent about Swaraj, but each one of us probably interpreted the word in his or her own way. To most of the younger men it meant political independence, or something like it, and a democratic form of government, and we said so in our public utterances. Many of us also thought that inevitably this would result in a lessening of the burdens that crushed the workers and the peasantry. But it was obvious that to most of our leaders Swaraj meant something much less than independence. Gandhiji was delightfully vague on the subject, and he did not encourage clear thinking about it either. But he always spoke, vaguely but definitely, in terms of the under-dog, and this brought great comfort to many of us, although, at the same time, he was full of assurances to the top-dog also. Gandhiji's stress was never on the intellectual approach to a problem but on character and piety. He did succeed amazingly in giving backbone and character to the Indian people. There were many, however, who developed neither much backbone nor character, but who imagined that a limp body and a flabby look might be the outward semblance of piety.

It was this extraordinary stiffening-up of the masses that filled us with confidence. A demoralized, backward, and broken-up people suddenly straightened their backs and lifted their heads and took part in disciplined, joint action on a country-wide scale. This action itself, we felt, would give irresistible power to the masses. We ignored the necessity of thought behind the action: we forgot that without a conscious ideology and objective the energy and enthusiasm of the masses must end largely in smoke. To some extent the revivalist element in our movement carried us on; a feeling that non-violence as conceived for political or economic movements or for righting wrongs was a new message which our people were destined to give to the world. We became victims to the curious illusion of all peoples and all nations that in some way they are a chosen race. Non-violence was the moral equivalent of war and of all violent struggle. It was not merely an ethical alternative, but it was effective also. Few of us, I think, accepted Gandhiji's old ideas about machinery and modern civilization. We thought that even he looked upon them as Utopian and as largely inapplicable to modern conditions. Certainly most of us were not prepared to reject the achievements of modern civilization, although we may have felt that some variation to suit Indian conditions was possible. Personally, I have always felt attracted towards big machinery and fast travelling. Still there can be no doubt that Gandhiji's ideology influenced many people and made them critical of the machine and all its consequences. So, while some looked to the future, others looked back to the past. And, curiously, both felt that the joint action they were indulging in was worthwhile, and this made it easy to bear sacrifice and face self-denial.

I became wholly absorbed and wrapt in the movement, and large numbers of other people did likewise. I gave up all my other associations and contacts, old friends, books, even newspapers, except in so far as they dealt with the work in hand. I had kept up till then some reading of current books and had tried to follow the developments of world affairs. But there was no time for this now. In spite of the strength of my family bonds, I almost forgot my family, my wife, my daughter. It was only long afterwards that I realized what a burden and a trial I must have been to them in those days, and what amazing patience and tolerance my wife had shown towards me. I lived in offices and committee meetings and crowds. "Go to the villages" was the slogan, and we trudged many a mile across fields and visited distant villages and addressed peasant meetings. I experienced the thrill of mass-feeling, the power of influencing the mass. I began to understand a little the psychology of the crowd, the difference between the city masses and the peasantry, and I felt at home in the dust and discomfort, the pushing and jostling of large gatherings, though their want of discipline often irritated me. Since those days I have sometimes had to face hostile and angry crowds, worked up to a state when a spark would light a flame, and I found that that early experience and the confidence it begot in me stood me in good stead. Always I went straight to the crowd and trusted it, and so far I have always had courtesy and appreciation from it, even though there was no agreement. But crowds are fickle, and the future may have different experiences in store for me.

I took to the crowd and the crowd took to me, and yet I never lost myself in it; always I felt apart from it. From my separate mental perch I looked at it critically, and I never ceased to wonder how I, who was so different in every way from those thousands who surrounded me, different in habits, in desires, in mental and spiritual outlook, how I had managed to gain goodwill and a measure of confidence from these people. Was it because they took me for something other than I was? Would they bear with me when they knew me better? Was I gaining their goodwill under false pretences? I tried to be frank and straightforward to them; I even spoke harshly to them sometimes and criticized many of their pet beliefs and customs, but still they put up with me. And yet I could not get rid of the idea that their affection was meant not for me as I was, but for some fanciful image of me that they had formed. How long could that false image endure? And why should it be allowed to endure? And when it fell down and they saw the reality, what then?

I am vain enough in many ways, but there could be no question of vanity with these crowds of simple folk. There was no posing about them, no vulgarity, as in the case of many of us of the middle classes who consider ourselves their betters. They were dull certainly, uninteresting individually, but in the mass they produced a feeling of overwhelming pity and a sense of ever-impending tragedy.

Very different were our conferences where our chosen workers, including myself, performed on the platform. There was sufficient posing there and no lack of vulgarity in our flamboyant addresses. All of us must have been to some extent guilty of this, but some of the minor Khilafat leaders probably led the rest. It is not easy to behave naturally on a platform before a large audience, and few of us had previous experience of such publicity. So we tried to look as, we imagined, leaders should look, thoughtful and serious, with no trace of levity or frivolity. When we walked or talked or smiled we were conscious of thousands of eyes staring at us and we reacted accordingly. Our speeches were often very eloquent but, equally often, singularly pointless. It is difficult to see oneself as other's see one. And so, unable to criticize myself, I took to watching carefully the ways of others, and I found considerable amusement in this occupation. And then the terrible thought would strike me that I might perhaps appear equally ludicrous to others.

Right through the year 1921 individual Congress workers were being arrested and sentenced, but there were no mass arrests. The Ali Brothers had received long sentences for inciting the Indian Army to disaffection. Their words, for which they had been sentenced, were repeated at hundreds of platforms by thousands of persons. I was threatened in the summer with proceedings for sedition because of some speeches I had delivered. No such step, however, was taken then. The end of the year brought matters to a head. The Prince of Wales was coming to India, and the Congress had proclaimed a boycott of all the functions in connection with his visit. Towards the end of November the Congress volunteers in Bengal were declared illegal and this was followed by a similar declaration for the United Provinces. Deshbandhu Das gave a stirring message to Bengal: "I feel the handcuffs on my wrists and the weight of iron chains on my body. It is the agony of bondage. The whole of India is a vast prison. The work of the Congress must be carried on. What matters it whether I am taken or left? What matters it whether I am dead or alive?" In the U.P. we took up the challenge and not only announced that our volunteer organization would continue to function, but published lists of names of volunteers in the daily newspapers. The first list was headed by my father's name. He was not a volunteer but, simply for the purpose of defying the Government order, he joined and gave his name. Early in December, a few days before the Prince came to our province, mass arrests began.

We knew that matters had at last come to a head; the inevitable conflict between the Congress and the Government was about to break out. Prison was still an unknown place, the idea of going there still a novelty. I was sitting rather late one day in the Congress office at Allahabad trying to clear up arrears of work. An excited clerk told me that the police had come with a search warrant and were surrounding the office building. I was, of course, a little excited also, for it was my first experience of the kind, but the desire to show off was strong, the wish to appear perfectly cool and collected, unaffected by the comings and goings of the police. So I asked a clerk to accompany the police officer in his search round the office rooms, and insisted on the rest of the staff carrying on their usual work and ignoring the police. A little later a friend and a colleague, who had been arrested just outside the office, came to me, accompanied by a policeman, to bid me good-bye. I was so full of the conceit that I must treat these novel occurrences as everyday happenings that I treated my colleague in a most unfeeling manner. Casually I asked him and the policeman to wait till I had finished the letter I was writing. Soon news came of other arrests in the city. I decided at last to go home and see what was happening there. I found the inevitable police searching part of the large house and learnt that they had come to arrest both father and me.

Nothing that we could have done would have fitted in so well with our programme of boycotting the Prince's visit. Wherever he was taken he was met with *hartals* and deserted streets. Allahabad, when he came, seemed to be a city of the dead; Calcutta, a few days later, suddenly put a temporary stop to all the activities of a great city. It was hard on the Prince of Wales; he was not to blame, and there was no feeling against him whatever. But the Government of India had tried to exploit his personality to prop up their decaying prestige.

There was an orgy of arrests and convictions, especially in the United Provinces and in Bengal. All the prominent Congress leaders and workers in these provinces were arrested, and ordinary volunteers by the thousand went to prison. They were, at first, largely city men and there seemed to be an inexhaustible supply of volunteers for prison. The U.P. Provincial Congress Committee was arrested *en bloc* (fifty-five members) as they were actually holding a committee meeting. Many people, who had so far taken no part in any Congress or political activity, were carried away by the wave of enthusiasm and insisted on being arrested. There were cases of Government clerks, returning from their offices in the evening, being swept away by this current and landing in gaol instead of their homes. Young men and boys would crowd inside the police lorries and refuse to come out. Every evening we could hear from inside the gaol, lorry after lorry arriving outside heralded by our slogans and shouts. The gaols were crowded and the gaol officials were at their wits' ends at this extraordinary phenomenon. It happened sometimes that a police lorry would bring, according to the warrant accompanying it, a certain number of prisoners—no names were or could be mentioned. Actually, a larger number than that mentioned would emerge from the lorry and the gaol officials did not know how to meet this novel situation. There was nothing in the *Jail Manual* about it.

Gradually the Government gave up the policy of indiscriminate arrests; only noted workers were picked out. Gradually also the first flush of enthusiasm of the people cooled down and, owing to the absence in prison of all the trusted workers, a feeling of indecision and helplessness spread. But the change was superficial only, and there was still thunder in the air and the atmosphere was tense and pregnant with revolutionary possibilities. During the months of December 1921 and January 1922 it is estimated that about 30,000 persons were sentenced to imprisonment in connection with the non-cooperation movement. But though most of the prominent men and workers were in prison, the leader of the whole struggle, Mahatma Gandhi, was still out, issuing from day to day messages and directions which inspired the people, as well as checking many an undesirable activity. The Government had not touched him so far, for they feared the consequences, the reactions on the Indian Army and the police.

Suddenly, early in February 1922, the whole scene shifted, and we in prison learnt, to our amazement and consternation, that Gandhiji had stopped the aggressive aspects of our struggle, that he had suspended civil resistance. We read that this was because of what had happened near the village of Chauri Chaura where a mob of villagers had retaliated on some policemen by setting fire to the police-station and burning half a dozen or so policemen in it.

We were angry when we learnt of this stoppage of our struggle at a time when we seemed to be consolidating our position and advancing on all fronts. But our disappointment and anger in prison could do little good to any one, and civil resistance stopped and non-co-operation wilted away. After many months of strain and anxiety the Government breathed again, and for the first time had the opportunity of taking the initiative. A few weeks later they arrested Gandhiji and sentenced him for a long term of imprisonment.

12

NON-VIOLENCE AND THE DOCTRINE
OF THE SWORD

The sudden suspension of our movement after the Chauri Chaura incident was resented, I think, by almost all the prominent Congress leaders—other than Gandhiji of course. My father (who was in gaol at the time) was much upset by it. The younger people were naturally even more agitated. Our mounting hopes tumbled to the ground, and this mental reaction was to be expected. What troubled us even more were the reasons given for this suspension and the consequences that seemed to flow from them. Chauri Chaura may have been and was a deplorable occurrence and wholly opposed to the spirit of the non-violent movement; but were a remote village and a mob of excited peasants in an out-of-the-way place going to put an end, for some time at least, to our national struggle for freedom? If this was the inevitable consequence of a sporadic act of violence, then surely there was something lacking in the philosophy and technique of a non-violent struggle. For it seemed to us to be impossible to guarantee against the occurrence of some such untoward incident. Must we train the three hundred and odd millions of India in the theory and practice of non-violent action before we could go forward? And, even so, how many of us could say that under extreme provocation from the police we would be able to remain perfectly peaceful? But even if we succeeded, what of the numerous *agents provocateurs,* stool pigeons, and the like who crept into our movement and indulged in violence themselves or induced others to do so? If this was the sole condition of its function, then the non-violent method of resistance would always fail.

We had accepted that method, the Congress had made that method its own, because of a belief in its effectiveness. Gandhiji had placed it before the country not only as the right method but as the most effective one for our purpose. In spite of its negative name it was a dynamic method, the very opposite of a meek submission to a tyrant's will. It was not a coward's refuge from action, but the brave man's defiance of evil and national subjection. But what was the use of the bravest and the strongest if a few odd persons—maybe even our opponents in the guise of friends—had the power to upset or end our movement by their rash behaviour?

Gandhiji had pleaded for the adoption of the way of nonviolence, of peaceful non-co-operation, with all the eloquence and persuasive power which he so abundantly possessed. His language had been simple and unadorned, his voice and appearance cool and clear and devoid of all emotion, but behind that outward covering of ice there was the heat of a blazing fire and concentrated passion, and the words he uttered winged their way to the innermost recesses of our minds and hearts, and created a strange ferment there. The way he pointed out was hard and difficult, but it was a brave path, and it seemed to lead to the promised land of freedom. Because of that promise we pledged our faith and marched ahead. In a famous article—"The Doctrine of the Sword"—he had written in 1920:

> I do believe that when there is only a choice between cowardice and violence, I would advise violence . . . I would rather have India resort to arms in order to defend her honour than that she should in a cowardly manner become or remain a helpless victim to her own dishonour. But I believe that non-violence is infinitely superior to violence, forgiveness is more manly than punishment. क्षमा वीरस्य भूषणम्
>
> Forgiveness adorns a soldier. But abstinence is forgiveness only when there is power to punish; it is meaningless when it pretends to proceed from a helpless creature. A mouse hardly forgives a cat when it allows itself to be torn to pieces by her . . . But I do not believe India to be helpless, I do not believe myself to be a helpless creature . . .
>
> Let me not be misunderstood. Strength does not come from physical capacity. It comes from an indomitable will . . .
>
> I am not a visionary. I claim to be a practical idealist. The religion of non-violence is not meant merely for the Rishis and saints. It is meant for the common people as well. Non-violence is the law of our species as violence is the law of the brute. The spirit lies dormant in the brute and he knows no law but that of physical might. The dignity of man requires obedience to a higher law—to the strength of the spirit.
>
> I have therefore ventured to place before India the ancient law of self-

sacrifice. For Satyagrah and its off-shoots, non-co-operation and civil resistance, are nothing but new names for the law of suffering. The Rishis who discovered the law of non-violence in the midst of violence, were greater geniuses than Newton. They were themselves greater warriors than Wellington. Having themselves known the use of arms, they realized their uselessness and taught a weary world that its salvation lay not through violence but through non-violence.

Non-violence in its dynamic condition means conscious suffering. It does not mean meek submission to the will of the evil-doer, but it means the putting of one's whole soul against the will of the tyrant. Working under this law of our being, it is possible for a single individual to defy the whole might of an unjust empire to save his honour, his religion, his soul and lay the foundation for that empire's fall or regeneration.

And so I am not pleading for India to practise non-violence because it is weak. I want her to practise non-violence being conscious of her strength and power ... I want India to recognize that she has a soul that cannot perish, and that can rise triumphant above any physical weakness and defy the physical combination of a whole world ...

I isolate this non-co-operation from Sinn Feinism, for, it is so conceived as to be incapable of being offered side by side with violence. But I invite even the school of violence to give this peaceful non-co-operation a trial. It will not fail through its inherent weakness. It may fail because of poverty of response. Then will be the time for real danger. The high-souled men, who are unable to suffer national humiliation any longer, will want to vent their wrath. They will take to violence. So far as I know, they must perish without delivering themselves or their country from the wrong. If India takes up the doctrine of the sword, she may gain momentary victory. Then India will cease to be the pride of my heart. I am wedded to India because I owe my all to her. I believe absolutely that she has a mission for the world.

We were moved by these arguments, but for us and for the National Congress as a whole the non-violent method was not, and could not be, a religion or an unchallengeable creed or dogma. It could only be a policy and a method promising certain results, and by those results it would have to be finally judged. Individuals might make of it a religion or incontrovertible creed. But no political organization, so long as it remained political, could do so.

Chauri Chaura and its consequences made us examine these

implications of non-violence as a method, and we felt that, if Gandhiji's argument for the suspension of civil resistance was correct, our opponents would always have the power to create circumstances which would necessarily result in our abandoning the struggle. Was this the fault of the non-violent method itself or of Gandhiji's interpretation of it? After all, he was the author and originator of it, and who could be a better judge of what it was and what it was not? And without him where was our movement?

Many years later, just before the 1930 Civil Disobedience movement began, Gandhiji, much to our satisfaction, made this point clear. He stated that the movement should not be abandoned because of the occurrence of sporadic acts of violence. If the non-violent method of struggle could not function because of such almost inevitable happenings, then it was obvious that it was not an ideal method for all occasions, and this he was not prepared to admit. For him the method, being the right method, should suit all circumstances and should be able to function, at any rate in a restricted way, even in a hostile atmosphere. Whether this interpretation, which widened the scope of non-violent action, represented an evolution in his own mind or not I do not know.

As a matter of fact even the suspension of civil resistance in February 1922 was certainly not due to Chauri Chaura alone, although most people imagined so. That was only the last straw. Gandhiji has often acted almost by instinct; by long and close association with the masses he appears to have developed, as great popular leaders often do, a new sense which tells him how the mass feels, what it does and what it can do. He reacts to this instinctive feeling and fashions his action accordingly, and later, for the benefit of his surprised and resentful colleagues, tries to clothe his decision with reasons. This covering is often very inadequate, as it seemed after Chauri Chaura. At that time our movement, in spite of its apparent power and the widespread enthusiasm, was going to pieces. All organization and discipline was disappearing; almost all our good men were in prison, and the masses had so far received little training to carry on by themselves. Any unknown man who wanted to do so could take charge of a Congress Committee and, as a matter of fact, large numbers of undesirable men, including *agents provocateurs*, came to the front and even controlled some local Congress and Khilafat organizations. There was no way of checking them.

This kind of thing is, of course, to some extent almost inevitable in such a struggle. The leaders must take the lead in going to prison, and trust to others to carry on. All that can be done is to train the masses in some simple kinds of activity and, even more so, to abstain from certain other kinds of activity. In 1930 we had already spent several years in giving some such training, and the Civil Disobedience movement then and in 1932 was a very powerful and organized affair. This was lacking in 1921 and 1922, and there was little behind the excitement and enthusiasm of the people. There is little doubt that if the movement had continued there would have been growing sporadic violence in many places. This would have been crushed by Government in a bloody manner and a reign of terror established which would have thoroughly demoralized the people.

These were probably the reasons and influences that worked in Gandhiji's mind, and granting his premises and the desirability of carrying on with the technique of non-violence, his decision was right. He had to stop the rot and build anew. From another and an entirely different view-point his decision might be considered wrong, but that view-point had nothing to do with the non-violent method. It was not possible to have it both ways. To invite a bloody suppression of the movement in that particular sporadic way and at that stage would not, of course, have put an end to the national movement, for such movements have a way of rising from their ashes. Temporary set-backs are often helpful in clarifying issues and in giving backbone; what matters is not a set-back or apparent defeat, but the principles and ideals: If these principles can be kept untarnished by the masses, then recovery comes soon. But what were our principles and objectives in 1921 and 1922? A vague Swaraj with no clear ideology behind it and a particular technique of non-violent struggle. The latter method would naturally have gone if the country had taken to sporadic violence on any big scale, and as to the former, there was little to hold on to. The people generally were not strong enough to carry on the struggle for long and, in spite of almost universal discontent with foreign rule and sympathy with the Congress, there was not enough backbone or organization. They could not last. Even the crowds that went to prison did so on the spur of the moment, expecting the whole thing to be over very soon.

It may be, therefore, that the decision to suspend civil resistance in

1922 was a right one, though the manner of doing it left much to be desired and brought about a certain demoralization.

It is possible, however, that this sudden bottling up of a great movement contributed to a tragic development in the country. The drift to sporadic and futile violence in the political struggle was stopped, but the suppressed violence had to find a way out, and in the following years this perhaps aggravated the communal trouble. The communalists of various denominations, mostly political reactionaries, had been forced to lie low because of the overwhelming mass support for the non-co-operation and civil disobedience movement. They emerged now from their retirement. Many others, secret service agents and people who sought to please the authorities by creating communal friction, also worked on the same theme. The Moplah rising and its extraordinarily cruel suppression—what a horrible thing was the baking to death of the Moplah prisoners in the closed railway vans!—had already given a handle to those who stirred the waters of communal discord. It is just possible that if civil resistance had not been stopped and the movement had been crushed by Government, there would have been less communal bitterness and less superfluous energy left for the subsequent communal riots.

Before civil resistance was called off an incident occurred which might have led to different results. The first wave of civil resistance amazed and frightened the Government. It was then that Lord Reading, the Viceroy, said in a public speech that he was troubled and perplexed. The Prince of Wales was in India, and his presence added greatly to the Government's responsibility. An attempt was made by the Government in December 1921, soon after the mass arrests at the beginning of the month, to come to some understanding with the Congress. This was especially in view of the Prince's forthcoming visit to Calcutta. There were some informal talks between representatives of the Bengal Government and Deshbandhu Das, who was in gaol then. A proposal seems to have been made, that a small round table conference might take place between the Government and the Congress. This proposal appears to have fallen through because Gandhiji insisted that Maulana Mohamad Ali, who was then in prison in Karachi, should be present at this conference. Government would not agree to this.

Mr C.R. Das did not approve of Gandhiji's attitude in this matter and, when he came out of prison later, he publicly criticized him and said that he had blundered. Most of us (we were in gaol) do not know the details of what took place then, and it is difficult to judge without all the facts. It seems, however, that little good could have come out of the conference at that stage. It was an effort on the part of Government to tide over somehow the period of the Prince's visit to Calcutta. The basic problems that faced us would have remained. Nine years later, when the nation and the Congress were far stronger, such a conference took place without any great results. But apart from this, it seems to me that Gandhiji's insistence on Mohamad Ali's presence was perfectly justified. Not only as a Congress leader but as the leader of the Khilafat movement—and the Khilafat question was then an important plank in the Congress programme—his presence was essential. No policy or manoeuvre can ever be a right one if it involves the forsaking of a colleague. The fact that Government were not prepared to release him from gaol itself shows that there was no likelihood of any results from a conference.

Both my father and I had been sentenced to six months' imprisonment on different charges and by different courts. The trials were farcical and, as was our custom, we took no part in them. It was easy enough, of course, to find enough material in our speeches or other activities for a conviction. But the actual choice was amusing. Father was tried as a member of an illegal organization, the Congress Volunteers, and to prove this a form with his signature in Hindi was produced. The signature was certainly his, but, as it happened, he had hardly ever signed in Hindi before, and very few persons could recognize his Hindi signature. A tattered gentleman was then produced who swore to the signature. The man was quite illiterate, and he held the signature upside down when he examined it. My daughter, aged four at the time, had her first experience of the dock during father's trial, as he held her in his arms throughout.

My offence was distributing notices for a *hartal*. This was no offence under the law then, though I believe it is one now, for we are rapidly advancing towards Dominion Status. However, I was sentenced. Three months later I was informed in the prison, where I was with my father and others, that some revising authority had come to the conclusion that I was wrongly sentenced and I was to be discharged. I was surprised, as no one had taken any step on my behalf. The suspension of civil resistance had apparently galvanized the revising judges into activity. I was sorry to go out, leaving my father behind.

I decided to go almost immediately to Gandhiji in Ahmedabad. Before I arrived there he had been arrested, and my interview with him took place in Sabarmati Prison. I was present at his trial. It was a memorable occasion, and those of us who were present are not likely ever to forget it. The judge, an Englishman, behaved with dignity and feeling. Gandhiji's statement to the court was a most moving one, and we came away, emotionally stirred, and with the impress of his vivid phrases and striking images in our mind.

I came back to Allahabad. I felt unhappy and lonely outside the prison when so many of my friends and colleagues were behind prison bars. I found that the Congress organization was not functioning well and I tried to put it straight. In particular I interested myself in the boycott of foreign cloth. This item of our programme still continued in spite of the withdrawal of civil resistance. Nearly all the cloth merchants in Allahabad had pledged themselves not to import or purchase foreign cloth, and had formed an association for the purpose. The rules of this association laid down that any infringement would be punished by a fine. I found that several of the big dealers had broken their pledges and were importing foreign cloth. This was very unfair to those who stuck to their pledges. We remonstrated with little result, and the cloth dealers' association seemed to be powerless to take action. So we decided to picket the shops of the erring merchants. Even a hint of picketing was enough for our purpose. Fines were paid, pledges were taken afresh. The money from the fines went to the cloth merchants' association.

Two or three days later I was arrested, together with a number of colleagues who had taken part in the negotiations with the merchants. We were charged with criminal intimidation and extortion! I was further charged with some other offences, including sedition. I did not defend myself, but I made a long statement in court. I was sentenced on at least three counts, including intimidation and extortion, but the sedition charge was not proceeded with, as it was probably considered that I had already got as much as I deserved. As far as I remember there were three sentences, two of which were for eighteen months and were concurrent. In all, I think, I was sentenced to a year and nine months. That was my second sentence. I went back to prison after about six weeks spent outside it.

13

LUCKNOW DISTRICT GAOL

Imprisonment for political offences was not a new thing in the India of 1921. From the time of the Bengal partition agitation especially, there had always been a continuous stream of men going to prison, sentenced often to very long terms. There had been internments without trial also. The greatest Indian leader of the day, Lokamanya Tilak, was sentenced in his declining years to six years' imprisonment. The Great War speeded up this process of internment and imprisonment, and conspiracy cases became frequent, usually resulting in death sentences or life terms. The Ali brothers and M. Abul Kalam Azad were among the war-time internees. Soon after the war, martial law in the Punjab took a heavy toll, and large numbers were sentenced in conspiracy cases or summary trials. So political imprisonment had become a frequent enough occurrence in India, but so far it had not been deliberately courted. It had come in the course of a person's activities, or perhaps because the secret police did not fancy him, and every effort was made to avoid it by means of a defence in the law court. In South Africa, of course, a different example had been set by Gandhiji and thousands of his followers in their campaign of Satyagraha.

But still in 1921 prison was an almost unknown place, and very few knew what happened behind the grim gates that swallowed the new convict. Vaguely we imagined that its inhabitants were desperate people and dangerous criminals. In our minds the place was associated with isolation, humiliation, and suffering, and, above all, the fear of the unknown. Frequent references to gaol-going from 1920 onwards, and the march of many of our comrades to prison, gradually accustomed us to the idea and took away the edge from that almost involuntary feeling of repugnance and reluctance. But no amount of previous mental preparation could prevent the tension and nervous excitement that filled us when we first entered the iron gates. Since those days, thirteen years ago, I imagine that at least 300,000 men and women of India have entered those gates for political offences, although often enough the actual charge has been under some other section of the criminal code. Thousands of these have gone in and out many a time; they have got to know well what to expect inside: they have tried to adapt themselves to the strange life there, as far as one can adapt oneself to an existence full of abnormality and a dull suffering and a dreadful monotony. We grow accustomed to it, as one grows accustomed to almost anything; and yet every time that we enter those gates again, there is a bit of the old excitement, a feeling of tension, a quickening of the pulse. And the eyes turn back involuntarily to take a last good look outside at the greenery and wide spaces, and people and conveyances moving about, and familiar faces that they may not see again for a long time.

My first term in gaol, which ended rather suddenly after three months, was a hectic period both for us and the gaol staff. The gaol officials were half paralyzed by the influx of the new type of convict. The number itself of these newcomers, added to from day to day, was extraordinary and created an impression of a flood which might sweep away the old traditional landmarks. More upsetting still was the type of the newcomer. It belonged to all classes, but had a high proportion of the middle class. All these classes, however, had this in common: they differed entirely from the ordinary convict, and it was not easy to treat them in the old way. This was recognized by the authorities, but there was nothing to take the place of the existing rules; there were no precedents and no experience. The average Congress prisoner was not very meek and mild, and even inside the gaol walls numbers gave him a feeling of strength. The agitation outside, and the new interest of the public in what transpired inside the prisons, added to this. In spite of this somewhat aggressive attitude, our general policy was one of co-operation with the gaol authorities. But for our help, the troubles of the officials would have been far greater. The gaoler would come to us frequently and ask us to visit some of the barracks containing our volunteers in order to soothe them or get them to agree to something.

We had come to prison of our own accord, many of the volunteers indeed having pushed their way in almost uninvited. There was thus hardly any question of any one of them trying to escape. If he had any desire to go out, he could do so easily by expressing regret for his action or giving an undertaking that he would refrain from such activity in future. An attempt to escape would only bring a measure of ignominy, and in itself was tantamount to a withdrawal from political activity of the civil resistance variety. The superintendent of our prison in Lucknow fully appreciated this and used to tell the gaoler (who was a Khan Sahib) that if he could succeed in allowing some of the Congress prisoners to escape he, the superintendent, would recommend him to Government for the title of Khan Bahadur.

Most of our fellow-prisoners were kept in huge barracks in the inner circle of the prison. About eighteen of us, selected I suppose for better treatment, were kept in an old weaving shed with a large open space attached. My father, two of my cousins, and I had a small shed to ourselves, about 20 feet by 16. We had considerable freedom in moving about from one barrack to another. Frequent interviews with relatives outside were allowed. Newspapers came, and the daily news of fresh arrests and the developments of our struggle kept up an atmosphere of excitement. Mutual discussions and talks took up a lot of time, and I could do little reading or other solid work. I spent the mornings in a thorough cleaning and washing of our shed, in washing father's and my own clothes, and in spinning. It was winter, the best time of year in North India. For the first few weeks we were allowed to open classes for our volunteers, or such of them as were illiterate, to teach them Hindi and Urdu and other elementary subjects. In the afternoons we played volley-ball.[1]

Gradually restrictions grew. We were stopped from going outside our enclosure and visiting the part of the gaol where most of our volunteers were kept. The classes naturally stopped. I was discharged about that time.

I went out early in March, and six or seven weeks later, in April, I returned. I found that the conditions had greatly changed. Father had been transferred to the Naini Tal Gaol and, soon after his departure, new rules were enforced. All the prisoners in the big weaving shed, where I had been kept previously, were transferred to the inner gaol

---

1. A ridiculous story has appeared in the Press, and, though contradicted, continues to appear from time to time. According to this, Sir Harcourt Butler, the then Governor of the U.P., sent champagne to my father in prison. Sir Harcourt sent my father nothing at all in prison; nobody sent him champagne or any other alcoholic drink; and indeed he had given up alcohol in 1920 after the Congress took to non-co-operation, and was not taking any such drinks at that time.

and kept in the barracks (single halls) there. Each barrack was practically a gaol within a gaol, and no communications were allowed between different barracks. Interviews and letters were now restricted to one a month. The food was much simpler, though we were allowed to supplement it from outside.

In the barrack in which I was kept there must have been about fifty persons. We were all crowded together, our beds being about three or four feet from each other. Fortunately almost everybody in that barrack was known to me, and there were many friends. But the utter want of privacy, all day and night, became more and more difficult to endure. Always the same crowd looking on, the same petty annoyances and irritations, and no escape from them to a quiet nook. We bathed in public and washed our clothes in public, and ran round and round the barrack for exercise, and talked and argued till we had largely exhausted each other's capacity for intelligent conversation. It was the dull side of family life, magnified a hundred-fold, with few of its graces and compensations, and all this among people of all kinds and tastes. It was a great nervous strain for all of us, and often I yearned for solitude. In later years I was to have enough of this solitude and privacy in prison, when for months I would see no one except an occasional gaol official. Again I lived in a state of nervous tension, but this time I longed for suitable company. I thought then sometimes, almost with envy, of my crowded existence in the Lucknow District Gaol in 1922, and yet I knew well enough that of the two I preferred the solitude, provided at least that I could read and write.

And yet I must say that the company was unusually decent and pleasant, and we got on well together. But all of us, I suppose, got a little bored with the others occasionally and wanted to be away from them and have a little privacy. The nearest approach to privacy that I could get was by leaving my barrack and sitting in the open part of the enclosure. It was the monsoon season and it was usually possible to do so because of the clouds. I braved the heat and an occasional drizzle even, and spent as much time as possible outside the barrack.

Lying there in the open, I watched the skies and the clouds and I realized, better than I had ever done before, how amazingly beautiful were their changing hues.

To watch the changing clouds, like clime in clime;
Oh! sweet to lie and bless the luxury of time.

Time was not a luxury for us, it was more of a burden. But the time I spent in watching those ever-shifting monsoon clouds was filled with delight and a sense of relief. I had the joy of having made almost a discovery, and a feeling of escape from confinement. I do not know why that particular monsoon had that great effect on me; no previous or subsequent one has moved me in that way. I had seen and admired many a fine sunrise and sunset in the mountains and over the sea, and bathed in its glory, and felt stirred for the time being by its magnificence. Having seen it, I had almost taken it for granted and passed on to other things. But in gaol there were no sunrises or sunsets to be seen, the horizon was hidden from us, and late in the morning the hot-rayed sun emerged over our guardian walls. There were no colours anywhere, and our eyes hardened and grew dull at seeing always that same drab view of mud-coloured wall and barrack. They must have hungered for some light and shade and colouring, and when the monsoon clouds sailed gaily by, assuming fantastic shapes, and playing in a riot of colour, I gasped in surprised delight and watched them almost as if I was in a trance. Sometimes the clouds would break, and one saw through an opening in them that wonderful monsoon phenomenon, a dark blue of an amazing depth, which seemed to be a portion of infinity.

The restrictions on us gradually grew in number, and stricter rules were enforced. The Government, having got the measure of our movement, wanted us to experience the full extent of its displeasure with our temerity in having dared to challenge it. The introduction of new rules or the manner of their enforcement led to friction between the gaol authorities and the political prisoners. For several months nearly all of us—we were some hundreds at the time in that particular gaol—gave up our interviews as a protest. Evidently it was thought that some of us were the trouble-makers, and so seven of us were transferred to a distant part of the gaol, quite cut off from the main barracks. Among those who were thus separated were Purushottam Das Tandon, Mahadev Desai, George Joseph, Balkrishna Sharma, Devadas Gandhi and I.

We were sent to a smaller enclosure, and there were some disadvantages in living there. But on the whole I was glad of the change. There was no crowding here; we could live in greater quiet and with more privacy. There was more time to read or do other work. We were cut off completely from our colleagues in other parts of the gaol as well as from the outside world, for newspapers were now stopped for all political prisoners.

Newspapers did not come to us, but some news from outside trickled through, as it always manages to trickle through in prison. Our monthly interviews and letters also brought us odd bits of information. We saw that our movement was at a low ebb outside. The magic moment had passed and success seemed to retire into the dim future. Outside, the Congress was split into two factions—the pro-changers and no-changers. The former, under the leadership of Deshbandhu Das and my father, wanted the Congress to take part in the new elections to the central and provincial councils and, if possible, to capture these legislatures; the latter, led by C. Rajagopalachari, opposed any change of the old programme of non-co-operation. Gandhiji was, of course, in prison at the time. The fine ideals of the movement which had carried us forward, as on the crest of an advancing tide, were being swamped by petty squabbles and intrigues for power. We realized how much easier it was to do great and venturesome deeds in moments of enthusiasm and excitement than to carry on from day to day when the glow was past. Our spirits were damped by the news from outside, and this, added to the various humours that prison produces, increased the strain of life there. But still there remained within us an inner feeling of satisfaction, that we had preserved our self-respect and dignity, that we had acted rightly whatever the consequences. The future was dim, but, whatever shape it might take, it seemed that it would be the lot of many of us to spend a great part of our lives in prison. So we talked amongst ourselves, and I remember particularly a conversation with George Joseph in which we came to this conclusion. Since those days Joseph has drifted far apart from us and has even become a vigorous critic of our doings. I wonder if he ever remembers that talk we had on an autumn evening in the Civil Ward of the Lucknow District Gaol?

We settled down to a routine of work and exercise. For exercise we used to run round and round the little enclosure, or two of us would draw water, like two bullocks yoked together, pulling a huge leather bucket from a well in our yard. In this way we watered a small vegetable garden in our enclosure. Most of us used to spin a little daily. But reading was my principal occupation during those winter days and long evenings. Almost always, whenever the superintendent visited us, he found me reading. This devotion to reading seemed to get on his nerves a little, and he remarked on it once, adding that, so far as he was concerned, he had practically finished his general reading at the age of twelve! No doubt this abstention on his part had been of use to that gallant English colonel in avoiding troublesome thoughts, and perhaps it helped him subsequently in rising to the position of Inspector-General of Prisons in the United Provinces.

The long winter evenings and the clear Indian sky attracted us to the stars and, with the help of some charts, we spotted many of them. Nightly we would await their appearance and greet them with the satisfaction of seeing old acquaintances.

So we passed our time, and the days lengthened themselves into weeks, and the weeks became months. We grew accustomed to our routine existence. But in the world outside the real burden fell on our womenfolk, our mothers and wives and sisters. They wearied with the long waiting, and their very freedom seemed a reproach to them when their loved ones were behind prison bars.

Soon after our first arrest in December 1921 the police started paying frequent visits to Anand Bhawan, our house in Allahabad. They came to realize the fines which had been imposed on father and me. It was the Congress policy not to pay fines. So the police came day after day and attached and carried away bits of furniture. Indira, my four-year-old daughter, was greatly annoyed at this continuous process of despoilation and protested to the police and expressed her strong displeasure. I am afraid those early impressions are likely to colour her future views about the police force generally.

In the gaol every effort was made to keep us apart from the ordinary non-political convicts, special gaols being as a rule reserved for politicals. But complete segregation was impossible, and we often came into touch with those prisoners and learnt from them, as well as directly, the realities of prison life in those days. It was a story of violence and widespread graft and corruption. The food was quite amazingly bad; I tried it repeatedly and found it quite uneatable. The staff was usually wholly incompetent and was paid very low salaries, but it had every opportunity to add to its income by extorting money on every conceivable occasion from the prisoners or their relatives. The duties and responsibilities of the gaoler and his assistants and the warders, as laid down by the Gaol Manual, were so many and so various that it was quite impossible for any person to discharge them conscientiously or competently. The general policy of the prison administration in the United Provinces (and probably in other provinces) had absolutely nothing to do with the reform of the prisoner or of teaching him good habits and useful trades. The object of prison labour was to harass the convict.[1] He was to be frightened and broken into blind submission; the idea was that he should carry away from prison a fear and a horror of it, so that he might avoid crime and a return to prison in the future.

There have been some changes in recent years for the better. Food has improved a little, so also clothing and other matters. This was largely due to the agitation carried on outside by political prisoners after their discharge. Non-co-operation also resulted in a substantial increase in the warders' salaries to give them an additional inducement to remain loyal to the *Sarkar*. A feeble effort is also made now to teach reading and writing to the boys and younger prisoners. But all these changes, welcome us they are, barely scratch the problem, and the old spirit remains much the same.

The great majority of the political prisoners had to put up with this regular treatment for ordinary prisoners. They had no special privileges or other treatment, but being more aggressive and intelligent than the others, they could not easily be exploited, nor could money be made

---

1. Article 987 of the United Provinces Gaol Manual, which has now been removed from the new edition, stated that:
   "Labour in a gaol should be considered primarily as a means of punishment and not of employment only; neither should the question of its being highly remunerative have much weight, the object of paramount importance being that prison work should be irksome and laborious and a cause of dread to evil-doers." This might be compared with the following articles of the Russian S.F.S.R. Criminal Code:
   Article 9.— "The measures of social defence do not have for their object the infliction of physical suffering nor the lowering of human dignity, nor are they meant to avenge or to punish."
   Article 26.— "Sentences, being a measure of protection, must be free from any element of torture, and must not cause the criminal needless or superfluous suffering."

out of them. Because of this they were naturally not popular with the staff, and when occasion offered itself a breach of gaol discipline by any of them was punished severely. For such a breach a young boy of fifteen or sixteen, who called himself Azad, was ordered to be flogged. He was stripped and tied to the whipping triangle, and as each stripe fell on him and cut into his flesh, he shouted "Mahatma Gandhi ki Jai". Every stripe brought forth the slogan till the boy fainted. Later, that boy was to become one of the leaders of the group of Terrorists in North India.

14

OUT AGAIN

One misses many things in prison, but perhaps most of all one misses the sound of women's voices and children's laughter. The sounds one usually hears are not of the pleasantest. The voices are harsh and minatory, and the language brutal and largely consisting of swear-words. Once I remember being struck by a new want. I was in the Lucknow District Gaol and I realized suddenly that I had not heard a dog bark for seven or eight months.

On the last day of January 1923 all of us politicals in the Lucknow Gaol were discharged. There must have been between 100 and 200 'special class' prisoners in Lucknow then. All those who had been sentenced to a year or less in December 1921 or the beginning of 1922 had already served out their sentences. Only those with longer sentences, and a few who had come back a second time, remained. This sudden release took us by surprise, as there had been no previous intimation of an amnesty. The local Provincial Council had passed a resolution favouring a political amnesty, but the executive Government seldom pays heed to such demands. As it happened, however, the time was propitious from the point of view of Government. The Congress was doing nothing against the Government, and Congressmen were engrossed in mutual squabbles. There were not many well-known Congress people left in gaol and so the gesture was made.

There is always a feeling of relief and a sense of glad excitement in coming out of the prison gate. The fresh air and open expanses, the moving street scene, and the meeting with old friends, all go to the head and slightly intoxicate. Almost, there is a touch of hysteria in one's first reactions to the outer world. We felt exhilarated, but this was a passing sensation, for the state of Congress politics was discouraging enough. In the place of ideals there were intrigues, and various cliques were trying to capture the Congress machinery by the usual methods which have made politics a hateful word to those who are at all sensitive.

My own inclination was wholly against Council entry, because this seemed to lead inevitably to compromising tactics and to a continuous watering down of our objective. But there really was no other political programme before the country. The no-changers laid stress on a 'constructive programme', which in effect was a programme of social reform, and its chief merit was that it brought our workers in touch with the masses. This was not likely to satisfy those who believed in political action, and it was inevitable that after a wave of direct action, which had not succeeded, there should be a phase of parliamentary activity. Even this activity was envisaged by Deshbandhu Das and my father, the leaders of the new movement, as one of obstruction and defiance and not of co-operation and construction.

Mr C.R. Das had always favoured entry into the legislatures for the purpose of carrying on the national struggle there also. My father had more or less the same outlook, his acceptance of the Council boycott in 1920 was partly a subordination of his own view-point to Gandhiji's. He wanted to throw his full weight into the struggle, and the only way to do it then was to accept the Gandhi formula *in toto*. The minds of many of the younger people were full of the tactics of Sinn Fein in so far as they had captured the parliamentary seats and then refused to enter the House of Commons. I remember pressing Gandhiji in the summer of 1920 to adopt this variant of the boycott, but in such matters he was adamant. Mohamad Ali was in Europe then on a Khilafat deputation. On his return he also expressed his regret at the method of boycott adopted; he would have preferred the Sinn Fein way. But it was quite immaterial what other individuals thought in the matter, as ultimately Gandhiji's view was bound to prevail. He was the author of the movement, and it was felt that he must be given freedom as to the details. His chief objections to the Sinn Fein method were (apart from its association with violence) that it would not he understood by the masses as much as a straight call to boycott the polling-booths and the voting. To get elected and then not to go to the Councils would create confusion in the mass mind. Further, that once our people got elected they would be drawn towards the Councils and it would be difficult for them to keep out of them. There was not enough discipline and power in our movement to keep them out for long, and a demoralizing dribble would set in towards the many direct and indirect ways of taking advantage of

Government patronage through the Councils.

These were weighty arguments and, indeed, we saw many of them justified in the middle 'twenties when the Swaraj Party went into the Councils. And yet one cannot help wondering what would have happened if the Congress had set itself to capture the legislatures in 1920. There can be no doubt that, supported as it was by the Khilafat Committee, it would have won almost every elective seat in the provincial Councils as well as in the central Assembly. Today (August 1934) there is again talk of the Congress putting up candidates for the Assembly, and a Parliamentary Board has been set up. But much has happened since 1920 to deepen the fissures in our social and political fabric, and whatever may be the measure of success of the Congress in the coming elections, it can hardly be what it might have been in 1920.

On my discharge from gaol I co-operated with a few others who were trying to bring about an understanding between the rival groups. We met with little success, and I was fed up with the pro-change and no-change politics. As secretary of the U.P. Provincial Congress Committee I devoted myself to the work of Congress organization. There was much to be done after the shake-up of the past year. I worked hard, but I worked with little purpose. Mentally I was at a loose end. Soon a new field of activity opened out before me. Within a few weeks of my release I was pitchforked into the headship of the Allahabad Municipality. This election was so unexpected that forty-five minutes before the event no one had mentioned my name, or perhaps even thought of me, in this connection. But at the last moment it was felt on the Congress side that I was the only person of their group who was certain of success.

It so happened that year that leading Congressmen all over the country became presidents of municipalities. Mr C.R. Das became the first Mayor of Calcutta, Mr Vithalbhai Patel the President of Bombay Corporation, Sardar Vallabbhai Patel of Ahmedabad. In the United Provinces most of the big municipalities had Congressmen for their chairman.

Municipal work in all its varied forms began to interest me, and I gave more and more time to it. Some of its problems fascinated me. I studied the subject and developed ambitious notions of municipal reform. I was to find out later that there is little room for ambition or startling development in Indian municipalities as they are constituted today. Still, there was room for work and a cleaning and speeding-up of the machine, and I worked hard enough at it. Just then my Congress work was growing, and in addition to the provincial secretaryship I was made the All-India Secretary also. These various jobs often made me work fifteen hours a day, and the end of the day found me thoroughly exhausted.

On my return home from gaol the first letter that met my eyes was one from Sir Grimwood Mears, the then Chief Justice of the Allahabad High Court. The letter had been written before my discharge, but evidently in the knowledge that it was coming. I was a little surprised at the cordiality of his language and his invitation to me to visit him frequently. I hardly knew him. He had just come to Allahabad in 1919 when I was drifting away from legal practice. I think I argued only one case before him, and that was my last one in the High Court. For some reason or other he developed a partiality for me without knowing much about me. He had an idea—he told me so later—that I would go far, and he wanted to be a wholesome influence on me to make me appreciate the British view-point. His method was subtle. He was of the opinion, and there are many Englishmen who still think so, that the average 'extremist' politician in India had become anti-British because in the social sphere he had been treated badly by Englishmen. This had led to resentment and bitterness and extremism. There is a story, which has been repeated by responsible persons, to the effect that my father was refused election to an English club and this made him anti-British and extremist. The story is wholly without foundation and is a distortion of an entirely different incident.[1] But to many an Englishman such instances, whether true or not, afford a simple and sufficient explanation of the origins of the nationalist movement. As a matter of fact neither my father nor I had any particular grievance on this score. As individuals we had usually met with courtesy from the Englishman and we got on well with him, though, like all Indians, we were no doubt racially conscious of subjection, and resented it bitterly. I must confess that even today I get on very well with an Englishman, unless he happens to be an official and wants to patronize me, and even then there is no lack of humour in our contacts. Probably I have more in common with him than the Liberals or others who co-operate with him politically in India.

---

1. See the footnote in Chapter 37 for a fuller account of this incident.

Sir Grimwood's idea was to root out this original cause of bitterness by friendly intercourse and frank and courteous treatment. I saw him several times. On the pretext of objecting to some municipal tax he would come to see me and discuss other matters. On one occasion he made quite an onslaught on the Indian Liberals—timid, weak-kneed opportunists with no character or backbone, he called them, and his language was stronger and full of contempt. "Do you think we have any respect for them?" he said. I wondered why he spoke to me in this way; probably because he thought that this kind of talk might please me. And then he led up the conversation to the new Councils and their Ministers and the opportunities these Ministers had for serving their country. Education was one of the most vital problems before the country. Would not an Education Minister, with freedom to act as he chose, have a worthy opportunity to mould the destinies of millions, the chance of a lifetime? Suppose, he went on, a man like you, with intelligence, character, ideals, and the energy to push them through, was in charge of education for the province, could you not perform wonders? And he assured me, adding that he had seen the Governor recently, that I would be given perfect freedom to work out my policy. Then realizing, perhaps, that he had gone too far, he said that he could not, of course, commit anybody officially, and the suggestion he had made was a personal one.

I was diverted by Sir Grimwood's diplomatic and roundabout approach to the proposal he had made. The idea of my associating myself with the Government as a Minister was unthinkable for me; indeed, it was hateful to me. But I have often yearned, then as well as in later years, for a chance to do some solid, positive, constructive work. Destruction and agitation and non-co-operation are hardly normal activities for human beings. And yet, such is our fate, that we can only reach the land where we can build after passing through the deserts of conflict and destruction. And it may be that most of us will spend our energies and our lives in struggling and panting through those shifting sands, and the building will have to be done by our children or our children's children.

Ministries were going cheap in those days, in the United Provinces at least. The two Liberal Ministers, who had functioned throughout the non-co-operation period, had gone. When the Congress movement threatened the existing order, the Government tried to exploit the Liberal

Ministers in fighting Congress. They were respected then and treated with honour by the executive government, for it was something to hold them up in those days of trouble, as supporters of the Government. They thought, perhaps, that this respect and honour were due to them as a right, not realizing that this was but a reaction on the part of Government to the mass attack of the Congress. When that attack was drawn off the value of the Liberal Ministers fell heavily in the eyes of Government, and the respect and honour were suddenly conspicuous by their absence. The Ministers resented this, but this availed them little, and soon they were forced to resign. Then began a search for new Ministers, and this was not immediately successful. The handful of Liberals in the Council kept aloof in sympathy with their colleagues who had been unceremoniously thrown out. Of the others, mostly zamindars, there were few who could be called even moderately educated. The Congress having boycotted the Councils, a curious assortment of people had got in.

There is a story of a person who was offered a ministership in the U.P. about this time, or perhaps a little later. He is reported to have replied that he was not vain enough to consider himself an unusually clever man, but he did think himself to be moderately intelligent and, perhaps, a little above the average, and he hoped that he had that reputation. Did the Government want him to accept a ministership and thus proclaim himself to the world to be a damned fool?

This protest had some justification. The Liberal Ministers had been narrow-minded with no broad vision of politics or social affairs, but that was the fault of the sterile Liberal creed. They had, however, the ability of professional men, and they did their routine work conscientiously. Some of those who followed them in office came from the ranks of the zamindars, and their education, even in the formal sense, had been strictly limited. I think they might justly have been called literate, and nothing more. It almost seemed that the Governor chose these gentlemen and put them in high office to display the utter incapacity of Indians. Of them it might well have been said that:

Fortune advanced thee that all might aver
That nothing is impossible to her.[2]

---

2. Richard Garnett.

Educated or not, these Ministers had the zamindar vote with them, and they could give delightful garden parties to the high officials. What worthier use could be made of the money that came to them from their starving tenantry?

DOUBT AND CONFLICT

I occupied myself with many activities and sought thereby to keep away from the problems that troubled me. But there was no escape from them, no getting away from the questions that were always being formed in my mind and to which I could find no satisfactory answer. Action now was partly an attempt to run away from myself; no longer was it a wholehearted expression of the self as it had been in 1920 and 1921. I came out of the shell that had protected me then and looked round at the Indian scene as well as at the world outside. I found many changes that I had not so far noticed, new ideas, new conflicts, and instead of light I saw a growing confusion. My faith in Gandhiji's leadership remained, but I began to examine some parts of his programme more critically. But he was in prison and beyond our reach, and his advice could not be taken. Neither of the two Congress parties then functioning—the Council party and the No-changers—attracted me. The former was obviously veering towards reformism and constitutionalism, and these seemed to me to lead to a blind alley. The No-changers were supposed to be the ardent followers of the Mahatma, but like most disciples of the great, they prized the letter of the teaching more than the spirit. There was nothing dynamic about them, and in practice most of them were inoffensive and pious social reformers. But they had one advantage. They kept in touch with the peasant masses, while the Swarajists in the Councils were wholly occupied with parliamentary tactics.

Deshbandhu Das tried, soon after my discharge from prison, to convert me to the Swarajist creed. I did not succumb to his advocacy, though I was by no means clear as to what I should do. It is curious and rather remarkable, but characteristic of him, that my father, who was at the time very keen on the Swaraj Party, never tried to press me or influence me in that direction. It was obvious that he would have been very pleased if I had joined him in his campaign, but with extraordinary consideration for me, he left me to myself so far as this subject was concerned.

During this period there grew up a close friendship between my father and Mr C.R. Das. It was something much more than political *camaraderie*. There was a warmth and intimacy in it that I was not a little surprised to notice, since intimate friendships are perhaps rarely formed at advanced ages. My father had a host of acquaintances, and had the gift of laughing his way through them, but he was chary of friendship, and in later years he had grown rather cynical. And yet between him and Deshbandhu the barriers seemed to fall, and they took each other to heart. My father was nine years older, but was, physically, probably the stronger and the healthier of the two. Though both had the same background of legal training and success at the Bar, they differed in many ways. Mr Das, in spite of being a lawyer, was a poet and had a poet's emotional outlook—I believe he has written fine poetry in Bengali. He was an orator, and he had a religious temperament. My father was more practical and prosaic: he was a great organizer, and he had little of religion in him. He had always been a fighter, ready to receive and give hard blows. Those whom he considered fools he suffered not at all, or at any rate not gladly; and opposition he could not tolerate. It seemed to him a challenge requiring the use of a broom. The two, my father and Deshbandhu, unlike in some ways as they were, fitted in and made a remarkable and effective combination for the leadership of a party, each in some measure supplying the other's deficiencies. And between the two of them there was absolute confidence, so much so that each had authorized the other to use his name for any statement or declaration, even without previous reference or consultation.

It was this personal factor that went a long way to establish the Swaraj Party firmly and give it strength and prestige in the country. From the earliest days there were fissiparous tendencies in it, for many careerists and opportunists had been drawn into it by the possibilities of personal advancement through the Councils. There were also some genuine moderates in it who were inclined to more co-operation with the Government. As soon as these tendencies appeared on the surface after the elections, they were denounced by the Party leadership. My father declared that he would not hesitate 'to cut off a diseased limb' from the Party, and he acted up to this declaration.

From 1923 onwards I found a great deal of solace and happiness in family life, though I gave little time to it. I have been fortunate in my family relationships, and in times of strain and difficulty they have soothed me and sheltered me. I realized, with some shame at my own unworthiness in this respect, how much I owed to my wife for her splendid behaviour since 1920. Proud and sensitive as she was, she had not only put up with my vagaries but brought me comfort and solace when I needed them most.

Our style of living had undergone some change since 1920. It was much simpler, and the number of servants had been greatly reduced. Even so, it was not lacking in any essential comfort. Partly to get rid of superfluities and partly to raise money for current expenditure, many things had been sold off—horses and carriages, and household articles which did not fit in with our new style of living. Part of our furniture had been seized and sold by the police. For lack of furniture and gardeners, our house lost its prim and clean appearance, and the garden went wild. For nearly three years little attention had been paid to house or garden. Having become accustomed to a lavish scale of expenditure, father disliked many economies. He decided therefore to go in for chamber practice in his spare time and thus earn some money. He had very little spare time, but, even so, he managed to earn a fair amount.

I felt uncomfortable and a little unhappy at having to depend financially on father. Ever since I had given up my legal practice I had practically no income of my own, except a trifle from some dividends on shares. My wife and I did not spend much. Indeed, I was quite surprised to find how little we spent. This was one of the discoveries made by me in 1921 which brought me great satisfaction. Khadi clothes and third-class railway travelling demand little money. I did not fully realize then, living as we did with father, that there are innumerable other household expenses which mount up to a considerable figure. Anyhow, the fear of not having money has never troubled me; I suppose I could earn enough in case of necessity, and we can do with relatively little.

We were not much of a burden on father, and even a hint of this kind would have pained him greatly. Yet I disliked my position, and for the next three years I thought over the problem without finding a solution. There was no great difficulty in my finding paying work, but the acceptance of any such work necessitated my giving up or, at any rate, my curtailing the public work I was doing. So far I had given all my working time to Congress work and Municipal work. I did not like to withdraw from them for the sake of making money. So I refused offers, financially very advantageous, from big industrial firms. Probably they were willing to pay heavily, not so much for my competence as for the opportunity to exploit my name. I did not like the idea of being associated with big-industry in this way. To go back to the profession of law was also out of the question for me. My dislike for it had grown and kept on growing.

A suggestion was made in the 1924 Congress that the General Secretaries should be paid. I happened to be one of the secretaries then, and I welcomed the proposal. It seemed to me quite wrong to expect whole-time work from anyone without paying him a maintenance allowance at least. Otherwise some person with private means has to be chosen, and such gentlemen of leisure are not perhaps always politically desirable, nor can they be held responsible for the work. The Congress would not have paid much; our rates of payment were low enough. But there is in India an extraordinary and thoroughly unjustified prejudice against receiving salaries from public funds (though not from the State), and my father strongly objected to my doing so. My co-secretary, who was himself in great need of money, also considered it below his dignity to accept it from the Congress. And so I, who had no dignity in the matter and was perfectly prepared to accept a salary, had to do without it.

Once only I spoke to father on the subject and told him how I disliked the idea of my financial dependence. I put it to him as gently and indirectly as possible so as not to hurt him. He pointed out to me how foolish it would be of me to spend my time, or most of it, in earning a little money, instead of doing public work. It was far easier for him to earn with a few days' work all that my wife and I would require for a year. The argument was weighty, but it left me unsatisfied. However, I continued to act in consonance with it.

These family affairs and financial worries carried us from the beginning of 1923 to the end of 1925. Meanwhile the political situation had been changing and, almost against my will, I was dragged into various combinations and acceptance of responsible office in the All-India Congress. The position in 1923 was a peculiar one. Mr C.R. Das had been the President of the preceding Congress at Gaya. As such, he was the *ex-officio* Chairman of the All-India Congress Committee for the year 1923. But in this Committee there was a majority against him and the Swarajist policy, though the majority was a small one, and the two groups were pretty evenly balanced. Matters came to a head in the early summer of 1923 at a meeting of the A.I.C.C. in Bombay. Mr Das resigned from the chairmanship, and a small centre group emerged and formed the new Working Committee. This centre group had no backing whatever in the A.I.C.C., and could only exist with the goodwill of one of the two main parties. Allied to either, it could just defeat the other. Dr Ansari was the new President, and I was one of the secretaries.

We soon got into trouble on both sides. Gujrat, which was a no-change stronghold, refused to carry out some of the directions of the central office. Late in the summer of the same year another meeting of the A.I.C.C. was held, this time in Nagpur, where the National Flag Satyagraha was being carried on. Our Working Committee, representing the unfortunate Centre Group, came to an end here after a brief and inglorious career. It had to go because it represented nobody in particular, and it tried to boss it over those who held the real power in the Congress organization. The resignation was brought about by the failure of an attempt to censure Gujrat for its indiscipline. I remember how gladly I sent in my resignation and how relieved I felt. Even a short experience of party manoeuvres had been too much for me, and I was quite shocked at the way some prominent Congressmen could intrigue.

At this meeting Mr C.R. Das accused me of being 'cold-blooded'. I suppose he was right; it depends on the standard used for comparison. Compared to many of my friends and colleagues I am cold-blooded. And yet I have always been afraid of being submerged in or swept away by too much sentiment or emotion or temper. For years I have tried my hardest to become 'cold-blooded', and I fear that the success that has attended me in this respect has been superficial only.

16

AN INTERLUDE AT NABHA

The tug-of-war between the Swarajists and the No-changers went on, the former gradually gaining. Another stage, marking a Swarajist advance, was reached at a special session of the Congress held at Delhi in the autumn of 1923. It was immediately after this Congress that I had a strange and unexpected adventure.

The Sikhs, and especially the Akalis among them, had been coming into repeated conflict with the Government in the Punjab. A revivalist movement among them had taken it upon itself to purge their Gurdwaras by driving out corrupt Mahants and taking possession of the places of worship and the property belonging to them. The Government intervened and there was conflict. The Gurdwara movement was partly due to the general awakening caused by non-co-operation, and the methods of the Akalis were modelled on non-violent Satyagraha. Many incidents took place, but chief among them was the famous Guru-ka-Bagh struggle, where scores of Sikhs, many of them ex-soldiers, allowed themselves to be brutally beaten by the police without raising their hands or turning back from their mission. India was startled by this amazing display of tenacity and courage. The Gurdwara Committee was declared illegal by the Government, and the struggle continued for some years and ended in the victory of the Sikhs. The Congress was naturally sympathetic, and for some time it had a special liaison officer in Amritsar to keep in close touch with the Akali movement.

The incident to which I am going to refer had little to do with this general Sikh movement, but there is no doubt that it occurred because of this Sikh upheaval. The rulers of two Sikh States in the Punjab, Patiala and Nabha, had a bitter, personal quarrel which resulted ultimately in the deposition of the Maharaja of Nabha by the Government of India. A British Administrator was appointed to rule the Nabha State. This deposition was resented by the Sikhs, and they agitated against it both in Nabha and outside. In the course of this agitation, a religious ceremony, at a place called Jaito in Nabha State, was stopped by the new Administrator. To protest against this, and with the declared object of continuing the interrupted ceremony, the Sikhs began sending *jathas* (batches of men) to Jaito. These *jathas* were stopped, beaten by the police, arrested, and usually carried to an out-of-the-way place in the jungle and left there. I had been reading accounts of these beatings from time to time, and when I learnt at Delhi, immediately after the Special Congress, that another *jatha* was going and I was invited to come and see what happened, I gladly accepted the invitation. It meant the loss of only a day to me, as Jaito was near Delhi. Two of my Congress colleagues— A. T. Gidwani and K. Santanum of Madras—accompanied me. The *jatha* marched most of the way. It was arranged that we should go to the nearest railway station and then try to reach by road the Nabha boundary near Jaito just when the *jatha* was due to arrive there. We arrived in time, having come in a country cart, and followed the *jatha*, keeping apart from it. On arrival at Jaito the *jatha* was stopped by the police, and immediately an order was served on me, signed by the English Administrator, calling upon me not to enter Nabha territory, and if I had entered it, to leave it immediately. A similar order was served on Gidwani and Santanum, but without their names being mentioned, as the Nabha authorities did not know them. My colleagues and I told the police officer that we were there not as part of the *jatha* but as spectators, and it was not our intention to break any of the Nabha laws. Besides, when we were already in the Nabha territories there could be no question of our not entering them, and obviously we could not vanish suddenly into thin air. Probably the next train from Jaito went many hours later. So for the present, we told him, we proposed to remain there. We were immediately arrested and taken to the lock-up. After our removal the *jatha* was dealt with in the usual manner.

We were kept the whole day in the lock-up and in the evening we were marched to the station. Santanum and I were handcuffed together, his left wrist to my right one, and a chain attached to the handcuff was held by the policeman leading us. Gidwani, also handcuffed and chained, brought up the rear. This march of ours down the streets of Jaito town reminded me forcibly of a dog being led on by a chain. We felt somewhat irritated to begin with, but the humour of the situation dawned upon us, and on the whole we enjoyed the experience. We did not enjoy the night that followed. This was partly spent in crowded third-class compartments in slow-moving trains, with, I think, a change at midnight, and partly in a lock-up at Nabha. All this time, till the forenoon of next day, when we were finally delivered up at the Nabha Gaol, the joint handcuff and the heavy chain kept us company. Neither of us could move at all without the other's co-operation. To be handcuffed to another person for a whole night and part of a day is not an experience I should like to repeat.

In Nabha Gaol we were all three kept in a most unwholesome and insanitary cell. It was small and damp, with a low ceiling which we could almost touch. At night we slept on the floor, and I would wake up with a start, full of horror, to find that a rat or a mouse had just passed over my face.

Two or three days later we were taken to court for our case, and the most extraordinary and Gilbertian proceedings went on there from day to day. The magistrate or judge seemed to be wholly uneducated. He knew no English, of course, but I doubt if he knew how to write the court language, Urdu. We watched him for over a week, and during all this time he never wrote a line. If he wanted to write anything he made the court reader do it. We put in a number of small applications. He did not pass any orders on them at the time. He kept them and produced them the next day with a note written by somebody else on them. We did not formally defend ourselves. We had got so used to not defending cases in court during the non-co-operation movement that the idea of defence, even when it was manifestly permissible, seemed almost indecent. But I gave the court a long statement containing the facts, as well as my own opinion about Nabha ways, especially under British administration.

Our case was dragging on from day to day although it was a simple enough affair. Suddenly there was a diversion. One afternoon after the court had risen for the day we were kept waiting in the building; and late in the evening, at about 7 p.m., we were taken to another room where a person was sitting by a table and there were some other people about. One man, our old friend the police officer who had arrested us at Jaito, was there, and he got up and began making a statement. I inquired where we were and what was happening. I was informed that it was a court-room and we were being tried for conspiracy. This was an entirely different proceeding from the one we had so far attended, which was for breach of the order not to enter Nabha territory. It was evidently thought that the maximum sentence for this breach being only six months was not enough punishment for us and a more serious charge was necessary. Apparently three were not enough for conspiracy, and so a fourth man, who had absolutely nothing to do with us, was arrested and put on his trial with us. This unhappy man, a Sikh, was not known to us, but we had just seen him in the fields on our way to Jaito.

The lawyer in me was rather taken aback by the casualness with which a conspiracy trial had been started. The case was a totally false one, but decency required that some formalities should be observed. I pointed out to the judge that we had had no notice whatever and that we might have wanted to make arrangements for our defence. This did not worry him at all. It was the Nabha way. If we wanted to engage a lawyer for our defence we could chose some one in Nabha. When I suggested that I might want some lawyer from outside I was told that this was not permitted under the Nabha rules. We were further enlightened about the peculiarities of Nabha procedure. In some disgust we told the judge to do what he liked, but so far as we were concerned we would take no part in the proceedings. I could not wholly adhere to this resolve. It was difficult to listen to the most astounding lies about us and remain silent, and so occasionally we expressed our opinion, briefly but pointedly, about the witnesses. We also gave the court a statement in writing about the facts. This second judge, who tried the conspiracy case, was more educated and intelligent than the other one.

Both these cases went on and we looked forward to our daily visits to the two courts-rooms, for that meant a temporary escape from the foul cell in gaol. Meanwhile, we were approached, on behalf of the Administrator, by the Superintendent of the gaol, and told that if we would express our regret and give an undertaking to go away from Nabha, the proceedings against us would be dropped. We replied that there was nothing to express regret about, so far as we were concerned; it was for the administration to apologize to us. We were also not prepared to give any undertaking.

About a fortnight after our arrest the two trials at last ended. All this time had been taken up by the prosecution, for we were not defending. Much of it had been wasted in long waits, for every little difficulty that arose necessitated an adjournment or a reference to some authority behind the scenes—probably the English Administrator. On the last day when the prosecution case was closed we handed in our written statements. The first court adjourned and, to our surprise, returned a little later with a bulky judgment written out in Urdu. Obviously this huge judgment could not have been written during the interval. It had been prepared before our statements had been handed in. The judgment was not read out; we were merely told that we had been awarded the maximum sentence of six months for breach of the order to leave Nabha territory.

In the conspiracy case we were sentenced the same day to either eighteen months or two years, I forget which. This was to be in addition to the sentence for six months. Thus we were given in all either two years or two and a half years.

Right through our trial there had been any number of remarkable incidents which gave us some insight into the realities of Indian State administration, or rather the British administration of an Indian State. The whole procedure was farcical. Because of this I suppose no newspaperman or outsider was allowed in court. The police did what they pleased, and often ignored the judge or magistrate and actually disobeyed his directions. The poor magistrate meekly put up with this, but we saw no reason why we should do so. On several occasions I had to stand up and insist on the police behaving and obeying the magistrate. Sometimes there was an unseemly snatching of papers by the police, and the magistrate, being incapable of action or of introducing order in his own court, we had partly to do his job! The poor magistrate was in an unhappy position. He was afraid of the police, and he seemed to be a little frightened of us, too, for our arrest had been noised in the press. If this was the state of affairs when more or less prominent politicians like us were concerned, what, I wonder, would be the fate of others less known?

My father knew something of Indian States, and so he was greatly upset at my unexpected arrest in Nabha. Only the fact of arrest was known; little else in the way of news could leak out. In his distress he even telegraphed to the Viceroy for news of me. Difficulties were put in the way of his visiting me in Nabha, but he was allowed at last to interview me in prison. He could not be of any help to me, as I was not defending myself, and I begged him to go back to Allahabad and not to worry. He returned, but he left a young lawyer colleague of ours, Kapil Dev Malaviya, in Nabha to watch the proceedings. Kapil Dev's knowledge of law and procedure must have been considerably augmented by his brief experience of the Nabha Courts. The police tried to deprive him forcibly in open court of some papers that he had.

Most of the Indian States are well known for their backwardness and their semi-feudal conditions. They are personal autocracies, devoid even of competence or benevolence. Many a strange thing occurs there which never receives publicity. And yet their very inefficiency lessens the evil in some ways and lightens the burden on their unhappy people. For this is reflected in a weak executive, and it results in making even tyranny and injustice inefficient. That does not make tyranny more bearable, but it does make it less far-reaching and widespread. The assumption of direct British control over an Indian State has a curious result in changing this equilibrium. The semi-feudal conditions are retained, autocracy is kept, the old laws and procedure are still supposed to function, all the restrictions on personal liberty and association and expression of opinion (and these are all-embracing) continue, but one change is made which alters the whole background. The executive becomes stronger and a measure of efficiency is introduced, and this leads to a tightening-up of all the feudal and autocratic bonds. In course of time the British administration would no doubt change some of the archaic customs and methods, for they come in the way of efficient government as well as commercial penetration. But to begin with they take full advantage of them to tighten their hold on the people who have now to put up not only with feudalism and autocracy, but with an efficient enforcement of them by a strong executive.

I saw something of this in Nabha. The State was under a British Administrator, a member of the Indian Civil Service, and he had the full powers of an autocrat, subject only to the Government of India. And yet at every turn we were referred to Nabha laws and procedure to justify the denial of the most ordinary rights. We had to face a combination of feudalism and the modern bureaucratic machine with the disadvantages of both and the advantages of neither.

So our trial was over and we had been sentenced. We did not know what the judgments contained, but the solid fact of a long sentence had a sobering effect. We asked for copies of the judgments, and were told to apply formally for them.

That evening in gaol the Superintendent sent for us and showed us an order of the Administrator under the Criminal Procedure Code suspending our sentences. There was no condition attached, and the legal result of that order was that the sentences ended so far as we were concerned. The Superintendent then produced a separate order called an Executive Order, also issued by the Administrator, asking us to leave Nabha and not to return to the State without special permission. I asked for the copies of the two orders, but they were refused. We were then escorted to the railway station and released there. We did not know a soul in Nabha, and even the city gates had been closed for the night. We found that a train was leaving soon for Ambala, and we took this. From Ambala I went on to Delhi and Allahabad.

From Allahabad I wrote to the Administrator requesting him to send me copies of his two orders, so that I might know exactly what they were, also copies of the two judgments. He refused to supply any of these copies. I pointed out that I might decide to file an appeal, but he persisted in his refusal. In spite of repeated efforts I have never had the opportunity to read these judgments, which sentenced me and my two colleagues to two years or two and a half years. For aught I know, these sentences may still be hanging over me, and may take effect whenever the Nabha authorities or the British Government so choose.

The three of us were discharged in this 'suspended' way, but I could never find out what had happened to the fourth member of the alleged conspiracy, the Sikh who had been tacked on to us for the second trial. Very likely he was not discharged. He had no powerful friends or public interest to help him and, like many another person, he sank into the oblivion of a State prison. He was not forgotten by us. We did what we could and this was very little, and, I believe, the Gurdwara Committee interested itself in his case also. We found out that he was one of the old 'Komagata Maru' lot, and he had only recently come out of prison after a long period. The police do not believe in leaving such people out, and so they tacked him on to the trumped-up charge against us.

All three of us—Gidwani, Santanum and I—brought an unpleasant companion with us from our cell in Nabha Gaol. This was the typhus germ, and each one of us had an attack of typhoid. Mine was severe and for a while dangerous enough, but it was the lightest of the three, and I was only bed-ridden for about three or four weeks, but the other two were very seriously ill for long periods.

There was yet another sequel to this Nabha episode. Probably six months, or more, later Gidwani was acting as the Congress representative in Amritsar, keeping in touch with the Sikh Gurdwara Committee. The Committee sent a special *jatha* of 500 persons to Jaito, and Gidwani decided to accompany it as an observer to the Nabha border. He had no intention of entering Nabha territory. The *jatha* was fired on by the police near the border, and many persons were, I believe, killed and wounded. Gidwani went to the help of the wounded when he was pounced upon by the police and taken away. No proceedings in court were taken against him. He was simply kept in prison for the best part of a year when, utterly broken in health, he was discharged.

Gidwani's arrest and confinement seemed to me to be a monstrous abuse of executive authority. I wrote to the Administrator (who was still the same English member of the I.C.S.) and asked him why Gidwani had been treated in this way. He replied that Gidwani had been imprisoned because he had broken the order not to enter Nabha territory without permission. I challenged the legality of this as well as, of course, the propriety of arresting a man who was giving succour to the wounded, and I asked the Administrator to send me or publish a copy of the order in question. He refused to do so. I felt inclined to go to Nabha myself and allow the Administrator to treat me as he had treated Gidwani. Loyalty to a colleague seemed to demand it. But many friends thought otherwise and dissuaded me. I took shelter behind the advice of friends, and made of it a pretext to cover my own weakness. For, after all, it was my weakness and disinclination to go to Nabha Gaol again that kept me away, and I have always felt a little ashamed of thus deserting a colleague. As often with us all, discretion was preferred to valour.

17

COCONADA AND M. MOHAMAD ALI

In December 1923 the annual session of the Congress was held at Coconada in the South. Maulana Mohamad Ali was the President and, as was his wont, he delivered an enormously long presidential address. But it was an interesting one. He traced the growth of political and communal feeling among the Muslims and showed how the famous Muslim deputation to the Viceroy in 1908, under the leadership of the Aga Khan, which led to the first official declaration in favour of separate electorates, was a command performance and had been engineered by the Government itself.

Mohamad Ali induced me, much against my will, to accept the All-India Congress secretaryship for his year of presidentship. I had no desire to accept executive responsibility, when I was not clear about future policy. But I could not resist Mohamad Ali, and both of us felt that some other secretary might not be able to work as harmoniously with the new President as I could. He had strong likes and dislikes, and I was fortunate enough to be included in his 'likes'. A bond of affection and mutual appreciation tied us to each other. He was deeply and, as I considered, most irrationally religious, and I was not, but I was attracted by his earnestness, his over-flowing energy and keen intelligence. He had a nimble wit, but sometimes his devastating sarcasm hurt, and he lost many a friend thereby. It was quite impossible for him to keep a clever remark to himself, whatever the consequences might be.

We got on well together during his year of office, though we had many little points of difference. I introduced in our A.I.C.C. office a practice of addressing all our members by their names only, without any prefixes or suffixes, honorific titles and the like. There are so many of these in India—Mahatma, Maulana, Pandit, Shaikh, Syed, Munshi, Moulvi, and latterly Sriyut and Shri, and, of course, Mr and Esquire—and they are so abundantly and often unnecessarily used that I wanted to set a good example. But I was not to have my way. Mohamad Ali sent me a frantic telegram directing me 'as president' to revert to our old practice and, in particular, always to address Gandhiji as Mahatma.

Another frequent subject for argument between us was the Almighty. Mohamad Ali had an extraordinary way of bringing in some reference to God even in Congress resolutions, either by way of expressing gratitude or some kind of prayer. I used to protest, and then he would shout at me for my irreligion. And yet, curiously enough, he would tell me later that he was quite sure that I was fundamentally religious, in spite of my superficial behaviour or my declarations to the contrary. I have often wondered how much truth there was in his statement. Perhaps it depends on what is meant by religion and religious.

I avoided discussing this subject of religion with him, because I knew we would only irritate each other, and I might hurt him. It is always a difficult subject to discuss with convinced believers of any creed. With most Muslims it is probably an even harder matter for discussion, since no latitude of thought is officially permitted to them. Ideologically, theirs is a straight and narrow path, and the believer must not swerve to the right or the left. Hindus are somewhat different, though not always so. In practice they may be very orthodox; they may, and do, indulge in the most out-of-date, reactionary and even pernicious customs, and yet they will usually be prepared to discuss the most radical ideas about religion. I imagine the modern Arya Samajists have not, as a rule, this wide intellectual approach. Like the Muslims, they follow their own straight and narrow path. There is a certain philosophical tradition among the intelligent Hindus, which, though it does not affect practice, does make a difference to the ideological approach to a religious question. Partly, I suppose, this is due to the wide and often conflicting variety of opinions and customs that are included in the Hindu fold. It has, indeed, often been remarked that Hinduism is hardly a religion in the usual sense of the word. And yet, what amazing tenacity it has got, what tremendous power of survival! One may even be a professing atheist—as the old Hindu philosopher, Charvaka, was—and yet no one dare say that he has ceased to be a Hindu. Hinduism clings on to its children, almost despite them. A Brahman I was born, and a Brahman I seem to remain whatever I might say or do in regard to religion or social custom. To the Indian world I am 'Pandit' so and so, in spite of my desire not to have this or any other honorific title attached to my name. I remember meeting a Turkish scholar once in Switzerland, to whom I had sent previously a letter of introduction in which I had been referred to as 'Pandit Jawaharlal Nehru'. He was surprised and a little disappointed to see me for, as he told me, the 'Pandit' had led him to expect a reverend and scholarly gentleman of advanced years.

So Mohamad Ali and I did not discuss religion. But he did not possess the virtue of silence, and some years later (I think this was in 1925 or early in 1926) he could not repress himself on this subject any more. He burst out one day, as I was visiting him in his house in Delhi, and said that he insisted on discussing religion with me. I tried to dissuade him, pointing out that our view-points were very different, and we were not likely to make much impression on each other. But he was not going to be diverted. "We must have it out," he said. "I suppose you think that I am a fanatic. Well, I am going to show you that I am not." He told me that he had studied the subject of religion deeply and extensively. He pointed out shelves full of books on various religions, especially Islam and Christianity, and including some modern books like H.G. Wells's *God, the Invisible King*. During the long years of his war-time internment, he had gone through the Quran repeatedly, and consulted all the commentaries on it. As a result of this study he found out, so he told me, that about 97 per cent of what was contained in the Quran was entirely reasonable, and could be justified even apart from the Quran. The remaining 3 per cent, was not prima facie acceptable to his reason. But was it more likely that the Quran, which was obviously right in regard to 97 per cent, was also right in regard to the remaining 3 per cent, than that his feeble reasoning faculty was right and the Quran wrong? He came to the conclusion that the chances were heavily in favour of the Quran, and so he accepted it as 100 per cent correct.

The logic of this argument was not obvious, but I had no wish to argue. What followed really surprised me. Mohamad Ali said that he was quite certain that if any one read the Quran with an open and receptive mind, he would be convinced of its truth. He knew (he added) that Bapu (Gandhiji) had read it carefully, and he must, therefore, have been convinced of the truth of Islam. But his pride of heart had kept him from declaring this.

After his year of presidentship, Mohamad Ali gradually drifted away from the Congress, or, perhaps, as he would have put it, the Congress drifted away from him. The process was a slow one, and he continued to attend Congress and A.I.C.C. meetings, and take vigorous part in them for several years more. But the rift widened, estrangement grew. Perhaps no particular individual or individuals were to blame for this; it was an inevitable result of certain objective conditions in the country. But it was an unfortunate result, which hurt many of us. For, whatever the differences on the communal question might have been, there were very few differences on the political issue. He was devoted to the idea of Indian independence. And because of this common political outlook, it was always possible to come to some mutually satisfactory arrangement with him on the communal issue. There was nothing in common, politically, between him and the reactionaries who pose as the champions of communal interests.

It was a misfortune for India that he left the country for Europe in the summer of 1928. A great effort was then made to solve the communal problem, and it came very near success. If Mohamad Ali had been here then, it is just conceivable that matters would have shaped differently. But by the time he came back the break had already taken place and, inevitably, he found himself on the other side.

Two years later, in 1930, when large numbers of our people were in prison and the Civil Disobedience movement was in full swing, Mohamad Ali ignored the Congress decision, and attended the Round Table Conference. I was hurt by his going. I believe that in his own heart he was unhappy about it, and there is enough evidence of this in his activities in London. He felt that his real place was in the fight in India, not in the futile conference chamber in London. And if he had returned to his country he would, I feel sure, have joined that struggle. Physically, he was a doomed man, and for years past the grip of disease was tightening upon him. In London his overwhelming anxiety to achieve, to do something worthwhile, when rest and treatment was what he needed, hastened his end. The news of his death came to me in Naini Prison as a blow.

I met him for the last time on the occasion of the Lahore Congress in December 1929. He was not pleased with some parts of my presidential address, and he criticized it vigorously. He saw that the Congress was going ahead, and becoming politically more aggressive. He was aggressive enough himself, and, being so, he disliked taking a back-seat and allowing others to be in the front. He gave me solemn warning: "I warn you, Jawahar, that your present colleagues will desert you. They will leave you in the lurch in a crisis. Your own Congressmen will send you to the gallows." A dismal prophecy!

The Coconada Congress, held in December 1923, had a special interest for me, because the foundations of an all-India volunteer organization, the Hindustani Seva Dal, were laid there. There had been no lack of volunteer organizations even before, both for organizational work and for gaol-going. But there was little discipline, little cohesion. Dr N.S. Hardiker conceived the idea of having a well-disciplined all-India corps trained to do national work under the general guidance of the Congress. He pressed me to co-operate with him in this, and I gladly did so, for the idea appealed to me. The beginnings were made at Coconada. We were surprised to find later how much opposition there was to the Seva Dal among leading Congressmen. Some said that this was a dangerous departure, as it meant introducing a military element in the Congress, and the military arm might over-power the civil authority! Others seemed to think that the only discipline necessary was for the volunteer to obey orders issued from above, and for the rest it was hardly desirable for volunteers even to walk in step. At the back of the mind of some was the notion that the idea of having trained and drilled volunteers was somehow inconsistent with the Congress principle of non-violence. Hardiker, however, devoted himself to this task, and by the patient labour of years he demonstrated how much more efficient and even non-violent our trained volunteers could be.

Soon after my return from Coconada, in January 1924, I had a new kind of experience in Allahabad. I write from memory, and I am likely to get mixed up about dates. But I think that was the year of the *Kumbh,* or the *Ardh-Kumbh,* the great bathing *mela* held on the banks of the Ganges at Allahabad. Vast numbers of pilgrims usually turn up, and most of them bathe at the confluence of the Ganges and the Jumna—the *Triveni,* it is called, as the mythical Saraswati is also supposed to join the other two. The Ganges river-bed is about a mile wide, but in winter the river shrinks and leaves a wide expanse of sand exposed, which is very useful for the camps of the pilgrims. Within this river-bed, the Ganges frequently changes its course. In 1924 the current of the Ganges was such that it was undoubtedly dangerous for crowds to bathe at the *Triveni.*

With certain precautions, and the control of the numbers bathing at a time, the danger could be greatly lessened.

I was not at all interested in this question, as I did not propose to acquire merit by bathing in the river on the auspicious days. But I noticed in the Press that a controversy was going on between Pandit Madan Mohan Malaviya and the Provincial Government, the latter (or the local authorities) having issued orders prohibiting all bathing at the junction of the rivers. This was objected to by Malaviyaji, as, from the religious point of view, the whole point was to bathe at that confluence. The Government was perfectly justified in taking precautions to prevent accidents and possible serious loss of life, but, as usual, it set about its work in the most wooden and irritating way possible.

On the big day of the Kumbh, I went down to the river early in the morning to see the *mela,* with no intention of bathing. On arrival at the river bank, I learnt that Malaviyaji had sent some kind of polite ultimatum to the District Magistrate, asking him for permission to bathe at the *Triveni.* Malaviyaji was agitated, and the atmosphere was tense. The Magistrate refused permission. Thereupon Malaviyaji decided to offer Satyagraha, and, accompanied by about two hundred others, he marched towards the junction of the rivers. I was interested in these developments and, on the spur of the moment, joined the Satyagraha band. A tremendous barrier had been erected right across the open space, to keep away people from the confluence. When we reached this high palisade, we were stopped by the police, and a ladder we had was taken away from us. Being non-violent Satyagrahis, we sat down peacefully on the sands near the palisade. And there we sat for the whole morning and part of the afternoon. Hour after hour went by, the sun became stronger, the sand hotter, and all of us hungrier. Foot and mounted police stood by on both sides of us. I think the regular cavalry was also there. Most of us grew impatient, and said that something should be done. I believe the authorities also grew impatient, and decided to force the pace. Some order was given to the cavalry, who mounted their horses. It struck me (I do not know if I was right) that they were going to charge us and drive us away in this fashion. I did not fancy the idea of being chased by mounted troopers, and, anyhow, I was fed up with sitting there. So I suggested to those sitting near me that we might as well cross over the palisade, and I mounted it. Immediately scores of others did likewise, and some even pulled out a few stakes, thus making a passage-way. Somebody gave me a national flag, and I stuck it on top of the palisade, where I continued to sit. I grew rather excited, and thoroughly enjoyed myself, watching the people clambering up or going through and the mounted troopers trying to push them away. I must say that the cavalry did their work as harmlessly as possible. They waved about their wooden staffs, and pushed people with them, but refrained from causing much injury. Faint memories of revolutionary barricades came to me.

At last I got down on the other side and, feeling very hot after my exertions, decided to have a dip in the Ganges. On coming back, I was amazed to find that Malaviyaji and many others were still sitting on the other side of the palisade as before. But the mounted troopers and the foot police now stood shoulder to shoulder between the Satyagrahis and the palisade. So I went (having got out by a roundabout way) and sat down again near Malaviyaji. For some time we sat on, and I noticed that Malaviyaji was greatly agitated; he seemed to be trying to control some strong emotion. Suddenly, without a hint to any one, he dived in the most extraordinary way through the policemen and the horses. For any one, that would have been a surprising dive, but for an old and physically weak person like Malaviyaji, it was astounding. Anyhow, we all followed him; we all dived. After some effort to keep us back the cavalry and the police did not interfere. A little later they were withdrawn.

We half expected some proceedings to be taken against us by the Government, but nothing of the kind happened. Government probably did not wish to take any steps against Malaviyaji, and so the smaller fry got off too.

18

MY FATHER AND GANDHIJI

Early in 1924 there came suddenly the news of the serious illness of Gandhiji in prison, followed by his removal to a hospital and an operation. India was numbed with anxiety; we held our breaths almost and waited, full of fear. The crisis passed, and a stream of people began to reach Poona from all parts of the country to see him. He was still in hospital, a prisoner under guard, but he was permitted to see a limited number of friends. Father and I visited him in the hospital.

He was not taken back from the hospital to the prison. As he was convalescing, Government remitted the rest of his sentence and discharged him. He had then served about two years out of the six years to which he had been sentenced. He went to Juhu, by the sea-side near Bombay, to recuperate.

Our family also trekked to Juhu, and established itself in a tiny little cottage by the sea. We spent some weeks there, and I had, after a long gap, a holiday after my heart, for I could indulge in swimming and running and riding on the beach. The main purpose of our stay, however, was not holiday-making, but discussions with Gandhiji. Father wanted to explain to him the Swarajist position, and to gain his passive co-operation at least, if not his active sympathy. I was also anxious to have some light thrown on the problems that were troubling me. I wanted to know what his future programme of action was going to be.

The Juhu talks, so far as the Swarajists were concerned, did not succeed in winning Gandhiji, or even in influencing him to any extent. Behind all the friendly talk, and the courteous gestures, the fact remained that there was no compromise. They agreed to differ, and statements to this effect were issued to the Press.

I also returned from Juhu a little disappointed, for Gandhiji did not resolve a single one of my doubts. As is usual with him, he refused to look into the future, or lay down any long-distance programme. We were to carry on patiently 'serving' the people, working for the constructive and social reform programme of the Congress, and await the time for aggressive activity. The real difficulty, of course, was that even when that time came, would not some incident like Chauri Chaura upset all our calculations and again hold us up? To that he gave no answer then. Nor was he at all definite in regard to our objective. Many of us wanted to be clear in our own minds what we were driving at, although the Congress did not then need to make a formal declaration on the subject. Were we going to hold out for independence and some measure of social change, or were our leaders going to compromise for something very much less? Only a few months before, I had stressed independence in my presidential address at the U.P. Provincial Conference. This Conference was held in the autumn of 1923, a little after my return from Nabha. I was just recovering from the illness with which Nabha Gaol had presented me and I was unable to attend the Conference; but my address, written under fever in bed, went to it.

While some of us wanted to make the issue of independence clear in the Congress, our friends the Liberals had drifted so far from us—or perhaps the drifting had been done by us—that they publicly gloried in the pomp and power of the Empire, although that Empire might treat our countrymen as a doormat, and its dominions keep our countrymen as helots or refuse them all admittance. Mr Sastri had become an Imperial Envoy, and Sir Tej Bahadur Sapru had proudly declared at the Imperial Conference in London in 1923: "I can say with pride that it is my country that makes the Empire imperial."

A vast ocean seemed to separate us from these Liberal leaders; we lived in different worlds, we spoke in different languages, and our dreams—if they ever had dreams—had nothing in common. Was it not necessary then to be clear and precise about our goal?

But such thoughts were then confined to a few. Precision is not loved by most people, especially in a nationalist movement which by its very nature is vague and somewhat mystical. In the early months of 1924, public attention was largely concentrated on the Swarajists in the Legislative Assembly and the Provincial Councils. What were these groups going to do after their brave talk about "opposition from within" and wrecking the Councils? Some fine gestures took place. The budget for the year was rejected by the Assembly; a resolution demanding a round-table discussion to settle the terms of Indian freedom was passed. The

Bengal Council, under Deshbandhu's leadership, also bravely voted down supplies. But both in the Assembly and in the provinces, the Viceroy or the Governor certified the budgets and they became law. There were some speeches, some excitement in the legislatures, a momentary feeling of triumph among the Swarajists, headlines in the Press, and nothing more. What else could they do? They could repeat their tactics, but the novelty wore off, the excitement vanished, and the public mind grew accustomed to budgets and laws being certified by the Viceroy or Governor. The next step, of course, was beyond the competence of the Swarajists inside the Councils. It lay outside the Council chamber.

Some time in the middle of that year (1924) a meeting of the All-India Congress Committee was held at Ahmedabad. At this meeting, unexpectedly, a sharp conflict appeared between Gandhiji and the Swarajists, and there were some dramatic situations. The initiative was taken by Gandhiji. He proposed a fundamental alteration in the Congress constitution, changing the franchise and the rules for membership. So far, every one who subscribed to the first article of the Congress constitution, which laid down the objective of Swaraj and peaceful methods, and paid four annas could become a member. He now wanted to limit membership to those who gave a certain amount of self-spun yarn instead of the four annas. This was a serious limitation of the franchise, and the A.I.C.C. was certainly not competent to do this. But Gandhiji has seldom cared for the letter of a constitution when this has come in his way. I was shocked at what I considered a violence to our constitution, and I offered to the Working Committee my resignation from the secretaryship. But some new developments took place and I did not press it. In the A.I.C.C. the proposal was fiercely resisted by my father and Mr Das, and ultimately, to show their entire disapproval of it, they marched out with a goodly number of their followers just before the voting. Even then some people, opposed to the resolution, still remained present in the Committee. The resolution was passed by a majority, but ultimately it was withdrawn. For Gandhiji had been tremendously affected by the walk-out of the Swarajists and the unbending attitude on this subject of Deshbandhu and my father. He was emotionally worked up, and a chance remark of a member upset him and he broke down. It was obvious that he had been cut to the quick. He addressed the Committee in a most feeling manner and reduced a number of members to tears. It was a moving and extraordinary sight.[1]

I could never make out why he was so keen on that exclusive form of spinning franchise then, for he must have known that it would be bitterly opposed. Probably he wanted the Congress to consist only of people who were believers in his constructive programme of Khadi, etc., and was prepared to drive out the others or make them conform. But although he had the majority with him, he weakened in his resolve and began to compromise with the others. During the next three or four months, to my amazement, he changed several times on this question. He seemed to be completely at sea, unable to find his bearings. That was the one idea that I did not associate with him, and hence my surprise. The question itself was not, so it seemed to me, a very vital one. The idea of labour being made the qualification for franchise was a very desirable one, but in the restricted form in which it came up, it lost some of its meaning.

I came to the conclusion that Gandhiji's difficulties had been caused

---

1. The above account was written in prison from memory. I find now that my memory was defective and I had overlooked an important aspect of the A.I.C.C. discussions, thus giving a wrong impression of what happened. What moved Gandhiji was a resolution relating to a young Bengali terrorist (Gopinath Saha) which was moved in the meeting and was ultimately lost. The resolution, so far as I remember, condemned his deed but expressed sympathy for his motives. More than the resolution itself, the speeches accompanying it distressed Gandhiji, and it was this feeling that many people in the Congress were not serious about its profession of non-violence that upset him. Writing of this meeting in *Young India* soon after, he said: "I had a bare majority always for the four resolutions. But it must be regarded by me as a minority. The house was fairly evenly divided. The Gopinath Saha resolution clinched the issue. The speeches, the result and the scenes I witnessed after were a perfect eye-opener ... Dignity vanished after the Gopinath Saha resolution. It was before this house that I had to put my last resolution. As the proceedings went on, I must have become more and more serious. I felt like running away from the oppressive scene. I dreaded having to move a resolution in my charge ... I do not know that I have made it clear that no speaker had any malice in him. What preyed upon my mind was the fact of unconscious irresponsibility and disregard of the Congress creed or policy of non-violence ... That there were seventy Congress representatives to support the resolution was a staggering revelation." This incident, with Gandhiji's commentary on it, is very significant, as it shows the extreme importance attached by Gandhiji to non-violence, and the reactions on him of any attempt, even though this might be unconscious and indirect, to challenge it. Much that he has subsequently done is probably due fundamentally to some such reactions. Non-violence has been, and is, the sheet-anchor of his policy and activities.

because he was moving in an unfamiliar medium. He was superb in his special field of Satyagrahic direct action, and his instinct unerringly led him to take the right steps. He was also very good in working himself and making others work quietly for social reform among the masses. He could understand absolute war or absolute peace. Anything in between he did not appreciate. The Swarajist programme, of struggle and opposition inside Councils, left him cold. If a person wants to go to the legislature, let him do so with the object of co-operating with the authorities for better legislation, etc., and not for the sake of opposition. If he does not want to do so, let him stay out. The Swarajists adopted neither of these positions, and hence his difficulty in dealing with them.

Ultimately he adjusted himself to them. The spinning franchise became an alternative form, the old four-anna franchise remaining. He almost blessed the Swarajist work in the legislatures, but for himself he kept severely aloof. It was said that he had retired from politics, and the British Government and its officers believed that his popularity was waning and that he was a spent force. Das and Nehru, it was said, had driven Gandhi into the background; they seemed to dominate the political scene. Such remarks, with suitable variations, have been repeated many times in the course of the last fifteen years, and they have demonstrated every time how singularly ignorant our rulers are about the feelings of the Indian people. Ever since Gandhiji appeared on the Indian political scene, there has been no going back in popularity for him, so far as the masses are concerned. There has been a progressive increase in his popularity, and this process still continues. They may not carry out his wishes, for human nature is often weak, but their hearts are full of goodwill for him. When objective conditions help they rise in huge mass movements, otherwise they lie low. A leader does not create a mass movement out of nothing, as if by a stroke of the magician's wand. He can take advantage of the conditions themselves when they arise; he can prepare for them, but not create them.

But it is true to say that there is a waning and a waxing of Gandhiji's popularity among the intelligentsia. In moments of forward-going enthusiasm they follow him; when the inevitable reaction comes they grow critical. But even so the great majority of them bow down to him. Partly this has been due to the absence of any other effective programme. The Liberals and various groups resembling them, like the Responsivists, do not count; those who believe in terroristic violence are completely out of court in the modern world and are considered ineffective and out of date. The socialist programme is still little known, and it frightens the upper-class members of the Congress.

After a brief political estrangement in the middle of 1924, the old relations between my father and Gandhiji were resumed and they grew even more cordial. However much they differed from one another, each had the warmest regard and respect for the other. What was it that they so respected? Father has given us a glimpse into his mind in a brief Foreword he contributed to a booklet called *Thought Currents*, containing selections from Gandhiji's writings:

"I have heard," he writes, "of saints and supermen, but have never had the pleasure of meeting them, and must confess to a feeling of scepticism about their real existence. I believe in men and things manly. The 'Thought Currents' preserved in this volume have emanated from a man and are things manly. They are illustrative of two great attributes of human nature—Faith and Strength . . .

"'What is all this going to lead to?' asks the man with neither faith nor strength in him. The answer 'to victory or death' does not appeal to him . . . Meanwhile the humble and lowly figure standing erect . . . on the firm footholds of faith unshakable and strength unconquerable, continues to send out to his countrymen his message of sacrifice and suffering for the motherland. That message finds echo in millions of hearts . . ."

And he finishes up by quoting Swinburne's lines:

Have we not men with us royal,
Men the masters of things?

Evidently he wanted to stress the fact that he did not admire Gandhiji as a saint or a Mahatma, but as a man. Strong and unbending himself, he admired strength of spirit in him. For it was clear that this little man of poor physique had something of steel in him, something rock-like which did not yield to physical powers, however great they might be. And in spite of his unimpressive features, his loin-cloth and bare body, there was a royalty and a kinginess in him which compelled a willing obeisance from others. Consciously and deliberately meek and humble, yet he was full of power and authority, and he knew it, and at times he was imperious enough, issuing commands which had to be obeyed. His calm, deep eyes would hold one and gently probe into the depths; his voice, clear and limpid, would purr its way into the heart and evoke an emotional response. Whether his audience consisted of one person or a thousand, the charm and magnetism of the man passed on to it, and each one had a feeling of communion with the speaker. This feeling had little to do with the mind, though the appeal to the mind was not wholly ignored. But mind and reason definitely had second place. This process of 'spell-binding' was not brought about by oratory or the hypnotism of silken phrases. The language was always simple and to the point and seldom was an unnecessary word used. It was the utter sincerity of the man and his personality that gripped; he gave the impression of tremendous inner reserves of power. Perhaps also it was a tradition that had grown up about him which helped in creating a suitable atmosphere. A stranger, ignorant of this tradition and not in harmony with the surroundings, would probably not have been touched by that spell, or, at any rate, not to the same extent. And yet one of the most remarkable things about Gandhiji was, and is, his capacity to win over, or at least to disarm, his opponents.

Gandhiji had little sense of beauty or artistry in man-made objects, though he admired natural beauty. The Taj Mahal was for him an embodiment of forced labour and little more. His sense of smell was feeble. And yet in his own way he had discovered the art of living and had made of his life an artistic whole. Every gesture had meaning and grace, without a false touch. There were no rough edges or sharp corners about him, no trace of vulgarity or commonness, in which, unhappily, our middle classes excel. Having found an inner peace, he radiated it to others and marched through life's tortuous ways with firm and undaunted step.

How different was my father from him! But in him too there was strength of personality and a measure of kingliness, and the lines of Swinburne he had quoted would apply to him also. In any gathering in which he was present he would inevitably be the centre and the hub. Whatever the place where he sat at table it would become, as an eminent English judge said later, the head of the table. He was neither meek nor mild, and, again unlike Gandhiji, he seldom spared those who differed from him. Consciously imperious, he evoked great loyalty as well as bitter opposition. It was difficult to feel neutral about him; one had to like him or dislike him. With a broad forehead, tight lips and a determined chin, he had a marked resemblance to the busts of the Roman Emperors in the museums in Italy. Many friends in Italy who saw his photograph with us remarked on this resemblance. In later years especially, when his head was covered with silver hair—unlike me, he kept his hair to the end—there was a magnificence about him and a grand manner, which is sadly to seek in this world of today. I suppose I am partial to him, but I miss his noble presence in a world full of pettiness and weakness. I look round in vain for that grand manner and splendid strength that was his.

I remember showing Gandhiji a photograph of father's some time in 1924, when he was having a tug-of-war with the Swaraj Party. In this photograph father had no moustache, and, till then, Gandhiji had always seen him with a fine moustache. He started almost on seeing this photograph and gazed long at it, for the absence of the moustache brought out the hardness of the mouth and the chin, and he said, with a somewhat dry smile, that now he realized what he had to contend against. The face was softened, however, by the eyes and by the lines that frequent laughter had made. But sometimes the eyes glittered.

Father had taken to the work in the Assembly like a duck to water. It suited his legal and constitutional training, and, unlike Satyagraha and its offshoots, he knew the rules of this game. He kept his party strictly disciplined and even induced other groups and individuals to give support. But soon he had to face difficulties with his own people. During the early days of the Swaraj Party, it had to contend against the No-changers in the Congress, and many undesirables were taken in to increase its strength within the Congress. Then came the elections, and these demanded funds which had to come from the rich. So these rich folk had to be kept in good humour, and some were even asked to become Swarajist candidates. "Politics," says an American socialist (quoted by Sir Stafford Cripps), "is the gentle art of getting votes from the poor and campaign funds from the rich by promising to protect each from the other."

All these elements weakened the Party from the very beginning. Work in the Assembly and the Councils necessitated daily compromises with other and more moderate groups, and no crusading spirit or principles could long survive this. Gradually a decline in the discipline and temper of the Party set in, and the weaker elements and the opportunists began to give trouble. The Swaraj Party had invaded the legislatures with the declared object of "opposition from within". But two could play at this game, and the Government decided to have a hand in it by creating opposition and disruption within the ranks of the Swarajists. High office and patronage in innumerable ways was placed in the way of the weaker brethren. They had just to pick them up. Their ability and their qualities of statesmanship and sweet reasonableness were praised. A pleasant and agreeable atmosphere was created round them— so different from the dust and tumult of the field and market-place.

The general tone of the Swarajists went down. Individuals here and there began to slip away to the other side. My father shouted and thundered and talked about cutting 'the diseased limb'. But this threat has no great effect when the limb is eager to walk away by itself. Some Swarajists became ministers, some became Executive Councillors in the provinces later. A number formed a separate group calling themselves 'Responsivists' or 'Responsive Co-operators', a name originally used by Lokamanya Tilak in entirely different circumstances. As used now it seemed to mean: take a job when you have the chance and make the best of it. The Swaraj Party carried on in spite of these defections, but father and Mr Das became a little disgusted with the turn of events and somewhat weary of what seemed to be their profitless work in the legislatures. To add to this weariness of spirit was the growing Hindu-Muslim tension in North India, leading occasionally to riots.

Some Congressmen who had been to prison with us in 1921 and 1922 were now ministers and holders of high offices in the Government. In 1921 we had had the satisfaction of being declared unlawful and being sentenced to prison by a Government of which some Liberals (also old-time Congressmen) were members. In future we were going to have the additional solace of being imprisoned and outlawed by some of our own old colleagues in some provinces at least. These new ministers and Executive councillors were far more efficient for this job than the Liberals had been. They knew us and our weaknesses and how to exploit them; they were well acquainted with our methods; and they had some experience of crowds and the feelings of the masses. Like the Nazis, they had flirted with revolutionary methods before changing sides, and could apply this knowledge to suppress more efficiently their old colleagues of the Congress than either the official hierarchy or the Liberal ministers in their ignorance could have done.

In December 1924 the Congress session was held at Belgaum, and Gandhiji was President. For him to become the Congress President was something in the nature of an anticlimax, for he had long been the permanent super-president. I did not like his presidential address. It struck me as being very uninspiring. At the end of the session I was again elected, at Gandhiji's instance, the working secretary of the A.I.C.C. for the next year. In spite of my own wishes in the matter, I was gradually becoming a semi-permanent secretary of the Congress.

In the summer of 1925 my father was unwell and his asthma troubled him greatly. He went with the family to Dalhousie in the Himalayas, and I joined him for a short while later. We made a little trip from Dalhousie to Chamba in the interior of the Himalayas. It was a June day when we arrived, and we were a little tired after our journey by mountain paths. A telegram came. It told us that Chitta Ranjan Das had died. For a long time father sat still without a word, bowed down with grief. It was a cruel blow to him, and I had seldom seen him so affected. The one person who had grown to be a closer and dearer comrade to him than anyone else had suddenly gone and left him to shoulder the burden alone. That burden had been growing, and both he and Deshbandhu had grown aweary of it and of the weakness of their people. Deshbandhu's last speech at the Faridpur Conference was the speech of a person who is a little tired.

We left Chamba the next morning and tramped back over the mountains to Dalhousie, and from there to the distant railhead by car, and then to Allahabad and Calcutta.

19

COMMUNALISM RAMPANT

My illness in the autumn of 1923, after my return from Nabha prison, when I had a bout with the typhus germ, was a novel experience for me. I was unused to illness or lying in bed with fever or physical weakness. I was a little proud of my health, and I objected to the general valetudinarian attitude that was fairly common in India. My youth and good constitution pulled me through, but, after the crisis was over, I lay long in bed in an enfeebled condition, slowly working my way to health. And during this period I felt a strange detachment from my surroundings and my day-to-day work, and I viewed all this from a distance, apart. I felt as if I had extricated myself from the trees and could see the wood as a whole; my mind seemed clearer and more peaceful than it had previously been. I suppose this experience, or something like it, is common enough to those who have passed through severe illness. But for me it was in the nature of a spiritual experience— I use the word not in a narrow religious sense—and it influenced me considerably. I felt lifted out of the emotional atmosphere of our politics and could view the objectives and the springs that had moved me to action more clearly. With this clarification came further questioning for which I had no satisfactory answer. But more and more I moved away from the religious outlook on life and politics. I cannot write much about that experience of mine; it was a feeling I cannot easily express. It was eleven years ago, and only a faded impression of it remains in the mind now. But I remember well that it had a lasting effect on me and on my way of thinking, and for the next two years or more I went about my work with something of that air of detachment.

Partly, no doubt, this was due to developments which were wholly outside my control and with which I did not fit in. I have referred already to some of the political changes. Far more important was the progressive deterioration of Hindu-Muslim relations, in North India especially. In the bigger cities a number of riots took place, brutal and callous in the extreme. The atmosphere of distrust and anger bred new causes of dispute which most of us had never heard of before. Previously a fruitful source of discord had been the question of cow sacrifice, especially on the Bakr-id day. There was also tension when Hindu and Muslim festivals clashed, as, for instance, when the Moharram fell on the days when the Ram Lila was celebrated. The Moharram revived the memory of a past tragedy and brought sorrow and tears; the Ram Lila was a festival of joy and the celebration of the victory of good over evil. The two did not fit in. Fortunately they came together only once in about thirty years, for the Ram Lila is celebrated according to the solar calendar at a fixed time of the year, while the Moharram moves round the seasons, following a lunar year.

But now a fresh cause of friction arose, something that was ever present, ever recurring. This was the question of music before mosques. Objection was taken by the Muslims to music or any noise which interfered with their prayers in their mosques. In every city there are many mosques, and five times every day they have prayers, and there is no lack of noises and processions (including marriage and funeral processions). So the chances of friction were always present. In particular, objection was taken to processions and noises at the time of the sunset prayer in the mosques. As it happens, this is just the time when evening worship takes place in the Hindu temples, and gongs are sounded and the temple bells ring. *Arti*, this is called, and *arti-namaz* disputes now assumed major proportions.

It seems amazing that a question which could be settled with mutual consideration for each other's feelings and a little adjustment should give rise to great bitterness and rioting. But religious passions have little to do with reason or consideration or adjustments, and they are easy to fan when a third party in control can play off one group against another.

One is apt to exaggerate the significance of these riots in a few northern cities. Most of the towns and cities and the whole of rural India carried on peacefully, little affected by these happenings, but the newspapers naturally gave great prominence to every petty communal disturbance. It is perfectly true, however, that communal tension and bitterness increased in the city masses. This was pushed on by the communal leaders at the top, and it was reflected in the stiffening up of the political communal demands. Because of the communal tension,

Muslim political reactionaries, who had taken a back seat during all these years of non-co-operation, emerged into prominence, helped in the process by the British Government. From day to day new and more far-reaching communal demands appeared on their behalf, striking at the very root of national unity and Indian freedom. On the Hindu side also political reactionaries were among the principal communal leaders, and, in the name of guarding Hindu interests, they played definitely into the hands of the Government. They did not succeed, and indeed they could not, however much they tried by their methods, in gaining any of the points on which they laid stress: they succeeded only in raising the communal temper of the country.

The Congress was in a quandary. Sensitive to and representative of national feeling as it was, these communal passions were bound to affect it. Many a Congressman was a communalist under his national cloak. But the Congress leadership stood firm and, on the whole, refused to side with either communal party, or rather with any communal group, for now the Sikhs and other smaller minorities were also loudly voicing their particular demands. Inevitably this led to denunciation from both the extremes.

Long ago, right at the commencement of non-co-operation or even earlier, Gandhiji had laid down his formula for solving the communal problem. According to him, it could only be solved by goodwill and the generosity of the majority group, and so he was prepared to agree to everything that the Muslims might demand. He wanted to win them over, not to bargain with them. With foresight and a true sense of values he grasped at the reality that was worthwhile; but others who thought they knew the market price of everything, and were ignorant of the true value of anything, stuck to the methods of the market-place. They saw the cost of purchase with painful clearness, but they had no appreciation of the worth of the article they might have bought.

It is easy to criticize and blame others, and the temptation is almost irresistible to find some excuse for the failure of one's plans. Was not the failure due to the deliberate thwarting of others, rather than to an error in one's own way of thinking or acting? We cast the blame on the Government and the communalists, the latter blame the Congress. Of course, there was thwarting of us, deliberate and persistent thwarting, by the Government and their allies. Of course, British governments in the past and the present have based their policy on creating divisions in our ranks. Divide arid rule has always been the way of empires, and the measure of their success in this policy has been also the measure of their superiority over those whom they thus exploit. We cannot complain of this or, at any rate, we ought not to be surprised at it. To ignore it and not to provide against it is in itself a mistake in one's thought.

How are we to provide against it? Not surely by bargaining and haggling and generally adopting the tactics of the market-place, for whatever offer we make, however high our bid might be, there is always a third party which can bid higher and, what is more, give substance to its words. If there is no common national or social outlook, there will not be common action against the common adversary. If we think in terms of the existing political and economic structure and merely wish to tamper with it here and there, to reform it, to 'Indianise' it, then all real inducement for joint action is lacking. The object then becomes one of sharing in the spoils, and the third and controlling party inevitably plays the dominant role and hands out its gifts to the prize boys of its choice. Only by thinking in terms of a different political framework—and even more so a different social framework—can we build up a stable foundation for joint action. The whole idea underlying the demand for independence was this: to make people realize that we were struggling for an entirely different political structure and not just an Indianised edition (with British control behind the scenes) of the present order, which Dominion Status signifies. Political independence meant, of course, political freedom only, and did not include any social change or economic freedom for the masses. But it did signify the removal of the financial and economic chains which bind us to the City of London, and this would have made it easier for us to change the social structure. So I thought then. I would add now that I do not think it is likely that real political freedom will come to us by itself. When it comes it will bring a large measure of social freedom also.

But almost all our leaders continued to think within the narrow steel frame of the existing political, and of course the social, structure. They faced every problem—communal or constitutional—with this background and, inevitably, they played into the hands of the British Government, which controlled completely that structure. They could not do otherwise, for their whole outlook was essentially reformist and not revolutionary, in spite of occasional experiments with direct action. But the time had gone by when any political or economic or communal problem in India could be satisfactorily solved by reformist methods. Revolutionary outlook and planning and revolutionary solutions were demanded by the situation. But there was no one among the leaders to offer these.

The want of clear ideals and objectives in our struggle for freedom undoubtedly helped the spread of communalism. The masses saw no clear connection between their day-to-day sufferings and the fight for swaraj. They fought well enough at times by instinct, but that was a feeble weapon which could be easily blunted or even turned aside for other purposes. There was no reason behind it, and in periods of reaction it was not difficult for the communalists to play upon this feeling and exploit it in the name of religion. It is nevertheless extraordinary how the *bourgeois* classes, both among the Hindus and the Muslims, succeeded, in the sacred name of religion, in getting a measure of mass sympathy and support for programmes and demands which had absolutely nothing to do with the masses, or even the lower middle class. Every one of the communal demands put forward by any communal group is, in the final analysis, a demand for jobs, and these jobs could only go to a handful of the upper middle class. There is also, of course, the demand for special and additional seats in the legislatures, as symbolizing political power, but this too is looked upon chiefly as the power to exercise patronage. These narrow political demands, benefiting at the most a small number of the upper middle classes, and often creating barriers in the way of national unity and progress, were cleverly made to appear the demands of the masses of that particular religious group. Religious passion was hitched on to them in order to hide their barrenness.

In this way political reactionaries came back to the political field in the guise of communal leaders, and the real explanation of the various steps they took was not so much their communal bias as their desire to obstruct political advance. We could only expect opposition from them politically, but still it was a peculiarly distressing feature of an unsavoury situation to find to what lengths they would go in this respect. Muslim communal leaders said the most amazing things and seemed to care not at all for Indian nationalism or Indian freedom; Hindu communal leaders, though always speaking apparently in the name of nationalism, had little to do with it in practice and, incapable of any real action, sought to humble themselves before the Government, and did that too in vain. Both agreed in condemning socialistic and such-like "subversive" movements; there was a touching unanimity in regard to any proposal affecting vested interests. Muslim communal leaders said and did many things harmful to political and economic freedom, but as a group and individually they conducted themselves before the Government and the public with some dignity. That could hardly be said of the Hindu communal leaders.

There were many Muslims in the Congress. Their numbers were large, and included many able men, and the best-known and most popular Muslim leaders in India were in it. Many of those Congress Muslims organized themselves into a group called the 'Nationalist Muslim Party', and they combated the communal Muslim leaders. They did so with some success to begin with, and a large part of the Muslim intelligentsia seemed to be with them. But they were all upper middle class folk, and there were no dynamic personalities amongst them. They took to their professions and their businesses, and lost touch with the masses. Indeed, they never went to their masses. Their method was one of drawing-room meetings and mutual arrangements and pacts, and at this game their rivals, the communal leaders, were greater adepts. Slowly the latter drove the Nationalist Muslims from one position to another, made them give up, one by one, the principles for which they stood. Always the Nationalist Muslims tried to ward off further retreat and to consolidate their position by adopting the policy of the 'lesser evil', but always this led to another retreat and another choice of the 'lesser evil'. There came a time when they had nothing left to call their own, no fundamental principle on which they stood except one, and that had been the very sheet-anchor of their group: joint electorates. But again the policy of the lesser evil presented the fatal choice to them, and they emerged from the ordeal minus that sheet-anchor. So today they stand divested of every shred of principle or practice on the basis of which they formed their group, and which they had proudly nailed to their masthead—of everything, all, except their name!

The collapse and elimination of the Nationalist Muslims as a group—as individuals they are, of course, still important leaders of the Congress—forms a pitiful story. It took many years, and the last chapter has only been written this year (1934). In 1923 and subsequent years they were a strong group, and they took up an aggressive attitude against the Muslim communalists. Indeed, on several occasions, Gandhiji was prepared to agree to some of the latter's demands, much as he disliked them, but his own colleagues, the Muslim Nationalist leaders, prevented this and were bitter in their opposition.

During the middle 'twenties many attempts were made to settle the communal problem by mutual talks and discussions—'Unity Conferences' they were called. The most notable of these was the conference convened by M. Mohamad Ali, the Congress president for the year, in 1924, and held in Delhi under the shadow of Gandhiji's twenty-one-day fast. There were many earnest and well-meaning people at these conferences, and they tried hard to come to an agreement. Some pious and good resolutions were passed, but the basic problem remained unsolved. It could not be solved by those conferences, for a solution could not be reached by a majority of votes but by virtual unanimity, and there were always extremists of various groups present whose idea of a solution was a complete submission of all others to their views. Indeed, one was led to doubt whether some of the prominent communalists desired a solution at all. Many of them were political reactionaries, and there was no common ground between them and those who desired radical political change.

But the real difficulties went deeper and were not just the result of individual back-sliding. The Sikhs were now loudly advancing their communal demands, and an extraordinarily complicated triangle was created in the Punjab. The Punjab, indeed, became the crux of the matter, and the fear of each group of the others produced a background of passion and prejudice. In some provinces agrarian trouble—Hindu zamindars and Muslim tenants in Bengal—appeared under communal guise. In the Punjab and Sind, the banker and richer classes generally were Hindus, the debtors were Muslim agriculturists, and all the feeling of the impoverished debtors against the creditor, out for his pound of flesh, went to swell the communal tide. As a rule, the Muslims were the poorer community, and the Muslim communal leaders managed to exploit the antagonism of the have-nots against the haves for communal purposes, though, strangely enough, these purposes had nothing whatever to do with the betterment of those have-nots. Because of this, these Muslim communal leaders did represent some mass elements, and gained strength thereby. The Hindu communal leaders, in an economic sense, represented the rich banker and professional classes; they had little backing among the Hindu masses although, on occasions, they had their sympathy.

The problem, therefore, is getting a little mixed up with economic groupings, though unhappily this fact is not realized. It may develop into more obvious conflicts between economic classes, but if that time comes, the present-day communal leaders, representing the upper classes of all groups, will hasten to patch up their differences in order to face jointly the common class foe. Even under present conditions it should not be difficult to arrive at a political solution, but only if, and it is a big if, the third party was not present.

The Delhi Unity Conference of 1924 was hardly over when a Hindu-Muslim riot broke out in Allahabad. It was not a big riot, as such riots go, in so far as casualties were concerned, but it was painful to have these troubles in one's home town. I rushed back with others from Delhi to find that the actual rioting was over; but the aftermath, in the shape of bad blood and court cases, lasted a long time. I forget why the riot had begun. That year, or perhaps later, there was also some trouble over the Ram Lila celebrations at Allahabad. Probably because of restrictions about music before mosques, these celebrations, involving huge processions as they did, were abandoned as a protest. For about eight years now the Ram Lila has not been held in Allahabad, and the greatest festival of the year for hundreds of thousands in the Allahabad district has almost become a painful memory. How well I remember my visits to it when I was a child! How excited we used to get! And the vast crowds that came to see it from all over the district and even from other towns. It was a Hindu festival, but it was an open-air affair, and Muslims also swelled the crowds, and there was joy and lightheartedness everywhere. Trade flourished. Many years afterwards when, as a grown-up, I visited it I was not excited, and the procession and the tableaux rather bored me. My standards of art and amusement had gone up. But even then, I saw how the great crowds appreciated and enjoyed the show. It was carnival time for them. And now, for eight or nine years, the children of Allahabad, not to mention the grown-ups, have had no chance of seeing this show and having a bright day of joyful excitement in the dull routine of their lives. And all because of trivial disputes and conflicts! Surely religion and the spirit of religion have much to answer for. What kill-joys they have been!

20

MUNICIPAL WORK

For two years I carried on, but with an ever-increasing reluctance, with the Allahabad Municipality. My term of office as chairman was for three years. Before the second year was well begun, I was trying to rid myself of the responsibility. I had liked the work, and given a great deal of my time and thought to it. I had met with a measure of success and gained the goodwill of all my colleagues. Even the Provincial Government had overcome its political dislike of me to the extent of commending some of my municipal activities. And yet I found myself hedged in, obstructed and prevented from doing anything really worth while.

It was not deliberate obstruction on anybody's part; indeed, I had a surprising amount of willing co-operation. But on the one side, there was the Government machine; on the other, the apathy of the members of the municipality as well as the public. The whole steel-frame of municipal administration, as erected by Government, prevented radical growth or innovation. The financial policy was such that the municipality was always dependent on the Government. Most radical schemes of taxation or social development were not permissible under the existing municipal laws. Even such schemes as were legally permissible had to be sanctioned by Government, and only the optimists, with a long stretch of years before them, could confidently ask for and await this sanction. It amazed me to find out how slowly and laboriously and inefficiently the machinery of Government moved when any job of social construction, or of nation building was concerned. There was no slowness or inefficiency, however, when a political opponent had to be curbed or struck down. The contrast was marked.

The department of the Provincial Government dealing with Local Self-government was presided over by a Minister; but, as a rule, this presiding genius was supremely ignorant of municipal affairs or, indeed, of any public affairs. Indeed, he counted for little and was largely ignored by his own department, which was run by the permanent officials of the Indian Civil Service. These officials were influenced by the prevailing conception of high officials in India that government was primarily a police function. Some idea of authoritarian paternalism coloured this conception, but there was hardly any appreciation of the necessity of social services on a large scale.

Government is always a creditor of the municipalities, and, next to the police view, it is the creditor's view that it takes of them. Are the debt instalments paid regularly? Is the municipality thoroughly solvent, and has it got a substantial balance in hand? All very necessary and relevant questions, but it is often overlooked that the municipality has some positive functions to perform—education, sanitation, etc.—and that it is not merely an organization for borrowing money and paying it back at regular intervals. The social services provided by Indian municipalities are few enough, but even these are curtailed where there is financial stringency, and usually the first to suffer is education. The ruling classes are not personally interested in municipal schools; their children go to more up-to-date and expensive private schools, often receiving grants-in-aid from the State.

Most Indian cities can be divided into two parts: the densely crowded city proper, and the widespread area with bungalows and cottages, each with a fairly extensive compound or garden, usually referred to by the English as the 'Civil Lines'. It is in these Civil Lines that the English officials and businessmen, as well as many upper middle class Indians, professional men, officials, etc., live. The income of the municipality from the city proper is greater than that from the Civil Lines, but the expenditure on the latter far exceeds the city expenditure. For the far wider area covered by the Civil Lines requires more roads, and they have to be repaired, cleaned-up, watered, and lighted; and the drainage, the water supply, and the sanitation system have to be more widespread. The city part is always grossly neglected, and, of course, the poorer parts of the city are almost ignored; it has few good roads, and most of the narrow lanes are ill-lit and have no proper drainage or sanitation system. It puts up with all these disabilities patiently and seldom complains; and when it does complain, nothing much happens. Nearly all the Big Noises and Little Noises live in the Civil Lines.

To equalize the burden a little and to encourage improvements, I wanted to introduce a tax on land values. But hardly had I made the suggestion when a protest came from a Government official, I think it was the District Magistrate, who pointed out that this would be in contravention of various enactments or conditions of land tenure. Such a tax would obviously have fallen more heavily on the owners of the bungalows in the Civil Lines. But Government approves thoroughly of an indirect tax like the octroi which crushes trade, raises prices of all goods, including foodstuffs, and falls most heavily on the poor. And this most unsocial and harmful levy has been the mainstay of most Indian municipalities, though, I believe, it is very slowly disappearing in the larger cities.

As chairman of the Municipality I had thus to deal with, on the one side, an impersonal authoritarian government machine which jogged along laboriously in the old ruts and obstinately refused either to move faster or in a different direction; and on the other, were my colleagues, the members, most of whom were equally in the ruts. Some of them were idealists, and took to their work with enthusiasm, but taken as a whole there was no vision, no passion for change or betterment. The old ways were good enough, why try experiments which might not come off? Even the idealists and enthusiasts gradually succumbed to the narcotic effects of dull routine. But one subject could always be relied upon to infuse vigour into the members—the subject of patronage and appointments. This interest did not always result in greater efficiency.

Year after year government resolutions and officials and some newspapers criticize municipalities and local boards, and point out their many failings. And from this the moral is drawn that democratic institutions are not suited to India. Their failings are obvious enough, but little attention is paid to the framework within which they have to function. This framework is neither democratic nor autocratic; it is a cross between the two, and has the disadvantages of both. That a central government should have certain powers of supervision and control may be admitted, but this can only fit in with a popular local body if the central government itself is democratic and responsive to public needs. Where this is not so, there will either be a tussle between the two or a tame submission to the will of the central authority, which thus exercises power without in any way shouldering responsibility. This is obviously unsatisfactory, and it takes away from the reality of popular control. Even the members of the Municipal Board look more to the central authority than to their constituents, and the public also often ignores the Board. Real social issues hardly ever come before the Board, chiefly because they lie outside its functions, and its most obvious activities are tax-collecting, which do not make it excessively popular.

The franchise for the local bodies is also limited, and should be greatly lowered and extended. Even a great city corporation like the Bombay Corporation is, I believe, elected on a very restricted franchise. Some time back a resolution asking for wider franchise was actually defeated in the Corporation itself. Evidently the majority of councillors were satisfied with their lot and saw no reason to change it or risk it.

Whatever the reasons, the fact remains that our local bodies are not, as a rule, shining examples of success and efficiency, though they might, even so, compare with some municipalities in advanced democratic countries. They are not usually corrupt; they are just inefficient, and their weak point is nepotism, and their perspectives are all wrong. All this is natural enough; for democracy, to be successful, must have a background of informed public opinion and a sense of responsibility. Instead, we have an all-pervading atmosphere of authoritarianism, and the accompaniments of democracy are lacking. There is no mass educational system, no effort to build up public opinion based on knowledge. Inevitably public attention turns to personal or communal or other petty issues.

The main interest of Government in municipal administration is that 'politics' should be kept out. Any resolution of sympathy with the national movement is frowned upon; textbooks which might have a nationalist flavour are not permitted in the municipal schools, even pictures of national leaders are not allowed there. A national flag has to be pulled down on pain of suppression of the municipality. Lately a concerted attempt seems to have been made by several Provincial Governments to hound out Congressmen from the service of the municipal corporations and boards. Usually, pressure was enough to bring this about, accompanied as it was with the threat of withholding various Government grants for municipal education or other purposes. But in some cases, notably that of the Calcutta Corporation, legislation has been promoted to keep out all persons who may have gone to prison in connection with civil disobedience or any other political movement against the Government. The object was purely political; there was no question of incompetence or unfitness for the job.

These few instances show how much freedom our municipal and district boards have, how little democratic they are. The attempt to keep out political opponents from all municipal and local services—of course they did not go in for direct government service—deserves a little attention. It is estimated that about 300,000 persons have gone to prison at various times during the past fourteen years; and there can be no doubt that, politics apart, these 300,000 included some of the most dynamic and idealistic, the most socially minded and selfless people in India. They had push and energy and the ideal of service to a cause. They were thus the best material from which a public department or utility service could draw its employees. And yet Government has made every effort, even to the extent of passing laws, to keep out these people, and so to punish them and those who sympathized with them. It prefers and pushes on the lap-dog breed, and then complains of the inefficiency of our local bodies. And although politics are said to be outside the province of local bodies, Government has no objection whatever to their indulging in politics in support of itself. Teachers in local board schools have been practically compelled, for fear of losing their jobs, to go out in the villages to do propaganda on behalf of Government.

During the last fifteen years Congress workers have had to face many difficult positions; they have shouldered heavy responsibilities; they have, after all, combated, not without success, a powerful and entrenched Government. This hard course of training has given them self-reliance and efficiency and strength to persevere; it has provided them with the very qualities of which a long and emasculating course of authoritarian government had deprived the Indian people. Of course, the Congress movement, like all mass movements, had, and has, many undesirables— fools, inefficients, and worse people. But I have no doubt whatever that an average Congress worker is likely to be far more efficient and dynamic than another person of similar qualifications.

There is one aspect of this matter which Government and its advisers perhaps do not appreciate. The attempt to deprive Congress workers of all jobs and to shut avenues of employment to them is welcomed by the real revolutionary. The average Congressman is notoriously not a revolutionary, and after a period of semi-revolutionary action he resumes his humdrum life and activities. He gets entangled either in his business or profession or in the mazes of local politics. Larger issues seem to fade off in his mind, and revolutionary ardour, such as it was, subsides. Muscle turns to fat, and spirit to a love of security. Because of this inevitable tendency of middle-class workers, it has always been the effort of advanced and revolutionary-minded Congressmen to prevent their comrades from entering the constitutional mazes of the legislatures and the local bodies, or accepting whole-time jobs which prevent them from effective action. The Government has, however, now come to their help to some extent by making it a little more difficult for the Congress worker to get a job, and it is thus likely that he will retain some of his revolutionary ardour or even add to it.

After a year or more of municipal work I felt that I was not utilizing my energies to the best advantage there. The most I could do was to speed-up work and make it a little more efficient. I could not push through any worthwhile change. I wanted to resign from the chairmanship, but all the members of the Board pressed me to stay. I had received uniform kindness and courtesy from them, and I found it hard to refuse. At the end of my second year, however, I finally resigned.

This was in 1925. In the autumn of that year my wife fell seriously ill, and for many months she lay in a Lucknow hospital. The Congress was held that year at Cawnpore, and, somewhat distracted, I rushed backwards and forwards between Allahabad, Cawnpore, and Lucknow. (I was still General Secretary of the Congress.)

Further treatment in Switzerland was recommended for my wife. I welcomed the idea, for I wanted an excuse to go out of India myself. My mind was befogged, and no clear path was visible; and I thought that, perhaps, if I was far from India I could see things in better perspective and lighten up the dark corners of my mind.

At the beginning of March 1926 we sailed, my wife, our daughter and I, from Bombay for Venice. With us on the same boat went also my sister and brother-in-law, Ranjit S. Pandit. They had planned their European trip long before the question of our going had arisen.

21

IN EUROPE

I was going back to Europe after more than thirteen years—years of war, and revolution, and tremendous change. The old world I knew had expired in the blood and horror of the War and a new world awaited me. I expected to remain in Europe for six or seven months or, at most, till the end of the year. Actually our stay lengthened out to a year and nine months.

It was a quiet and restful period for both my mind and body. We spent it chiefly in Switzerland, in Geneva, and in a mountain sanatorium at Montana. My younger sister, Krishna, came from India and joined us early in the summer of 1926, and remained with us till the end of our stay in Europe. I could not leave my wife for long, and so I could only pay brief visits to other places. Later, when my wife was better, we travelled a little in France, England, and Germany. On our mountain-top, surrounded by the winter snow, I felt completely cut off from India as well as the European world. India, and Indian happenings, seemed especially far away. I was a distant onlooker, reading, watching, following events, gazing at the new Europe, its politics, economics, and the far freer human relationships, and trying to understand them. When we were in Geneva I was naturally interested in the activities of the League of Nations and the International Labour Office.

But with the coming of winter, the winter sports absorbed my attention; for some months they were my chief occupation and interest. I had done ice-skating previously, but ski-ing was a new experience, and I succumbed to its fascination. It was a painful experience for a long time, but I persisted bravely, in spite of innumerable falls, and I came to enjoy it.

Life was very uneventful on the whole. The days went by and my wife gradually gained strength and health. We saw few Indians; indeed, we saw few people apart from the little colony living in that mountain resort. But in the course of the year and three-quarters that we spent in

Europe, we came across some Indian exiles and old revolutionaries whose names had been familiar to me.

There was Shyamji Krishnavarma living with his ailing wife high up on the top floor of a house in Geneva. The aged couple lived by themselves with no whole-time servants, and their rooms were musty and suffocating, and everything had a thick layer of dust. Shyamji had plenty of money, but he did not believe in spending it. He would even save a few centimes by walking instead of taking the tram. He was suspicious of all comers, presuming them, until the contrary was proved, to be either British agents or after his money. His pockets bulged with ancient copies of his old paper, the *Indian Sociologist*, and he would pull them out and point with some excitement to some article he had written a dozen years previously. His talk was of the old days, of India House at Hampstead, of the various persons that the British Government had sent to spy on him, and how he had spotted them and outwitted them. The walls of his rooms were covered with shelves full of old books, dust-laden and neglected, looking down sorrowfully on the intruder. Books and papers also littered the floor; they seemed to have remained so for days and weeks, and even months past. Over the whole place there hung an atmosphere of gloom, an air of decay; life seemed to be an unwelcome stranger there, and, as one walked through the dark and silent corridors, one almost expected to come across, round the corner, the shadow of death. With relief one came out of that flat and breathed the air outside.

Shyamji desired to make some arrangement about his money, to create some trust for a public purpose, preferably for the education of Indians in foreign countries. He suggested that I might be one of the trustees, but I showed no keenness for shouldering this responsibility. I had no desire to get mixed up with his financial affairs; and, besides, I felt that if I showed any undue interest he would immediately suspect me of coveting his money. No one knew how much he had. It was rumoured that he had lost greatly in the German inflation.

Occasionally prominent Indians used to pass through Geneva. Those who came to the League of Nations were of the official variety, and Shyamji would not, of course, go anywhere near them. But the Labour Office sometimes brought non-officials of note, even prominent Congressmen, and Shyamji would try to meet them. It was interesting to watch their reactions to him. Invariably they felt uncomfortable, and tried to avoid him in public, and excused themselves, whenever they could, in private. He was not considered a safe person with whom to be associated or seen with.

And so Shyamji and his wife lived their lonely life without children or relatives or friends, with hardly any associations, hardly any human contacts. He was a relic of the past, and had really outlived his day. He did not fit in with the present, and the world passed him by, ignoring him. But there was still some of the old fire in his eyes, and though there was little in common between him and me, I could not withhold my sympathy and consideration for him.

Recently the newspapers reported his death, followed soon after by the death of the gentle Gujrati old lady who had been his life-long companion in exile in foreign lands. It was stated that a large sum of money was left by her for the training of Indian women abroad.

Another well-known person whose name I had often heard, but whom I met for the first time in Switzerland, was Raja Mahendra Pratap. He was (and, I suppose, is still) a delightful optimist, living completely in the air and refusing to have anything to do with realities. I was a little taken aback when I first saw him. He appeared in strange composite attire, which might have been suitable in the highlands of Tibet or in the Siberian plains, but was completely out of place at Montreux in the summer. It was a kind of semi-military costume, with high Russian boots, and there were numerous large pockets, all bulging with papers, photographs, etc. There was a letter from Bethman-Hollweg, the German Chancellor, an autographed picture of the Kaiser, a fine scroll from the Dalai Lama of Tibet, and innumerable documents and pictures. It was amazing how much those various pockets contained. He told us that once he had lost a dispatch-box, containing valuable papers, in China, and ever since then he had considered it safer to carry his papers on his person! Hence the numerous pockets.

Mahendra Pratap was full of stories of his wanderings and adventures in Japan, China, Tibet, and Afghanistan. He had led a varied life, and the record of it was an interesting one. His latest enthusiasm was for a 'Happiness Society' which he had himself founded, and which had for its motto: "Be Happy". Apparently this society had met with greatest success in Latvia (or was it Lithuania?).

His idea of propaganda was to send out periodically large numbers of post cards containing a printed message from him to members of various conferences that met in Geneva or elsewhere. These messages were signed by him, but the name given was an extraordinary one—long and varied. 'Mahendra Pratap' had been reduced to initials, but many other names had been added, each addition representing apparently some favoured country he had visited. In this way he emphasized his international and cosmopolitan character, and, fittingly, the final description below this unique name was "Servant of Mankind". It was difficult to take Mahendra Pratap seriously. He seemed to be a character out of medieval romance, a Don Quixote who had strayed into the twentieth century. But he was absolutely straight and thoroughly earnest.

In Paris we saw old Madame Cama, rather fierce and terrifying as she came up to you and peered into your face, and, pointing at you, asked abruptly who you were. The answer made no difference (probably she was too deaf to hear it) for she formed her own impressions and stuck to them, despite facts to the contrary.

Then there was Moulvi Obeidulla, whom I met for a short while in Italy. He seemed to me to be clever, but rather in the sense of possessing an ability for old-style political manoeuvring. He was not in touch with modern ideas. He had produced a scheme for the 'United States' or 'United Republics of India', which was quite an able attempt to solve the communal problem. He told me of some of his past activities in Istanbul (it was still called Constantinople then) and, not attaching much importance to them, I soon forgot about them. Some months later he met Lala Lajpat Rai and, apparently, repeated the same story to him. Lalaji was vastly impressed and exercised about it, and that story, with many unjustifiable inferences and amazing deductions, played an important part in the Indian Council elections that year. Moulvi Obeidulla later went to the Hedjaz, and for years past no news of him has come my way.

Another Moulvi, but a different type entirely, was Barkatulla whom I first met in Berlin. He was a delightful old man, very enthusiastic and very likeable. He was rather simple, not very intelligent, but still trying to imbibe new ideas and to understand the present-day world. He died in San Francisco in 1927, while we were in Switzerland. I was grieved to learn of his passing away.

In Berlin there was quite a number of those who had formed an

Indian group in war-time, but the group had long gone to pieces. They had fallen out and quarrelled amongst themselves, each suspecting the other of betrayal. That seems to be the fate of political exiles everywhere. Many of these Berlin Indians had settled down to sedate middle-class occupations—when these could be had, and that was not often in post-war Germany—and had ceased to be in any way revolutionary. They even avoided politics.

The story of this old war-time group was interesting. Most of them were students in various German universities in that fateful summer of 1914. They lived a common life with the German students, sang their songs, joined in their games, drank beer with them, and approached their culture with sympathy and consideration. The War was no concern of theirs, but they could not help being moved to some extent by the wave of nationalistic hysteria that swept over Germany. Their feeling was really anti-British, and not pro-German, and their Indian nationalism inclined them to the enemies of Britain. Soon after the outbreak of the War a few other Indians, more consciously revolutionary, drifted into Germany through Switzerland. These people formed themselves into a committee, and sent for Hardayal, who was on the west coast of the United States at the time. Hardayal came some months later, but meanwhile the Committee had become quite important. This importance had been thrust upon them by the German Government, who were, naturally, anxious to exploit all anti-British feelings to their own advantage. The Indians, on their part, wanted to take advantage of the international situation for their own nationalistic purposes, and had no intention of allowing themselves to be exploited purely for Germany's advantage. They did not have much choice in the matter, but they felt that they had something to give which the German authorities were keen on having, and this gave them a handle to bargain with. They insisted on assurances and pledges for Indian freedom. The German Foreign Office seems to have entered into a regular treaty with them, in which it pledged itself to acknowledge Indian independence in case of victory, and it was on this pledge and condition, and many other minor conditions, that the Indian group promised support in the war. The Committee was officially honoured in every way, and its representatives were treated almost on the footing of foreign ambassadors.

This sudden importance, thrust on a small group consisting mainly of inexperienced young men, went to the heads of some of them. They felt that they were playing a historic role, that they were involved in great and epoch-making undertakings. Many of them had exciting adventures, hair-breadth escapes. In the later stages of the war, their importance visibly lessened, and they began to be ignored. Hardayal, who had come over from America, had long been discarded. He did not fit in with the Committee at all, and both the Committee and the German Government considered him unreliable, and quietly pushed him aside. Years later, when I was in Europe in 1926 and 1927, I was surprised to find with what bitterness and resentment most of the old Indian residents in Europe thought of Hardayal. He lived at the time in Sweden. I did not meet him.

The War ended, and with it ended finally the Indian Committee in Berlin. Life became a dreary affair for them after the failure of all their hopes. They had gambled for high stakes and lost. In any event, life would have seemed a humdrum affair after the high adventure and importance of those wartime years. But even a secure, humdrum life was not to be had for the asking. They could not return to India, and defeated Germany after the War was not an easy place to live in. It was a hard struggle. A few of them were later allowed by the British Government to return to India, but many had to stay on in Germany. Their position was peculiar. They were, apparently, citizens of no State. They had no proper passports. Travel outside Germany was hardly possible, even residence in Germany was full of difficulties and was at the mercy of the local police. It was a life of insecurity and hardship, and day-today worry; of continual anxiety to find the wherewithal to eat and live.

The Nazi regime since early in 1933 has added to their misfortunes, unless they fall in completely with the Nazi doctrine. Non-Nordic, and especially Asiatic, foreigners are not welcome in Germany; they are only suffered to exist so long as they behave. Hitler has pointedly declared himself in favour of British imperialist rule in India, no doubt because he wants to gain the goodwill of Britain, and he does not wish to encourage any Indians who may have displeased the British Government.

One of the exiles in Berlin whom we met, a prominent member of the old war-time group, was Champakraman Pillai. He was rather pompous, and young Indian students had given him an irreverent title. He could think in terms of nationalism only, and shrunk away from the social or economic approach to a question. With the German Nationalists, the Steelhelmets, he was perfectly at home. He was one of the very few Indians in Germany who got on with the Nazis. A few months back, in gaol, I read of his death in Berlin.

An entirely different type of person was Virendranath Chattopadhyaya, member of a famous family in India. Popularly known as Chatto, he was a very able and a very delightful person. He was always hard up, his clothes were very much the worse for wear, and often he found it difficult to raise the wherewithal for a meal. But his humour and lightheartedness never left him. He had been some years senior to me during my educational days in England. He was at Oxford when I went to Harrow. Since those days he had not returned to India, and, sometimes, a fit of homesickness came to him, when he longed to be back. All his home-ties had long been severed, and it is quite certain that if he came to India he would soon feel unhappy and out of joint. But in spite of the passage of many years and long wandering, the pull of the home remains. No exile can escape the malady of his tribe, that consumption of the soul, as Mazzini called it.

I must say that I was not greatly impressed by most of the Indian political exiles that I met abroad, although I admired their sacrifice, and sympathized with their sufferings and present difficulties, which are very real. I did not meet many of them; there are so many spread out all over the world. Only a few are known to us even by reputation, and the others have dropped out of the Indian world and been forgotten by their countrymen whom they sought to serve. Of the few I met, the only persons who impressed me intellectually were V. Chattopadhyaya and M.N. Roy. Roy I met for a brief half-hour in Moscow. He was a leading Communist then, although, subsequently, his communism drifted away from the orthodox Comintern brand. Chatto was not, I believe, a regular Communist, but he was communistically inclined. Roy has been in an Indian prison for more than three years now.

There were many other Indians floating about the face of Europe, talking a revolutionary language, making daring and fantastic suggestions, asking curious questions. They seemed to have the impress of the British Secret Service upon them.

We met, of course, many Europeans and Americans. From Geneva we went on a pilgrimage many a time (the first time with a letter of introduction from Gandhiji) to the Villa Olga at Villeneuve, to see Romain Rolland. Another precious memory is that of Ernst Toller, the young German poet and dramatist, now, under Nazi rule, no longer a German; and of Roger Baldwin, of the Civil Liberties Union of New York. In Geneva we also made friends with Dhan Gopal Mukerji, the author, who has settled down in America.

Before going to Europe I had met Frank Buchman, of the Oxford Group Movement, in India. He had given me some of the literature of his movement, and I had read it with amazement. Sudden conversions and confessions, and a revivalist atmosphere generally, seemed to me to go ill with intellectuality. I could not make out how some persons, who seemed obviously intelligent, should experience these strange emotions and be affected by them to a great extent. I grew curious. I met Frank Buchman again, in Geneva, and he invited me to one of his international house-parties, somewhere in Rumania, I think, this one was. I was sorry I could not go and look at this new emotionalism at close quarters. My curiosity has thus remained unsatisfied, and the more I read of the growth of the Oxford Group Movement, the more I wonder.

22

CONTROVERSIES IN INDIA

Soon after our arrival in Switzerland, the General Strike broke out in England. I was vastly excited, and my sympathies were naturally all on the strikers' side. The collapse of the strike, after a few days, came almost as a personal blow. Some months later I happened to visit England for a few days. The miners' struggle was still on, and London lay in semi-darkness at night. I paid a brief visit to a mining area—I think it was somewhere in Derbyshire. I saw the haggard and pinched faces of the men and women and children and, more revealing still, I saw many of the strikers and their wives being tried in the local or county court. The magistrates were themselves directors or managers of the coal mines, and they tried the miners and sentenced them for trivial offences under certain emergency regulations. One case especially angered me: three or four women, with babies in their arms, were brought up in the dock for the offence of having jeered at the blacklegs. The young mothers (and their babies) were obviously miserable and undernourished; the long struggle had told upon them and enfeebled them, and embittered them against the scabs who seemed to take the bread from their mouths.

One reads often about class justice, and in India nothing is commoner than this, but somehow I had not expected to come across such a flagrant example of it in England. It came as a shock. Another fact that I noticed with some surprise was the general atmosphere of fear among the strikers. They had definitely been terrorized by the police and the authorities, and they put up very meekly, I thought, with rather offensive treatment. It is true that they were thoroughly exhausted after a long struggle, their spirit was near breaking-point, their comrades of other trade unions had long deserted them. But still, compared to the poor Indian worker, there was a world of difference. The British miners had still a powerful organization, the sympathy of a nation-wide, and indeed world-wide, trade union movement, publicity, and resources of many kinds. All these were lacking to the Indian worker. And yet that frightened and terrorized look in the two had a strange resemblance.

In India that year there were the triennial elections to the Legislative Assembly and the Provincial Councils. I was not interested in them, but some echoes of fierce controversies managed to reach me in Switzerland. I learnt of a new party having been formed by Pandit Madan Mohan Malaviya and Lala Lajpat Rai to oppose the Swaraj Party or the regular Congress Party in the legislature, as it now was. The Nationalist Party, this was called. I could not make out, and I still do not know, what grounds of principle separated the new party from the old. Indeed, most present-day Indian parties in the legislature are like Tweedledum and Tweedledee; no real principles separate them. The Swaraj Party, for the first time, brought a new and aggressive element in the Councils, and it stood for a more extreme political policy than the others. But the difference was one of degree, not of kind.

The new Nationalist Party represented a more moderate outlook, and was definitely more to the right than was the Swaraj Party. It was also wholly a Hindu party working in close cooperation with the Hindu Mahasabha. Pandit Malaviya's leadership of it was easy to understand, for it represented as nearly as possible his own public attitude. He had, because of old associations, continued to remain in the Congress, but his intellectual outlook was not dissimilar to that of the Liberals or Moderates. He had not taken kindly to non-co-operation and the new direct action methods of the Congress, and had had no share in shaping Congress policy. Although greatly respected and always welcome to it, he was not really of the new Congress. He was not a member of its small executive, the Working Committee. He did not carry out the Congress mandates, especially in regard to the legislatures. He was also the most popular leader of the Hindu Mahasabha, and, in regard to communal matters, his policy differed from that of the Congress. To Congress he had that sentimental attachment to an organization with which he had been connected almost from the very beginning, partly to an emotional pull in the direction of the freedom struggle, for he saw that the Congress was the only organization doing anything effective about it. His heart was thus often in the Congress camp, especially in times of struggle; his head was in other camps. Inevitably this led to a continual conflict within him, and occasionally to a simultaneous attempt to march in opposite directions. The result was public confusion; but nationalism is a confusing medley, and Malaviyaji was a nationalist alone and not concerned with social or economic change. He was, and is, a supporter of the old orthodox order culturally, socially, economically; the Indian princes and the taluqadars and big zamindars consider him rightly as a benevolent friend. The sole change he desires, and desires passionately, is the complete elimination of foreign control in India. The political training and reading of his youth still influence his mind greatly, and he looks upon this dynamic, revolutionary, post-war world of the twentieth century with the spectacles of a semi-static-nineteenth century, of T.H. Green and John Stuart Mill and Gladstone and Morley, and a three- or four-thousand-year background of old Hindu culture and sociology. It is a curious combination, bristling with contradictions, but he has an amazing confidence in his own capacity to resolve contradictions. His long record of public service in various fields from early youth upwards, his success in establishing a great institution like the Benares Hindu University, his manifest sincerity and earnestness, his impressive oratory, and his gentle nature and winning personality, have endeared him to the Indian public, particularly the Hindu public, and though many may not agree with him or follow him in politics, they yield him respect and affection. Both by his age and his long public record he is the Nestor of Indian politics, but a Nestor who seems a little out of date, and very much out of touch, with the modern world. His voice commands attention, but the language he speaks is no longer understood or heeded by many.

It was natural, therefore, for Malaviyaji not to join the Swaraj Party, which was too advanced politically for him and required a disciplined adherence to the Congress policy. He wanted something more to the right and greater latitude, both politically and communally, and he got this in a new party, of which he was the founder and leader.

It is not so easy to understand Lala Lajpat Rai's adherence to this new party, though his inclination was also somewhat to the right as well as towards a more communal orientation. I had met Lalaji in Geneva that summer, and from our talks I had not gathered that he contemplated taking up an aggressive attitude against the Congress Party. How this happened I have still no idea. But in the course of the election campaign, he made certain vague charges, which showed how his mind had been working. He accused the Congress leaders of intriguing with people outside India. He further accused them of some such intrigue in establishing a Congress branch in Kabul. I do not think he ever specified his charges or went into any details, in spite of repeated requests.

I remember that when I read in the Indian papers that reached me in Switzerland about Lalaji's charges I was astounded. As Congress Secretary, I knew all about our organization; I had myself been instrumental in getting the Kabul Committee affiliated (Deshbandhu Das had taken the initiative in the matter); and though I did not then know (as I do not now know) the details of the charges, I could say from their general nature that they could have no foundation so far as the Congress was concerned. I do not know how Lalaji was misled in the matter. He may have relied on various rumours, and I think he must have been influenced by the talk he had recently had with Moulvi Obeidulla, although there was nothing in that talk which seemed extraordinary to me. But elections are extraordinary phenomena. They have a curious way of upsetting tempers and ordinary standards. The more I see of them the more I wonder, and a wholly undemocratic distaste of them grows within me.

But, personalities apart, the rise of the Nationalist Party, or some such party, was inevitable owing to the growing communal temper of the country. On the one side, there were the Muslim fears of a Hindu majority; on the other side, Hindu resentment at being bullied, as they conceived it, by the Muslims. Many a Hindu felt that there was too much of the stand-up-and-deliver about the Muslim attitude, too much of an attempt to extort special privileges with the threat of going over to the other side. Because of this, the Hindu Mahasabha rose to some importance, representing as it did Hindu nationalism, Hindu communalism opposing Muslim communalism. The aggressive activities of the Mahasabha acted on and stimulated still further this Muslim communalism, and so action and reaction went on, and in the process the communal temperature of the country went up. Essentially this was a question between the majority group in the country and a big minority. But, curiously enough, in some parts of the country the position was reversed. In the Punjab and Sind the Hindus as well as the Sikhs were in a minority, the Muslims in a majority; and these provincial minorities had as much fear of being crushed by a hostile majority in those provinces as the Muslims had in the whole of India. Or, to be more accurate, the middle-class job-seekers in each group were afraid of being ousted by the other group, and to some extent the holders of vested interests were afraid of radical changes affecting those interests.

The Swaraj Party suffered because of this growth of communalism. Some of its Muslim members dropped off and joined the communal organizations, and some of its Hindu members drifted off to the Nationalist Party. Malaviyaji and Lala Lajpat Rai made a powerful combination so far as the Hindu electorate was concerned, and Lalaji had great influence in the Punjab, the storm centre of communalism. On the side of the Swaraj Party or Congress, the chief burden of fighting the elections fell on my father. C.R. Das was no longer there to share it with him. He enjoyed a fight, or at any rate never shirked it, and the growing strength of the opposition made him throw all his great energy into the election campaign. He received and gave hard blows; little grace was shown or quarter given by either party. That election left a trail of bitter memories.

The Nationalist Party met with a great measure of success, but this success definitely lowered the political tone of the Legislative Assembly. The centre of gravity moved more to the right. The Swaraj Party had itself been the right wing of the Congress. In its attempts to add to its strength, it had allowed many a doubtful person to creep in, and had suffered in quality because of this. The Nationalist Party followed the same policy, only on a lower plane, and a motley crew of title-holders, big landholders, industrialists and others, who had little to do with politics, came into its ranks.

The end of that year 1926 was darkened by a great tragedy, which sent a thrill of horror all over India. It showed to what depths communal passion could reduce our people. Swami Shraddhanand was assassinated by a fanatic as he lay in bed. What a death for a man who had bared his chest to the bayonets of the Gurkhas and marched to meet their fire! Nearly eight years earlier he, an Arya Samajist leader, had stood in the pulpit of the great Jame Masjid of Delhi and preached to a mighty gathering of Muslims and Hindus of unity and India's freedom. And that great multitude had greeted him with loud cries of *Hindu-Musalman-ki-jai*, and outside in the streets they had jointly sealed that cry with their blood. And now he lay dead, killed by a fellow-countryman, who thought, no doubt, that he was doing a meritorious deed, which would lead him to paradise.

Always I have admired sheer physical courage, the courage to face physical suffering in a good cause, even unto death. Most of us, I suppose, admire it. Swami Shraddhanand had an amazing amount of that fearlessness. His tall and stately figure, wrapped in a sanyasin's robe, perfectly erect in spite of advanced years, eyes flashing, sometimes a shadow of irritation or anger at the weakness of others passing over his face—how I remember that vivid picture, and how often it has come back to me!

23

THE OPPRESSED MEET AT BRUSSELS

Towards the end of 1926 I happened to be in Berlin, and I learnt there of a forthcoming Congress of Oppressed Nationalities, which was to be held at Brussels. The idea appealed to me, and I wrote home, suggesting that the Indian National Congress might take official part in the Brussels Congress. My suggestion was approved, and I was appointed the Indian Congress representative for this purpose.

The Brussels Congress was held early in February 1927. I do not know who originated the idea. Berlin was at the time a centre which attracted political exiles and radical elements from abroad; it was gradually catching up with Paris in that respect. The Communist element was also strong there. Ideas of some common action between oppressed nations *inter se*, as well as between them and the Labour left wing, were very much in the air. It was felt more and more that the struggle for freedom was a common one against the thing that was imperialism; and joint deliberation and, where possible, joint action were desirable. The colonial Powers—England, France, Italy, etc.—were naturally hostile to any such attempts being made, but Germany was, since the War, no longer a colonial Power, and the German Government viewed with a benevolent neutrality the growth of agitation in the colonies and dependencies of other Powers. This was one of the reasons which made Berlin a centre for advanced and disaffected elements from abroad. Among these the most prominent and active were the Chinese belonging to the left wing of the Kuo-Min-Tang, which was then sweeping across China, and the old feudal elements seemed to be rolling down before its irresistible advance. Even the Imperialist powers lost their aggressive habits and minatory tone before this new phenomenon. It appeared that the solution of the problem of China's unity and freedom could not long be delayed. The Kuo-Min-Tang was flushed with success, but it knew the difficulties that lay ahead, and it wanted to strengthen itself by international propaganda. Probably it was the left wing of the party, co-operating with Communists and near-Communists abroad, that laid stress on this propaganda, both to strengthen China's national position abroad and its own position in the Party ranks at home. The Party had not split up at the time into two or more rival and bitterly hostile groups, and presented, to all outward seeming, a united front.

The European representatives of the Kuo-Min-Tang, therefore, welcomed the idea of the Congress of Oppressed Nationalities; perhaps they even originated the idea jointly with some other people. Some Communists and near-Communists were also at the back of the proposal right from the beginning, but, as a whole, the Communist element kept in the background. Active support and help also came from Latin America, which was chafing at the time at the economic imperialism of the United States. Mexico, with a radical President and policy, was eager to take the lead in a Latin American *bloc* against the United States; and Mexico, therefore, took great interest in the Brussels Congress. Officially the Government could not take part, but it sent one of its leading diplomats to be present as a benevolent observer.

There were also present at Brussels representatives from the national organizations of Java, Indo-China, Palestine, Syria, Egypt, Arabs from North Africa, and African Negroes. Then there were many left-wing Labour organizations represented, and several well-known men, who had played a leading part in European Labour struggles for a generation, were present. Communists were there also, and they took an important part in the proceedings; they came not as Communists, but as representatives of trade union or similar organizations.

George Lansbury was elected president, and he delivered an eloquent address. That in itself was proof that the Congress was not so rabid after all, nor was it merely hitched on to the star of Communism. But there is no doubt that the gathering was friendly towards the Communists, and, even though agreement might be lacking on some matters, there appeared to be several common grounds for action.

Mr Lansbury agreed to be president also of the permanent organization that was formed—the League Against Imperialism. But he repented of his rash behaviour soon, or perhaps his colleagues of the British Labour Party did not approve of it. The Labour Party was 'His Majesty's Opposition' then, soon to blossom out as 'His Majesty's Government', and future Cabinet Ministers cannot dabble in risky and revolutionary politics. Mr Lansbury resigned from the presidentship on the ground of being too busy for it; he even resigned from the membership of the League. I was hurt by this sudden change in a person whose speech I had admired only two or three months earlier. The League Against Imperialism had, however, quite a number of distinguished persons as its patrons. Einstein was one of them, and Madame Sun Yat Sen and, I think, Romain Rolland. Many months later Einstein resigned, as he disagreed with the pro-Arab policy of the League in the Arab-Jewish quarrels in Palestine.

The Brussels Congress, as well as the subsequent Committee meetings of the League, which were held in various places from time to time, helped me to understand some of the problems of colonial and dependent countries. They gave me also an insight into the inner conflicts of the Western Labour world. I knew something about them already; I had read about them, but there was no reality behind my knowledge, as there had been no personal contacts. I had some such contacts now, and sometimes had to face problems which reflected these inner conflicts. As between the Labour worlds of the Second International and the Third International, my sympathies were with the latter. The whole record of the Second International from the War onwards filled me with distaste, and we in India had had sufficient personal experience of the methods of one of its strongest supports—the British Labour Party. So I turned inevitably with goodwill towards Communism, for, whatever its faults, it was at least not hypocritical and not imperialistic. It was not a doctrinal adherence, as I did not know much about the fine points of Communism, my acquaintance being limited at the time to its broad features. These attracted me, as also the tremendous changes taking place in Russia. But Communists often irritated me by their dictatorial ways, their aggressive and rather vulgar methods, their habit of denouncing everybody who did not agree with them. This reaction was no doubt due, as they would say, to my own *bourgeois* education and up-bringing.

It was curious how, in our League Against Imperialism Committee meetings, I would usually be on the side of the Anglo-American members on petty matters of argument. There was a certain similarity in our outlook in regard to method at least. We would both object to declamatory and long-winded resolutions, which resembled manifestos. We preferred something simpler and shorter, but the Continental tradition was against this. There was often difference of opinion between the Communist elements and the non-Communists. Usually we agreed on a compromise. Later on, some of us returned to our homes and could not attend any further Committee meetings.

The Brussels Congress was viewed with some consternation by the Foreign and Colonial Offices of the Imperialist powers. 'Angur', the well-known writer of the British Foreign Office, has given a somewhat sensational, and occasionally ludicrous, account of it in one of his books. The Congress itself was probably full of international spies, many of the delegates even representing various secret services. We had an amusing instance of this. An American friend of mine, who was in Paris, had a visit from a Frenchman who belonged to the French secret service. It was quite a friendly visit to enquire about certain matters. When he had finished his enquiries he asked the American if he did not recognize him, for they had met previously. The American looked hard, but he had to admit that he could not place him at all. The secret service agent then told him that he had met him at the Brussels Congress as a Negro delegate, with his face, hands, etc., all blacked over!

One of the meetings of the Committee of the League Against Imperialism took place at Cologne, and I attended it. After the meeting was over we were asked to go to Dusseldorf, near by, to attend a Sacco-Vanzetti meeting. As we were returning from that meeting, we were asked to show our passports to the police. Most of the people had their passports with them, but I had left mine at the hotel in Cologne, as we had only come for a few hours to Dusseldorf. I was thereupon marched to a police-station. Fortunately for me I had companions in distress—an Englishman and his wife, who also had left their passport in Cologne. After about an hour's wait, during which probably telephonic enquiries were made, the police chief was graciously pleased to allow us to depart.

The League Against Imperialism veered more towards Communism in later years, though at no time, so far as I know, did it lose its individual character. I could only remain in distant touch with it by means of correspondence. In 1931, because of my part in the Delhi truce between the Congress and the Government of India, it grew exceedingly angry with me, and excommunicated me with bell, book, and candle—or to be more accurate, it expelled me by some kind of a resolution. I must confess that it had great provocation, but it might have given me some chance of explaining my position.

In the summer of 1927 my father came to Europe. I met him at Venice, and during the next few months we were often together. All of us—my father, my wife, my young sister, and I—paid a brief visit to Moscow in November during the tenth anniversary celebrations of the Soviet. It was a very brief visit, just three or four days in Moscow, decided upon at the last moment. But we were glad we went, for even that glimpse was worthwhile. It did not, and could not, teach us much about the new Russia, but it did give us a background for our reading. To my father all such Soviet and collectivist ideas were wholly novel. His whole training had been legal and constitutional, and he could not easily get out of that framework. But he was definitely impressed by what he saw in Moscow.

We were in Moscow when the announcement about the Simon Commission was first made. We first read about it in a Moscow sheet. A few days afterwards, father was appearing in the Privy Council in London in an Indian appeal with Sir John Simon as a colleague. It was an old zamindari case in the earlier stages of which, many years previously, I had also appeared. I had no further interest in it, but at Sir John Simon's suggestion I accompanied my father on one occasion to Sir John's chambers for a consultation.

The year 1927 was drawing to an end, and our stay in Europe had been unduly prolonged. Probably we would have returned home sooner but for father visiting Europe. It was our intention to spend some time in south-eastern Europe and Turkey and Egypt on our way back. But there was no time for this then, and I was eager to be back in time for the next Congress session which was going to be held in Madras at Christmas-time. We sailed from Marseilles, my wife, sister, daughter and I, early in December for Colombo. My father remained in Europe for another three months.

24

RETURN TO INDIA AND PLUNGE BACK INTO POLITICS

I was returning from Europe in good physical and mental condition. My wife was not yet wholly recovered, but she was far better, and that relieved me of anxiety on her score. I felt full of energy and vitality, and the sense of inner conflict and frustration that had oppressed me so often previously was, for the time being, absent. My outlook was wider, and nationalism by itself seemed to me definitely a narrow and insufficient creed. Political freedom, independence, were no doubt essential, but they were steps only in the right direction; without social freedom and a socialistic structure of society and the State, neither the country nor the individual could develop much. I felt I had a clearer perception of world affairs, more grip on the present-day world, ever changing as it was. I had read largely, not only on current affairs and politics, but on many other subjects that interested me, cultural and scientific. I found the vast political, economic, and cultural changes going on in Europe and America a fascinating study. Soviet Russia, despite certain unpleasant aspects, attracted me greatly, and seemed to hold forth a message of hope to the world. Europe, in the middle 'twenties, was trying to settle down in a way; the great depression was yet to come. But I came back with the conviction that this settling down was superficial only, and big eruptions and mighty changes were in store for Europe and the world in the near future.

To train and prepare our country for these world events—to keep in readiness for them, as far as we could—seemed to be the immediate task. The preparation was largely an ideological one. First of all, there should be no doubt about the objective of political independence. This should be clearly understood as the only possible political goal for us; something radically different from the vague and confusing talk of Dominion Status. Then there was the social goal. It would be too much,

I felt, to expect the Congress to go far in this direction just then. The Congress was a purely political and nationalistic body, unused to thinking on other lines. But a beginning might be made. Outside the Congress, in labour circles and among the young, the idea could be pushed on much further. For this purpose I wanted to keep myself free from Congress office, and I had a vague idea also of spending some months in remote rural areas to study their conditions. But this was not to be, and events were to drag me again into the heart of Congress politics.

Immediately on our arrival in Madras I was caught in the whirl. I presented a bunch of resolutions to the Working Committee—resolutions on Independence, War Danger, association with the League against Imperialism, etc.—and nearly all of these were accepted and made into official Working Committee resolutions. I had to put them forward at the open session of the Congress, and, to my surprise, they were all almost unanimously adopted. The Independence resolution was supported even by Mrs Annie Besant. This all-round support was very gratifying, but I had an uncomfortable feeling that the resolutions were either not understood for what they were, or were distorted to mean something else. That this was so became apparent soon after the Congress, when a controversy arose on the meaning of the Independence resolution.

These resolutions of mine were somewhat different from the usual Congress resolutions; they represented a new outlook. Many Congressmen no doubt liked them, some had a vague dislike for them, but not enough to make them oppose. Probably the latter thought that they were academic resolutions, making little difference either way, and the best way to get rid of them was to pass them and move on to something more important. The Independence resolution thus did not represent then, as it did a year or two later, a vital and irrepressible urge on the part of the Congress; it represented a widespread and growing sentiment.

Gandhiji was in Madras and he attended the open Congress sessions, but he did not take any part in the shaping of policy. He did not attend the meetings of the Working Committee of which he was a member. That had been his general political attitude in the Congress since the dominance of the Swaraj Party. But he was frequently consulted, and little of importance was done without his knowledge. I do not know how far the resolutions I put before the Congress met with his approval.

I am inclined to think that he disliked them, not so much because of what they said, but because of their general trend and outlook. He did not, however, criticize them on any occasion. My father was, of course, away in Europe at the time.

The unreality of the Independence resolution came out in that very session of the Congress, when another resolution condemning the Simon Commission and appealing for its boycott was considered. As a corollary to this it was proposed to convene an All-Parties Conference, which was to draw up a constitution for India. It was manifest that the moderate groups, with whom co-operation was sought, could never think in terms of Independence. The very utmost they could go to was some form of Dominion Status.

I stepped back into the Congress secretaryship. There were personal considerations—the desire of the President for the year, Dr M. A. Ansari, who was an old and dear friend—and the fact that, as many of my resolutions had been passed, I ought to see them through. It was true that the resolution on the All-Parties Conference had partly neutralized the effect of my resolutions. Still, much remained. The real reason for my accepting office again was my fear that the Congress might, through the instrumentality of the All-Parties Conference, or because of other reasons, slide back to a more moderate and compromising position. It seemed to be in a hesitant mood, swinging alternately from one extreme to another. I wanted to prevent, as far as I could, the swing back to Moderation and to hold on to the Independence objective.

The National Congress always attracts a large number of side-shows at its annual sessions. One of the side-shows at Madras was a Republican Conference which held its first (and last) sessions that year. I was asked to preside. The idea appealed to me, as I considered myself a republican. But I hesitated, as I did not know who was at the back of the new venture, and I did not want to associate myself with mushroom growths. I presided, eventually, but later I repented of this, for the Republican Conference turned out to be, like so many others, a still-born affair. For several months I tried, and tried in vain, to get the text of the resolutions passed by it. It is amazing how many of our people love to sponsor new undertakings and then ignore them and leave them to shift for themselves. There is much in the criticism that we are not a persevering lot.

Before we had dispersed from Madras after the Congress, news came of the death of Hakim Ajmal Khan at Delhi. As an ex-president of the Congress he was one of its elder statesmen; but he was something more also, and he occupied a unique place in the Congress leadership. Brought up as he was, entirely in the old conservative way, with no touch of modernism in it, and steeped in the culture of imperial Delhi of Moghal days, it was a delight to watch his fine courtesy and hear his unhurried voice and listen to his dry humour. He was, in his manners, a typical aristocrat of the old order, with princely look and princely ways, and even his face bore a marked resemblance to the miniatures of the Moghal sovereigns. Such a person would not ordinarily take to the rough-and-tumble of politics; and Britishers in India have often sighed for persons of this old type when the new breed of agitators has troubled them. Hakim Sahab had also little to do with politics in his early days. As the head of a famous family of physicians, he was busy with his enormous practice. But even during the latter part of the War events, and the influence of his old friend and colleague, Dr M.A. Ansari, were driving him to the Congress; and subsequent happenings—Martial Law in the Punjab and the Khilafat question—moved him deeply, and he turned with approval to the new Gandhian technique of non-co-operation. He brought a rare quality and precious gifts to the Congress—he became a link between the old order and the new, and gave the support of the former to the national movement; and thus he produced a harmony between the two, and gave strength and a certain stolidity to the advance guard of the movement. He brought the Hindus and Muslims much nearer to each other, for both honoured him and were influenced by his example. To Gandhiji he became a trusted friend, whose advice in regard to Hindu-Muslim matters was the final word for him. My father and Hakimji had naturally taken to each other.

Last year I was accused by some leaders of the Hindu Mahasabha of my ignorance of Hindu sentiments because of my defective education and general background of 'Persian' culture. What culture I possess, or whether I possess any at all, is a little difficult for me to say. Persian, as a language, unhappily, I do not even know. But it is true that my father had grown up in an Indo-Persian cultural atmosphere, which was the legacy in north India of the old Delhi court, and of which, even in these degenerate days, Delhi and Lucknow are the two chief centres. Kashmiri Brahmans had a remarkable capacity for adaptation, and coming down to the Indian plains and finding that this Indo-Persian culture was predominant at the time, they took to it, and produced a number of fine scholars in Persian and Urdu. Later they adapted themselves with equal rapidity to the changing order, when a knowledge of English and the elements of European culture became necessary. But even now there are many distinguished scholars in Persian among the Kashmiris in India— Sir Tej Bahadur Sapru and Raja Narendra Nath, to mention two of them.

Hakim Sahab and my father had thus much in common, and they even discovered old family connections. They became great friends and addressed each other as *Bhai Sahab*—brother. Politics was the least of their many bonds. In his domestic habits Hakimji was extraordinarily conservative; he could not, or his family people could not, get out of old habits. I have never seen such amazingly strict *purdah*, or seclusion of women, as existed in his family. And yet Hakimji was firmly convinced that no nation advanced unless the women of that country freed themselves. He impressed this upon me, and told me how much he admired the part Turkish women had played in their freedom struggle. It was chiefly because of Turkish women, he said, that Kemal Pasha had succeeded.

The death of Hakim Ajmal Khan was a great blow to the Congress; it meant the removal of one of its stoutest supports. For all of us there has been since then something lacking in a visit to Delhi, for Delhi was so closely associated with Hakimji and his house in Billimaran.

The year 1928 was, politically, a full year, with plenty of activity all over the country. There seemed to be a new impulse moving the people forward, a new stir that was equally present in the most varied groups. Probably the change had been going on gradually during my long absence from the country; it struck me as very considerable on my return. Early in 1926 India was still quiescent, passive, perhaps not fully recovered from the effort of 1919-1922; in 1928 she seemed fresh, active, and full of suppressed energy. Everywhere there was evidence of this: among the industrial workers, the peasantry, middle class youth, and the intelligentsia generally.

The Trade Union movement had grown greatly, and the All-India Trade Union Congress, established seven or eight years previously, was already a strong and representative body. It had not only grown in numbers and in organization, but its ideology was becoming more militant and extreme. Strikes were frequent, and class-consciousness was growing. The textile industry and the railways were the best organized, and of these the strongest and most advanced unions were the Girni Kamgar Union of Bombay and the G.I.P. Railway Union. The growth of labour organization had inevitably brought the seeds of internal conflict and disruption from the West, and hardly had the Indian Trade Union Movement established itself when it threatened to split up into rival and hostile camps. There were those who adhered to the Second International, and those who favoured the Third; those who were moderately reformist in their outlook, and those who were frankly revolutionary and out for radical changes. In between the two there were various shades and degrees of opinion and, as is unfortunately the case in all mass organizations, of opportunism.

The peasantry was also astir. This was noticeable in the United Provinces and especially in Oudh, where large gatherings of protesting tenants became common. It was realized that the new Oudh tenancy law, which gave a life-tenure and had promised a great deal, made little difference to the hard lot of the peasant. In Gujrat a conflict on a big scale developed between the peasantry and the Government because of the attempt of the latter to increase revenue—Gujrat being an area of peasant-proprietors where Government deals directly with the peasants. This struggle was the Bardoli Satyagraha under the leadership of Sardar Vallabhbhai Patel. It was gallantly carried through to the admiration of the rest of India. The Bardoli peasantry met with a considerable measure of success; the real success of their campaign, however, lay in the effect it produced amongst the peasantry all over India. Bardoli became a sign and a symbol of hope and strength and victory to the Indian peasant.

Another very noticeable feature of the India of 1928 was the growth of the Youth Movement. Everywhere youth leagues were being established, youth conferences were being held. They were a very varied lot, from semi-religious groups to others discussing revolutionary ideology and technique; but whatever their origin and auspices, such gatherings of youth always began to discuss the vital social and economic problems of the day, and generally, their tendency was for root-and-branch change.

From the purely political point of view the year was noted for the boycott of the Simon Commission and (what was called the constructive side of the boycott) the All-Parties Conference. The moderate groups co-operated with the Congress in this boycott, and it was remarkably successful. Wherever the Commission went it was greeted by hostile crowds and the cry of "Simon go back", and thus vast numbers of the Indian masses became acquainted not only with Sir John Simon's name but with two words of the English language, the only two they knew. These words must have become a hated obsession for the members of the Commission. The story is related that once, when they were staying at the Western Hostel in New Delhi, the refrain seemed to come to them in the night out of the darkness. They were greatly irritated at being pursued in this way, even at night. As a matter of fact, the noise that disturbed them came from the jackals that infest the waste places of the imperial capital.

The All-Parties Conference had no difficulty at all in settling the main principles of the constitution; they were to be of the democratic parliamentary variety, and almost anyone could draw them up. The real difficulty, and the only difficulty, came from the communal or minorities issue, and as the Conference had within its fold the representatives of all the extreme communal organizations, an agreement became extraordinarily difficult. It was a repetition of the old infructuous Unity Conferences. My father, who had returned from Europe in the spring, took great interest in the Conference. Ultimately, as a last resource, a small committee was appointed, with my father as chairman, to draft the constitution and make a full report on the communal issue. This Committee came to be known as the Nehru Committee, and their subsequent report, as the Nehru Report. Sir Tej Bahadur Sapru was also a member of this Committee, and was responsible for part of the Report.

I was not a member of this Committee, but as Congress Secretary I had much to do with it. It was an awkward situation for me, for I thought it wholly futile to draw up detailed paper constitutions when the real problem was the conquest of power. Another difficulty for me was the inevitable limitations by this mixed Committee of our goal to what was called Dominion Status and was, in fact, even less. For me the real importance of the Committee lay in the possibility of its finding a way out of the communal *impasse*. I did not expect a final solution of this question by some pact or agreement—that solution would only come by a diversion of interest to social and economic issues—but there was the possibility that even a temporary pact, if accepted by a sufficient number of people, would help to ease the situation and thus succeed in diverting interest to other issues. So I did not wish to obstruct the work of the Committee and I gave such help as I could.

Success seemed almost within grasp. Only two or three points remained to settle, and of these the really important one was the Punjab, where there was the Hindu-Muslim-Sikh triangle. The Committee in their report considered the question of the Punjab from a novel point of view, and supported their recommendation with the help of some revealing figures of the distribution of population. But all this was in vain. Fear and mistrust remained on either side, and the little step to cross the short distance that remained was not taken.

The All-Parties Conference met at Lucknow to consider the report of their Committee. Again some of us were in a dilemma, for we did not wish to come in the way of a communal settlement, if that was possible, and yet we were not prepared to yield on the question of independence. We begged that the conference leave this question open so that each constituent part could have liberty of action on this issue—the Congress adhering to independence and the more moderate groups to Dominion Status. But my father had set his heart on the Report and he would not yield, nor perhaps could he under the circumstances. I was thereupon asked by our Independence group in the conference—and this was a large one—to make a statement to the Conference on its behalf, dissociating ourselves completely from everything that lowered the objective of independence. But we made it further clear that we would not be obstructive, as we did not wish to come in the way of the communal statement.

This was not a very effective line to adopt on such a major issue; at best it was a negative gesture. A positive side was given to our attitude by our founding that very day the Independence for India League.

The All-Parties Conference gave me another and a greater shock by adding to the Fundamental Rights in the proposed constitution, at the instance of the Oudh taluqadars, a clause guaranteeing their vested rights in their taluqas. The whole constitution was, of course, based on the idea of private property, but it did seem to me an outrage to make the property rights in the huge semi-feudal estates one of the irremovable foundations of the constitution. This made it clear that the Congress leadership, and much more so the non-Congress people, preferred the company of the landed magnates to that of the socially advanced groups in their own ranks. It was obvious that a wide gulf separated us from many of our leaders, and it seemed a little absurd for me to carry on as General Secretary of the Congress under these circumstances. I offered my resignation on the ground of having been one of the founders of the Independence for India League. But the Working Committee would not agree to it and told me (as well as Subhas Bose, who had also offered to resign on the same ground) that we could carry on with the League without any conflict with the Congress policy. Indeed, the Congress had already declared for independence. And again I agreed. It was surprising how easy it was to win me over to a withdrawal of my resignation. This happened on many occasions, and as neither party really liked the idea of a break, we clung to every pretext to avoid it.

Gandhiji took no part in these All-Party Conference or Committee meetings. He was not even present at the Lucknow Conference.

Meanwhile the Simon Commission had been moving about, pursued by black flags and hostile crowds shouting, "Go back." Occasionally there were minor conflicts between the police and the crowds. Lahore brought matters to a head and suddenly sent a thrill of indignation throughout the country. The anti-Simon Commission demonstration there was headed by Lala Lajpat Rai, and as he stood by the road-side in front of the thousands of demonstrators he was assaulted and beaten on his chest with a baton by a young English police officer. There had been no attempt whatever on the part of the crowd; much less on the part of Lalaji, to indulge in any methods of violence. Even so, as he stood peacefully by, he and many of his companions were severely beaten by the police. Anyone who takes part in street demonstrations runs the risk of a conflict with the police, and, though our demonstrations were almost always perfectly peaceful, Lalaji must have known of this risk and taken it consciously. But still, the manner of the assault, the needless brutality of it, came as a shock to vast numbers of people in India. Those were the days when we were not used to lathi charges by the police; our sensitiveness had not been blunted by repeated brutality. To find that even the greatest of our leaders, the foremost and most popular man in the Punjab, could be so treated seemed little short of monstrous, and a dull anger spread all over the country, especially in north India. How helpless we were, how despicable when we could not even protect the honour of our chosen leaders!

The physical injury to Lalaji had been serious enough, as he had been hit on the chest and he had long suffered from heart disease. Probably, in the case of a healthy young man the injury would not have been great, but Lalaji was neither young nor healthy. What effect this physical injury had on his death a few weeks later it is hardly possible to say definitely, though his doctors were of opinion that it hastened the end. But I think that there can be no doubt that the mental shock which accompanied the physical injury had a tremendous effect on Lalaji. He felt angry and bitter, not so much at the personal humiliation, as at the national humiliation involved in the assault on him.

It was this sense of national humiliation that weighed on the mind of India, and when Lalaji's death came soon after, inevitably it was connected with the assault, and sorrow itself gave pride of place to anger and indignation. It is well to appreciate this, for only so can we have some understanding of subsequent events, of the phenomenon of Bhagat Singh, and of his sudden and amazing popularity in north India. It is very easy and very fatuous to condemn persons or acts without seeking to understand the springs of action, the causes that underlie them. Bhagat Singh was not previously well known; he did not become popular because of an act of violence, an act of terrorism. Terrorists have flourished in India, off and on, for nearly thirty years, and at no time, except in the early days in Bengal, did any of them attain a fraction of that popularity which came to Bhagat Singh. This is a patent fact which cannot be denied; it has to be admitted. And another fact, which is equally obvious, is that terrorism, in spite of occasional recrudescence, has no longer any real appeal for the youth of India. Fifteen years' stress on non-violence has changed the whole background in India and made the masses much more indifferent to, and even hostile to, the idea of terrorism as a method of political action. Even the classes from which the terrorists are usually drawn, the lower middle-classes and intelligentsia, have been powerfully affected by the Congress propaganda against, methods of violence. Their active and impatient elements, who think in terms of revolutionary action, also realize fully now that revolution does not come through terrorism, and that terrorism is an outworn and profitless method which comes in the way of real revolutionary action. Terrorism is a dying thing in India and elsewhere, not because of Government coercion, which can only suppress and bottle up, not eradicate, but because of basic causes and world events. Terrorism usually represents the infancy of a revolutionary urge in a country. That stage passes, and with it passes terrorism as an important phenomenon. Occasional outbursts may continue because of local causes or individual suppressions. India has undoubtedly passed that stage, and no doubt even the occasional outbursts will gradually die out. But this does not mean that all people in India have ceased to believe in methods of violence. They have, very largely, ceased to believe in individual violence and terrorism but many, no doubt, still think that a time may come when organized, violent methods may be necessary for gaining freedom, as they have often been necessary in other countries. That is today an academic issue which time alone will put to the test; it has nothing to do with terroristic methods.

Bhagat Singh thus did not become popular because of his act of terrorism, but because he seemed to vindicate, for the moment, the honour of Lala Lajpat Rai, and through him of the nation. He became a symbol; the act was forgotten, the symbol remained, and within a few months each town and village of the Punjab, and to a lesser extent in the rest of northern India, resounded with his name. Innumerable songs grew up about him, and the popularity that the man achieved was something amazing.

A short time after the Simon Commission beating, Lala Rajpat Rai attended a meeting of the All-India Congress Committee in Delhi. He bore marks of injuries, and was still suffering from the after-effects. The meeting was held after the Lucknow All-Parties Conference, and the question of Independence came up for discussion in some form or other. I forget the exact point that was in issue, but I remember speaking at some length, and pointing out that the time had come for the Congress to choose between a revolutionary outlook, which involved radical changes in our political and social structure, and a reformist objective and method. The speech had no importance, and I would have forgotten it but for the fact that Lalaji replied to it in the Committee, and criticized some parts of it. One of his warnings was to the effect that we should expect nothing from the British Labour Party. That warning was not necessary so far as I was concerned, for I was not an admirer of the official leadership of British Labour; the only thing that could surprise me in regard to it would have been to find it supporting the struggle for India's freedom, or doing anything effectively anti-imperialist or likely to lead to socialism.

On returning to Lahore, Lalaji reverted to the subject of my speech at the A.I.C.C. meeting, and began a series of articles on various issues connected with it in his weekly journal *The People.* Only the first article appeared; before the second could come out in the next week's issue, he was dead. That first unfinished article of his, perhaps his last writing for publication. has had a melancholy interest for me.

·

25

EXPERIENCE OF LATHI CHARGES

The assault on Lala Lajpat Rai, and his subsequent death, increased the vigour of the demonstrations against the Simon Commission in the places which it subsequently visited. It was due in Lucknow, and the local Congress Committee made extensive preparations for its 'reception'. Huge processions, meetings, and demonstrations were organized many days in advance, both as propaganda and as rehearsals for the actual show. I went to Lucknow, and was present at some of these. The success of these preliminary demonstrations, which were perfectly orderly and peaceful, evidently nettled the authorities, and they began to obstruct and issue orders against the taking out of processions in certain areas. It was in this connection that I had a new experience, and my body felt the baton and *lathi* blows of the police.

Processions had been prohibited, ostensibly to avoid any interference with the traffic. We decided to give no cause for complaint on this score, and arranged for small groups of sixteen, as far as I can remember, to go separately, along unfrequented routes to the meeting place. Technically, this was no doubt a breach of the order, for sixteen with a flag were a procession. I led one of the groups of sixteen and, after a big gap, came another such group under the leadership of my colleague, Govind Ballabh Pant. My group had gone perhaps about 200 yards, the road was a deserted one, when we heard the clatter of horses' hoofs behind us. We looked back to find a bunch of mounted police, probably two or three dozen in number, bearing down upon us at a rapid pace. They were soon right upon us, and the impact of the horses broke up our little column of sixteen. The mounted policemen then started belabouring our volunteers with huge batons or truncheons and, instinctively, the volunteers sought refuge on the side-walks, and some even entered the petty shops. They were pursued and beaten down. My own instinct had urged me to seek safety when I saw the horses charging down upon us; it was a discouraging sight. But then, I suppose, some other instinct held me to my place and

I survived the first charge, which had been checked by the volunteers behind me. Suddenly I found myself alone in the middle of the road; a few yards away from me, in various directions, were the policemen beating down our volunteers. Automatically, I began moving slowly to the side of the road to be less conspicuous, but again I stopped and had a little argument with myself, and decided that it would be unbecoming for me to move away. All this was a matter of a few seconds only, but I have the clearest recollections of that conflict within me and the decision, prompted by my pride, I suppose, which could not tolerate the idea of my behaving like a coward. Yet the line between cowardice and courage was a thin one, and I might well have been on the other side. Hardly had I so decided, when I looked round to find that a mounted policeman was trotting up to me, brandishing his long new baton. I told him to go ahead, and turned my head away—again an instinctive effort to save the head and face. He gave me two resounding blows on the back. I felt stunned, and my body quivered all over but, to my surprise and satisfaction, I found that I was still standing. The police force was withdrawn soon after, and made to block the road in front of us. Our volunteers gathered together again, many of them bleeding and with split skulls, and we were joined by Pant and his lot, who had also been belaboured, and all of us sat down facing the police. So we sat for an hour or so, and it became dark. On the one side, various high officials gathered; on the other, large crowds began to assemble as the news spread. Ultimately, the officials agreed to allow us to go by our original route, and we went that way with the mounted policemen, who had charged us and belaboured us, going ahead of us as a kind of escort.

I have written about this petty incident in some detail because of its effect on me. The bodily pain I felt was quite forgotten in a feeling of exhilaration that I was physically strong enough to face and bear *lathi* blows. And a thing that surprised me was that right through the incident, even when I was being beaten, my mind was quite clear and I was consciously analysing my feelings. This rehearsal stood me in good stead the next morning, when a stiffer trial was in store for us. For the next morning was the time when the Simon Commission was due to arrive, and our great demonstration was going to take place.

My father was at Allahabad at the time, and I was afraid that the news of the assault on me, when he read about it in the next morning's papers, would upset him and the rest of the family. So I telephoned to him late in the evening to assure him that all was well, and that he should not worry. But he did worry and, finding it difficult to sleep over it, he decided at about midnight to come over to Lucknow. The last train had gone, and so he started by motor-car. He had some bad luck on the way, and it was nearly five in the morning by the time he had covered the journey of 146 miles and reached Lucknow, tired out and exhausted.

That was about the time when we were getting ready to go in procession to the station. The previous evening's incidents had the effect of rousing up Lucknow more than anything that we could have done, and even before the sun was out, vast numbers of people made their way to the station. Innumerable little processions came from various parts of the city, and from the Congress office started the main procession, consisting of several thousands, marching in fours. We were in this main procession. We were stopped by the police as we approached the station. There was a huge open space, about half a mile square, in front of the station (this has now been built over by the new station) and we were made to line up on one side of this *maidan*, and there our procession remained, making no attempt to push our way forward. The place was full of foot and mounted police, as well as the military. The crowd of sympathetic onlookers swelled up, and many of these persons managed to spread out in twos and threes in the open space. Suddenly we saw in the far distance a moving mass. They were two or three long lines of cavalry or mounted police, covering the entire area, galloping down towards us, and striking and riding down the numerous stragglers that dotted the *maidan*. That charge of galloping horsemen was a fine sight, but for the tragedies that were being enacted on the way, as harmless and very much surprised sightseers went under the horses' hoofs. Behind the charging lines these people lay on the ground, some still unable to move, others writhing in pain, and the whole appearance of that *maidan* was that of a battlefield. But we did not have much time for gazing on that scene or for reflections; the horsemen were soon upon us, and their front line clashed almost at a gallop with the massed ranks of our processionists. We held our ground, and, as we appeared to be unyielding, the horses had to pull up at the last moment and reared up on their hind legs with their front hoofs quivering in the air over our heads. And then began a beating of us, and battering with *lathis* and long batons both by the mounted and the foot police. It was a tremendous hammering, and the clearness of vision that I had had the evening before left me. All I knew was that I had to stay where I was, and must not yield or go back. I felt half blinded with the blows, and sometimes a dull anger seized me and a desire to hit out. I thought how easy it would be to pull down the police officer in front of me from his horse and to mount up myself, but long training and discipline held and I did not raise a hand, except to protect my face from a blow. Besides, I knew well enough that any aggression on our part would result in a ghastly tragedy, the firing and shooting down of large numbers of our men.

After what seemed a tremendous length of time, but was probably only a few minutes, our line began to yield slowly, step by step, without breaking up. This left me somewhat isolated, and more exposed at the sides. More blows came, and then I was suddenly lifted off my feet from behind and carried off, to my great annoyance. Some of my young colleagues, thinking that a dead-set was being made at me, had decided to protect me in this summary fashion.

Our processionists lined up again about a hundred feet behind our original line. The police also withdrew and stood in a line, fifty feet apart from us. So we remained, when the cause of all this trouble, the Simon Commission, secretly crept away from the station in the far distance, more than half a mile away. But, even so, they did not escape the black flags or demonstrators. Soon after, we came back in full procession to the Congress office, and there dispersed, and I went on to father, who was anxiously waiting for us.

Now that the excitement of the moment had passed, I felt pains all over my body and great fatigue. Almost every part of me seemed to ache, and I was covered with contused wounds and marks of blows. But fortunately I was not injured in any vital spot. Many of our companions were less fortunate, and were badly injured. Govind Ballabh Pant, who stood by me, offered a much bigger target, being six foot-odd in height, and the injuries he received then have resulted in a painful and persistent malady which prevented him for a long time from straightening his back or leading an active life. I emerged with a somewhat greater conceit of my physical condition and powers of endurance. But the memory that endures with me, far more than that of the beating itself, is that of many of the faces of those policemen, and especially of the officers, who were attacking us. Most of the real beating and battering was done by European sergeants, the Indian rank and file were milder in their methods. And those faces, full of hate and blood-lust, almost mad, with no trace of sympathy or touch of humanity! Probably the faces on our side just then were equally hateful to look at, and the fact that we were mostly passive did not fill our minds and hearts with love for opponents, or add to the beauty of our countenances. And yet, we had no grievance against each other; no quarrel that was personal, no ill-will. We happened to represent, for the time being, strange and powerful forces which held us in thrall and cast us hither and thither, and, subtly gripping our minds and hearts, roused our desires and passions and made us their blind tools. Blindly we struggled, not knowing what we struggled for and whither we went. The excitement of action held us; but, as it passed, immediately the question arose: To what end was all this? To what end?

26

TRADE UNION CONGRESS

The Simon Commission boycott and the All Parties Conference bulked largely politically in the country that year, but my own interest and activities lay largely in other directions. As working General Secretary of the Congress, I was busy in looking after and strengthening its organization, and I was particularly interested in directing people's attention to social and economic changes. The position gained in Madras in regard to Independence had also to be consolidated, especially as the tendency of the All Parties Conference was to pull us back. With this purpose in view I travelled a great deal and addressed many important gatherings. I presided, I think, over four provincial conferences in 1928—in the Punjab, in Malabar in the South, in Delhi, and in the United Provinces—as well as over Youth Leagues and Students' Conferences in Bengal and Bombay. From time to time I visited rural areas in the U.P. and occasionally I addressed industrial workers. The burden of my speeches was always much the same though the form varied according to local circumstances and the stress depended on the kind of audience I happened to be addressing. Everywhere I spoke on political independence and social freedom and made the former a step towards the attainment of the latter. I wanted to spread the ideology of socialism especially among Congress workers and the intelligentsia, for these people, who were the backbone of the national movement, thought largely in terms of the narrowest nationalism. Their speeches laid stress on the glories of old times; the injuries, material and spiritual, caused by alien rule; the sufferings of our people; the indignity of foreign domination over us and our national honour demanding that we should be free; the necessity for sacrifice at the altar of the motherland. They were familiar themes which found an echo in every Indian heart, and the nationalist in me responded to them and was moved by them (though I was never a blind admirer of ancient times in India or elsewhere). But though the truth in them remained, they seemed to grow a little thin and threadbare with constant use, and their ceaseless repetition prevented the consideration of other problems and vital aspects of our struggle. They only fostered emotion and did not encourage thought. I was by no means a pioneer in the socialist field in India. Indeed I was rather backward and I had only advanced painfully, step by step, where many others had gone ahead blazing a trail. The workers' trade union movement was, ideologically, definitely socialist, and so were the majority of the Youth Leagues. A vague confused socialism was already part of the atmosphere of India when I returned from Europe in December 1927, and even earlier than that there were many individual socialists. Mostly they thought along Utopian lines, but Marxian theory was influencing them increasingly, and a few considered themselves as 100 per cent Marxists. This tendency was strengthened in India, as in Europe and America, by developments in the Soviet Union, and particularly the Five-Year Plan.

Such importance as I possessed as a socialist worker lay in the fact that I happened to be a prominent Congressman holding important Congress offices. There were many other well-known Congressmen who were beginning to think likewise. This was most marked in the U.P. Provincial Congress Committee, and in this Committee we even tried, as early as 1926, to draw up a mild socialist programme. We are a zamindari and taluqadari province, and the first question we had to face was that of the land. We declared that the existing land system must go and that there should be no intermediaries between the State and the cultivator. We had to proceed cautiously, as we were moving in an atmosphere which was, till then, unused to such ideas.

The next year, 1929, the U.P. Provincial Congress Committee went a step further and made a recommendation, definitely on socialist lines, to the All-India Congress Committee. This latter Committee, meeting in Bombay in the summer of 1929, adopted the preamble of the U.P. resolution and thus accepted the principle of socialism underlying the whole resolution. The consideration of the detailed programme given in the U.P. resolution was postponed for a later date. Most people seem to have forgotten these resolutions of the A.I.C.C. and the U.P.P.C.C. and imagine that the subject of socialism has suddenly cropped up in the Congress during the last year or so. It is true, however, that the A.I.C.C. passed that resolution without giving much thought to it and most members probably did not realize what they were doing.

The U.P. branch of the Independence for India League (consisting entirely of principal Congress workers in the province) was definitely socialistic and it went a little further than a mixed body like the Congress Committee could go. Indeed one of the objects of the Independence League was social freedom. We had hoped to build up a strong League organization all over India and utilize it for propaganda in favour of independence and socialism. Unhappily, and much to my disappointment, the League never got going except to some extent in the U.P. This was not because of lack of support in the country. But most of our workers were also prominent workers in the Congress, and, the Congress having adopted Independence in theory at least, they could always work through the Congress organization. Another reason was that some of the original sponsors of the League did not take it seriously enough as an organization to be developed. They looked upon it as something to be used for bringing pressure to bear on the Congress executive, or even for influencing the elections for the Congress Working Committee. So the Independence League languished, and as the Congress grew more aggressive, it drew all the dynamic elements towards itself and the League grew weaker. With the coming of the Civil Disobedience struggle in 1930, the League got merged into the Congress and disappeared.

In the second half of 1928 and in 1929 there was frequent talk of my arrest. I do not know what reality lay behind the press references and the numerous private warnings I received from friends who seemed to be in the know, but the warnings produced a feeling of uncertainty in me and I felt I was always on the verge of it. I did not mind this particularly as I knew that, whatever the future held for me, it could not be a settled life of routine. The sooner I got used to uncertainty and sudden changes and visits to prison the better. And I think that on the whole I succeeded in getting used to the idea (and to a much lesser extent my people also succeeded) and whenever arrest came I took it more casually than I might otherwise have done. So rumours of arrest were not without compensation; they gave a certain excitement and a bite to my daily existence. Every day of freedom was something precious, a day gained. As a matter of fact I had a long innings in 1928 and 1929, and arrest came at last as late as April 1930. Since then my brief periods outside prison have had a measure of unreality about them, and I have lived in my house as a stranger on a short visit, or moved about uncertainly, not knowing what the morrow would hold for me, and with the constant expectation of a call back to gaol.

As 1928 approached its appointed end, the Calcutta Congress drew near. My father was to preside over it. He was full of the All Parties Conference and of his Report to it and wanted to push this through the Congress. To this he knew that I was not agreeable, because I was not prepared to compromise on the Independence issue, and this irritated him. We did not argue about the matter much, but there was a definite feeling of mental conflict between us, an attempt to pull different ways. Differences of opinion we had often had before, vital differences which had kept us in different political camps. But I do not think that at any previous or subsequent occasion the tension had been so great. Both of us were rather unhappy about it. In Calcutta matters came to this, that my father made it known that if he could not have his way in the Congress—that is, if he could not have a majority for the resolution in favour of the All Parties Report—he would refuse to preside over the Congress. That was a perfectly reasonable and constitutional course to adopt. None the less it was disconcerting to many of his opponents who did not wish to force the issue to this extent. There has often been a tendency in the Congress, and elsewhere, I suppose, to criticize and condemn and yet shrink from accepting responsibility; there is always a hope that the criticism will make the other party change its course to our advantage without casting on us the burden of piloting the boat. Where responsibility is withheld from us and there is an irremovable and irresponsible executive, as there is in the Government of India today, criticism is all that is open to us (apart, of course, from action), and that criticism is bound to be negative criticism. Even so, if that negative criticism is to be effective, there must be behind it the mental preparation and preparedness to assume full control and responsibility whenever the opportunity offers itself—control over every department of government, civil and military, internal and foreign. To ask for partial control only, as, for instance, the Liberals do in the matter of the army, is to confess our inability to run the show and to take the sting out of the criticism.

This attitude of criticism and condemnation and yet a shrinking back from the natural consequences thereof, has been frequent in the case of Gandhiji's critics. There have been a number of people in the Congress who dislike many of his activities and criticize them strongly but who are not prepared to drive him out of the Congress. This attitude is easy to understand but it is hardly fair to either party.

Some such difficulties arose at the Calcutta Congress. There were negotiations between the two groups, and a compromise formula was announced, and then this fell through. It was all rather confusing and not very edifying. The main resolution of the Congress, as it was finally adopted, accepted the All Parties Report but intimated that if the British Government did not agree to that constitution within a year, the Congress would revert to Independence. It was an offer of a year's grace and a polite ultimatum. The resolution was no doubt a come-down from the ideal of independence, for the All Parties Report did not even ask for full Dominion Status. And yet it was probably a wise resolution in the sense that it prevented a split when no one was ready for it, and kept the Congress together for the struggle that began in 1930. It was clear enough that the British Government were not going to accept the All Parties Constitution within a year. The struggle was inevitable and, as matters stood in the country, no such struggle could be at all effective without Gandhiji's lead.

I had opposed the resolution in the open Congress, though I did so half-heartedly. And yet I was again elected General Secretary! Whatever happened I managed to stick on to the secretaryship, and in the Congress sphere I seemed to act the part of the famous Vicar of Bray. Whatever president sat on the Congress throne, still I was secretary in charge of the organization.

A few days before the Calcutta Congress, the All-India Trade Union Congress was held at Jharia, the centre of the coal mine area. I attended and participated in it for the first two days and then had to go away to Calcutta. It was my first Trade Union Congress and I was practically an outsider, though my activities amongst the peasantry, and lately amongst the workers, had gained for me a measure of popularity with the masses. I found the old tussle going on between the reformists and the more advanced and revolutionary elements. The main points in issue were the question of affiliation to one of the Internationals, as well as to the League against Imperialism and the Pan-Pacific Union, and the desirability of sending representatives to the International Labour Office Conference at Geneva. More important than these questions was the vast difference in outlook between the two sections of the Congress. There was the old trade union group, moderate in politics and indeed distrusting the intrusion of politics in industrial matters. They believed in industrial action only and that too of a cautious character, and aimed at the gradual betterment of workers' conditions. The leader of this group was N.M. Joshi, who had often represented Indian labour at Geneva. The other group was more militant, believed in political action, and openly proclaimed its revolutionary outlook. It was influenced, though by no means controlled, by some Communists and near-Communists. Bombay textile labour had been captured by this group, and under their leadership there had been a great, and partly successful, textile strike in Bombay. A new and powerful textile union had risen in Bombay, the Girni Kamgar Union, which dominated the labour situation in Bombay. Another powerful union under the influence of the advanced group was the G.I.P. Railway Union.

Ever since the inception of the Trade Union Congress the executive and the office had been in the control of N.M. Joshi and his close colleagues, and Joshi had been responsible for building up the movement. The radical group, though more powerful in the rank and file, had little opportunity of influencing policy at the top. This was an unsatisfactory position and it did not reflect the true state of affairs. There was dissatisfaction and friction and a desire on the part of the radical elements to seize power in the T.U.C. At the same time there was a disinclination to carry matters too far, for a split was feared. The trade union movement was still in its early youth in India; it was weak and was largely being run by non-worker leaders. Always, under such circumstances, there is a tendency for outsiders to exploit workers and this was obvious enough in the Indian T.U.C. and labour unions. N.M. Joshi had, however, proved himself, by years of work, a sound and earnest trade unionist, and even those who considered him politically backward and moderate, acknowledged the worth of his services to the Indian Labour movement. This could be said of few others, moderate or advanced.

My own sympathies at Jharia were with the advanced group but, being a newcomer, I felt a little at sea in these domestic conflicts of the T.U.C. and I decided to keep aloof from them. After I had left Jharia the annual T.U.C. elections took place, and I learnt at Calcutta that I had been elected president for the next year. I had been put forward by the moderate group, probably because they felt that I stood the best chance of defeating the other candidate who was an actual worker (on the railways) and who had been put forward by the radical group. If I had been present at Jharia on the day of the election I am sure that I would have withdrawn in favour of the worker candidate. It seemed to me positively indecent that a newcomer and a non-worker should be suddenly thrust into the presidentship. This was in itself a measure of the infancy and weakness of the trade union movement in India.

Nineteen twenty-eight had been full of labour disputes and strikes; 1929 carried on likewise. Bombay textile labour, miserable and militant, took the lead in these strikes. There was a big general strike in the Bengal Jute Mills. There were also strikes in the Iron Works at Jamshedpur, and, I think, on the railways. A long drawn out struggle, bravely carried on for many months, took place in the Tin Plate Works in Jamshedpur. In spite of great public sympathy, the workers were crushed by the powerful company (connected with the Burma Oil Company) owning these works.

Altogether the two years were full of industrial unrest, and the conditions of labour were deteriorating. The post-war years had been boom years for industry in India and the most stupendous profits had been made. For five or six years the average dividend in the jute or cotton mills exceeded a hundred per cent, and was often 150 per cent, per annum. All these huge profits went to the owners and shareholders, and the workers continued as before. The slight rise in wages was usually counterbalanced by a rise in prices. During these days when millions were being made feverishly, most of the workers continued to live in the most miserable of hovels, and even their womenfolk had hardly clothes to wear. The conditions in Bombay were bad enough, but perhaps even worse was the lot of the jute workers, within an hour's drive of the palaces of Calcutta. Semi-naked women, wild and unkempt, working away for the barest pittance, so that a broad river of wealth should flow ceaselessly to Glasgow and Dundee, as well as to some pockets in India.

In the boom years all went well for industry, though the workers carried on as before and profited little. But when the boom passed and it was not so easy to make large profits, the burden, of course, fell on the workers. The old profits were forgotten; they had been consumed. And if profits were not now sufficient, how could industry run? And so there was industrial unrest and labour troubles and the gigantic strikes in

Bombay which impressed everybody and frightened both the employers and Government. The Labour Movement was becoming class-conscious, militant and dangerous, both in ideology and in organization. The political situation was also developing fast, and, though the two were separate and unconnected, they were partly parallel, and the Government could not contemplate the future with any satisfaction.

In March 1929 the Government struck suddenly at organized labour by arresting some of its most prominent workers from the advanced groups. The leaders of the Bombay Girni Kamgar Union were taken, as well as labour leaders from Bengal, the U.P. and the Punjab. Some of these were communists, others were near-communists, yet others were just trade unionists. This was the beginning of the famous Meerut trial which lasted for four years and a half.

A defence committee was formed for the Meerut accused, of which my father was chairman, Dr Ansari and others, including myself, were members. We had a difficult task. Money was not easy to collect; it seemed that the moneyed people had no great sympathy for communists and socialists and labour agitators. And lawyers would only sell their services for a full pound of somebody's flesh. We had some eminent lawyers on our Committee, my father and others, and they were always available for consultation and general guidance. That did not cost us anything, but it was not possible for them to sit down in Meerut for months at a time. The other lawyers whom we approached seemed to look upon the case as a means of making as much money as possible.

Apart from the Meerut Case I have been connected with some other defence committees—in M.N. Roy's case and others. On each occasion I have marvelled at the cupidity of men of my own profession. My first big shock came during the Punjab Martial Law trials in 1919 when a very eminent leader of the profession insisted on his full fee—and it was a huge fee—from the victims of Martial Law, one of them even a fellow-lawyer, and many of these people had to borrow money or sell property to pay him. My later experiences were even more painful. We had to collect money, often in coppers from the poorest workers, and pay out fat cheques to lawyers. It went against the grain. And the whole process seemed so futile for, whether we defended a political or labour case or not, the result was likely to be the same. In a case like the Meerut trial a defence was, of course, obviously called for from many points of view.

The Meerut Case Defence Committee did not have an easy time with the accused. There were different kinds of people among these, with different types of defences, and often there was an utter absence of harmony among them. After some months we wound up the formal committee, but we continued to help in our individual capacities. The development of the political situation was absorbing more and more of our attention, and in 1930 all of us were ourselves in gaol.

27

THUNDER IN THE AIR

The 1929 Congress was going to be held in Lahore. After ten years it had come back to the Punjab, and people's minds leapt over that decade and went back to the events of 1919—Jallianwala Bagh, martial law with all its humiliations, the Congress sessions at Amritsar, to be followed by the beginnings of non-co-operation. Much had happened during this decade and India's face had changed, but there was no lack of parallels. Political tension was growing; the atmosphere of struggle was developing fast. The long shadow of the conflict to come lay over the land.

The Legislative Assembly and the Provincial Councils had long ceased to interest anyone, except the handful who moved in their sacred orbits. They carried on in their humdrum way, providing some kind of a cloak— a torn and tattered affair—to the authoritarian and despotic nature of the Government, an excuse to some people to talk of India's parliament, and allowances to their members. The last successful effort of the Assembly to draw attention to itself was when it passed a resolution in 1928 refusing its co-operation to the Simon Commission.

There had also been subsequently a conflict between the Chair and the Government. Vithalbhai Patel, the Swarajist President of the Assembly, had become a thorn in the tender side of the Government on account of his independence (of them) and attempts were made to clip his wings. Such happenings attracted attention but, on the whole, the public mind was now concentrated on events outside. My father was thoroughly disillusioned with Council work, and often expressed his opinion that nothing more could be got out of the legislatures at that stage. He wanted to get out of them himself if an opportunity presented itself. Constitutionally minded as he was and used to legal methods and procedure, force of circumstances had driven him to the painful conclusion that the so-called constitutional methods were ineffective and futile in India. He would justify this to his own legalist mind by saying that there was no constitution in India, nor was there any real rule of law when laws, in the shape of ordinances and the like, appeared suddenly, like rabbits from a conjurer's hat, at the will of an individual or a dictating group. In temperament and habit he was far from being a revolutionary, and if there had been anything like *bourgeois* democracy, he would undoubtedly have been a pillar of the constitution. But, as it was, talk of constitutional agitation in India, with a parade of a sham parliament, began to irritate him more and more.

Gandhiji was still keeping away from politics, except for the part he played at the Calcutta Congress. He was, however, in full touch with developments and was often consulted by the Congress leaders. His main activity for some years had been khadi propaganda, and with this object he had undertaken extensive tours all over India. He took each province by turn and visited every district and almost every town of any consequence, as well as remote rural areas. Everywhere he attracted enormous crowds, and it required a great deal of previous staff-work to carry through his programme. In this manner he has repeatedly toured India and got to know every bit of the vast country from the north to the far south, from the eastern mountains to the western sea. I do not think any other human being has ever travelled about India as much as he has done.

In the past there were great wanderers who were continually on the move, pilgrim souls with the *wanderlust*, but their means of locomotion were slow, and a life-time of such wandering could hardly compete with a year by railway and motor-car. Gandhiji went by railway and automobile, but he did not confine himself to them; he tramped also. In this way he gathered his unique knowledge of India and her people, and in this way also scores of millions saw him and came into personal touch with him.

He came to the United Provinces in 1929 on his khadi tour, and spent many weeks in these provinces during the hottest part of the year. I accompanied him occasionally for a few days at a time and, despite previous experience, could not help marvelling at the vast crowds he attracted. This was especially noticeable in our eastern districts, like Gorakhpur, where the swarms of human beings reminded one of hordes of locusts. As we motored through the rural areas, we would have gatherings of from 10,000 to 25,000 every few miles, and the principal meeting of the day might even exceed a hundred thousand. There were no broadcasting facilities, except rarely in a few big cities, and it was manifestly impossible to be heard by these crowds. Probably they did not expect to hear anything; they were satisfied if they saw the Mahatma. Gandhiji usually addressed them briefly, avoiding undue strain; it would have been quite impossible to carry on otherwise in this fashion from hour to hour and day to day.

I did not accompany him throughout his U.P. tour as I could be of no special use to him, and there was no point in my adding to the number of the touring party. I had no objection to crowds, but there was not sufficient inducement to get pushed and knocked about and my feet crushed—the usual fate of people accompanying Gandhiji. I had plenty of other work to do, and had no desire to confine myself to khadi propaganda, which seemed to me a relatively minor activity in view of the developing political situation. To some extent I resented Gandhiji's pre-occupation with non-political issues, and I could never understand the background of his thought. In those days he was collecting funds for khadi work, and he would say frequently that he wanted money for *Daridranarayan*, the 'Lord of the Poor', or 'God that resides in the Poor'; meaning thereby, presumably, that he wanted it to help the poor to find employment and work in cottage industries. But behind that word there seemed to be a glorification of poverty; God was especially the Lord of the poor; they were His chosen people. That, I suppose, is the usual religious attitude everywhere. I could not appreciate it, for poverty seemed to me a hateful thing, to be fought and rooted out and not to be encouraged in any way. This inevitably led to an attack on a system which tolerated and produced poverty, and those who shrunk from this had of necessity to justify poverty in some way. They could only think in terms of scarcity and could not picture a world abundantly supplied with the necessaries of life; probably, according to them, the rich and the poor would always be with us.

Whenever I had occasion to discuss this with Gandhiji he would lay stress on the rich treating their riches as a trust for the people; it was a view-point of considerable antiquity, and one comes across it frequently in India as well as medieval Europe. I confess that I have always been wholly unable to understand how any person can reasonably expect this to happen, or imagine that therein lies the solution of the social problem.

The Legislative Assembly, as I have said above, was becoming a somnolent affair and few people took interest in its dreary activities. A rude awakening came to it one day when Bhagat Singh and B.K. Dutt threw two bombs from the visitors' gallery on to the floor of the House. No one was seriously hurt, and probably the bombs were intended, as was stated by the accused later, to make a noise and create a stir, and not to injure.

They did create a stir both in the Assembly and outside. Other activities of Terrorists were not so innocuous. A young English police officer, who was alleged to have hit Lala Lajpat Rai, was shot down and killed in Lahore. In Bengal and elsewhere there seemed to be a recrudescence of terrorist activity. A number of conspiracy cases were launched, and the number of detenus—people kept in prison or otherwise detained without trial or conviction—rapidly increased.

In the Lahore conspiracy case some extraordinary scenes were enacted in the court by the police, and a great deal of public attention was drawn to the case because of this. As a protest against the treatment given to them in court and in prison, there was a hunger-strike on the part of most of the prisoners. I forget the exact reason why it began, but ultimately the question involved became the larger one of treatment of prisoners, especially Politicals. This hunger-strike went on from week to week and created a stir in the country. Owing to the physical weakness of the accused, they could not be taken to court, and the proceedings had to be adjourned repeatedly. The Government of India thereupon initiated legislation to allow court proceedings to continue even in the absence of the accused or their counsel. The question of prison treatment had also to be considered by them.

I happened to be in Lahore when the hunger-strike was already a month old. I was given permission to visit some of the prisoners in the prison, and I availed myself of this. I saw Bhagat Singh for the first time, and Jatindranath Das and a few others. They were all very weak and bed-ridden, and it was hardly possible to talk to them much. Bhagat Singh had an attractive, intellectual face, remarkably calm and peaceful. There seemed to be no anger in it. He looked and talked with great gentleness, but then I suppose that any one who has been fasting for a month will look spiritual and gentle. Jatin Das looked milder still, soft and gentle like a young girl. He was in considerable pain when I saw him. He died later, as a result of fasting, on the sixty-first day of the hunger-strike.

Bhagat Singh's chief ambition seemed to be to see, or at least to have news of, his uncle, Sardar Ajit Singh, who had been deported, together with Lala Lajpat Rai, in 1907. For many years he had been an exile abroad. There were some vague reports that he had settled in South America, but I do not think anything definite is known about him. I do not even know if he is alive or dead.

Jatin Das's death created a sensation all over the country. It brought the question of the treatment of political prisoners to the front, and Government appointed a committee on the subject. As a result of the deliberations of this committee, new rules were issued creating three classes of prisoners. No special class of political prisoners was created. These new rules, which seemed to promise a change for the better, as a matter of fact made little difference, and the position remained, and still remains, highly unsatisfactory.

As the summer and monsoon months gradually shaded off into the autumn, the Provincial Congress Committees busied themselves with the election of the President for the Lahore session of the Congress. This election is a lengthy process, and used to go on from August to October. In 1929 there was almost unanimity in favour of Gandhiji. This desire to have him as President for a second time did not, of course, push him any higher in the Congress hierarchy, for he had been a kind of super-president for many years. It was generally felt, however, that as a struggle was impending, and he was bound to be the *de facto* leader of it, he might as well be the *de jure* head of the Congress for the occasion. Besides, there was really no other person outstanding enough and obvious enough for the presidentship.

So Gandhiji was recommended for the presidentship by the Provincial Committees. But he would have none of it. His refusal, though emphatic, seemed to leave some room for argument, and it was hoped that he would reconsider it. A meeting of the All-India Congress Committee was held in Lucknow to decide finally, and almost to the last hour all of us thought that he would agree. But he would not do so, and at the last moment he pressed my name forward. The A.I.C.C. was somewhat taken aback by his final refusal, and a little irritated at being placed in a difficult and invidious position. For want of any other person, and in a spirit of resignation, they finally elected me.

I have seldom felt quite so annoyed and humiliated as I did at that election. It was not that I was not sensible of the honour, for it was a great honour, and I would have rejoiced if I had been elected in the ordinary way. But I did not come to it by the main entrance or even a side entrance; I appeared suddenly by a trap-door and bewildered the audience into acceptance. They put a brave face on it, and, like a necessary pill, swallowed me. My pride was hurt, and almost I felt like handing back the honour. Fortunately I restrained myself from making an exhibition of myself, and stole away with a heavy heart.

Probably the person who was happiest about this decision was my father. He did not wholly like my politics, but he liked me well enough, and any good thing that came my way pleased him. Often he would criticize me and speak a little curtly to me, but no person who cared to retain his goodwill could run me down in his presence.

My election was indeed a great honour and a great responsibility for me; it was unique in that a son was immediately following his father in the presidential chair. It was often said that I was the youngest President of the Congress—I was just forty when I presided. This was not true. I think Gokhale was about the same age, and Maulana Abul Kalam Azad (though he is a little older than me) was probably just under forty when he presided. But Gokhale was considered one of the elder statesmen even when he was in his late thirties, and Abul Kalam Azad has especially cultivated a look of venerable age to give a suitable background to his great learning. As statesmanship has seldom been considered one of my virtues, and no one has accused me of possessing an excess of learning, I have escaped so far the accusation of age, though my hair has turned grey and my looks betray me.

The Lahore Congress drew near. Meanwhile events were marching, step by step, inevitably, pushed onward, so it seemed, by some motive force of their own. Individuals, for all the brave show they put up, played a very minor role. One had the feeling of being a cog in a great machine which swept on relentlessly.

Hoping perhaps to check this onward march of destiny, the British Government took a forward step, and the Viceroy, Lord Irwin, made an announcement about a forthcoming Round Table Conference. It was an ingeniously worded announcement, which could mean much or very little, and it seemed to many of us obvious that the latter was the more likely contingency. And in any event, even if there was more in the announcement, it could not be anywhere near what we wanted. Hardly had this Viceregal announcement been made when, almost with indecent haste, so it seemed, a "Leaders' Conference" was arranged at Delhi, and people from various groups were invited to it. Gandhiji was there, so was my father; Vithalbhai Patel (still President of the Assembly) was also there, and Moderate leaders like Sir Tej Bahadur Sapru and others. A joint resolution or manifesto was agreed to, accepting the Viceroy's declaration subject to some conditions, which, it was stated, were vital and must be fulfilled. If these conditions were accepted by Government, then co-operation was to be offered. These conditions[1] were solid enough and would have made a difference.

It was a triumph to get such a resolution agreed to by representatives of all the groups, moderate and advanced. For the Congress it was a come-down; as a common measure of agreement it was high. But there was a fatal catch in it. The conditions were looked upon from at least two different view-points. The Congress people considered them to be essential, the *sine qua non*, without which there could be no co-operation. For them they represented the minimum required. This was made clear by a subsequent meeting of the Congress Working Committee, which further stated that this offer was limited to the date of the next Congress. For the Moderate groups they were a desirable maximum which should be stated, but which could not be insisted on to the point of refusal of co-operation. For them the conditions, though called vital, were not really conditions.

And so it happened that later on, though none of these conditions were satisfied and most of us lay in gaol, together with scores of thousands of others, our Moderate and Responsivist friends, who had signed that manifesto with us, gave their full co-operation to our gaolers.

---

1. The conditions were:
   (1) All discussions at the proposed conference to be on the basis of full Dominion Status for India.
   (2) There should be a predominant representation of Congressmen at the conference.
   (3) A general amnesty of political prisoners.
   (4) The Government of India to be carried on from now onwards, as far as is possible under existing conditions, on the lines of a Dominion government.

Most of us suspected that this would happen—though hardly to the extent it did happen—but there was some hope that this joint action, whereby the Congress people had to some extent curbed themselves, would also result in curbing the propensities of the Liberals and others to indiscriminate and almost invariable co-operation with the British Government. A more powerful motive for some of us, who heartily disliked the compromising resolution, was to keep our own Congress ranks well knit together. On the eve of a big struggle we could not afford to split up the Congress. It was well known that Government was not likely to accept the conditions laid down by us, and our position would thus be stronger and we could easily carry our Right Wing with us. It was only a question of a few weeks; December and the Lahore Congress were near.

And yet that joint manifesto was a bitter pill for some of us. To give up the demand for independence, even in theory and even for a short while, was wrong and dangerous; it meant that it was just a tactical affair, something to bargain with, not something which was essential and without which we could never be content. So I hesitated and refused to sign the manifesto (Subhas Bose had definitely refused to sign it), but, as was not unusual with me, I allowed myself to be talked into signing. Even so, I came away in great distress, and the very next day I thought of withdrawing from the Congress presidentship, and wrote accordingly to Gandhiji. I do not suppose that I meant this seriously, though I was sufficiently upset. A soothing letter from Gandhiji and three days of reflection calmed me.

Just prior to the Lahore Congress, a final attempt was made to find some basis of agreement between Congress and the Government. An interview with Lord Irwin, the Viceroy, was arranged. I do not know who took the initiative in arranging this interview, but I imagine that Vithalbhai Patel was the prime mover. Gandhiji and my father were present at the interview, representing the Congress view-point, and I think also present were Mr Jinnah, Sir Tej Bahadur Sapru and President Patel. The interview came to nothing; there was no common ground, and the two main parties—the Government and Congress—were far apart from each other. So now nothing remained but for the Congress to go ahead. The year of grace given at Calcutta was ending; independence was to be declared once for all the objective of the Congress, and the necessary steps taken to carry on the struggle to attain it.

During these final weeks prior to the Lahore Congress I had to attend to important work in another field. The All-India Trade Union Congress was meeting at Nagpur, and, as President for the year, I had to preside over it. It was very unusual for the same person to preside over both the National Congress and the Trade Union Congress within a few weeks of each other. I had hoped that I might be a link between the two and bring them closer to each other—the National Congress to become more socialistic, more proletarian, and organized Labour to join the national struggle.

It was, perhaps, a vain hope, for nationalism can only go far in a socialistic or proletarian direction by ceasing to be nationalism. Yet I felt that, *bourgeois* as the outlook of the National Congress was, it did represent the only effective revolutionary force in the country. As such, Labour ought to help it and co-operate with it and influence it, keeping, however, its own identity and ideology distinct and intact. And I hoped that the course of events and the participation in direct action would inevitably drive the Congress to a more radical ideology and to face social and economic issues. The development of the Congress during recent years had been in the direction of the peasant and the village. If this development continued, it might in course of time become a vast peasant organization, or, at any rate, an organization in which the peasant element predominated. Already in many of our U.P. District Congress Committees the peasantry were strongly represented, though the middle-class intelligentsia held the leadership in their hands.

There was thus a possibility of the eternal conflict between the village and the city influencing the relations of the National Congress with the T.U.C. The contingency was remote, as the present National Congress is run by middle-class people and is controlled by the city, and, so long as the question of national freedom is not solved, its nationalism will dominate the field and be the most powerful sentiment in the country. Still it seemed to me obviously desirable to bring the Congress nearer to organized labour, and in U.P. we even invited delegates to our Provincial Congress Committee from the provincial branch of the T.U.C. Many Congressmen also took prominent part in Labour activities.

The advanced sections of Labour, however, fought shy of the National Congress. They mistrusted its leaders, and considered its ideology *bourgeois* and reactionary, which indeed it was, from the Labour point of view. The Congress was, as its very name implied, a nationalist organization.

Throughout 1929 Trade Unions in India were agitated over a new issue—the appointment of a Royal Commission on Labour in India, known as the Whitley Commission. The Left Wing was in favour of a boycott of the Commission, the Right Wing in favour of co-operation, and the personal factor came in, as some of the Right Wing leaders were offered membership of the Commission. In this matter, as in many others, my sympathies were with the Left, especially as this was also the policy of the National Congress. It seemed absurd to co-operate with official Commissions when we were carrying on, or going to carry on, a direct action struggle.

At the Nagpur T.U. Congress, this question of the boycott of the Whitley Commission became a major issue, and on this, as well as on several other matters in dispute, the Left Wing triumphed. I played a very undistinguished role at this Congress. Being a newcomer in the Labour field and still feeling my way, I was a little hesitant. Generally, I expressed my views in favour of the more advanced groups, but I avoided acting with any group, and played the part more of an impartial speaker than a directing president. I was thus an almost passive spectator of the breaking-up of the T.U.C. and the formation of a new moderate organization. Personally, I felt that the Right groups were not justified in breaking away, and yet some of the leaders of the Left had forced the pace and given them every pretext to depart. Between the quarrels of the Right and Left, a large Centre group felt a little helpless. Perhaps given a right lead, it could have curbed the two and avoided the break-up of the T.U.C., and, even if the break came, it would not have had the unfortunate consequences which resulted.

As it was, the Trade Union Movement in India suffered a tremendous blow from which it has not yet recovered. The Government had already started its campaign against the advanced wings of the Labour movement, and the Meerut case was among the first fruits thereof. This campaign continued. The employers also thought the moment opportune to push their advantage home. The world depression had already begun in that winter of 1929-30, and buffeted by this, and attacked on every side, and with their own trade union organizations at their lowest ebb, the Indian working class had a very hard time, and were the helpless witnesses of a progressive deterioration in their own condition. The Trade Union Congress experienced another split in the course of the next year or two, when a Communist faction broke off. Thus there were in theory three federations of Trade Unions in India—a Moderate group, the main T.U.C., and a Communist group. In practice they were all weak and ineffective, and their mutual quarrels disgusted the rank-and-file workers. I was out of all this from 1930 onwards, as I was mostly in prison. During my short periods outside I learnt that attempts at unity were being made. They were not successful.[2] The Moderate group of unions gained strength by the adhesion of railway workers to them. They had one advantage over the other groups, as Government recognized them and accepted their recommendations for the Labour Conferences at Geneva. The lure of a visit to Geneva pulled some Labour leaders to them, and they brought their unions with them.

2. Subsequent efforts to bring about Trade Union unity have been more successful, and the various groups are now working in some co-operation with each other.

28

INDEPENDENCE AND AFTER

The Lahore Congress remains fresh in my memory—a vivid patch. That is natural, for I played a leading role there, and, for a moment, occupied the centre of the stage; and I like to think sometimes of the emotions that filled me during those crowded days. I can never forget the magnificent welcome that the people of Lahore gave me, tremendous in its volume and its intensity. I knew well that this overflowing enthusiasm was for a symbol and an idea, not for me personally; yet it was no little thing for a person to become that symbol, even for a while, in the eyes and hearts of great numbers of people, and I felt, exhilarated and lifted out of myself. But my personal reactions were of little account, and there were big issues at stake. The whole atmosphere was electric and surcharged with the gravity of the occasion. Our decisions were not going to be mere criticisms or protests or expressions of opinion, but a call to action which was bound to convulse the country and affect the lives of millions.

What the distant future held for us and our country, none dare prophesy; the immediate future was clear enough, and it held the promise of strife and suffering for us and those who were dear to us. This thought sobered our enthusiasms and made us very conscious of our responsibility. Every vote that we gave became a message of farewell to ease and comfort and domestic happiness and the intercourse of friends, and an invitation to lonely days and nights and physical and mental distress.

The main resolution on Independence, and the action to be taken in furtherance of our freedom struggle, was passed almost unanimously, barely a score of persons, out of many thousands, voting against it. The real voting took place on a side issue, which came in the form of an amendment. This amendment was defeated and the voting figures were announced and the main resolution declared carried, by a curious coincidence, at the stroke of midnight on December 31st, as the old year yielded place to the new. Thus even as the year of grace, fixed by the

Calcutta Congress, expired, the new decision was taken and preparations for the struggle launched. The wheels had been set moving, but we were still in darkness as to how and when we were to begin. The All-India Congress Committee had been authorized to plan and carry out our campaign, but all knew that the real decision lay with Gandhiji.

The Lahore Congress was attended by large numbers of people from the Frontier Province near by. Individual delegates from this province had always come to the Congress sessions, and for some years past Khan Abdul Ghaffar Khan had been attending and taking part in our deliberations. In Lahore for the first time a large batch of earnest young men from the Frontier came into touch with all-India political currents. Their fresh minds were impressed, and they returned with a sense of unity with the rest of India in the struggle for freedom and full of enthusiasm for it. They were simple but effective men of action, less given to talk and quibbling than the people of any other province in India, and they started organizing their people and spreading the new ideas. They met with success, and the men and women of the Frontier, the latest to join in India's struggle, played an outstanding and remarkable part from 1930 onwards.

Immediately after the Lahore Congress, and in obedience to its mandate, my father called upon the Congress members of the Legislative Assembly and the Provincial Councils to resign from their seats. Nearly all of them came out in a body, a very few refusing to do so, although this involved a breach of their election promises.

Still we were vague about the future. In spite of the enthusiasm shown at the Congress session, no one knew what the response of the country would be to a programme of action. We had burned our boats and could not go back, but the country ahead of us was an almost strange and uncharted land. To give a start to our campaign, and partly also to judge the temper of the country, January 26th was fixed as Independence Day, when a pledge of independence was to be taken all over the country.

And so, full of doubt about our programme, but pushed on by enthusiasm and the desire to do something effective, we waited for the march of events. I was in Allahabad during the early part of January; my father was mostly away. It was the time of the great annual fair, the Magh Mela; probably it was the special Kumbh year, and hundreds of thousands of men and women were continually streaming into Allahabad, or holy Prayag, as it was to the pilgrims. They were all kinds of people, chiefly peasants, also labourers, shopkeepers, artisans, merchants, businessmen, professional people—indeed, it was a cross-section of Hindu India. As I watched these great crowds and the unending streams of people going to and from the river, I wondered how they would react to the call for civil resistance and peaceful direct action. How many of them knew or cared for the Lahore decisions? How amazingly powerful was that faith which had for thousands of years brought them and their forebears from every corner of India to bathe in the holy Ganga! Could they not divert some of this tremendous energy to political and economic action to better their own lot? Or were their minds too full of the trappings and traditions of their religion to leave room for other thought? I knew, of course, that these other thoughts were already there, stirring the placid stillness of ages. It was the movement of these vague ideas and desires among the masses that had caused the upheavals of the past dozen years and had changed the face of India. There was no doubt about their existence and of the dynamic energy behind them. But still doubt came and questions arose to which there was no immediate answer. How far had these ideas spread? What strength lay behind them, what capacity for organized action, for long endurance?

Our house attracted crowds of pilgrims. It lay conveniently situated near one of the places of pilgrimage, Bharadwaj, where in olden times there was a primitive university, and on the days of the mela an endless stream of visitors would come to us from dawn to dusk. Curiosity, I suppose, brought most of them, and the desire to see well-known persons they had heard of, especially my father. But a large proportion of those who came were politically inclined, and asked questions about the Congress and what it had decided and what was going to happen; and they were full of their own economic troubles and wanted to know what they should do about them. Our political slogans they knew well, and all day the house resounded with them. I started the day by saying a few words to each group of twenty or fifty or a hundred as it came, one after the other, but soon this proved an impossible undertaking, and I silently saluted them when they came. There was a limit to this, too, and then I tried to hide myself. It was all in vain. The slogans became louder and louder, the verandas of the house were full of these visitors of ours, each door and window had a collection of prying eyes. It was impossible to work or talk or feed or, indeed, do anything. This was not only embarrassing, it was annoying and irritating. Yet there they were, these people looking up with shining eyes full of affection, with generations of poverty and suffering behind them, and still pouring out their gratitude and love and asking for little in return, except fellow-feeling and sympathy. It was impossible not to feel humbled and awed by this abundance of affection and devotion.

A dear friend of ours was staying with us at the time, and often it became impossible to carry on any conversation with her, for every five minutes or less I had to go out to say a word or two to a crowd that had assembled, and in between we listened to the slogans and shouting outside. She was amused at my plight and a little impressed, I think, by what she considered my great popularity with the masses. (As a matter of fact the principal attraction was my father, but, as he was away, I had to face the music.) She turned to me suddenly and asked me how I liked this hero-worship. Did I not feel proud of it? I hesitated a little before answering, and this led her to think that she had, perhaps, embarrassed me by too personal a question. She apologized. She had not embarrassed me in the least, but I found the question difficult to answer. My mind wandered away, and I began to analyse my own feelings and reactions. They were very mixed.

It was true that I had achieved, almost accidentally as it were, an unusual degree of popularity with the masses; I was appreciated by the intelligentsia; and to young men and women I was a bit of a hero, and a halo of romance seemed to surround me in their eyes. Songs had been written about me, and the most impossible and ridiculous legends had grown up. Even my opponents had often put in a good word for me and patronizingly admitted that I was not lacking in competence or in good faith.

Only a saint, perhaps, or an inhuman monster could survive all this, unscathed and unaffected, and I can place myself in neither of these categories. It went to my head, intoxicated me a little, and gave me confidence and strength. I became (I imagine so, for it is a difficult task to look at oneself from outside) just a little bit autocratic in my ways, just a shade dictatorial. And yet I do not think that my conceit increased markedly. I had a fair measure of my abilities, I thought, and I was by no means humble about them. But I knew well enough that there was nothing at all remarkable about them, and I was very conscious of my failings. A habit of introspection probably helped me to retain my balance and view many happenings connected with myself in a detached manner. Experience of public life showed me that popularity was often the handmaiden of undesirable persons; it was certainly not an invariable sign of virtue or intelligence. Was I popular then because of my failings or my accomplishments? Why indeed was I popular?

Not because of intellectual attainments, for they were not extraordinary, and, in any event, they do not make for popularity. Not because of so-called sacrifices, for it is patent that hundreds and thousands in our own day in India have suffered infinitely more, even to the point of the last sacrifice. My reputation as a hero is entirely a bogus one, and I do not feel at all heroic, and generally the heroic attitude or the dramatic pose in life strikes me as silly. As for romance, I should say that I am the least romantic of individuals. It is true that I have some physical and mental courage, but the background of that is probably pride: personal, group, and national, and a reluctance to be coerced into anything.

I had no satisfactory answer to my question. Then I proceeded along a different line of inquiry. I found that one of the most persistent legends about my father and myself was to the effect that we used to send our linen weekly from India to a Paris laundry. We have repeatedly contradicted this, but the legend persists. Anything more fantastic and absurd it is difficult for me to imagine, and if anyone is foolish enough to indulge in this wasteful snobbery, I should have thought he would get a special mention for being a prize fool.

Another equally persistent legend, often repeated in spite of denial, is that I was at school with the Prince of Wales. The story goes on to say that when the Prince came to India in 1921 he asked for me; I was then in gaol. As a matter of fact, I was not only not at school with him, but I have never had the advantage of meeting him or speaking to him.

I do not mean to imply that my reputation or popularity, such as they are, depend on these or similar legends. They may have a more secure foundation, but there is no doubt that the superstructure has a thick covering of snobbery, as is evidenced by these stories. At any rate, there is the idea of mixing in high society and living a life of luxury and then renouncing it all, and renunciation has always appealed to the Indian mind. As a basis for a reputation this does not at all appeal to me. I prefer the active virtues to the passive ones, and renunciation and sacrifice for their own sakes have little appeal for me. I do value them from another point of view—that of mental and spiritual training—just as a simple and regular life is necessary for the athlete to keep in good physical condition. And the capacity for endurance and perseverance in spite of hard knocks is essential for those who wish to dabble in great undertakings. But I have no liking or attraction for the ascetic view of life, the negation of life, the terrified abstention from its joys and sensations. I have not consciously renounced anything that I really valued; but then values change.

The question that my friend had asked me still remained unanswered: did I not feel proud of this hero-worship of the crowd? I disliked it and wanted to run away from it, and yet I had got used to it, and when it was wholly absent, I rather missed it. Neither way brought satisfaction, but, on the whole, the crowd had filled some inner need of mine. The notion that I could influence them and move them to action gave me a sense of authority over their minds and hearts; and this satisfied, to some extent, my will to power. On their part, they exercised a subtle tyranny over me, for their confidence and affection moved inner depths within me and evoked emotional responses. Individualist as I was, sometimes the barriers of individuality seemed to melt away, and I felt that it would be better to be accursed with these unhappy people than to be saved alone. But the barriers were too solid to disappear, and I peeped over them with wondering eyes at this phenomenon which I failed to understand.

Conceit, like fat on the human body, grows imperceptibly, layer upon layer, and the person whom it affects is unconscious of the daily accretion. Fortunately the hard knocks of a mad world tone it down or even squash it completely, and there has been no lack of these hard knocks for us in India during recent years. The school of life has been a difficult one for us, and suffering is a hard taskmaster.

I have been fortunate in another respect also—the possession of family members and friends and comrades, who have helped me to retain a proper perspective and not to lose my mental equilibrium. Public functions, addresses by municipalities and local boards and other public bodies, processions and the like, used to be a great strain on my nerves and my sense of humour and reality. The most extravagant and pompous language would be used, and everybody would look so solemn and pious that I felt an almost uncontrollable desire to laugh, or to stick out my tongue, or stand on my head, just for the pleasure of shocking and watching the reactions on the faces at that august assembly! Fortunately for my reputation and for the sober respectability of public life in India, I have suppressed this mad desire and usually behaved with due propriety. But not always. Sometimes there has been an exhibition on my part in a crowded meeting, or more often in processions, which I find extraordinarily trying. I have suddenly left a procession, arranged in our honour, and disappeared in the crowd, leaving my wife or some other person to carry on, perched up in a car or carriage, with that procession.

This continuous effort to suppress one's feelings and behave in public is a bit of a strain, and the usual result is that one puts on a glum and solid look on public occasions. Perhaps because of this I was once described in an article in a Hindu magazine as resembling a Hindu widow! I must say that, much as I admire Hindu widows of the old type, this gave me a shock. The author evidently meant to praise me for some qualities he thought I possessed—a spirit of gentle resignation and renunciation and a smileless devotion to work. I had hoped that I possessed—and, indeed, I wish that Hindu widows would possess—more active and aggressive qualities and the capacity for humour and laughter. Gandhiji once told an interviewer that if he had not had the gift of humour he might have committed suicide, or something to this effect. I would not presume to go so far, but life certainly would have been almost intolerable for me but for the humour and light touches that some people gave to it.

My very popularity and the brave addresses that came my way, full (as is, indeed, the custom of all such addresses in India) of choice and flowery language and extravagant conceits, became subjects for raillery in the circle of my family and intimate friends. The high-sounding and pompous words and titles that were often used for all those prominent in the national movement, were picked out by my wife and sisters and others and bandied about irreverently. I was addressed as *Bharat Bhushan*—'Jewel of India'; *Tyagamurti*—'O Embodiment of Sacrifice'; and this light-hearted treatment soothed me, and the tension of those solemn public gatherings, where I had to remain on my best behaviour, gradually relaxed. Even my little daughter joined in the game. Only my mother insisted on taking me seriously, and she never wholly approved of any sarcasm or raillery at the expense of her darling boy. Father was amused; he had a way of quietly expressing his deep understanding and sympathy.

But all these shouting crowds, and dull and wearying public functions, and interminable arguments, and the dust and tumble of politics touched me on the surface only, though sometimes the touch was sharp and pointed. My real conflict lay within me, a conflict of ideas, desires and loyalties, of subconscious depths struggling with outer circumstances, of an inner hunger unsatisfied. I became a battleground, where various forces struggled for mastery. I sought an escape from this; I tried to find harmony and equilibrium, and in this attempt I rushed into action. That gave me some peace; outer conflict relieved the strain of the inner struggle.

Why am I writing all this sitting here in prison? The quest is still the same, in prison or outside, and I write down my past feelings and experiences in the hope that this may bring me some peace and psychic satisfaction.

29

CIVIL DISOBEDIENCE BEGINS

Independence day came, January 26th, 1930, and it revealed to us, as in a flash, the earnest and enthusiastic mood of the country. There was something vastly impressive about the great gatherings everywhere, peacefully and solemnly taking the pledge of independence[1] without any speeches or exhortation. This celebration gave the necessary impetus to Gandhiji, and he felt, with his sure touch on the pulse of the people, that the time was ripe for action. Events followed then in quick succession, like a drama working up to its climax.

As Civil Disobedience approached and electrified the atmosphere, our thoughts went back to the movement of 1921-22 and the manner of its sudden suspension after Chauri Chaura. The country was more disciplined now, and there was a clearer appreciation of the nature of the struggle. The technique was understood to some extent, but more important still from Gandhiji's point of view, it was fully realized by every one that he was terribly in earnest about non-violence. There could be no doubt about that now as there probably was in the minds of some people ten years before. Despite all this, how could we possibly be certain that an outbreak of violence might not occur in some locality either spontaneously or as the result of an intrigue? And if such an incident occurred, what would be its effect on our civil disobedience movement? Would it be suddenly wound up as before? That prospect was most disconcerting.

Gandhiji probably thought over this question also in his own way, though the problem that seemed to trouble him, as far as I could gather from scraps of conversation, was put differently.

The non-violent method of action to bring about a change for the better was to him the only right method and, if rightly pursued, an infallible method. Must it be said that this method required a specially

---

1. This pledge is given in Appendix A (p. 637)

favourable atmosphere for its functioning and success, and that it should not be tried if outward conditions were not suited to it? That led to the conclusion that the non-violent method was not meant for all contingencies, and was thus neither a universal nor an infallible method. This conclusion was intolerable for Gandhiji, for he firmly believed that it was a universal and infallible method. Therefore, necessarily, it must function even though the external conditions were unfavourable, and even in the midst of strife and violence. The way of its functioning might be varied to suit varying circumstances, but to stop it would be a confession of failure of the method itself.

Perhaps his mind worked in some such way, but I cannot be sure of his thoughts. He did give us the impression that there was a slightly different orientation to his thinking, and that Civil Disobedience, when it came, need not be stopped because of a sporadic act of violence. If, however, the violence became in any way part of the movement itself, then it ceased to be a peaceful civil disobedience movement, and its activities had to be curtailed or varied. This assurance went a long way in satisfying many of us. The great question that hung in the air now was—how? How were we to begin? What form of civil disobedience should we take up that would be effective, suited to the circumstances, and popular with the masses? And then the Mahatma gave the hint.

Salt suddenly became a mysterious word, a word of power. The Salt Tax was to be attacked, the salt laws were to be broken. We were bewildered and could not quite fit in a national struggle with common salt. Another surprising development was Gandhiji's announcement of his 'Eleven Points'. What was the point of making a list of some political and social reforms—good in themselves, no doubt—when we were talking in terms of independence? Did Gandhiji mean the same thing when he used this term as we did, or did we speak a different language? We had no time to argue for events were on the move. They were moving politically before our eyes from day to day in India; and, hardly realized by us at the time, they were moving fast in the world and holding it in the grip of a terrible depression. Prices were falling, and the city dwellers welcomed this as a sign of the plenty to come, but the farmer and the tenant saw the prospect with alarm.

Then came Gandhiji's correspondence with the Viceroy and the beginning of the Dandi Salt March from the Ashram at Sabarmati. As people followed the fortunes of this marching column of pilgrims from day to day, the temperature of the country went up. A meeting of the All-India Congress Committee was held at Ahmedabad to make final arrangements for the struggle that was now almost upon us. The Leader in the struggle was not present, for he was already tramping with his pilgrim band to the sea, and he refused to return. The A.I.C.C. planned what should be done in case of arrests, and large powers were given to the President to act on behalf of the Committee, in case it could not meet, to nominate members of the Working Committee in place of those arrested, and to nominate a successor for himself with the same powers. Similar powers were given by Provincial and local Congress Committees to their presidents.

Thus was inaugurated a regime when so-called 'dictators' flourished and controlled the struggle on behalf of the Congress. Secretaries of State for India and Viceroys and Governors have held up their hands in horror and proclaimed how vicious and degraded was the Congress because it believed in dictatorships; they, of course, being convinced adherents of democracy. Occasionally the Moderate Press in India has also preached to us the virtues of democracy. We listened to all this in silence (because we were in prison) and in amazement. Brazen-faced hypocrisy could hardly go further. Here was India being governed forcibly under an absolute dictatorship with Ordinance laws and suppression of every kind of civil liberty, and yet our rulers talked unctuously of democracy. Even normally, where was the shadow of democracy in India? It was no doubt natural for the British Government to defend its power and vested interests in India and to suppress those who sought to challenge its authority. But its assertion that all this was the democratic method was worthy of record for future generations to admire and ponder over.

The Congress had to face a situation when it would be impossible for it to function normally; when it would be declared an unlawful organization, and its committees could not meet for consultation or any action, except secretly. Secrecy was not encouraged by us, as we wanted to keep our struggle a perfectly open one, and thus to keep up our tone and influence the masses. But even secret work did not take us far. All our leading men and women at the centre, as well as in the provinces and in local areas, were bound to be arrested. Who was then to carry on? The only course open to us was, after the fashion of an army in action, to make arrangements for new commanders to be appointed as old ones were disabled. We could not sit down in the field of battle and hold committee meetings. Indeed, we did so sometimes, but the object of this, and the inevitable result, was to have the whole committee arrested *en bloc*. We did not even have the advantage of a general staff sitting safely behind the lines, or a civilian cabinet in still greater safety elsewhere. Our general staffs and cabinets had to keep, by the very nature of our struggle, in the most advanced and exposed positions, and they were arrested and removed in the early stages. And what was the power we conferred on our 'dictators'? It was an honour for them to be put forward as symbols of the national determination to carry on the struggle; but the actual authority they had was largely confined to 'dictating' themselves to prison. They could only function at all when the committee they represented could not meet on account of *force majeure*; and wherever and whenever that committee could meet, the 'dictator' lost his individual authority, such as it was. He or she could not tackle any basic problems or principles; only minor and superficial phases of the movement could be affected by the 'dictator'. Congress 'dictatorships' were really stepping-stones to prison; and from day to day this process went on, new persons taking the place of those who were disabled.

And so, having made our final preparations, we bade good-bye to our comrades of the All-India Congress Committee at Ahmedabad, for none knew when or how we would meet again, or whether we would meet at all. We hastened back to our posts to give the finishing touches to our local arrangements, in accordance with the new directions of the A.I.C.C., and, as Sarojini Naidu said, to pack up our toothbrushes for the journey to prison.

On our way back, father and I went to see Gandhiji. He was at Jambusar with his pilgrim band and we spent a few hours with him there, and then saw him stride away with his party to the next stage in the journey to the salt sea. That was my last glimpse of him then as I saw him, staff in hand, marching along at the head of his followers, with firm step and a peaceful but undaunted look. It was a moving sight.

At Jambusar my father had decided, in consultation with Gandhiji, to make a gift of his old house in Allahabad to the nation and to rename this Swaraj Bhawan. On his return to Allahabad he made the announcement, and actually handed over charge to the Congress people; part of the large house being converted into a hospital. He was unable to go through the legal formalities at the time, and, a year and half later, I created a trust of the property, in accordance with his wishes.

April came, and Gandhiji drew near to the sea, and we waited for the word to begin civil disobedience by an attack on the salt laws. For months past we had been drilling our volunteers, and Kamala and Krishna (my wife and sister) had both joined them and donned male attire for the purpose. The volunteers had, of course, no arms or even sticks. The object of training them was to make them more efficient in their work and capable of dealing with large crowds. The 6th of April was the first day of the National Week, which is celebrated annually in memory of the happenings in 1919, from Satyagraha Day to Jallianwala Bagh. On that day Gandhiji began the breach of the salt laws at Dandi beach, and three or four days later permission was given to all Congress organizations to do likewise and begin Civil Disobedience in their own areas.

It seemed as though a spring had been suddenly released; and all over the country, in town and village, salt manufacture was the topic of the day, and many curious expedients were adopted to produce salt. We knew precious little about it, and so we read it up where we could, and issued leaflets giving directions, and collected pots and pans and ultimately succeeded in producing some unwholesome stuff, which we waved about in triumph, and often auctioned for fancy prices. It was really immaterial whether the stuff was good or bad; the main thing was to commit a breach of the obnoxious Salt Law, and we were successful in that, even though the quality of our salt was poor. As we saw the abounding enthusiasm of the people and the way salt-making was spreading like a prairie fire, we felt a little abashed and ashamed for having questioned the efficacy of this method when it was first proposed by Gandhiji. And we marvelled at the amazing knack of the man to impress the multitude and make it act in an organized way.

I was arrested on the 14th of April as I was entraining for Raipur in the Central Provinces, where I was going to attend a conference. That very day I was tried in prison and sentenced to six months' imprisonment under the Salt Act. In anticipation of arrest I had nominated (under the new powers given to me by the A.I.C.C.) Gandhiji to act as Congress

President in my absence, but, fearing his refusal, my second nomination was for father. As I expected, Gandhiji would not agree, and so father became the acting-President of the Congress. He was in poor health, nevertheless he threw himself into the campaign with great energy; and, during those early months, his strong guidance and enforcement of discipline was of tremendous benefit to the movement. The movement benefited greatly, but it was at the cost of such health and physical fitness as had remained in him.

Those were days of stirring news—processions and *lathi* charges and firing, frequent *hartals* to celebrate noted arrests, and special observances, like Peshawar Day, Garhwali Day, etc. For the time being the boycott of foreign cloth and all British goods was almost complete. When I heard that my aged mother and, of course, my sisters used to stand under the hot summer sun picketing before foreign cloth shops, I was greatly moved. Kamala did so also, but she did something more. She threw herself into the movement in Allahabad city and district with an energy and determination which amazed me, who thought I had known her so well for so many years. She forgot her ill-health and rushed about the whole day in the sun, and showed remarkable powers of organization. I heard of this vaguely in gaol. Later, when my father joined me there, I was to learn from him how much he had himself appreciated Kamala's work, and especially her organizing capacity. He did not at all fancy my mother or the girls rushing about in the hot sun, but, except for an occasional remonstrance, he did not interfere.

The biggest news of all that came to us in those early days was of the occurrences in Peshawar on April 23rd, and subsequently all over the Frontier Province. Anywhere in India such a remarkable exhibition of disciplined and peaceful courage before machine-gun firing would have stirred the country. In the Frontier Province it had an additional significance, for the Pathans, noted for their courage, were not noted for their peaceful nature; and these Pathans had set an example which was unique in India. In the Frontier Province also occurred the famous incident of the refusal to fire on the civil population by the Garhwali soldiers. They refused to fire because of a soldier's distaste for firing on an unarmed crowd, and because, no doubt, of sympathy with the crowd. But even sympathy is not usually enough to induce a soldier to take the grave step of refusing to obey his officer's orders. He knows the consequences. The Garhwalis probably did so (in common with some other regiments elsewhere whose disobedience did not receive publicity) because of a mistaken notion that the British power was collapsing. Only when such an idea takes possession of the soldier does he dare to act according to his own sympathies and inclinations. Probably for a few days or weeks the general commotion and civil disobedience led some people to think that the last days of British rule had come, and this influenced part of the Indian Army. Soon it became obvious that no such thing was going to happen in the near future, and then there was no more disobedience in the army. Care was also taken not to put them in compromising positions.

Many strange things happened in those days, but undoubtedly the most striking was the part of the women in the national struggle. They came out in large numbers from the seclusion of their homes and, though unused to public activity, threw themselves into the heart of the struggle. The picketing of foreign cloth and liquor shops they made their preserve. Enormous processions consisting of women alone were taken out in all the cities; and, generally, the attitude of the women was more unyielding than that of the men. Often they became Congress 'dictators' in provinces and in local areas.

The breach of the Salt Act soon became just one activity, and civil resistance spread to other fields. This was facilitated by the promulgation of various ordinances by the Viceroy prohibiting a number of activities. As these ordinances and prohibitions grew, the opportunities for breaking them also grew, and civil resistance took the form of doing the very thing that the ordinance was intended to stop. The initiative definitely remained with the Congress and the people, and as each ordinance law failed to control the situation from the point of view of government, fresh ordinances were issued by the Viceroy. Many of the Congress Working Committee members had been arrested, but it continued to function with new members added on to it, and each official ordinance was countered by a resolution of the Working Committee giving directions as to how to meet it. These directions were carried out with surprising uniformity all over this country—with one exception, the one relating to the publication of newspapers.

When an ordinance was issued for the further control of the Press and the demand of security from newspapers, the Working Committee called upon the Nationalist Press to refuse to give any security, and to stop publication instead. This was a hard pill to swallow for the newspapermen, for just then the public demand for news was very great. Still the great majority of newspapers—some Moderate papers excepted—stopped publication, with the result that all manner of rumours began to spread. But they could not hold out for long, the temptation was too great, and the sight of their moderate rivals picking up their business too irritating. So most of them drifted back to publication.

Gandhiji had been arrested on May 5th. After his arrest big raids on the salt pans and depots were organized on the west coast. There were very painful incidents of police brutality during these raids. Bombay then occupied the centre of the picture with its tremendous *hartals* and processions and *lathi* charges. Several emergency hospitals grew up to treat the victims of these *lathi* charges. Much that was remarkable happened in Bombay, and being a great city it had the advantage of publicity. Occurrences of equal importance in small towns and the rural areas received no publicity.

In the latter half of June my father went to Bombay, and with him went my mother and Kamala. They had a great reception, and during their stay there occurred some of the fiercest of the *lathi* charges. These were, indeed, becoming frequent occurrences in Bombay. A fortnight or so later an extraordinary all-night ordeal took place there, when Malaviyaji and members of the Working Committee, at the head of a huge crowd, spent the night facing the police, who blocked their way.

On his return from Bombay father was arrested on June 30th, and Syed Mahmud was arrested with him. They were arrested as acting-President and Secretary of the Working Committee, which was declared unlawful. Both of them were sentenced to six months. My father's arrest was probably due to his having issued a statement defining the duties of a soldier or policeman in the event of an order to fire on civil populations being given. The statement was strictly a legal affair, and contained the present British Indian law on this point. Nevertheless, it was considered a provocative and dangerous document.

The Bombay visit had been a great strain on father, and from early morning to late at night he was kept busy, and he had to take the responsibility for every important decision. He had long been unwell, but now he returned fagged out, and decided, at the urgent advice of his doctors, to take complete rest immediately. He arranged to go to Mussoorie and packed up for it, but the day before he intended leaving for Mussoorie, he appeared before us in our barrack in Naini Central Prison.

30

IN NAINI PRISON

I had gone back to gaol after nearly seven years, and memories of prison life had somewhat faded. I was in Naini Central Prison, one of the big prisons of the province, and I was to have the novel experience of being kept by myself. My enclosure was apart from the big enclosure containing the gaol population of between 2200 and 2300. It was a small enclosure, circular in shape, with a diameter of about one hundred feet, and with a circular wall about fifteen feet high surrounding it. In the middle of it was a drab and ugly building containing four cells. I was given two of these cells, connecting with each other, one to serve as a bathroom and lavatory. The others remained unoccupied for some time.

After the exciting and very active life I had been leading outside, I felt rather lonely and depressed. I was tired out, and for two or three days I slept a great deal. The hot weather had already begun, and I was permitted to sleep at night in the open, outside my cell in the narrow space between the inner building and the enclosing wall. My bed was heavily chained up, lest I might take it up and walk away, or, more probably, to avoid the bed being used as a kind of scaling ladder to climb the wall of the enclosure. The nights were full of strange noises. The convict overseers, who guarded the main wall, frequently shouted to each other in varying keys, sometimes lengthening out their cries till they sounded like the moaning of a distant wind; the night-watchmen in the barracks were continually counting away in a loud voice the prisoners under their charge and shouting out that all was well; and several times a night some gaol official, going his rounds, visited our enclosure and shouted an enquiry to the warder on duty. As my enclosure was some distance away from the others, most of these voices reached me indistinctly, and I could not make out at first what they were. At times I felt as if I was on the verge of the forest, and the peasantry were shouting to keep the wild animals away from their fields; sometimes it seemed the forest itself and the beasts of the night were keeping up their nocturnal chorus.

Was it my fancy, I wonder, or is it a fact that a circular wall reminds one more of captivity than a rectangular one? The absence of corners and angles adds to the sense of oppression. In the daytime that wall even encroached on the sky and only allowed a glimpse of a narrow-bounded portion. With a wistful eye I looked

> Upon that little tent of blue
> Which prisoners call the sky,
> And at every drifting cloud that went
> With sails of silver by.

At night that wall enclosed me all the more, and I felt as if I was at the bottom of a well. Or else that part of the star-lit sky that I saw ceased to be real and seemed part of an artificial planetarium.

My barrack and enclosure were popularly known throughout the gaol as the *Kuttaghar*—the Dog House. This was an old name which had nothing to do with me. The little barrack had been built originally, apart from all others, for especially dangerous criminals who had to be isolated. Latterly it had been used for political prisoners, detenus, and the like who could thus be kept apart from the rest of the gaol. In front of the enclosure, some distance away, was an erection that gave me a shock when I first had a glimpse of it from my barrack. It looked like a huge cage, and men went round and round inside it. I found out later that it was a water-pump worked by human labour, as many as sixteen persons being employed at a time. I got used to it as one gets used to everything, but it has always seemed to me one of the most foolish and barbarous ways of utilizing human labour-power. And whenever I pass it I think of the zoo.

For some days I was not permitted to go outside my enclosure for exercise or any other purpose. I was later allowed to go out for half an hour in the early mornings, when it was almost dark, and to walk or run under the main wall. That early morning hour had been fixed for me so that I might not come in contact with, or be seen by, the other prisoners. I liked that outing, and it refreshed me tremendously. In order to compress as much open-air exercise as I could in the short time at my disposal, I took to running, and gradually increased this to over two miles daily.

I used to get up very early in the morning, about four, or even half-past three, when it was quite dark. Partly this was due to going to bed early, as the light provided was not good for much reading. I liked to watch the stars, and the position of some well-known constellation would give me the approximate time. From where I lay I could just see the Pole Star peeping over the wall, and as it was always there, I found it extraordinarily comforting. Surrounded by a revolving sky, it seemed to be a symbol of cheerful constancy and perseverence.

For a month I had no companion, but I was not alone, as I had the warder and the convict overseers and a convict cook and cleaner in my enclosure. Occasionally other prisoners came there on some business, most of them being convict overseers—C.O.s—serving out long sentences. 'Lifers'—convicts sentenced for life—were common. Usually a life-sentence was supposed to terminate after twenty years, or even less, but there were many in prison then who had served more than twenty years already. I saw one very remarkable case in Naini. Prisoners carry about, attached to their clothes at the shoulder, little wooden boards giving information about their convictions and mentioning the date when release was due. On the board of one prisoner I read that his date of release was 1996! He had already, in 1930, served out several years, and he was then a person of middle age. Probably he had been given several sentences and they had been added up one after the other; the total, I think, amounting to seventy-five years.

For years and years many of these 'lifers' do not see a child or woman, or even animals. They lose touch with the outside world completely, and have no human contacts left. They brood and wrap themselves in angry thoughts of fear and revenge and hatred; forget the good of the world, the kindness and joy, and live only wrapped up in the evil, till gradually even hatred loses its edge and life becomes a soulless thing, a machine-like routine. Like automatons they pass their days, each exactly like the other, and have few sensations, except one—fear! From time to time the prisoner's body is weighed and measured. But how is one to weigh the mind and the spirit which wilt and stunt themselves and wither away in this terrible atmosphere of oppression? People argue against the death penalty, and their arguments appeal to me greatly. But when I see the long drawn-out agony of a life spent in prison, I feel that it is perhaps better to have that penalty rather than to kill a person slowly and by degrees. One of the 'lifers' came up to me once and asked me: "What of us lifers? Will Swaraj take us out of this hell?"

Who are these lifers? Many of them come in gang cases, when large numbers, as many as fifty or 100, may be convicted *en bloc*. Some. of these are probably guilty, but I doubt if most of those convicted are really guilty; it is easy to get people involved in such cases. An approver's evidence, a little identification, is all that is needed. Dacoities are increasing nowadays and the prison population goes up year by year. If people starve, what are they to do? Judges and magistrates wax eloquent about the increase of crime, but are blind to the obvious economic causes of it.

Then there are the agriculturists who have a little village riot over some land dispute, *lathis* fly about, and somebody dies—result, many people in gaol for life or for a long term. Often all the menfolk in a family will be imprisoned in this way, leaving the women to carry on as best they can. Not one of these is a criminal type. Generally they are fine young men, considerably above the average villager, both physically and mentally. A little training, some diversion of interest to other subjects and jobs, and these people would be valuable assets to the country.

Indian prisons contain, of course, hardened criminals, persons who are aggressively anti-social and dangerous to the community. But I have been amazed to find large numbers of fine types in prison, boys and men, whom I would trust unhesitatingly. I do not know what the proportion of real criminals to non-criminal types is, and probably no one in the prison department has ever even thought of this distinction. Some interesting figures are given on this subject by Lewis E. Lawes, the Warden of Sing Sing Prison in New York. He says of his prison population that, to his knowledge, 50 per cent are not criminally inclined at all; that 25 per cent are the products of circumstances and environment; that of the remaining 25 per cent, only a possible half, that is 12.5 per cent, are aggressively anti-social. It is a well-known fact that real criminality flourishes more in the big cities and centres of modern civilization than in the undeveloped countries. American gangsterdom is notorious, and Sing Sing has a special reputation as a prison where some of the worst criminals go. And yet, according to its warden, only 12.5 per cent of its prisoners are really bad. I think it may very safely be said that this proportion is far less in an Indian prison. A more sensible economic policy, more employment, more education would soon empty out our prisons. But of course to make that successful, a radical plan, affecting the whole of our social fabric, is essential. The only other real alternative is what the British Government is doing: increasing its police forces and enlarging its prisons in India. The number of persons sent to gaol in India is appalling. In a recent report issued by the Secretary of the All-India Prisoners' Aid Society, it is stated that in the Bombay Presidency alone 128,000 persons were sent to gaol in 1933, and the figure for Bengal for the same year was 124,000.[1] I do not know the figures for all the provinces, but if the total for two provinces exceeds a quarter of a million, it is quite possible that the All-India total approaches the million mark. This figure does not, of course, represent the permanent gaol population, for a large number of persons get short sentences. The permanent population will be very much less, but still it must be enormous. Some of the major provinces in India are said to have the biggest prison administrations in the world. U.P. is among those supposed to have this doubtful honour, and very probably it is, or was, one of the most backward and reactionary administrations. Not the least effort is made to consider the prisoner as an individual, a human being, and to improve or look after his mind. The one thing the U.P. administration excels in is keeping its prisoners. There are remarkably few attempts to escape, and I doubt if one in ten thousand succeeds in escaping.

One of the most saddening features of the prisons is the large number of boys, from fifteen upwards, who are to be found in them. Most of them are bright-looking lads who, if given the chance, might easily make good. Lately some beginnings have been made to teach them the elements of reading and writing but, as usual, these are absurdly inadequate and inefficient. There are very few opportunities for games or recreation, no newspapers of any kind are permitted nor are books encouraged. For twelve hours or more all prisoners are kept locked up in their barracks or cells with nothing whatever to do in the long evenings.

Interviews are only permitted once in three months, and so are letters—a monstrously long period. Even so, many prisoners cannot take advantage of them. If they are illiterate, as most are, they have to rely

---

1. The *Statesman*, 11 December 1934.

on some gaol official to write on their behalf; and the latter, not being keen on adding to his other work, usually avoids it. Or, if a letter is written, the address is not properly given and the letter does not reach. Interviews are still more difficult. Almost invariably they depend on a gratification for some gaol official. Often prisoners are transferred to different gaols, and their people cannot trace them. I have met many prisoners who had lost complete touch with their families for years, and did not know what had happened. Interviews, when they do take place after three months or more, are most extraordinary. A number of prisoners and their interviewers are placed together on either side of a barrier, and they all try to talk simultaneously. There is a great deal of shouting at each other, and the slight human touch that might have come from the interview is entirely absent.

A very small number of prisoners, ordinarily not exceeding one in a thousand (Europeans excepted), are given some extra privileges in the shape of better food and more frequent interviews and letters. During a big political civil resistance movement, when scores of thousands of political prisoners go to gaol, this figure of special class prisoners goes up slightly, but even so it is very low. About 95 per cent of these political prisoners, men and women, are treated in the ordinary way and are not given even these facilities.

Some individuals, sentenced for revolutionary activities for life or long terms of imprisonment, are often kept in solitary confinement for long periods. In U.P., I believe, all such persons are automatically kept in solitary cellular confinement. Ordinarily, this solitary confinement is awarded as a special punishment for a prison offence. But in the case of these persons—usually young boys—they are kept alone although their behaviour in gaol might be exemplary. Thus an additional and very terrible punishment is added by the Gaol Department to the sentence of the court, without any reason therefor. This seems very extraordinary, and hardly in conformity with any rule of law. Solitary confinement, even for a short period, is a most painful affair; for it to be prolonged for years is a terrible thing. It means the slow and continuous deterioration of the mind, till it begins to border on insanity; and the appearance of a look of vacancy, or a frightened animal type of expression. It is the killing of the spirit by degrees, the slow vivisection of the soul. Even if a man survives it, he becomes abnormal and an absolute misfit in the world. And the question always arises—was this man guilty at all of any act or offence? Police methods in India have long been suspect; in political matters they are doubly so.

European or Eurasian prisoners, whatever their crime or status, are automatically placed in a higher class and get better food, lighter work and more interviews and letters. A weekly visit from a clergyman keeps them in touch with outside affairs. The parson brings them foreign illustrated and humorous papers, and communicates with their families when necessary.

No one grudges the European convicts these privileges, for they are few enough, but it is a little painful to see the utter absence of any human standard in the treatment of others—men and women. The convict is not thought of as an individual human being, and so he or she is seldom treated as such. One sees in prison the inhuman side of the State apparatus of administrative repression at its worst. It is a machine which works away callously and unthinkingly, crushing all that come in its grip, and the gaol rules have been purposely framed to keep this machine in evidence. Offered to sensitive men and women, this soulless regime is a torture and an anguish of the mind. I have seen long-term convicts sometimes breaking down at the dreariness of it all, and weeping like little children. And a word of sympathy and encouragement, so rare in this atmosphere, has suddenly made their faces light up with joy and gratitude.

And yet among the prisoners themselves there were often touching instances of charity and good comradeship. A blind 'habitual' prisoner was once discharged after thirteen years. After this long period he was going out, wholly unprovided for, into a friendless world. His fellow convicts were eager to help him, but they could not do much. One gave his shirt deposited in the gaol office, another some other piece of clothing. A third had that very morning received a new pair of *chappals* (leather sandals) and he had shown them to me with some pride. It was a great acquisition in prison. But when he saw this blind companion of many years going out bare-footed, he willingly parted with his new *chappals*. I thought then that there appeared to be more charity inside the gaol than outside it.

That year 1930 was full of dramatic situations and inspiring happenings; what surprised most was the amazing power of Gandhiji to inspire and enthuse a whole people. There was something almost hypnotic about it, and we remembered the words used by Gokhale about him: how he had the power of making heroes out of clay. Peaceful civil disobedience as a technique of action for achieving great national ends seemed to have justified itself, and a quiet confidence grew in the country, shared by friend and opponent alike, that we were marching towards victory. A strange excitement filled those who were active in the movement, and some of this even crept inside the gaol. "*Swaraj* is coming!" said the ordinary convicts; and they waited impatiently for it, in the selfish hope that it might do them some good. The warders, coming in contact with the gossip of the bazaars, also expected that *Swaraj* was near; the petty gaol official grew a little more nervous.

We had no daily newspapers in prison, but a Hindi weekly brought us some news, and often this news would set our imagination afire. Daily *lathi* charges, sometimes firing, martial law at Sholapur with sentences of ten years for carrying the national flag. We felt proud of our people, and especially of our womenfolk, all over the country. I had a special feeling of satisfaction because of the activities of my mother, wife and sisters, as well as many girl cousins and friends; and though I was separated from them and was in prison, we grew nearer to each other, bound by a new sense of comradeship in a great cause. The family seemed to merge into a larger group, and yet to retain its old flavour and intimacy. Kamala surprised me, for her energy and enthusiasm overcame her physical ill-health and, for some time at least, she kept well in spite of strenuous activities.

The thought that I was having a relatively easy time in prison, at a time when others were facing danger and suffering outside, began to oppress me. I longed to go out, and as I could not do that, I made my life in prison a hard one, full of work. I used to spin daily for nearly three hours on my own *charkha*; for another two or three hours I did *newar* weaving, which I had especially asked for from the gaol authorities. I liked these activities. They kept me occupied without undue strain or requiring too much attention, and they soothed the fever of my mind. I read a great deal, and otherwise busied myself with cleaning up, washing my clothes, etc. The manual labour I did was of my own choice as my imprisonment was 'simple'.

And so, between thought of outside happenings and my gaol routine,

I passed my days in Naini Prison. Watching the working of an Indian prison, it struck me that it was not unlike the British government of India. There is great efficiency in the apparatus of government, which goes to strengthen the hold of the Government on the country, and little or no care for the human material of the country. Outwardly the prison must appear efficiently run, and to some extent this was true. But no one seemed to think that the main purpose of the prison must be to improve and help the unhappy individuals who come to it. Break them!— that is the idea, so that by the time they go out, they may not have the least bit of spirit left in them. And how is the prison controlled, and the convicts kept in check and punished? Very largely with the help of the convicts themselves, some of whom are made convict-warders (C.Ws.) or convict-overseers (C.O.s.), and are induced to cooperate with the authorities because of fear, and in the hope of rewards and special remissions. There are relatively few paid non-convict warders; most of the guarding inside the prison is done by convict warders and C.O.s. A widespread system of spying pervades the prison, convicts being encouraged to become stool pigeons and to spy on each other; and no combination or joint action is, of course, permitted among the prisoners. This is easy to understand, for only by keeping them divided up could they be kept in check.

Outside, in the government of our country, we see much of this duplicated on a larger, though less obvious, scale. But there the C.W.s. or C.O.s. are known differently. They have impressive titles, and their liveries of office are more gorgeous. And behind them, as in prison, stands the armed guard with weapons ever ready to enforce conformity.

How important and essential is a prison to the modern State! The prisoner at least begins to think so, and the numerous administrative and other functions of the government appear almost superficial before the basic functions of the prison, the police, the army. In prison one begins to appreciate the Marxian theory, that the State is really the coercive apparatus meant to enforce the will of a group that controls the government.

For a month I was alone in my barrack. Then a companion came— Narmada Prasad Singh—and his coming was a relief. Two and a half months later, on the last day of June 1930, our little enclosure was the scene of unusual excitement. Unexpectedly, early in the morning, my father and Dr Syed Mahmud, were brought there. They had both been arrested in Anand Bhawan, while they were actually in their beds, that morning.

31

NEGOTIATIONS AT YERAVDA

My father's arrest was accompanied by, or immediately preceded by, the declaration of the Congress Working Committee as an unlawful body. This led to a new development outside—the Committee would be arrested *en bloc* when it was having a meeting. Substitute members were added to it, under the authority given to the Acting-Presidents, and in this way several women became acting members. Kamala was one of them.

Father was in very poor health when he came to gaol, and the conditions in which he was kept there were of extreme discomfort. This was not intentional on the part of the Government, for they were prepared to do what they could to lessen those discomforts. But they could not do much in Naini Prison. Four of us were now crowded together in the four tiny cells of my barrack. It was suggested by the superintendent of the prison that father might be kept in some other part of the gaol where he might have a little more room, but we preferred to be together, so that some of us could attend personally to his comforts.

The monsoon was just beginning and it was not particularly easy to keep perfectly dry even inside the cells, for the rainwater came through the roof occasionally and dripped in various places. At night it was always a problem where to put father's bed, in the little 10 feet, by 5 feet. veranda attached to our cell, in order to avoid the rain. Sometimes he had fever. The gaol authorities ultimately decided to build an additional veranda, a fine broad one, attached to our cell. This veranda was built and it was a great improvement, but father did not profit by it much, as he was discharged soon after it was ready. Those of us who continued to live in that barrack took full advantage of it later.

Towards the end of July there was a great deal of talk about Sir Tej Bahadur Sapru and Mr M.R. Jayakar, endeavouring to bring about peace between the Congress and the Government. We read about it in a daily newspaper, which was supplied as a special favour to father. We read in this paper the correspondence that had passed between the Viceroy, Lord Irwin, and Messrs Sapru and Jayakar, and then we learnt that the so-called 'peacemakers' had visited Gandhiji. We did not know at all what had induced them to take this initiative, or what they were driving at. Later we were told by them that they had been encouraged to proceed in the matter because of a brief statement that father had agreed to in Bombay a few days before his arrest. The statement had been drafted by Mr Slocombe (a correspondent of the London *Daily Herald* then in India) after a conversation with my father, and had been approved by the latter. This statement[1] considered the possibility of the Congress withdrawing the civil disobedience campaign, subject to the Government agreeing to a number of conditions. It was a vague and tentative affair, and it made it quite clear that even those vague conditions could not be considered till father had a chance of consulting Gandhiji and me. I came in as the President of the Congress for the year. I remember father mentioning it to me in Naini, after his arrest, and adding that he was rather sorry that he had given such a vague statement in a hurry, as it was possible that it might be misunderstood. It was indeed misunderstood, as even the most exact and explicit statements are likely to be, by people whose way of thinking is entirely different.

Sir Tej Bahadur Sapru and Mr Jayakar suddenly descended on us in Naini Prison, on July 27th, with a note from Gandhiji. On that day and

---

1. Statement, dated Bombay, June 25, 1930, agreed to by Pandit Motilal Nehru: "If in certain circumstances the British Government and the Government of India, although unable to anticipate the recommendations that may in perfect freedom be made by the Round Table Conference or the attitude which the British Parliament may reserve for such recommendations, would nevertheless be willing to give a private assurance that they would support the demand for full responsible government for India, subject to such mutual adjustments and terms of transfer as are required by the special needs and conditions of India and by her long association with Great Britain and as may be decided by the Round Table Conference; Pandit Motilal Nehru would undertake to take personally such an assurance—or the indication received from a responsible third party that such an assurance would be forthcoming—to Mr Gandhi and to Pandit Jawaharlal Nehru. If such an assurance were offered and accepted it would render possible a general measure of conciliation which would entail the simultaneous calling off of the civil disobedience movement, the cessation of the Government's present repressive policy and a general measure of amnesty for political prisoners, and would be followed by Congress participation in the Round Table Conference on terms to be mutually agreed upon."

the next we had long interviews with them, which were very exhausting for father as he was actually feverish then. We talked and argued in a circle, hardly understanding each other's language or thought, so great was the difference in political outlook. It was obvious to us that there was not the faintest chance of any peace between the Congress and the Government as matters stood. We refused to make any suggestions without first consulting our colleagues of the Working Committee, especially Gandhiji. And we wrote something to this effect to Gandhiji.

Eleven days later, on August 8th, Dr Sapru came to see us again with the Viceroy's reply. The Viceroy had no objection to our going to Yeravda (the prison in Poona where Gandhiji was kept) but he and his Council could not allow us to meet Sardar Vallabhbhai Patel, Maulana Abul Kalam Azad and other members of the Working Committee who were outside and were still carrying on an active campaign against the Government. Dr Sapru asked us if we were prepared to go to Yeravda under these circumstances. We told him that we had and could have no objection to going to see Gandhiji at any time, but as we could not meet our other colleagues there was no chance of our deciding anything finally. That very day's paper (or perhaps that of the day before) had given the news of a fierce *lathi* charge in Bombay, and the arrest there of Vallabhbhai Patel, Malaviyaji, Tasadduk Sherwani and others as permanent or acting members of the Working Committee. We pointed out to Dr Sapru that this had not improved matters, and we asked him to make the position quite clear to the Viceroy. Dr Sapru, however, said that there would be no harm in our meeting Gandhiji as soon as possible. We had previously pointed out to him that in case we were sent to Yeravda, our colleague, Dr Syed Mahmud, who was with us at Naini, should also go there as he was the Congress secretary.

Two days later, on August 10th, the three of us—father, Mahmud and I—were sent by a special train from Naini to Poona. Our train did not stop at the big stations; we rushed past them, stopping at the small wayside ones. Still news of us travelled ahead, and large crowds gathered both at the stations where we stopped and at those where we did not stop. We reached Kirkee, near Poona, late at night on the 11th.

We expected to be kept in the same barrack as Gandhiji or, at least, to see him soon. That was the arrangement made by the Superintendent of Yeravda prison, but at the last moment he had to change his arrangements because of some instructions received through the police officer who had accompanied us from Naini. Lt. Col. Martin, the Superintendent, would not tell us the secret, but a little subtle questioning by father made it clear to us that the idea was that we should not meet Gandhiji (for the first time, at least) except in the presence of Messrs. Sapru and Jayakar. It was feared that a previous meeting between us might stiffen our attitude, or make us hold together more firmly than otherwise. So that night and the whole of the next day and night, we were kept apart in a separate barrack, and father was exceedingly irritated at this. It was tantalizing and annoying to be there and not to be allowed to see Gandhiji, to meet whom he had come all the way from Naini. On the forenoon of the 13th we were told that Sir Tej Bahadur Sapru and Mr Jayakar had arrived, and Mr Gandhi had joined them in the prison office, and we were asked to go there ourselves. Father refused to go, and only agreed after various explanations and apologies, and on condition that we should see Gandhiji alone first. At our joint request later, Vallabhbhai Patel and Jairamdas Doulatram, who had both been brought to Yeravda, as well as Sarojini Naidu, who was kept in the Women's Prison opposite, were allowed to join our conference. That evening father, Mahmud and I were moved to Gandhiji's enclosure and there we remained for the rest of our stay in Yeravda. Vallabhbhai Patel and Jairamdas Doulatram were also brought there for those few days to enable us to consult together.

Our conferences in the prison office with Messrs. Sapru and Jayakar lasted three days, the 13th, 14th and 15th August, and we exchanged letters giving expression to our views and indicating the minimum conditions necessary to enable us to withdraw civil disobedience and offer co-operation to the Government. These letters were subsequently published in the newspapers.[2]

The strain of these conferences had told on father, and on the 16th he suddenly got high fever. This delayed our return, and we started back on the night of the 19th, again by special train, for Naini. Every effort was made by the Bombay Government to provide a comfortable journey for father, and even in Yeravda, during our brief stay there, his comforts were studied. I remember an amusing incident on the night of our

---

2. The letter containing these minimum conditions is given in Appendix B. (p. 639).

arrival at Yeravda. Colonel Martin, the Superintendent, asked father what kind of food he would like. Father told him that he took very simple and light food, and then he enumerated his various requirements from early morning tea in bed to dinner at night. (In Naini we used to get food for him daily from home.) The list father gave in all innocence and simplicity consisted certainly of light foods, but it was impressive. Very probably at the Ritz or the Savoy it would have been considered simple and ordinary food, as father himself was convinced that it was. But in Yeravda Prison it seemed strange and far away and most inappropriate. Mahmud and I were highly amused to watch the expression on Colonel Martin's face as he listened to father's numerous and expensive requirements in the way of food. For a long time he had had in his keeping the greatest and most famous of India's leaders, and all that he had required in the way of food was goat's milk, dates, and perhaps oranges occasionally. The new type of leader that had come to him was very different.

During our journey back from Poona to Naini we again rushed by the big stations and stopped in out-of-the-way places. But the crowds were larger still, filling the platforms and sometimes even swarming over the railway lines, especially at Harda, Itarsi and Sohagpur. Accidents were narrowly averted.

Father's condition was rapidly deteriorating. Many doctors came to examine him, his own doctors as well as doctors sent on behalf of the Provincial Government. It was obvious that gaol was the worst place for him and there could be no proper treatment there. And yet, when a suggestion was made by some friend in the Press that he should be released because of his illness, he was irritated, as he thought that people might think that the suggestion came from him. He even went to the length of sending a telegram to Lord Irwin, saying that he did not want to be released as a special favour. But his condition was growing worse from day to day; he was losing weight rapidly, and physically he was a shadow of himself. On 8th September he was discharged after exactly ten weeks of prison.

Our barrack became a dull and lifeless place after his departure. There was so much to be done when he was with us, little services to add to his comfort, and all of us—Mahmud, Narmada Prasad and I—filled our days with this joyful service. I had given up newar weaving, I spun very little, and I did not have much time for books either. And now that he was gone, we reverted rather heavily and joylessly to the old routine. Even the daily newspaper stopped after father's release. Four or five days later my brother-in-law, Ranjit S. Pandit, was arrested, and he joined us in our barrack.

A month later, on October 11th, I was discharged on the expiry of six months' sentence. I knew I would have little freedom, for the struggle was going on and becoming more intense. The attempts of the 'peacemakers'—Messrs. Sapru and Jayakar—had failed. On the very day I was discharged one or two more ordinances were announced. I was glad to be out and eager to do something effective during my short spell of freedom.

Kamala was in Allahabad then, busy with her Congress work; father was under treatment at Mussoorie, and my mother and sisters were with him. I spent a busy day and a half in Allahabad before going up to Mussoorie myself with Kamala. The great question before us then, was whether a no-tax campaign in the rural areas should be started or not. The time for rent collection and payment of revenue was close at hand, and, in any event, collections were going to be difficult because of the tremendous fall in the prices of agricultural produce. The world slump was now very evident in India.

It seemed an ideal opportunity for a no-tax campaign, both as a part of the general civil disobedience movement and, independently, on its own merits. It was manifestly impossible both for landlords and tenants to pay up the full demand out of that year's produce. They had to fall back on old reserves, if they had any, or borrow. The zamindars usually had something to fall back upon, or could borrow more easily. The average tenant, always on the verge of destitution and starvation, had nothing to fall back upon. In any democratic country, or where the agriculturists were properly organized and had influence, it would have been quite impossible, under those circumstances, to make them pay much. In India their influence was negligible, except in so far as the Congress, in some parts of the country, stood for them; and except, of course, for the ever-present fear of peasant risings when the situation became intolerable for them. But they had been trained for generations past to stand almost anything without much murmuring.

In Gujrat, and in some other parts, there were no-tax campaigns in progress at the time, but they were almost wholly political campaigns, started as parts of the civil disobedience movement. These were areas where the *ryotwari* system prevailed and the peasant proprietors dealt directly with the Government. Their non-payment of revenue affected the State immediately. The United Provinces were different, for we were a zamindari and taluqadari area, and there were middlemen between the cultivator and the State. If the tenants stopped paying their rent the landlord suffered immediately. A class issue also was thus raised. The Congress, as a whole, was a purely nationalist body, and included many middling zamindars and a few of the larger ones also. Its leaders were terribly afraid of doing anything which might raise this class issue or irritate the zamindar elements. So, right through the first six months of civil disobedience, they avoided calling for a general no-tax campaign in the rural areas, although conditions for this seemed to me to be ripe. I was not afraid of raising the class issue in this way or any other way, but I recognized that the Congress, being what it was, could not then patronize class conflict. It could, however, call upon both parties, zamindars and tenants, not to pay. The average zamindar would probably pay up the revenue demanded from him by the Government, but that would be his fault.

When I came out of gaol in October, both political and economic conditions seemed to me to be crying out for a no-tax campaign in rural areas. The economic difficulties of the agriculturists were obvious enough. Politically, our civil disobedience activities, though still flourishing everywhere, were getting a bit stale. People went on going to gaol in small numbers, and sometimes in large groups, but the sting had gone from the atmosphere. The cities and the middle classes were a bit tired of the *hartals* and processions. Obviously something was needed to liven things up, a fresh infusion of blood was necessary. Where could this come from except from the peasantry?—and the reserve stocks there were enormous. It would again become a mass movement touching the vital interests of the masses, and, what was to me very important, would raise social issues.

We discussed these matters, my colleagues and I, during the brief day and a half I was at Allahabad. At short notice we convened a meeting there of the executive of our Provincial Congress Committee, and, after long debate, we decided to sanction a no-tax campaign, making it permissive for any district to take it up. We did not declare it ourselves in any part of the province, and the Executive Council made it apply to zamindars as well as tenants, to avoid the class issue if possible. We knew, of course, that the main response would come from the peasantry.

Having got this permission to go ahead, our district of Allahabad wanted to take the first step. We decided to convene a representative kisan or peasants' conference of the district a week later, to give the new campaign a push. I felt that I had done a good first day's work after release from gaol. I added to it a big mass meeting in Allahabad city, where I spoke at length. It was for this speech that I was subsequently convicted again.

And then, on October 13th, Kamala and I went off to Mussoorie to spend three days with father. He was looking just a little better, and I was happy to think that he had turned the corner and was getting well. I remember those quiet and delightful three days well; it was good to be back in the family. Indira, my daughter, was there; and my three little nieces, my sister's daughters. I would play with the children and sometimes we would march bravely round the house in a stately procession, led, flag in hand, by the youngest, aged three or four, singing *Jhanda uncha rahe hamara*, our flag song. And those three days were the last I was to have with father before his fatal illness came to snatch him away from me.

Expecting my re-arrest soon, and desiring perhaps to see a little more of me, father suddenly decided to return to Allahabad also. Kamala and I were going down from Mussoorie on 17th October to be in time for the Peasant Conference at Allahabad on the 19th. Father arranged to start with the others on the 18th, the day after us.

We had a somewhat exciting journey back, Kamala and I. At Dehra Dun an order under Section 144 Criminal Procedure Code was served on me almost as I was leaving. At Lucknow we got off for a few hours, and I learnt that another order under Section 144 awaited me there, but it was not actually served on me, as the police officer could not reach me owing to the large crowds. I was presented with an address by the Municipality, and then we left by car for Allahabad, stopping at various places *en route* to address some peasant gatherings. We reached Allahabad on the night of the 18th.

The morning of the 19th brought yet another order under Section

144 for me! The Government was evidently hot on my trail and my hours were numbered. I was anxious to attend the kisan conference before my re-arrest. We called this conference a private one of delegates only, and so it was, and did nor allow outsiders to come in. It was very representative of Allahabad District, and, as far as I remember, about 1,600 delegates were present. The conference decided very enthusiastically to start the no-tax campaign in the district. There was some hesitation among our principal workers, some doubt about the success of such a venture, for the influence and the power of the big zamindars to terrorise, backed as this was by the Government, was very great, and they wondered if the peasantry would be able to withstand this. But there was no hesitation or doubt in the minds of the sixteen hundred and odd peasants of all degrees who were present, or at any rate it was not apparent. I was one of the speakers at the conference. I do not know if thereby I committed a breach of the Section 144 order which had forbidden me from speaking in public.

I then went to the station to receive my father and the rest of the family. The train was late, and, immediately after their arrival, I left them to attend a public meeting, a joint affair of the peasants, who had come from the surrounding villages, and the townspeople. Kamala and I were returning from this meeting, thoroughly tired out, after 8 p.m. I was looking forward to a talk with father, and I knew that he was waiting for me, for we had hardly spoken to each other since his return. On our way back our car was stopped almost in sight of our house, and I was arrested and carried off across the river Jumna to my old quarters in Naini. Kamala went on, alone, to Anand Bhawan to inform the waiting family of this new development; and, at the stroke of nine, I re-entered the great gate of Naini Prison.

32

THE NO-TAX CAMPAIGN IN THE
UNITED PROVINCES

After eight days' absence I was back again in Naini, and I rejoined Syed Mahmud, Narmada Prasad and Ranjit Pandit in the same old barrack. Some days afterwards I was tried in prison on a number of charges, all based on various parts of that one speech I had delivered at Allahabad, the day after my discharge. As usual with us, I did not defend myself, but made a brief statement in court. I was sentenced for sedition under Section 124A to 18 months' rigorous imprisonment and a fine of Rs 500; under the Salt Act of 1882 to six months and a fine of Rs 100; and under Ordinance VI of 1930 (I forget what this Ordinance was about) also to six months and a fine of Rs 100. As the last two were concurrent, the total sentence was two years' rigorous imprisonment and, in addition, five months in default of fines. This was my fifth term.

My re-arrest and conviction had some effect on the tempo of the civil disobedience movement for a while; it put on a little spurt and showed greater energy. This was largely due to father. When news was brought to him by Kamala of my arrest, he had a slightly unpleasant shock. Almost immediately he pulled himself together and banged a table in front of him, saying that he had made up his mind to be an invalid no longer. He was going to be well and to do a man's work, and not submit weakly to illness. It was a brave resolve, but unhappily no strength of will could overcome and crush that deep-seated disease that was eating into him. Yet for a few days it worked a marked change, to the surprise of those who saw him. For some months past, ever since he was at Yeravda, he had been bringing up blood in his sputum. This stopped quite suddenly after this resolve of his, and for some days it did not reappear. He was pleased about it, and he came to see me in prison and mentioned this fact to me in some triumph. It was unfortunately a brief respite, for the blood came later in greater quantities and the disease reasserted itself. During this interval he worked with his old energy and gave a push to the civil disobedience movement all over India. He conferred with many people from various places and issued detailed instructions. He fixed one day (it was my birthday in November!) for an all-India celebration at which the offending passages from my speech, for which I had been convicted, were read out at public meetings. On that day there were numerous *lathi* charges and forcible dispersals of processions and meetings, and it was estimated that, on that day alone, about five thousand arrests were made all over the country. It was a unique birthday celebration.

Ill as he was, this assumption of responsibility and pouring out of energy was very bad for father, and I begged of him to take absolute rest. I realized that such rest might not be possible for him in India, for his mind would always be occupied with the ups and downs of our struggle and, inevitably, people would go to him for advice. So I suggested to him to go for a short sea voyage towards Rangoon, Singapore, and the Dutch Indies, and he rather liked the idea. It was arranged that a doctor friend might accompany him on the voyage. With this object in view he went to Calcutta, but his condition grew slowly worse and he was unable to go far. In a Calcutta suburb he remained for seven weeks, and the whole family joined him there, except Kamala, who remained in Allahabad for most of the time, doing Congress work.

My re-arrest had probably been hastened because of my activities in connection with the no-tax campaign. As a matter of fact few things could have been better for that campaign than my arrest on that particular day, immediately after the kisan conference, while the peasant delegates were still in Allahabad. Their enthusiasm grew because of it, and they carried the decisions of the conference to almost every village in the district. Within a couple of days the whole district knew that the no-tax campaign had been inaugurated, and everywhere there was a joyful response to it.

Our chief difficulty in those days was one of communication, of getting people to know what we were doing or what we wanted them to do. Newspapers would not publish our news for fear of being penalized and suppressed by Government; printing presses would not print our leaflets and notices; letters and telegrams were censored and often stopped. The only reliable method of communication open to us was to send couriers with despatches, and even so our messengers were sometimes arrested. The method was an expensive one and required a great deal of organization. It was organized with some success, and the provincial centres were in constant touch with headquarters as well as with their principal district centres. It was not difficult to spread any information in the cities. Many of these issued unauthorized news-sheets, usually cyclostyled, daily or weekly, and there was always a great demand for them. For our public notifications, one of the city methods was by beat of drum; this resulted usually in the arrest of the drummer. This did not matter, as arrests were sought, not avoided. All these methods suited the cities and were not easily applicable to the rural areas. Some kind of touch was kept up with principal village centres by means of messengers and cyclostyled notices, but this was not satisfactory, and it took time for our instructions to percolate to distant villages.

The kisan conference at Allahabad got over this difficulty. Delegates had come to it from practically every important village in the district and, when they dispersed, they carried the news of the fresh decisions affecting the peasantry, and of my arrest in connection with them, to every part of the district. They became, sixteen hundred of them, effective and enthusiastic propagandists for the no-tax campaign. The initial success of the movement thus became assured, and there was no doubt that the peasantry as a whole in that area would not pay their rent to begin with, and not at all unless they were frightened into doing so. No one, of course, could say what their powers of endurance would be in face of official or zamindari violence and terrorism.

Our appeal had been addressed both to zamindars and tenants not to pay; in theory it was not a class appeal. In practice most of the zamindars did pay their revenue, even some who sympathized with the national struggle. The pressure on them was great and they had more to lose. The tenantry, however, stood firm and did not pay, and our campaign thus became practically a no-rent campaign. From the Allahabad district it spread to some other districts of the United Provinces. In many districts it was not formally adopted or declared, but in effect tenants withheld their rents or, in many cases, were wholly unable to pay them owing to the fall in prices. As it happened, neither Government nor the big zamindars took any widespread action to terrorise the recalcitrant tenantry for several months. They were not sure of their ground, as they had the political struggle with civil disobedience on the one side, and the economic slump, resulting in agricultural distress, on the other. The two merged into each other, and the Government was always afraid of an agrarian upheaval. With the Round Table Conference in session in London, they were not keen on adding to their troubles in India or on giving a still more striking demonstration of 'strong' government.

The no-tax movement in the United Provinces had one important result so far as this province was concerned. It shifted the centre of gravity of our struggle from the urban to the rural areas, and it thereby revitalized the movement and put it on a broader and more enduring basis. Though our city people became bored and tired, and our middle-class workers were obviously rather stale, the movement itself in the U.P. was as strong, or even stronger, than it had been at any other time. In the other provinces this change-over from urban to rural, from political to economic issues, did not take place to the same extent, and consequently they continued to be dominated by the cities and to suffer increasingly from the weariness of the middle-class elements. Even the city of Bombay, which had all along played a prominent part in the movement, began to grow a little stale. Defiance of authority would go on there and elsewhere, and arrests would continue, but all this seemed somewhat artificial. The organic element had gone. This was natural enough, as it is impossible to keep the masses at a certain revolutionary pitch for long periods. Ordinarily, this was a question of days, but civil disobedience had the remarkable capacity for lengthening this period to many months, and even then of carrying on at a lower pitch for an indefinite period.

Government repression grew. Local Congress Committees, Youth Leagues, etc., which had rather surprisingly carried on so far, were declared illegal and suppressed. The treatment of political prisoners in gaols became worse. Government was especially irritated when people returned to gaol for a second sentence soon after their discharge. This failure to bend in spite of punishment hurt the morale of the rulers. In November or early December 1930 there were some cases of flogging of political prisoners in U.P. prisons, apparently for offences against gaol discipline. News of this reached us in Naini Prison and upset us—since then we have got used to this, as well as many worse happenings in India—for flogging seemed to me to be an undesirable infliction, even on hardened criminals of the worst type. For young, sensitive boys and for technical offences of discipline, it was barbarous. We four in our barrack wrote to the Government about it, and, not receiving any reply for about two weeks, we decided to take some definite step to mark our protest at the floggings and our sympathy with the victims of this barbarity. We undertook a complete fast for three days—72 hours. This was not much as fasts go, but none of us was accustomed to fasting, and did not know how we would stand it. My previous fasts had seldom exceeded 24 hours.

We went through that fast without any great difficulty, and I was glad to find out that it was not such an ordeal as I feared. Very foolishly I carried on my strenuous exercises—running, jerks, etc.—right through that fast. I do not think that did me much good, especially as I had been feeling a little unwell previously. Each one of us lost seven to eight pounds in weight during those three days. This was in addition to the fifteen to twenty-six pounds that each had lost in the previous months in Naini.

Quite apart from our fasting, there was a fair amount of agitation outside against the flogging, and I believe that the U.P. Government issued orders to its Gaol Department not to indulge in it in future. But these orders were not to remain unchanged for long, and a little more than a year later there was going to be no lack of flogging in the gaols of the United Provinces and the other provinces.

Except for these occasional alarms, we lived a quiet life in prison. The weather was agreeable, for winter in Allahabad is very pleasant. Ranjit Pandit was an acquisition to our barrack, for he knew much about gardening, and soon that dismal enclosure of ours was full of flowers and was gay with colour. He even arranged in that narrow, restricted space a miniature golf course!

One of the welcome excitements of our prison existence at Naini was the passage of aeroplanes over our heads. Allahabad is one of the ports of call for all the great airlines between East and West, and the giant planes going to Australia, Java, and French Indo-China would pass almost directly above our heads at Naini. Most stately of all were the Dutch liners flying to and from Batavia. Sometimes, if we were lucky, we saw a plane in the early winter morning, when it was still dark and the stars were visible. The great liner was brightly lit up, and at both ends it had red lights. It was a beautiful sight, as it sailed by, against the dark background of the early morning sky.

Pandit Madan Mohan Malaviya was also transferred to Naini from some other gaol. He was kept separately, not in our barrack, but we met him daily, and perhaps I saw more of him there than I had done outside. He was a delightful companion, full of vitality and a youthful interest in things. He even started, with Ranjit's help, to learn German, and he showed quite a remarkable memory. He was in Naini when news of the floggings came, and he was greatly upset and wrote to the Acting-Governor of the Province. Soon afterwards he fell ill.

He was unable to bear the cold in the conditions that prevailed in prison. His illness grew serious, and he had to be removed to the city hospital, and later to be discharged before his term was over. Happily, he recovered in hospital.

The New Year's Day, the first of January 1931, brought us the news of Kamala's arrest. I was pleased, for she had so longed to follow many of her comrades to prison. Ordinarily, if they had been men, both she and my sister and many other women would have been arrested long ago. But at that time the Government avoided, as far as possible, arresting women, and so they had escaped for so long. And now she had her heart's desire! How glad she must be, I thought. But I was apprehensive, for she was always in weak health, and I feared that prison conditions might cause her much suffering.

As she was arrested, a pressman who was present asked her for a message, and, on the spur of the moment and almost unconsciously, she gave a little message that was characteristic of her: "I am happy beyond measure and proud to follow in the footsteps of my husband. I hope the people will keep the flag flying." Probably she would not have said just that if she had thought over the matter, for she considers herself a champion of woman's right against the tyranny of man. But at that moment the Hindu wife in her came uppermost and even man's tyranny was forgotten.

My father was in Calcutta and was far from well, but news of Kamala's arrest and conviction shook him up, and he decided to return to Allahabad. He sent on my sister Krishna immediately to Allahabad, and followed himself, with the rest of the family, a few days later. On the 12th of January he came to see me in Naini. I saw him after nearly two months, and I had a shock which I could conceal with difficulty. He seemed to be unaware of the dismay that his appearance had produced in me, and told me that he was much better than he had lately been in Calcutta. His face was swollen up, and he seemed to think that this was due to some temporary cause.

That face of his haunted me. It was so utterly unlike him. For the first time a fear began to creep in my mind that there was real danger for him ahead. I had always associated him with strength and health, and I could not think of death in connection with him. He had always laughed at the idea of death, made fun of it, and told us that he proposed to live for a further long term of years. Latterly I had noticed that whenever an old friend of his youth died, he had a sense of loneliness, of being left by himself in strange company, and even a hint of an approaching end. But generally this mood passed and his overflowing vitality asserted itself, and we of his family had grown so used to his rich personality and the all-embracing warmth of his affection, that it was difficult for us to think of the world without him.

I was troubled by that look of his and my mind was full of forebodings. Yet I did not think that any danger to him lay in the near future. I was myself, for some unknown reason, keeping poor health just then.

Those were the last days of the first Round Table Conference, and we were a little amused—and I am afraid our amusement had a touch of disdain in it—at the final flourishes and gestures. Those speeches and platitudes and discussions seemed unreal and futile, but one reality stood out: that even in the hour of our country's sorest trial, and when our men and women had behaved so wonderfully, there were some of our countrymen who were prepared to ignore our struggle and give their moral support to the other side. It became clearer to us than it had been before how, under the deceptive cover of nationalism, conflicting economic interests were at work, and how those with vested interests were trying to preserve them for the future in the name of this very nationalism. The Round Table Conference was an obvious collection of these vested interests. Many of them had opposed our struggle; some had silently stood aside, reminding us, however, from time to time that "they also serve who only stand and wait." But the waiting period came to a sudden end when London beckoned, and they trooped up to ensure the safety of their own particular interests and to share in such further spoils as might be forthcoming. This general lining up in London was hastened by a realization that the Congress was going increasingly to the Left and the masses were influencing it more and more. Instinctively, it was felt that if a root and branch political change came in India, it would mean the dominance, or at least the emergence into importance, of various mass elements, and these would inevitably press towards radical social changes and thus endanger those vested interests. The Indian vested interests drew back from this, to them, alarming prospect, and this led them to oppose any far-reaching political change. They wanted the British to remain in India as a deciding factor, to preserve the existing social structure and the existing vested interests. This was the real thought that underlay the insistence on Dominion Status. A well-known Indian Liberal leader once got rather irritated with me for insisting that, as an essential part of a settlement with Great Britain, the British Army should withdraw immediately from India and the Indian Army must be put under Indian democratic control. He went to the length of saying that even if the British Government agreed to do this, he would oppose it with all his might. He opposed this obvious and essential preliminary to any kind of national freedom, therefore, not because it was difficult of achievement under existing circumstances, but because he considered it undesirable. Partly, it may be thought, this was due to fear of external invasion, and he wanted the British Army to protect us from this. Quite apart from the possibility or otherwise of such an invasion, it seems a humiliating thought for any Indian of spirit to ask for an outsider's protection. But I do not think this is the real reason behind the desire to keep the strong arm of the British in India; the British are required to preserve Indian vested interests against Indians themselves, against undiluted democracy, against an upsurge of the masses.

So the Indian Round Table Delegates, not only the declared reactionaries and communalists, but even those who called themselves progressives and nationalists, found much in common between themselves and the British Government. Nationalism indeed seemed to us a term of wide and varied reach, if it included in its embrace both those who went to gaol in India in furtherance of the struggle for freedom and those who shook hands and lined up with our gaolers and discussed a common policy with them. There were others also in our country, brave nationalists, fluent of speech, who encouraged the *Swadeshi* movement in every way, telling us that therein lay the heart of *Swaraj,* and calling upon their countrymen to further it even at a sacrifice. Fortunately the movement brought no sacrifice to them; it increased their businesses and their dividends. And while many went to prison or faced the *lathi*, they sat in their counting houses counting out their money. Later, when aggressive nationalism became a little more risky, they toned down their speeches, and condemned the 'extremists', and made pacts and agreements with the other party.

We did not really mind or care what the Round Table Conference did. It was far away, unreal and shadowy, and the struggle lay here in our towns and villages. We had no illusions about the speedy termination of our struggle or about the dangers ahead, and yet the events of 1930 had given us a certain confidence in our national strength and stamina, and with that confidence we faced the future.

One incident in December or early January had pained us greatly. Mr Srinivas Sastri, in a speech at Edinburgh (where, I think, the freedom of the city was presented to him), referred with some contempt to those who were going to prison in India in the civil disobedience movement. That speech, and especially the occasion for it, hurt us to the quick. For though we differed from Mr Sastri greatly in politics, we respected him.

Mr Ramsay MacDonald had wound up the Round Table Conference with one of his usual brotherly speeches, and this seemed to contain an implied appeal to the Congress to give up its evil ways and join the happy throng. Just about that time—the middle of January 1931—the Congress Working Committee met at Allahabad, and, among other matters, this speech and appeal were also considered. I was in Naini Prison then, and I heard of the proceedings on my release. Father had just returned from Calcutta, and, though he was very ill, he insisted on the members gathering round his bed and discussing this subject there. Some one made a suggestion in favour of a gesture to Mr MacDonald and toning down civil disobedience. This excited father greatly, and he sat up in bed and declared that he would not compromise till the national objective had been gained, and that he would carry on the struggle, even if he was the sole person left to do so. This excitement was very bad for him, and as his temperature shot up, the doctors succeeded at last in removing the visitors and leaving him alone.

Largely at his instance, the Working Committee passed an uncompromising resolution. Before this was published, a cable came from Sir Tej Bahadur Sapru and Mr Srinivas Sastri addressed to father, requesting the Congress, through him, not to come to any decision till they had had an opportunity of a discussion. They were already on their way home. A reply was sent to the effect that a resolution had already been passed by the Working Committee, but this would be withheld from the Press till Messrs. Sapru and Sastri had arrived and had a discussion.

Inside the prison we did not know of these developments outside. But we knew that something was afoot and we were rather worried. What filled our minds much more was the approach of January 26th, the first anniversary of Independence Day, and we wondered how this would be celebrated. It was observed, as we learnt subsequently, all over the country by the holding of mass meetings which confirmed the resolution of independence, and passed an identical resolution called the "Resolution of Remembrance".[1] The organization of this celebration was a remarkable feat, for newspapers and printing presses were not available, nor could the post or telegraph be utilized. And yet an identical resolution, in the particular language of the province concerned, was passed at large gatherings held at more or less the same times at innumerable places, urban and rural, throughout the country. Most of these gatherings were held in defiance of the law and were forcibly dispersed by the police.

January 26th found us in Naini Prison musing of the year that was past and of the year that was to come. In the forenoon I was told suddenly that my father's condition was serious and that I must go home immediately. On enquiry, I was informed that I was being discharged. Ranjit also accompanied me.

That evening, many other persons were discharged from various prisons throughout India. These were the original and substitute members of the Congress Working Committee. The Government was giving us a chance to meet and consider the situation. So, in any event, I would have been discharged that evening. Father's condition hastened my release by a few hours. Kamala also was discharged that day from her Lucknow prison after a brief gaol life of 26 days. She too was a substitute member of the Working Committee.

---

1. This resolution is given in Appendix C (p. 642).

33

DEATH OF MY FATHER

I saw father after two weeks, for he had visited me at Naini on January 12th when his appearance had given me a shock. He had now changed for the worse, and his face was even more swollen. He had some little difficulty in speaking, and his mind was not always quite clear. But his old will remained, and this held on and kept the body and mind functioning.

He was pleased to see Ranjit and me. A day or two later Ranjit (who did not come in the category of Working Committee members) was taken back to Naini Prison. This upset father, and he was continually asking for him and complaining that when so many people were coming to see him from distant parts of India, his own son-in-law was kept away. The doctors were worried by this insistence, and it was obvious that it was doing father no good. After three or four days, I think at the doctors' suggestion, the U.P. Government released Ranjit.

On January 26th, the same day that I was discharged, Gandhiji was also discharged from Yeravda Prison. I was anxious to have him in Allahabad, and when I mentioned his release to father, I found that he was eager to see him. The very next day Gandhiji started from Bombay after a stupendous mass meeting of welcome there, such as even Bombay had not seen before. He arrived at Allahabad late at night, but father was lying awake, waiting for him, and his presence and the few words he uttered had a markedly soothing effect on father. To my mother also his coming brought solace and relief.

The various Working Committee members, original and substitute, who had been released, were meanwhile at a loose end and were waiting for directions about a meeting. Many of them, anxious about father, wanted to come to Allahabad immediately. It was decided therefore to summon them all forthwith to a meeting at Allahabad. Two days later thirty or forty of them arrived, and their meetings took place in Swaraj Bhawan next to our house. I went to these meetings from time to time, but I was much too distraught to take any effective part in them, and I have at present no recollection whatever of what their decisions were. I suppose they were in favour of a continuance of the civil disobedience movement.

All these old friends and colleagues who had come, many of them freshly out of prison and expecting to go back again soon, wanted to visit father and to have what was likely to be a last glimpse and a last farewell of him. They came to him in twos and threes in the mornings and evenings, and father insisted on sitting up in an easy-chair to receive his old comrades. There he sat, massively and rather expressionlessly, for the swelling on his face prevented much play of expression. But as one old friend came after another and comrade succeeded comrade, there was a glitter in his eye and recognition of them, and his head bowed a little and his hands joined in salutation. And though he could not speak much, sometimes he would say a few words, and even then his old humour did not leave him. There he sat like an old lion mortally wounded and with his physical strength almost gone, but still very leonine and kingly. As I watched him, I wondered what thoughts passed through his head, or was he past taking interest in our activities? He was evidently often struggling with himself, trying to keep a grip of things which threatened to slip away from his grasp. To the end this struggle continued, and he did not give in, occasionally speaking to us with extreme clarity. Even when a constriction in his throat made it difficult for him to make himself understood, he took to writing on slips of paper what he wanted to say.

He took practically no interest in the Working Committee meetings which were taking place next door. A fortnight earlier they would have excited him, but now he felt that he was already far away from such happenings. "I am going soon, Mahatmaji," he said to Gandhiji, "and I shall not be here to see Swaraj. But I know that you have won it and will soon have it."

Most of the people who had come from other cities and provinces departed. Gandhiji remained, and a few intimate friends and near relatives, and the three eminent doctors, old friends of his, to whom, he used to say, he had handed over his body for safe keeping—M.A. Ansari, Bidhan Chandra Roy, and Jivraj Mehta. On the morning of February 4th he seemed to be a little better, and it was decided to take advantage of this and remove him to Lucknow, where there were facilities for deep X-ray treatment which Allahabad did not possess. That very day we took him by car, Gandhiji and a large party following us. We went slowly, but he was nevertheless exhausted. The next day he seemed to be getting over the fatigue, and yet there were some disquieting symptoms. Early next morning, February 6th, I was watching by his bedside. He had had a troublesome and restless night; suddenly I noticed that his face grew calm and the sense of struggle vanished from it. I thought that he had fallen asleep, and I was glad of it. But my mother's perceptions were keener, and she uttered a cry. I turned to her and begged her not to disturb him as he had fallen asleep. But that sleep was his last long sleep, and from it there was no awakening.

We brought his body that very day by car to Allahabad. I sat in that car and Ranjit drove it, and there was Hari, father's favourite personal servant. Behind us came another car containing my mother and Gandhiji, and then other cars. I was dazed all that day, hardly realizing what had happened, and a succession of events and large crowds kept me from thinking. Great crowds in Lucknow, gathered together at brief notice— the swift dash from Lucknow to Allahabad sitting by the body, wrapped in our national flag, and with a big flag flying above—the arrival at Allahabad, and the huge crowds that had gathered for miles to pay homage to his memory. There were some ceremonies at home, and then the last journey to the Ganga with a mighty concourse of people. As evening fell on the river bank on that winter day, the great flames leapt up and consumed that body which had meant so much to us who were close to him as well as to millions in India. Gandhiji said a few moving words to the multitude, and then all of us crept silently home. The stars were out and shining brightly when we returned, lonely and desolate.

Many thousands of messages of sympathy came to my mother and to me. Lord and Lady Irwin also sent my mother a courteous message. This tremendous volume of goodwill and sympathy took away somewhat the sting from our sorrow, but it was, above all, the wonderfully soothing and healing presence of Gandhiji that helped my mother and all of us to face that crisis in our lives.

I found it difficult to realize that he had gone. Three months later I was in Ceylon with my wife and daughter, and we were spending a few quiet and restful days at Nuwara Eliya. I liked the place, and it struck me suddenly that it would suit father. Why not send for him? He must be tired out, and rest would do him good. I was on the point of sending a telegram to him to Allahabad.

On our return to Allahabad from Ceylon the post brought one day a remarkable letter. The envelope was addressed to me in father's handwriting, and it bore innumerable marks and stamps of different post offices. I opened it in amazement to find that it was, indeed, a letter from father to me, only it was dated the 28th February, 1926. It was delivered to me in the summer of 1931, thus taking five and a half years in its journey. The letter had been written by father at Ahmedabad on the eve of my departure for Europe with Kamala in 1926. It was addressed to me to Bombay care of the Italian Lloyd steamer on which we were travelling. Apparently it just missed us there, and then it visited various places, and perhaps lay in many pigeon-holes till some enterprising person sent it on to me. Curiously enough, it was a letter of farewell.

34

THE DELHI PACT

On the day and almost at the very hour of my father's death, a large group of the Indian members of the Round Table Conference landed in Bombay. Mr Srinivasa Sastri and Sir Tej Bahadur Sapru, and perhaps some others whom I do not remember, came direct to Allahabad. Gandhiji and some members of the Congress Working Committee were already there. There were some private meetings at our house at which an account was given of what the R.T.C. had done. At the very commencement, however, there was a little incident. Mr Sastri, entirely of his own accord, expressed regret for what he had said at Edinburgh. He added that he was much influenced always by his surroundings and his 'exuberant verbosity' was apt to run away with him.

The Round Table Delegates did not tell us anything of importance about the R.T.C. that we did not know already. They did tell us of various intrigues behind the scenes, of what Lord So-and-So said or Sir Somebody did in private. Our Liberal friends in India have always seemed to me to attach more importance to private talks and gossip with and about high officials than to principles or to the realities of the Indian situation. Our informal discussions with the Liberal leaders did not lead to anything, and our previous opinions were only confirmed that the R.T.C. decisions had not the least value. Some one then suggested—I forget who he was—that Gandhiji should write to the Viceroy and ask for an interview and have a frank talk with him. He agreed to do so, although I do not think that he expected much in the way of result. But, on principle, he was always willing to go out of his way to meet and discuss anything with his opponents. Being absolutely convinced of the rightness of his own position he hoped to convince the other party; but it was perhaps something more than intellectual conviction that he aimed at. He was always after a psychological change, a breaking of the barriers of anger and distrust, an approach to the other's goodwill and fine feelings. He knew that if this change took place, conviction became far easier, or even if there was no conviction, opposition was toned down and the sting was taken out of the conflict. In his personal dealings with individuals hostile to him, he had gained many a victory; it was remarkable how, by sheer force of personality, he would win over an opponent. Many a critic and a scoffer had been overwhelmed by this personality and became an admirer, and even though the criticism continued, it could never again have a trace of mockery.

Conscious of this power, Gandhiji always welcomed a meeting with those who disagreed with him. But it was one thing to deal with individuals on personal or minor issues; it was quite another matter to come up against an impersonal thing like the British Government representing triumphant imperialism. Realizing this, Gandhiji went to the interview with Lord Irwin with no high expectation. The Civil Disobedience movement was still going on, though it had toned down because there was much talk of *pourparlers* with Government.

The interview was arranged without delay, and Gandhiji went off to Delhi, telling us that if there were any serious conversations with the Viceroy regarding a provisional settlement, he would send for the members of the Working Committee. A few days later we were all summoned to Delhi. For three weeks we remained there, meeting daily and having long and exhausting discussions. Gandhiji had frequent interviews with Lord Irwin, but sometimes there was a gap of three or four days, probably because the Government of India was communicating with the India Office in London. Sometimes apparently small matters or even certain words would hold up progress. One such word was 'suspension' of civil disobedience. Gandhiji had all along made it clear that civil disobedience could not be finally stopped or given up, as it was the only weapon in the hands of the people. It could, however, be suspended. Lord Irwin objected to this word and wanted finality about the word, to which Gandhiji would not agree. Ultimately the word 'discontinued' was used. There were also prolonged discussions about the picketing of foreign cloth and liquor shops. Most of our time was spent on considering provisional arrangements for a pact, and little attention was given to fundamental matters. Probably it was thought that these basic matters could be considered later under more favourable conditions when a provisional settlement had been made and the day-to-day struggle discontinued. We looked upon those talks as leading up to an armistice, which might then be followed by further conversations on the real matters in issue.

Delhi attracted in those days all manner of people. There were many foreign journalists, especially Americans, and they were somewhat annoyed with us for our reticence. They would tell us that they got much more news about the Gandhiji-Irwin conversations from the New Delhi Secretariat than from us, which was a fact. Then there were many people of high degree who hurried to pay their respects to Gandhiji, for was not the Mahatma's star in the ascendant? It was very amusing to see these people, who had kept far away from Gandhiji and the Congress and often condemned them, now hastening to make amends. The Congress seemed to have made good, and no one knew what the future might hold. Anyway, it was safer to keep on good terms with the Congress and its leaders. A year later yet another change was witnessed in them, and they were shouting their deep abhorrence of the Congress and all its works and their utter dissociation from it.

Even the communalists were stirred by events, and sensed with some apprehension that they might not occupy a very prominent place in the coming order. And so, many of them came to the Mahatma and assured him that they were perfectly willing to come to terms on the communal issue and, if only he would take the initiative, there would be no difficulty about a settlement.

A ceaseless stream of people, of high and low degree, came to Dr Ansari's house, where Gandhiji and most of us were staying, and in our leisure moments we watched them with interest and profit. For some years our chief contacts had been with the poor in towns and villages and those who were down and out in gaols. The very prosperous gentlemen who came to visit Gandhiji showed us another side of human nature, and a very adaptable side, for wherever they sensed power and success, they turned to it and welcomed it with the sunshine of their smiles. Many of them were staunch pillars of the British Government in India. It was comforting to know that they would become equally staunch pillars of any other government that might flourish in India.

Often in those days I used to accompany Gandhiji in his early morning walks in New Delhi. That was usually the only time one had a chance of talking to him, for the rest of the day was cut up into little bits, each minute allotted to somebody or something. Even the early morning walk was sometimes given over to an interviewer, usually from abroad, or to a friend, come for a personal consultation. We talked of many matters, of the past, of the present, and especially of the future. I remember how he surprised me with one of his ideas about the future of the Congress. I had imagined that the Congress, as such, would automatically cease to exist with the coming of freedom. He thought that the Congress should continue, but on one condition: that it passed a self-denying ordinance, laying it down that none of its members could accept a paid job under the State, and if any one wanted such a post of authority in the State, he would have to leave the Congress. I do not at present remember how he worked this out, but the whole idea underlying it was that the Congress by its detachment and having no axe to grind, could exercise tremendous moral pressure on the Executive as well as other departments of the Government, and thus keep them on the right track.

Now this is an extraordinary idea which I find it difficult to grasp, and innumerable difficulties present themselves. It seems to me that such an assembly, if it could be conceived, would be exploited by some vested interest. But practicality apart, it does help one to understand a little the background of Gandhiji's thought. It is the very opposite of the modern idea of a party which is built up to seize the State power in order to refashion the political and economic structure according to certain pre-conceived ideas; or that kind of party, found often enough nowadays, whose function seems to be (to quote Mr R.H. Tawney) to offer the largest possible number of carrots to the largest number of donkeys.

Gandhiji's conception of democracy is definitely a metaphysical one. It has nothing to do with numbers or majority or representation in the ordinary sense. It is based on service and sacrifice, and it uses moral pressure. In a recent statement[1] he defines a democrat. He claims to be 'a born democrat'. "I make that claim, if complete identification with the poorest of mankind, longing to live no better than they, and a corresponding conscious effort to approach that level to the best of one's ability, can entitle one to make it." He further discusses democracy:

Let us recognize the fact that the Congress enjoys the prestige of a democratic character and influence not by the number of delegates and

---

1. Dated September 17, 1934.

visitors it has drawn to its annual function, but by an ever-increasing amount of service it has rendered. Western democracy is on its trial, if it has not already proved a failure. May it be reserved to India to evolve the true science of democracy by giving a visible demonstration of its success.

Corruption and hypocrisy ought not to be the inevitable products of democracy, as they undoubtedly are today. Nor is bulk a true test of democracy. True democracy is not inconsistent with a few persons representing the spirit, the hope and the aspirations of those whom they claim to represent. I hold that democracy cannot be evolved by forcible methods. The spirit of democracy cannot be imposed from without; it has to come from within.

This is certainly not Western democracy, as he himself says; but, curiously enough, there is some similarity to the communist conception of democracy, for that, too, has a metaphysical touch. A few communists will claim to represent the real needs and desires of the masses, even though the latter may themselves be unaware of them. The mass will become a metaphysical conception with them, and it is this that they claim to represent. The similarity, however, is slight and does not take us far; the differences in outlook and approach are far greater, notably in regard to methods and force.

Whether Gandhiji is a democrat or not, he does represent the peasant masses of India; he is the quintessence of the conscious and subconscious will of those millions. It is perhaps something more than representation; for he is the idealized personification of those vast millions. Of course, he is not the average peasant. A man of the keenest intellect, of fine feeling and good taste, wide vision; very human, and yet essentially the ascetic who has suppressed his passions and emotions, sublimated them and directed them in spiritual channels; a tremendous personality, drawing people to himself like a magnet, and calling out fierce loyalties and attachments—all this so utterly unlike and beyond a peasant. And yet withal he is the great peasant, with a peasant's outlook on affairs, and with a peasant's blindness to some aspects of life. But India is peasant India, and so he knows his India well and reacts to her lightest tremors, and gauges a situation accurately and almost instinctively, and has a knack of acting at the psychological moment.

What a problem and a puzzle he has been not only to the British

Government but to his own people and his closest associates! Perhaps in every other country he would be out of place today, but India still seems to understand, or at least appreciate, the prophetic-religious type of man, talking of sin and salvation and non-violence. Indian mythology is full of stories of great ascetics, who, by the rigour of their sacrifices and self-imposed penance, built up a 'mountain of merit' which threatened the dominion of some of the lesser gods and upset the established order. These myths have often come to my mind when I have watched the amazing energy and inner power of Gandhiji, coming out of some inexhaustible spiritual reservoir. He was obviously not of the world's ordinary coinage; he was minted of a different and rare variety, and often the unknown stared at us through his eyes.

India, even urban India, even the new industrial India, had the impress of the peasant upon her, and it was natural enough for her to make this son of hers, so like her and yet so unlike, an idol and a beloved leader. He revived ancient and half-forgotten memories, and gave her glimpses of her own soul. Crushed in the dark misery of the present, she had tried to find relief in helpless muttering and in vague dreams of the past and the future, but he came and gave hope to her mind and strength to her much-battered body, and the future became an alluring vision. Two-faced like Janus, she looked both backwards into the past and forward into the future, and tried to combine the two.

Many of us had cut adrift from this peasant outlook, and the old ways of thought and custom and religion had become alien to us. We called ourselves moderns, and thought in terms of 'progress', and industrialization and a higher standard of living and collectivization. We considered the peasant's viewpoint reactionary, and some, and a growing number, looked with favour towards socialism and communism. How came we to associate ourselves with Gandhiji politically, and to become, in many instances, his devoted followers? The question is hard to answer, and to one who does not know Gandhiji, no answer is likely to satisfy. Personality is an indefinable thing, a strange force that has power over the souls of men, and he possesses this in ample measure, and to all who come to him he often appears in a different aspect. He attracted people, but it was ultimately intellectual conviction that brought them to him and kept them there. They did not agree with his philosophy of life, or even with many of his ideals. Often they did not understand him. But the action that he proposed was something tangible which could be understood and appreciated intellectually. Any action would have been welcome after the long tradition of inaction which our spineless politics had nurtured; brave and effective action with an ethical halo about it had an irresistible appeal, both to the intellect and the emotions. Step by step he convinced us of the rightness of the action, and we went with him, although we did not accept his philosophy. To divorce action from the thought underlying it was not perhaps a proper procedure and was bound to lead to mental conflict and trouble later. Vaguely we hoped that Gandhiji, being essentially a man of action and very sensitive to changing conditions, would advance along the line that seemed to us to be right. And in any event the road he was following was the right one thus far, and if the future meant a parting it would be folly to anticipate it.

All this shows that we were by no means clear or certain in our minds. Always we had the feeling that while we might be more logical, Gandhiji knew India far better than we did, and a man who could command such tremendous devotion and loyalty must have something in him that corresponded to the needs and aspirations of the masses. If we could convince him, we felt that we could also convert these masses. And it seemed possible to convince him for, in spite of his peasant outlook, he was the born rebel, a revolutionary out for big changes, whom no fear of consequences could stop.

How he disciplined our lazy and demoralized people and made them work—not by force or any material inducement, but by a gentle look and a soft word and, above all, by personal example! In the early days of Satyagraha in India, as long ago as 1919, I remember how Umar Sobani of Bombay called him the 'beloved slave-driver'. Much had happened in the dozen years since then. Umar had not lived to see these changes, but we who had been more fortunate looked back from those early months of 1931 with joy and elation. Nineteen-thirty had, indeed, been a wonder year for us, and Gandhiji seemed to have changed the face of our country with his magic touch. No one was foolish enough to think that we had triumphed finally over the British Government. Our feeling of elation had little to do with the Government. We were proud of our people, of our womenfolk, of our youth, of our children for the part they had played in the movement. It was a spiritual gain, valuable at any time and to any people, but doubly so to us, a subject and down-trodden people.

And we were anxious that nothing should happen to take this away from us.

To me, personally, Gandhiji had always shown extraordinary kindness and consideration, and my father's death had brought him particularly near to me. He had always listened patiently to whatever I had to say, and had made every effort to meet my wishes. This had, indeed, led me to think that perhaps some colleagues and I could influence him continuously in a socialist direction, and he had himself said that he was prepared to go step by step as he saw his way to do so. It seemed to me almost inevitable then that he would accept the fundamental socialist position, as I saw no other way out from the violence and injustice and waste and misery of the existing order. He might disagree about the methods but not about the ideal. So I thought then, but I realize now that there are basic differences between Gandhiji's ideals and the socialist objective.

To go back to Delhi in February 1931. The Gandhi-Irwin talks went on from time to time, and then they came to a sudden stop. For several days Gandhiji was not sent for by the Viceroy, and it seemed to us that the break had come. The members of the Working Committee prepared to leave Delhi for their respective provinces. Before leaving we conferred together about our future plans and civil disobedience (which was in theory still going on). We felt certain that as soon as the break was definitely announced we would have no further opportunity of meeting and conferring together. We expected arrest, and we had been told, and it seemed likely, that the Government would launch a fierce offensive against the Congress; something much fiercer than we had so far had. So we met together at what we thought was our final meeting, and we passed various resolutions to guide the movement in the future. One resolution had a certain significance. So far, the practice had been for each Acting-President to nominate his successor in case of arrest, and also to fill by nomination the vacancies in the Working Committee. The substitute Working Committees hardly functioned and had little authority to take the initiative in any matter. They could only go to prison. There was always a risk, however, that this continuous process of substitution might place the Congress in a false position. There were obvious dangers to it. The Working Committee in Delhi, therefore, decided that in future there should be no nominations of acting-Presidents or substitute members. So long as any members (or member) of the original Committee were out of gaol they would function as the full Committee. When all of them were in prison, then there would be no Committee functioning, but, we said rather grandiloquently, the powers of the Working Committee would then vest in each man and woman in the country, and we called upon them to carry on the struggle uncompromisingly.

This resolution was a brave lead for a continuance of the fight, and it left no loophole for compromise. It was also a recognition of the fact that it was becoming increasingly difficult for our headquarters to keep in touch with all parts of the country and to issue instructions regularly. This was inevitable, as most of our workers were well-known men and women, and they worked openly. They could always be arrested. During 1930 a secret courier service had been built up to carry instructions, bring reports, and do inspection work. This worked well, and it demonstrated to us that we could organize secret information work of this kind with great success. But to some extent it did not fit in with our open movement, and Gandhiji was averse to it. In the absence of instructions from headquarters we had to place the responsibility for carrying on the work on local people, as otherwise they would simply wait helplessly for directions from above and do nothing. When possible, of course, instructions were sent.

So we passed this resolution and other resolutions (none of them were published or became effective because of subsequent events) and packed up to go. Just then another summons came from Lord Irwin, and the conversations were resumed.

On the night of the 4th of March we waited till midnight for Gandhiji's return from the Viceroy's house. He came back about 2 a.m., and we were woken up and told that an agreement had been reached. We saw the draft. I knew most of the clauses, for they had been often discussed, but, at the very top, Clause 2[2] with its reference to safeguards, etc., gave me a tremendous shock. I was wholly unprepared for it. I said

2. Clause 2 of the Delhi Settlement (dated March 5, 1931): "As regards constitutional questions, the scope of future discussion is stated, with the assent of His Majesty's Government, to be with the object of considering further the scheme for the constitutional Government of India discussed at the Round Table Conference. Of the scheme there outlined, Federation is an essential part; so also are Indian responsibility

nothing then, and we all retired.

There was nothing more to be said. The thing had been done, our leader had committed himself; and even if we disagreed with him, what could we do? Throw him over? Break from him? Announce our disagreement? That might bring some personal satisfaction to an individual, but it made no difference to the final decision. The Civil Disobedience movement was ended for the time being at least, and not even the Working Committee could push it on now, when the Government could declare that Mr Gandhi had already agreed to a settlement. I was perfectly willing, as were our other colleagues, to suspend civil disobedience and to come to a temporary settlement with the Government. It was not an easy matter for any of us to send our comrades back to gaol, or to be instrumental in keeping many thousands in prison who were already there. Prison is not a pleasant place to spend our days and nights, though many of us may train ourselves for it and talk light-heartedly of its crushing routine. Besides, three weeks or more of conversations between Gandhiji and Lord Irwin had led the country to expect that a settlement was coming, and a final break would have been a disappointment. So all of us in the Working Committee were decidedly in favour of a provisional settlement (for obviously it could be nothing more), provided that thereby we did not surrender any vital position.

So far as I was concerned I was not very much concerned with many of the points that had given rise to great argument. Two matters interested me above all others. One was that our objective of independence should in no way be toned down, and the second was the effect of the settlement on our U.P. agrarian situation. Our no-tax or no-rent campaign had so far been a great success, and in certain areas hardly any collections had been made. The peasantry were in fine mettle, and world agricultural conditions and prices were worse than ever, making it difficult for them to pay. Our no-tax campaign had been both political and economic. If there was a provisional settlement with the Government, civil disobedience would be withdrawn and the political basis for the no-tax campaign would go. But what of the economic side, of the terrible

---

and reservations or safeguards in the interests of India, for such matters as, for instance, defence; external affairs; the position of minorities; the financial credit of India, and the discharge of obligations."

fall in prices, and of the inability of most of the peasants to pay anything like the demand? Gandhiji had made this point quite clear to Lord Irwin. He had stated that while the no-tax campaign would be withdrawn, we could not advise the peasantry to pay beyond their capacity. This matter could not be discussed in detail with the Government of India as it was a provincial matter. We were assured that the Provincial Government would gladly confer with us on the subject and would do everything in its power to relieve the distress of the peasantry. It was a vague assurance, but, under the circumstances, it was difficult to have anything more definite. This matter was thus, for the time being, disposed of.

The other and vital question of our objective, of independence, remained. And now I saw in that Clause 2 of the settlement that even this seemed to be jeopardized. Was it for this that our people had behaved so gallantly for a year? Were all our brave words and deeds to end in this? The independence resolution of the Congress, the pledge of January 26, so often repeated? So I lay and pondered on that March night and in my heart there was a great emptiness as of something precious gone, almost beyond recall.

> This is the way the world ends,
> Not with a bang, but a whimper.

35

KARACHI CONGRESS

Gandhiji learnt indirectly of my distress, and the next morning he asked me to accompany him in his usual walk. We had a long talk, and he tried to convince me that nothing vital had been lost, no surrender of principle made. He interpreted Clause 2 of the agreement in a particular way so as to make it fit in with our demand for independence, relying chiefly on the words in it: "in the interests of India." The interpretation seemed to me to be a forced one, and I was not convinced, but I was somewhat soothed by his talk. The merits of the agreement apart, I told him that his way of springing surprises upon us frightened me; there was something unknown about him which, in spite of the closest association for fourteen years, I could not understand at all and which filled me with apprehension. He admitted the presence of this unknown element in him, and said that he himself could not answer for it or foretell what it might lead to.

For a day or two I wobbled, not knowing what to do. There was no question of opposing or preventing that agreement then. That stage was past, and all I could do was to dissociate myself theoretically from it, though accepting it as a matter of fact. That would have soothed my personal vanity, but how did it help the larger issue? Would it not be better to accept gracefully what had been done, and put the most favourable interpretation upon it, as Gandhiji had done? In an interview to the Press immediately after the agreement he had stressed that interpretation and that we stood completely by independence. He went to Lord Irwin and made this point quite clear, so that there might be no misapprehension then or in the future. In the event of the Congress sending any representative to the Round Table Conference, he told him, it could only be on this basis and to advance this claim. Lord Irwin could not, of course, admit the claim, but he recognized the right of the Congress to advance it.

So I decided, not without great mental conflict and physical distress, to accept the agreement and work for it wholeheartedly. There appeared to me to be no middle way.

In the course of Gandhiji's interviews with Lord Irwin prior to the agreement, as well as after, he had pleaded for the release of political prisoners other than the civil disobedience prisoners. The latter were going to be discharged as part of the agreement itself. But there were thousands of others, both those convicted after trial and detenus kept without any charge, trial or conviction. Many of these detenus had been kept so for years, and there had always been a great deal of resentment all over India, and especially in Bengal which was most affected, at this method of imprisonment without trial. Like the Chief of the General Staff in *Penguin Island* (or was it in the Dreyfus case?) the Government of India believed that no proofs are the best proofs. No proofs cannot be disproved. The detenus were alleged by the Government to be actual or potential revolutionaries of the violent type. Gandhiji had pleaded for their release, not necessarily as part of the agreement, but as eminently desirable in order to relieve political tension and establish a more normal atmosphere in Bengal. But the Government was not agreeable to this.

Nor did the Government agree to Gandhiji's hard pleading for the commutation of Bhagat Singh's death sentence. This also had nothing to do with the agreement, and Gandhiji pressed for it separately because of the very strong feeling all over India on this subject. He pleaded in vain.

I remember a curious incident about that time, which gave me an insight into the mind of the terrorist group in India. This took place soon after my discharge from prison, either a little before father's death or a few days after. A stranger came to see me at our house, and I was told that he was Chandrashekhar Azad. I had never seen him before, but I had heard of him ten years earlier, when he had non-co-operated from school and gone to prison during the N.C.O. movement in 1921. A boy of fifteen or so then, he had been flogged in prison for some breach of gaol discipline. Later he had drifted towards the terrorists, and he became one of their prominent men in north India. All this I had heard vaguely, and I had taken no interest in these rumours. I was surprised, therefore, to see him. He had been induced to visit me because of the general expectation (owing to our release) that some negotiations between the Government and the Congress were likely. He wanted to know if, in case of a settlement, his group of people would have any peace. Would they still be considered, and treated, as outlaws; hunted out from place to place, with a price on their heads, and the prospect of the gallows ever before them? Or was there a possibility of their being allowed to pursue peaceful vocations? He told me that as far as he was concerned, as well as many of his associates, they were convinced now that purely terrorist methods were futile and did no good. He was not, however, prepared to believe that India would gain her freedom wholly by peaceful methods. He thought that some time in the future a violent conflict might take place, but this would not be terrorism. He ruled out terrorism as such, so far as the question of Indian freedom was concerned. But then, he added, what was he to do when no chance was given him to settle down, as he was being hounded all the time? Many of the terroristic acts that had occurred recently, according to him, were purely in self-defence.

I was glad to learn from Azad, and I had confirmation of this subsequently, that the belief in terrorism was dying down. As a group notion, indeed, it had practically gone, and individual and sporadic cases were probably due to some special reason, act of reprisal, or individual aberration, and not to a general idea. This did not mean, of course, that the old terrorists or their new associates had become converts to nonviolence, or admirers of British rule. But they did not think in terms of terrorism as they used to. Many of them, it seems to me, have definitely the fascist mentality.

I tried to explain to Chandrashekhar Azad what my philosophy of political action was, and tried to convert him to my view-point. But I had no answer to his basic question: what was he to do now? Nothing was likely to happen that would bring him, or his like, any relief or peace. All I could suggest was that he should use his influence to prevent the occurrence of terrorist acts in the future, for these could only injure the larger cause as well as his own group.

Two or three weeks later, while the Gandhi–Irwin talks were going on, I heard at Delhi that Chandrashekhar Azad had been shot down and killed by the police in Allahabad. He was recognized in the day-time in a park, and was surrounded by a large force of police. He tried to defend himself from behind a tree; there was quite a shooting-match, and he injured one or two policemen before he was shot down.

I left Delhi soon after the provisional settlement was arrived at, and went to Lucknow. We had taken immediate steps to stop civil disobedience all over the country, and the whole Congress organization had responded to our new instructions with remarkable discipline. We had many people in our ranks who were dissatisfied, many fire-brands, and we had no means of compelling them to desist from the old activities. But without a single exception known to me, the huge organization accepted in practice the new role, though many criticized it. I was particularly interested in the reactions in our province, as the no-tax campaign was going strong in some areas there. Our first job was to see that the civil disobedience prisoners were discharged. Thousands of these were discharged from day to day, and after some time only a number of disputed cases were left in prison; apart, of course, from the thousands of detenus and those convicted for violent activities, who were not released.

These discharged prisoners, when they went home to their town or villages, were naturally welcomed back by their people. There were often decorations and buntings, and processions, and meetings, and speeches and addresses of welcome. It was all very natural and to be expected, but the change was sudden from the time when the police *lathi* was always in evidence, and meetings and processions were forcibly dispersed. The police felt rather uncomfortable, and probably there was a feeling of triumph among many of our people who came out of gaol. There was little enough reason to be triumphant, but a coming out of gaol always brings a feeling of elation (unless the spirit has been crushed in gaol), and mass gaol deliveries add very much to this exhilaration.

I mention this fact here, because in later months great exception was taken by the Government to this 'air of triumph', and it was made a charge against us! Brought up and living always in an authoritarian atmosphere, with a military notion of government and with no roots or supports in the people, nothing is more painful to them than a weakening of what they consider their prestige. None of us, so far as I know, had given the least thought to the matter, and it was with great surprise that we learnt later that Government officials, from the heights of Simla to the plains below, were simmering with anger and wounded pride at this impudence of the people. The newspapers that echo their views have not got over it yet; and even now, three and a half years later, they refer with almost a visible shudder to those bold, bad days when, according to them, Congressmen went about in triumph as if they had won a great victory. These outbursts on the part of the Government and its friends in the Press, came as a revelation to us. They showed what a state of nerves they had been in, what suppressions they had put up with, resulting in all manner of complexes. It was extraordinary that a few processions and a few speeches of our rank-and-file men should so upset them.

As a matter of fact there was in Congress ranks then, and even less in the leadership, no idea of having 'defeated' the British Government. But there was a feeling of triumph amongst us at our own people's sacrifices and courage. We were a little proud of what the country had done in 1930; it raised us in our self-esteem, gave us confidence, and even our littlest volunteer straightened himself and held up his head at the thought of this. We also felt that this great effort, which had attracted world attention, had brought enormous pressure on the British Government, and had taken us nearer our goal. All this had nothing to do with defeating the Government, and indeed many of us were fully conscious of the fact that the Government had done rather well in the Delhi Pact. Those of us who pointed out that we were far from our goal, and big and difficult struggles lay ahead, were accused by friends of the Government of war-mongering and going behind the spirit of the Delhi Pact.

In the United Provinces we had now to face the agrarian problem. Our policy now was one of co-operation, as far as possible, with the British Government and immediately we put ourselves in touch with the U.P. Provincial Government. After a long interval—for a dozen years we had had no official dealings with them—I visited some of the high officials of the province to discuss the agrarian question. We also carried on a lengthy correspondence on the subject. Our Provincial Congress Committee appointed one of our leading men, Govind Ballabh Pant, as a special liaison officer to keep in continuous touch with the Provincial Government. The facts of the agrarian crisis, of the tremendous fall in agricultural prices, and of the inability of the average peasant to pay the rent demanded, were admitted. The question was, what remissions should be given, and in this matter the initiative lay with the Provincial Government. Ordinarily the Government dealt with the landlords alone, and not with their tenants direct, and it was for the landlords to reduce or remit rents. But the landlords refused to do any such thing, so long as the Government did not remit part of their revenue demand; and in any event they were not, as a rule, keen on giving remissions to their tenantry.

So the decision rested with the Government.

The Provincial Congress Committee had told the peasantry that the no-tax campaign was off, and they should pay as much of their rent as they could. But, as their representatives, they had demanded heavy remissions. For a long time Government took no action. Probably it was handicapped by the absence on leave or special duty of the Governor, Sir Malcolm Hailey. Prompt and far-reaching action was necessary, but the acting Governor and his colleagues hesitated to commit themselves, and preferred to delay matters till the return of Sir Malcolm Hailey in the summer. This indecision and delay made a difficult situation worse, and resulted in much suffering for the tenantry.

I had a little breakdown in health soon after the Delhi Pact. Even in gaol I had been unwell, and then the shock of father's death, followed immediately by the long strain of the Delhi negotiations, proved too much for my physical health. I recovered somewhat for the Karachi Congress.

Karachi is far to the north-west of India, difficult of access, and partly cut off from the rest of the country by desert regions. But it attracted a great gathering from distant parts, and truly represented the temper of the country at the moment. There was a feeling of quiet, but deep satisfaction at the growing strength of the national movement in India; pride in the Congress organization which had so far worthily responded to the heavy calls made on it, and fully justified itself by its disciplined sacrifice; a confidence in our people, and a restrained enthusiasm. At the same time there was a heavy sense of responsibility at the tremendous problems and perils ahead; our words and resolutions were now the preludes to action on a national scale, and could not be lightly uttered or passed. The Delhi Pact, though accepted by the great majority, was not popular or liked, and there was a fear that it might lead us to all manner of compromising situations. Somehow it seemed to take away from the clarity of the issues before the country. On the very eve of the Congress, a new element of resentment had crept in—the execution of Bhagat Singh. This feeling was especially marked in North India, and Karachi, being itself in the north, had attracted large numbers of people from the Punjab.

The Karachi Congress was an even greater personal triumph for Gandhiji than any previous Congress had been. The president, Sardar

Vallabhbhai Patel, was one of the most popular and forceful men in India with the prestige of victorious leadership in Gujrat, but it was the Mahatma who dominated the scene. The Congress also had a strong contingent of 'Redshirts' from the Frontier Province under the leadership of Abdul Ghaffar Khan. These Redshirts were popular and drew a cheer wherever they went, for India had been impressed by their extraordinary and peaceful courage in the face of great provocation from April 1930 onwards. The name 'Redshirts' led some people to think, quite wrongly, that they were Communists or left-wing labourites. As a matter of fact their name was "Khudai Khidmatgar", and this organization had allied itself to the Congress (later in 1931 they were to become integral parts of the Congress organization). They were called Redshirts simply because of their rather primitive uniforms, which were red. They had no economic policy in their programme, which was nationalistic and also dealt with social reform.

The principal resolution at Karachi dealt with the Delhi Pact and the Round Table Conference. I accepted it, of course, as it emerged from the Working Committee, but when I was asked by Gandhiji to move it in the open Congress, I hesitated. It went against the grain, and I refused at first, and then this seemed a weak and unsatisfactory position to take up. Either I was for it or against it, and it was not proper to prevaricate or leave people guessing in the matter. Almost at the last moment, a few minutes before the resolution was taken up in the open Congress, I decided to sponsor it. In my speech I tried to lay before the great gathering quite frankly what my feelings were and why I had wholeheartedly accepted that resolution and pleaded with them to accept it. That speech, made on the spur of the moment and coming from the heart, and with little of ornament or fine phrasing in it, was probably a greater success than many of my other efforts, which had followed a more careful preparation.

I spoke on other resolutions, too, notably on the Bhagat Singh resolution and the one on Fundamental Rights and Economic Policy. The latter resolution interested me especially, partly because of what it contained, and even more so because it represented a new outlook in the Congress. So far the Congress had thought along purely nationalist lines, and had avoided facing economic issues, except in so far as it encouraged cottage industries and *swadeshi* generally. In the Karachi resolution it took a step, a very short step, in a socialist direction by advocating nationalization of key industries and services, and various other measures to lessen the burden on the poor and increase it on the rich. This was not socialism at all, and a capitalist state could easily accept almost everything contained in that resolution.

This very mild and prosaic resolution evidently made the big people of the Government of India furiously to think. Perhaps they even pictured, with their usual perspicacity, the red gold of the Bolsheviks stealing its way into Karachi and corrupting the Congress leaders. Living in a kind of political harem, cut off from the outer world, and surrounded by an atmosphere of secrecy, their receptive minds love to hear tales of mystery and imagination. And then these stories are given out in little bits in a mysterious manner, through favoured newspapers, with a hint that much more could be seen if only the veil were lifted. In this approved and well-practised manner, frequent references have been made to the Karachi resolution on Fundamental Rights, etc., and I can only conclude that they represent the Government view of this resolution. The story goes that a certain mysterious individual with communist affiliations drew up this resolution, or the greater part of it, and thrust it down upon me at Karachi; that thereupon I issued an ultimatum to Mr Gandhi to accept this or to face my opposition on the Delhi Pact issue, and Mr Gandhi accepted it as a sop to me, and forced it down on a tired Subjects Committee and Congress on the concluding day.

The name of the 'mysterious individual' has, so far as I know, not been directly mentioned, but numerous hints make it quite clear who is meant. Not being myself used to ways of mystery and roundabout methods of expression, I might as well state that this person seems to be M.N. Roy. It would be interesting to know, and instructive to the big ones of Simla and Delhi to find out, what M.N. Roy or any other person 'communistically inclined' thinks of that very innocent Karachi resolution. It may surprise them to discover that any such person is rather contemptuous of the resolution because, according to him, it is a typical product of a *bourgeois* reformist mentality.

So far as Mr Gandhi is concerned, I have had the privilege of knowing him pretty intimately for the last seventeen years, and the idea of my presenting ultimatums to him or bargaining with him seems to me monstrous. We may accommodate ourselves to each other; or we may, on a particular issue, part company, but the methods of the market-place can never affect our mutual dealings.

The idea of getting the Congress to pass a resolution of this kind was an old one. For some years the U.P. Provincial Congress Committee had been agitating in the matter, and trying to get the A.I.C.C. to accept a socialist resolution. In 1929 it succeeded to some extent in getting the A.I.C.C. to accept the principle. Then followed civil disobedience. During my early morning talks in Delhi with Gandhiji in February and March 1931, I had referred to this matter, and he had welcomed the idea of having a resolution on economic matters. He asked me to bring the matter up at Karachi, and to draft a resolution and show it to him there. I did so at Karachi, and he made various changes and suggestions. He wanted both of us to agree on the wording, before we asked the Working Committee to consider it. I had to make several drafts, and this delayed matters for a few days, and we were otherwise very much occupied with other matters. Ultimately Gandhiji and I agreed on a draft, and this was placed before the Working Committee, and later before the Subjects Committee. It is perfectly true that it was a new subject for the Subjects Committee and some members were surprised. However, it was easily passed by the Committee and the Congress, and was referred to the A.I.C.C. for further elucidation and enlargement on the lines laid down.

While I was drafting this resolution various people, who used to come to my tent, were sometimes consulted by me about it. But M.N. Roy had absolutely nothing to do with it, and I knew well enough that he would disapprove of it and laugh at it.

I had come across M.N. Roy in Allahabad some days before coming to Karachi. He turned up suddenly one evening at our house, and though I had no notion that he was in India, I recognized him immediately, having seen him in Moscow in 1927. He saw me at Karachi also, but that was probably for not more than five minutes. During the past few years Roy had written a great deal in condemnation of me politically, and he had often succeeded in hurting me a little. There was a great deal of difference between us, and yet I felt attracted towards him, and when later he had been arrested and was in trouble, I wanted to do what little I could (and that was little enough) to help him. I was attracted to him by his remarkable intellectual capacity; I was also attracted to him because he seemed such a lonely figure, deserted by everybody. The British

Government was naturally after him; nationalist India was not interested in him; and those who called themselves Communists in India condemned him as a traitor to the cause. I knew that after many years' residence in Russia and close co-operation with the Comintern, he had parted with them or, perhaps, been made to part. Why this happened I did not know, nor do I know still, except very vaguely, what his present views or his differences with the orthodox Communists are. But this desertion of a man like him by almost everybody pained me, and, against my usual habit, I joined the Defence Committee. Since that summer in 1931, over three years ago now, he has been in prison, unwell and practically in solitary confinement.

One of the final acts of the Congress session at Karachi was to elect a new Working Committee. This is elected by the All-India Congress Committee, but a convention has grown up that the suggestions of the President for the year (made in consultation with Gandhiji and sometimes other colleagues) are accepted by the A.I.C.C. The Karachi election of the Working Committee led to an untoward result, which none of us anticipated then. Some Muslim members of the A.I.C.C. objected to this election, in particular to one (Muslim) name in it. Perhaps they also felt slighted because no one of their group had been chosen. In an all-India committee of fifteen it was manifestly impossible to have all interests represented, and the real dispute, about which we knew nothing, was an entirely personal and local one in the Punjab. The result was that the protestant group gradually drifted away from the Congress in the Punjab, and joined others in an 'Ahrar Party' or 'Majlis-e-Ahrar'. Some of the most active and popular Muslim Congress workers in the Punjab joined this, and it attracted large numbers of Punjab Muslims to it. It represented chiefly the lower middle-class elements and it had numerous contacts with the Muslim masses. It thus became a powerful organization, far stronger than the decrepit Muslim communal organizations of upper-class folk, which functioned in the air or, rather, in drawing-rooms and committee rooms. Inevitably, the Ahrars drifted towards communalism, but because of their touch with the Muslim masses they remained a live body with a vague economic outlook. They played an important part later in Muslim agitations in Indian States, notably Kashmir, where economic ills and communalism were strangely and unhappily mixed together. The defection of some of the leaders of the Ahrar Party from the Congress was a serious loss for the Congress in the Punjab. But we did not know of this at Karachi; the realization came slowly in later months. This defection did not, of course, come because of resentment at the election of the Congress Working Committee. That was just a straw showing the drift of the wind; the real causes lay deeper.

While we were all at Karachi news had come of the Hindu-Muslim riots at Cawnpore, to be followed, soon after, by the report of the murder of Ganesh Shankar Vidyarthi by a frenzied mob of persons whom he was trying to help. Those terrible and brutal riots were bad enough, but Ganeshji's death brought them home to us as nothing else could have done. He was known to thousands in that Congress camp, and to all of us of the U.P. he was the dearest of comrades and friend, brave and intrepid, far-sighted and full of wise counsel, never downhearted, quietly working away and scorning publicity and office and the limelight. In the pride of his youth he willingly offered his life for the cause he loved and served, and foolish hands struck him down, and deprived Cawnpore and the province of the brightest of their jewels. There was gloom over our U.P. camp in Karachi when this news came; the glory seemed to have departed. And yet there was pride in him, that he had faced death so unfalteringly and died so gloriously.

36

A SOUTHERN HOLIDAY

My doctors urged me to take some rest and go for a change, and I decided to spend a month in Ceylon. India, huge as the country is, did not offer a real prospect of change or mental rest, for wherever I might go, I would probably come across political associates and the same problems would pursue me. Ceylon was the nearest place within reach of India, and so to Ceylon we went—Kamala, Indira and I. That was the first holiday I had had since our return from Europe in 1927, the first time since then that my wife and daughter and I holidayed together peacefully with little to distract our attention. There has been no repetition of that experience, and sometimes I wonder if there will be any.

And yet we did not really have much rest in Ceylon, except for two weeks at Nuwara Eliya. We were fairly overwhelmed by the hospitality and friendliness of all classes of people there. It was very pleasant to find all this goodwill, but it was often embarrassing also. At Nuwara Eliya groups of labourers, tea-garden workers and others would come daily, walking many miles, bringing gracious gifts with them—wild flowers, vegetables, home-made butter. We could not, as a rule, even converse together; we merely looked at each other and smiled. Our little house was full of these precious gifts of theirs, which they had given out of their poverty, and we passed them on to the local hospital and orphanages.

We visited many of the famous sights and historical ruins of the island, and Buddhist monasteries, and the rich tropical forests. At Anuradhapura, I liked greatly an old seated statue of the Buddha. A year later, when I was in Dehra Dun Gaol, a friend in Ceylon sent me a picture of this statue, and I kept it on my little table in my cell. It became a precious companion for me, and the strong, calm features of Buddha's statue soothed me and gave me strength and helped me to overcome many a period of depression.

Buddha has always had a great appeal for me. It is difficult for me to analyse this appeal, but it is not a religious appeal, and I am not interested in the dogmas that have grown up round Buddhism. It is the personality that has drawn me. So also the personality of Christ has attracted me greatly.

I saw many Buddhist *bhikkus* (monks) in their monasteries and on the highways, meeting with respect wherever they went. The dominant expression of almost all of them was one of peace and calm, a strange detachment from the cares of the world. They did not have intellectual faces, as a rule, and there was no trace of the fierce conflicts of the mind on their countenances. Life seemed to be for them a smooth-flowing river moving slowly to the great ocean. I looked at them with some envy, with just a faint yearning for a haven, but I knew well enough that my lot was a different one, cast in storms and tempests. There was to be no haven for me, for the tempests within me were as stormy as those outside. And if perchance I found myself in a safe harbour, protected from the fury of the winds, would I be contented or happy there?

For a little while the harbour was pleasant, and one could lie down and dream and allow the soothing and enervating charm of the tropics to steal over one. Ceylon fitted in with my mood then, and the beauty of the island filled me with delight. Our month of holiday was soon over, and it was with real regret that we bade good-bye. So many memories come back to me of the land and her people; they have been pleasant companions during the long, empty days in prison. One little incident lingers in my memory; it was near Jaffna, I think. The teachers and boys of a school stopped our car and said a few words of greeting. The ardent, eager faces of the boys stood out, and then one of their number came to me, shook hands with me, and without question or argument, said: "I will not falter." That bright young face with shining eyes, full of determination, is imprinted in my mind. I do not know who he was; I have lost trace of him. But somehow I have the conviction that he will remain true to his word and will not falter when he has to face life's difficult problems.

From Ceylon we went to South India, right to the southern tip at Cape Comorin. Amazingly peaceful it was there. And then through Travancore, Cochin, Malabar, Mysore, Hyderabad—mostly Indian States, some the most progressive of their kind, some the most backward. Travancore and Cochin educationally far in advance of British India; Mysore probably ahead industrially; Hyderabad almost a perfect feudal relic. We received courtesy and welcome everywhere, both from the people and the authorities, but behind that welcome I could sense the anxiety of the latter lest our visit might lead the people to think dangerously. Mysore and Travancore seemed to give some civil liberty and opportunities of political work at the time; in Hyderabad even this was wholly absent; and I felt, in spite of the courtesy that surrounded us, stifled and suffocated. Latterly the Mysore and Travancore governments have withdrawn even the measure of civil liberty and political activity that they had previously permitted.

In Bangalore, in the Mysore State, I had hoisted at a great gathering a national flag on an enormous iron pole. Not long after my departure this pole was broken up into bits, and the Mysore government made the display of the flag an offence. This ill-treatment and insult of the flag I had hoisted pained me greatly.

In Travancore today even the Congress has been made an unlawful association, and no one can enrol ordinary members for it, although in British India it is now lawful since the withdrawal of civil disobedience. Thus both Mysore and Travancore are crushing ordinary peaceful political activity and have taken back some facilities they had previously allowed. They have moved backwards. Hyderabad had no necessity for going back or withdrawing facilities, for it had never moved forward at all or given any facility of the kind. Political meetings are unknown in Hyderabad, and even social and religious gatherings are looked upon with suspicion, and special permission has to be taken for them. There are no newspapers worthy of the name issued there, and, in order to prevent the germs of corruption from coming from outside, a large number of newspapers published in other parts of India are prevented entry. So strict is this policy of exclusion that even Moderate journals are excluded.

In Cochin we visited the quarter of the 'White Jews', as they are called, and saw one of the services in their old tabernacle. The little community is very ancient and very unique. It is dwindling in numbers. The part of Cochin they live in, we were told, resembled ancient Jerusalem. It certainly had an ancient look about it.

We also visited, along the backwaters of Malabar, some of the towns inhabited chiefly by Christians belonging to the Syrian churches. Few people realize that Christianity came to India as early as the first century after Christ, long before Europe turned to it, and established a firm hold in South India. Although these Christians have their religious head in Antioch or somewhere in Syria, their Christianity is practically indigenous and has few outside contacts.

To my surprise, we also came across a colony of Nestorians in the South; I was told by their bishop that there were ten thousand of them. I had laboured under the impression that the Nestorians had long been absorbed in other sects, and I did not know that they had ever flourished in India. But I was told that at one time they had a fairly large following in India, extending as far north as Benares.

We had gone to Hyderabad especially to pay a visit to Mrs Sarojini Naidu and her daughters, Padmaja and Leilamani. During our stay with them a small *purdanashin* gathering of women assembled at their house to meet my wife, and Kamala apparently addressed them. Probably she spoke of women's struggle for freedom against man-made laws and customs (a favourite topic of hers) and urged the women not to be too submissive to their menfolk. There was an interesting sequel to this two or three weeks later, when a distracted husband wrote to Kamala from Hyderabad and said that since her visit to that city his wife had behaved strangely. She would not listen to him and fall in with his wishes, as she used to, but would argue with him and even adopt an aggressive attitude.

Seven weeks after we had sailed from Bombay for Ceylon we were back in that city, and immediately I plunged again into the whirlpool of Congress politics. There were meetings of the Working Committee to consider vital problems—a rapidly-changing and developing situation in India, the U.P. agrarian impasse, the phenomenal growth of the 'Redshirt' movement in the Frontier province under Khan Abdul Ghaffar Khan's leadership, Bengal in an extreme state of tension and suppressed anger and unrest, the ever-present communal problem, and petty local conflicts, over a variety of issues, between Congressmen and Government officials, involving mutual charges of breaches of the Delhi Pact. And then there was the ever-recurring question: was the Congress to be represented at the second Round Table Conference? Should Mahatma Gandhi go there?

37

FRICTION DURING TRUCE PERIOD

Should Gandhiji go to London for the Round Table Conference or not? Again and again the question arose, and there was no definite answer. No one knew till the last moment—not even the Congress Working Committee or Gandhiji himself. For the answer depended on many things, and new happenings were constantly giving a fresh turn to the situation. Behind that question and answer lay real and difficult problems.

We were told repeatedly, on behalf of the British Government and their friends, that the Round Table Conference had already laid down the framework of the constitution, that the principal lines of the picture had been drawn, and all that remained was the filling of this picture. But the Congress did not think so, and so far as it was concerned, the picture had to be drawn or painted from the very beginning on an almost blank canvas. It was true that by the Delhi agreement the federal basis had been approved and the idea of safeguards accepted. But a federation had long seemed to many of us the best solution of the Indian constitutional problem, and our approval of this idea did not mean our acceptance of the particular type of federation envisaged by the first Round Table Conference. A federation was perfectly compatible with political independence and social change. It was far more difficult to fit in the idea of safeguards and, ordinarily, they would mean a substantial diminution of sovereignty, but the qualifying phrase "in the interests of India" helped us to get over this difficulty to some extent at least, though not perhaps very successfully. In any event, the Karachi Congress had made it clear that an acceptable constitution must provide for full control of defence, foreign affairs, and financial and economic policy, and an examination of the question of India's indebtedness to foreign (meaning largely British) interests before liabilities were undertaken; and the fundamental rights resolution had also indicated some of the political and economic changes desired. All this was incompatible with many of the Round Table Conference decisions, as well as with the existing framework of administration in India.

The gulf between the Congress view-point and that of the British Government was immense, and it seemed exceedingly unlikely that it could be bridged at that stage. Very few Congressmen expected any measure of agreement between the Congress and the Government at the Round Table Conference, and even Gandhiji, optimistic as he always is, could not look forward to much. And yet he was never hopeless and was determined to try to the very end. All of us felt that whether success came or not, the effort had to be made, in continuation of the Delhi agreement. But there were two vital considerations which might have barred our participation in the second Round Table Conference. We could only go if we had full freedom to place our view-point in its entirety before the Round Table Conference, and were not prevented from doing so by being told that the matter had already been decided, or for any other reason. We could also be prevented from being represented at the Round Table Conference by conditions in India. A situation might have developed here which precipitated a conflict with Government, or in which we had to face severe repression. If this took place in India and our very house was on fire, it would have been singularly out of place for any representative of ours to ignore the fire and talk academically of constitutions and the like in London.

The situation was developing swiftly in India. This was noticeable all over the country, and especially so in Bengal, the United Provinces, and the Frontier Province. In Bengal the Delhi agreement had made little difference, and the tension continued and grew worse. Some civil disobedience prisoners were discharged, but thousands of politicals, who were technically not civil disobedience prisoners, remained in prison. The detenus also continued in gaol or detention camps. Fresh arrests were frequently made for 'seditious' speeches or other political activities, and generally it was felt that the Government offensive had continued without any abatement. For the Congress, the Bengal problem has been an extraordinarily difficult one because of the existence of terrorism. Compared to the normal Congress activities and civil disobedience, these terroristic activities were, in extent and importance, very little. But they made a loud noise and attracted great attention. They also helped in making it difficult for Congress work to function as in most other provinces, for terrorism produced an atmosphere which was not favourable to peaceful direct action. Inevitably they invited the severest repression from the Government, and this fell with considerable impartiality on terrorist and non-terrorist alike.

It was difficult for the police and the local executive authorities not to make use of the special laws and ordinances (meant for the terrorists) for Congressmen, labour and peasant workers and others whose activities they disapproved of. It is possible than the real offence of many of the detenus, kept now for years without charge or trial or conviction, was not terroristic activity but other effective political activity. They have been given no chance of proving or disproving anything, or even of knowing what their sins are. They are not tried in court, presumably because the police have not sufficient evidence against them to secure a conviction, although it is well known that the British-Indian laws for offences against the State are amazingly thorough and comprehensive, and it is difficult to escape from their close meshes. It often happens that a person is acquitted by the law courts and is immediately arrested again and thereafter treated as a detenu.

The Congress Working Committee felt very helpless before this intricate problem of Bengal. They were continually oppressed by it, and some Bengal matter was always coming up before them in different forms. They dealt with it as best they could, but they knew well that they were not really tackling the problem. So, rather weakly, they simply allowed matters to drift there; it is a little difficult to say what else they could have done, placed as they were. This attitude of the Working Committee was much resented in Bengal, and an impression grew up there that the Congress executive, as well as the other provinces, were ignoring Bengal. In the hour of her trial Bengal seemed to be deserted. This impression was entirely wrong, for the whole of India was full of sympathy for the people of Bengal, but it did not know how to translate this sympathy into effective help. And, besides, every part of India had to face its own troubles.

In the United Provinces the agrarian situation was becoming worse. The Provincial Government temporized with the problem and delayed a decision about rent and revenue remissions, and forcible collections were begun. There were wholesale ejectments and attachments. While we were in Ceylon there had taken place two or three agrarian riots when forcible attempts were made to collect rents. The riots were petty in themselves, but unhappily they resulted in the death of the landlord or his agent. Gandhiji had gone to Naini Tal (also when I was in Ceylon) to discuss the agrarian situation with the Governor of U.P., Sir Malcolm Hailey, without much result. When the Government announced its remissions, they fell far short of expectations, and in the rural areas there was a continuous and an ever-growing uproar. As the pressure of landlord plus government grew on the peasantry, and thousands of tenants were ejected from their holdings and had their little property seized, a situation developed which in most other countries would have resulted in a big peasant rising. I think it was very largely the efforts of the Congress which kept the tenants from indulging in violent activity. But there was an abundance of violence against them.

There was one bright side to this agrarian upheaval and distress. Owing to the very low prices of agricultural produce, the poorer classes, including the peasants, unless they were dispossessed, had more to eat than they had had for a long time. In the Frontier Province, as in Bengal, the Delhi Pact brought no peace. There was a permanent state of tension there, and government was a military affair, with special laws and ordinances and heavy punishments for trivial offences. To oppose this state of affairs, Abdul Ghaffar Khan led a great agitation, and he soon became a bugbear to the Government. From village to village he went striding along, carrying his six-feet-three of Pathan manhood, and establishing centres of the 'Redshirts'. Wherever he or his principal lieutenants went, they left a trail of their 'Redshirts' behind, and the whole province was soon covered by branches of the 'Khudai Khidmatgar'. They were thoroughly peaceful and, in spite of vague allegations, not a single definite charge of violence against them has been established. But whether they were peaceful or not, they had the tradition of war and violence behind them, and they lived near the turbulent frontier, and this rapid growth of a disciplined movement, closely allied to the Indian national movement, thoroughly upset the Government. I do not suppose they ever believed in its professions of peace and non-violence. But even if they had done so, their reactions to it would only have been of fright and annoyance. It represented too much of actual and potential power for them to view it with equanimity.

Of this great movement the unquestioned head was Khan Abdul

Ghaffar Khan—"Fakhr-e-Afghan", "Fakr-e-Pathan", the 'Pride of the Pathans', 'Gandhi-e-Sarhad', the 'Frontier Gandhi', as he came to be known. He had attained an amazing popularity in the Frontier Province by sheer dint of quiet, persevering work, undaunted by difficulties or Government action. He was, and is, no politician as politicians go; he knows nothing of the tactics and manoeuvres of politics. A tall, straight man, straight in body and mind, hating fuss and too much talk, looking forward to freedom for his Frontier Province people within the framework of Indian freedom, but vague about, and uninterested in, constitutions and legal talk. Action was necessary to achieve anything, and Mahatma Gandhi had taught a remarkable way of peaceful action which appealed to him. For action, organization was necessary; therefore, without further argument or much drafting of rules for his organization, he started organizing—and with remarkable success.

He was especially attracted to Gandhiji. At first his shyness and desire to keep in the background made him keep away from him. Later they had to meet to discuss various matters, and their contacts grew. It was surprising how this Pathan accepted the idea of non-violence, far more so in theory than many of us. And it was because he believed in it that he managed to impress his people with the importance of remaining peaceful in spite of provocation. It would be absurd to say that the people of the Frontier Province have given up all thoughts of ever indulging in violence, just as it would be absurd to say this of the people generally in any province. The masses are moved by waves of emotion, and no one can predict what they might do when so moved. But the self-discipline that the frontier people showed in 1930 and subsequent years has been something amazing.

Government officials and some of our very timid countrymen look askance at the 'Frontier Gandhi'. They cannot take him at his word, and can only think in terms of deep intrigue. But the past years have brought him and other frontier comrades very near to Congress workers in other parts of India, and between them there has grown up a close comradeship and mutual appreciation and regard. Abdul Ghaffar Khan has been known and liked for many years in Congress circles. But he has grown to be something more than an individual comrade; more and more he has come to be, in the eyes of the rest of India, the symbol of the courage and sacrifice of a gallant and indomitable people, comrades of ours in a common struggle.

Long before I had heard of Abdul Ghaffar Khan, I knew his brother, Dr Khan Sahib. He was a student at St. Thomas's Hospital in London when I was at Cambridge, and later, when I was eating my Bar dinners at the Inner Temple he and I became close friends, and hardly a day went by, when I was in London, when we did not meet. I returned to India, leaving him in England, and he stayed on for many more years, serving as a doctor in war-time. I saw him next in Naini Prison.

The frontier 'Redshirts' co-operated with the Congress, but they were an organization apart. It was a peculiar position. The real connecting link was Abdul Ghaffar Khan. This question was fully considered by the Working Committee in consultation with the Frontier Province leaders in the summer of 1931, and it was decided to absorb the 'Redshirts' into the Congress. The 'Redshirt' movement thus became part of the Congress organization.

It was Gandhiji's wish to go to the Frontier Province immediately after the Karachi Congress, but the Government did not encourage this at all. Repeatedly, in later months, when Government officials complained of the doings of the 'Red-shirts', he pressed to be allowed to go there to find out for himself, but to no purpose. Nor was my going there approved. In view of the Delhi agreement, it was not considered desirable by us to enter the Frontier Province against the declared wish of the Government.

Yet another of the problems before the Working Committee was the communal problem. There was nothing new about this, although it had a way of reappearing in novel and fantastic attire. The Round Table Conference gave it an added importance at the time, as it was obvious that the British Government would keep it in the forefront and subordinate all other issues to it. The members of the Conference, all nominees of the Government, had been mainly chosen in order to give importance to the communal and sectional interests, and to lay stress on these divergences rather than on the common interests. The Government had even refused, pointedly and aggressively, to nominate any leader of the Nationalist Muslims. Gandhiji felt that if the Conference, at the instance of the British Government, became entangled in the communal issue right at the beginning, the real political and economic issues would not get proper consideration. Under these circumstances, his going to the Conference would be of little use. He put it to the Working

Committee, therefore, that he should only go to London if some understanding on the communal issue was previously arrived at between the parties concerned. His instinct was perfectly justified, but nevertheless the Committee overruled him and decided that he must not refuse to go merely on the ground that we had failed to solve the communal problem. An attempt was made by the Committee, in consultation with representatives of various communities, to put forward a proposed solution. This had no great success.

These were some of the major problems before us during that summer of 1931, besides a large number of minor issues. From all over the country we were continually receiving complaints from local Congress Committees pointing out breaches of the Delhi Pact by local officials. The more important of these were forwarded by us to the Government, which, in its turn, brought charges against Congressmen of violation of the Pact. So charges and counter-charges were made, and later they were published in the Press. Needless to say, this did not result in the improvement of the relations between the Congress and the Government.

And yet this friction on petty matters was by itself of no great importance. Its importance lay in its revealing the development of a more fundamental conflict, something which did not depend on individuals but arose from the very nature of our national struggle and the want of equilibrium of our agrarian economy, something that could not be liquidated or compromised away without a basic change. Our national movement had originally begun because of the desire of our upper middle classes to find means of self-expression and self-growth, and behind it there was the political and economic urge. It spread to the lower middle classes and became a power in the land; and then it began to stir the rural masses who were finding it more and more difficult to keep up, as a whole, even their miserable rock-bottom standard of living. The old self-sufficient village economy had long ceased to exist. Auxiliary cottage industries, ancillary to agriculture, which had relieved somewhat the burden on the land, had died off, partly because of State policy, but largely because they could not compete with the rising machine industry. The burden on land grew and the growth of Indian industry was too slow to make much difference to this. Ill-equipped and almost unawares, the overburdened village was thrown into the world market and was tossed about hither and thither. It could not compete on even terms. It was backward in its methods of production, and its land system, resulting in a progressive fragmentation of holdings, made radical improvement impossible. So the agricultural classes, both landlords and tenants, went downhill, except during brief periods of boom. The landlords tried to pass on the burden to their tenantry, and the growing pauperization of the peasantry—both the petty landholders and the tenants—drew them to the national movement. The agricultural proletariat, the large numbers of landless labourers in rural areas, were also attracted; and for all these rural classes 'nationalism' or 'swaraj' meant fundamental changes in the land system, which would relieve or lessen their burdens and provide land for the landless. These desires found no clear expression either in the peasantry or in the middle-class leaders of the national movement.

The Civil Disobedience movement of 1930 happened to fit in unbeknown to its own leaders at first, with the great world slump in industry and agriculture. The rural masses were powerfully affected by this slump, and they turned to the Congress and civil disobedience. For them it was not a matter of a fine constitution drawn up in London or elsewhere, but of a basic change in the land system, especially in the zamindari areas. The zamindari system, indeed, seemed to have outlived its day and had no stability left in it. But the British Government, situated as it was, could not venture to undertake a radical change of this land system. Even when it had appointed the Royal Agricultural Commission, the terms of reference to it barred a discussion of the question of ownership of land or the system of land tenure.

Thus the conflict lay in the very nature of things in India then, and it could not be charmed away by phrases or compromises. Only a solution of the basic problem of land (not to mention other vital national issues) could resolve that conflict. And of this solution through the instrumentality of the British Government there was no possibility. Temporary measures might alleviate the distress for a while; severe repression might frighten and prevent public expression of it; but neither helped in the solution of the problem.

The British Government, like most governments I suppose, has an idea that much of the trouble in India is due to 'agitators'. It is a singularly inept notion. India has had a great leader during the past fifteen years who has won the affection and even adoration of her millions, and has seemed to impose his will on her in many ways. He has played a vitally important part in her recent history, and yet more important than he were the people themselves who seemed to follow blindly his behests. The people were the principal actors, and behind them, pushing them on, were great historical urges which prepared them and made them ready to listen to their leader's piping. But for that historical setting and political and social urges, no leaders or agitators could have inspired them to action. It was Gandhiji's chief virtue as a leader that he could instinctively feel the pulse of the people and know when conditions were ripe for growth and action.

In 1930 the national movement in India fitted in for a while with the growing social forces of the country, and because of this a great power came to it, a sense of reality, as if it was indeed marching step by step with history. The Congress represented that national movement, and this power and strength were reflected in the growth of Congress prestige. This was something vague, incalculable, indefinable, but nevertheless very much present. The peasantry, of course, turned to the Congress and gave it its real strength; the lower middle class formed the backbone of its fighting ranks. Even the upper *bourgeoisie*, troubled by this new atmosphere, thought it safer to be friendly with the Congress. The great majority of the textile mills in India signed undertakings prescribed by the Congress, and were afraid of doing things which might bring on them the displeasure of the Congress. While people argued fine legal points in London at the first R.T.C., the reality of power seemed to be slowly and imperceptibly flowing towards the Congress as representing the people. This illusion grew even after the Delhi Pact, not because of vainglorious speeches, but because of the events of 1930 and after. Indeed, probably the persons who were most conscious of the difficulties and dangers ahead were the Congress leaders, and they took every care not to minimize them.

This vague sense of a dual authority growing in the country was naturally most irritating to the Government. It had no real basis in fact, as physical power rested completely with the authorities, but that it existed psychologically there was no doubt. For an authoritarian, irremovable government this was an impossible situation, and it was this subtle atmosphere that really got on their nerves, and not a few odd village speeches or processions of which they complained later. A clash, therefore, seemed inevitable; for the Congress could hardly commit voluntary *hara-kiri*, and the Government could not tolerate this atmosphere of duality, and was bent on crushing the Congress. This clash was deferred because of the second Round Table Conference. For some reason or other the British Government was very keen on having Gandhiji in London, and avoided, as far as possible, doing anything to prevent this.

And yet the sense of conflict grew, and we could feel the hardening on the side of Government. Soon after the Delhi Pact, Lord Irwin had left India and Lord Willingdon had come in his place as Viceroy. A legend grew up that the new Viceroy was a hard and stern person and not so amenable to compromise as his predecessor. Many of our politicians have inherited a 'liberal' habit of thinking of politics in terms of persons rather than of principles. They do not realize that the broad imperial policy of the British Government does not depend on the personal views of the Viceroys. The change of Viceroys, therefore, did not and could not make any difference, but, as it happened, the policy of Government gradually changed owing to the development of the situation. The Civil Service hierarchy had not approved of pacts and dealings with the Congress; all their training and authoritarian conceptions of government were opposed to this. They had an idea that they had added to the Congress influence and Gandhiji's prestige by dealing with him almost as an equal and it was about time that he was brought down a peg or two. The notion was a very foolish one, but then the Indian Civil Service is not known for the originality of its conceptions. Whatever the reason, the Government stiffened its back and tightened its hold, and it seemed to tell us, in the words of the old prophet: My little finger is thicker than my father's loins. Whereas he chastised you with whips, I will chastise you with scorpions.

But the time for chastisement was not yet. If possible the Congress was to be represented at the second Round Table Conference. Twice Gandhiji went to Simla to have long conversations with the Viceroy and other officials. They discussed many of the points at issue, especially the 'Redshirt' movement in the Frontier and the U.P. Agrarian situation, the two problems, apart from Bengal, which seemed to be worrying the Government most.

Gandhiji had sent for me from Simla, and I had occasion to meet some of the Government of India officials also. My talks were limited to the U.P. They were frank talks, and the real conflicts, which lay behind the petty charges and countercharges, were discussed. I remember being told that the Government had been in a position in February 1931 to crush the Civil Disobedience movement absolutely within three months at the most. They had perfected their machinery of repression and only a push had to be given to it; a button pressed. But preferring, if possible, a settlement by agreement to one imposed by force, they had decided to try the experiment of mutual talks which had led to the Delhi agreement. If the agreement had not come off, the button was always there, and could have been pressed at a moment's notice. And there seemed to be a hint that the button might have to be pressed in the not distant future if we did not behave. It was all said very courteously and very frankly, and both of us knew that, quite apart from us and whatever we might say or do, conflict was inevitable. Another high official paid a compliment to the Congress. We were for the moment discussing wider problems of a non-political nature, and he told me that, politics apart, the Congress had done a great service to India. The usual charge brought against Indians was that they were not good organizers, but during 1930 the Congress had done a wonderful bit of organizing, despite enormous difficulties and opposition.

Gandhiji's first visit to Simla was inconclusive in so far as the question of going to the Round Table Conference was concerned. The second visit took place in the last week of August. A final decision had to be taken one way or the other, but still he found it difficult to make up his mind to leave India. In Bengal, in the Frontier Province, and in the U.P., he saw trouble ahead, and he did not want to go unless he had some assurance of peace in India. At last some kind of an agreement was arrived at with the Government embodied in a statement and some letters that were exchanged. This was done at the very last moment to enable him to travel by the liner that was carrying the delegates to the R.T.C. Indeed, it was after the last moment, in a sense, as the last train had gone. A special train from Simla to Kalka was arranged, and other trains were delayed to make the connections,

I accompanied him from Simla to Bombay, and there, one bright morning towards the end of August, I waved good-bye to him as he was carried away to the Arabian Sea and the far West. That was my last glimpse of him for two years.

38

THE ROUND TABLE CONFERENCE

In a recent book an English journalist, who claims to have seen a great deal of Mr Gandhi both in India and at the Round Table Conference in London, writes as follows:

> The leaders on board the Mooltan knew that there was a conspiracy against Mr Gandhi within the Congress Working Committee. They knew that, when the time was ripe, Congress might expel him. But Congress, by expelling Mr Gandhi, would expel in all probability half its members; and that was the half Sir Tej Bahadur Sapru and Mr Jayakar wished to attach to the Liberal cause. They never disguised the fact that Mr Gandhi was, in their own words, 'muddle-headed'. It was worth winning a 'muddle-headed' leader when he could bring with him a million 'muddle-headed' followers.[1]

---

1. From Glorney Bolton's *The Tragedy of Gandhi*. I have taken this extract from a review of the book, as I have had no opportunity so far of reading the book itself. I hope that I am not doing an injustice thereby to the author or to the persons mentioned in the quotation . . . Since writing the above I have read the book. Many of the statements of Mr Bolton and the inferences he draws are, to my thinking, wholly unjustified. There are also a number of errors of fact, especially in regard to what the Working Committee did or did not do during the Delhi Pact negotiations and after. There is also a curious assumption that Mr Vallabhbhai Patel got the Congress presidentship in 1931, and thereby the leadership of the Congress, in rivalry with Mr Gandhi. As a matter of fact, during the last fifteen years Mr Gandhi has been a far bigger person in the Congress (and, of course, in the country) than any Congress President could possibly be. He has been the president-maker, and invariably his suggestions have been followed. Repeatedly he refused to preside and preferred that some of his colleagues and lieutenants should do so. I became president of the Congress entirely because of him. He had actually been elected, but he withdrew and forced my election. Mr Vallabhbhai Patel's election was not normal. We had just come out of prison, and the Congress Committees were still illegal bodies, and could not function in the ordinary way. The Working Committee, therefore, took it upon itself to elect the President of the Karachi Congress. The whole Committee, including Mr Vallabhbhai Patel, begged Mr Gandhi to accept the presidentship and thus to be the titular head, as he was the real head, of the Congress during the coming critical year.

I do not know how far this quotation represents the views of Sir Tej Bahadur Sapru, Mr Jayakar, or the other members of the R.T.C. on their way to London in 1931. But it does seem to me an astonishing thing that any person, journalist or 'leader', with the least acquaintance with Indian politics, could have made such a statement. I was astounded to read it; I had not heard of it previously even as a suggestion, though that is not difficult to understand, as I have been in prison for most of the time since then.

Who were the conspirators and what were they after? It was sometimes stated that the President, Vallabhbhai Patel, and I were among the extremists of the Working Committee, and, therefore, I suppose, we must have been numbered among the leaders of the conspiracy. Perhaps in the whole of India Gandhiji has had no more loyal colleague than Vallabhbhai, a man strong and unbending in his work, and yet devoted to him personally and to his ideals and policy. I could not claim to have

---

He would not agree, and insisted on Mr Vallabhbhai Patel accepting it. I remember that it was pointed out to him at the time that he wanted to be Mussolini all the time while others were made by him temporary kings and figureheads. It is not possible to deal with various other misapprehensions of Mr Bolton in a footnote. One somewhat personal matter I should, however, like to refer to. He seems to be convinced that the turning-point in my father's political career was his non-election by a European club, and that this led him not only to radical ways but to an avoidance of English society. This story, though often repeated, is wholly untrue. The real facts have little importance, but I am giving them here to clear up this mystery. In his early days at the Bar, he became a favourite of Sir John Edge, who was then the Chief Justice of the Allahabad High Court. Sir John suggested to him that he should join the Allahabad (European) Club, and wanted to propose his name himself. My father thanked him for his kindly suggestion, but pointed out that there was bound to be trouble, as many English people would object to him as an Indian and might vote against him. Any subaltern could blackball him, and he would rather not offer himself for election under these circumstances. Sir John even suggested that he would get the Brigadier-General commanding the Allahabad area to second my father's name. Ultimately, however, the matter dropped, and my father's name was not proposed, as he made it clear that he was not prepared to risk an insult. This incident, far from embittering him against English people, drew him to Sir John Edge, and most of his English friendships and connections grew up in subsequent years. This occurred in the 'nineties, and it was nearly a quarter of a century later that he became the radical politician and non-co-operator. The change was not sudden, but the Punjab Martial Law hurried up the process, and Mr Gandhi's influence at the right moment made a difference. Even then he had no deliberate intention of giving up social contacts with Englishmen. But where Englishmen are largely officials, non-co-operation and civil disobedience inevitably prevent such contacts.

accepted these ideals in the same way, but I had had the privilege of working with Gandhiji in the closest association, and the idea of intriguing against him in any way is a monstrous one. Indeed, that applied to the whole Working Committee. That Committee was practically his creation; he had nominated it, in consultation with a few colleagues, and the election itself was a formal matter. The backbone of the Committee consisted of members who had served on it for many years and had come to be considered almost as permanent members. There were political differences amongst them, differences in outlook and in temper; but years of association, the joint shouldering of burdens and the facing of common perils, had welded them together. Between them had grown up friendship and camaraderie and regard for each other. They formed not a coalition but an organic unity, and it was inconceivable for any one to intrigue against the other. Gandhiji dominated the Committee, and every one looked to him for guidance. That had been so for many years; it was even more marked in 1931 after the great success that had attended our struggle in 1930.

What could have been the purpose of the 'extremists' in the Working Committee to try to 'expel' him? Perhaps it was thought that he was considered too compromising a person and was, therefore, an encumbrance. But without him where was the struggle, where was Civil Disobedience and Satyagraha? He was part of the living movement; indeed, he was the movement itself. So far as that struggle was concerned everything depended on him. The national struggle, of course, was not his creation, nor did it depend on any individual; it had deeper roots. But that particular phase of the struggle, of which civil disobedience was the symbol, was singularly dependent on him. Parting with him meant winding up that movement and building anew on fresh foundations. That would have been a difficult enough proposition at any time; in 1931 it was unthinkable for anyone.

It is amusing to think how, according to some people, some of us were conspiring to drive him out of the Congress in 1931. Why should we conspire when a gentle hint to him was sufficient? A mere suggestion from him that he would retire has always been enough to upset the Working Committee as well as the country. He was so much part of our struggle that the very thought that he might leave us was unbearable. We hesitated to send him to London, because in his absence the burden in

India would fall on us, and we did not welcome the prospect. We were so used to shifting it on to his shoulders. For many of us, in the Working Committee and outside, the bonds that tied us to Gandhiji were such that even failure with him seemed preferable to the winning of some temporary advantage without him.

Whether Gandhiji is 'muddle-headed' or not we can leave to our Liberal friends to decide. It is undoubtedly true that his politics are sometimes very metaphysical and difficult to understand. But he had shown himself a man of action, a man of wonderful courage, and a man who could often deliver the goods; and if 'muddle-headedness' yields such practical results perhaps it compares not unfavourably with the 'practical politics' that begin and end in the study and in select circles. True, his millions of followers were 'muddle-headed'. They knew nothing of politics and constitutions; they could think only in terms of their human needs, of food and shelter and clothing and land.

It has always seemed to me very remarkable how eminent foreign journalists, trained in the observation of human nature, go wrong in India. Is it because of the ineradicable impression of their childhood that the East is utterly different and cannot be judged by ordinary standards? Or is it, in the case of Englishmen, the kink of empire that governs their vision and distorts their view? They will believe almost anything, however unlikely it might be, without any surprise, for everything is deemed to be possible in the mysterious East. They publish books sometimes containing able surveys and acute bits of observation and, in between, amazing lapses.

I remember reading, just on the eve of Gandhiji's departure for Europe in 1931, an article by a well-known Paris correspondent (at the time) of a London newspaper. The article was about India, and in the course of it he referred to an incident which, according to him, took place in 1921 during the non-co-operation days when the Prince of Wales visited India. It was stated that in some place (probably it was Delhi) Mahatma Gandhi burst in dramatically and unannounced on the Prince, fell on his knees, clasped the Prince's feet and, weeping copiously, begged him to give peace to this unhappy land. None of us, not even Gandhiji, had heard of this remarkable story, and I wrote to the journalist pointing this out to him. He expressed regret, but added that he had got it from a reliable source. What astonished me was that he should have given credence, without any attempt at an enquiry, to a story on the face of it highly improbable, and which no one who knew anything about Mr Gandhi, the Congress, or India could believe. It is, unhappily, true that there are many Englishmen in India who, in spite of long residence, know nothing about the country or about the Congress or about Gandhiji. The story was an incredible and ridiculous one, comparable perhaps to a fanciful account of the Archbishop of Canterbury suddenly bursting in upon Mussolini, standing on his head, and waving his legs in the air in token of greeting.

A recent report in a newspaper gives another type of story. It is stated that Gandhiji has got huge funds, running into millions of pounds, secretly deposited with friends, and the Congress is after this money. It (the Congress) is afraid that if Gandhiji retires from its membership it might lose these hoards. The story is on the face of it absurd, for he never keeps funds personally or secretly, and whatever he has collected he hands over to a public organization. He has the *bania's* instinct for careful accounting, and all his collections are publicly audited.

This rumour is probably based on the story of the famous crore of rupees which were collected by the Congress in 1921. This sum, which sounds big but was not much if spread out all over India, was utilized for national universities and schools, promotion of cottage industries and especially khaddar, untouchability work and a variety of other constructive schemes. Much of it was tied up in ear-marked funds, which still exist, and are used for their special purposes. The rest of the collections were left with the local committees, and spent for Congress organizational and political work. The non-co-operation movement was financed by it, as well as Congress work for a few years after. We have been taught by Gandhiji, as well as by the poverty of the country, to carry on our political movement with exceedingly limited means. Most of our work has been wholly voluntary, and where payment has been made it has been on a starvation scale. The best of our workers, university graduates with families to support, have been paid less than the unemployment allowance in England. I doubt if any political or labour movement on a large scale has been run anywhere with so little money as the Congress movement during the last fifteen years. And all Congress funds and accounts have been publicly audited from year to year, no part of them being secret, except during the civil disobedience periods, when the Congress was an illegal organization.

Gandhiji had gone to London as the sole representative of the Congress to the Round Table Conference. We had decided, after long debate, not to have additional representatives. Partly this was due to our desire to have our best men in India at a very critical time, when the most tactful handling of the situation was necessary. We felt that, in spite of the R.T.C. meeting in London, the centre of gravity lay in India, and developments in India would inevitably have their reactions in London. We wanted to check untoward developments, and to keep our organization in proper condition. This was, however, not the real reason for our sending only one representative. If we had thought it necessary and advisable, we would certainly have sent others also. Deliberately we refrained from doing so.

We were not joining the Round Table Conference to talk interminably about the petty details of a constitution. We were not interested in those details at that stage, and they could only be considered when some agreement on fundamental matters had been arrived at with the British Government. The real question was how much power was to be transferred to a democratic India. Any solicitor almost could do the drafting and the settlement of details afterwards. The Congress position was a fairly simple one on these basic matters, and there was no great room for argument over it. It seemed to us that the dignified course would be for one representative, and that one our leader, to go and explain that position, to show the essential reasonableness of it and the inevitability of it, and to try to win over, if he could, the British Government to it. That was very difficult, we knew; hardly possible as matters stood then, but then we had no other alternative. We could not give up that position and our principles and ideals, to which we were pledged and in which we firmly believed. If by a strange chance a basis of agreement was found on those fundamentals, the rest followed easily enough. Indeed, it had been settled between us that, in case of such an agreement, Gandhiji would immediately summon to London some or even all the members of the Working Committee, so that we could then share the work of detailed negotiation. We were to keep ourselves in readiness for that summons, and even travel by air if necessary. We could thus be with him within ten days of the call.

But if there was no initial agreement on fundamentals, then the question of further and detailed negotiations did not arise, nor was it necessary for additional Congress representatives to go to the R.T.C. So we decided to send Gandhiji only. One other member of the Working Committee, Mrs Sarojini Naidu, also attended the R.T.C., but she did not do so as a Congress representative. She was invited as a representative of Indian womanhood, and the Working Committee permitted her to go as such.

The British Government had, however, no intention of falling in with our wishes in the matter. Their policy was to postpone the consideration of fundamental questions and to make the Conference exhaust itself, more or less, on minor and immaterial matters. Even when major matters were considered, the Government held its hand, refused to commit itself, and promised to express its opinion after mature consideration later on. Their trump card was, of course, the communal issue and they played it for all it was worth. It dominated the Conference.

The great majority of the Indian members of the Conference fell in, most of them willingly, some unwillingly, with this official manoeuvring. They were a motley assembly. Few of them represented any but themselves. Some were able and respected; of many others this could not be said. As a whole they represented, politically and socially, the most reactionary elements in India. So backward and reactionary were they that the Indian Liberals, so very moderate and cautious in India, shone as progressives in their company. They represented groups of vested interests in India who were tied up with British imperialism, and looked to it for advancement or protection. The most prominent representation came from various 'minority' and 'majority' groups on the communal issue. This consisted of a number of upper-class irreconcilables who, it was notorious, could never agree amongst themselves. Politically they were thorough reactionaries, and their sole interest seemed to be to gain a communal advantage, even though that might involve a surrender of political advance. Indeed they proclaimed that they would not agree to having any greater measure of political freedom unless and until their communal demands were satisfied. That was an extraordinary sight, and it revealed with painful clarity the depths to which a subject people could fall, and how they could be made pawns in the imperialist game. It was true that the Indian people could not be said to be represented by that crowd of highnesses, lords, knights and others of high degree. The members of the Round Table Conference had been nominated by the

British Government, and, from its own point of view, the Government had chosen well. And yet the mere fact that the British authorities could use and exploit us so, showed the weakness of our people, and the strange facility with which they could be side-tracked and made to undo each other's efforts. Our upper classes were still wrapped up in the ideology of our imperialist rulers, and played their game. Was it because they did not see through it? Or did they, knowing its real significance, accept it knowingly because of their fear of democracy and freedom in India?

It was fitting that in this assembly of vested interests—imperialist, feudal, financial, industrial, religious, communal—the leadership of the British Indian delegation should usually fall to the Aga Khan, who in his own person happened to combine all these interests in some degree. Closely associated as he has been with British imperialism and the British ruling class for over a generation, residing chiefly in England, he could thoroughly appreciate and represent our rulers' interests and view-point. He would have been an able representative of Imperialist England at that Round Table Conference. The irony of it was that he was supposed to represent India.

The scales were terribly loaded against us at that Conference and, little as we expected from it, we watched its proceedings with amazement and ever-growing disgust. We saw the pitiful and absurdly inadequate attempts to scratch the surface of national and economic problems, the pacts and intrigues and manoeuvres, the joining of hands of some of our own countrymen with the most reactionary elements of the British Conservative Party, the endless talk over petty issues, the deliberate shelving of all that really mattered, the continuous playing into the hands of the big vested interests and especially British imperialism, the mutual squabbles, varied by feasting and mutual admiration. It was all jobbery— big jobs, little jobs, jobs and seats for the Hindus, for the Muslims, for the Sikhs, for the Anglo-Indians, for the Europeans; but all jobs for the upper classes, the masses had no look-in. Opportunism was rampant, and different groups seemed to prowl about like hungry wolves waiting for their prey—the spoils under the new constitution. The very conception of freedom had taken the form of large-scale jobbery— 'indianisation' it was called—more jobs for Indians in the army, in the civil services, etc. No one thought in terms of independence, of real freedom, of a transfer of power to a democratic India, of the solution of any of the vital and urgent economic problems facing the Indian people. Was it for this that India had struggled so manfully? Must we exchange this murky air for the rare atmosphere of fine idealism and sacrifice?

In that gilded and crowded hall Gandhiji sat, a very lonely figure. His dress, or absence of it, distinguished him from all others, but there was an even vaster difference between his thought and outlook and that of the well-dressed folk around him. His was an extraordinarily difficult position in that Conference, and we wondered from afar how he could tolerate it. But with amazing patience he carried on, and made attempt after attempt to find some basis of agreement. One characteristic gesture he made, which suddenly showed up how communalism really covered political reaction. He did not like many of the communal demands put forward on behalf of the Muslim delegates to the Conference; he thought, and his own Muslim Nationalist colleagues thought so, that some of these demands were a bar to freedom and democracy. But still he offered to accept the whole lot of them, without question or argument, if the Muslim delegates there joined forces with him and the Congress on the political issue, that is, on independence.

That offer was a personal offer because he could not, situated as he was, bind down the Congress. But he promised to urge Congress to agree to it, and no one who knew his position in the Congress could doubt that he would succeed in getting Congress approval. The offer, however, was not accepted, and indeed it is a little difficult to imagine the Aga Khan standing for Indian independence. This demonstrated that the real trouble was not communal, although the communal issue loomed large before the Conference. It was political reaction that barred all progress and sheltered itself behind the communal issue. By careful selection of its nominees for the Conference, the British Government had collected these reactionary elements, and by controlling the procedure, they had made the communal issue the major issue, and an issue on which no agreement was possible between the irreconcilables gathered there.

The British Government succeeded in its endeavour, and thereby demonstrated that it still has not only the physical strength to uphold its Empire, but also the cunning and statecraft to carry on the imperial tradition for a while longer. The people of India failed, although the Round Table Conference neither represented them nor was it a measure of their strength. They failed because they had no ideological background of what they were striving for, and could be easily misled and side-tracked. They failed because they did not feel themselves strong enough to discard the vested interests that encumbered their progress. They failed because of an excess of religiosity, and the ease with which communal feelings could be roused. They failed, in short, because they were not advanced enough and strong enough to succeed.

There was no question of failure or success at this Round Table Conference itself. Little was expected of it, and yet it made a difference. The previous conference, the first of its kind, had attracted very little attention in India or elsewhere for the Civil Disobedience movement absorbed attention. The nominees of the British Government who went to the Conference of 1930 often went to the accompaniment of black flags and uncomplimentary slogans. But in 1931 all was different, and it was different because Gandhiji went as the representative of the Congress, and as a leader whom millions followed. This gave prestige to the Conference, and India followed its career with far greater interest; and any failure, whatever the cause, redounded now to the discredit of India. We understood then why the British Government had attached so much importance to Gandhiji's participation in it.

The Conference itself, with all its scheming and opportunism and futile meandering, was no failure for India. It was constituted so as to fail, and the people of India could hardly be made responsible for its failing. But it succeeded in diverting world attention from real issues in India, and, in India itself, it produced disillusion and depression and a sense of humiliation. It gave a handle to reactionary forces to raise their heads again.

Success or failure was to come to the people of the country by events in India itself. The powerful nationalist movement could not fade away, because of distant manoeuvring in London. Nationalism represented a real and immediate need of the middle classes and peasantry, and by its means they sought to solve their problems. The movement could thus either succeed, fulfil its function, and give place to some other movement, which would carry the people further on the road to progress and freedom, or else it could be forcibly suppressed for the time being. That struggle was to come in India soon after, and was to result in temporary disablement. The second Round Table Conference could not affect this struggle much, but it did create an atmosphere somewhat unfavourable to it.

39

AGRARIAN TROUBLES IN THE UNITED PROVINCES

As one of the General Secretaries of the Congress and a member of the Working Committee, I was in touch with All-India politics and occasionally had to do some touring also, though I avoided this as far as possible. As our burdens and responsibilities grew, the meetings of the Working Committee became longer and longer, till they developed into a regular sessions of two weeks at a time. It was no longer a question of merely passing resolutions of criticism, but of controlling numerous different kinds of constructive activities of a vast and many-sided organization, and of tackling, from day to day, difficult problems on whose handling depended conflict or otherwise on a nation-wide scale.

My chief activities, however, lay in the United Provinces where the agrarian situation absorbed Congress attention. The U.P. Provincial Congress Committee consisted of over a hundred and fifty members, and met every two or three months. Its Executive Council, consisting of about fifteen members, met frequently and was in charge of its agrarian department.

In the second half of the year 1931, a special Agrarian Committee was appointed by this Council. It is interesting to find that several zamindars were prominently associated with the Council and this Committee throughout, and all steps were taken with their approval. Indeed, the President of our Provincial Committee for the year (and consequently the *ex-officio* head of the Executive Council and the Agrarian Committee) was Tasadduq Ahmad Khan Sherwani, who belongs to a well-known zamindari family. The General Secretary, Sri Prakasa, as well as several leading members of the Council were also zamindars, or were members of zamindari families. The remaining members were middle-class professional people. There was not a single tenant or poor peasant representative in our provincial executive. Peasants were to be found in our District Committees, but they seldom survived the various elections which ultimately resulted in the formation of the Executive Council for the province, which was a body entirely dominated by the middle-class intelligentsia with a strong zamindari leaven in it. It was thus far from being an extreme body in any sense of the word, and certainly not so on the agrarian issue.

My own position in the province was that of a member of the Executive Council and its Agrarian Committee, and nothing more. I took a prominent part in our consultations and our other work, but in no sense did I take the leading part. Indeed no one can be said to have played the leading part in our province, as we had long accustomed ourselves to corporate and joint action, stress being always laid on the organization and not on the individual. The president for the year was our temporary head, and represented us, but even he had no special authority.

I also functioned locally as a member of the Allahabad District Congress Committee. This Committee, under the leadership of its president, Purushottam Das Tandon, played an important part in the development of the agrarian situation. In 1930 it had given the lead in starting the no-tax campaign in the province. This was not because Allahabad district was the area affected most by the agricultural depression; the Taluqadari districts of Oudh were much worse off. But Allahabad district was better organized and more politically conscious, because Allahabad city was a centre of political activity and many prominent workers were frequently visiting the surrounding villages.

Immediately after the Delhi Pact of March 1931, we had hastened to send workers and notices to the rural areas, informing the peasantry that civil disobedience and the movement were off. On political grounds there was no bar to their payment of rent, and we advised them to pay. But we added that in view of the tremendous fall in prices we were of the opinion that big remissions should be given to them, and we proposed that we should jointly try to obtain these. Even in normal times the rent was often an almost unbearable burden; with the slump in prices it was impossible to make full payment or even anything approaching it. We held conferences with representatives of the peasantry and, as a tentative proposal, suggested a general remission of 50 per cent, and in some cases more than that.

We tried to separate the agrarian issue entirely from the general question of civil disobedience. We wanted, at any rate in 1931, to consider it from the economic plane only, divorced from the political. This was difficult, as the two were anyhow intimately connected, and in the past had been closely associated. We, as a Congress organization, were also definitely political. For the moment we tried to function as a kind of peasants' Union (with non-peasants and even zamindars in control!) but we could not and did not desire to give up our political character, and the Government looked upon everything we did as political. The shadow of future civil disobedience also lay ahead of us, and if this materialized there could be no doubt that economics and politics would march together, hand in hand.

In spite of all these obvious hindrances, it was our effort throughout, from the time of the Delhi Pact onwards, to keep the agrarian question apart from the political struggle. The real reason for this was that the Delhi Pact did not put an end to it, and we wanted to make this perfectly clear to the Government as well as the people. In the course of the Delhi conversations, Gandhiji had, I believe, assured Lord Irwin that even if he did not go to the Round Table Conference he would not resume civil disobedience while the Conference was sitting. He would ask the Congress to give the Conference every chance, and to await its result. But even then Gandhiji made it clear that this assurance did not apply to any local economic struggle that might be forced on us. The U.P. agrarian situation was before us all then, because organized action had been taken in U.P.; as a matter of fact the peasantry all over India had been similarly affected. During the Simla talks Gandhiji repeated this point, and mention was made of it in the published correspondence.[1]

---

1. The following letters were integral parts of the Simla Agreement of August 27, 1931:

Mr Gandhi to Mr Emerson, Secretary, Home Department, Government of India.
Simla,
August 27, 1931.
"Dear Mr Emerson,
"I have to acknowledge with thanks your letter of even date, enclosing a new draft. Sir Cowasji has also communicated to me the amendments suggested by you. My colleagues and I have carefully considered the amended draft, which we are prepared to accept, subject to the following remarks:
"In paragraph 4, it is not possible for me on behalf of the Congress to subscribe to

On the very eve of sailing for Europe, he made it clear that, quite apart from the Round Table Conference and the political issues, it might be necessary for the Congress to protect the people's, and especially the peasantry's, rights in economic struggles. He had no desire to indulge in such a struggle; he wanted to avoid it; but, if it became inevitable, it must

---

the position taken up by the Government. For we feel that where, in the opinion of the Congress, a grievance arising out of the working of the Settlement is not redressed, an inquiry is a necessity of the case, because of the fact that civil disobedience remains under suspension during the pendency of the Delhi Pact. But if the Government of India and Local Governments are not prepared to grant an inquiry, my colleagues and I have no objection to the clause remaining. The result will be that, whilst the Congress will not press for an inquiry in regard to 'the other matters hitherto raised' on its behalf, if unfortunately any grievance is so acutely felt that it becomes the paramount duty of the Congress to seek some method of relief, in the absence of an inquiry, in the shape of defensive direct action, the Congress should be held free to adopt such remedy, notwithstanding the suspension of civil disobedience.

"I need hardly assure the Government that it would be the constant endeavour of the Congress to avoid direct action and to gain relief by discussion, persuasion, and the like. The statement of the Congress position given here has become necessary in order to avoid any possible misunderstanding in the future or a charge of breach of faith on the part of the Congress. In the event of a successful issue to the present discussions, I assume that the communique, this letter, and your reply would be simultaneously published.

"Yours sincerely,

"M.K. Gandhi."

Mr Emerson to Mr Gandhi.

Simla,
August 27, 1931.

Dear Mr Gandhi,

"I write to thank you for your letter of today's date, in which you accept the draft communique, subject to the observations contained in your letter. The Governor-General-in-Council has noted that it is not the intention of the Congress to press for any inquiry into those matters hitherto raised by them, but that while you give an assurance that it will be the constant endeavour of the Congress to avoid direct action, and to gain relief by discussion, persuasion, and the like, you wish to make clear the position of the Congress in regard to any future action that they may decide to take. I am to say that the Governor-General-in-Council shares your hope that no resort to direct action will be taken. In regard to the general position of Government, I am to refer you to the letter of His Excellency the Viceroy dated August 19 to your address. I am to say that the communiqué, your letter of today's date, and this reply will be published simultaneously by Government.

"Yours sincerely,

"H.W. Emerson."

be undertaken. We could not desert the masses. His point was that the Delhi Pact, which applied to general and political civil disobedience, did not bar this.

I mention this because the charge has been repeatedly brought against the U.P. Provincial Congress Committee and its leaders that they broke the Delhi Pact by re-starting a no-tax campaign. Conveniently for its makers, this charge was brought when those who were charged and could have answered it were all locked up in gaol and every newspaper and press was strictly censored. Quite apart from the fact that the U.P. Committee never started a no-tax campaign in 1931, the point which I wish to make clear is that even such a campaign for an economic purpose, and apart from civil disobedience, would have been no breach of the Delhi Pact. Whether it was justified or not on the merits was another matter; but the peasantry were as much entitled to start it as the workers of a factory are to strike for an economic grievance. This was our position throughout from Delhi to Simla, and it was not only understood but appreciated by the Government.

The agricultural slump of 1929 and onwards came as a climax to a steadily worsening situation. For many years past world agricultural prices had tended to go up, and Indian agriculture, tacked on to the world market, had shared in this tendency. The disproportion in the development of industry and agriculture all over the world had everywhere sent up agricultural prices. As these prices went up in India, the Government revenue and the landlord's rent went up also, so that the actual cultivator hardly profited by this upward tendency. On the whole, the peasantry, except in some favoured areas, deteriorated. In the United Provinces rent went up much faster than revenue, the proportion of relative increase of these two during the first thirty years of this century being nearly (to quote from memory) five to one. Thus while the Government's income from land increased substantially, the landlord's income increased far more, and the tenant remained, as ever, at starvation level. Even where prices fell or there were local natural calamities—drought, floods, locusts, hail, etc.—the rent and revenue remained at the original figures, some remissions being granted very hesitatingly, for the season only. The level of the rents was at the best of times much too high; at other times it became unbearable without recourse to the money-lender. Agricultural debt grew.

All the agricultural classes—landlords, peasant proprietors, tenants—
became the victims of the money-lender, who fulfilled, under existing
conditions, an indispensable function in the primitive village economy.
He exploited that function very much to his own advantage, and his
stranglehold grew on the land and those connected with it. There were
few checks on him. The law helped him, and he stuck to the letter of his
bond and claimed, and received, his pound of flesh. Gradually land passed
to him both from many of the smaller landlords and the peasant
proprietors, and the money-lender blossomed out himself as a proprietor
of land on a large scale, a big zamindar, one of the landed gentry. The
peasant proprietor, who had so far cultivated his own land, now became
almost a serf of the bania-zamindar or *sahukar.* The tenant's position was
even worse. He was also a *sahukar's* serf or he joined the increasing army
of the dispossessed landless proletariat. The financier or banker who
thus developed into a landowner had no living contacts with the soil or
the tenantry. He was usually a city dweller, where he carried on his
banking business, and he delegated the collection of rent to agents who
did the work with the callousness and inhumanity of machines.

The progressive growth of agricultural indebtedness was in itself
evidence of the unsoundness and instability of the land system. The vast
majority of the population had no reserves of any kind, physical or
material, no power of resistance, and lived on the verge of starvation.
They could not stand any unusual occurrence of an unfavourable
character. An epidemic would sweep away millions. In 1929 and 1930 it
was estimated by the officially-appointed Provincial Banking Inquiry
Committee that the agricultural indebtedness of India (including Burma)
was 860 crores of rupees. This figure included the debts of landlords,
peasant proprietors and tenants, but it was mainly the debt of actual
cultivators. Government currency policy has entirely favoured the creditor
classes, and this has added to the heavy burden of the debt. Thus the
fixing of the rupee ratio at one shilling and sixpence, instead of sixteen
pence, in spite of vehement Indian opposition, meant increasing the
agricultural debt by 12.5 per cent, or by about 107 crores.[2]

---

2. The figure of Rs 860 crores for the agricultural indebtedness of India is probably a
   gross under-estimate, and, in any event, it must have gone up considerably during the
   last four or five years. The Punjab part of the figure, estimated by the Punjab Provincial

After the post-war spurt in prices there was a gradual but continuing decline, and agrarian conditions worsened. On top of this came the catastrophe of 1929 and after.

Our contention in the United Provinces in 1931 was that rents should correspond with prices; that is to say, that rent should be reduced to a figure which prevailed in the past when prices were as low as in 1931. Approximately this was so thirty years earlier, about 1901. This was a rough test and its application was not easy as there were many classes of tenants—occupancy, non-occupancy, sub-tenants, etc.—and the worst sufferers were the lowest grade of tenants. The only other test—and this was undoubtedly the fairest—was to find out the capacity of the tenant to pay after making allowances for his cost of production and living wage. But according to this latter test, however low the living expenses are kept, a very large number of holdings in India become wholly uneconomic, and, as we showed by some instances in U.P. in 1931, many could not pay any rent at all without selling property (if there was any to be sold) or borrowing money at a high rate of interest.

Our U.P. Congress Committee's first and tentative proposal was a general remission of 50 per cent, for all occupancy tenants, and a higher percentage for the other tenants who were worse off. When Gandhiji came to the U.P. in May 1931 and visited the Governor, Sir Malcolm Hailey, there was some difference of opinion between them and they could not agree. Soon afterwards he (Gandhiji) issued appeals to the zamindars and tenants of U.P. In the latter appeal he asked the tenants to pay as much as they could and suggested some figure, which was a somewhat higher figure than the one we had previously given. Our Provincial Committee accepted Gandhiji's figure, but that did not help matters much, as Government would not agree to it.

The Provincial Government was in a difficult position. The land tax was its chief source of income, and it could not permit this to vanish

Banking Inquiry Committee in 1929, was Rs 135 crores. The report of the Select Committee on the Punjab Relief from Indebtedness Bill (presented in October 1934) states that "the debt burden of the agriculturists is stupendous, being modestly estimated at Rs 200 crores." This new figure is almost 50 per cent in excess of the Banking Inquiry Committee's estimate. If this rate of increase holds good for the other provinces also, the present (1934) all-India figure for agricultural indebtedness should be over 1200 crores of rupees (a crore = ten millions).

away or reduce it very greatly without facing bankruptcy. On the other hand, it had a wholesome fear of an agrarian upheaval and wanted to soothe the tenantry, as far as it could, by substantial rent remissions. It was not easy to have it both ways. Between the State and the cultivator stood the zamindar, from the economic point of view a useless and unnecessary addition, and it might have been possible to protect and help both the State and the cultivator at his expense. But the British Government, constituted as it is, could not for political reasons alienate one of the few classes which clung on to it.

At last the Provincial Government announced the remissions both for the landlords and the tenants. These were based on some complicated system, and it was not easy at first to make out what they were. It was clear, however, that they were far from enough. Besides, they related to the current demand and said nothing at all about the arrears due from the tenant or his debts. It was obvious that if the tenant was not in a position to pay the rent for the current half-year, much less could he pay arrears for past years or old debts. As a rule, it was the landlord's custom to credit all realizations to past arrears. This procedure was dangerous from the tenant's point of view, for he could always be proceeded against and dispossessed of his land on the ground of non-payment of some part of the amount due from him.

The Provincial Congress Executive was put in an extraordinarily difficult position. We were convinced that the tenants were being treated very unfairly and yet we were helpless in the matter. We did not want to take the responsibility of advising the tenants not to pay. We went on repeating that they should pay as much as they could and generally sympathizing with them in their misfortunes and trying to hearten them. We agreed with them that the demand, even after the remissions, was too much for them.

The machinery of coercion, legal as well as illegal, began to move. Ejectment suits brought against thousands, attachments of cows, bullocks, personal property, beatings by agents of landlords. Large numbers of tenants paid part of the demand; according to them, this was as much as they could pay then. Very probably in some instances they could have paid more, but it was quite obvious that for the great majority this was a heavy burden. These part payments did not save them. The steam-roller of the law went on advancing, pitilessly crushing all that came in its way. Ejectment suits were decreed, even though part payment had taken place; attachments and sale of cattle and personal property continued. The tenants could not have been worse off if they had not paid at all. Indeed, they would have been slightly better off, for they would have saved that much money at least.

They came to us in large numbers, complaining bitterly, telling us that they had followed our advice and paid what they could, and this was the consequence. In Allahabad district alone many thousands had been dispossessed, and some proceeding or other had been launched against many thousands of others. The District Congress Committee office was surrounded all day by a distraught crowd. My own house was equally besieged, and often I felt like running away and hiding myself somewhere, anywhere, to escape this dreadful predicament. Many tenants who came to us bore marks of injury, said to have been inflicted by zamindars' agents. We had them treated in hospital. What could they do? What could we do? We sent long letters to the U.P. Government. Our Committee had appointed Govind Ballabh Pant as our liaison officer to keep in touch with the Provincial Government at Naini Tal or Lucknow. He was constantly writing to the Government. Our provincial President, Tasadduq A.K. Sherwani, also wrote from time to time, and so did I.

Another difficulty arose with the approach of the monsoon in June-July. That was the tilling and sowing season. Were the tenants, who had been dispossessed, to sit idle and watch their land lie fallow in front of them? This was very difficult for a peasant; it went against the grain. The dispossession in many cases was legal and technical and not an actual moving away. A court decree had been passed and nothing else had been done. Or were they to plough the land and thereby commit an offence of criminal trespass, perhaps leading to a petty riot? To watch others till their old land was also very difficult for the peasants to tolerate. They came to us for advice. What advice could we give?

I put this difficulty to a high official in the Government of India, when I visited Simla with Gandhiji during that summer, and I asked him what advice he would give if he was in our position. His answer was a revealing one. He said that if a peasant who had been dispossessed asked him this question he would simply refuse to answer him! Even he was not prepared to tell the peasant straight off *not* to till his land, although he had been legally dispossessed. It was easy for him, sitting on the Simla heights, to pass orders on files as if he was dealing with an abstract problem in mathematics. He, or the provincial bosses at Naini Tal, were not brought into touch with the human factor, nor did they see the human misery involved.

We were also told at Simla that we should give only one advice to the peasantry: that they should pay the full demand or as much as they could. We should in fact act almost as the agents of the landlords. As a matter of fact we had said something like it when we asked them to pay as much as they could. We had added no doubt that they should not sell up their cattle or incur additional debt. And we had seen the result.

It was a terrible summer for all of us, and the strain of it was great. The Indian peasant has an amazing capacity to bear misfortune, and he has always had more than his share of it—famine, flood, disease, and continuous grinding poverty—and when he could endure it no longer, he would quietly and almost uncomplainingly lie down in his thousands or millions and die. That was his way of escape. Nothing happened in 1931 to compare with the periodical great misfortunes that had visited him. But, somehow, the events of 1931 did not seem to him part of Nature's inscrutable plans, and, therefore, to be patiently endured; they were the work of man, he thought, and so he resented them. His new political education was bearing fruit. For us, too, these happenings of 1931 were especially painful because we held ourselves partly responsible for them. Had not the peasants largely followed our advice in the matter? And yet I am quite convinced that, but for our constant help, the condition of the peasantry would have been far worse. We held them together and they remained a force to be reckoned with, and because of this they obtained greater remissions than they otherwise would have done. Even the coercion and ill-treatment to which they were subjected, bad as it was, was not unusual for these unhappy people. The difference was partly one of degree (as there was much more of it now) and partly a question of publicity. Ordinarily, ill-treatment and even torture of a tenant by a zamindar's agent in a village is almost taken for granted, and few persons outside that area hear of it, unless the victim dies. It was different now because of our organization and the new consciousness of the peasantry which made them hang together and report all mishaps to the Congress offices.

As the summer advanced, the attempts at forcible collections toned down and coercive proceedings lessened. What troubled us now was the question of the great number of the ejected tenants. What was to be done to them? We were pressing the Government to help them to get back their holdings, which, in the majority of cases, were lying vacant. More important still was the question of the future. The remissions that had been so far granted were for the past season only, and nothing had yet been decided about the future. From October onwards the season for the next collections would begin. What would happen then? Would we have to go through the same terrible round again? The Provincial Government appointed a small committee, consisting of its own officials and some zamindar members of the local Council, to consider this. There was no representative of the peasantry on it. At the last moment, when the Committee had actually begun its work, Govind Ballabh Pant was asked by Government to join it on our behalf. He did not think it worthwhile to join at that late stage, when important decisions had already been made.

The U.P. Provincial Congress Committee had also appointed a small committee to collect various agrarian data, past and present, and to report on the existing situation. This committee submitted a long report containing an able survey of agrarian conditions in the U.P. and an analysis of the havoc caused by the agricultural slump in prices. Their recommendations were far-reaching. The report, which was published in book form, was signed by Govind Ballabh Pant, Rafi Ahmad Kidwai, and Venkatesh Narayan Tewary.

Long before this report came out, Gandhiji had gone to London for the Round Table Conference. He had gone with great hesitation, and one of the reasons for this hesitation was the U.P. agrarian situation. He had in fact almost decided that, in the event of not going to London for the Round Table Conference, he would come to U.P. and devote himself to this complex problem. The last Simla conversations with the Government dealt, *inter alia*, with U.P. After his departure for England we kept him fully informed of developments. I used to write to him, during the first month or two, every week both by the air mail and the ordinary mail. During the latter part of his stay I was not so regular, as we expected him to return soon. He had given us to understand that, at the very latest, he would be back within three months, that is, some time in November, and we had hoped that no crisis would arise in India till then. Above all, we wanted to avoid crises and conflicts with Government in his absence. When, however, his return was delayed and the agrarian situation began to develop rapidly, we sent him a long cablegram informing him of the latest developments and pointing out to him how our hands were being forced. He replied by cable that he was helpless in the matter and could not do anything for us then, and told us to go ahead according to our lights.

The Working Committee was also kept fully informed by the Provincial Congress Executive. I was always there to give them first-hand information, but, as matters were taking a serious turn, the Committee also conferred with our Provincial President, Tasadduq Sherwani, and the Allahabad District President, Purushottam Das Tandon.

The Government Agrarian Committee issued its report and made certain recommendations, which were both complicated and vague, and left a great deal to local officers. On the whole, the proposed remissions were bigger than in the past season, but we felt that they were not enough. We objected to the principles underlying the recommendations as well as to their application. Also, the report dealt with the future only and ignored past arrears, debt, and the question of the large number of dispossessed tenants. What were we to do? Just advise the peasantry to pay as much as they could, as we had done in the spring and summer, and face the same consequences? That advice, we had seen, was the most foolish of all and could not be repeated. Either the peasants should make a great effort and pay the revised demand in full, if they could at all do so, or they should not pay at all for the present and await developments. To pay part of the rent demanded was neither here nor there; the tenants exhausted their financial resources and, at the same time, lost their land.

Our Provincial Congress Executive considered the position long and earnestly and decided that the Government proposals were not favourable enough to be accepted as they were, although they were an improvement on the summer's remissions. There was still a possibility of their being varied to the peasantry's advantage, and we pressed Government accordingly. But we felt that there was little hope, and the conflict we had tried to avoid seemed to approach with some rapidity. The attitude of the Provincial Government as well as the Government of India towards the Congress organization had been progressively changing and becoming more frigid. To our long letters we received brief replies referring us to local officials. It was obvious that the policy of Government was not to encourage us in any way. One grievance and difficulty of the Government was the possibility of Congress prestige going up because of the grant of remissions to the peasantry. Through long habit, it could only think in terms of prestige, and the idea that the masses might give the credit for the remissions to the Congress irritated it, and it wanted to avoid this as far as possible.

Meanwhile, reports were coming to us from Delhi and elsewhere that the Government of India were on the point of launching a big offensive against the whole Congress movement. The little finger was going to function more vigorously now and the scorpions were going to chastise us. We even received many details of the proposed action. Some time in November, I think, Dr Ansari sent me (as well as separately to Vallabhbhai Patel, the Congress President) a message confirming many of the previous reports received by us, and especially giving details of the proposed ordinances for the Frontier and the United Provinces. Bengal had, I believe, already received the gift of a new ordinance or, perhaps, was about to receive it. Dr Ansari's message was amply confirmed even in its details many weeks later, when the new ordinances appeared as if to meet a new situation. It was generally supposed that Government had delayed action because of the unforeseen prolongation of the Round Table Conference. They wished to avoid wholesale repression in India while the members of the Round Table Conference whispered sweet nothings into each other's ears.

So tension grew, and all of us had a feeling that events were marching ahead despite our little selves, and none could stop them from their predestined course. All we could do was to prepare ourselves to face them and to play our parts, individually and together, in the drama— more likely the tragedy—of life. But we hoped still that Gandhiji would be back before the curtain went up on this clash of forces, and would take the responsibility on his shoulders for peace or war. None of us was prepared to shoulder that burden in his absence.

In the United Provinces, the Government took another step which produced a commotion in the rural areas. Remission slips were distributed to the tenants, stating how much remission had been allowed, and containing a threat that unless the amount now due was paid up within

a month (sometimes the period mentioned was shorter), the remission
would be cancelled and the full sum realized by legal process, which
meant ejectment, attachment of property, etc. In normal years the tenants
usually paid up their rent in instalments in the course of two or three
months. Even this usual period was thus not allowed. The whole
countryside was suddenly faced by a crisis, and, slip in hand, the tenants
rushed about protesting and complaining and asking for advice. It was a
very foolish threat on the part of the Government or their local officials,
and it was not, we were told later, meant seriously. But it lessened the
chances of a peaceful settlement very greatly and led inevitably, step by
step, to conflict.

The choice had to be made very soon now by the peasants and by
the Congress; we could not postpone our decision till Gandhiji's return.
What were we to do? What advice to give? Could we reasonably ask the
peasants to pay up the sum demanded within the short period allowed
when we knew that many of them could not possibly do so? And then
what of the arrears due from them? Would they not run the risk of
dispossession even if they paid a large part of the sum demanded, or
even, the full current demand, which might be credited to arrears?

The Allahabad District Congress Committee, with its strong peasant
contingent, showed fight. It decided that it could not possibly advise the
peasants to pay. It was told, however, that it could not take any aggressive
step without the formal permission of the Provincial Executive as well
as of the All-India Working Committee. The matter was, therefore, referred
to the Working Committee, and both Tasadduq Sherwani and Purushottam Das Tandon were present to place the case for the province and
the district. The question before us related to Allahabad district only and
it was a purely economic issue, but we realized that, in the state of
political tension then existing, it might have far-reaching consequences.
Should the Allahabad District Committee be permitted to advise the
peasants in the district to withhold payment of rent or revenue for the
time being and pending further negotiation and better terms? This was
the narrow issue and we wanted to confine ourselves to it, but could we
do so? The Working Committee wanted to strain every nerve to prevent
a break with Government before Gandhiji's return, and, in particular, it
wanted to avoid a break on an economic issue which might develop
into a class issue. The Committee, though politically advanced, was not

so socially, and it disliked the raising of the tenant *versus* zamindar question. Being socialistically inclined, I was not considered a very safe person to advise on economic and social matters. I myself felt that the Working Committee should realize that the U.P. situation was such that even our more moderate and right wing members were being forced by events to take action, in spite of all their disinclination for it. I welcomed, therefore, the presence of Sherwani and others from our province at our Committee meeting, for Sherwani (our Provincial President) was by no means a fire-brand. Constitutionally he was a right winger in the Congress, both politically and socially, and, at the beginning of the year, he had been prejudiced against the agrarian policy of the U.P. Congress Committee. But when he became the head of that Committee himself and had to shoulder the burden, he realized that there was no other alternative for us. Every subsequent step taken by the Provincial Committee was in the closest co-operation with him and, indeed, often through him, as President.

Tasadduq Sherwani's pleading before the Working Committee, therefore, produced great effect on the members—a much greater effect than mine would have done. With great hesitation, but feeling that they could not refuse it, they gave the U.P. Committee authority to permit in any area the suspension of payment of rent and revenue. But, at the same time, they pressed the U.P. people to avoid this step if they could and to carry on negotiations with the Provincial Government.

These negotiations were carried on for a while with little result. Some improvement was made, I believe, in the Allahabad district figures for remissions. It might have been possible, under ordinary circumstances, to arrive at a settlement or at least to avoid open conflict. The differences were being narrowed down. But the circumstances were very unusual, and on both sides—the Government and the Congress—there was the feeling of the inevitability of an approaching conflict, and there was no reality behind our negotiations. Every step taken by either party seemed to indicate a desire to manoeuvre for a position. The Government's preparations for this could be and were in fact carried on and perfected in secret. Our strength lay entirely in the morale of the people, and this could not be prepared or raised by secret activities. Some of us—and I was one of the guilty ones—had often repeated in our public speeches that the struggle for freedom was far from over, and that we would have to face many trials and difficulties in the near future. We had asked our people to keep themselves in readiness for them, and because of this we had been criticized as war-mongers. As a matter of fact, there was a marked reluctance on the part of our middle class Congress workers to face facts, and they hoped that somehow or other a conflict would be avoided. Gandhiji's presence in London also distracted the attention of the newspaper-reading classes. And yet in spite of this passivity of the intelligentsia, events marched ahead, especially in Bengal, the Frontier Province and U.P., and in November it began to dawn on many people that a crisis was approaching.

The U.P. Provincial Congress Committee, afraid of being forestalled by events, made some domestic arrangements in the event of conflict taking place. The Allahabad Committee held a big Peasant Conference, which passed a tentative resolution stating that, in case better terms were not obtained, they would have to advise the peasants to withhold payment of rent and revenue. This resolution irritated the Provincial Government greatly, and, treating it as a *casus belli*, it refused to have any further dealings with us. That attitude again produced its reactions on the Provincial Congress, which interpreted it as a sign of the coming storm and hastened its own preparations. In Allahabad there was yet another Peasant Conference, when a stronger and more definite resolution asking the peasantry to withhold payment pending further negotiations and better terms, was passed. The attitude taken up even then, and to the end, was not one of a 'no-rent' campaign but a 'fair-rent' campaign, and we went on asking for negotiations, though the other party had ostentatiously walked away. The Allahabad resolution applied to zamindar and tenant alike, but we knew that in effect it applied to tenants and some petty zamindars only.

This was the position in U.P. towards the end of November and the beginning of December 1931. Meanwhile in Bengal and the Frontier Province matters had also marched to a head, and in Bengal a new and terribly comprehensive ordinance had been applied. All these were signs of war, not of peace, and the question arose: when would Gandhiji return? Would he reach India before the Government started its great offensive, for which it had prepared so long? Or would he return to find many of his colleagues in prison and the struggle launched? We learnt that he was on his way back and would reach Bombay in the last week of the year. Each one of us, every prominent worker in the Congress at headquarters or in the provinces, wanted to avoid that struggle till his return. Even from the point of view of the struggle itself it was desirable for us to meet him, to have his advice and his directions. It was a race in which we were helpless. The initiative lay with the British Government.

40

THE END OF THE TRUCE

In spite of my preoccupation in the United Provinces, I had long been anxious to visit the two other storm centres, the Frontier Province and Bengal. I wanted to study the situation on the spot and to meet old colleagues, many of whom I had not seen for nearly two years. But, above all, I wanted to pay my homage to the spirit and courage of the people of these provinces and their sacrifices in the national struggle. The Frontier Province was beyond reach for the time being, for the Government of India did not approve of any prominent Congressman visiting it, and we had no desire to go in view of this disapproval, and thus create an impasse.

In Bengal the situation was deteriorating and, much as I was attracted to the province, I hesitated before going. I realized that I would be helpless there and could do little good. A deplorable and long-standing dispute between two groups of Congressmen in the province had long frightened outside Congressmen and kept them away, for they were afraid of getting involved in it on one side or the other. This was a feeble and ostrich-like policy, and did not help either in soothing Bengal or in solving her problems. Some time after Gandhiji had gone to London two incidents suddenly concentrated all-India attention on the situation in Bengal. These two took place in Hijli and Chittagong.

Hijli was a special detention camp gaol for detenus. It was officially announced that a riot had taken place inside the camp, the detenus had attacked the staff, and the latter had been forced to fire on them. One detenu was killed by this firing and many were wounded. A local official enquiry, held immediately after, absolved the staff from all blame for this firing and its consequences. But there were many curious features, and some facts leaked out which did not fit in with the official version, and vehement demands were made for a fuller enquiry. Contrary to the usual official practice in India, the Government of Bengal appointed an Enquiry Committee consisting of high judicial officers. It was a purely official committee, but it took evidence and considered the matter fully, and its findings were against the staff of the Detention Camp Gaol. It was held that the fault was largely that of the staff, and the firing was unjustified. The previous Government communiqués issued on the subject were thus entirely falsified.

There was nothing very extraordinary about the Hijli occurrence. Unhappily such incidents or accidents are not rare in India, and one frequently reads of 'gaol riots' and of the gallant suppression of unarmed and helpless prisoners within the gaol by armed warders and others. Hijli was unusual in so far as it exposed, and exposed officially, the utter one-sided-ness, and even the falsity of Government communiqués on such occurrences. Little credence had been attached to these communiqués in the past, but now they were completely found out.

Since the Hijli affair a large number of gaol 'occurrences' involving sometimes firing, sometimes the use of other kinds of force by the staff, have taken place all over India. Strangely enough in these 'gaol riots' only the prisoners seem to get hurt. Almost invariably an official communiqué has been issued accusing the prisoners of various misdeeds and absolving the staff. Very rarely some departmental punishments have been awarded to the staff. All demands for a full enquiry have been curtly refused, a departmental enquiry being deemed sufficient. Evidently the lesson of Hijli was well learnt by Government, that it is unsafe to have proper and impartial enquiries, and the best judge is the accuser himself. Is it surprising that the people also should learn the lesson of Hijli, that Government communiqués tell us what the Government wants them to believe and not what actually happens?

The Chittagong affair was much more serious. A terrorist shot down and killed a Muslim police inspector. This was followed by a Hindu-Muslim riot, or so it was called. It was patent, however, that it was something much more than that; something different from the usual communal riot. It was obvious that the terrorist's act had nothing to do with communalism; it was directed against a police officer, regardless of whether he was a Hindu or Muslim. Yet it is true that there was some Hindu-Muslim rioting afterwards. How this started, what was the occasion for it, has not been cleared up, although very serious charges have been made by responsible public men. Another feature of the rioting was the part taken by definite groups of other people, Anglo-Indians, chiefly railway employees, and other Government employees, who are alleged to have indulged in reprisals on a large scale. J.M. Sen-Gupta and other noted leaders of Bengal made specific allegations in regard to the occurrences in Chittagong, and challenged an enquiry or even a suit for defamation, but the Government preferred to take no such step.

These somewhat unusual occurrences in Chittagong drew pointed attention to two dangerous possibilities. Terrorism had been condemned from many points of view; even modern revolutionary technique condemned it. But one of its possible consequences had always especially frightened me, and that was the danger of sporadic and communal violence spreading in India. I am not enough of a 'timid Hindu' to be afraid of violence as such, although I certainly dislike it. But I do feel that the disruptive forces in India are still very great, and sporadic violence would certainly give them strength and make the process of building up a united and disciplined nation a much harder task than it is. When people murder in the name of religion, or to reserve a place for themselves in Paradise, it is a dangerous thing to accustom them to the idea of terroristic violence. Political murder is bad. And yet the political terrorist can be reasoned with and won over to other ways, because presumably the end he is striving for is an earthly one, not personal but national. Religious murder is worse, for it deals with things of the other world, and one cannot even attempt to reason about such matters. Sometimes the dividing line between the two is very thin and almost disappears, and political murder, by a metaphysical process, becomes semi-religious.

The Chittagong murder of a police official by a terrorist, and its consequences, made one realize very vividly the dangerous possibilities of terroristic activity and the enormous harm it might do to the cause of Indian unity and freedom. The reprisals that followed also showed us that fascist methods had appeared in India. Since then there have been many instances, notably in Bengal, of such reprisals, and the fascist spirit has undoubtedly spread in the European and Anglo-Indian community. Some of the Indian hangers-on of British imperialism have also imbibed it.

It is a curious thing, but the Terrorists themselves, or many of them, also have this fascist outlook, but it looks in a different direction. Their nationalist-fascism faces the imperialist-fascism of the Europeans, Anglo-Indians, and some upper class Indians.

I went to Calcutta for a few days in November 1931. I had a very crowded programme, and, apart from meeting individuals and groups privately, addressed a number of mass meetings. In all these meetings I discussed the question of terrorism, and tried to show how wrong and futile and harmful it was for Indian freedom. I did not abuse the Terrorists, nor did I call them 'dastardly' or 'cowardly', after the fashion of some of our countrymen who have themselves seldom, if ever, yielded to the temptation of doing anything brave or involving risk. It has always seemed to me a singularly stupid thing to call a man or woman, who is constantly risking his life, a coward. And the reaction of it on that man is to make him a little more contemptuous of his timid critics who shout from a distance and are incapable of doing anything.

On my last evening in Calcutta, a little before I was due to go to the station for my departure, two young men called on me. They were very young, about twenty, with pale, nervous faces and brilliant eyes. I did not know who they were, but soon I guessed their errand. They were very angry with me for my propaganda against terroristic violence. They said that it was producing a bad effect on young men, and they could not tolerate my intrusion in this way. We had a little argument; it was a hurried one, for the time for my departure was at hand. I am afraid our voices and our tempers rose, and I told them some hard things; and as I left them, they warned me finally that if I continued to misbehave in the future they would deal with me as they had dealt with others.

And so I left Calcutta, and as I lay in my berth in the train that night I was long haunted by the excited faces of these two boys. Full of life and nervous energy they were; what good material if only they turned the right way! I was sorry that I had dealt with them hurriedly and rather brusquely, and wished I had had the chance of long conversation with them. Perhaps I could have convinced them to apply their bright young lives to other ways, ways of serving India and freedom, in which there was no lack of opportunity for daring and self-sacrifice. Often I have thought of them in these after years. I never found out their names, nor did I have any other trace of them; and I wonder, sometimes, if they are dead or in some cell in the Andaman Islands.

It was December. The second Peasant Conference took place in Allahabad, and then I hurried south to Karnataka to fulfil a long promise made to my old comrade of the Hindustani Seva Dal, Doctor N.S.

Hardiker. The Seva Dal, the volunteer wing of the national movement, had all along been an auxiliary of the Congress, though its organization was quite separate. In the summer of 1931, however, the Working Committee decided to absorb it completely into the Congress organization, and to make it the Volunteer Department of the Congress. This was done, and Hardiker and I were put in charge of it. The headquarters of the Dal continued in the Karnataka province at Hubli, and Hardiker induced me to visit the place for various functions connected with the Dal. He then took me about on tour for a few days in Karnataka, and I was amazed at the tremendous enthusiasm of the people everywhere. On my way back I visited Sholapur of Martial Law fame.

That tour in Karnataka assumed the character of a farewell performance for me; my speeches became swan-songs, though they were rather aggressive and, I am afraid, not musical. News from U.P. was definite and clear, the Government had struck, and struck hard. On my way to Karnataka from Allahabad I had gone to Bombay with Kamala. She was again ill, and I arranged for her treatment in Bombay. It was in Bombay, almost immediately after our arrival from Allahabad, that we learnt that the Government of India had promulgated a special Ordinance for the United Provinces. They had decided not to wait for Gandhiji's arrival, although he was already on the high seas, and was due in Bombay soon. The Ordinance was supposed to deal with the agrarian agitation, but it was so extraordinarily wide-flung and far-reaching that it made all political or public activity impossible. It provided even for the punishment of parents and guardians for the sins of their children and wards—a reversal of the old Biblical practice.

It was about this time that we read the report of the interview alleged to have been given by Gandhiji in Rome to the *Giornale d'Italia*. This came as a surprise, as it was unlike him to give an interview of this kind casually in Rome. On closer examination we found many words and phrases in it which were quite foreign to him, and it was patent to us, even before the denial came, that the interview could not have been given as published. We thought that there had been a great deal of distortion of something that he had said. Then came his emphatic contradiction of it, and his statement that he had never given any interview at all in Rome. It was evident to us that some one had played a trick on him. But to our amazement British newspapers and public men refused to believe him, and contemptuously referred to him as a liar. This hurt and angered.

I was eager to go back to Allahabad and to give up the Karnataka tour. I felt that my place was with my comrades in U.P. and to be far away when so much was happening at home was an ordeal. I decided, however, in favour of adhering to the Karnataka programme. On my return to Bombay some friends advised me to stay on for Gandhiji's arrival, which was due exactly a week later. But this was impossible. From Allahabad came news of Purushottam Das Tandon's arrest and other arrests. There was, besides, our Provincial Conference which had been fixed at Etawah for that week. And so I decided to go to Allahabad and to return to Bombay six days later, if I was free, to meet Gandhiji and to attend a meeting of the Working Committee. I left Kamala bed-ridden in Bombay.

Even before I had reached Allahabad, at Chheoki station, an order under the new Ordinance was served on me. At Allahabad station another attempt was made to serve a duplicate of that order on me; at my house a third attempt was made by a third person. Evidently no risks were being taken. The order interned me within the municipal limits of Allahabad, and I was told that I must not attend any public meeting or function, or speak in public, or write anything in a newspaper or leaflet. There were many other restrictions. I found that a similar order had been served on many of my colleagues, including Tasadduq Sherwani. The next morning I wrote to the District Magistrate (who had issued the order) acknowledging receipt of it and informing him that I did not propose to take my orders from him as to what I was to do or not to do. I would carry on with my ordinary work in the ordinary way, and in the course of this work I proposed to return to Bombay soon to meet Mr Gandhi, and take part in the meeting of the Working Committee, of which I was the secretary.

A new problem confronted us. Our U.P. Provincial Conference had been fixed to meet at Etawah that week. I had come from Bombay with the intention of suggesting a postponement, as it clashed somewhat with Gandhiji's arrival, and in order to avoid conflict with the Government. But before my return to Allahabad a peremptory message had come from the U.P. Government to our President, Sherwani, enquiring if our conference would consider the agrarian question, for if so, they would prohibit the conference itself. It was patent that the main purpose of the conference was to discuss the agrarian question which was agitating the whole province; to meet and not to discuss it would be the height of absurdity and self-stultification. And in any event our President or anyone else had no authority to tie down the conference. Quite apart from the Government's threat it was the intention of some of us to postpone the conference, but this threat made a difference. Many of us were rather obstinate in such matters, and the idea of being dictated to by Government was not pleasant. After long argument we decided to swallow our pride and to postpone the conference. We did so because almost at any cost we wanted still to avoid the development of the conflict, which had already begun, till Gandhiji's arrival. We did not want him to be confronted with a situation in which he was powerless to take the helm. In spite of our postponement of our Provincial Conference there was a great display of the police and military at Etawah, some stray delegates were arrested, and the Swadeshi Exhibition there was seized by the military.

Sherwani and I decided to leave Allahabad for Bombay on the morning of December 26th. Sherwani had been especially invited to the Working Committee meeting to confer on the U.P. situation. Both of us had been served with orders under the Ordinance not to leave Allahabad city. The Ordinance was said to be directed against the suspension of rent activities in the rural areas of Allahabad and some other U.P. districts. It was easy to understand that the Government should prevent us from visiting these rural areas. But it was obvious that we could not carry on this agrarian agitation in the city of Bombay; and the Ordinance, if it was really meant for the agrarian situation only, should have welcomed our departure from the province. Ever since the promulgation of the Ordinance our general policy had been a defensive one, and we had avoided coming to grips with it, although there had been individual cases of disobedience of orders. So far as the U.P. Congress was concerned, it was clear that they wanted to avoid or postpone conflict with the Government for the present at least. Sherwani and I were going to Bombay where Gandhiji and the Working Committee would consider these matters, and no one knew—certainly I was by no means sure—what their ultimate decisions might be.

All these considerations made me think that we would be permitted to go to Bombay, and the technical breach of the order of internment would, for the moment at least, be tolerated by Government. And yet in my bones I felt otherwise.

As we got into the train we read in the morning's papers of the new Frontier Province Ordinance and the arrest of Abdul Ghaffar Khan and Doctor Khan Sahib and others. Very soon our train, the Bombay Mail, came to a sudden halt at a wayside station, Iradatganj, which is not one of its usual stopping places, and police officials mounted up to arrest us. A Black Maria waited by the railway line, and Sherwani and I mounted this closed prisoners' van and were bumped away to Naini. The Superintendent of Police, an Englishman, who had arrested us on that morning of Boxing Day looked glum and unhappy. I am afraid we had spoiled his Christmas.

And so to prison!

Absent thee from felicity a while,
And for a season draw thy breath in pain.

41

ARRESTS, ORDINANCES, PROSCRIPTIONS

Two days after our arrest Gandhiji landed in Bombay, and it was only then that he learnt of the latest developments. He had heard in London of the Bengal Ordinance, and had been much upset by it. He now found that fresh Christmas gifts awaited him in the shape of the U.P. and Frontier Ordinances, and some of his closest colleagues in the Frontier Province and U.P. had been arrested. The die seemed to be cast and all hope of peace gone, but still he made an effort to find a way out, and sought an interview with the Viceroy, Lord Willingdon, for the purpose. The interview, he was informed from New Delhi, could only take place on certain conditions—these conditions being that he must not discuss recent events in Bengal, U.P. and the Frontier, the new Ordinances, and the arrests under them. (I write from memory, and have not got the text of the Viceregal reply before me.) What exactly Gandhiji or any Congress leader was officially supposed to discuss with the Viceroy, apart from these forbidden subjects which were agitating the country, passes one's comprehension. It was absolutely clear now that the Government of India had determined to crush the Congress, and would have no dealings with it. The Working Committee had no choice left but to resort to civil disobedience. They expected arrest at any moment, and they wanted to give a lead to the country before their enforced departure. Even so, the civil disobedience resolution was passed tentatively, and another attempt was made by Gandhiji to see the Viceroy, and he sent him a second telegram asking for an unconditional interview. The reply of the Government was to arrest Gandhiji as well as the Congress President, and to press the button which was to let loose fierce repression all over the country. It was clear that whoever else wanted or did not want the struggle, the Government was eager and over-ready for it.

We were in gaol, of course, and all this news came to us vaguely and disjointedly. Our trial was postponed to the New Year, and so we had, as under-trials, more interviews than a convict could have. We heard of the great discussion that was going on as to whether the Viceroy should or should not have agreed to the interview, as if it really mattered either way. This question of the interview shadowed all other matters. It was stated that Lord Irwin would have agreed to the interview, and if he and Gandhiji had met all would have been well. I was surprised at the extraordinarily superficial view that the Indian Press took of the situation and how they ignored realities. Was the inevitable struggle between Indian Nationalism and British Imperialism—in the final analysis, two irreconcilables—to be reduced to the personal whims of individuals? Could the conflict of two historical forces be removed by smiles and mutual courtesy? Gandhiji was driven to act in one way, because Indian Nationalism could not commit *hara-kiri* or submit willingly to foreign dictation in vital matters; the British Viceroy of India had to act in a particular way to meet the challenge of this Nationalism and to endeavour to protect British interest, and it made not the slightest difference who the Viceroy was at the time. Lord Irwin would have acted exactly as Lord Willingdon did, for either of them was but the instrument of British imperialist policy and could only make some minor deviations from the line laid down. Lord Irwin, indeed, was subsequently a member of the British Government, and he associated himself fully with the official steps taken in India. To praise or condemn individual Viceroys for British policy in India seems to me a singularly inept thing to do, and our habit of indulging in this pastime can only be due to an ignorance of the real issues or to a deliberate evasion of them.

January 4th, 1932, was a notable day. It put a stop to argument and discussion. Early that morning Gandhiji and the Congress President, Vallabhbhai Patel, were arrested and confined without trial as State prisoners. Four new ordinances were promulgated giving the most far-reaching powers to magistrates and police officers. Civil liberty ceased to exist, and both person and property could be seized by the authorities. It was a declaration of a kind of state of siege for the whole of India, the extent and intensity of application being left to the discretion of the local authorities.[1]

On that 4th of January also our trial took place in Naini Prison under the U.P. Emergency Powers Ordinance, as it was called. Sherwani was sentenced to six months' rigorous imprisonment and a fine of Rs 150; I was sentenced to two years' rigorous imprisonment and a fine of Rs 500 (in default six months more). Our offences were identical; we had been served with identical orders of internment in Allahabad city; we had committed the same breach of them by attempting to go together to Bombay; we had been arrested and tried together under the same section, and yet our sentences were very dissimilar. There was, however, one difference: I had written to the District Magistrate and informed him of my intention to go to Bombay in defiance of the order; Sherwani had given no such formal notice, but his proposed departure was equally well known, and had been mentioned in the Press. Immediately after the sentence Sherwani asked the trying magistrate, to the amusement of those present and the embarrassment of the magistrate, if his smaller sentence was due to communal considerations.

Quite a lot happened on that fateful day, January 4th, all over the country. Not far from where we were, in Allahabad city, huge crowds came in conflict with the police and military, and there were the usual *lathi* charges involving deaths and other casualties. The gaols began to fill with civil disobedience prisoners. To begin with, these prisoners went to the district gaols, and Naini and the other great central prisons received only the overflows. Later, all the gaols filled up, and huge temporary camp gaols were established.

Very few came to our little enclosure in Naini. My old companion, Narmada Prasad, joined us, and Ranjit Pandit and my cousin, Mohanlal Nehru. A surprising addition to our little brotherhood of Barrack No. 6 was Bernard Aluvihare, a young friend from Ceylon, who had just returned from England after being called to the Bar. He had been told by my sister not to get mixed up with our demonstrations; but, in a moment of enthusiasm, he joined a Congress procession—and a Black Maria carried him to prison.

---

1. Sir Samuel Hoare, Secretary of State for India, stated in the House of Commons on March 24, 1932: "I admit that the Ordinances that we have approved are very drastic and severe. They cover almost every activity of Indian life."

The Congress had been declared illegal—the Working Committee at the top, the Provincial Committees, and innumerable local committees. Together with the Congress all manner of allied or sympathetic or advanced organizations had been declared unlawful—kisan sabhas and peasant unions, youth leagues, students' associations, advanced political organizations, national universities and schools, hospitals, swadeshi concerns, libraries. The lists were indeed formidable, and contained many hundreds of names for each major province. The all-India total must have run into several thousands, and this very number of outlawed organizations was in itself a tribute to the Congress and the National Movement.

My wife lay in Bombay, ill in bed, fretting at her inability to take part in civil disobedience. My mother and both my sisters threw themselves into the movement with vigour, and soon both the sisters were in gaol with a sentence of a year each. Odd bits of news used to reach us through newcomers to prison or through the local weekly paper that we were permitted to read. We could only guess much that was happening, for the press censorship was strict, and the prospect of heavy penalties always faced newspapers and news agencies. In some provinces it was an offence even to mention the name of a person arrested or sentenced.

So we sat in Naini Prison cut off from the strife outside, and yet wrapped up in it in a hundred ways; busying ourselves with spinning or reading or other activities, talking sometimes of other matters, but thinking always of what was happening beyond the prison walls. We were out of it, and yet in it. Sometimes the strain of expectation was very great; or there was anger at something wrongly done; disgust at weakness or vulgarity. At other times we were strangely detached, and could view the scene calmly and dispassionately, and feel that petty individual errors or weaknesses mattered little when vast forces were at play and the mills of the gods were grinding. We would wonder what the morrow would bring of strife and tumult, and gallant enthusiasm and cruel repression and hateful cowardice—and what was all this leading to? Whither were we going? The future was hid from us, and it was as well that it was hidden; even the present was partly covered by a veil, so far as we were concerned. But this we knew: that there was strife and suffering and sacrifice in the present and on the morrow.

Men will renew the battle in the plain
To-morrow; red with blood will Xanthus be;
Hector and Ajax will be there again;
Helen will come upon the wall to see.

Then we shall rust in shade, or shine in strife,
And fluctuate 'tween blind hopes and blind despairs.
And fancy that we put forth all our life,
And never know how with the soul it fares.[2]

2. Matthew Arnold.

42

BALLYHOO

Those early months of 1932 were remarkable, among other things, for an extraordinary exhibition of ballyhoo on the part of the British authorities. Officials, high and low, shouted out how virtuous and peaceful they were, and how sinful and pugnacious was the Congress. They stood for democracy while the Congress favoured dictatorships. Was not its President called a dictator? In their enthusiasm for a righteous cause they forgot trifles like Ordinances, and suppression of all liberties, and muzzling of newspapers and presses, imprisonment of people without trial, seizure of properties and monies, and the many other odd things that were happening from day to day. They forgot also the basic character of British rule in India. Ministers of Government (our own countrymen) grew eloquent on how Congressmen were 'grinding their axes'—in prison—while they laboured for the public good on paltry salaries of a few thousand rupees per month. The lower magistracy not only sentenced us to heavy terms but lectured to us in the process, and sometimes abused the Congress and individuals connected with it. Even Sir Samuel Hoare, from the serene dignity of his high office as Secretary of State for India, announced that though dogs barked the caravan moved on. He forgot for the moment that the dogs were in gaol and could not easily bark there, and those left outside were effectively muzzled.

Most surprising of all, the Cawnpore Communal Riots were laid at the door of the Congress. The horrors of these truly horrible riots were laid bare, and it was repeatedly stated that the Congress was responsible for them. As it happened, the Congress had played the only decent part in them, and one of its noblest sons lay dead, mourned by every group and community in Cawnpore. The Karachi session of the Congress, immediately on hearing of the riots, appointed an Enquiry Committee, and this Committee made a most exhaustive enquiry. After many months of labour, it issued a voluminous report, which was promptly proscribed by the Government, and printed copies were seized and, I suppose, destroyed. This attempt to suppress the results of an enquiry has not prevented our official critics and the British-owned Press from repeating from time to time that the riots were due to Congress work. No doubt, in this and other matters, the truth will prevail in the end, but sometimes the lie has a long start.

> When all its work is done, the lie shall rot;
> The truth is great and shall prevail,
> When none cares whether it prevails or not.

It was all very natural, I suppose, this exhibition of a hysterical war mentality, and no one could expect truth or restraint under the circumstances. But it did seem to go beyond expectation, and was surprising in its intensity and abandon. It was some indication of the state of nerves of the ruling group in India, and of how they had been repressing themselves in the past. Probably the anger was not caused by anything we had done or said, but by the realization of their own previous fear of losing their empire. Rulers who are confident of their own strength do not give way in this manner. The contrast between this picture and the other was very marked. For on the other side silence reigned, not the silence of voluntary and dignified restraint, but the silence of prison and of fear and an all-pervasive censorship. But for this enforced gagging, no doubt the other side would have also excelled in hysterical outbursts and exaggeration and abuse. One outlet, however, there was— unauthorized news sheets which were issued in various towns from time to time.

The British-owned Anglo-Indian newspapers in India joined in this game of ballyhoo with gusto, and gave utterance and publicity to many a thought which perhaps they had nurtured and repressed in secret for long. Ordinarily they have to be a little careful of what they say, for many of their readers are Indians, but the crisis in India swept away these restraints and gave us a glimpse of the minds of all, English and Indian alike. There are few Anglo-Indian newspapers left in India; one by one they have dropped out. Several of those that remain are high-class journals, both in the news they supply and their general get-up. Their leading articles on world affairs, though always representing the conservative view-point, are able and show knowledge and grasp.

Undoubtedly as newspapers they are probably the best in India. But on Indian political problems there is a sudden fall, and their treatment of them is amazingly one-sided; and, in times of crisis, this partiality often becomes hysteria and vulgarity. They represent faithfully the Government of India, and the continuous propaganda they do for it has not the merit of being unobtrusive.

Compared to these selected few Anglo-Indian newspapers, the Indian newspapers are usually poor stuff. Their financial resources are limited, and there is little attempt on the part of their owners to improve them. They carry on their day-to-day life with difficulty, and the unhappy editorial staff has no easy time. Their get-up is poor, their advertisements often of the most objectionable kind, and their general attitude to life and politics sentimental and hysterical. Partly, I suppose, this is due to the fact that we are a sentimental race; partly because the medium (of the English newspapers) is a foreign tongue and it is not easy to write simply and, at the same time, forcefully. But the real reason is that all of us suffer from any number of complexes due to long depression and subjection, and every outlet is apt to be surcharged with emotion.

Among the Indian-owned English newspapers, *The Hindu* of Madras is probably the best, so far as get-up and news service are concerned. It always reminds me of an old maiden lady, very prim and proper, who is shocked if a naughty word is used in her presence. It is eminently the paper of the *bourgeois*, comfortably settled in life. Not for it is the shady side of existence, the rough and tumble and conflict of life. Several other newspapers of moderate views have also this 'old maiden lady' standard. They achieve it, but without the distinction of *The Hindu* and, as a result, they become astonishingly dull in every respect.

It was evident that the Government had long prepared its blow, and it wanted it to be as thorough and staggering as possible right at the beginning. In 1930 it was always attempting, by fresh Ordinances, to catch up an ever-worsening situation. The initiative remained then with the Congress. The 1932 methods were different, and Government began with an offensive all along the line. Every conceivable power was given and taken under a batch of all-India and provincial Ordinances; organizations were outlawed; buildings, property, automobiles, bank accounts were seized; public gatherings and processions forbidden, and newspapers and printing presses fully controlled. On the other hand, unlike 1930, Gandhiji was definitely desirous of avoiding civil disobedience just then, and most of the members of the Working Committee thought likewise. Some of them, including myself, thought that a struggle was inevitable, however much we disliked it, and should therefore be prepared for, and in the United Provinces and the Frontier Province a growing tension had directed people's minds to the approaching conflict. But, on the whole, the middle classes and the intelligentsia were not thinking then in terms of struggle although they could not wholly ignore the possibility. Somehow, they hoped that this struggle would be avoided on Gandhiji's return; the wish was obviously father to the thought. Thus the initiative early in 1932 was definitely with the Government, and Congress was always on the defensive. Local Congress leaders in many places were taken by surprise by the rapid developments leading to the Ordinances and civil disobedience. In spite of this there was a remarkable response to the Congress call, and there was no lack of civil resisters. Indeed I think that there can be little doubt that the resistance offered to the British Government in 1932 was far greater than in 1930, although in 1930 there was more show and publicity, especially in the big cities. In spite of this greater endurance shown by the people in 1932, and their remaining overwhelmingly peaceful, the initial push of inspiration was far less than in 1930. It was as if we entered unwillingly to battle. There was a glory about it in 1930 which had faded a little two years later. The Government countered Congress with every resource at its command; India lived practically under martial law, and Congress never really got back the initiative or any freedom of action. The first blows stunned it, and most of its *bourgeois* sympathizers who had been its principal supporters in the past. Their pockets were hit, and it became obvious that those who joined the civil disobedience movement, or were known to help it in any way, stood to lose not only their liberty, but perhaps all their property. This did not matter so much to us in U.P., where the Congress was a poor man's concern; but in the big cities, like Bombay, it made a great deal of difference. It meant absolute ruin for the merchant class and great loss to professional people. The mere threat of this (and it was sometimes carried out) paralysed these well-to-do city classes. I learnt later of a timid but prosperous merchant, who had little to do with politics, except perhaps to give an occasional donation, being threatened by the police with a fine of five lakhs of rupees, besides a long term of imprisonment. Such threats were fairly common, and were by no means empty talk, for the police were all-powerful then and instances occurred daily of threats being translated into action.

I do not think any Congressman has a right to object to the procedure adopted by the Government, although the violence and coercion used by the Government against an overwhelmingly non-violent movement was certainly most objectionable from any civilized standards. If we choose to adopt revolutionary direct action methods, however non-violent they might be, we must expect every resistance. We cannot play at revolution in a drawing-room, but many people want to have the advantage of both. For a person to dabble in revolutionary methods, he must be prepared to lose everything he possesses. The prosperous and the well-to-do are therefore seldom revolutionaries, though individuals may play the fool in the eyes of the worldly-wise and be dubbed traitors to their own class.

Other methods had to be adopted, of course, to deal with the masses, who had no cars or banking accounts or other property worth seizing, and on whom the real burden of the struggle lay. One interesting result of the ruthlessness of Government action in all directions was to whip up that crowd of people, who might be called (to borrow a word from a recent book) 'Governmentarians', into activity. Some of them had recently begun to flirt with the Congress, not knowing what the future might bring. But Government could not tolerate this, and no passive loyalty was enough. In the words of Frederick Cooper of Mutiny fame the authorities "would brook nothing short of absolute, active, and positive loyalty. Government could not condescend to exist upon the moral sufferance of its subjects." A year ago Mr Lloyd George referred to his old colleagues, the leaders of the British Liberal Party who had joined the National Government, as "specimens of those changeable reptiles who adapt their hue to their environments". The new environment in India tolerated no neutral hues, and so some of our countrymen appeared in the brightest of approved colours and, with song and feasting, they declared their love and admiration for our rulers. They had nothing to fear from the Ordinances and the numerous prohibitions and inhibitions and curfew orders and sunset laws; for had it not been officially stated that all this was meant for the disloyal and the seditious, and the loyal need have no cause for alarm? And so they could view the turmoil and conflict all round them with a measure of equanimity, devoid of that fear that gripped many of their countrymen. With Chloe (in *The Faithful Shepherdess*) they might perhaps have agreed when she said:

For from one cause of fear I am most free,
It is impossible to ravish me,
I am so willing.

The Government had somehow got hold of the idea that Congress was going to exploit women in the struggle by filling the gaols with them, in the hope that women would be well treated or would get light sentences. It was a fantastic notion, as if any one likes to push his womenfolk into prison. Usually when girls or women took an active part in the campaign, it was in spite of their fathers or brothers or husbands, or at any rate not with their full co-operation. Government, however, decided to discourage women by long sentences and bad treatment in prison. Soon after my sisters' arrest and conviction, a number of young girls, mostly 15 or 16 years old, met in Allahabad to discuss what they could do. They had no experience, but were full of enthusiasm and wanted advice. They were arrested as they were meeting in a private house, and each of them was sentenced to two years' rigorous imprisonment. This was a minor incident, one of many that were occurring all over India from day to day. Most of the girls and women who were sentenced had a very bad time in prison, even worse than the men had. I heard of many painful instances, but the most extraordinary account that I saw was one prepared by Miraben (Madeleine Slade) giving her experiences, together with those of other civil disobedience prisoners, in a Bombay gaol.

In the United Provinces our struggle was centred in the rural areas. Owing to the unceasing pressure of the Congress, as representing the peasantry, fairly substantial remissions had been promised, though we did not think them enough. Immediately after our arrest additional remissions were announced. It was curious that this announcement did not come earlier, for it could have made a great deal of difference. It would have been difficult for us to reject it offhand. But then Government was very anxious that the Congress should not get the credit for these remissions, and so on the one side they wanted to crush the Congress, and on the other to give as much as possible remissions to the peasants to keep them quiet. It was noticeable that the remissions were highest wherever the Congress pressure had been greatest.

These remissions, considerable as they were, did not solve the agrarian problem, but they did ease the situation greatly. They took the edge off the peasantry's resistance, and from the point of view of our larger struggle, weakened us at the moment. That struggle brought suffering to scores of thousands of peasants in U.P., and many were completely ruined by it. But the pressure of that struggle brought millions of peasants almost the highest possible remissions under the existing system, and saved them (the consequences of civil disobedience and its offshoots apart) from a tremendous amount of harassment. These petty seasonal gains for the peasants do not amount to much, but I have no doubt that, such as they were, they were largely due to the persistent efforts of the U.P. Congress Committee on behalf of the peasantry. The general body of the peasantry benefited temporarily, but the bravest of them were among the casualties in that struggle.

When the U.P. Special Ordinance was issued in December 1931 an explanatory statement accompanied it. This statement, as well as the statements accompanying other Ordinances, contained many half-truths and untruths which were to serve as propaganda. It was all part of the initial ballyhoo, and we had no chance to answer them or even contradict their glaring errors. One particularly glaring attempt, in which a falsehood was sought to be fastened on Sherwani, was corrected by him just before his arrest. These various statements and apologies of Government made curious reading. They showed how rattled Government was, how its nerve was shaken. Reading the other day of a decree issued by the Bourbon Charles III of Spain, banishing the Jesuits from his realm, I was forcibly reminded of these decrees and ordinances of the British Government in India and of the reasons given for them. In this decree, issued in February 1767, the King justified his action by "extremely grave reasons relative to my duty to maintain subordination, tranquillity, and justice among my subjects, and other urgent, just, and necessary reasons which I reserve in my royal breast."

So the real reasons for the Ordinances remained locked up in the Viceregal breast or in the imperialist breasts of his counsellors, though they were obvious enough. The reasons given out officially helped us to understand the new technique of propaganda which the British Government in India was perfecting. Some months later we learnt of semi-official pamphlets and leaflets being widely distributed all over the rural areas containing quite an astonishing number of misrepresentations and, in particular, hinting at the fact that the Congress had caused the fall in agricultural prices which had hurt the peasantry so much. This was a remarkable tribute to the power of the Congress, which could bring about a world depression! But the lie was spread persistently and assiduously, in the hope that the prestige of the Congress might suffer.

In spite of all this, the response of the peasantry in some of the principal districts of U.P. to the call for civil disobedience, which inevitably got mixed up with the dispute about fair rent and remissions, was very fine. It was a far bigger and more disciplined response than in 1930. To begin with there was good humour about it too. A delightful story came to us of a visit of a police party to the village Bakulia in Rae Bareli district. They had gone to attach goods for non-payment of rent. The village was relatively prosperous, and its residents were men of some spirit. They received the revenue and police officials with all courtesy and, leaving the doors of all the houses open, invited them to go wherever they wanted to. Some attachments of cattle, etc., were made. The villagers then offered *pan supari* to the police and revenue officials, who retired looking very small and rather shamefaced! But this was a rare and unusual occurrence, and very soon there was little of humour or charity or human kindness to be seen. Poor Bakulia could not escape punishment for its spirit because of its humour.

For many months in these particular districts rent was withheld by the tenantry, and it was only early in summer probably that collections began to dribble in. Large numbers of arrests were of course made, but this was almost in spite of Government's policy. Generally arrests were confined to special workers and village leaders. The others were merely beaten. Beating was found to be superior to prison as well as shooting. It could be repeated whenever necessary and, taking place in remote rural areas, attracted little outside attention; nor did it add to the swelling number of prisoners. There were of course large numbers of ejectments, attachments and sale of cattle and property. With terrible anguish, the peasants watched the little they possessed being taken away and disposed of for ridiculous prices.

Swaraj Bhawan had been seized by the Government, in common with numerous other buildings all over the country. All the valuable equipment and material belonging to the Congress Hospital, which was functioning in Swaraj Bhawan, was also seized. For a few days the hospital ceased functioning altogether, but then an open-air dispensary was established in a park near by. Later the hospital, or rather dispensary, moved to a small house adjoining Swaraj Bhawan, and there it functioned for nearly two and a half years.

There was some talk of our dwelling-house, Anand Bhawan, also being taken possession of by the Government, for I had refused to pay a large amount due as income tax. This tax had been assessed on father's income in 1930, and he had not paid it that year because of civil disobedience. In 1931, after the Delhi Pact, I had an argument with the income tax authorities about it, but ultimately I agreed to pay and did pay an instalment. Just then came the Ordinances, and I decided to pay no more. It seemed to me utterly wrong, and even immoral, for me to ask the peasants to withhold payment of rent and revenue and to pay income tax myself. I expected, therefore, that our house would be attached by the Government. I disliked this idea intensely, as it would have meant my mother being turned out; our books, papers, goods and chattels and many things that we valued for personal and sentimental reasons going into strange hands and perhaps being lost; and our National Flag being pulled down and the Union Jack put up instead. At the same time I was attracted to the idea of losing the house. I felt that this would bring me nearer to the peasantry, who were being dispossessed, and would hearten them. From the point of view of our movement it was certainly a desirable thing. But the Government decided otherwise and did not touch the house, perhaps because of consideration for my mother, perhaps because they judged rightly that it would give an impetus to civil disobedience. Many months afterwards some odd railway shares of mine were discovered and attached, for non-payment of income tax. My motor-car, as well as my brother-in-law's, had been previously attached and sold.

One feature of these early months pained me greatly. This was the hauling down of our National Flag by various municipalities and public bodies, and especially by the Calcutta Corporation which was said to have a majority of Congress members. The flag was taken down under pressure from the police and the Government, which threatened severe action in case of non-compliance. This action would have probably meant a suspension of the municipality or punishment of its members. Organizations with vested interests are apt to be timid, and perhaps it was inevitable that they should act as they did, but nevertheless it hurt. That flag had become a symbol to us of much that we held dear, and under its shadow we had taken many a pledge to protect its honour. To pull it down with our own hands, or to have it pulled down at our behest, seemed not only a breaking of that pledge but almost a sacrilege. It was a submission of the spirit, a denial of the truth in one; an affirmation, in the face of superior physical might, of the false. And those who submitted in this way lowered the morale of the nation, and injured its self-respect.

It was not that they were expected to behave as heroes, and rush into the fire. It was wrong and absurd to blame anyone for not being in the front rank and courting prison, or other suffering or loss. Each one had many duties and responsibilities to shoulder, and no one else had a right to sit in judgment on him. But to sit or work in the background is one thing; to deny the truth, or what one conceives to be the truth, is a more serious matter. It was open to members of municipalities, when called upon to do anything against the national interest, to resign from their seats. As a rule they preferred to remain in those seats.

> But bees, on flowers alighting, cease their hum—
> So, settling upon places, Whigs grow dumb![1]

Perhaps it is unjust to criticize anyone for his behaviour during a sudden crisis which threatens to overwhelm him. The nerve of the bravest fails them sometimes, as the World War demonstrated over and again. Earlier still, in the great *Titanic* disaster of 1912, famous people, who could never have been associated with cowardice, escaped by bribing the crew, leaving others to drown. Very recently the fire on the *Morro Castle* revealed a shameful state of affairs. No one knows how he will behave in a similar crisis when the primeval instincts overpower reason

---

1. Thomas Moore.

and restraint. So we may not blame. But that should not prevent us from noting that falling away from right conduct, and from taking care in future that the steering-wheel of the ship of the nation is not put in hands that tremble and fail when the need is greatest. Worse still is the attempt to justify this failure and call it right conduct. That, surely, is a greater offence than the failure itself.

All struggles between rival forces depend greatly on morale and nerve. Even the bloodiest war depends upon them: "In the final event battles are won by nerves," said Marshal Foch. Much more so are nerve and morale necessary in a non-violent struggle, and anyone who, by his conduct, impairs that morale and shakes the nation's nerve, does a serious disservice to the cause.

The months went by bringing their daily toll of good news and bad, and we adapted ourselves in our respective prisons, to our dull and monotonous routine. The National Week came—April 6th to 13th— and we knew that this would witness many an unusual happening. Much, indeed, happened then; but for me everything else paled before one occurrence. In Allahabad my mother was in a procession which was stopped by the police and later charged with *lathis*. When the procession had been halted some one brought her a chair, and she was sitting on this on the road at the head of the procession. Some people who were especially looking after her, including my secretary, were arrested and removed, and then came the police charge. My mother was knocked down from her chair, and was hit repeatedly on the head with canes. Blood came out of an open wound in the head; she fainted, and lay on the roadside, which had now been cleared of the processionists and public. After some time she was picked up and brought by a police officer in his car to Anand Bhawan.

That night a false rumour spread in Allahabad that my mother had died. Angry crowds gathered together, forgot about peace and non-violence, and attacked the police. There was firing by the police, resulting in the death of some people.

When the news of all this came to me some days after the occurrence (for we had a weekly paper), the thought of my frail old mother lying bleeding on the dusty road obsessed me, and I wondered how I would have behaved if I had been there. How far would my non-violence have carried me? Not very far, I fear, for that sight would have made me forget the long lesson I had tried to learn for more than a dozen years; and I would have recked little of the consequences, personal or national.

Slowly she recovered, and when she came to see me next month in Bareilly Gaol she was still bandaged up. But she was full of joy and pride at having shared with our volunteer boys and girls the privilege of receiving cane and *lathi* blows. Her recovery, however, was more apparent than real, and it seems that the tremendous shaking that she received at her age upset her system entirely and brought into prominence deep-seated troubles, which a year later assumed dangerous proportions.

IN BAREILLY AND DEHRA DUN GAOLS

After six weeks in Naini Prison I was transferred to the Bareilly District Gaol. I was again keeping indifferent health and, much to my annoyance, I used to get a daily rise in temperature. After four months spent in Bareilly, when the summer temperature was almost at its highest, I was again transferred, this time to a cooler place, Dehra Dun Gaol, at the foot of the Himalayas. There I remained, without a break, for fourteen and a half months, almost to the end of my two-year term. News reached me, of course, from interviews and letters and selected newspapers, but I was wholly out of touch with much that was happening and had only a hazy notion of the principal events.

When I was discharged I was kept busy with personal affairs as well as the political situation as I found it then. After a little more than five months of freedom I was brought back to prison, and here I am still. Thus, during the last three years I have been mostly in prison and out of touch with events, and I have had little opportunity of making myself acquainted in any detail with all that has happened during this period. I have still the vaguest of knowledge as to what took place behind the scenes at the second Round Table Conference, which was attended by Gandhiji. I have had no chance so far of a talk with him on this subject, nor of discussing with him or others much that has happened since.

I do not know enough of those years 1932 and 1933 to trace the development of our national struggle. But I knew the stage and the background well and the actors also, and had an instinctive appreciation of many a little thing that happened. I could thus form a fair notion of the general course of the struggle. For the first four months or so civil disobedience functioned strongly and aggressively, and then there was a gradual decline with occasional bursts. A direct action struggle can only remain at a revolutionary pitch for a very short time. It cannot remain static; it has to go up or down. Civil disobedience, after the first flush, went down slowly, but it could carry on at a lower level for long periods.

In spite of outlawry, the All-India Congress organization continued to function with a fair measure of success. It kept in touch with its provincial workers, sent instructions, received reports, occasionally gave financial assistance.

The provincial organizations also continued with more or less success. I do not know much about other provinces during those years when I was in prison, but I gathered some information about U.P. activities after my release. The U.P. Congress office functioned regularly right through 1932 and till the middle of 1933, when civil disobedience was first suspended by the then acting Congress president, on the advice of Gandhiji. During this period frequent directions were sent to districts, printed or cyclostyled bulletins issued regularly, district work inspected from time to time, and our National Service workers paid their allowances. Much of this work was necessarily secret work; but the secretary of the Provincial Committee in charge of the office, etc., was always working as such, publicly, till he was arrested and removed and another took his place.

Our experience of 1930 and 1932 showed that it was easily possible for us to organize a secret network of information all over India. Without much effort, and in spite of some opposition, good results were produced. But many of us had the feeling that secrecy did not fit in with the spirit of civil disobedience, and produced a damping effect on the mass consciousness. As a small part of a big open mass-movement it was useful, but there was always the danger, especially when the movement was declining, of a few more or less ineffective secret activities taking the place of the mass-movement. Gandhiji condemned all secrecy in July 1933.

Agrarian no-tax movements flourished for some time in Gujrat and Karnataka, apart from U.P. In both Gujrat and Karnataka there were peasant proprietors who refused to pay their revenue to the Government, and suffered greatly because of this. Some effort, necessarily inadequate, was made on behalf of the Congress to help the sufferers and relieve the misery caused by the ejectments and confiscation of property. In U.P. no effort to help the dispossessed tenantry in this way was made by the Provincial Congress. The problem here was a much vaster one (tenants are far more numerous than peasant proprietors), the area was much bigger, and the provincial resources were very limited. It was quite impossible for us to help scores of thousands who had suffered because of the campaign, and equally difficult for us to draw a line between them and the vast numbers who were always on the starvation line. To help a few thousands only would have led to trouble and bad blood So we decided not to give financial assistance, and we broadcasted this fact right at the beginning, and our position was thoroughly appreciated by the peasantry. It was wonderful how much they put up with without complaint or murmur. Of course, we tried to help individuals where we could, especially the wives and children of workers who went to prison. Such is the poverty of this unhappy country that even one rupee per month was a godsend.

Right through this period the U.P. Provincial Committee (which was, of course, a proscribed body) continued to pay the usual meagre allowances to its paid workers; and if they went to prison, as all of them did in turn, to support their families. This was a major item in its budget. Then came the charge for printing and duplicating leaflets and bulletins; this also was a heavy charge. Travelling expenses formed another principal item, and some grants had to be given to the less prosperous districts. In spite of all these and other expenses during a period of intensive mass-struggle against a powerful and entrenched government, the total expenditure of the U.P. Provincial Committee for twenty months from January 1932 to the end of August 1933 were about Rs 63,000, that is about Rs 3,140 per month. (This figure does not include the separate expenditure of some of the strong and more prosperous district committees like Allahabad, Agra, Cawnpore, Lucknow.) As a province, U.P. kept in the very forefront of the struggle right through 1932 and 1933, and I think, considering the results obtained, it is remarkable how little it spent. It would be interesting to compare with this modest figure the provincial Government's special expenditure to crush civil disobedience. I imagine (though I have no knowledge) that some of the other major Congress provinces spent much more. But Behar was, from the Congress view-point, an even poorer province than its neighbour, the U.P., and yet its part in the struggle was a splendid one.

So, gradually, the civil disobedience movement declined; but still it carried on, not without distinction. Progressively it ceased to be a mass movement. Apart from the severity of Government repression, the first severe blow to it came in September 1932 when Gandhiji fasted for the first time on the Harijan issue. That fast roused mass consciousness, but it directed it in another direction. Civil disobedience was finally killed for all practical purposes by the suspension of it in May 1933. It continued after that more in theory than in practice. It is no doubt true that, even without that suspension, it would have gradually petered out. India was numbed by the violence and harshness of repression. The nervous energy of the nation as a whole was for the moment exhausted, and it was not being re-charged. Individually there were still many who could carry on civil resistance, but they functioned in a somewhat artificial atmosphere.

It was not pleasant for us in prison to learn of this slow decay of a great movement. And yet very few of us had expected a flashing success. There was always an odd chance that something flashing might happen if there was an irrepressible upheaval of the masses. But that was not to be counted upon, and so we looked forward to a long struggle with ups and downs and many a stalemate in between, and a progressive strengthening of the masses in discipline and united action and ideology. Sometimes in those early days of 1932 I almost feared a quick and spectacular success, for this seemed to lead inevitably to a compromise leaving the 'Governmentarians' and opportunists at the top. The experience of 1931 had been revealing. Success to be worthwhile should come when the people generally were strong enough and clear enough in their ideas to take advantage of it. Otherwise the masses would fight and sacrifice and, at the psychological moment, others would step in gracefully and gather the spoils. There was grave danger of this, because in the Congress itself there was a great deal of loose thinking and no clear ideas as to what system of government or society we were driving at. Some Congressmen, indeed, did not think of changing the existing system of government much, but simply of replacing the British or alien element in it by the *swadeshi* brand.

The 'Governmentarians' of the pure variety did not matter much, for their first article of faith was subservience to the State authority whatever it was. But even the Liberals and Responsivists accepted the ideology of the British Government almost completely; and their occasional criticism, such as it was, was thus wholly ineffective and valueless. It was well known that they were legalists at any price, and as such they could not welcome civil resistance. But they went much further, and more or less ranged themselves on the side of the Government. They were almost silent and rather frightened spectators of the complete suppression of civil liberties of all kinds. It was not merely a question of civil disobedience being countered and suppressed by the Government, but of all political life and public activity being stopped, and hardly a voice was raised against this. Those who usually stood for these liberties were involved in the struggle itself and they took the penalties for refusing to submit to the State's coercion. Others were cowed into abject submission, and hardly raised their voices in criticism. Mild criticism, when it was indulged in, was apologetic in tone and was accompanied by strong denunciation of the Congress and those who were carrying on the struggle.

In Western countries a strong public opinion has been built up in favour of civil liberties, and any limitation of them is resented and opposed. (Perhaps this is past history now.) There are large numbers of people who, though not prepared to participate in strong and direct action themselves, care enough for the liberty of speech and writing, Assembly and Organization, person and Press, to agitate for them ceaselessly and thus help to check the tendency of the State to encroach upon them. The Indian Liberals claim to some extent to carry on the traditions of British Liberalism (although they have nothing in common with them except the name), and might have been expected to put up some intellectual opposition to the suppression of these liberties, for they suffered from this also. But they played no such part. It was not for them to say with Voltaire: "I disagree absolutely with what you say, but I will defend to the death your right to say it."

It is not perhaps fair to blame them for this, for they have never stood out as the champions of democracy or liberty, and they had to face a situation in which a loose word might have got them into trouble. It is more pertinent to observe the reactions of those ancient lovers of liberty, the British Liberals, and the new socialists of the British Labour Party to repression in India. They managed to contemplate the Indian scene with a certain measure of equanimity, painful as it was, and sometimes their satisfaction at the success of the "scientific application of repression," as a correspondent of the *Manchester Guardian* put it, was evident. Recently the National Government of Great Britain has sought to pass a Sedition Bill, and a great deal of criticism has been directed to it, especially from Liberals and Labourites on the ground, *inter alia*, that it restricts free speech and gives magistrates the right of issuing warrants for searches. Whenever I read this criticism I sympathized with it, and I had at the same time the picture of India before me, where the actual laws in force today are approximately a hundred times worse than the British Sedition Bill seeks to enact. I wondered how it was that Britishers who strain at a gnat in England could swallow a camel in India without turning a hair. Indeed I have always wondered at and admired the astonishing knack of the British people of making their moral standards correspond with their material interests, and of seeing virtue in everything that advances their imperial designs. Mussolini and Hitler are condemned by them in perfect good faith and with righteous indignation for their attacks on liberty and democracy; and, in equal good faith, similar attacks and deprivation of liberty in India seem to them as necessary, and the highest moral reasons are advanced to show that true disinterested behaviour on their part demands them.

While fire raged all over India and men's and women's souls were put to the test, far away in London the chosen ones foregathered to draw up a constitution for India. There was the third Round Table Conference in 1932 and numerous committees, and large numbers of members of the Legislative Assembly angled for membership of these committees so that they might thus combine public duty with private pleasure. Quite a crowd went at the public expense. Later, in 1933, came the Joint Committee with its Indian assessors, and again free passages were provided by a benevolent Government to those who went as witnesses. Many people crossed the seas again at public cost in their earnest desire to serve India, and some, it was stated, even haggled for more passage money.

It was not surprising to see these representatives of vested interests, frightened by the mass movements of India in action, gathering together in London under the aegis of British imperialism. But it hurt the nationalism in us to see any Indian behave in this way when the mother country was involved in a life-and-death struggle. And yet from one point of view it seemed to many of us a good thing, for it separated once and for all, as we thought (wrongly, it now appears), the reactionary from the progressive elements in India. This sifting would help in the political education of the masses, and make it clearer still to all concerned, that only through independence could we hope to face social issues and raise the burdens from the masses.

But it was surprising to find how far these people had alienated themselves, not only in their day-to-day lives, but morally and mentally, from the Indian masses. There were no links with them, no understanding of them or of that inner urge which was driving them to sacrifice and suffering. Reality for these distinguished statesmen consisted of one thing—British imperial power, which could not be successfully challenged and therefore should be accepted with good or bad grace. It did not seem to strike them that it was quite impossible for them to solve India's problem or draw up a real live constitution without the goodwill of the masses. Mr J.A. Spender, in his recent *Short History of Our Times*, refers to the failure of the Irish Joint Conference of 1910 which sought to end the constitutional crisis. He says that the political leaders who were trying to find a constitution in the midst of a crisis were like men trying to insure a house when it is on fire. The fire in India in 1932 and 1933 was far greater than in Ireland in 1910, and even though the flames die down, the burning embers will remain for a long time, hot and unquenchable as India's will to freedom.

In India there was an amazing growth of the spirit of violence in official circles. The tradition was an old one, and the country had been governed by the British mainly as a police State. The overriding outlook even of the civilian ruler had been military; there was always a touch of a hostile army occupying alien and conquered soil. This mentality grew because of the serious challenge to the existing order. The occasional acts of terrorism in Bengal or elsewhere fed this official violence, and gave it some justification for its own acts. The various ordinances and the Government policy gave such tremendous power to the executive and the police, that in effect India was under Police Raj and there were hardly any checks.

To a greater or less degree all the provinces of India went through this fire of fierce repression, but the Frontier Province and Bengal suffered most. The Frontier Province had always been a predominantly military area, administered under semi-military regulations. Its strategic position was important, and the 'Redshirt' movement had thoroughly upset the Government. Military columns were very much in evidence in the 'pacification' of the province, and in dealing with 'recalcitrant villages'.

It was a common practice all over India to impose heavy collective fines on villages, and occasionally (in Bengal especially) on towns. Punitive police were often stationed, and police excesses were inevitable when they had enormous powers and no checks. We had typical instances of the lawlessness and disorderliness of law and order.

Parts of Bengal presented the most extraordinary spectacle. Government treated the whole populations (or, to be exact, the Hindu population) as hostile, and everyone—man, woman, boy or girl between 12 and 25—had to carry identity cards. There were externments and internments in the mass, dress was regulated, schools were regulated or closed, bicycles were not allowed, movements had to be reported to the police, curfew, sunset law, military marches, punitive police, collective fines, and a host of other rules and regulations. Large areas seemed to be in a continuous state of siege, and the inhabitants were little better than ticket-of-leave men and women under the strictest surveillance. Whether, from the point of view of the British Government, all these amazing provisions and regulations were necessary or not, it is not for me to judge. If they were not necessary, then that Government must be held guilty of a grave offence in oppressing and humiliating and causing great loss to the populations of whole areas. If they were necessary then surely that is the final verdict on British rule in India.

The spirit of violence pursued our people even within the gaols. The class division of prisoners was a farce, and often a torture for those who were put in an upper class. Very few went to these upper classes, and many a sensitive man and woman had to submit to conditions which were a continuing agony. The deliberate policy of Government seems to have been to make the lot of political prisoners worse than that of ordinary convicts. An Inspector-General of Prisons went to the length of issuing a confidential circular to all the prisons, pointing out that Civil Disobedience prisoners must be "dealt with grimly".[1] Whipping became a frequent gaol punishment. On April 27, 1933, the Under Secretary for India stated in the House of Commons "that Sir Samuel

---

1. This circular was dated June 30, 1932, and it contained the following: "The Inspector-General impresses upon Superintendents and gaol subordinates the fact that there is no justification for preferential treatment in favour of Civil Disobedience Movement prisoners as such. This class require to be kept in their places and dealt with grimly."

Hoare was aware that over 500 persons in India were whipped during 1932 for offences in connection with the civil disobedience movement." It is not clear if this figure includes the many whippings in prisons for breaches of gaol discipline. As news of frequent whippings came to us in prison in 1932, I remembered our protest and our three-day fast in December 1930 against one or two odd instances of whipping. I had felt shocked then at the brutality of it, and now I was still shocked and there was a dull pain inside me, but it did not strike me that I should protest and fast again. I felt much more helpless in the matter. The mind gets blunted to brutality after a while. A bad thing has only to continue for long for the world to get used to it.

The hardest of labour was given to our men in prison—mills, oil-presses, etc.—and their lot was made as unbearable as possible in order to induce them to apologize and be released on an undertaking being given to Government. That was considered a great triumph for the gaol authorities.

Most of these gaol punishments fell to the lot of boys and young men, who resented coercion and humiliation. A fine and spirited lot of boys they were, full of self-respect and 'pep' and the spirit of adventure, the kind that in an English public school or university would have received every encouragement and praise. Here in India their youthful idealism and pride led them to fetters and solitary confinement and whipping.

The lot of our womenfolk in prison was especially hard and painful to contemplate. They were mostly middle class women, accustomed to a sheltered life, and suffering chiefly from the many repressions and customs produced by a society dominated to his own advantage by man. The call of freedom had always a double meaning for them, and the enthusiasm and energy with which they threw themselves into the struggle had no doubt their springs in the vague and hardly conscious, but nevertheless intense, desire to rid themselves of domestic slavery also. Excepting a very few, they were classed as ordinary prisoners and placed with the most degraded of companions, and often under horrid conditions. I was once lodged in a barrack next to a female enclosure, a wall separating us. In that enclosure there were, besides other convicts, some women political prisoners, including one who had been my hostess and in whose house I had once stayed. A high wall separated us, but it did not prevent me from listening in horror to the language and curses which our friends had to put up with from the women convict warders.

It was very noticeable that the treatment of political prisoners in 1932 and 1933 was worse than it had been two years earlier, in 1930. This could not have been due merely to the whims of individual officers, and the only reasonable inference seems to be that this was the deliberate policy of the Government. Even apart from political prisoners, the United Provinces Gaol Department had had the reputation in those years of being very much against anything that might savour of humanity. We had an interesting instance of this from an unimpeachable source. A distinguished gaol visitor, a gallant knight, not a rebel and a sedition-monger like us, but one whom the Government had delighted to honour, paid us a visit once in prison. He told us that some months earlier he had visited another gaol, and in his inspection note had described the gaoler as a "humane disciplinarian". The gaoler in question begged him not to say anything about his humanity, as this was at a discount in official circles. But the knight insisted, as he could not conceive that any harm would befall the gaoler because of his description. Result: soon after the gaoler was transferred to a distant and out-of-the-way place, which was in the nature of a punishment to him.

Some gaolers, who were considered to be particularly fierce and unscrupulous, were promoted and given titles. Graft is such a universal phenomenon in gaols that hardly any one keeps clear of it. But my own experience, and that of many of my friends, has been that the worst offenders among the gaol staff are usually those who pose as strict disciplinarians.

I have been fortunate in gaol and outside, and almost every one I have come across has given me courtesy and consideration, even when perhaps I did not deserve them. One incident in gaol, however, caused me and my people much pain. My mother, Kamala and Indira, my daughter, had gone to interview my brother-in-law, Ranjit Pandit, in the Allahabad District Gaol and, for no fault of theirs, they were insulted and hustled out by the gaoler. I was grieved when I learnt of this, and the reaction of the Provincial Government to it shocked me. To avoid the possibility of my mother being insulted by gaol officials, I decided to give up all interviews. For nearly seven months, while I was in Dehra Dun Gaol, I had no interview.

44

PRISON HUMOURS

Two of us were transferred together from the Bareilly District Gaol to the Dehra Dun Gaol—Govind Ballabh Pant and I. To avoid the possibility of a demonstration, we were not put on the train at Bareilly, but at a wayside station 50 miles out. We were taken secretly by motor-car at night, and, after many months of seclusion, that drive through the cool night air was a rare delight.

Before we left Bareilly Gaol, a little incident took place which moved me then and is yet fresh in my memory. The Superintendent of Police of Bareilly, an Englishman, was present there, and, as I got into the car, he handed to me rather shyly a packet which he told me contained old German illustrated magazines. He said that he had heard that I was learning German and so he had brought these magazines for me. I had never met him before, nor have I seen him since. I do not even know his name. This spontaneous act of courtesy and the kindly thought that prompted it touched me and I felt very grateful to him.

During that long midnight drive I mused over the relations of Englishmen and Indians, of ruler and ruled, of official and non-official, of those in authority and those who have to obey. What a great gulf divided the two races, and how they distrusted and disliked each other. But more than the distrust and the dislike was the ignorance of each other, and, because of this, each side was a little afraid of the other and was constantly on its guard in the other's presence. To each, the other appeared as a sour-looking, unamiable creature, and neither realized that there was decency and kindliness behind the mask. As the rulers of the land, with enormous patronage at their command, the English had attracted to themselves crowds of cringing place-hunters and opportunists, and they judged of India from these unsavoury specimens. The Indian saw the Englishman function only as an official with all the inhumanity of the machine and with all the passion of a vested interest trying to preserve itself. How different was the behaviour of a person acting as an individual and obeying his own impulses, from his behaviour as an official or a unit in an army. The soldier, stiffening to attention, drops his humanity, and, acting as an automaton, shoots and kills inoffensive and harmless persons who have done him no ill. So also, I thought, the police officer who would hesitate to do an unkindness to an individual would, the day after, direct a *lathi* charge on innocent people. He would not think of himself as an individual then, nor will he consider as individuals those crowds whom he beats down or shoots.

As soon as one begins to think of the other side as a mass or a crowd, the human link seems to go. We forget that crowds also consist of individuals, of men and women and children, who love and hate and suffer. An average Englishman, if he was frank, would probably confess that he knows some quite decent Indians, but they are exceptions, and as a whole Indians are a detestable crowd. The average Indian would admit that some Englishmen whom he knows were admirable, but, apart from these few, the English were an overbearing, brutal, and thoroughly bad lot. Curious how each person judges of the other race, not from the individual with whom he has come in contact, but from others about whom he knows very little or nothing at all.

Personally, I have been very fortunate and, almost invariably, I have received courtesy from my own countrymen as well as from the English. Even my gaolers and the policemen, who have arrested me or escorted me as a prisoner from place to place, have been kind to me, and much of the bitterness of conflict and the sting of gaol life has been toned down because of this human touch. It was not surprising that my own countrymen should treat me so, for I had gained a measure of notoriety and popularity among them. Even for Englishmen I was an individual and not merely one of the mass, and, I imagine, the fact that I had received my education in England, and especially my having been to an English public school, brought me nearer to them. Because of this, they could not help considering me as more or less civilized after their own pattern, however perverted my public activities appeared to be. Often I felt a little embarrassed and humiliated because of this special treatment when I compared my lot with that of most of my colleagues.

Despite all these advantages that I had, gaol was gaol, and the oppressive atmosphere of the place was sometimes almost unbearable. The very air of it was full of violence and meanness and graft and untruth; there was either cringing or cursing. A person who was at all sensitive was in a continuous state of tension. Trivial occurrences would upset one. A piece of bad news in a letter, some item in the newspaper, would make one almost ill with anxiety or anger for a while. Outside there was always relief in action, and various interests and activities produced an equilibrium of the mind and body. In prison there was no outlet and one felt bottled up and repressed, and, inevitably, one took one-sided and rather distorted views of happenings. Illness in gaol was particularly distressing.

And yet I managed to accustom myself to the gaol routine, and with physical exercise and fairly hard mental work kept fit. Whatever the value of work and exercise might be outside, they are essential in gaol, for without them one is apt to go to pieces. I adhered to a strict time-table and, in order to keep up to the mark, I carried on with as many normal habits as I could, such as the daily shave (I was allowed a safety razor). I mention this minor matter because, as a rule, people gave it up and slacked in other ways. After a hard day's work, the evening found me pleasantly tired and sleep was welcomed.

And so the days passed, and the weeks and the months. But sometimes a month would stick terribly and would not end, or so it seemed. And sometimes I would feel bored and fed up and angry with almost everything and everybody—with my companions in prison, with the gaol staff, with people outside for something they had done or not done, with the British Empire (but this was a permanent feeling), and above all with myself. I would become a bundle of nerves, very susceptible to various humours caused by gaol life. Fortunately I recovered soon from these humours.

Interview days were the red-letter days in gaol. How one longed for them and waited for them and counted the days! And after the excitement of the interview there was the inevitable reaction and a sense of emptiness and loneliness. If, as sometimes happened, the interview was not a success, because of some bad news which upset me, or some other reason, I would feel miserable afterwards. There were gaol officials present of course at the interviews, but two or three times at Bareilly there was in addition a C.I.D. man present with paper and pencil, eagerly taking down almost every word of the conversation. I found this exceedingly irritating, and these interviews were complete failures.

And then I gave up these precious interviews because of the treatment my mother and wife had received in the course of an interview in the Allahabad Gaol and afterwards from the Government. For nearly seven months I had no interview. It was a dreary time for me, and when at the end of that period I decided to resume interviews and my people came to see me, I was almost intoxicated with the joy of it. My sister's little children also came to see me, and when a tiny one wanted to mount on my shoulder, as she used to do, it was more than my emotions could stand. That touch of home life, after the long yearning for human contacts, upset me.

When interviews stopped, the fortnightly letters from home or from some other gaol (for both my sisters were in prison) became all the more precious and eagerly expected. If the letter did not come on the appointed day I was worried. And yet when it did come, I almost hesitated to open it. I played about with it as one does with an assured pleasure, and at the back of my mind there was also a trace of fear lest the letter contain any news or reference which might annoy me. Letter writing and receiving in gaol were always serious incursions on a peaceful and unruffled existence. They produced an emotional state which was disturbing, and for a day or two afterwards one's mind wandered and it was difficult to concentrate on the day's work.

In Naini Prison and Bareilly Gaol I had several companions. In Dehra Dun there were three of us to begin with—Govind Ballabh Pant, Kunwar Anand Singh of Kashipur and I—but Pantji was discharged after a couple of months on the expiry of his six months. Two others joined us later. By the beginning of January 1933 all my companions had left me and I was alone. For nearly eight months, till my discharge at the end of August, I lived a solitary life in Dehra Dun Gaol with hardly any one to talk to, except some member of the gaol staff for a few minutes daily. This was not technically solitary confinement, but it was a near approach to it, and it was a dreary period for me. Fortunately I had resumed my interviews, and they brought some relief. As a special favour, I suppose, I was allowed to receive fresh flowers from outside and to keep a few photographs, and they cheered me greatly. Ordinarily, flowers and photographs are not permitted, and on several occasions I have not been allowed to receive the flowers that had been sent for me. Attempts to brighten up the cells were not encouraged, and I remember a superintendent of a gaol once objecting to the manner in which a companion of mine, whose cell was next to mine, had arranged his toilet articles. He was told that he must not make his cell look attractive and "luxurious". The articles of luxury were: a tooth brush, tooth paste, fountain-pen ink, a bottle of hair oil, a brush and comb, and perhaps one or two other little things.

One begins to appreciate the value of the little things of life in prison. One's belongings are so few and they cannot easily be added to or replaced, and one clings to them and gathers up odd bits of things which, in the world outside, would go to the waste-paper basket. The property sense does not leave one even when there is nothing worthwhile to own and keep.

Sometimes a physical longing would come for the soft things of life—bodily comfort, pleasant surroundings, the company of friends, interesting conversation, games with children ... A picture or a paragraph in a newspaper would bring the old days vividly before one, carefree days of youth, and a nostalgia would seize one, and the day would be passed in restlessness.

I used to spin a little daily, for I found some manual occupation soothing and a relief from too much intellectual work. My main occupation, however, was reading and writing. I could not have all the books I wanted, as there were restrictions and a censorship, and the censors were not always very competent for the job. Spengler's *Decline of the West* was held up because the title looked dangerous and seditious. But I must not complain, for I had, on the whole, a goodly variety of books. Again I seem to have been a favoured person, and many of my colleagues (A Class prisoners) had the greatest difficulty in getting books on current topics. In Benares Gaol, I was told, even the official White Paper, containing the British Government's constitutional proposals, was not allowed in, as it dealt with political matters. The only books that British officials heartily recommended were religious books or novels. It is wonderful how dear to the heart of the British Government is the subject of religion and how impartially it encourages all brands of it.

When the most ordinary civil liberties have been curtailed in India, it is hardly pertinent to talk of a prisoner's rights. And yet the subject is worthy of consideration. If a court of law sentences a person to imprisonment, does it follow that not only his body but also his mind should be incarcerated? Why should not the minds of prisoners be free even though their bodies are not? Those in charge of the prison administrations in India will no doubt be horrified at such a question, for their capacity for new ideas and sustained thought is usually limited. Censorship is bad enough at any time and is partisan and stupid. In India it deprives us of a great deal of modern literature and advanced journals and newspapers. The list of proscribed books is extensive and is frequently added to. To add to all this, the prisoner has to suffer a second and a separate censorship, and thus many books and newspapers that can be legally purchased and read outside the prison may not reach him.

Some time ago this question arose in the United States, in the famous Sing Sing Prison of New York, where some Communist newspapers had been banned. The feeling against Communists is very strong among the ruling classes in America, but in spite of this the prison authorities agreed that the inmates of the prison could receive any publication which they desired, including Communist newspapers and magazines. The sole exception made by the Warden was in the case of cartoons which he regarded as inflammatory.

It is a little absurd to discuss this question of freedom of mind in prison in India when, as it happens, the vast majority of the prisoners are not allowed any newspapers or writing materials. It is not a question of censorship but of total denial. Only A Class (or in Bengal, Division I) prisoners are allowed writing materials as a matter of course, and not even all these are allowed daily newspapers. The daily newspaper allowed is of the Government's choice. B and C Class prisoners, politicals and non-politicals, are not supposed to have writing materials. The former may sometimes get them as a very special privilege, which is frequently withdrawn. Probably the proportion of A Class prisoners to the others is one to a thousand, and they might well be excluded in considering the lot of prisoners in India. But it is well to remember that even these favoured A Class convicts have far less privileges in regard to books and newspapers than the ordinary prisoners in most civilized countries.

For the rest, the 999 in every thousand, two or three books are permitted at a time, but conditions are such that they cannot always take advantage of this privilege. Writing or the taking of notes of books read are dangerous pastimes in which they must not indulge. This deliberate discouragement of intellectual development is curious and revealing.

From the point of view of reclaiming a prisoner and of making him a fit citizen, his mind should be approached and diverted, and he should be made literate and taught some craft. But this point of view has perhaps not struck the prison authorities in India. Certainly it has been conspicuous by its absence in the United Provinces. Recently attempts have been made to teach reading and writing to the boys and young men in prison, but they are wholly ineffective, and the men in charge of them have no competence. Sometimes it is said that convicts are averse to learning. My own experience has been the exact opposite, and I found many of them, who came to me for the purpose, to have a perfect passion for learning to read and write. We used to teach such convicts as came our way, and they worked hard; and sometimes when I woke up in the middle of the night I was surprised to find one or two of them sitting by a dim lantern inside their barrack, learning their lessons for the next day.

So I occupied myself with my books, going from one type of reading to another, but usually sticking to 'heavy' books. Novels made one feel mentally slack, and I did not read many of them. Sometimes I would weary of too much reading, and then I would take to writing. My historical series of letters to my daughter kept me occupied right through my two-year term, and they helped me very greatly to keep mentally fit. To some extent I lived through the past I was writing about and almost forgot about my gaol surroundings.

Travel books were always welcome—records of old travellers, Hiuen Tsang, and Marco Polo, and Ibn Battuta and others, and moderns like Sven Hedin, with his journeys across the deserts of Central Asia, and Roerich, finding strange adventures in Tibet. Picture books also, especially of mountains and glaciers and deserts, for in prison one hungers for wide spaces and seas and mountains. I had some beautiful picture books of Mont Blanc, the Alps, and the Himalayas, and I turned to them often and gazed at the glaciers when the temperature of my cell or barrack was 115°F. or even more. An atlas was an exciting affair. It brought all manner of past memories and dreams of places we had visited and places we had wanted to go to. And the longing to go again to those haunts of past days, and visit all the other inviting marks and dots that represented great cities, and cross the shaded regions that were mountains, and the blue patches that were seas, and to see the beauties of the world, and

watch the struggles and conflicts of a changing humanity—the longing
to do all this would seize us and clutch us by the throat, and we would
hurriedly and sorrowfully put the atlas by, and return to the well-known
walls that surrounded us and the dull routine that was our daily lot.

45

ANIMALS IN PRISON

For fourteen and a half months I lived in my little cell or room in the Dehra Dun Gaol, and I began to feel as if I was almost a part of it. I was familiar with every bit of it; I knew every mark and dent on the whitewashed walls and on the uneven floor and the ceiling with its moth-eaten rafters. In the little yard outside I greeted little tufts of grass and odd bits of stone as old friends. I was not alone in my cell, for several colonies of wasps and hornets lived there, and many lizards found a home behind the rafters, emerging in the evenings in search of prey. If thoughts and emotions leave their traces behind in the physical surroundings, the very air of that cell must be thick with them, and they must cling to every object in that little space.

I had had better cells in other prisons, but in Dehra Dun I had one privilege which was very precious to me. The gaol proper was a very small one, and we were kept in an old lock-up outside the gaol walls, but within the gaol compound. This place was so small that there was no room to walk about in it, and so we were allowed, morning and evening, to go out and walk up and down in front of the gate, a distance of about a hundred yards. We remained in the gaol compound, but this coming outside the walls gave us a view of the mountains and the fields and a public road at some distance. This was not a special privilege for me; it was common for all the A and B Class prisoners kept at Dehra Dun. Within the compound, but outside the gaol walls, there was another small building called the European Lock-up. This had no enclosing wall, and a person inside the cell could have a fine view of the mountains and the life outside. European convicts and others kept here were also allowed to walk in front of the gaol gate every morning and evening.

Only a prisoner who has been confined for long behind high walls can appreciate the extraordinary psychological value of these outside walks and open views. I loved these outings, and I did not give them up even during the monsoon, when the rain came down for days in torrents and I had to walk in ankle-deep of water. I would have welcomed the outing in any place, but the sight of the towering Himalayas near by was an added joy which went a long way to removing the weariness of prison. It was my good fortune that during the long period when I had no interviews, and when for many months I was quite alone, I could gaze at these mountains that I loved. I could not see the mountains from my cell, but my mind was full of them and I was ever conscious of their nearness, and a secret intimacy seemed to grow between us.

> Flocks of birds have flown high and away;
> A solitary drift of cloud, too, has gone, wandering on.
> And I sit alone with Ching-ting Peak, towering beyond,
> We never grow tired of each other, the mountain and I.

I am afraid I cannot say with the poet, Li T'ai Po, that I never grew weary, even of the mountain; but that was a rare experience, and, as a rule, I found great comfort in its proximity. Its solidity and imperturbability looked down upon me with the wisdom of a million years, and mocked at my varying humours and soothed my fevered mind.

Spring was very pleasant in Dehra, and it was a far longer one than in the plains below. The winter had denuded almost all the trees of their leaves, and they stood naked and bare. Even four magnificent peepal trees, which stood in front of the gaol gate, much to my surprise, dropped nearly all their leaves. Gaunt and cheerless they stood there, till the spring air warmed them up again and sent a message of life to their innermost cells. Suddenly there was a stir both in the peepals and the other trees, and an air of mystery surrounded them as of secret operations going on behind the scenes; and I would be startled to find little bits of green peeping out all over them. It was a gay and cheering sight. And then, very rapidly, the leaves would come out in their millions and glisten in the sunlight and play about in the breeze. How wonderful is the sudden change from bud to leaf!

I had never noticed before that fresh mango leaves are reddish-brown, russet coloured, remarkably like the autumn tints on the Kashmir hills. But they change colour soon and become green.

The monsoon rains were always welcome, for they ended the summer heat. But one could have too much of a good thing, and Dehra Dun is one of the favoured haunts of the rain god. Within the first five or six weeks of the break of the monsoon we would have about fifty or sixty inches of rain, and it was not pleasant to sit cooped up in a little narrow place trying to avoid the water dripping from the ceiling or rushing in from the windows.

Autumn again was pleasant, and so was the winter, except when it rained. With thunder and rain and piercing cold winds, one longed for a decent habitation and a little warmth and comfort. Occasionally there would be a hailstorm, with hailstones bigger than marbles coming down on the corrugated iron roofs and making a tremendous noise, something like an artillery bombardment.

I remember one day particularly; it was the 24th of December, 1932. There was a thunderstorm and rain all day, and it was bitterly cold. Altogether it was one of the most miserable days, from the bodily point of view, that I have spent in gaol. In the evening it cleared up suddenly, and all my misery departed when I saw all the neighbouring mountains and hills covered with a thick mantle of snow. The next day—Christmas Day—was lovely and clear, and there was a beautiful view of snow-covered mountains.

Prevented from indulging in normal activities we became more observant of nature's ways. We watched also the various animals and insects that came our way. As I grew more observant I noticed all manner of insects living in my cell or in the little yard outside. I realized that while I complained of loneliness, that yard, which seemed empty and deserted, was teeming with life. All these creeping or crawling or flying insects lived their life without interfering with me in any way, and I saw no reason why I should interfere with them. But there was continuous war between me and bed-bugs, mosquitos, and, to some extent, flies. Wasps and hornets I tolerated, and there were hundreds of them in my cell. There had been a little tiff between us when, inadvertently I think, a wasp had stung me. In my anger I tried to exterminate the lot, but they put up a brave fight in defence of their temporary home, which probably contained their eggs, and I desisted and decided to leave them in peace if they did not interfere with me any more. For over a year after that I lived in that cell surrounded by these wasps and hornets, and they never attacked me, and we respected each other.

Bats I did not like, but I had to endure them. They flew soundlessly in the evening dusk, and one could just see them against the darkening sky. Eerie things; I had a horror of them. They seemed to pass within an inch of one's face, and I was always afraid that they might hit me. Higher up in the air passed the big bats, the flying-foxes.

I used to watch the ants and the white ants and other insects by the hour. And the lizards as they crept about in the evenings and stalked their prey and chased each other, wagging their tails in a most comic fashion. Ordinarily they avoided wasps, but twice I saw them stalk them with enormous care and seize them from the front. I do not know if this avoidance of the sting was intentional or accidental.

Then there were squirrels, crowds of them if trees were about. They would become very venturesome and come right near us. In Lucknow Gaol I used to sit reading almost without moving for considerable periods, and a squirrel would climb up my leg and sit on my knee and have a look round. And then it would look into my eyes and realize that I was not a tree or whatever it had taken me for. Fear would disable it for a moment, and then it would scamper away. Little baby squirrels would sometimes fall down from the trees. The mother would come after them, roll them up into a little ball, and carry them off to safety. Occasionally the baby got lost. One of my companions picked up three of these lost baby squirrels and looked after them. They were so tiny that it was a problem how to feed them. The problem was, however, solved rather ingeniously. A fountain-pen filler, with a little cotton wool attached to it, made an efficient feeding bottle.

Pigeons abounded in all the gaols I went to, except in the mountain prison of Almora. There were thousands of them, and in the evenings the sky would be thick with them. Sometimes the gaol officials would shoot them down and feed on them. There were mainas, of course; they are to be found everywhere. A pair of them nested over my cell door in Dehra Dun, and I used to feed them. They grew quite tame, and if there was any delay in their morning or evening meal they would sit quite near me and loudly demand their food. It was amusing to watch their signs and listen to their impatient cries.

In Naini there were thousands of parrots, and large numbers of them lived in the crevices of my barrack walls. Their courtship and love-making was always a fascinating sight, and sometimes there were fierce quarrels between two male parrots over a lady parrot, who sat calmly by waiting for the result of the encounter and ready to grant her favours to the winner.

Dehra Dun had a variety of birds, and there was a regular jumble of singing and lively chattering and twittering, and high above it all came the koel's plaintive call. During the monsoon and just before it the Brain-Fever bird visited us, and I realized soon why it was so named. It was amazing the persistence with which it went on repeating the same notes, in daytime and at night, in sunshine and in pouring rain. We could not see most of these birds, we could only hear them as a rule, as there were no trees in our little yard. But I used to watch the eagles and the kites gliding gracefully high up in the air, sometimes swooping down and then allowing themselves to be carried up by a current of air. Often a horde of wild duck would fly over our heads.

There was a large colony of monkeys in Bareilly Gaol and their antics were always worth watching. One incident impressed me. A baby monkey managed to come down into our barrack enclosure and he could not mount up the wall again. The warder and some convict overseers and other prisoners caught hold of him and tied a bit of string round his neck. The parents (presumably) of the little one saw all this from the top of the high wall, and their anger grew. Suddenly one of them, a huge monkey, jumped down and charged almost right into the crowd which surrounded the baby monkey. It was an extraordinary brave thing to do, for the warder and C.O.s had sticks and *lathis* and they were brandishing them about, and there was quite a crowd of them. Reckless courage triumphed, and the crowd of humans fled, terrified, leaving their sticks behind them! The little monkey was rescued.

We had often animal visitors that were not welcome. Scorpions were frequently found in our cells, especially after a thunderstorm. It was surprising that I was never stung by one, for I would come across them in the most unlikely places—on my bed, or sitting on a book which I had just lined up. I kept a particularly black and poisonous-looking brute in a bottle for some time, feeding him with flies, etc., and then when I tied him up on a wall with a string he managed to escape. I had no desire to meet him loose again, and so I cleaned my cell out and hunted for him everywhere, but he had vanished.

Three or four snakes were also found in my cells or near them. News of one of them got out, and there were headlines in the Press. As a matter of fact I welcomed the diversion. Prison life is dull enough, and everything that breaks through the monotony is appreciated. Not that I appreciate or welcome snakes, but they do not fill me with terror as they do some people. I am afraid of their bite, of course, and would protect myself if I saw a snake. But there would be no feeling of repulsion or overwhelming fright. Centipedes horrify me much more; it is not so much fear as instinctive repulsion. In Alipore Gaol in Calcutta I woke in the middle of the night and felt something crawling over my foot. I pressed a torch I had and I saw a centipede on the bed. Instinctively and with amazing rapidity I vaulted clear out of that bed and nearly hit the cell wall. I realized fully then what Pavlov's reflexes were.

In Dehra Dun I saw a new animal, or rather an animal which was new to me. I was standing at the gaol gate talking to the gaoler when we noticed a man outside carrying a strange animal. The gaoler sent for him, and I saw something between a lizard and a crocodile, about two feet long with claws and a scaly covering. This uncouth animal, which was very much alive, had been twisted round in a most peculiar way forming a kind of knot, and its owner had passed a pole through this knot and was merrily carrying it in this fashion. He called it a "Bo." When asked by the gaoler what he proposed to do with it, he replied with a broad smile that he would make *bhujji*—a kind of curry—out of it! He was a forest-dweller. Subsequently I discovered from reading F. W. Champion's book—*The Jungle in Sunlight and Shadow*—that this animal was the Pangolin.

Prisoners, especially long-term convicts, have to suffer most from emotional starvation. Often they seek some emotional satisfaction by keeping animal pets. The ordinary prisoner cannot keep them, but the convict overseers have a little more freedom and the gaol staff usually does not object. The commonest pets were squirrels and, strangely, mongooses. Dogs are not allowed in gaols, but cats seem to be encouraged. A little kitten made friends with me once. It belonged to a gaol official, and when he was transferred he took it away with him. I missed it. Although dogs are not allowed, I got tied up with some dogs accidentally in Dehra Dun. A gaol official had brought a bitch, and then he was transferred, and he deserted her. The poor thing became a homeless wanderer, living under culverts, picking up scraps from the warders, usually starving. As I was being kept in the lock-up outside the gaol proper, she used to come to me begging for food. I began to feed her regularly, and she gave birth to a litter of pups under a culvert. Many of these were taken away, but three remained and I fed them. One of the puppies fell ill with a violent distemper, and gave me a great deal of trouble. I nursed her with care, and sometimes I would get up a dozen times in the course of the night to look after her. She survived, and I was happy that my nursing had pulled her round.

I came in contact with animals far more in prison than I had done outside. I had always been fond of dogs, and had kept some, but I could never look after them properly as other matters claimed my attention. In prison I was grateful for their company. Indians do not, as a rule, approve of animals as household pets. It is remarkable that in spite of their general philosophy of non-violence to animals, they are often singularly careless and unkind to them. Even the cow, that favoured animal, though looked up to and almost worshipped by many Hindus and often the cause of riots, is not treated kindly. Worship and kindliness do not always go together.

Different countries have adopted different animals as symbols of their ambition or character—the eagle of the United States of America and of Germany, the lion and bulldog of England, the fighting-cock of France, the bear of old Russia. How far do these patron animals mould national character? Most of them are aggressive, fighting animals, beasts of prey. It is not surprising that the people who grow up with these examples before them should mould themselves consciously after them and strike up aggressive attitudes, and roar, and prey on others. Nor is it surprising that the Hindu should be mild and non-violent, for his patron animal is the cow.

46

STRUGGLE

Outside, the struggle went on, and brave men and women continued to defy peacefully a powerful and entrenched government, though they knew that it was not for them to achieve in the present or the near future. And repression without break and with ever-increasing intensity, demonstrated the basis of British rule in India. There was no camouflage about it now, and this at least was some satisfaction to us. Bayonets were triumphant, but a great warrior had once said that "you can do everything with bayonets save sit on them." It was better that we should be governed thus, we thought, than that we should sell our souls and submit to spiritual prostitution. We were physically helpless in prison, but we felt we served our cause even there, and served it better than many outside. Should we, because of our weakness, sacrifice the future of India to save ourselves? It was true that the limits of human vitality and human strength were narrow, and many an individual was physically disabled, or died, or fell out of the ranks, or even betrayed the cause. But the cause went on despite setbacks; there could be no failure if ideals remained undimmed and spirits undaunted. Real failure was a desertion of principle, a denial of our right, and an ignoble submission to wrong. Self-made wounds always took longer to heal than those caused by an adversary.

There was often a weariness at our weaknesses and at a world gone awry, and yet there was a measure of pride for our achievement. For our people had indeed behaved splendidly, and it was good to feel oneself to be a member of a gallant band.

During those years of civil disobedience two attempts were made to hold open Congress sessions, one at Delhi and the other at Calcutta. It was obvious that an illegal organization could not meet normally and in peace, and any attempt at an open session meant conflict with the police. The meetings were in fact dispersed forcibly with the help of the *lathi* by the police, and large numbers of people were arrested. The extraordinary thing about these gatherings was the fact that thousands came from all parts of India as delegates to these illegal gatherings. I was glad to learn that people from the United Provinces played a prominent part in both of them. My mother also insisted on going to the Calcutta session at the end of March 1933. She was arrested, however, together with Pandit Malaviya and others, and detained in prison for a few days at Asansol, on the way to Calcutta. I was amazed at the energy and vitality she showed, frail and ailing as she was. Prison was really of little consequence to her; she had gone through a harder ordeal. Her son and both her daughters and others whom she loved spent long periods in prison, and the empty house where she lived had become a nightmare to her.

As our struggle toned down and stabilized itself at a low level there was little of excitement in it, except at long intervals. My thoughts travelled more to other countries, and I watched and studied, as far as I could in gaol, the world situation in the grip of the great depression. I read as many books as I could find on the subject, and the more I read the more fascinated I grew. India with her problems and struggles became just a part of this mighty world drama, of the great struggle of political and economic forces that was going on everywhere, nationally and internationally. In that struggle my own sympathies went increasingly towards the communist side.

I had long been drawn to socialism and communism, and Russia had appealed to me. Much in Soviet Russia I dislike—the ruthless suppression of all contrary opinion, the wholesale regimentation, the unnecessary violence (as I thought) in carrying out various policies. But there was no lack of violence and suppression in the capitalist world, and I realized more and more how the very basis and foundation of our acquisitive society and property was violence. Without violence it could not continue for many days. A measure of political liberty meant little indeed when the fear of starvation was always compelling the vast majority of people everywhere to submit to the will of the few, to the greater glory and advantage of the latter.

Violence was common in both places, but the violence of the capitalist order seemed inherent in it; whilst the violence of Russia, bad though it was, aimed at a new order based on peace and co-operation and real freedom for the masses. With all her blunders, Soviet Russia had triumphed over enormous difficulties and taken great strides towards this new order. While the rest of the world was in the grip of the depression and going backward in some ways, in the Soviet country a great new world was being built up before our eyes. Russia, following the great Lenin, looked into the future and thought only of what was to be, while other countries lay numbed under the dead hand of the past and spent their energy in preserving the useless relics of a bygone age. In particular, I was impressed by the reports of the great progress made by the backward regions of Central Asia under the Soviet regime. In the balance, therefore, I was all in favour of Russia, and the presence and example of the Soviets was a bright and heartening phenomenon in a dark and dismal world.

But Soviet Russia's success or failure, vastly important as it was as a practical experiment in establishing a communist state, did not affect the soundness of the theory of communism. The Bolsheviks may blunder or even fail because of national or international reasons, and yet the communist theory may be correct. On the basis of that very theory it was absurd to copy blindly what had taken place in Russia, for its application depended on the particular conditions prevailing in the country in question and the stage of its historical development. Besides, India, or any other country, could profit by the triumphs as well as the inevitable mistakes of the Bolsheviks. Perhaps the Bolsheviks had tried to go too fast because, surrounded as they were by a world of enemies, they feared external aggression. A slower tempo might avoid much of the misery caused in the rural areas. But then the question arose if really radical results could be obtained by slowing down the rate of change. Reformism was an impossible solution of any vital problem at a critical moment when the basic structure had to be changed, and however slow the progress might be later on, the initial step must be a complete break with the existing order, which had fulfilled its purpose and was now only a drag on future progress.

In India, only a revolutionary plan could solve the two related questions of the land and industry as well as almost every other major problem before the country. "There is no graver mistake," as Mr Lloyd George says in his *War Memoirs*, "than to leap the abyss in two jumps."

Russia apart, the theory and philosophy of Marxism lightened up many a dark corner of my mind. History came to have a new meaning for me. The Marxist interpretation threw a flood of light on it, and it became an unfolding drama with some order and purpose, howsoever unconscious, behind it. In spite of the appalling waste and misery of the past and the present, the future was bright with hope, though many dangers intervened. It was the essential freedom from dogma and the scientific outlook of Marxism that appealed to me. It was true that there was plenty of dogma in official communism in Russia and elsewhere, and frequently heresy hunts were organized. That seemed to be deplorable, though it was not difficult to understand in view of the tremendous changes taking place rapidly in the Soviet countries when effective opposition might have resulted in catastrophic failure.

The great world crisis and slump seemed to justify the Marxist analysis. While all other systems and theories were groping about in the dark, Marxism alone explained it more or less satisfactorily and offered a real solution.

As this conviction grew upon me, I was filled with a new excitement and my depression at the non-success of civil disobedience grew much less. Was not the world marching rapidly towards the desired consummation? There were grave dangers of wars and catastrophes, but at any rate we were moving. There was no stagnation. Our national struggle became a stage in the longer journey, and it was as well that repression and suffering were tempering our people for future struggles and forcing them to consider the new ideas that were stirring the world. We would be the stronger and the more disciplined and hardened by the elimination of the weaker elements. Time was in our favour.

And so I studied carefully what was happening in Russia, Germany, England, America, Japan, China, France, Spain, Italy and Central Europe, and tried to understand the tangled web of current affairs. I followed with interest the attempts of each country separately, and of all of them together, to weather the storm. The repeated failures of international conferences to find a solution for political and economic ills and the problem of disarmament reminded me forcibly of a little, but sufficiently troublesome, problem of our own—the communal problem. With all the goodwill in the world, we have so far not solved the problem; and, in spite of a widespread belief that failure would lead to world catastrophe, the great statesmen of Europe and America have failed to pull together. In either case the approach was wrong, and the people concerned did not dare to go the right way.

In thinking over the troubles and conflicts of the world, I forgot to some extent my own personal and national troubles. I would even feel buoyant occasionally at the fact that I was alive at this great revolutionary period of the world's history. Perhaps I might also have to play some little part in my own corner of the world in the great changes that were to come. At other times I would find the atmosphere of conflict and violence all over the world very depressing. Worse still was the sight of intelligent men and women who had become so accustomed to human degradation and slavery that their minds were too coarsened to resent suffering and poverty and inhumanity. Noisy vulgarity and organized humbug flourished in this stifling moral atmosphere, and good men were silent. The triumph of Hitler and the Brown Terror that followed was a great shock, though I consoled myself that it could only be temporary. Almost one had the feeling of the futility of human endeavour. The machine went on blindly, what could a little cog in it do?

But still the communist philosophy of life gave me comfort and hope. How was it to be applied to India? We had not solved yet the problem of political freedom, and the nationalistic outlook filled our minds. Were we to jump to economic freedom at the same time or take them in turn, however short the interval might be? World events as well as happenings in India were forcing the social issue to the front, and it seemed that political freedom could no longer be separated from it.

The policy of the British Government in India had resulted in ranging the socially reactionary classes in opposition to political independence. That was inevitable, and I welcomed the clearer demarcation of the various classes and groups in India. But was this fact appreciated by others? Apparently not by many. It was true that there were a handful of orthodox Communists in some of the big cities and they were hostile to, and bitterly critical of, the national movement. The organized Labour movement, especially in Bombay and, to a lesser extent, in Calcutta, was also socialistic in a loose kind of way, but it was broken up into bits and suffering from the depression. Vague communistic and socialistic ideas had spread among the intelligentsia, even among intelligent Government officials. The younger men and women of the Congress, who used to read Bryce on Democracies and Morley and Keith and Mazzini, were now reading, when they could get them, books on socialism and communism and Russia. The Meerut Conspiracy Case had helped greatly in directing people's minds to these new ideas, and the world crisis had compelled attention. Everywhere there was in evidence a new spirit of enquiry, a questioning, and a challenge to existing institutions. The general direction of the mental wind was obvious, but still it was a gentle breeze, unsure of itself. Some people flirted with Fascist ideas. A clear and definite ideology was lacking. Nationalism still was the dominating thought.

It seemed clear to me that nationalism would remain the outstanding urge, till some measure of political freedom was attained. Because of this the Congress had been, and was still (apart from certain Labour circles), the most advanced organization in India, as it was far the most powerful. During the past thirteen years, under Gandhiji's leadership, it had produced a wonderful awakening of the masses and, in spite of its vague *bourgeois* ideology, it had served a revolutionary purpose. It had not exhausted its utility yet, and was not likely to do so till the nationalist urge gave place to a social one. Future progress, both ideological and in action, must therefore be largely associated with the Congress, though other avenues could also be used.

To desert the Congress seemed to me thus to cut oneself adrift from the vital urge of the nation, to blunt the most powerful weapon we had, and perhaps to waste energy in ineffective adventurism. And yet, was the Congress, constituted as it was, ever likely to adopt a really radical social solution? If such an issue was placed before it, the result was bound to be to split it into two or more parts, or at least to drive away large sections from it. That in itself was not undesirable or unwelcome if the issues became clearer and a strongly-knit group, either a majority or minority in the Congress, stood for a radical social programme.

But Congress at present meant Gandhiji. What would he do? Ideologically he was sometimes amazingly backward, and yet in action he had been the greatest revolutionary of recent times in India. He was a unique personality, and it was impossible to judge him by the usual standards, or even to apply the ordinary canons of logic to him. But because he was a revolutionary at bottom and was pledged to political independence for India, he was bound to play an uncompromising role till that independence was achieved. And in this very process he would release tremendous mass energies and would himself, I half hoped, advance step by step towards the social goal.

The orthodox Communists in India and outside have for many years past attacked Gandhiji and the Congress bitterly, and imputed all manner of base motives to the Congress leaders. Many of their theoretical criticisms of Congress ideology were able and pointed, and subsequent events partly justified them. Some of the earlier Communist analyses of the general Indian political situation turned out to be remarkably correct. But as soon as they leave their general principles and enter into details, and especially when they consider the rôle of the Congress, they go hopelessly astray. One of the reasons for the weakness in numbers as well as influence of the Communists in India is that, instead of spreading a scientific knowledge of communism and trying to convert people's minds to it, they have largely concentrated on abuse of others. This has reacted on them and done them great injury. Most of them are used to working in labour areas, where a few slogans are usually enough to win over the workers. But mere slogans are not enough for the intellectual, and they have not realized that in India today the middle class intellectual is the most revolutionary force. Almost in spite of the orthodox Communists, many intellectuals have been drawn to communism, but even so there is a gulf between them.

According to the Communists, the objective of the Congress leaders has been to bring mass pressure on the Government in order to obtain industrial and commercial concessions in the interests of Indian capitalists and zamindars. The task of the Congress is "to harness the economic and political discontent of the peasantry, the lower middle class and the industrial working class to the chariot of the mill-owners and financiers of Bombay, Ahmedabad and Calcutta." The Indian capitalists are supposed to sit behind the scenes and issue orders to the Congress Working Committee first to organize a mass movement and, when it becomes too vast and dangerous, to suspend it or side-track it. Further, that the Congress leaders really do not want the British to go away, as they are required to control and exploit a starving population, and the Indian middle class do not feel themselves equal to this.

It is surprising that able Communists should believe this fantastic analysis, but believing this as they apparently do, it is not surprising that they should fail so remarkably in India. Their basic error seems to be that they judge the Indian National Movement from European Labour standards, and used as they are to the repeated betrayals of the labour movement by the labour leaders, they apply the analogy to India. The

Indian National Movement is obviously not a labour or proletarian movement. It is a *bourgeois* movement, as its very name implies, and its objective so far has been, not a change of the social order, but political independence. This objective may be criticized as not far-reaching enough, and nationalism itself may be condemned as out of date. But accepting the fundamental basis of the movement, it is absurd to say that the leaders betray the masses because they do not try to upset the land system or the capitalist system. They never claimed to do so. Some people in the Congress, and they are a growing number, want to change the land system and the capitalist system, but they cannot speak in the name of the Congress.

It is true that the Indian capitalist classes (not the big zamindars and taluqadars) have profited greatly by the national movement because of British and other foreign boycotts, and the push given to swadeshi. This was inevitable, as every national movement encourages home industries and preaches boycotts. As a matter of fact the Bombay mill industry in a body, during the continuance of civil disobedience and when we were preaching the boycott of British goods, had the temerity to conclude a pact with Lancashire. From the point of view of the Congress, this was a gross betrayal of the national cause, and it was characterized as such. The representative of the Bombay mill-owners in the Assembly also consistently ran down the Congress and 'extremists' while most of us were in gaol.

The part that many capitalist elements have played in India during the past few years has been scandalous, even from the Congress and nationalist view-point. Ottawa may have benefited temporarily some small groups, but it was bad in the interest of Indian industry as a whole, and made it even more subservient to British capital and industry. It was harmful to the masses, and it was negotiated while our struggle was being carried on, and many thousands were in prison. Every Dominion wrung out the hardest terms from England, but India had the privilege of making almost a gift to her. During the last few years also financial adventurers have trafficked in gold and silver at India's expense.

As for the big zamindars and taluqadars, they ranged themselves completely against the Congress in the Round Table Conference, and they openly and aggressively declared themselves on the side of the Government right through civil disobedience. It was with their help that Government passed repressive legislation in various provinces embodying the Ordinances. And in the United Provinces Council the great majority of the zamindar members voted against the release of civil disobedience prisoners.

The idea that Gandhiji was forced to launch seemingly aggressive movements in 1921 and 1930 because of mass pressure, is also absolutely wrong. Mass stirrings there were, of course, but on both occasions it was Gandhiji who forced the pace. In 1921 he carried the Congress almost single-handed, and plunged it into non-co-operation. In 1930 it would have been quite impossible to have any aggressive and effective direct action movement if he had resisted it in any way.

It is very unfortunate that foolish and ill-informed criticisms of a personal nature are made, because they divert attention from the real issues. To attack Gandhiji's *bona fides* is to injure oneself and one's own cause, for to the millions of India he stands as the embodiment of truth, and anyone who knows him at all realizes the passionate earnestness with which he is always seeking to do right.

Communists in India have associated with the industrial workers of the big towns. They have little knowledge of, or contact with, the rural areas. The industrial workers, important as they are, and likely to be more so in the future, must take second place before the peasants, for the problem of today in India is the problem of the peasantry. Congress workers, on the other hand, have spread all over these rural areas and, in the ordinary course, the Congress must develop into a vast peasant organization. Peasants are seldom revolutionary after their immediate objective is attained, and it is likely that some time in the future the usual problem of city *versus* village and industrial worker *versus* peasant will rise in India also.

It has been my privilege to be associated very closely with a large number of Congress leaders and workers, and I could not wish for a finer set of men and women. And yet I have differed from them on vital issues, and often I have felt a little weary at finding that they do not appreciate or understand something that seems to me quite obvious. It was not due to want of intelligence, somehow we moved in different ideological grooves. I realized how difficult it is to cross these boundaries suddenly. They constitute different philosophies of life, and we grow into them gradually and unconsciously. It is futile to blame the other party. Socialism involves a certain psychological outlook on life and its problems. It is more than mere logic. So also are the other outlooks based on heredity, upbringing, the unseen influences of the past and our present environments. Only life itself with its bitter lessons forces us along new paths and ultimately, which is far harder, makes us think differently. Perhaps we may help a little in this process. And perhaps

On rencontre sa destinée
Souvent par les chemins q'on prend pour l'éviter.

47

WHAT IS RELIGION?

Our peaceful and monotonous routine in gaol was suddenly upset in the middle of September 1932 by a bombshell. News came that Gandhiji had decided to "fast unto death" in disapproval of the separate electorates given by Mr Ramsay MacDonald's Communal Award to the Depressed Classes. What a capacity he had to give shocks to people! Suddenly all manner of ideas rushed into my head; all kinds of possibilities and contingencies rose up before me and upset my equilibrium completely. For two days I was in darkness with no light to show the way out, my heart sinking when I thought of some results of Gandhiji's action. The personal aspect was powerful enough, and I thought with anguish that I might not see him again. It was over a year ago that I had seen him last on board ship on the way to England. Was that going to be my last sight of him?

And then I felt annoyed with him for choosing a side-issue for his final sacrifice—just a question of electorate. What would be the result on our freedom movement? Would not the larger issues fade into the background, for the time being at least? And if he attained his immediate object and got a joint electorate for the Depressed Classes, would not that result in a reaction and a feeling that something has been achieved and nothing more need be done for a while? And was not his action a recognition, and in part an acceptance, of the Communal Award and the general scheme of things as sponsored by the Government? Was this consistent with Non-Co-operation and Civil Disobedience? After so much sacrifice and brave endeavour, was our movement to tail off into something insignificant?

I felt angry with him at his religious and sentimental approach to a political question, and his frequent references to God in connection with it. He even seemed to suggest that God had indicated the very date of the fast. What a terrible example to set!

If Bapu died! What would India be like then? And how would her politics run? There seemed to be a dreary and dismal future ahead, and despair seized my heart when I thought of it. So I thought and thought, and confusion reigned in my head, and anger and hopelessness, and love for him who was the cause of this upheaval. I hardly knew what to do, and I was irritable and short-tempered with everybody, and most of all with myself.

And then a strange thing happened to me. I had quite an emotional crisis, and at the end of it I felt calmer and the future seemed not so dark. Bapu had a curious knack of doing the right thing at the psychological moment, and it might be that his action—impossible to justify as it was from my point of view—would lead to great results, not only in the narrow field in which it was confined, but in the wider aspects of our national struggle. And even if Bapu died our struggle for freedom would go on. So whatever happened, one must keep ready and fit for it. Having made up my mind to face even Gandhiji's death without flinching, I felt calm and collected and ready to face the world and all it might offer.

Then came news of the tremendous upheaval all over the country, a magic wave of enthusiasm running through Hindu society, and untouchability appeared to be doomed. What a magician, I thought, was this little man sitting in Yeravda Prison, and how well he knew how to pull the strings that move people's hearts!

A telegram from him reached me. It was the first message I had received from him since my conviction, and it did me good to hear from him after that long interval. In this telegram he said:

> During all these days of agony you have been before mind's eye. I am most anxious to know your opinion. You know how I value your opinion. Saw Indu (and) Sarup's children. Indu looked happy and in possession of more flesh. Doing very well. Wire reply. Love.

It was extraordinary, and yet it was characteristic of him, that in the agony of his fast and in the midst of his many preoccupations, he should refer to the visit of my daughter and my sister's children to him, and even mention that Indira had put on flesh! (My sister was also in prison then and all these children were at school in Poona.) He never forgets the seemingly little things in life which really mean so much.

News also came to me just then that some settlement had been reached over the electorate issue. The superintendent of the gaol was good enough to allow me to send an answer to Gandhiji, and I sent him the following telegram:

> Your telegram and brief news that some settlement reached filled me with relief and joy. First news of your decision to fast caused mental agony and confusion, but ultimately optimism triumphed and I regained peace of mind. No sacrifice too great for suppressed downtrodden classes. Freedom must be judged by freedom of lowest but feel danger of other issues obscuring only goal. Am unable to judge from religious view point. Danger your methods being exploited by others but how can I presume to advise a magician. Love.

A 'pact' was signed by various people gathered in Poona, and with unusual speed the British Prime Minister accepted it and varied his previous award accordingly, and the fast was broken. I disliked such pacts and agreements greatly, but I welcomed the Poona Pact apart from its contents.

The excitement was over and we reverted to our gaol routine. News of the Harijan movement and of Gandhiji's activities from prison came to us, and I was not very happy about it. There was no doubt that a tremendous push had been given to the movement to end untouchability and raise the unhappy depressed classes, not so much by the pact as by the crusading enthusiasm created all over the country. That was to be welcomed. But it was equally obvious that civil disobedience had suffered. The country's attention had been diverted to other issues, and many Congress workers had turned to the Harijan cause. Probably most of these people wanted an excuse to revert to safer activities which did not involve the risk of gaol going or, worse still, *lathi* blows and confiscations of property. That was natural, and it was not fair to expect all the thousands of our workers to keep always ready for intense suffering and the break-up and destruction of their homes. But still it was painful to watch this slow decay of our great movement. Civil disobedience was, however, still going on, and occasionally there were mass demonstrations like the Calcutta Congress in March–April 1933. Gandhiji was in Yeravda Prison, but he had been given certain privileges to meet people and issue directions for the Harijan movements. Somehow this took away from the sting of his being in prison. All this depressed me.

Many months later, early in May 1933, Gandhiji began his twenty-one-day fast. The first news of this had again come as a shock to me, but I accepted it as an inevitable occurrence and schooled myself to it. Indeed I was irritated that people should urge him to give it up, after he had made up his mind and declared it to the public. For me the fast was an incomprehensible thing and, if I had been asked before the decision had been taken, I would certainly have spoken strongly against it. But I attached great value to Gandhiji's word, and it seemed to me wrong for anyone to try to make him break it, in a personal matter which, to him, was of supreme importance. So, unhappy as I was, I put up with it.

A few days before beginning his fast he wrote to me, a typical letter which moved me very much. As he asked for a reply I sent him the following telegram:

> Your letter. What can I say about matters I do not understand. I feel lost in strange country where you are the only familiar landmark and I try to grope my way in dark but I stumble. Whatever happens my love and thoughts will be with you.

I had struggled against my utter disapproval of his act and my desire not to hurt him. I felt, however, that I had not sent him a cheerful message, and now that he was bent on undergoing his terrible ordeal, which might even end in his death, I ought to cheer him up as much as I could. Little things make a difference psychologically, and he would have to strain every nerve to survive. I felt also that we should accept whatever happened, even his death, if unhappily it should occur, with a stout heart. So I sent him another telegram:

> Now that you are launched on your great enterprise may I send you again love and greetings and assure you that I feel more clearly now that whatever happens it is well and whatever happens you win.

He survived the fast. On the first day of it he was discharged from prison, and on his advice Civil Disobedience was suspended for six weeks.

Again I watched the emotional upheaval of the country during the fast, and I wondered more and more if this was the right method in politics. It seemed to be sheer revivalism, and clear thinking had not a ghost of a chance against it. All India, or most of it, stared reverently at the Mahatma and expected him to perform miracle after miracle and put an end to untouchability and get swaraj and so on—and did precious little itself! And Gandhiji did not encourage others to think; his insistence was only on purity and sacrifice. I felt that I was drifting further and further away from him mentally, in spite of my strong emotional attachment to him. Often enough he was guided in his political activities by an unerring instinct. He had the flair for action, but was the way of faith the right way to train a nation? It might pay for a short while, but in the long run?

And I could not understand how he could accept, as he seemed to do, the present social order, which was based on violence and conflict. Within me also conflict raged, and I was torn between rival loyalties. I knew that there was trouble ahead for me, when the enforced protection of gaol was removed. I felt lonely and homeless, and India, to whom I had given my love and for whom I had laboured, seemed a strange and bewildering land to me. Was it my fault that I could not enter into the spirit and ways of thinking of my countrymen? Even with my closest associates I felt that an invisible barrier came between us and, unhappy at being unable to overcome it, I shrank back into my shell. The old world seemed to envelop them, the old world of past ideologies, hopes and desires. The new world was yet far distant.

Wandering between two worlds, one dead,
The other powerless to be born,
With nowhere yet to rest his head.

India is supposed to be a religious country above everything else, and Hindu and Muslim and Sikh and others take pride in their faiths and testify to their truth by breaking heads. The spectacle of what is called religion, or at any rate organized religion, in India and elsewhere has filled me with horror, and I have frequently condemned it and wished to make a clean sweep of it. Almost always it seems to stand for blind belief and reaction, dogma and bigotry, superstition and exploitation, and the preservation of vested interests. And yet I knew well that there was something else in it, something which supplied a deep inner craving of human beings. How else could it have been the tremendous power it has been and brought peace and comfort to innumerable tortured souls? Was that peace merely the shelter of blind belief and absence of questioning, the calm that comes from being safe in harbour, protected from the storms of the open sea, or was it something more? In some cases certainly it was something more.

But organized religion, whatever its past may have been, today is very largely an empty form devoid of real content. Mr G.K. Chesterton has compared it (not his own particular brand of religion, but others!) to a fossil which is the form of an animal or organism from which all its own organic substance has entirely disappeared, but which has kept its shape, because it has been filled up by some totally different substance. And even where something of value still remains, it is enveloped by other and harmful contents.

That seems to have happened in our Eastern religions as well as in the Western. The Church of England is perhaps the most obvious example of a religion which is not a religion in any real sense of the word. Partly that applies to all organized Protestantism, but the Church of England has probably gone further because it has long been a State political department.[1]

---

1. In India the Church of England has been almost indistinguishable from the Government. The officially paid (out of Indian revenues) priests and chaplains are the symbols of the imperial power just as the higher services are. The Church has been, on the whole, a conservative and reactionary force in Indian politics and generally opposed to reform or advance. The average missionary is usually wholly ignorant of India's past history and culture and does not take the slightest trouble to find out what it was or is. He is more interested in pointing out the sins and failings of the heathen. Of course, there have been many fine exceptions. India does not possess a more devoted friend than Charlie Andrews, whose abounding love and spirit of service and overflowing friendliness it is a joy to have. The Christa Seva Sangh of Poona contains some fine Englishmen, whose religion has led them to understand and serve and not to patronize, and who have devoted themselves with all their great gifts to a selfless service of the Indian people. There are many other English churchmen whose memory is treasured in India.

The Archbishop of Canterbury, speaking in the House of Lords on December 12, 1934, referred to the preamble of the Montagu-Chelmsford reforms of 1919 and said that "he sometimes thought the great declaration had been somewhat hastily made, and supposed that it was one of the hasty, generous gestures after the War, but

Many of its votaries are undoubtedly of the highest character, but it is remarkable how that Church has served the purposes of British imperialism and given both capitalism and imperialism a moral and Christian covering. It has sought to justify, from the highest ethical standards, British predatory policy in Asia and Africa, and given that extraordinary and enviable feeling of being always in the right to the English. Whether the Church has helped in producing this attitude of smug rectitude or is itself a product of it, I do not know. Other less favoured countries on the Continent of Europe and in America often accuse the English of hypocrisy—*perfide Albion* is an old taunt—but the accusation is probably the outcome of envy at British success, and certainly no other imperialist Power can afford to throw stones at England, for its own record is equally shady. No nation that is consciously hypocritical could have the reserves of strength that the British have repeatedly shown, and the brand of 'religion' which they have adopted has apparently helped them in this by blunting their moral susceptibilities where their own interests were concerned. Other peoples and nations have often behaved far worse than the British have done, but they have never succeeded, quite to the same extent, in making a virtue of what profited them. All of us find it remarkably easy to spot the mote in the other's eye and overlook the beam in our own, but perhaps the British excel at this performance.[2]

---

the goal set could not be withdrawn." It is worthy of note that the head of the English Church should take such an exceedingly conservative view of Indian politics. A step, which was considered wholly insufficient by Indian opinion and which, because of this, led to non-co-operation and all its consequences, is considered by the Archbishop as "hasty and generous." It is a comforting doctrine from the point of view of the English ruling classes, and, no doubt, this conviction of their own generosity, even to the point of rashness, must produce a righteous glow of satisfaction.

2. A recent instance of how the Church of England indirectly influences politics in India has come to my notice. At a provincial conference of the U.P. Indian Christians held at Cawnpore on the 7th November, 1934, the Chairman of the Reception Committee, Mr E.V. David, said: "As Christians we are bound by our religion to loyalty to the King, who is the Defender of our Faith." Inevitably that meant support of British imperialism in India. Mr David further expressed his sympathies with some of the views of the 'die-hard' Conservative elements in England in regard to the I.C.S., the police, and the whole proposed constitution, which, according to them, might endanger Christian missions in India.

Protestantism tried to adapt itself to new conditions and wanted to have the best of both worlds. It succeeded remarkably so far as this world was concerned, but from the religious point of view it fell, as an organized religion, between two stools, and religion gradually gave place to sentimentality and big business. Roman Catholicism escaped this fate, as it stuck on to the old stool, and, so long as that stool holds, it will flourish. Today it seems to be the only living religion, in the restricted sense of the word, in the West. A Roman Catholic friend sent me in prison many books on Catholicism and Papal Encyclicals and I read them with interest. Studying them, I realized the hold it had on such large numbers of people. It offered, as Islam and popular Hinduism offer, a safe anchorage from doubt and mental conflict, an assurance of a future life which will make up for the deficiencies of this life.

I am afraid it is impossible for me to seek harbourage in this way. I prefer the open sea, with all its storms and tempests. Nor am I greatly interested in the after life, in what happens after death. I find the problems of this life sufficiently absorbing to fill my mind. The traditional Chinese outlook, fundamentally ethical and yet irreligious or tinged with religious scepticism, has an appeal for me, though in its application to life I may not agree. It is the *Tao*, the path to be followed and the way of life that interests me; how to understand life, not to reject it but to accept it, to conform to it and to improve it. But the usual religious outlook does not concern itself with this world. It seems to me to be the enemy of clear thought, for it is based not only on the acceptance without demur of certain fixed and unalterable theories and dogmas, but also on sentiment and emotion and passion. It is far removed from what I consider spiritual and things of the spirit, and it deliberately or unconsciously shuts its eyes to reality lest reality may not fit in with preconceived notions. It is narrow and intolerant of other opinions and ideas; it is self-centred and egotistic, and it often allows itself to be exploited by self-seekers and opportunists.

This does not mean that men of religion have not been and are not still often of the highest moral and spiritual type. But it does mean that the religious outlook does not help, and even hinders, the moral and spiritual progress of a people, if morality and spirituality are to be judged by this world's standards, and not by the hereafter. Usually religion becomes an asocial quest for God or the Absolute, and the religious man is concerned far more with his own salvation than with the good of society. The mystic tries to rid himself of self, and in the process usually becomes obsessed with it. Moral standards have no relation to social needs, but are based on a highly metaphysical doctrine of sin. And organized religion invariably becomes a vested interest and thus inevitably a reactionary force opposing change and progress.

It is well known that the Christian Church in the early days did not help the slaves to improve their social status. The slaves became the feudal serfs of the Middle Ages of Europe because of economic conditions. The attitude of the Church, as late as two hundred years ago (in 1727), was well exemplified in a letter written by the Bishop of London to the slave-owners of the southern colonies of America.[3]

"Christianity," wrote the Bishop, "and the embracing of the gospel does not make the least alteration in Civil property or in any of the duties which belong to civil relations; but in all these respects it continues Persons just in the same State as it found them. The Freedom which Christianity gives is Freedom from the bondage of Sin and Satan and from the Dominion of Men's Lusts and Passions and inordinate Desires; but as to their outward condition, whatever that was before, whether bond or free, their being baptized and becoming Christians makes no manner of change in them."

No organized religion today will express itself in this outspoken manner, but essentially its attitude to property and the existing social order will be the same.

Words are well known to be, by themselves, very imperfect means of communication, and are often understood in a variety of ways. No word perhaps in any language is more likely to be interpreted in different ways by different people as the word 'religion' (or the corresponding words in other languages). Probably to no two persons will the same complex of ideas and images arise on hearing or reading this word. Among these ideas and images may be those of rites and ceremonial, of sacred books, of a community of people, of certain dogmas, of morals, reverence, love, fear, hatred, charity, sacrifice, asceticism, fasting, feasting, prayer, ancient history, marriage, death, the next world, of riots and the

---

3. This letter is quoted in Reinhold Niebuhr's *Moral Man and Immoral Society* (p. 78), a book which is exceedingly interesting and stimulating.

breaking of heads, and so on. Apart from the tremendous confusion caused by this immense variety of images and interpretations, almost invariably there will be a strong emotional response which will make dispassionate consideration impossible. The word 'religion' has lost all precise significance (if it ever had it) and only causes confusion and gives rise to interminable debate and argument, when often enough entirely different meanings are attached to it. It would be far better if it was dropped from use altogether and other words with more limited meanings were used instead, such as: theology, philosophy, morals, ethics, spirituality, metaphysics, duty, ceremonial, etc. Even these words are vague enough, but they have a much more limited range than 'religion.' A great advantage would be that these words have not yet attached to themselves, to the same extent, the passions and emotions that surround and envelop the word 'religion.'

What then is religion (to use the word in spite of its obvious disadvantages)? Probably it consists of the inner development of the individual, the evolution of his consciousness in a certain direction which is considered good. What that direction is will again be a matter for debate. But, as far as I understand it, religion lays stress on this inner change and considers outward change as but the projection of this inner development. There can be no doubt that this inner development powerfully influences the outer environment. But it is equally obvious that the outer environment powerfully influences the inner development. Both act and interact on each other. It is a commonplace that in the modern industrial West outward development has far outstripped the inner, but it does not follow, as many people in the East appear to imagine, that because we are industrially backward and our external development has been slow, therefore our inner evolution has been greater. That is one of the delusions with which we try to comfort ourselves and try to overcome our feeling of inferiority. It may be that individuals can rise above circumstances and environment and reach great inner heights. But for large groups and nations a certain measure of external development is essential before the inner evolution can take place. A man who is the victim of economic circumstances, and who is hedged and restricted by the struggle to live, can very rarely achieve inner consciousness of any high degree. A class that is downtrodden and exploited can never progress inwardly. A nation which is politically and economically subject to another and hedged and circumscribed and exploited can never achieve inner growth. Thus even for inner development external freedom and a suitable environment become necessary. In the attempt to gain this outer freedom and to change the environment so as to remove all hindrances to inner development, it is desirable that the means should be such as not to defeat the real object in view. I take it that when Gandhiji says that the means are more important than the end, he has something of this kind in view. But the means should be such as lead to the end, otherwise they are wasted effort, and they might even result in even greater degradation, both outer and inner.

"No man can live without religion," Gandhiji has written somewhere. "There are some who in the egotism of their reason declare that they have nothing to do with religion. But that is like a man saying that he breathes, but that he has no nose." Again he says: "My devotion to truth has drawn me into the field of politics; and I can say without the slightest hesitation, and yet in all humility, that those who say that religion has nothing to do with politics do not know what religion means." Perhaps it would have been more correct if he had said that most of these people who want to exclude religion from life and politics mean by that word 'religion' something very different from what he means. It is obvious that he is using it in a sense—probably moral and ethical more than any other—different from that of the critics of religion. This use of the same word with different meanings makes mutual comprehension still more difficult.

A very modern definition of religion, with which the men of religion will not agree, is that of Professor John Dewey. According to him, religion is "whatever introduces genuine perspective into the piecemeal and shifting episodes of existence"; or again "any activity pursued in behalf of an ideal end against obstacles, and in spite of threats of personal loss, because of conviction of its general and enduring value, is religious in quality." If this is religion, then surely no one can have the slightest objection to it.

Romain Rolland also has stretched religion to mean something which will probably horrify the orthodox of organized religions. In his *Life of Ramkrishna*, he says:

. . . many souls who are or who believe they are free from all religious belief, but who in reality live immersed in a state of super-rational consciousness, which they term Socialism, Communism, Humanitarianism, Nationalism and even Rationalism. It is the quality of thought and not its object which determines its source and allows us to decide whether or not it emanates from religion. If it turns fearlessly towards the search for truth at all costs with single-minded sincerity prepared for any sacrifice, I should call it religious; for it presupposes faith in an end to human effort higher than the life of existing society, and even higher than the life of humanity as a whole. Scepticism itself, when it proceeds from vigorous natures true to the core, when it is an expression of strength and not of weakness, joins in the march of the Grand Army of the religious Soul.

I cannot presume to fulfil the conditions laid down by Romain Rolland, but on these terms I am prepared to be a humble camp-follower of the Grand Army.

48

THE 'DUAL POLICY' OF THE BRITISH GOVERNMENT

The Harijan movement was going on, guided by Gandhiji from Yeravda Prison and later from outside. There was a great agitation for removing the barriers to temple entry, and a Bill to that effect was introduced in the Legislative Assembly. And then the remarkable spectacle was witnessed of an outstanding leader of the Congress going from house to house in Delhi, visiting the members of the Assembly and canvassing for their votes for this Temple Entry Bill. Gandhiji himself sent an appeal through him to the Assembly members. And yet civil disobedience was still going on and people were going to prison, and the Assembly had been boycotted by the Congress and all our members had withdrawn from it. The rump that remained and the others who had filled the vacancies had distinguished themselves in this crisis by opposition to the Congress and support of the Government. A majority of them had helped the Government to pass repressive legislation giving some permanence to the extraordinary provisions of the Ordinances. They had swallowed the Ottawa Pact, they had fed and feasted with the great ones in Delhi and Simla and London, and joined in the thank-offerings for British rule in India, and prayed for the success of what was called the 'Dual Policy' in India.

I was amazed at Gandhiji's appeal, under the circumstances then existing, and even more so by the strenuous efforts of Rajagopalachariar, who, a few weeks before, had been the acting-President of the Congress. Civil Disobedience, of course, suffered by these activities, but what hurt me more was the moral side. To me, for Gandhiji or any Congress leader to countenance such activities appeared immoral and almost a breach of faith with the large numbers of people in gaol or carrying on the struggle. But I knew that his way of looking at it was different.

The Government attitude to this Temple Entry Bill, then and

subsequently, was very revealing. It put every possible difficulty in the way of its promoters, went on postponing it and encouraging opposition to it, and then finally declared its own opposition to it, and killed it. That, to a greater or lesser extent, has been its attitude to all measures of social reform in India, and on the plea of non-interference with religion, it has prevented social progress. But this, it need hardly be said, has not prevented it from criticizing our social evils and encouraging others to do so. By a fluke, the Sarda Child Marriage Restraint Bill became law, but the subsequent history of this unhappy Act showed more than anything else how much averse to enforcing any such measure the Government was. The Government that could produce ordinances overnight, creating novel offences and providing for vicarious punishment, and could send scores of thousands of people to prison for breach of their provisions, apparently quailed at the prospect of enforcing one of its regular laws like the Sarda Act. The effect of the Act was first to increase tremendously the very evil it was intended to combat, for people rushed to take advantage of the intervening six months of grace which the Act very foolishly allowed. And then it was discovered that the Act was more or less of a joke and could be easily ignored without any steps being taken by Government. Not even the slightest attempt at propaganda was made officially, and most people in the villages never knew what the Act was. They heard distorted accounts of it from Hindu and Muslim village preachers, who themselves seldom knew the correct facts.

This extraordinary spirit of toleration of social evils in India which the British Government has shown is obviously not due to any partiality for them. It is true that they do not very much care about their removal, for these evils do not interfere with their business of governing India and exploiting her resources. There is also always the danger of irritating various people by proposing social reforms, and, having to face enough anger and irritation on the political plane, the British Government has no desire whatever to add to its troubles. But latterly the position has become worse from the point of view of the social reformer, for the British are becoming more and more the silent bulwarks of these evils. This is due to their close association with the most reactionary elements in India. As opposition to their rule increases they have to seek strange allies, and today the firmest champions of British rule in India are the extreme communalists and the religious reactionaries and obscurantists.

The Muslim communal organizations are notoriously reactionary from every point of view—political, economic, social. The Hindu Mahasabha rivals them, but it is left far behind in this backward-moving race by the Sanatanists, who combine religious obscurantism of an extreme type with fervent, or at any rate loudly expressed, loyalty to British rule.

If the British Government was quiescent and took no steps to popularize the Sarda Act and to enforce it, why did not the Congress or other non-official organizations carry on propaganda in favour of it? This question is often put by British and other foreign critics. So far as the Congress is concerned, it has been engaged during the last fifteen years, and especially since 1930, in a fierce life-and-death struggle for national freedom with the British rulers. The other organizations have no real strength or contact with the masses. Men and women of ideals and force of character and influence among the masses were drawn into the Congress and spent much of their time in British prisons.

Other organizations could seldom go beyond the passing of resolutions by select people who feared the mass touch. They functioned in a gentlemanly way or, like the All-India Women's Association, in a lady-like way, and the spirit of aggressive propaganda was not theirs. Besides, they too were paralysed by the terrible repression of all public activities by the Ordinances and the laws that followed them. Martial law may crush revolutionary activity, but at the same time it paralyses civilization and most civilized activities.

But the real reason why the Congress and other non-official organizations cannot do much for social reform goes deeper. We suffer from the disease of nationalism, and that absorbs our attention and it will continue to do so till we get political freedom. As Bernard Shaw has said: "A conquered nation is like a man with cancer; he can think of nothing else . . . There is indeed no greater curse to a nation than a nationalist movement, which is only the agonizing symptom of a suppressed natural function. Conquered nations lose their place in the world's march because they can do nothing but strive to get rid of their nationalist movements by recovering their national liberty."

Past experience shows us that we can make little social progress under present conditions, in spite of apparent transfers of subjects to elected ministers. The tremendous inertia of the Government is always helpful to the conservative elements, and for generations past the British

Government has crushed initiative and ruled despotically, or paternally, as it has itself called it. It does not approve of any big organized effort by non-officials, and suspects ulterior motives. The Harijan movement, in spite of every precaution taken by its organizers, has occasionally come in conflict with officials. I am sure that if the Congress started a nation-wide propaganda for the greater use of soap it would come in conflict with Government in many places.

I do not think it is very difficult to convert the masses to social reform if the State takes the matter in hand. But alien rulers are always suspect, and they cannot go far in the process of conversion. If the alien element was removed and economic changes were given precedence, an energetic administration could easily introduce far-reaching social reforms.

But social reform and the Sarda Act and the Harijan Movement did not fill our minds in prison, except in so far as I felt a little irritated by the Harijan Movement because it had come in the way of civil disobedience. Early in May 1933 Civil Disobedience had been suspended for six weeks, and we waited anxiously for further developments. That suspension had given a final blow to the movement, for one cannot play fast and loose with a national struggle and switch it on and off at will. Even before the suspension the leadership of the movement had been singularly weak and ineffective. There were petty conferences being held, and all manner of rumours spread which militated against active work. Some of the acting-Presidents of the Congress were very estimable men, but it was unkindness to them to make them generals of an active campaign. There was too much of a hint of tiredness about them, of a desire to get out of a difficult position. There was some discontent against this vacillation and indecision in high quarters, but it was difficult to express it in an organized way, as all Congress bodies were unlawful.

Then came Gandhiji's twenty-one-day fast, his discharge from prison, and the suspension of civil disobedience for six weeks. The fast was over, and very slowly he recovered from it. In the middle of June the period of suspension of civil disobedience was extended by another six weeks. Meanwhile the Government had in no way toned down its aggression. In the Andaman Islands political prisoners (those convicted in Bengal for acts of revolutionary violence were sent there) were on hunger-strike on the question of treatment, and one or two of them died—

starved to death. Others lay dying. People who addressed meetings in India in protest of what was happening in the Andamans were themselves arrested and sentenced. We were not only to suffer, but we were not even to complain, even though prisoners died by the terrible ordeal of the hunger-strike, having no other means of protest open to them. Some months later, in September 1933 (when I was out of prison), an appeal was issued over a number of signatures including Rabindra Nath Tagore, C.F. Andrews, and many other well-known people, mostly unconnected with the Congress, asking for more humanitarian treatment of the Andamans' prisoners, and preferably for their transfer to Indian gaols. The Home Member of the Government of India expressed his great displeasure at this statement, and criticized the signatories strongly for their sympathy for the prisoners. Later, as far as I can remember, the expression of such sympathy was made a punishable offence in Bengal.

Before the second six weeks of suspension of civil disobedience were over, news came to us in Dehra Dun Gaol that Gandhiji had called an informal conference at Poona. Two or three hundred people met there and, on Gandhiji's advice, mass civil disobedience was suspended, but individual civil disobedience was permitted, and all secret methods were barred. The decisions were not very inspiring, but I did not particularly object to them so far as they went. To stop mass civil disobedience was to recognize and stabilize existing conditions, for, in reality, there was no mass movement then. Secret work was merely a pretence that we were carrying on, and often it demoralized, having regard to the character of our movement. To some extent it was necessary in order to send instructions and keep contacts, but civil disobedience itself could not be secret.

What surprised me and distressed me was the absence of any real discussion at Poona of the existing situation and of our objectives. Congressmen had met together after nearly two years of fierce conflict and repression, and much had happened meanwhile in the world at large and in India, including the publication of the White Paper containing the British Government's proposals for constitutional reform. We had to put up during this period with enforced silence, and on the other side there had been ceaseless and perverted propaganda to obscure the issues. It was frequently stated, not only by supporters of the Government but by Liberals and others, that the Congress had given up its objective of independence. The least that should have been done, I thought, was to lay stress on our political objective, to make it clear again, and, if possible, to add to it social and economic objectives Instead of this, the discussion seems to have been entirely confined to the relative merits of mass and individual civil disobedience, and the desirability or otherwise of secrecy. There was also some strange talk of 'peace' with the Government. Gandhiji sent a telegram to the Viceroy, as far as I remember, asking for an interview, to which the Viceroy replied with a 'No', and then Gandhiji sent a second telegram mentioning something about 'honourable peace'. Where was this elusive peace that was being sought, when the Government was triumphantly trying to crush the nation in every way, and people were starving to death in the Andamans? But I knew that, whatever happened, it was Gandhiji's way always to offer the olive branch.

Repression was going on in full swing, and all the special laws suppressing public activities were in force. In February 1933 even a memorial meeting on my father's death anniversary was prohibited by the police, although it was a non-Congress meeting, and such a good Moderate as Sir Tej Bahadur Sapru was to have presided over it. And as a vision of future favours to come we had been presented with the White Paper.

This was a remarkable document, a perusal of which left one gasping for breath. India was to be converted into a glorified Indian State, with a dominating influence of the States' feudal representatives in the Federation. But in the States themselves no outside interference would be tolerated, and undiluted autocracy would continue to prevail there. The real imperial links, the chains of debt, would bind us for ever to the City of London, and the currency and monetary policy would also be controlled, through a Reserve Bank, by the Bank of England. There would be an impregnable defence of all vested rights, and additional vested interests were going to be created. Our revenues were mortgaged up to the hilt for the benefit of these vested interests. The great imperial services, which we love so much, would continue uncontrolled and untouched, to train us for further instalments of self-government. There was going to be Provincial Autonomy, but the Governor would be a benevolent and all-powerful dictator keeping us in order. And high above all would sit the All-Highest, the supreme Dictator, the Viceroy, with complete powers to do what he will and check when he desires. Truly, the genius of the British ruling class for colonial government was never more in evidence, and well may the Hitlers and Mussolinis admire them and look with envy on the Viceroy of India.

Having produced a constitution which tied up India hand and foot, a collection of 'special responsibilities' and safeguards were added as additional fetters, making the unhappy country a prisoner incapable of movement. As Mr Neville Chamberlain said: "They had done their best to surround the proposals with all the safeguards the wit of man could devise."

Further, we were informed that for these favours we would have to pay heavily—to begin with a lump sum of a few crores, and then annual payment. We could not have the blessings of Swaraj without adequate payment. We had been suffering under the delusion that India was poverty-stricken and already had too heavy a burden to carry, and we had looked to freedom to lighten it. That had been for the masses the urge for freedom. But it now appeared that the burden was to become heavier.

This Gilbertian solution of the Indian problem was offered with true British grace, and we were told how generous our rulers were. Never before had an imperial Power of its own free will offered such power and opportunities to a subject people. And a great debate arose in England between the donors and those who, horrified at such generosity, objected to it. This was the outcome of the many comings and goings between India and England during three years, of the three Round Table Conferences, and innumerable committees and consultations.

But the visits to England were not over yet. There was the joint Select Committee of the British Parliament which was going to sit in judgment on the White Paper, and Indians went to it as a kind of assessors and as witnesses. There were also many other committees sitting in London, and there was an undignified scramble behind the scenes for membership of any committee which meant a free passage to and stay in the heart of the Empire. Brave men, undaunted by the petrifying provisions of the White Paper, undertook to face the perils of the sea voyage or the air journey, and the greater dangers of a stay in London city in order to attempt, with all the eloquence and power of persuasion at their command, to vary the provisions of the White Paper. They knew and said that the task was an almost hopeless one, but they were no quitters, and would continue to have their say even though there was no one to listen to them. One of them, a leader of the Responsivists, stuck on till the bitter end, when all others had left, probably having interview after interview and dinner after dinner with the men in authority in London, so that he might impress upon them what political changes he desired. When at last he returned to his native land, he informed an expectant public that, with the well-known tenacity of the Marathas, he had refused to give up his job, and had stayed on in London to have his say to the very end.

I remember a frequent complaint of my father's that his Responsivist friends had no sense of humour. He often got into trouble with them because of his humorous remarks, which were not appreciated by them at all, and then he had to explain and soothe—a tiring operation. And I thought of the fine fighting spirit of the Marathas, not only in the past but in the present during our national struggles, and of the great and indomitable Tilak, who would not bend though he break.

The Liberals utterly disliked the White Paper. They also had no liking for the repression that was going on from day to day in India, and sometimes though rarely, even protested against it, always making it clear that they condemned the Congress and all its works. They would suggest to Government occasionally to release some prominent Congressman from prison—they could only think in terms of individuals they knew. The argument advanced, both by the Liberals and Responsivists, was that so-and-so should be released as there was no longer any danger to the public peace. And then it is always open to the Government to re-arrest that person if he misbehaves, and Government could do so with more justification. Some people in England also were good enough to plead for the release of some members of the Working Committee, or special individuals, on these grounds. We could not help being grateful to people who were interested in us while we were in prison, but we felt also sometimes that it would be a good thing if we were saved from our well-meaning friends. We did not doubt their good intentions, but it was obvious that they had adopted completely the ideology of the British Government, and between them and us there was a wide chasm.

The Liberals did not like much that was happening in India; they were unhappy about it, and yet what were they to do? It was unthinkable for them to take any effective action against Government. Merely to preserve themselves as a separate entity they had to retreat further away from the masses and the active elements in the population; to drift to the Right, till their ideology was hardly distinguishable from that of the Government. Small in numbers, and with no mass influence, they could not make any difference to a mass struggle. But among them were some distinguished and well-known persons who were personally respected. And these leaders, as well as the Liberal and Responsivist groups as a whole, did an inestimable service to the British Government at a moment of grave crisis by a moral support of the official policy. Even the coercion and lawlessness of Government profited by the lack of effective criticism and occasional acquiescence and approval of the Liberals. Thus the Liberals and Responsivists gave a moral sanction to the fierce and unprecedented coercion that was going on in the country at a time when the Government was hard put to it to justify it.

The White Paper was bad, very bad, so said the Liberal leaders. What was to be done about it? At the Liberal Federation meeting held in Calcutta in April 1933, Mr Srinivasa Sastri, the most eminent of the Liberal leaders, pleaded that however unsatisfactory the constitutional changes might be they should work them. "This is no time to stand by and let things pass," he said. The only action that apparently was conceivable to him was to accept what was given and to try to work it. The alternative to this was doing nothing. Further he added: "If we have wisdom, experience, moderation, power of persuasion, quiet influence, and real efficiency—if we have these virtues, this is the time to display them in the fullest strength." "Shining words" was the Calcutta *Statesman's* comment on this eloquent appeal.

Mr Sastri is always eloquent, and has the orator's love of fine words and their musical use. But he is apt to be carried away by his enthusiasms, and the word-magic that he creates blurs his meaning to others and perhaps to himself. It is worthwhile examining this appeal he made at Calcutta in April 1933 during the continuance of the Civil Disobedience Movement. Fundamental principles and objectives apart, two points seem to me worthy of note. The first is that whatever happens, however much we might be insulted, crushed, humiliated, and exploited by the British Government, we must submit to it. The line can never be drawn beyond which we must not go. A worm may turn, but not the Indian people if they followed Mr Sastri's advice. There is no other way according to him. This means that, so far as he is concerned, submission to and acceptance of the British Government's decisions is tantamount to a religion (if I may use that unfortunate word). It is the fate—*Kismet*—to which all of us have to bow whether we want to or not.

It must be noted that he was not giving advice on a definite, known situation. The 'constitutional changes' were still in the making, though one had a fair notion that they would be very bad. If he had said that, bad as the White Paper proposals are, having regard to all the circumstances, I am in favour of working them, should they be enacted, his advice might have been good or bad, but it had relation to existing facts. Mr Sastri went much further, and said that however unsatisfactory the constitutional changes might be his advice would hold. He was prepared to give a blank cheque to the British Government on the most vital matter from the nation's view-point. It is a little difficult for me to understand how any individual, group, or party, can take up this attitude of commitment to an unforeseen future, unless it has no principles or moral and political standards whatever, and has for its creed and policy invariable subservience to the ruler's mandates.

The second point that strikes me is one of pure tactics. The White Paper was one stage in the long march to the enactment of the new reforms. It was, from Government's point of view, an important stage, but many stages remained, and it was possible that it might be altered for better or worse during its subsequent journey. These alterations would obviously depend on the pressure brought to bear on the British Government and Parliament from various interests. In this tug-of-war it was conceivable that the desire to win over the Indian Liberals to its side might have influenced the Government and induced it to liberalize the proposals, or at least to resist encroachments. But Mr Sastri's emphatic declaration, long before the question of acceptance or rejection, working or not working the new reforms arose, made it clear to the Government that they could completely ignore the Indian Liberals. There was no question of winning them over. They would not desert the Government, even if they were pushed out. Looking at the matter from the Liberal view-point, as far as I can, Mr Sastri's speech at Calcutta seems to me to have been extraordinarily bad tactics and injurious to the Liberal cause.

I have ventured to write so much on Mr Sastri's old speech, not because of any intrinsic importance of that speech or the Liberal

Federation meeting, but because of my desire to understand the mentality and psychology of the Liberal leaders. They are able and estimable men, and yet, with the best will in the world, I have been wholly unable to appreciate why they act as they do. Another speech of Mr Sastri's, which I read in prison, influenced me greatly. He was addressing the Servants of India Society, of which he is president, at Poona in June 1933. He is reported to have pointed the danger in India if British influence were suddenly withdrawn, of political movements being marked by acute hatred, persecution, and oppression of one party by another. On the other hand, toleration having throughout been a feature of British political life, the more India's future is worked out in co-operation with Britain, the greater the likelihood of toleration prevailing in India. Being in prison, I have to rely on the summary of Mr Sastri's speech given by the *Statesman* of Calcutta. The *Statesman* added: "It is a pleasant doctrine, and we note that Doctor Moonje has been speaking in the same sense." Mr Sastri is further reported to have referred to the suppression of freedom in Russia, Italy, and Germany, and to the inhumanities and savageries that were being perpetrated there.

It struck me, when I read this, how extraordinarily similar was Mr Sastri's outlook in regard to Britain and India to that of the 'diehard' British Conservative. In matters of detail there were no doubt differences, but fundamentally the ideology was the same. Mr Winston Churchill could have expressed himself in identical language without doing any violence to his convictions. And yet Mr Sastri belongs to the Left wing of the Liberal party, and is the ablest of its leaders.

I am afraid I am wholly unable to accept Mr Sastri's reading of history, or his views on world affairs, and more particularly on Britain and India. Probably no foreigner, who is not an Englishman, will accept them; possibly many Englishmen of advanced views will disagree with him. It is his happy gift to see the world and his own country through the tinted glasses of the British ruling class. Nevertheless, it is remarkable that he should ignore in this speech the very unusual occurrences which had taken place from day to day in India during the previous eighteen months, and were taking place at the time the speech was delivered. He referred to Russia, Italy, and Germany, but not to the fierce repression and suppression of all liberties in his own country. He may not have known of all the terrible occurrences in the Frontier Province and in

Bengal—the 'rape of Bengal' as Rajendra Babu has called it in his recent Congress presidential address—as the heavy veil of censorship hid much of what was happening. But was he oblivious to the agony of India and the struggle for life and freedom that his people were waging against a powerful adversary? Did he not know of the police raj that prevailed over large areas, of conditions resembling martial law, of the Ordinances, of the hunger-strikes, and other sufferings in prison? Did he not realize that the very toleration and freedom for which he praised Britain had been crushed by Britain herself in India?

It did not matter whether he agreed with the Congress or not. He was perfectly entitled to criticize and condemn Congress policy. But as an Indian, as a lover of freedom, as a sensitive man, what were his reactions to the wonderful courage and sacrifice of his countrymen and countrywomen? Did he not feel any pain and anguish when our rulers played with a hatchet on India's heart? Was it nothing to him that scores of thousands were refusing to bend before the physical might of a proud empire, and preferred to see their bodies crushed, their homes broken, their dear ones suffer, rather than yield their souls? We put on a brave face in gaol or outside, and smiled and laughed, but we smiled often through our tears, and our laughter was sometimes near to crying.

Mr Verrier Elwin, a brave and generous Englishman, tells us what his reactions were. "It was a wonderful experience," he says of 1930, "to watch a whole nation throwing off its mental bonds of servitude and rising to its true dignity of fearless determination." And again: "The amazing discipline exhibited by most of the Congress volunteers during the Satyagraha struggle, a discipline to which one of the provincial Governors has borne generous testimony . . ."

Mr Srinivasa Sastri is an able and sensitive man who is widely respected by his countrymen, and it seems impossible that he would not react in the same way and feel for his countrymen during such a struggle. One would have expected him to raise his voice in denunciation of the suppression of all civil liberty and all public activities by the Government. One would further have hoped that he and his colleagues would personally visit the worst affected areas—Bengal and the Frontier—not in any way to help the Congress or civil disobedience, but to expose and thus check official and police excesses. This is usually done by the lovers of freedom and civil liberty in other countries. But instead of acting in this way, instead of trying to check the executive when it was riding rough-shod over India's men and woman and had done away with even the usual liberties; instead at least of finding out what was happening, he chose to give a certificate to the British for toleration and freedom just when both of these virtues were completely lacking under British rule in India. He gave them his moral backing and thus heartened and encouraged them in their task of repression. I am quite sure that he could not have meant this or realized the consequences of his action. But that his speech must have had this effect cannot be doubted. Why, then, should he think and act in this manner?

I have found no adequate answer to this question except that the Liberal leaders have cut themselves completely aloof from their countrymen as well as from all modern thought. The musty books that they read have shut out the people of India from their view, and they have developed a kind of narcissism. We went to gaol and our bodies were locked up in cells, but our minds ranged free and our spirits were undismayed. But they created mental prisons of their own fashioning, where they went round and round and from which they found no escape. They worshipped the God of Things as they are; and when things changed, as they do in this changing world, they were without rudder and compass, helpless in mind and body, without ideals or moral values. The choice for each one of us always is to go forward or be pushed; we cannot remain static in a dynamic universe. Afraid of change and movement, the Liberals were frightened at the tempests that surrounded them; weak of limb, they could not go forward, and so they were tossed hither and thither, clutching at every straw that came their way. They became the Hamlets of Indian politics, "sicklied o'er with the pale cast of thought", ever doubting, hesitating, and irresolute.

> The time is out of joint. O cursed spite!
> That ever I was born to set it right.

The *Servant of India*, a Liberal weekly, accused Congressmen, during the latter days of the Civil Disobedience Movement, of wanting to go to prison, and when they got there wanting to come out again. That, it said with some irritation, was the sole Congress policy. The Liberal alternative to that, apparently, was to send a deputation to England to wait on the British ministers, or to wait and pray for a change of

Government in England.

It was true, to some extent, that the Congress policy then was mainly one of defiance of the Ordinance laws and other repressive measures, and this led to gaol. It was also true that the Congress and the nation were exhausted after the long struggle and could not bring any effective pressure on the Government. But there was a practical and moral consideration.

Naked coercion, as India was experiencing, is an expensive affair for the rulers. Even for them it is a painful and nerve-shaking ordeal, and they know well that ultimately it weakens their foundations. It exposes continually the real character of their rule, both to the people coerced and the world at large. They infinitely prefer to put on the velvet glove to hide the iron fist. Nothing is more irritating and, in the final analysis, harmful to a Government than to have to deal with people who will not bend to its will, whatever the consequences. So even sporadic defiance of the repressive measures had value; it strengthened the people and sapped the morale of Government,

The moral consideration was even more important. In a famous passage Thoreau has said: "At a time when men and women are unjustly imprisoned the place for just men and women is also in prison." This advice may not appeal to Liberals and others, but many of us often feel that a moral life under existing conditions is intolerable, when, even apart from civil disobedience, many of our colleagues are always in prison and the coercive apparatus of the State is continually repressing us and humiliating us, as well as helping in the exploitation of our people. In our own country we move about as suspects, shadowed and watched, our words recorded lest they infringe the all-pervading law of sedition, our correspondence opened, the possibility of some executive prohibition or arrest always facing us. For us the choice is: abject submission to the power of the State, spiritual degradation, the denial of the truth that is in us, and our moral prostitution for purposes that we consider base—or opposition with all the consequences thereof. No one likes to go to gaol or to invite trouble. But often gaol is preferable to the other alternative. "The only real tragedy in life," as Bernard Shaw has written, "is the being used by personally minded men for purposes which you know to be base. All the rest is at the worst mere misfortune and mortality: this alone is misery, slavery, hell on earth."

49

THE END OF A LONG TERM

The time for my discharge was drawing near. I had received the usual remissions for 'good behaviour', and this had reduced my two-year term by three and a half months. My peace of mind, or rather the general dullness of the mind which prison produces, was being disturbed by the excitement created by the prospect of release. What must I do outside? A difficult question, and the hesitation I had in answering it took away from the joy of going out. But even that was a momentary feeling, and my long-suppressed energy was bubbling up and I was eager to be out.

The end of July 1933 brought a painful and very disturbing piece of news—the sudden death of J.M. Sen-Gupta. We had not only been close colleagues on the Congress Working Committee for many years, but he was also a link with my early Cambridge days. We met in Cambridge first—I was a freshman, and he had just taken his degree.

Sen-Gupta died under detention. He had been made a State prisoner on his return from Europe early in 1932, while he was yet on board ship in Bombay. Since then he had been a prisoner or a detenu, and his health had deteriorated. Various facilities were given to him by the Government, but evidently they could not check the course of the disease. His funeral in Calcutta was the occasion for a remarkable mass demonstration and tribute; it seemed that the long pent-up suffering soul of Bengal had found an outlet for a while at least.

So Sen-Gupta had gone. Subhas Bose, another State prisoner whose health had broken down by years of internment and prison, had at last been permitted by the Government to go to Europe for treatment. The veteran Vithabhbhai Patel also lay ill in Europe. And how many others had broken down in health or died, unable to stand the physical strain of gaol life and ceaseless activity outside! How many, though outwardly not much changed, had suffered deeper mental derangements and developed complexes on account of the abnormal lives they had been made to lead!

Sen-Gupta's death made me vividly aware of all this terrible, silent suffering going on throughout the country, and I felt weary and depressed. To what end was all this? To what end? I had been fortunate about my own health, and in spite of the strains and irregular life of Congress activity I had, on the whole, kept well. Partly, I suppose, this was due to a good constitution I had inherited, partly to my care of the body. Illness and weak health as well as too much fat seemed to me a most unbecoming state of affairs, and with the help of exercise, plenty of fresh air, and simple food, I managed to keep away from them. My own experience has been that a vast proportion of the ailments of the Indian middle classes are caused by wrong feeding; the food is both rich and excessive. (This applies only to those who can afford such wasteful habits.) The fond mother lays the firm foundation of life-long indigestion by over-feeding the child with sweets and other so-called dainties. The child is also muffled up in too many clothes. The English people in India also seem to eat far too much, although their food is less rich. Probably they have improved a little from the older generation which used to consume enormous quantities of food, hot and strong.

I have cared little for food fads, and have only avoided overeating and rich foods. Like nearly all Kashmiri Brahmans our family was a meat-eating one, and from childhood onwards I had always taken meat, although I never fancied it much. With the coming of Non-Co-operation in 1920 I gave up meat and became a vegetarian. I remained a vegetarian till a visit to Europe six years later, when I relapsed to meat-eating. On my return to India I became a vegetarian again, and since then I have been more or less a vegetarian. Meat-eating seems to agree with me well, but I have developed a distaste for it, and it gives me a feeling of coarseness.

My periods of ill-health, chiefly in prison in 1932, when for many months I got a rise of temperature every day, annoyed me, because they hurt my conceit of good health. And for the first time I did not think, as I used to do, in terms of abounding life and energy, but a spectre of a gradual decay and a wearing away rose up before me and alarmed me. I do not think I am particularly frightened of death. But a slow deterioration, bodily and mental, was quite another matter. However, my fears proved exaggerated, and I managed to get rid of the indisposition and bring my body under control. Long sun-baths during the winter helped me to get back my feeling of well-being. While my companions in prison would shiver in their coats and shawls, I would sit, bare-bodied, delightfully warmed up by the sun's embrace. This was only possible in North India during the winter, as elsewhere the sun is usually too hot.

Among my exercises one pleased me particularly—the *shirshasana*, standing on the head with the palms of the hands, fingers interlocked, supporting the back of the head, elbows on the floor, body vertical, upside down. I suppose physically this exercise is very good: I liked it even more for its psychological effect on me. The slightly comic position increased my good humour and made me a little more tolerant of life's vagaries.

My usual good health and the bodily sense of well-being have been of very great help to me in getting over periods of depression, which are inevitable in prison life. They have helped me also in accommodating myself to changing conditions in prison or outside. I have had many shocks, which at the time seemed to bowl me over, but to my own surprise I have recovered sooner than I expected. I suppose a test of my fundamental sobriety and sanity is the fact that I hardly know what a bad headache is, nor have I ever been troubled with insomnia. I have escaped these common diseases of civilization, as also bad eyesight, in spite of excessive use of the eyes for reading and writing, sometimes in a bad light in gaol. An eye specialist expressed his amazement last year at my good eyesight. Eight years before he had prophesied that I would have to take to spectacles in another year or two. He was very much mistaken, and I am still carrying on successfully without them. Although these facts might establish my reputation for sobriety and sanity, I might add that I have a horror of people who are inescapably and unchangingly sane and sober.

While I waited for my discharge from prison, the new form of civil disobedience for individuals was beginning outside. Gandhiji decided to give the lead and, after giving full notice to the authorities, he started on August 1st with the intention of preaching civil resistance to the Gujrat peasantry. He was immediately arrested, sentenced to one year, and sent back again to his cell in Yeravda. I was glad he had gone back. But soon a new complication arose. Gandhiji claimed the same facilities for carrying on Harijan work from prison as he had had before; the Government refused to grant them. Suddenly we heard that Gandhiji had started fasting again on this issue. It seemed an extraordinarily trivial matter for such a tremendous step. It was quite impossible for me to understand his decision, even though he might be completely right in his argument with the Government. We could do nothing, and we looked on, bewildered.

After a week of the fast his condition grew rapidly worse. He had been removed to a hospital, but he was still a prisoner and Government would not give in on the question of facilities for Harijan work. He lost the will to live (which he had during his previous fasts) and allowed himself to go down hill. The end seemed to be near. He said good-bye and even made dispositions about the few personal articles that were lying about him, giving some to the nurses. But the Government had no intention of allowing him to die on their hands, and that evening he was suddenly discharged. It was just in time to save him. Another day and perhaps it would have been too late. Probably a great deal of the credit for saving him should go to C.F. Andrews who had rushed to India, contrary to Gandhiji's advice.

Meanwhile I was transferred from Dehra Dun Gaol on August 23rd, and I returned to Naini Prison after more than a year and a half's residence in other gaols. Just then news came of my mother's sudden illness and her removal to hospital. On 30th August, 1933, I was discharged from Naini because my mother's condition was considered serious. Ordinarily I would have been released, at the latest, on September 12th when my term expired. I was thus given an additional thirteen days of remission by the Provincial Government.

50

A VISIT TO GANDHIJI

Immediately after my release, I hastened to Lucknow to my mother's bed-side, and I remained with her for some days. I had come out of prison after a fairly long period, and I felt detached and out of touch with my surroundings. I realized with a little shock, as we all do, that the world had gone on moving and changing while I lay stagnating in prison. Children and boys and girls growing up, marriages, births, deaths; love and hate, work and play, tragedy and comedy. New interests in life, new subjects for conversation, always there was a little element of surprise in what I saw and heard. Life seemed to have passed by, leaving me in a backwater. It was not a wholly pleasant feeling. Soon I would have adapted myself to my environment, but I felt no urge to do so. I realized that I was only having a brief outing outside prison, and would have to go back again before long. So why trouble myself about adaptation to something which I would leave soon?

Politically, India was more or less quiet; public activities were largely controlled and suppressed by the Government, and arrests occasionally took place. But the silence of India then was full of significance. It was the ominous silence which follows exhaustion after experiencing a period of fierce repression, a silence which is often very eloquent, but is beyond the ken of governments that repress. India was the ideal police state, and the police mentality pervaded all spheres of government. Outwardly all non-conformity was suppressed, and a vast army of spies and secret agents covered the land. There was an atmosphere of demoralization and an all-pervading fear among the people. Any political activity, especially in the rural areas, was immediately suppressed, and the various provincial governments were trying to hound out Congressmen from the service of municipalities and local boards. Every person who had been to prison as a civil resister was unfit, according to Government, for teaching in a municipal school or serving the municipality in any other way. Great pressure was brought to bear on municipalities, etc., and threats were held out that Government grants would be stopped, if the offending Congressmen were not dismissed. The most notorious example of this coercion took place in the Calcutta Corporation. Ultimately, I believe, the Bengal Government passed a law against the employment by the Corporation of persons who had been convicted for political offences.

Reports of Nazi excesses in Germany had a curious effect on British officials and their Press in India. They gave them a justification for all they had done in India, and it was pointed out to us, with a glow of conscious virtue, how much worse our lot would have been if the Nazis had had anything to do with us. New standards and records had been set up by the Nazis, and it was certainly not an easy matter to rival them. Perhaps our lot would have been worse; it is difficult for me to judge for I have not all the facts of the occurrences that have taken place in various parts of India during the past five years. The British Government in India believes in the charity that its right hand should not know what its left hand does, and so it has turned down every suggestion for an impartial enquiry, although such enquiries are always weighted on the official side. I think it is true that the average Englishman hates brutality, and I cannot conceive English people openly glorying in and repeating lovingly the word '*Brutalität*' (or its English equivalent) as the Nazis do. Even when they indulge in the deed, they are a little ashamed of it. But whether we are Germans or English or Indians, I am afraid our veneer of civilized conduct is thin enough, and when passions are aroused it rubs off and reveals something that is not good to look at. The Great War brutalized humanity terribly, and we saw the aftermath of this in that awful hunger blockade of Germany even after the Armistice—"one of the most senseless, brutal and hideous atrocities ever committed by any nation" as an English writer has described it. The years 1857 and 1858 have not been forgotten in India. Whenever the challenge to our own interests is made we forget our good breeding and society manners, and untruth becomes 'propaganda', and brutality 'scientific repression' and the preservation of 'law and order'.

It is not the fault of individuals or any particular people. More or less every one behaves so under similar circumstances. In India, and in every country under foreign domination, there is always a latent challenge to the ruling power, and from time to time this becomes more obvious and threatening. This challenge always develops the military virtues and vices in the ruling groups. We have had evidence of these military virtues and vices in a superlative degree in India during the last few years, because our challenge had become powerful and effective. But to some extent we have always to put up with the military mind (or absence of it) in India. That is one of the consequences of Empire, and it degrades both the parties involved. The degradation of Indians is obvious enough, the other degradation is more subtle, but in times of crisis it becomes patent. Then there is a third group, which has the misfortune to share in both types of degradation.

I have had ample leisure in gaol to read the speeches of high officials, their answers to questions in the Assembly and Councils, and Government statements. I noticed, during the last three years, a marked change coming over them, and this change became progressively more and more obvious. They became more threatening and minatory, developing more and more in the style of a sergeant-major addressing his men. A remarkable example of this was a speech delivered by the Commissioner of, I think, the Midnapur Division in Bengal in November or December 1933. *Vae victis* seems to run like a thread through these utterances. Non-official Europeans, in Bengal especially, go even further than the official variety, and both in their speeches and actions have shown a very decided Fascist tendency.

Yet another revealing instance of brutalization was the recent public hangings of some convicted criminals in Sind. Because crime was on the increase in Sind the authorities there decided to execute these criminals publicly, as a warning to others. Every facility was given to the public to attend and watch this ghastly spectacle, and it is said that many thousands came.

So after my discharge from prison, I surveyed political and economic conditions in India, and felt little enthusiasm at them. Many of my comrades were in prison, fresh arrests continued, all the Ordinance laws were in operation, censorship throttled the Press and upset our correspondence. A colleague of mine, Rafi Ahmad Kidwai, was greatly irritated at the vagaries of the censor regarding his correspondence. Letters would be held up and came very late, or would get lost, and this would upset his engagements. He wanted to appeal to the censor to do his job a little more efficiently, but who was he to write to? The censor was not a public official. He was probably some C.I.D. officer working secretly, whose existence and work were not even acknowledged openly. Rafi Ahmad solved the difficulty by writing to the censor, and addressing the envelope of this letter to himself! Sure enough the letter reached its proper destination, and there was some improvement afterwards in Rafi Ahmad's correspondence.

I had no desire to go back to prison. I had had enough of it. But I could not see how I could escape it under the existing circumstances, unless I decided to retire from all political activity. I had no such intention, and so I felt that I was bound to come into conflict with the Government. At any moment some order might be served on me to do something, or to abstain from doing something, and all my nature rebelled at being forced to act in a particular way. An attempt was being made to cow down and coerce the people of India. I was helpless, and could do nothing on the wider field, but, at any rate, I could refuse personally to be cowed down and coerced into submission.

Before I went back to prison I wanted to attend to certain matters. My mother's illness claimed my attention first of all. Very slowly she improved; the process was so slow that for a year she was bed-ridden. I was eager to see Gandhiji, who lay recovering from his latest fast in Poona. For over two years I had not met him. I also wanted to meet as many of my provincial colleagues as possible to discuss, not only the existing political situation in India, but the world situation as well as the ideas that filled my mind. I thought then that the world was going rapidly towards a catastrophe, political and economic and we ought to keep this in mind in drawing up our national programmes.

My household affairs also claimed my attention. I had ignored them completely so far, and I had not even examined my father's papers since his death. We had cut down our expenditure greatly, but still it was far more than we could afford. And yet it was difficult to reduce it further, so long as we lived in that house of ours. We were not keeping a car because that was beyond our means, and also because, at any moment, it could be attached by Government. Faced by financial difficulties, I was diverted by the large mail of begging letters that I received. (The censor passed the lot on.) There was a general and very erroneous impression, especially in South India, that I was a wealthy person.

Soon after my release my younger sister, Krishna, got engaged to be married and I was anxious to have the wedding early, before my enforced departure took place. Krishna herself had come out of prison a few months earlier after serving out a year.

As soon as my mother's health permitted it, I went to Poona to see Gandhiji. I was happy to see him again and to find that, though weak, he was making good progress. We had long talks. It was obvious that we differed considerably in our outlook on life and politics and economics, but I was grateful to him for the generous way in which he tried to come as far as he could to meet my view-point. Our correspondence, subsequently published, dealt with some of the wider issues that filled my mind, and though they were referred to in vague language, the general drift was clear. I was happy to have Gandhiji's declaration that there must be a de-vesting of vested interests, though he laid stress that this should be by conversion, not compulsion. As some of his methods of conversion are not far removed, to my thinking, from courteous and considerate compulsion, the difference did not seem to me very great. I had the feeling with him then, as before, that though he might be averse to considering vague theories, the logic of facts would take him, step by step, to the inevitability of fundamental social changes. He was a curious phenomenon—a person of the type of a medieval Catholic saint, as Mr Verrier Elwin has called him—and at the same time a practical leader with his pulse always on the Indian peasantry. Which way he might turn in a crisis it was difficult to say, but whichever way it was, it would make a difference. He might go the wrong way, according to our thinking, but it would always be a straight way. It was good to work with him, but if necessity arose then different roads would have to be followed.

For the present, I thought then, this question did not arise. We were in the middle of our national struggle and civil disobedience was still the programme, in theory, of the Congress, although it had been restricted to individuals. We must carry on as we are and try to spread socialistic ideas among the people, and especially among the more politically-conscious Congress workers, so that when the time came for another declaration of policy we might be ready for a notable advance. Meanwhile, Congress was an unlawful organization, and the British Government was trying to crush it. We had to meet that attack.

The principal problem which faced Gandhiji was a personal one. What was he to do himself? He was in a tangle. If he went to gaol again the same question of Harijan privileges would arise and, presumably, the Government would not give in, and he would fast again. Would the same round be repeated? He refused to submit to such a cat-and-mouse policy, and said that if he fasted again for those privileges, the fast would continue even though he was released. That meant a fast to death.

The second possible course before him was not to court imprisonment during the year of his sentence (ten and a half months of this remained still) and devote himself to Harijan work. But at the same time he would meet Congress workers and advise them when necessary.

A third possibility he suggested to me was that he should retire from the Congress altogether for a while, and leave it in the hands of the "younger generation," as he put it.

The first course, ending, as it seemed, in his death by starvation, was impossible for anyone of us to recommend. The third seemed very undesirable when the Congress was an illegal body. It would either result in the immediate withdrawal of civil disobedience and all forms of direct action and a going back to legality and constitutional activity, or to a Congress, outlawed and isolated, now even from Gandhiji, being crushed still further by Government. Besides, there was no question of any group taking possession of an illegal organization which could not meet and discuss any policy. By a process of exclusion we arrived thus at the second course of action suggested by him. Most of us disliked it, and we knew that it would give a heavy blow to the remains of civil disobedience. If the leader had himself retired from the fight, it was not likely that many enthusiastic Congress workers would jump into the fire. But there seemed no other way out of the tangle, and Gandhiji made his announcement accordingly.

We agreed, Gandhiji and I, though perhaps for different reasons, that the time was not yet for a withdrawal of civil disobedience and we must carry on even at a low-ebb. For the rest, I wanted to turn people's attention to socialistic doctrines and the world situation.

I spent a few days in Bombay on my way back. I was fortunate in catching Udai Shankar there and seeing his dancing. This was an unexpected treat which I enjoyed greatly. Theatres, music, cinema, talkies, radio and broadcasting—all this had been beyond my reach for many years, for even during my intervals of freedom I was too engrossed in other activities. I have only been once to a talkie so far, and the great names of cinema stars are names only to me. I have missed the theatre especially, and I have often read with envy of new productions in foreign countries. In northern India, even when I was out of gaol, there was little opportunity of seeing good plays, for there were hardly any within reach. I believe the Bengali, Gujrati and Marathi drama has made some progress; not so the Hindustani stage, which is, or was (for I do not know the latest developments) terribly crude and inartistic. I am told most of the Indian films, both silent and talkies, do not err on the side of artistry. They are usually operettes or melodramas, drawing upon some theme from old Indian history or mythology.

I suppose they supply what is most appreciated by the city people. The contrast between these crude and painful shows and the still surviving artistry of the folk-song and dance, and even village drama, is very marked. In Bengal, in Gujrat and in the south, one discovers sometimes, with a shock of pleasant surprise, how fundamentally, and yet unconsciously, artistic the mass of the village people are. Not so the middle classes; they seem to have lost their roots and have no aesthetic tradition to cling to. They glory in cheap and horrid prints made in bulk in Germany and Austria, and sometimes even rise to Ravi Varma's pictures. The harmonium is their favourite instrument. (I live in hope that one of the earliest acts of the Swaraj government will be to ban this awful instrument.) But perhaps the height of painful incongruity and violation of all artistic codes is met with in the houses of most big taluqadars in Lucknow or elsewhere. They have money to spend and a desire to show off, and they do so; and the people who visit them are the pained witnesses of the fulfilment of this desire.

Recently there has been an artistic awakening, led by the brilliant Tagore family, and its influence is already apparent all over India. But how can any art flourish widely when the people of the country are hampered and restricted and suppressed at every turn and live in an atmosphere of fear?

In Bombay I met many friends and comrades, some only recently out of prison. The socialistic element was strong there, and there was much resentment at recent happenings in the upper ranks of the Congress. Gandhiji was severely criticized for his metaphysical outlook applied to politics. With much of the criticism I was in agreement, but I was quite clear that, situated as we were, we had little choice in the matter and had to carry on. Any attempt to withdraw civil disobedience would have brought no relief to us, for the Government's offensive would continue and all effective work would inevitably lead to prison. Our national movement had arrived at a stage when it had to be suppressed by Government, or it would impose its will on the British Government. This meant that it had arrived at a stage when it was always likely to be declared illegal and, as a movement, it could not go back even if civil disobedience was withdrawn. The continuance of disobedience made little difference in practice, but it was an act of moral defiance which had value. It was easier to spread new ideas during a struggle than it would be when the struggle was wound-up for the time being, and demoralization ensued. The only alternative to the struggle was a compromising attitude to the British authority and constitutional action in the councils.

It was a difficult position, and the choice was not an easy one. I appreciated the mental conflicts of my colleagues, for I had myself had to face them. But I found there, as I have found elsewhere in India, some people who wanted to make high socialistic doctrine a refuge for inaction. It was a little irritating to find people, who did little themselves, criticize others who had shouldered the burden in the heat and dust of the fray, as reactionaries. These parlour Socialists are especially hard on Gandhiji as the arch-reactionary, and advance arguments which, in logic, leave little to be desired. But the little fact remains that this 'reactionary' knows India, understands India, almost is peasant India, and has shaken up India as no so-called revolutionary has done. Even his latest Harijan activities have gently but irresistibly undermined orthodox Hinduism and shaken it to its foundations. The whole tribe of the Orthodox have ranged themselves against him, and consider him their most dangerous enemy, although he continues to treat them with all gentleness and courtesy. In his own peculiar way he has a knack of releasing powerful forces which spread out, like ripples on the water's surface, and affect millions. Reactionary or revolutionary, he has changed the face of India, given pride and character to a cringing and demoralized people, built up strength and consciousness in the masses, and made the Indian problem a world problem. Quite apart from the objectives aimed at and its metaphysical implications, the method of non-violent non-co-operation or civil resistance is a unique and powerful contribution of his to India and the world, and there can be no doubt that it has been peculiarly suited to Indian conditions.

I think it is right that we should encourage honest criticism, and have as much public discussion of our problems as possible. It is unfortunate that Gandhiji's dominating position has to some extent prevented this discussion. There was always a tendency to rely on him and to leave the decision to him. This is obviously wrong, and the nation can only advance by reasoned acceptance of objectives and methods, and a co-operation and discipline based on them and not on blind obedience. No one, however great he may be, should be above criticism. But when criticism becomes a mere refuge for inaction there is something wrong with it. For socialists to indulge in this kind of thing is to invite condemnation from the public, for the masses judge by acts. "He who denies the sharp tasks of today," says Lenin, "in the name of dreams about soft tasks of the future becomes an opportunist. Theoretically it means to fail to base oneself on the developments now going on in real life, to detach oneself from them in the name of dreams."

Socialists and communists in India are largely nurtured on literature dealing with the industrial proletariat. In some selected areas, like Bombay or near Calcutta, large numbers of factory workers abound, but for the rest India remains agricultural, and the Indian problem cannot be disposed of, or treated effectively, in terms of the industrial workers. Nationalism and rural economy are the dominating considerations, and European socialism seldom deals with these. Pre-war conditions in Russia were a much nearer approach to India, but there again the most extraordinary and unusual occurrences took place, and it is absurd to expect a repetition of these anywhere else. I do believe that the philosophy of communism helps us to understand and analyse existing conditions in any country, and further indicates the road to future progress. But it is doing violence and injustice to that philosophy to apply it blindfold and without due regard to facts and conditions.

Life is anyhow a complex affair, and the conflicts and contradictions of life sometimes make one despair a little. It is not surprising that people should differ, or even that comrades with a common approach to problems should draw different conclusions. But a person who tries to hide his own weakness in high-sounding phrases and noble principles is apt to be suspect. A person who tries to save himself from prison by giving undertakings and assurances to the Government, or by other dubious conduct, and then has the temerity to criticize others, is likely to injure the cause he espouses.

Bombay being a vast cosmopolitan city had all manner of people. One prominent citizen, however, showed a perfectly remarkable catholicity in his political, economic, social and religious outlook. As a Labour leader, he was a Socialist; in politics generally he called himself a Democrat; he was a favourite of the Hindu Sabha and he promised to protect old religious and social customs and prevent the legislature from interfering; at election-time he became the nominee of the Sanatanists, those high priests at the shrine of the ancient mysteries. Not finding this varied and diverting career exhausting enough, he utilized his superfluous energy in criticizing Congress and condemning Gandhiji as reactionary. In co-operation with a few others he started a Congress Democratic Party, which incidentally had nothing to do with democracy, and was connected with Congress only in so far as it attacked that august body. Searching for fresh fields to conquer, he then attended the Geneva Labour Conference as a Labour delegate. One might almost think that he was qualifying for the Prime Ministership of a 'National' Government after the English fashion.

Few people can have had the advantage of such a varied outlook and activities. And yet among the critics of the Congress there were many who had experimented in various fields, and who kept a finger in many a pie. A few of these called themselves socialists, and they gave a bad name to socialism.

51

THE LIBERAL OUTLOOK

During my visit to Poona to see Gandhiji, I accompanied him one evening to the Servants of India Society's home. For an hour or so questions were put to him on political matters by some of the members of the Society, and he answered them. Mr Srinivasa Sastri, the President of the Society, was not there, nor was Pandit Hriday Nath Kunzru, probably the ablest of the other members, but some senior members were present. A few of us who were present on the occasion listened with growing amazement, for the questions related to the most trivial of happenings. Mostly they dealt with Gandhiji's old request for an interview with the Viceroy and the Viceroy's refusal. Was this the only important subject they could think of in a world full of problems, and when their own country was carrying on a hard struggle for freedom and hundreds of organizations were outlawed? There was the agrarian crisis and the industrial depression causing widespread unemployment. There were the dreadful happenings in Bengal and the Frontier and in other parts of India, the suppression of freedom of thought and speech and writing and assembly; and so many other national and international problems. But the questions were limited to unimportant happenings, and the possible reactions of the Viceroy and the Government of India to an approach by Gandhiji.

I had a strong feeling as if I had entered a monastery, the inhabitants of which had long been cut off from effective contact with the outside world. And yet our friends were active politicians, able men with long records of public service and sacrifice. They formed, with a few others, the real backbone of the Liberal Party. The rest of the Party was a vague, amorphous lot of people, who wanted occasionally to have the sensation of being connected with political activities. Some of these, especially in Bombay and Madras, were indistinguishable from Government officials.

The questions that a country puts are a measure of that country's political development. Often the failure of that country is due to the fact that it has not put the right question to itself. Our wasting our time and energy and tempers over the communal distribution of seats, or our forming parties on the Communal Award and carrying on a sterile controversy about it to the exclusion of vital problems, is a measure of our political backwardness. In the same way the questions that were put to Gandhiji that day in the Servants of India Society's home mirrored the strange mental state of that Society and of the Liberal Party. They seemed to have no political or economic principles, no wide outlook, and their politics seemed to be of the parlour or court variety—what high officials would do or would not do.

One is apt to be misled by the name 'Liberal Party'. The word elsewhere, and especially in England, stood for a certain economic policy—free trade and *laisser-faire*, etc.—and a certain ideology of individual freedom and civil liberties. The English Liberal tradition was based on economic foundations. The desire for freedom in trade and to be rid of the King's monopolies and arbitrary taxation, led to the desire for political liberty. The Indian Liberals have no such background. They do not believe in free trade, being almost all protectionists, and they attach little importance to civil liberties as recent events have shown. Their close contacts with and general support of the semi-feudal and autocratic Indian States, where even the beginnings of democracy and personal freedom are nonexistent, also distinguish them from the European type of Liberal. Indeed the Indian Liberals are not liberal at all in any sense of the word, or at most they are liberal only in spots and patches. What they exactly are it is difficult to say, for they have no firm positive basis of ideas, and, though small in numbers, differ from one another. They are strong only in negation. They see error everywhere and attempt to avoid it, and hope that in doing so they will find the truth. Truth for them indeed always lies between two extremes. By criticizing everything they consider extreme, they experience the feeling of being virtuous and moderate and good. This method helps them in avoiding painful and difficult processes of thought and in having to put forward constructive ideas. Capitalism, some of them vaguely feel, has not wholly succeeded in Europe, and is in trouble; on the other hand socialism is obviously bad, because it attacks vested interests. Probably some mystic solution will be found in the future, some half-way house, and meanwhile vested interests should be protected. If there was an argument as to whether the earth was flat or round, probably they would condemn both these extreme views and suggest tentatively that it might be square or elliptical.

Over trivial and unimportant matters they grow quite excited, and there is an amazing amount of houha and shouting. Consciously and sub-consciously they avoid tackling fundamental issues, for such issues require fundamental remedies and the courage of thought and action. Hence Liberal defeats and victories are of little consequence. They relate to no principle. The leading characteristic of the Party and the distinguishing feature, if it can be considered so, is thus moderation in everything, good or bad. It is an outlook on life and the old name—the Moderates—was perhaps the most suitable.

> In moderation placing all my glory
> While Tories call me Whig and Whigs a Tory.[1]

But moderation, however admirable it might be, is not a bright and scintillating virtue. It produces dullness, and so the Indian Liberals have unhappily become a 'Dull Brigade'—sombre and serious in their looks, dull in their writing and conversation, and lacking in humour. Of course there are exceptions, and the most notable of these is Sir Tej Bahadur Sapru who, in his personal life, is certainly not dull or lacking in humour and who enjoys even a joke against himself. But on the whole the Liberal group represents bourgeoisdom *in excelsis* with all its pedestrian solidity. The *Leader* of Allahabad, which is the leading Liberal newspaper, had a revealing editorial note last year. It stated that great and unusual men had always brought trouble to the world, and therefore it preferred the ordinary, mediocre kind of man. With a fine and frank gesture it nailed its flag to mediocrity.

Moderation and conservatism and a desire to avoid risks and sudden changes are often the inevitable accompaniments of old age. They do not seem quite so appropriate in the young, but ours is an ancient land, and sometimes its children seem to be born tired and weary, with all the lack-lustre and marks of age upon them. But even this old country is now convulsed by the forces of change, and the moderate outlook is

---

1. Alexander Pope.

bewildered. The old world is passing, and all the sweet reasonableness of which the Liberals are capable does not make any difference; they might as well argue with the hurricane or the flood or the earthquake. Old assumptions fail them, and they dare not seek for new ways of thought and action. Dr A. N. Whitehead, speaking of the European tradition, says: "The whole of this tradition is warped by the vicious assumption that each generation will substantially live amid the conditions governing the lives of its fathers, and will transmit those conditions to mould with equal force the lives of its children. We are living in the first period of human history for which the assumption is false." Dr Whitehead errs on the side of moderation in his analysis, for probably that assumption has always been untrue. If the European tradition has been conservative, how much more so has ours been? But the mechanics of history pay little attention to these traditions when the time for change comes. We watch helplessly and blame others for the failure of our plans. And that, as Mr Gerald Heard points out, is the "most disastrous of illusions, the projection that convinces itself that any failure in one's plans must be due not to a mistake in one's own thinking, but to a deliberate thwarting by some one else."

All of us suffer from this terrible illusion. I sometimes think that Gandhiji is not free from it. But we act at least and try to keep in touch with life, and by trial and error sometimes lessen the power of the illusion and stumble along. But the Liberals suffer most. For they do not act for fear of acting wrongly, they do not move for fear of falling, they keep away from all healthy contacts with the masses, and sit enchanted and self-hypnotized in their mental cells. Mr Srinivasa Sastri warned his fellow-Liberals a year and a half ago not to "stand by and let things pass." That warning had greater truth in it than he himself probably realized. Thinking always in terms of what the Government did, he was referring to the constitutional changes that were being hatched by various official committees. But the misfortune of the Liberals had been that they stood by and let things pass when their own people were marching ahead. They feared their own masses, and they preferred to alienate themselves from these masses rather than fall out with our rulers. Was it any wonder that they became strangers in their own land, and life went by and left them standing? When fierce struggles were waged for life and freedom by their countrymen, there was no doubt on which side of the barricade the Liberals stood. From the other side of that barricade they gave us good advice, and were full of moral platitudes, laying them on thick like sticky paint. Their cooperation with the British Government in the round table conferences and committees was a moral factor of value to the Government. A denial of it would have made a difference. It was remarkable that at one of these conferences even the British Labour Party kept away; not so our Liberals, who went in spite of an appeal by some Britishers to them not to do so.

We are all moderates or extremists in varying degrees, and for various objects. If we care enough for anything we are likely to feel strongly about it, to be extremist about it. Otherwise we can afford a gracious tolerance, a philosophical moderation, which really hides to some extent our indifference. I have known the mildest of Moderates to grow very aggressive and extremist when a suggestion was made for the sweeping away of certain vested interests in land. Our Liberal friends represent to some extent the prosperous and well-to-do. They can afford to wait for Swaraj, and need not excite themselves about it. But any proposal for radical social change disturbs them greatly, and they are no longer moderate or sweetly reasonable about it. Thus their moderation is really confined to their attitude towards the British Government, and they nurse the hope that if they are sufficiently respectful and compromising perhaps, as a reward for this behaviour, they might be listened to. Inevitably they have to accept the British view-point. Blue books become their passionate study, Erskine May's *Parliamentary Practice* and such-like books their constant companions, a new Government Report a matter for excitement and speculation. Liberal leaders returning from England make mysterious statements about the doings of the great ones in Whitehall, for Whitehall is the Valhalla of Liberals, Responsivists and other similar groups. In the old days it was said that good Americans when they died went to Paris, and it may be that the shades of good Liberals sometimes haunt the precincts of Whitehall.

I write of Liberals, but what I write applies to many of us also in the Congress. It applies even more to the Responsivists, who have outdistanced the Liberals in their moderation. There is a great deal of difference between the average Liberal and the average Congressman, and yet the dividing line is not clear and definite. Ideologically there is little to choose between the advanced Liberal and the moderate

Congressman. But, thanks to Gandhiji, every Congressman has kept some touch with the soil and the people of the country, and he has dabbled in action, and because of this he has escaped some of the consequences of a vague and defective ideology. Not so the Liberals: they have lost touch with both the old and the new. As a group they represent a vanishing species.

Most of us, I suppose, have lost the old pagan feeling and not gained the new insight. Not for us to "have sight of Proteus rising from the sea"; or "hear old Triton blow his wreathed horn." And very few of us are fortunate enough—

> To see a World in a Grain of Sand
> And a Heaven in a Wild Flower,
> Hold Infinity in the palm of your hand
> And Eternity in an hour.

Not for most of us, unhappily, to sense the mysterious life of Nature, to hear her whisper close to our ears, to thrill and quiver at her touch. Those days are gone. But though we may not see the sublime in Nature as we used to, we have sought to find it in the glory and tragedy of humanity, in its mighty dreams and inner tempests, its pangs and failures, its conflicts and misery, and, over all this, its faith in a great destiny and a realization of those dreams. That has been some recompense for us for all the heart-breaks that such a search involves, and often we have been raised above the pettiness of life. But many have not undertaken this search, and having cut themselves adrift from the ancient ways, find no road to follow in the present. They neither dream nor do they act. They have no understanding of human convulsions like the great French Revolution or the Russian Revolution. The complex, swift and cruel eruptions of human desires, long suppressed, frighten them. For them the Bastille has not yet fallen.

It is often said with righteous indignation that "Patriotism is not a monopoly of Congressmen." The same phrase is repeated again and again with a lack of originality which is somewhat distressing. I hope no Congressman has ever claimed a corner in this emotion. Certainly I do not think it is a Congress monopoly, and I would be glad to make a present of it to anyone who desired it. It is often enough the refuge of the opportunist and the careerist, and there are so many varieties of it to suit all tastes, all interests, all classes. If Judas had been alive today he would no doubt act in its name. Patriotism is no longer enough: we want something higher, wider and nobler.

Nor is moderation enough by itself. Restraint is good and is the measure of our culture, but behind that restraint there must be something to restrain and hold back. It has been, and is, man's destiny to control the elements, to ride the thunderbolt, to bring the raging fire and the rushing and tumbling waters to his use, but most difficult of all for him has been to restrain and hold in check the passions that consume him. So long as he will not master them, he cannot enter fully into his human heritage. But are we to restrain the legs that move not and the hands that are palsied?

I cannot resist the temptation to quote four lines of Roy Campbell's, written on some South African novelists. They seem to be equally applicable to various political groups in India:

> They praise the firm restraint with which you write.
> I'm with you there, of course.
> You use the snaffle and the curb all right,
> But where's the bloody horse?

Our Liberal friends tell us that they follow the narrow path of the golden mean, and steer themselves between the extremes of the Congress and the Government. They constitute themselves the judges of the failings of both, and congratulate themselves that they are free from either. They endeavour to hold the scales and, like the figure of Justice, I suppose, they keep their eyes closed or bandaged. Is it my fancy merely that takes me back through the ages and makes me listen to that famous cry: "Scribes and Pharisees . . . Ye blind guides, which strain at a gnat and swallow a camel!"

52

DOMINION STATUS AND
INDEPENDENCE

Most of those who have shaped Congress policy during the last seventeen years have come from the middle classes. Liberal or Congressmen, they have come from the same class and have grown up in the same environment. Their social life and contacts and friendships have been similar, and there was little difference to begin with between the two varieties of *bourgeois* ideals that they professed. Temperamental and psychological differences began to separate them, and they began to look in different directions—one group more towards the Government and the rich, upper middle class, the other towards the lower middle classes. The ideology still remained the same, the objectives did not differ, but behind the second group there was now the push of larger numbers from the market-place and the humbler professions as well as the unemployed intelligentsia. The tone changed; it was no longer respectful and polite, but strident and aggressive. Lacking strength to act effectively, some relief was found in strong language. Frightened by this new development, the moderate elements dropped out and sought safety in seclusion. Even so, the upper middle class was strongly represented in the Congress, though in numbers the little *bourgeoisie* was predominant. They were drawn not only by the desire for success in their national struggle, but because they sought an inner satisfaction in that struggle. They sought thereby to recover their lost pride and self-respect, and to rehabilitate their shattered dignity. It was the usual nationalist urge, and though this was common to all, it was here that the temperamental differences between the moderate and the extremist became evident. Gradually the lower middle class began to dominate the Congress, and later the peasantry made their influence felt.

As the Congress became more and more the representative of the rural masses, the gulf that separated it from the Liberals widened, and it became almost impossible for the Liberal to understand or appreciate the Congress view-point. It is not easy for the upper-class drawing-room to understand the humble cottage or the mud hut. Yet, in spite of these differences, both the ideologies were nationalist and *bourgeois*; the variation was one of degree, not of kind. In the Congress many people remained to the last who would have been quite at home in the Liberal group.

For many generations the British treated India as a kind of enormous country-house (after the old English fashion) that they owned. They were the gentry owning the house and occupying the desirable parts of it, while the Indians were consigned to the servants' hall and pantry and kitchen. As in every proper country-house there was a fixed hierarchy in those lower regions—butler, housekeeper, cook, valet, maid, footman, etc.—and strict precedence was observed among them. But between the upper and lower regions of the house there was, socially and politically, an impassable barrier. The fact that the British Government should have imposed this arrangement upon us was not surprising; but what does seem surprising is that we, or most of us, accepted it as the natural and inevitable ordering of our lives and destiny. We developed the mentality of a good country-house servant. Sometimes we were treated to a rare honour—we were given a cup of tea in the drawing-room. The height of our ambition was to become respectable and to be promoted individually to the upper regions. Greater than any victory of arms or diplomacy was this psychological triumph of the British in India. The slave began to think as a slave, as the wise men of old had said.

Times have changed, and the country-house type of civilization is not accepted willingly now, either in England or India. But still there remain people amongst us who desire to stick to the servants' halls and take pride in the gold braid and livery of their service. Others, like the Liberals, accept that country-house in its entirety, admire its architecture and the whole edifice, but look forward to replacing the owners, one by one, by themselves. They call this Indianization. For them the problem is one of changing the colour of the administration, or at most having a new administration. They never think in terms of a new State.

For them Swaraj means that everything continues as before, only with a darker shade. They can only conceive of a future in which they, or people like them, will play the principal role and take the place of the

English high officials; in which there are the same types of services, government departments, legislatures, trade, industry—with the I.C.S. at their jobs; the princes in their palaces, occasionally appearing in fancy dress or carnival attire with all their jewels glittering to impress their subjects; the landlords claiming special protection, and meanwhile harassing their tenants; the money-lender, with his money-bags, harassing both zamindar and tenant; the lawyer with his fees; and God in His heaven.

Essentially their outlook is based on the maintenance of the *status quo*, and the changes they desire can almost be termed personal changes. And they seek to achieve these changes by a slow infiltration with the goodwill of the British. The whole foundation of their politics and economics rests on the continuance and stability of the British Empire. Looking on this Empire as unshakable, at least for a considerable time, they adapt themselves to it, and accept not only its political and economic ideology but also, to a large extent, its moral standards, which have all been framed to secure the continuance of British dominance.

The Congress attitude differs fundamentally from this because it seeks a new State and not just a different administration. What that new State is going to be may not be quite clear to the average Congressman, and opinions may differ about it. But it is common ground in the Congress (except perhaps for a moderate fringe) that present conditions and methods cannot and must not continue, and basic changes are essential. Herein lies the difference between Dominion Status and Independence. The former envisages the same old structure, with many bonds visible and invisible tying us to the British economic system; the latter gives us, or ought to give us, freedom to erect a new structure to suit our circumstances.

It is not a question of an implacable and irreconcilable antagonism to England and the English people, or the desire to break from them at all costs. It would be natural enough if there was bad blood between India and England after what has happened. "The clumsiness of power spoils the key and uses the pick-axe," says Tagore, and the key to our hearts was destroyed long ago, and the abundant use of the pick-axe on us has not made us partial to the British. But if we claim to serve the larger cause of India and humanity we cannot afford to be carried away by our momentary passions. And even if we were so inclined the hard training which Gandhiji has given us for the last fifteen years would prevent us. I write this sitting in a British prison, and for months past my mind has been full of anxiety, and I have perhaps suffered more during this solitary imprisonment than I have done in gaol before. Anger and resentment have often filled my mind at various happenings, and yet as I sit here, and look deep into my mind and heart, I do not find any anger against England or the English people. I dislike British imperialism and I resent its imposition on India; I dislike the capitalist system; I dislike exceedingly and resent the way India is exploited by the ruling classes of Britain. But I do not hold England or the English people as a whole responsible for this, and even if I did, I do not think it would make much difference, for it is a little foolish to lose one's temper at or to condemn a whole people. They are as much the victims of circumstances as we are.

Personally, I owe too much to England in my mental makeup ever to feel wholly alien to her. And, do what I will, I cannot get rid of the habits of mind, and the standards and ways of judging other countries as well as life generally, which I acquired at school and college in England. All my predilections (apart from the political plane) are in favour of England and the English people, and if I have become what is called an uncompromising opponent of British rule in India, it is almost in spite of myself.

It is that rule, that domination, to which we object, and with which we cannot compromise willingly—not the English people. Let us by all means have the closest contacts with the English and other foreign peoples. We want fresh air in India, fresh and vital ideas, healthy co-operation; we have grown too musty with age. But if the English come in the role of a tiger they can expect no friendship or co-operation. To the tiger of imperialism there will only be the fiercest opposition, and today our country has to deal with that ferocious animal. It may be possible to tame the wild tiger of the forest and to charm away his native ferocity, but there is no such possibility of taming capitalism and imperialism when they combine and swoop down on an unhappy land.

For anyone to say that he or his country will not compromise is, in a sense, a foolish remark, for life is always forcing us to compromise. When applied to another country or people, it is completely foolish. But there is truth in it when it is applied to a system or a particular set of circumstances, and then it becomes something beyond human power to accomplish. Indian freedom and British imperialism are two incompatibles, and neither martial law nor all the sugar-coating in the world can make them compatible or bring them together. Only with the elimination of British imperialism from India will conditions be created which permit of real Indo-British cooperation.

We are told that independence is a narrow creed in the modern world, which is increasingly becoming inter-dependent, and therefore in demanding independence we are trying to put the clock back. Liberals and pacifists and even so-called socialists in Britain advance this plea and chide us for our narrow nationalism, and incidentally suggest to us that the way to a fuller national life is through the "British Commonwealth of Nations." It is curious how all roads in England—liberalism, pacifism, socialism, etc.—lead to the maintenance of the Empire. "The desire of a ruling nation to maintain the *status quo*," says Trotsky, "frequently dresses up as a superiority to 'nationalism', just as the desire of a victorious nation to hang on to its booty easily takes the form of pacifism. Thus MacDonald, in the face of Gandhi, feels as though he were an internationalist."

I do not know what India will be like or what she will do when she is politically free. But I do know that those of her people who stand for national independence today stand also for the widest internationalism. For a socialist, nationalism can have no meaning, but even many of the non-socialists in the advanced ranks of the Congress are confirmed internationalists. If we claim independence today it is with no desire for isolation. On the contrary, we are perfectly willing to surrender part of that independence, in common with other countries, to a real international order. Any imperial system, by whatever high-sounding name it may be called, is an enemy of such an order, and it is not through such a system that world co-operation or world peace can be reached.

Recent developments have shown all over the world how the various imperialist systems are isolating themselves more and more by autarchy and economic imperialism. Instead of the growth of internationalism we see a reversal of the process. The reasons for this are not difficult to discover, and they indicate the growing weakness of the present economic order. One of the results of this policy is that while it produces greater cooperation within the area of autarchy, it also means isolation from the rest of the world. For India, as we have seen by Ottawa and other decisions, it has meant a progressive lessening of our ties and contacts with other countries. We have become, even more than we were, the hangers-on of British industry; and the dangers of this policy, apart from the immediate harm it has done in various ways, are obvious. Thus Dominion Status seems to lead to isolation and not to wider international contacts.

Our friends the Indian Liberals, however, have an amazing knack of seeing the world, and more particularly their own country, through British spectacles of true-blue colour. Without trying to appreciate what the Congress says and why it says so, they repeat the old British argument of independence being narrower and less soul-lifting than Dominion Status. Internationalism means for them Whitehall, for they are singularly ignorant of other countries, partly because of the language difficulty, but even more so because they are quite content to ignore them. They are, of course, averse to direct action or any kind of aggressive politics in India. But it is curious to note that some of their leaders have no objection to such methods being adopted in other countries. They can appreciate and admire them from a distance, and some of the present-day dictators of Western countries receive their mental homage.

Names are apt to mislead, but the real question before us in India is whether we are aiming at a new State or merely at a new administration. The Liberal answer is clear; they want the latter, and nothing more, and even that is a distant and progressive ideal. The words 'Dominion Status' are mentioned from time to time, but their real objective for the time being is expressed in those mystic words "responsibility at the centre". Not for them the full-blooded words: Power, Independence, Freedom, Liberty; they sound dangerous. The lawyer's language and approach appeals to them far more, even though it may not enthuse the multitude. History has innumerable instances of individuals and groups facing perils and risking their lives for the sake of faith and freedom. It seems doubtful if anyone will ever deliberately give up a meal or sleep less soundly for "responsibility at the centre" or any other legal phrase.

This, then, is their objective, and this is to be reached not by 'direct action' or any other form of aggressive action but, as Mr Srinivasa Sastri put it, by a display of "wisdom, experience, moderation, power of persuasion, quiet influence and real efficiency." It is hoped that by our good behaviour and our good work we shall ultimately induce our rulers to part with power. In other words, they resist us today because either they are irritated against us on account of our aggressive attitude, or they doubt our capacity, or both. This seems a rather naïve analysis of imperialism and the present situation. That brilliant English writer, Professor R.H.Tawney, has written an appropriate and arresting passage dealing with the notion of gaining power in stages and with the co-operation of the ruling classes. He refers to the British Labour Party, but his words are even more applicable to India, for in England they have at least democratic institutions, where the will of the majority can, in theory, make itself felt. Professor Tawney writes:

> Onions can be eaten leaf by leaf, but you cannot skin a live tiger paw by paw; vivisection is its trade, and it does the skinning first . . .
>
> If there is any country where the privileged classes are simpletons, it is certainly not England. The idea that tact and amiability in presenting the Labour Party's case can hoodwink them into the belief that it is their case also, is as hopeless as an attempt to bluff a sharp solicitor out of a property of which he holds the title-deeds. The plutocracy consists of agreeable, astute, forcible, self-confident, and, when hard pressed, unscrupulous people, who know pretty well on which side their bread is buttered, and intend that the supply of butter shall not run short . . . If their position is seriously threatened, they will use every piece on the board, political and economic—the House of Lords, the Crown, the Press, disaffection in the Army, financial crisis, international difficulties, and even, as newspaper attacks on the pound in 1931 showed, the émigré trick of injuring one's country to protect one's pocket.

The British Labour Party is a powerful organization. It is backed by the Trade Unions, with their millions of paying members, and a highly developed co-operative organization, as well as many members and sympathizers among the professional classes. Britain has democratic parliamentary institutions based on adult suffrage, and a long tradition of civil liberty. In spite of all this, Mr Tawney is of opinion—and recent events have confirmed the soundness of this—that the Labour Party cannot hope to gain real power merely by smiling and persuasion, useful and desirable as both these approaches are. Mr Tawney suggests that even if the Labour Party obtained a majority in the House of Commons, it would still be powerless to make any radical change in face of the opposition of the privileged classes, who hold so many political, social, economic, financial and military citadels. In India, it need hardly be pointed out, conditions are very different. There are no democratic institutions or traditions. We have instead a well-established practice of ordinance and dictatorial rule and the suppression of the liberties of the person, of speech, writing, assembly and the Press. Nor have the Liberals any strong organization behind them. They have thus to rely on their smile alone.

Liberals are strongly opposed to any activity that is 'unconstitutional' or 'illegal'. In countries with democratic constitutions the word 'constitutional' has a wide significance. It controls the making of laws, it protects liberties, it checks the executive, it provides for the democratic methods of bringing about changes in the political and economic structure. But in India there is no such constitution and the word can mean no such thing.[1] To use it here is merely to introduce an idea which has no place in the India of today. The word 'constitutional' is often used here, strange to say, in support of the executive's more or less arbitrary actions. Or else it is used in the sense of 'legal'. It is far better to confine ourselves to the words 'legal' or 'illegal', though they are vague enough and vary from day to day.

A new ordinance or a new law creates new offences. To attend a public meeting may be an offence; so also to ride a bicycle, to wear certain clothes, not to be home by sunset, not to report oneself to the police daily—all these and numerous other acts are offences today in some part of India. A certain act may be an offence in one part of the country and not in another. When these laws can be promulgated by an irresponsible executive at the shortest notice, the word 'legal' simply means the will of that executive and nothing more. Ordinarily that will is obeyed, willingly or sullenly, because the consequences of disobedience are unpleasant. But for anyone to say that he will always obey it means

---

1. Mr C.Y. Chintamani, the eminent Liberal leader and editor-in-chief of the *Leader* newspaper, has himself laid stress on the lack of any kind of constitutional government in India, in his criticism in the U.P. Council, of the Report of the Parliamentary Joint Select Committee on India: "Better submit to the present unconstitutional government rather than to the more reactionary and further more unconstitutional government of the future."

abject submission to a dictatorship or irresponsible authority, the surrender of his conscience, and the impossibility of ever gaining freedom, so far as his activities are concerned.

In every democratic country today there is an argument going on as to whether radical economic changes can be brought about in the ordinary course through the constitutional machinery at their disposal. Many people are of opinion that this cannot be done, and some unusual and revolutionary method will have to be adopted. For our purpose in India the issue of this argument is immaterial, for we have no constitutional means of bringing about the changes we desire. If the White Paper or something like it is enacted, constitutional progress in many directions will be stopped completely. There is no way out except by revolution or illegal action. What then is one to do? Give up all idea of change and resign oneself to fate?

The position today in India is even more extraordinary. The Executive can and does prevent or restrict all manner of public activities. Any activity that is, in its opinion, dangerous for it is prohibited. Thus all effective public activity can be stopped, as it was stopped during the last three years. Submission to this means giving up all public work. That is an impossible position to take up.

No one can say that he will always and without fail act legally. Even in a democratic state occasions may arise when one's conscience compels one to act otherwise. In a despotically or arbitrarily governed country these occasions are bound to be more frequent; indeed, in such a state the law loses all moral justification.

"Direct action is allied to dictatorship and not democracy, and those who wish to bring about the triumph of democracy must eschew direct action," say the Liberals. This is confused thinking and loose writing. Sometimes direct action—e.g. a workers' strike—may even be legal. But probably political action was meant. In Germany today under Hitler what kind of action is possible? Either abject submission or illegal and revolutionary action. How could democracy be served there?

Indian Liberals often refer to democracy, but most of them have no desire to go near it. Sir P.S. Sivaswamy Iyer, one of the most prominent of Liberal leaders, said in May 1934: "In advocating the convention of a constituent assembly, the Congress places too much faith in the wisdom of the multitude, and does too little justice to the sincerity and ability of men who have taken part in various Round Table Conferences. I very much doubt whether the constituent assembly would have done better." Sir Sivaswamy's idea of democracy is thus something apart from the 'multitude', and fits in more with a collection of 'sincere and able' men nominated by the British Government. Further, he blesses the White Paper, for though "not fully satisfied" with it, he thought "it would be unwise for the country to oppose it wholesale". There appears to be no reason whatever why there should not be the most perfect co-operation between the British Government and Sir P.S. Sivaswamy Iyer.

The withdrawal of civil disobedience by the Congress was naturally welcomed by the Liberals. It was also not surprising that they should take credit for their wisdom in having kept aloof from this "foolish and ill-advised movement". "Did we not say so?" they told us. It was a strange argument. Because when we stood up and put up a good fight we were knocked down; therefore, the moral pointed out was that standing up is a bad thing. Crawling is best and safest. It is quite impossible to be knocked down or to fall from that horizontal position.

53

INDIA OLD AND NEW

It was natural and inevitable that Indian nationalism should resent alien rule. And yet it was curious how large numbers of our intelligentsia, to the end of the nineteenth century, accepted, consciously or unconsciously, the British ideology of empire. They built their own arguments on this, and only ventured to criticize some of its outward manifestations. The history and economics and other subjects that were taught in the schools and colleges were written entirely from the British imperial view-point, and laid stress on our numerous failings in the past and present and the virtues and high destiny of the British. We accepted to some extent this distorted version, and even when we resisted it instinctively we were influenced by it. At first there was no intellectual escape from it for we knew no other facts or arguments, and so we sought relief in religious nationalism, in the thought that at least in the sphere of religion and philosophy we were second to no other people. We comforted ourselves in our misfortune and degradation with the notion that though we did not possess the outward show and glitter of the West we had the real inner article, which was far more valuable and worth having. Vivekananda and others, as well as the interest of Western scholars in our old philosophies, gave us a measure of self-respect again and roused up our dormant pride in our past.

Gradually we began to suspect and examine critically British statements about our past and present conditions, but still we thought and worked within the framework of British ideology. If a thing was bad, it would be called 'un-British'; if a Britisher in India misbehaved, the fault was his, not that of the system. But the collection of this critical material of British rule in India, in spite of the moderate outlook of the authors, served a revolutionary purpose and gave a political and economic foundation to our nationalism. Dadabhai Naoroji's *Poverty and Un-British Rule in India*, and books by Romesh Dutt and William Digby and others, thus played a revolutionary role in the development of our nationalist thought. Further researches in ancient Indian history revealed brilliant and highly civilized periods in the remote past, and we read of these with great satisfaction. We also discovered that the British record in India was very different from what we had been led to believe from their history books.

Our challenge to the British version of history, economics, and administration in India grew, and yet we continued to function within the orbit of their ideology. That was the position of Indian nationalism as a whole at the turn of the century. That is still the position of the Liberal group and other small groups as well as a number of moderate Congressmen, who go forward emotionally from time to time, but intellectually still live in the nineteenth century. Because of that the Liberal is unable to grasp the idea of Indian freedom, for the two are fundamentally irreconcilable. He imagines that step by step he will go up to higher offices and will deal with fatter and more important files. The machinery of government will go on smoothly as before, only he will be at the hub, and somewhere in the background, without intruding themselves too much, will be the British Army to give him protection in case of need. That is his idea of Dominion Status within the Empire. It is a naïve notion impossible of achievement, for the price of British protection is Indian subjection. We cannot have it both ways, even if that was not degrading to the self-respect of a great country. Sir Frederick Whyte (no partisan of Indian nationalism) says in a recent book:[1] "He (the Indian) still believes that England will stand between him and disaster, and as long as he cherishes this delusion he cannot even lay the foundation of his own ideal of self-government." Evidently he refers to the Liberal or the reactionary and communal types of Indians, largely with whom he must have come into contact when he was President of the Indian Legislative Assembly. This is not the Congress belief, much less is it that of other advanced groups. They agree with Sir Frederick, however, that there can be no freedom till this delusion goes and India is left to face disaster, if that is her fate, by herself. The complete withdrawal of British military control of India will be the beginning of Indian freedom.

It is not surprising that the Indian intelligentsia in the nineteenth century should have succumbed to British ideology; what is surprising

---

1. Sir Frederick Whyte: *The Future of East and West.*

is that some people should continue to suffer that delusion even after the stirring events and changes of the twentieth century. In the nineteenth century the British ruling classes were the aristocrats of the world, with a long record of wealth and success and power behind them. This long record and training gave them some of the virtues as well as failings of aristocracy. We in India can comfort ourselves with the thought that we helped substantially during the last century and three-quarters in providing the wherewithal and the training for this superior state. They began to think themselves—as so many races and nations have done—the chosen of God and their Empire as an earthly Kingdom of Heaven; if their special position was acknowledged and their superiority not challenged, they were gracious and obliging, provided that this did them no harm. But opposition to them became opposition to the divine order, and as such was a deadly sin which must be suppressed.

M. André Siegfried has an interesting passage dealing with this aspect of British psychology.[2]

"*Par l'habitude héréditaire du pouvoir joint à la richesse, il a fini par contracter une manière d'être, aristocratique, curieusement imbue de droit divin ethnique et qui même a continué de s'accentuer quand déjà la suprematie britannique était contestée. Les jeunes générations de la fin du siècle . . . elles en arrivent à se dire, inconsciemment, que ce succès leur est dû . . .*

"*Cette façon d'interpréter les choses est intéressante à souligner, parce qu'elle éclaire, dans ce défilé particulièrement délicat, les réactions de la psychologie britannique. On n'aura pas manqué de le remarquer, c'est dans des causes extérieures que l'Angleterre croit trouver la source de ces difficultés: toujours, pour commencer, c'est la faute de quelqu'un, et si ce quelqu'un veut bien se réformer, l'Angleterre alors pourra retrouver sa prospérité . . . toujours cet instinct de vouloir changer les autres au lieu de se changer soi-même!*"

If this was the general British attitude to the rest of the world, it was most conspicuous in India. There was something fascinating about the British approach to the Indian problem, even though it was singularly irritating. The calm assurance of always being in the right and of having borne a great burden worthily, faith in their racial destiny and their own brand of imperialism, contempt and anger at the unbelievers and sinners who challenged the foundations of the true faith—there was something

---

2. In *La Crise Britannique au XXe Siècle*.

of the religious temper about this attitude. Like the Inquisitors of old, they were bent on saving us regardless of our desires in the matter. Incidentally they profited by this traffic in virtue, thus demonstrating the truth of the old proverb: "Honesty is the best policy". The progress of India became synonymous with the adaptation of the country to the imperial scheme and the fashioning of chosen Indians after the British mould. The more we accepted British ideals and objectives the fitter we were for 'self-government'. Freedom would be ours as soon as we demonstrated and guaranteed that we would use it only in accordance with British wishes.

Indians and Englishmen are, I am afraid, likely to disagree about the record of British rule in India. That is perhaps natural, but it does come as a shock when high British officials, including Secretaries of State for India, draw fanciful pictures of India's past and present and make statements which have no basis in fact. It is quite extraordinary how ignorant English people, apart from some experts and others, are about India. If facts elude them, how much more is the spirit of India beyond their reach? They seized her body and possessed her, but it was the possession of violence. They did not know her or try to know her. They never looked into her eyes, for theirs were averted and hers downcast through shame and humiliation. After centuries of contact they face each other, strangers still, full of dislike for each other.

And yet India with all her poverty and degradation had enough of nobility and greatness about her, and though she was overburdened with ancient tradition and present misery, and her eyelids were a little weary, she had "a beauty wrought out from within upon the flesh, the deposit little cell by cell, of strange thoughts and fantastic reveries and exquisite passions". Behind and within her battered body one could still glimpse a majesty of soul. Through long ages she had travelled and gathered much wisdom on the way, and trafficked with strangers and added them to her own big family, and witnessed days of glory and of decay, and suffered humiliation and terrible sorrow, and seen many a strange sight; but throughout her long journey she had clung to her immemorial culture, drawn strength and vitality from it, and shared it with other lands. Like a pendulum she had swung up and down; she had ventured with the daring of her thought to reach up to the heavens and unravel their mystery, and she had also had bitter experience of the pit of hell.

Despite the woeful accumulations of superstition and degrading custom that had clung to her and borne her down, she had never wholly forgotten the inspiration that some of the wisest of her children, at the dawn of history, had given her in the Upanishads. Their keen minds, ever restless and ever striving and exploring, had not sought refuge in blind dogma or grown complacent in the routine observance of dead forms or ritual and creed. They had demanded not a personal relief from suffering in the present or a place in a paradise to come, but light and understanding: "Lead me from the unreal to the real, lead me from darkness to light, lead me from death to immortality."[3] In the most famous of the prayers recited daily even today by millions, the *gayatri mantra*, the call is for knowledge, for enlightenment.

Though often broken up politically her spirit always guarded a common heritage, and in her diversity there was ever an amazing unity.[4] Like all ancient lands she was a curious mixture of the good and bad, but the good was hidden and had to be sought after, while the odour of decay was evident and her hot, pitiless sun gave full publicity to the bad.

There is some similarity between Italy and India. Both are ancient countries with long traditions of culture behind them, though Italy is a newcomer compared to India, and India is a much vaster country. Both are split up politically, and yet the conception of Italia, like that of India, never died, and in all their diversity the unity was predominant. In Italy the unity was largely a Roman unity, for that great city had dominated the country and been the fount and symbol of unity. In India there was no such single centre or dominant city, although Benares might well be called the Eternal City of the East, not only for India but also for Eastern Asia. But, unlike Rome, Benares never dabbled in empire or thought of temporal power. Indian culture was so widespread all over India that no part of the country could be called the heart of that culture. From Cape Comorin to Amaranath and Badrinath in the Himalayas, from Dwarka

---

3. *Brihadaranyak Upanishad*, i, 3, 27.
4. "The greatest of all the contradictions in India is that over this diversity is spread a greater unity, which is not immediately evident because it failed historically to find expression in any political cohesion to make the country one, but which is so great a reality, and so powerful, that even the Musulman world of India has to confess that it has been deeply affected by coming within its influence." Sir Frederick Whyte: *The Future of East and West*.

to Puri, the same ideas coursed, and if there was a clash of ideas in one place, the noise of it soon reached distant parts of the country.

Just as Italy gave the gift of culture and religion to Western Europe, India did so to Eastern Asia, though China was as old and venerable as India. And even when Italy was lying prostrate politically, her life coursed through the veins of Europe.

It was Metternich who called Italy a "geographical expression", and many a would-be Metternich has used that phrase for India, and, strangely enough, there is a similarity even in their geographical positions in the two continents. More interesting is the comparison of England with Austria, for has not England of the twentieth century been compared to Austria of the nineteenth, proud and haughty and imposing still, but with the roots that gave strength shrivelling up and decay eating its way into the mighty fabric.

It is curious how one cannot resist the tendency to give an anthropomorphic form to a country. Such is the force of habit and early associations. India becomes *Bharat Mata*, Mother India, a beautiful lady, very old but ever youthful in appearance, sad-eyed and forlorn, cruelly treated by aliens and outsiders, and calling upon her children to protect her. Some such picture rouses the emotions of hundreds of thousands and drives them to action and sacrifice. And yet India is in the main the peasant and the worker, not beautiful to look at, for poverty is not beautiful. Does the beautiful lady of our imaginations represent the bare-bodied and bent workers in the fields and factories? Or the small group of those who have from ages past crushed the masses and exploited them, imposed cruel customs on them and made many of them even untouchable? We seek to cover truth by the creatures of our imaginations and endeavour to escape from reality to a world of dreams.

And yet despite these different classes and their mutual conflicts there was a common bond which united them in India, and one is amazed at its persistence and tenacity and enduring vitality. What was this strength due to? Not merely the passive strength and weight of inertia and tradition, great as these always are. There was an active sustaining principle, for it resisted successfully powerful outside influences and absorbed internal forces that rose to combat it. And yet with all its strength it could not preserve political freedom or endeavour to bring about political unity. These latter do not appear to have been considered worth much trouble; their importance was very foolishly ignored, and we have suffered for this neglect. Right through history the old Indian ideal did not glorify political and military triumph, and it looked down upon money and the professional money-making class. Honour and wealth did not go together, and honour was meant to go, at least in theory, to the men who served the community with little in the shape of financial reward.

The old culture managed to live through many a fierce storm and tempest, but though it kept its outer form, it lost its real content. Today it is fighting silently and desperately against a new and all-powerful opponent—the *bania* civilization of the capitalist West. It will succumb to this newcomer, for the West brings science, and science brings food for the hungry millions. But the West also brings an antidote to the evils of this cut-throat civilization—the principles of socialism, of co-operation, and service to the community for the common good. This is not so unlike the old Brahman ideal of service, but it means the brahmanization (not in the religious sense, of course) of all classes and groups and the abolition of class distinctions. It may be that when India puts on her new garment, as she must, for the old is torn and tattered, she will have it cut in this fashion, so as to make it conform both to present conditions and her old thought. The ideas she adopts must become rooted in her soil.

54

THE RECORD OF BRITISH RULE

What has been the record of British rule in India? I doubt if it is possible for any Indian or Englishman to take an objective and dispassionate view of this long record. And even if this were possible, it would be still more difficult to weigh and measure the psychological and other immaterial factors. We are told that British rule "has given to India that which throughout the centuries she never possessed, a government whose authority is unquestioned in any part of the sub-continent";[1] it has established the rule of law and a just and efficient administration; it has brought to India Western conceptions of parliamentary government and personal liberties; and "by transforming British India into a single unitary state it has engendered amongst Indians a sense of political unity" and thus fostered the first beginnings of nationalism. That is the British case, and there is much truth in it, though the rule of law and personal liberties have not been evident for many years.

The Indian survey of this period lays stress on many other factors, and points out the injury, material and spiritual, that foreign rule has brought us. The view-point is so different that sometimes the very thing that is commended by the British is condemned by Indians. As Doctor Ananda Coomaraswamy writes: "One of the most remarkable features of British rule in India is that the greatest injuries inflicted upon the Indian people have the outward appearance of blessings."

As a matter of fact the changes that have taken place in India during the last century or more have been world changes common to most countries in the East and West. The growth of industrialism in Western Europe, and later on in the rest of the world, brought nationalism and the strong unitary state in its train everywhere. The British can take

---

1. The quotations are from the Report of the Joint Parliamentary Committee on Indian Constitutional Reform (1934).

credit for having first opened India's window to the West and brought her one aspect of Western industrialism and science. But having done so they throttled the further industrial growth of the country till circumstances forced their hands. India was already the meeting-place of two cultures, the western Asiatic culture of Islam and the eastern, her own product, which spread to the Far East. And now a third and more powerful impulse came from further west, and India became a focal point and a battle-ground for various old and new ideas. There can be no doubt that this third impulse would have triumphed and thus solved many of India's old problems, but the British, who had themselves helped in bringing it, tried to stop its further progress. They prevented our industrial growth, and thus delayed our political growth, and preserved all the out-of-date feudal and other relics they could find in the country. They even froze up our changing and to some extent progressing laws and customs at the stage they found them, and made it difficult for us to get out of their shackles. It was not with their goodwill or assistance that the *bourgeoisie* grew in India. But after introducing the railway and other products of industrialism they could not stop the wheel of change; they could only check it and slow it down, and this they did to their own manifest advantage.

"On this solid foundation the majestic structure of the Government of India rests, and it can be claimed with certainty that in the period which has elapsed since 1858 when the Crown assumed supremacy over all the territories of the East India Company, the educational and material progress of India has been greater than it was ever within her power to achieve during any other period of her long and chequered history."[2] This statement is not so self-evident as it appears to be, and it has often been stated that literacy actually went down with the coming of British rule. But even if the statement was wholly true, it amounts to a comparison of the modern industrial age with past ages. In almost every country in the world the educational and material progress has been tremendous during the past century because of science and industrialism, and it may be said with assurance of any such country that progress of this kind "has been greater than was ever within her power to achieve during any other period of her long and chequered history"—

2. Report of the Joint Parliamentary Committee (1934).

though perhaps that country's history may not be a long one in comparison with Indian history. Are we needlessly cantankerous and perverse if we suggest that some such technical progress would have come to us anyhow in this industrial age, and even without British rule? And, indeed, if we compare our lot with many other countries, may we not hazard the guess that such progress might have been greater, for we have had to contend against a stifling of that progress by the British themselves? Railways, telegraphs, telephones, wireless and the like are hardly tests of the goodness or beneficence of British rule. They were welcome and necessary, and because the British happened to be the agents who brought them first, we should be grateful to them. But even these heralds of industrialism came to us primarily for the strengthening of British rule. They were the veins and arteries through which the nation's blood should have coursed, increasing its trade, carrying its produce, and bringing new life and wealth to its millions. It is true that in the long-run some such result was likely, but they were designed and worked for another purpose—to strengthen the imperial hold and to capture markets for British goods—which they succeeded in achieving. I am all in favour of industrialization and the latest methods of transport, but sometimes, as I rushed across the Indian plains, the railway, that life-giver, has almost seemed to me like iron bands confining and imprisoning India.

The British conception of ruling India was the police conception of the State. Government's job was to protect the State and leave the rest to others. Their public finance dealt with military expenditure, police, civil administration, interest on debt. The economic needs of the citizens were not looked after, and were sacrificed to British interests. The cultural and other needs of the people, except for a tiny handful, were entirely neglected. The changing conceptions of public finance which brought free and universal education, improvement of public health, care of poor and feeble-minded, insurance of workers against illness, old age and unemployment, etc., in other countries, were almost entirely beyond the ken of the Government. It could not indulge in these spending activities for its tax system was most regressive, taking a much larger proportion of small incomes than of the larger ones, and its expenditure on its protective and administrative functions was terribly heavy and swallowed up most of the revenue.

The outstanding feature of British rule was their concentration on everything that went to strengthen their political and economic hold on the country. Everything else was incidental. If they built up a powerful central government and an efficient police force, that was an achievement for which they can take credit, but the Indian people can hardly congratulate themselves on it. Unity is a good thing, but unity in subjection is hardly a thing to be proud of. The very strength of a despotic government may become a greater burden for a people; and a police force, no doubt useful in many ways, can be, and has been often enough, turned against the very people it is supposed to protect. Bertrand Russell, comparing modern civilization with the old Greek, has recently written: "The only serious superiority of Greek civilization as compared to ours was the inefficiency of the police, which enabled a larger proportion of decent people to escape."

Britain's supremacy in India brought us peace, and India was certainly in need of peace after the troubles and misfortunes that followed the break-up of the Moghal empire. Peace is a precious commodity, necessary for any progress, and it was welcome to us when it came. But even peace can be purchased at too great a price, and we can have the perfect peace of the grave, and the absolute safety of a cage or of prison. Or peace may be the sodden despair of men unable to better themselves. The peace which is imposed by an alien conqueror has hardly the restful and soothing qualities of the real article. War is a terrible thing and to be avoided, but it does encourage some virtues, which, according to William James, the psychologist, are: fidelity, cohesiveness, tenacity, heroism, conscience, education, inventiveness, economy, and physical health and vigour. Because of this, James sought for a moral equivalent of war which, without the horrors of war, would encourage these virtues in a community. Perhaps if he had learnt of non-co-operation and civil disobedience he would have found something after his own heart, a moral and peaceful equivalent of war.

It is a futile task to consider the 'ifs' and possibilities of history. I feel sure that it was a good thing for India to come in contact with the scientific and industrial West. Science was the great gift of the West, and India lacked this, and without it she was doomed to decay. The manner of our contacts was unfortunate, and yet, perhaps, only a succession of violent shocks could shake us out of our torpor. From this point of view the Protestant, individualistic, Anglo-Saxon English were suitable, for they were more different from us than most other Westerners, and could give us greater shocks.

They gave us political unity and that was a desirable thing, but whether we had this unity or not, Indian nationalism would have grown and demanded that unity. The Arab world is today split up into a large number of separate states—independent, protected, mandatory and the like— but throughout all of them runs the desire for Arab unity. There can be no doubt that Arab nationalism would largely achieve this unity if Western imperialist powers did not stand in the way. But, as in India, it is the purpose of these powers to encourage disruptive tendencies and create minority problems which weaken and partly counteract the nationalist urge and give an excuse to the imperialist power to stay on and pose as the impartial arbitrator.

The political unity of India was achieved incidentally as a side-product of the Empire's advance. In later years, when that unity allied itself to nationalism and challenged alien rule, we witnessed the deliberate promotion of disunity and sectarianism, formidable obstacles to our future progress.

What a long time it is since the British came here, a century and three-quarters since they became dominant! They had a free hand, as despotic governments have, and a magnificent opportunity to mould India according to their desire. During these years the world has changed out of all recognition—England, Europe, America, Japan. The insignificant American colonies bordering the Atlantic in the eighteenth century constitute today the wealthiest, the most powerful and technically the most advanced nation; Japan, within a brief span, has undergone amazing changes; the vast territories of the U.S.S.R., where till only yesterday the dead hand of the Tsar's government suppressed and stifled all growth, now pulsate with a new life and build a new world before our eyes. There have been big changes in India also, and the country is very different from what it was in the eighteenth century—railways, irrigation works, factories, schools and colleges, huge government offices, etc., etc.

And yet, in spite of these changes, what is India like today? A servile state, with its splendid strength caged up, hardly daring to breathe freely, governed by strangers from afar; her people poor beyond compare, short-lived and incapable of resisting disease and epidemic; illiteracy rampant;

vast areas devoid of all sanitary or medical provision; unemployment on a prodigious scale, both among the middle classes and the masses. Freedom, democracy, socialism, communism are, we are told, the slogans of unpractical idealists, doctrinaires or knaves; the test must be one of the well-being of the people as a whole. That is indeed a vital test, and by that test India makes a terribly poor show today. We read of great schemes of unemployment relief and the alleviation of distress in other countries; what of our scores of millions of unemployed and the distress that is widespread and permanent? We read also of housing schemes elsewhere; where are the houses of hundreds of millions of our people, who live in mud huts or have no shelter at all? May we not envy the lot of other countries where education, sanitation, medical relief, cultural facilities, and production advance rapidly ahead, while we remain where we were, or plod wearily along at the pace of a snail? Russia in a brief dozen years of wonderful effort has almost ended illiteracy in her vast territories, and has evolved a fine and up-to-date system of education, in touch with the life of the masses. Backward Turkey, under the Ataturk, Mustapha Kemal's leadership, has also made giant strides towards widespread literacy. Fascist Italy, on the very threshold of its career, attacked illiteracy with vigour. Gentile, the Education Minister, called for "a frontal attack on illiteracy. That gangrenous plague, which is rotting our body politic, must be extirpated with a hot iron." Hard words, unseemly for a drawing-room, but they show the conviction and energy behind the thought. We are politer here and use more rounded phrases. We move warily and exhaust our energies in commissions and committees.

Indians have been accused of talking too much and doing little. It is a just charge. But may we not express our wonder at the inexhaustible capacity of the British for committees and commissions, each of which, after long labour, produces a learned report—"a great State document"— which is duly praised and pigeon-holed? And so we get the sensation of moving ahead, of progress, and yet have the advantage of remaining where we were. Honour is satisfied, and vested interests remain untouched and secure. Other countries discuss how to get on; we discuss checks and brakes and safeguards lest we go too fast.

"The Imperial splendour became the measure of the people's poverty," so we are told (by the Joint Parliamentary Committee 1934) of the Moghal times. It is a just observation, but may we not apply the same measure today? What of New Delhi today with its Viceregal pomp and pageantry, and the Provincial Governors with all their ostentation? And all this with a background of abject and astonishing poverty. The contrast hurts, and it is a little difficult to imagine how sensitive men can put up with it. India today is a poor and dismal sight behind all the splendours of the imperial frontage. There is a great deal of patchwork and superficiality, and behind it the unhappy petty *bourgeoisie,* crushed more and more by modern conditions. Further back come the workers, living miserably in grinding poverty, and then the peasant, that symbol of India, whose lot it is to be "born to Endless Night".

> Bowed by the weight of centuries he leans
> Upon his hoe and gazes on the ground,
> The emptiness of ages on his face,
> And on his back the burden of the world.
>
> Through this dread shape the suffering ages look.
> Time's tragedy is in that aching stoop,
> Through this dread shape humanity betrayed,
> Plundered, profaned and disinherited,
> Cries protest to the powers that made the world,
> A protest that is also prophecy.[1]

It would be absurd to cast the blame for all India's ills on the British. That responsibility must be shouldered by us, and we may not shirk it; it is unseemly to blame others for the inevitable consequences of our own weaknesses. An authoritarian system of government, and especially one that is foreign, must encourage a psychology of subservience and try to limit the mental outlook and horizon of the people. It must crush much that is finest in youth—enterprise, spirit of adventure, originality, 'pep'— and encourage sneakishness, rigid conformity, and a desire to cringe and please the bosses. Such a system does not bring out the real service mentality, the devotion to public service or to ideals; it picks out the least public-spirited persons whose sole objective is to get on in life. We

---

1. These extracts are from the American poet, E. Markham's poem: *The Man with the Hoe.*

see what a class the British attract to themselves in India! Some of them are intellectually keen and capable of good work. They drift to government service or semi-government service because of lack of opportunity elsewhere, and gradually they tone down and become just parts of the big machine, their minds imprisoned by the dull routine of work. They develop the qualities of a bureaucracy—"a competent knowledge of clerkship and the diplomatic art of keeping office". At the highest they have a passive devotion to the public service. There is, or can be, no flaming enthusiasm. That is not possible under a foreign government.

But apart from these, the majority of petty officials are not an admirable lot, for they have only learnt to cringe to their superiors and bully their inferiors. The fault is not theirs. That is the training the system gives them. And if sycophancy and nepotism flourish, as they often do, is it to be wondered at? They have no ideals in service; the haunting fear of unemployment and consequent starvation pursues them, and their chief concern is to hold on to their jobs and get other jobs for their relatives and friends. Where the spy and that most odious of creatures, the informer, always hover in the background, it is not easy to develop the more desirable virtues in a people.

Recent developments have made it even more difficult for sensitive, public-spirited men to join government service. The Government does not want them, and they do not wish to associate with it too closely, unless compelled by economic circumstance.

But, as all the world knows, it is the White Man who bears the burden of Empire, not the Brown. We have various imperial services to carry on the imperial tradition, and a sufficiency of safeguards to protect their special privileges, all, we are told, in the interests of India. It is remarkable how the good of India seems to be tied up with the obvious interests and advancement of these services. If any privilege or prize post of the Indian Civil Service is taken away, we are told that inefficiency and corruption will result. If the reserved jobs for the Indian Medical Service are reduced, this becomes a "menace to India's health". And of course if the British element in the army is touched, all manner of terrible perils confront us.

I think there is some truth in this: that if the superior officials suddenly went away and left their departments in charge of their subordinates there would be a fall in efficiency. But that is because the whole system has been built this way, and the subordinates are not by any means the best men, nor have they ever been made to shoulder responsibility. I feel convinced that there is abundant good material in India, and it could be available within a fairly short period if proper steps were taken. But that means a complete change in our governmental and social outlook. It means a new State.

As it is we are told that whatever changes in the constitutional apparatus may come our way, the rigid framework of the great services which guard and shelter us will continue as before. Hierophants of the sacred mysteries of government, they will guard the temple and prevent the vulgar from entering its holy precincts. Gradually, as we make ourselves worthy of the privilege, they will remove the veils one after another, till, in some future age, even the holy of holies stands uncovered to our wondering and reverent eyes.

Of all these imperial services the Indian Civil Service holds first place, and to it must largely go the credit or discredit for the functioning of government in India. We have been frequently told of the many virtues of this service, and its greatness in the imperial scheme has almost become a maxim. Its unchallenged position of authority in India with the almost autocratic power that this gives, as well as the praise and boosting which it receives in ample measure, cannot be wholly good for the mental equilibrium of any individual or group. With all my admiration for the Service, I am afraid I must admit that it is peculiarly susceptible, both individually and as a whole, to that old and yet somewhat modern disease, paranoia.

It would be idle to deny the good qualities of the I.C.S., for we are not allowed to forget them, but so much bunkum has been and is said about the Service that I sometimes feel that a little debunking would be desirable. The American economist, Veblen, has called the privileged classes the "kept classes". I think it would be equally true to call the I.C.S., as well as the other imperial services, the "kept services". They are a very expensive luxury.

Major D. Graham Pole, formerly a Labour member of the British Parliament and one who is greatly interested in Indian affairs, writing in the *Modern Review* some time ago stated that "no one has ever tried to dispute the fact that the I.C.S. is a most able and efficient service." As similar statements are frequently made in England and believed, it is worthwhile examining this. It is always unsafe to make such positive and definite statements which can easily be disproved, and Major Graham Pole is entirely wrong in imagining that the fact has not been disputed. It has been frequently challenged and disputed, and long ago even Mr G.K. Gokhale said many hard things about the I.C.S. The average Indian—Congressman or non-Congressman—would certainly join issue with Major Graham Pole. And yet it is possible that both may be partly right and may be thinking of different qualifications. Ability and efficiency for what? If this ability and efficiency are to be measured from the point of view of strengthening the British Empire in India and helping it to exploit the country, the I.C.S. may certainly claim to have done well. If, however, the test is the well-being of the Indian masses, they have signally failed, and their failure becomes even more noticeable when one sees the enormous distance that separates them in regard to income and standards of living from the masses they are meant to serve, and from whom ultimately their varied emoluments come.

It is perfectly true that the service has, as a whole, kept up a certain standard, though that standard is necessarily one of mediocrity, and has occasionally thrown up exceptional men. More could hardly be expected of any such service. It embodied essentially the British Public School spirit, with all its good and bad points (though many of the members of the I.C.S. now are not public school men). Though it kept up a good standard, it disapproved strongly of nonconformity with the type, and special abilities of individual members lost themselves in the dull routine of the day's work, and to some extent in the fear of appearing different from the others. There were many earnest members, many with a conception of service, but it was service of the Empire, and India came only as a bad second. Trained and circumstanced as they were, they could only act in that way. Because they were few in numbers, surrounded by an alien and often unfriendly people, they held together and kept up a certain standard. The prestige both of race and office demanded this. And because they had largely autocratic powers, they resented all criticism, considered it one of the major sins, became more and more intolerant and pedagogic, and developed many of the failings of irresponsible rulers. They were self-satisfied and self-sufficient, narrow and fixed minds, static in a changing world, and wholly unsuited to a progressive environment.

When abler and more adaptable minds than theirs tackled the Indian problem they resented this, called them offensive names, suppressed them and threw every possible obstacle in their way. And when post-war changes brought dynamic conditions, they were wholly at sea and unable to adapt themselves to them. Their limited hidebound education had not fitted them for such emergencies and novel situations. They had been spoilt by a long spell of irresponsibility. As a group they had practically absolute power, subject only in theory to a control by the British Parliament. "Power corrupts," Lord Acton has told us, "and absolute power corrupts absolutely."

They were, on the whole, reliable officers in their limited way, doing their day-to-day work fairly competently, without brilliance. But their very training was such that a wholly unexpected situation found them wanting, although their self-confidence, their methodical nature, and their *esprit de corps* helped them to tide over immediate difficulties. The famous Mesopotamia muddle exposed the British Indian Government for its inefficiency and 'woodenness', but many a similar muddle does not see the light of day. Even their reaction to Civil Disobedience was crude. To shoot and club may dispose of the opponents for a while, but it does not solve any problem, and it undermines that very feeling of superiority which it is meant to protect. It was not surprising that they had recourse to violence to meet a growing and aggressive nationalist movement. That was inevitable, for empires rest on that and they had been taught no other way of meeting opposition. But the fact that excessive and unnecessary violence was used showed that they had lost all grip of the situation, and no longer possessed the self-control and restraint which they seemed to have in normal times. Nerves frequently gave way and even in their public utterances there was a trace of hysteria. The calm confidence of other days was gone. A crisis has a pitiless way of showing us all up and exposing our innermost weaknesses. Civil Disobedience was such a crisis and test, and very few on either side of the barricade—Congress or Government—survived fully that test. In a crisis the number of men and women of really first-class calibre is found to be small, says Mr Lloyd George, and "the rest do not count in a crisis. The hummocks that look like eminences in fine weather are quickly submerged in a great flood when the highest peaks alone are visible above the surface of the waters."

The I.C.S. were intellectually and emotionally not prepared for what happened. The original training of many of their members was classical, which gave them a certain culture and a certain charm. It was an old-world attitude, suitable for the Victorian Age, but utterly out of place under modern conditions. They lived in a narrow, circumscribed world of their own—Anglo-Indian—which was neither England nor India. They had no appreciation of the forces at work in contemporary society. In spite of their amusing assumption of being the trustees and guardians of the Indian masses, they knew little about them and even less about the new aggressive *bourgeoisie*. They judged Indians from the sycophants and office-seekers who surrounded them and dismissed others as agitators and knaves. Their knowledge of post-war changes all over the world, and especially in the economic sphere, was of the slightest, and they were too much in the ruts to adjust themselves to changing conditions. They did not realize that the order they represented was out of date under modern conditions, and that they were approaching as a group more and more the type which T.S. Eliot describes in *The Hollow Men*.

And yet that order will continue so long as British imperialism continues, and this is powerful enough still and has able and resourceful leaders. The British Government in India is like a tooth that is decaying, but is still strongly imbedded. It is painful, but it cannot be easily pulled out. The pain is likely to continue, and even grow worse, till the tooth is taken out or falls out itself.

The Public School type has had its day even in England, and does not occupy the same place as it did, although it is still prominent in public affairs. In India it is still more out of place, and it can never fit in or co-operate with an aggressive nationalism, much less with those working for social change.

There are of course many excellent men, both English and Indian, in the I.C.S. but, so long as the present system prevails their excellence will be devoted to objects which are not beneficial to the Indian people. Some Indian members of the Service are so overcome by this Public School spirit that they become *plus royaliste que le roi*. I remember meeting a youthful Indian member of the I.C.S. who had a very high opinion of himself which unfortunately I could not share. He pointed out to me the many virtues of his Service, and ended up by the unanswerable argument in favour of the British Empire—was it not better than the

Roman Empire and the Empires of Chengiz Khan and Timur?

The underlying assumption of the I.C.S. is that they discharge their duties most efficiently, and therefore they can lay every stress on their claims, and the claims are many and varied. If India is poor, that is the fault of her social customs, her *banias* and money-lenders, and above all, her enormous population. The greatest *bania* of all, the British Government in India, is conveniently ignored. And what they propose to do about this population I do not know, for in spite of a great deal of help received from famines, epidemics, and a high death-rate generally, the population is still overwhelming. Birth-control is proposed and I, for one, am entirely in favour of the spread of the knowledge and methods of birth-control. But the use of these methods itself requires a much higher standard of living for the masses, some measure of general education, and innumerable clinics all over the country. Under present conditions birth-control methods are completely out of reach for the masses. The middle classes can profit by them as, I believe, they are doing to a growing extent.

But this argument of over-population is deserving of further notice. The problem today all over the world is not one of lack of food or lack of other essentials, but actually lack of mouths to feed, or, to put it differently, lack of capacity to buy food, etc., for those who are in need. Even in India, considered apart, there is no lack of food, and though the population has gone up, the food supply has increased and can increase more proportionately than the population. Then again the much advertised increase of population in India has been (except in the last decade) at a much lower rate than in most Western countries. It is true that in future the difference will be greater, for various forces are tending to lessen or even stop population increase in Western countries. But limiting factors are likely to check population increase in India also soon.

Whenever India becomes free, and in a position to build her new life as she wants to, she will necessarily require the best of her sons and daughters for this purpose. Good human material is always rare, and in India it is rarer still because of our lack of opportunities under British rule. We shall want the help of many foreign experts in many departments of public activity, particularly in those which require special technical and scientific knowledge. Among those who have served in the I.C.S. or other imperial services there will be many, Indians or foreigners, who will be necessary and welcome to the new order. But of one thing I am quite sure, that no new order can be built up in India so long as the spirit of the I.C.S. pervades our administration and our public services. That spirit of authoritarianism is the ally of imperialism, and it cannot co-exist with freedom. It will either succeed in crushing freedom or will be swept away itself. Only with one type of state it is likely to fit in, and that is the fascist type. Therefore it seems to me quite essential that the I.C.S. and similar services must disappear completely, as such, before we can start real work on a new order. Individual members of these services, if they are willing and competent for the new job, will be welcome, but only on new conditions. It is quite inconceivable that they will get the absurdly high salaries and allowances that are paid to them today. The new India must be served by earnest, efficient workers who have an ardent faith in the cause they serve and are bent on achievement, and who work for the joy and glory of it, and not for the attraction of high salaries. The money motive must be reduced to a minimum. The need for foreign helpers will be considerable, but I imagine that the least wanted will be civil administrators who have no technical knowledge. There will be no lack of such people in India.

I have previously stated how the Indian Liberals, and other groups like them, have accepted British ideology with reference to the government of India. This is especially noticeable in regard to the Services, for their cry is for 'indianization' and not for radical change of the spirit and nature of the Services and the State structure. This is a vital matter on which it is impossible to give in, for Indian freedom is bound up not only with the withdrawal of British Forces and Services, but also with the elimination of the authoritarian spirit that inspired them, and a levelling down of their salaries and privileges. There is a great deal of talk of safeguards in these days of constitution-making. If these safeguards are to be in the interests of India, they should lay down, among other things, that the I.C.S. and similar services should cease to exist in their present form and with the powers and privileges they possess, and should have nothing to do with the new constitution.

Even more mysterious and formidable are the so-called Defence Services. We may not criticize them, we may not say anything about them, for what do we know about such matters? We must only pay and pay heavily without murmuring. A short while ago, in September 1934, Sir Philip Chetwode, the Commander-in-Chief in India, speaking in the Council of State at Simla, told Indian politicians, in pungent military language, to mind their own business and not interfere with his. Referring to the mover of an amendment to some proposition, he said: "Do he and his friends think that a war-worn and war-wise race like the British, who won their Empire at the point of the sword and have kept it by the sword ever since, are to be talked out of war wisdom which that experience brings to a nation by armchair critics . . .?" He made many other interesting remarks, and we were informed, lest we might think that he had spoken in the heat of the moment, that he had carefully written out his speech and spoke from a manuscript.

It is, of course, an impertinence for a layman to argue about military matters with a Commander-in-Chief, and yet perhaps even an armchair critic might be permitted to make a few observations. It is conceivable that the interests of those who hold the Empire by the sword and those over whose heads this shining weapon ever hangs, might differ. It is possible that an Indian army might be made to serve Indian interests or to serve imperial interests, and the two might differ or even conflict with each other. A politician and an armchair critic might also wonder if the claims of eminent generals for freedom from interference are valid after the experiences of the World War. They had a free field then to a large extent, and from all accounts they made a terrible mess of almost everything in every army—British, French, German, Austrian, Italian, Russian. Captain Liddell Hart, the distinguished British military historian and strategist, writes in his *History of the World War* that at one stage in the War while British soldiers fought the enemy, British generals fought one another. The national peril did not bring unity of thought or effort. The War, he continues, "has shattered our faith in idols, our hero-worshipping belief that great men are different clay from common men. Leaders are still necessary, perhaps more necessary, but our awakened realization of their common humanity is a safeguard against either expecting from them, or trusting in them, too much."

That arch-politician, Mr D. Lloyd George, has painted in his *War Memoirs* a terrible picture of the failings and blunders of the generals and admirals in the World War, blunders which cost the lives of hundreds of thousands of men. England and her allies won the War, but it was a "blood-stained stagger to victory"; the reckless and unintelligent handling of men and situations by the high officers brought England almost to the rim of catastrophe, and she and her allies were saved largely by the incredible folly of their foes. So writes the great War Premier of Britain, and he explains how he had to undertake surgical operations in order to get ideas into Lord Jellicoe's head, especially in regard to the proposal for having a convoy system. Of the French Marshal Joffre, he seems to think that his chief virtue was the possession of a resolute countenance which inspired a sense of strength. "That is what harassed people instinctively seek in trouble. They make the mistake of thinking that the seat of intelligence is in the chin."

But Mr Lloyd George's main indictment is against the British High Command itself, the Commander-in-Chief, Field-Marshal Haig. He demonstrates how Lord Haig's inordinate vanity and refusal to listen to politicians and others, made him conceal important facts from the British Cabinet itself, and led the British Army in France to one of its greatest disasters. And even when failure stared him in the face, obstinate to the last, he continued his ill-advised offensive for several months in that awful mud of Passchendaele and Cambrai, till 17,000 officers alone lay dead and dying, and 400,000 gallant British soldiers were 'casualties'. It is well that the 'Unknown Soldier' is honoured today after his death; his life was cheap, and he had little consideration when he was alive.

Politicians, like all other people, err frequently, but democratic politicians have to be sensitive and responsive to men and events, and they usually realize their mistakes and try to repair them. The soldier is bred in a different atmosphere, where authority reigns and criticism is not tolerated. So he resents the advice of others and when he errs, he errs thoroughly and persists in error. For him the chin is more important than the mind or brain. In India we have the advantage of having produced a mixed type, for the civil administration itself has grown up and lives in a semi-military atmosphere of authority and self-sufficiency, and possesses therefore to a great extent the soldier's chin and other virtues.

We are told that the process of 'indianization' of the army is being pushed on, and in another thirty years or more an Indian general might even appear on the Indian stage. It is possible that in not much more than a hundred years the process of indianization might be considerably advanced. One is apt to wonder how, in a moment of crisis, England built up a mighty army of millions within a year or two. If it had possessed our mentors, perhaps it would have proceeded more cautiously and warily. It is possible of course that the War would have been over long before this soundly-trained army was ready for it. One thinks also of the Russian Soviet armies growing out of almost nothing and facing and triumphing over a host of enemies, and today constituting one of the most efficient fighting machines in the world. They did not apparently possess "war-worn and war-wise" generals to advise them.

We have now a military academy at Dehra Dun where gentlemen cadets are trained to become officers. They are very smart on parade, we are told, and they will no doubt make admirable officers. But I wonder sometimes what purpose this training serves, unless it is accompanied by technical training. Infantry and cavalry are about as much use today as the Roman phalanx, and the rifle is little better than a bow and arrow in an age of air warfare, gas bombs, tanks, and powerful artillery. No doubt their trainers and mentors realize this.

What has been the record of British rule in India? Who are we to complain of its deficiencies when they were but the consequences of our own failings? If we lose touch with the river of change and enter a backwater, become self-centred and self-satisfied, and, ostrich-like, ignore what happens elsewhere, we do so at our peril. The British came to us on the crest of a wave of new impulse in the world, and represented mighty historic forces which they themselves hardly realized. Are we to complain of the cyclone that uproots us and hurls us about, or the cold wind that makes us shiver? Let us have done with the past and its bickering and face the future. To the British we must be grateful for one splendid gift of which they were the bearers, the gift of science and its rich offspring. It is difficult, however, to forget or view with equanimity the efforts of the British Government in India to encourage the disruptive, obscurantist, reactionary, sectarian, and opportunist elements in the country. Perhaps that too is a needed test and challenge for us, and before India is reborn it will have to go through again and again the fire that cleanses and tempers and burns up the weak, the impure and the corrupt.

55

A CIVIL MARRIAGE AND A QUESTION
OF SCRIPT

After spending about a week in Poona and Bombay in the middle of September 1933, I returned to Lucknow. My mother was still in hospital there, and was improving very slowly. Kamala was also in Lucknow, trying to attend on her, although she was not very well herself. My sisters used to come over from Allahabad for the week-ends. I remained in Lucknow for two or three weeks, and I had more leisure there than I was likely to have in Allahabad, my chief occupation being visits to the hospital twice daily. I utilized my spare hours in writing some articles for the Press, and these were widely published all over the country. A series of articles entitled "Whither India?", in which I had surveyed world affairs in relation to the Indian situation, attracted considerable attention. I learnt later that these articles were even reproduced in Persian translations in Teheran and Kabul. There was nothing novel or original in these articles for anyone in touch with recent developments and modern Western thought. But in India our people had been too engrossed in their domestic troubles to pay much attention to what was happening elsewhere. The reception given to my articles, as well as many other indications, showed that they were developing a wider outlook.

My mother was getting very tired of being in hospital, and we decided to take her back to Allahabad. One of the reasons for this was my sister Krishna's engagement, which had just then been announced. We wanted to have the marriage as soon as possible, before I was suddenly removed to prison again. I had no notion how long I would be allowed to remain out, as Civil Disobedience was still the official programme of the Congress, and the Congress itself and scores of other organizations were illegal.

We fixed the marriage for the third week of October in Allahabad. It was to be a civil ceremony. I was glad of this, though as a matter of fact we had no choice in the matter. The marriage was between two different castes, a Brahman and a non-Brahman, and under present British Indian Law no religious ceremony had validity for such a marriage. Fortunately a recently passed Civil Marriage Act came to our rescue.

There were two such Acts, the second one, under which my sister's marriage took place, being confined to Hindus and those belonging to allied faiths—Buddhists, Jains, Sikhs. But if either party does not belong to one of these faiths, by birth or conversion, then this second Act does not apply and the first Civil Marriage Act has to be resorted to. This first Act requires from both the parties a denunciation of all the leading religions, or at any rate a statement that they do not belong to them. This wholly unnecessary denunciation is a great nuisance. Many people, even though they are not religiously inclined, object to this statement and thus cannot take advantage of the Act. The orthodox of various faiths oppose all changes which would facilitate inter-marriages. The result is that they drive people either to make that statement of denunciation or to a patently superficial conversion to get within the law. Personally I should like to encourage inter-marriages, but whether they are encouraged or not, it is very necessary to have a permissive general civil marriage Act, applicable to persons of all religions, permitting them to marry without any denunciation or change of faith.

There was no fuss about my sister's wedding; it was a very simple affair. Ordinarily I dislike the fuss attendant on Indian marriages. In view of my mother's illness and, even more so, the fact that civil disobedience was still going on and many of our colleagues were in prison, anything in the nature of show was singularly out of place. Only a few relatives and local friends were invited. Many old friends of my father's were hurt because they felt, quite wrongly, that I had purposely ignored them.

The little invitation we issued for the wedding was written in Hindustani in the Latin script. This was an innovation, as such invitations are always either in the *nagri* or the Persian script, and the idea of writing Hindustani in the Latin script is almost unknown, except in army and missionary circles. I used the Latin script as an experiment, and I wanted to see the reactions of various people. It had a mixed reception, mostly unfavourable. The recipients were few: if a larger circle had been approached the reaction would have been still more unfavourable.

Gandhiji did not approve of what I had done.

I did not use the Latin script because I had become a convert to it, although it had long attracted me. Its success in Turkey and Central Asia had impressed me, and the obvious arguments in its favour were weighty. But even so I was not convinced, and even if I had been convinced, I knew well that it did not stand the faintest chance of being adopted in present-day India. There would be the most violent opposition to it from all groups, nationalist, religious, Hindu, Muslim, old and new. And I feel that the opposition would not be merely based on emotion. A change of script is a very vital change for any language with a rich past, for a script is a most intimate part of its literature. Change the script and different word-pictures arise, different sounds, different ideas. An almost insurmountable barrier is put up between the old literature and the new, and the former becomes almost a foreign language that is dead. Where there is no literature worth preserving this risk should be taken. In India I can hardly conceive of the change, for our literature is not only rich and valuable but is bound up with our history and our thought, and is intimately connected with the lives of our masses. It would be cruel vivisection to force such a change, and it would retard our progress in popular education.

But this question is not even an academic one in India today. The next step in script reform for us seems to me the adoption of a common script for the daughter languages of Sanskrit—Hindi, Bengali, Marathi and Gujrati. As it is, their scripts have a common origin and do not differ greatly, and it should not be difficult to strike a common mean. This would bring these four great sister languages much nearer to each other.

One of the legends about India which our English rulers have persistently circulated all over the world is that India has several hundred languages—I forget the exact number. For proof there is the census. Of these several hundred, it is an extraordinary fact that very few Englishmen know even one moderately well, in spite of a life-long residence in this country. They class the lot of these together and call them the 'Vernacular', the slave language (from the Latin *verna*, a home-born slave), and many of our people have, unknowingly, accepted this nomenclature. It is astonishing how English people spend a life-time in India without taking the trouble to learn the language well. They have evolved, with the help of their *khansamahs* and *ayahs,* an extraordinary jargon, a kind of pidgin-Hindustani, which they imagine is the real article. Just as they take their facts about Indian life from their subordinates and sycophants, they take their ideas about Hindustani from their domestic servants, who make a point of speaking their pidgin language to the sahib-log for fear that they would not understand anything else. They seem to be wholly ignorant of the fact that Hindustani, as well as the other Indian languages, have high literary merit and extensive literatures.

If the census tells us that India has two or three hundred languages, it also tells us, I believe, that Germany has about fifty or sixty languages. I do not remember anyone pointing out this fact in proof of the disunity or disparity of Germany. As a matter of fact, a census mentions all manner of petty languages, sometimes spoken by a few thousand persons only; and often dialects are classed, for scientific purposes, as different languages. India seems to me to have surprisingly few languages, considering its area. Compared to the same area in Europe, it is far more closely allied in regard to language, but because of widespread illiteracy, common standards have not developed and dialects have formed. The principal languages of India (excluding Burma) are Hindustani (of the two varieties, Hindi and Urdu), Bengali, Gujrati, Marathi, Tamil, Telugu, Malayalam and Canarese. If Assamese, Oriya, Sindhi, Pushtu and Punjabi are added, the whole country is covered, except for some hill and forest tribes. Of these, the Indo-Aryan languages, which cover the whole north, centre and west of India, are closely allied; and the southern Dravidian languages, though different, have been greatly influenced by Sanskrit and are full of Sanskrit words.

The eight principal languages mentioned above have all old and valuable literatures, and each of them is spoken today over a vast area, which is definite and clearly marked. Thus from the point of view of numbers speaking a language, these languages are among the major languages of the world. Fifty million people speak Bengali. As for Hindustani, with its variations, it is spoken, I imagine (I have no figures here), by about a hundred and forty millions in India, and it is partly understood by a vast number of others all over the country.[1] Such a

---

1. The following figures have been given by the advocates of Hindustani. I do not know if they are based on the last census of 1931 or the previous one of 1921. I

language has obviously enormous possibilities. It rests on the solid foundation of Sanskrit and it is closely allied to Persian. Thus it can draw from two rich sources, and of course, in recent years, it has drawn from English. The Dravidian country in the south is the only part where Hindustani comes as almost a foreign tongue, but the people there are making a great effort to learn it. Two years ago (in 1932) I saw some figures of a private voluntary society which had undertaken the teaching of Hindi in the south. During the previous fourteen years, since its formation, it was stated that 550,000 persons had learnt Hindi through its efforts in the Madras Presidency alone. For a voluntary effort, which is supported in no way by the State, this is remarkable, and most of the persons who learn Hindi themselves become missionaries in the cause.

I have no doubt whatever that Hindustani is going to be the common language of India. Indeed it is largely so today for ordinary purposes. Its progress has been hampered by foolish controversies about the script, *nagri* or Persian, and by the misdirected efforts of the two factions to use language which is either too Sanskritized or too Persianized. There is no way out of the script difficulty, for it arouses great heat and passion, except to adopt both officially, and allow people to use either. But an effort must be made to discourage the extreme tendencies and develop a middle literary language, on the lines of the spoken language in common use. With mass education this will inevitably take place. At present the

---

imagine they refer to the latter, and up-to-date figures would show a considerable increase under each head.

Hindustani (including western Hindi, Punjabi and Rajasthani)	139.3	millions
Bengali	49.3	"
Telugu	23.6	"
Marathi	18.8	"
Tamil	18.8	"
Canarese	10.3	"
Oriya	10.1	"
Gujrati	9.6	"
Total	279.8	"

Some languages like Pushtu, Assamese and, of course, Burmese, which is entirely different, linguistically and territorially, have been omitted from this list.

small middle-class groups, that are supposed to be the arbiters of literary taste and style, are terribly narrow-minded and conservative, each in its own way. They cling to antique forms that have no life in them and have few contacts with their own masses or with world literature.

The development and spread of Hindustani must not and will not conflict with the continued use and enrichment of the other great languages of India—Bengali, Gujrati, Marathi, Oriya and the Dravidian languages of the south. Some of these languages are already more wide-awake and intellectually alert than Hindustani, and they must remain the official languages for educational and other purposes in their respective areas. Only through them can education and culture spread rapidly among the masses.

Some people imagine that English is likely to become the *lingua franca* of India. That seems to me a fantastic conception, except in respect of a handful of upper-class intelligentsia. It has no relation to the problem of mass education and culture. It may be, as it is partly today, that English will become increasingly a language used for technical, scientific and business communications, and especially for international contacts. It is essential for many of us to know foreign languages in order to keep in touch with world thought and activities, and I should like our universities to encourage the learning of other languages besides English—French, German, Russian, Spanish, Italian. This does not mean that English should be neglected, but if we are to have a balanced view of the world we must not confine ourselves to English spectacles. We have already become sufficiently lop-sided in our mental outlook because of this concentration on one aspect and ideology, and even the most rabid of our nationalists hardly realize how much they are cribbed and confined by the British outlook in relation to India.

But however much we may encourage the other foreign languages, English is bound to remain our chief link with the outside world. That is as it should be. For generations past we have been trying to learn English, and we have achieved a fair measure of success in the endeavour. It would be folly to wipe the slate clean now and not to take full advantage of this long training. English also is today undoubtedly the most widespread and important world language, and it is gaining fast on the other languages. It is likely to become more and more the medium of international intercourse and radio broadcasting, unless 'American' takes its place. Therefore we must continue to spread the knowledge of English. It is desirable to learn it as well as possible, but it does not seem to me worthwhile for us to spend too much time and energy in appreciating the finer points of the language, as many of us do now. Individuals may do that, but to set it as an ideal for large numbers is to put a needless burden on them and prevent them from progressing in other directions.

I have been greatly attracted lately by 'Basic English', and it seems to me that this extreme simplification of English has a great future before it. It would be desirable for us to undertake the teaching of Basic English on an extensive scale rather than Standard English, which can be left to specialists and particular students.

I would personally like to encourage Hindustani to adapt and assimilate many words from English and other foreign languages. This is necessary, as we lack modern terms, and it is better to have well-known words rather than to evolve new and difficult words from the Sanskrit or Persian or Arabic. Purists object to the use of foreign words, but I think they make a great mistake, for the way to enrich our language is to make it flexible and capable of assimilating words and ideas from other languages.

I happened to go, soon after my sister's wedding, to Benares to visit an old friend and colleague, Shiva Prasad Gupta, who had been lying ill for over a year. He was in Lucknow Gaol when he had a sudden attack of paralysis, and he had been recovering from it very slowly ever since. During my Benares visit, a small Hindi literary society gave me an address and I had a pleasant informal talk with its members. I told them that I hesitated to speak to experts on subjects I knew little about, but still I made a few suggestions. I criticized the intricate and ornate language that was customary in Hindi writing, full of difficult Sanskrit words, artificial, and clinging to ancient forms. I ventured to suggest that this courtly style, addressed to a select audience, should be given up, and Hindi writers should deliberately write for the masses and in language understood by them. Mass contacts would give new life and sincerity to the language, and the writers themselves would catch some of the emotional energy of the mass and do far better work. Further, I suggested that if Hindi authors paid more attention to Western thought and literature, they would derive great benefit from it; it would be desirable to have translations from the classics of the European languages as well as from books dealing with modern ideas. I also mentioned that probably modern Bengali, Gujrati and Marathi were a little more advanced in these matters than modern Hindi, and certainly more creative work had been done in Bengali in recent years than in Hindi.

We had a friendly talk about these matters and then I came away. I had no idea that my remarks would be sent to the Press, but some one present sent a report to the Hindi papers.

And then there was a tremendous outcry in the Hindi Press against me and at my presumption in criticizing Hindi and comparing it, to its disadvantage, with Bengali, Gujrati and Marathi. I was called an ignoramus—which indeed I was in that particular subject—and many harder words were used to squash and suppress me. I had no time to follow the controversy and it went on, I am told, for months, till I was again in prison.

This incident was a revelation to me. It revealed the extraordinary sensitiveness of Hindi literary men and journalists, and their refusal to face a little honest criticism from one who wished them well. The inferiority complex was evidently at work. Self-criticism there was none at all, and critical standards were poor. It was not unusual for an author and his critic to fall out and accuse each other of personal motives. The whole outlook was narrow, *bourgeois* and parochial, and both the journalists and the authors seemed to write for each other and for a small circle, ignoring the vast public and its interests. It seemed to me an extraordinary pity and an unhappy waste of energy when the field was so vast and inviting.

Hindi literature has a fine past, but it cannot live for ever on its past. I feel sure that it has a great future, and that Hindi journalism will be a tremendous power in this country. But neither will progress much till it shakes itself free of narrow conventions and boldly addresses the masses.

56

COMMUNALISM AND REACTION

About the time of my sister's wedding came news of Vithalbhai J.
Patel's death in Europe. He had long been ailing, and it was because
of his ill-health that he had been released from prison in India. His
passing away was a painful event, and the thought of our veteran leaders
leaving us in this way, one after another, in the middle of our struggle,
was an extraordinarily depressing one. Many tributes were paid to
Vithalbhai, and most of these laid stress on his ability as a parliamentarian
and his success as President of the Assembly. This was perfectly true, and
yet this repetition irritated me. Was there any lack of good parliamentarians
in India or of people who could fill the Speaker's chair with ability?
That was the one job for which our lawyer's training had fitted us.
Vithalbhai had been something much more than that—he had been a
great and indomitable fighter for India's freedom.

During my visit to Benares in November I was invited to address the
students of the Hindu University. I gladly accepted this invitation and
addressed a huge gathering presided over by Pandit Madan Mohan
Malaviya, the Vice-Chancellor. In the course of my speech I had much
to say about communalism, and I denounced it in forcible language, and
especially condemned the activities of the Hindu Mahasabha. This was
not exactly a premeditated attack, but for a long time past my mind had
been full of resentment at the increasingly reactionary efforts of the
communalists of all groups, and as I warmed up to my subject, some of
this resentment came out. Deliberately I laid stress on the reactionary
character of the Hindu communalists, for there was no point in my
criticizing Muslims before a Hindu audience. At the moment, it did not
strike me that it was not in the best of taste to criticize the Hindu
Mahasabha at a meeting presided over by Malaviyaji, who had long
been one of its pillars. I did not think of this, as he had not had much to
do with it lately, and it almost seemed that the new aggressive leaders of
the Mahasabha had pushed him out. So long as he had been one of the

leading spirits, the Mahasabha, in spite of its communalism, had not been politically reactionary. But latterly this new development has become very patent, and I felt sure that Malaviyaji could not have anything to do with it and must have disapproved of it. Still, it was not quite right for me, as I realized later, to have taken an undue advantage of his invitation by making remarks which put him in an awkward position. I was sorry for this.

I was also sorry for a foolish error into which I had fallen. Some one sent us by post a copy of a resolution which, it stated, had recently been passed in Ajmer by a Hindu young men's organization. This resolution was most objectionable and I referred to it in my Benares speech. As a matter of fact no such resolution had been passed by any organization, and we had been the victims of a hoax.

My Benares speech, briefly reported, created an uproar. Used as I was to such outcries, I was quite taken aback by the vehemence of the attack of the Hindu Mahasabha leaders. These attacks were largely personal and seldom touched the point in issue. They overreached themselves, and soon I was glad of them, for they gave me an opportunity for having my say on the subject. I had been bursting with it for months past, even when I was in prison, but did not know how to tackle it. It was a hornets' nest, and though I was used to hornets, it was no pleasure to enter into controversies which degenerated into abuse. But now I had no choice, and I wrote what I considered a reasoned article on Hindu and Muslim communalism, showing how in neither case was it even *bona fide* communalism, but was political and social reaction hiding behind the communal mask. I happened to possess odd newspaper cuttings, which I had collected in prison, of various speeches and statements of communal leaders. Indeed I had so much material that I was hard put to it how to compress it in a newspaper article.

This article of mine was given great publicity in the Indian Press. But strange to say there was no response to it from either side—Hindu or Muslim communalists—although there was a great deal about both in my article. The Hindu Mahasabha leaders, who had denounced me in the most vigorous and varied language, now remained perfectly silent. From the Muslim side Sir Mohamad Iqbal endeavoured to correct some of my facts regarding the second Round Table Conference, but otherwise he did not say anything about my argument. It was in my reply to him that I suggested that a Constituent Assembly should decide both the political and communal issues. Later I wrote one or two additional articles on communalism. I was very much heartened, not only by the reception of all these articles, but by the visible effect they were producing on people who tried to think. I did not imagine, of course, that I could conjure away the passions that underlay the communal spirit. My object was to point out that the communal leaders were allied to the most reactionary elements in India and England, and were in reality opposed to political, and even more so to social advance. All their demands had no relation whatever to the masses. They were meant only to bring some advancement to the small groups at the top. It was my intention to carry on with this reasoned attack when prison claimed me again. The oft-repeated appeal for Hindu-Muslim unity, useful as it no doubt is, seemed to me singularly inane, unless some effort was made to understand the causes of the disunity. Some people, however, seem to imagine that by a frequent repetition of the magic formula, unity will ultimately emerge.

It is interesting to trace British policy since the Rising of 1857 in its relation to the communal question. Fundamentally and inevitably it has been one of preventing the Hindu and Muslim from acting together, and of playing off one community against another. After 1857 the heavy hand of the British fell more on the Muslims than on the Hindus. They considered the Muslims more aggressive and militant, possessing memories of recent rule in India, and therefore more dangerous. The Muslims had also kept away from the new education and had few jobs under the Government. All this made them suspect. The Hindus had taken far more kindly to the English language and clerkly jobs, and seemed to be more docile.

The new nationalism then grew up from above—the upper-class English-speaking intelligentsia—and this was naturally confined to the Hindus, for the Muslims were educationally very backward. This nationalism spoke in the gentlest and most abject of tones, and yet it was not to the liking of the Government, and they decided to encourage the Muslims more and keep them away from the new nationalist platform. Lack of English education was in itself a sufficient bar then, so far as the Muslims were concerned, but this was bound to go gradually. With foresight the British provided for the future, and in this task they were helped by an outstanding personality—Sir Syed Ahmad Khan.

Sir Syed was unhappy about the backward condition of his community, especially in education, and he was distressed at the lack of favour and influence it had in the eyes of the British Government. Like many of his contemporaries, he was a great admirer of the British, and a visit to Europe seems to have had a most powerful effect on him. Europe, or rather Western Europe, of the second half of the nineteenth century was at the height of its civilization, the unchallenged mistress of the world, with all the qualities that had made it great most in evidence. The upper classes were secure in their inheritance and adding to it, with little fear of a successful challenge. It was the age of a growing liberalism and a firm belief in a great destiny. It is not surprising that the Indians who went there were fascinated by this imposing spectacle. More Hindus went there to begin with and they returned admirers of Europe and England. Gradually they got used to the shine and glamour, and the first surprise wore off. But in Sir Syed's case that first surprise and fascination is very much in evidence. Visiting England in 1869, he wrote letters home giving his impressions. In one of these he stated: "The result of all this is that although I do not absolve the English in India of discourtesy, and of looking upon the natives of that country as animals and beneath contempt, I think they do so from not understanding us; and I am afraid I must confess that they are not far wrong in their opinion of us. Without flattering the English, I can truly say that the natives of India, high and low, merchants and petty shopkeepers, educated and illiterate, when contrasted with the English in education, manners and uprightness, are as like them as a dirty animal is to an able and handsome man. The English have reason for believing us in India to be imbecile brutes ... What I have seen, and seen daily, is utterly beyond the imagination of a native of India . . . All good things, spiritual and worldly, which should be found in man, have been bestowed by the Almighty on Europe, and especially on England."[1]

Greater praise no man could give to the British and to Europe, and it is obvious that Sir Syed was tremendously impressed. Perhaps also he used strong language and heightened the contrasts in order to shake up his own people out of their torpor and induce them to take a step forward. This step, he was convinced, must be in the direction of Western

---

1. This quotation has been taken from Hans Kohn's *History of Nationalism in the East.*

education; without that education his community would become more and more backward and powerless. English education meant government jobs, security, influence, honour. So to this education he turned all his energy, trying to win over his community to his way of thinking. He wanted no diversions or distractions from other directions; it was a difficult enough piece of work to overcome the inertia and hesitation of the Muslims. The beginnings of a new nationalism, sponsored by the Hindu *bourgeoisie*, seemed to him to offer such a distraction, and he opposed it. The Hindus, half a century ahead in Western education, could indulge in this pastime of criticizing the Government, but he had counted on the full co-operation of that Government in his educational undertakings and he was not going to risk this by any premature step. So he turned his back on the infant National Congress, and the British Government were only too willing to encourage this attitude.

Sir Syed's decision to concentrate on Western education for Muslims was undoubtedly a right one. Without that they could not have played any effective part in the building up of Indian nationalism of the new type, and they would have been doomed to play second fiddle to the Hindus with their better education and far stronger economic position. The Muslims were not historically or ideologically ready then for the *bourgeois* nationalist movement as they had developed no *bourgeoisie* as the Hindus had done. Sir Syed's activities, therefore, although seemingly very moderate, were in the right revolutionary direction. The Muslims were still wrapped up in a feudal antidemocratic ideology, while the rising middle class among the Hindus had begun to think in terms of the European liberals. Both were thoroughly moderate and dependent on British rule. Sir Syed's moderation was the moderation of the landlord-class to which the handful of well-to-do Muslims belonged. The Hindu's moderation was that of the cautious professional or businessman seeking an outlet for industry and investment. These Hindu politicians looked up to the shining lights of English liberalism—Gladstone, Bright, etc. I doubt if the Muslims did so. Probably they admired the Tories and the landed classes of England. Gladstone, indeed was their *bête noir* because of his repeated condemnation of Turkey and the Armenian massacres; and because Disraeli seemed to be more friendly to Turkey they—that is of course the handful who took interest in such matters—were to some extent partial to him.

Some of Sir Syed Ahmad Khan's speeches make strange reading today. At a speech delivered in Lucknow in December 1887 he seems to have criticised and condemned the very moderate demands of the National Congress which was holding its annual sessions just then. Sir Syed said: "...If Government fight Afghanistan or conquer Burma, it is no business of ours to criticize its policy ... Government has made a Council for making laws ... For this Council she selects from all Provinces those officials who are best acquainted with the administration and the condition of the people, and also some *Raises* who, on account of their high social position, are worthy of a seat in that assembly. Some people may ask—why should they be chosen on account of social position instead of ability? .. I ask you—Would our aristocracy like that a man of low caste or insignificant origin, though he be a B.A. or M.A. and have the requisite ability, should be in a position of authority above them and have power in making the laws that affect their lives and property? Never! ...None but a man of good breeding can the Viceroy take as his colleague, treat as his brother, and invite to entertainments at which he may have to dine with Dukes and Earls ... Can we say that the Government, in the method it has adopted for legislation, acts without regard to the opinions of the people? Can we say that we have no share in the making of the laws? Most certainly not."[2]

Thus spoke the leader and representative of the 'democracy of Islam' in India! It is doubtful if even the taluqadars of Oudh, or the landed magnates of Agra Province, Behar, or Bengal would venture to speak in this vein today. And yet Sir Syed was by no means unique in this. Many of the Congress speeches read equally strangely today. But it seems clear that the political and economic aspect of the Hindu-Muslim question then was this: the rising and economically better-equipped middle class (Hindu) was resisted and checked to some extent by part of the feudal landlord class (Muslim). The Hindu landlords were often closely connected with their *bourgeoisie*, and thus remained neutral or even sympathetic to the middle-class demands which were often influenced by them. The British, as always, sided with the feudal elements. The masses and the lower middle classes on either side were not in the picture at all.

---

2. Taken from Hans Kohn's *History of Nationalism in the East*.

Sir Syed's dominating and forceful personality impressed itself on the Indian Muslims, and the Aligarh College became the visible emblem of his hopes and desires. In a period of transition a progressive impulse may soon play out its part and be reduced to functioning as a brake. The Indian Liberals are an obvious example of this. They remind us often that they are the true heirs of the old Congress tradition and we of a later day are interlopers. True enough. But they forget that the world changes and the old Congress tradition has vanished with the snows of yester-year and only remain as a memory. So also Sir Syed's message was appropriate and necessary when it came, but it could not be the final ideal of a progressive community. It is possible that had he lived a generation later, he would himself have given another orientation to that message. Or other leaders could have re-interpreted his old message and applied it to changing conditions. But the very success that came to Sir Syed and the reverence that clung to his memory made it difficult for others to depart from the old faith; and, unhappily, the Muslims of India were strangely lacking in men of outstanding ability who could point a new way. Aligarh College did fine work, produced a large number of competent men, and changed the whole tone of the Muslim intelligentsia, but still it could not wholly get out of the framework in which it was built—a feudal spirit reigned over it, and the goal of the average student's ambition was government service. Not for him the adventures of the spirit or the quest of the stars: he was happy if he got a Deputy Collectorship. His pride was soothed by his being reminded that he was a unit in the great democracy of Islam, and in witness of this brotherhood, he wore jauntily on his head the red cap, called the Turkish fez, which the Turks themselves soon afterwards were going to discard utterly. Having assured himself of his inalienable right to democracy, which enabled him to feed and pray with his brother Muslims, he did not worry about the existence or otherwise of political democracy in India.

This narrow outlook and hankering after government service was not confined to the Muslim students of Aligarh and elsewhere. It was equally in evidence among the Hindu students who were far from being adventurous by nature. But circumstances forced many of them out of the rut. There were far too many of them and not enough jobs to go round, and so they became the *déclassé* intellectuals who are the backbone of national revolutionary movements.

The Indian Muslims had not wholly recovered from the cramping effects of Sir Syed Ahmad Khan's political message when the events of the early years of the twentieth century helped the British Government to widen the breach between them and the nationalist movement, now clamant and aggressive. Sir Valentine Chirol wrote in 1910 in his *Indian Unrest:* "It may be confidently asserted that never before have the Mohammadans of India as a whole identified their interests and their aspirations so closely as at the present day with the consolidation and permanence of British rule." Political prophecies are dangerous. Within five years after Sir Valentine wrote, the Muslim intelligentsia was trying hard to break through from the fetters that kept it back and to range itself beside the Congress. Within a decade the Indian Muslims seemed to have outstripped the Congress and were actually giving the lead to it. But these ten years were momentous years, and the Great War had come and gone and left a broken-down world as a legacy.

And yet Sir Valentine had superficially every reason to come to the conclusion he did. The Aga Khan had emerged as the leader of the Muslims, and that fact alone showed that they still clung to their feudal traditions, for the Aga Khan was no *bourgeois* leader. He was an exceedingly wealthy prince and the religious head of a sect, and from the British point of view he was very much a *persona grata* because of his close association with the British ruling classes. He was widely cultured, and lived mostly in Europe, the life of a wealthy English landed magnate and sportsman; he was thus far from being personally narrow-minded on communal or sectarian matters. His leadership of the Muslims meant the lining up of the Muslim landed classes as well as the growing *bourgeoisie* with the British Government; the communal problem was really secondary and was obviously stressed in the interests of the main objective. Sir Valentine Chirol tells us that the Aga Khan impressed upon Lord Minto, the Viceroy,

the Mahommedan view of the political situation created by the partition of Bengal, lest political concessions should be hastily made to the Hindus which would pave the way for the ascendancy of a Hindu majority equally dangerous to the stability of British rule and to the interests of the Mahommedan minority whose loyalty was beyond dispute.

But behind this superficial lining up with the British Government other forces were working. Inevitably the new Muslim *bourgeoisie* was feeling more and more dissatisfied with existing conditions and was being drawn towards the nationalist movement. The Aga Khan himself had to take notice of this and to warn the British in characteristic language. He wrote in the *Edinburgh Review* of January 1914 (that is, long before the War) advising the Government to abandon the policy of separating Hindus from Muslims, and to rally the moderate of both creeds in a common camp so as to provide a counterpoise to the radical nationalist tendencies of young India—both Hindu and Muslim. It was thus clear that he was far more interested in checking political change in India than in the communal interests of Muslims.

But the Aga Khan or the British Government could not stop the inevitable drift of the Muslim *bourgeoisie* towards nationalism. The World War hastened the process, and as new leaders arose the Aga Khan seemed to retire into the background. Even Aligarh College changed its tone, and among the new leaders the most dynamic were the Ali Brothers, both products of Aligarh. Doctor M.A. Ansari, Moulana Abul Kalam Azad, and a number of other *bourgeois* leaders now began to play an important part in the political affairs of the Muslims. So also, on a more moderate scale, Mr M.A. Jinnah. Gandhiji swept most of these leaders (not Mr Jinnah) and the Muslims generally into his non-co-operation movement, and they played a leading part in the events of 1919-23.

Then came the reaction, and communal and backward elements, both among the Hindus and the Muslims, began to emerge from their enforced retirement. It was a slow process, but it was a continuous one. The Hindu Mahasabha for the first time assumed some prominence, chiefly because of the communal tension, but politically it could not make much impression on the Congress. The Muslim communal organizations were more successful in regaining some of their old prestige among the Muslim masses. Even so a very strong group of Muslim leaders remained throughout with the Congress. The British Government meanwhile gave every encouragement to the Muslim communal leaders who were politically thoroughly reactionary. Noting the success of these reactionaries, the Hindu Mahasabha began to compete with them in reaction, thereby hoping to win the goodwill of the Government. Many of the progressive elements in the Mahasabha were driven out or left of their own accord, and it inclined more and more towards the upper middle classes, and especially the creditor and banker class.

The communal politicians on both sides, who were interminably arguing about percentages of seats in legislatures, thought only in terms of the patronage which influence in Government gives. It was a struggle for jobs for the middle-class intelligentsia. There were obviously not enough jobs to go round, and so the Hindu and Muslim communalists quarrelled about them, the former on the defensive, for they had most of the existing jobs, the latter always wanting more and more. Behind this struggle for jobs there was a much more important contest which was not exactly communal but which influenced the communal issue. On the whole the Hindus were, in the Punjab, Sind, and Bengal, the richer, creditor, urban class; the Muslims in these provinces were the poorer, debtor, rural class. The conflict between the two was therefore often economic, but it was always given a communal colouring. In recent months this has come out very prominently in the debates on various provincial bills for reducing the burden of rural debt, especially in the Punjab. The representatives of the Hindu Mahasabha have consistently opposed these measures and sided with the banker class.

The Hindu Mahasabha is always laying stress on its own irreproachable nationalism when it criticizes Muslim communalism. That the Muslim organizations have shown themselves to be quite extraordinarily communal has been patent to everybody. The Mahasabha's communalism has not been so obvious, as it masquerades under a nationalist cloak. The test comes when a national and democratic solution happens to injure upper-class Hindu interests, and in this test the Mahasabha has repeatedly failed. The separation of Sind has been consistently opposed by them in the economic interests of a minority and against the declared wishes of the majority.

But the most extraordinary exhibition of anti-nationalism and reaction, both on the part of Muslim and Hindu communalists, took place at the Round Table Conferences. The British Government had insisted on nominating only definitely communal Muslims, and these, under the leadership of the Aga Khan, actually went to the length of allying themselves with the most reactionary and, from the point of view not only of India but of all progressive groups, the most dangerous elements in British public life. It was quite extraordinary to see the close association of the Aga Khan and his group with Lord Lloyd and his party. They went a step further, and made pacts with the representatives of the European Association and others at the R.T.C. This was very depressing, for this Association has been and is, in India, the stoutest and the most aggressive opponent of Indian freedom.

The Hindu Mahasabha delegates responded to this by demanding, especially in the Punjab, all manner of checks on freedom—safeguards in the interests of the British. They tried to outbid the Muslims in their attempts to offer co-operation to the British Government, and, without gaining anything, damned their own case and betrayed the cause of freedom. The Muslims had at least spoken with dignity, the Hindu communalists did not even possess this.

The outstanding fact seems to me how, on both sides, the communal leaders represent a small upper-class reactionary group, and how these people exploit and take advantage of the religious passions of the masses for their own ends. On both sides every effort is made to suppress and avoid the consideration of economic issues. Soon the time will come when these issues can no longer be suppressed, and then, no doubt, the communal leaders on both sides will echo the Aga Khan's warning of twenty years ago for the moderates to join hands in a common camp against radical tendencies. To some extent that is already evident, for however much the Hindu and Muslim communalists attack each other in public they co-operate in the Assembly and elsewhere in helping Government to pass reactionary measures. Ottawa was one of the links which brought the three together.

Meanwhile it is interesting to notice that the Aga Khan's close association with the extreme Right wing of the Conservative party continues. In October 1934 he was the guest of honour at the British Navy League dinner, at which Lord Lloyd presided, and he supported wholeheartedly the proposals for further strengthening the British Navy, which Lord Lloyd had made at the Bristol Conservative Conference. An Indian leader was thus so anxious about imperial defence and the safety of England that he wanted to go further in increasing British armaments than even Mr Baldwin or the 'National' Government. Of course, this was all in the interest of peace.

The next month, in November 1934, it was reported that a film was privately shown in London, the object of which was "to link the Muslim world in lasting friendship with the British Crown".We were informed that the guests of honour on this occasion were the Aga Khan and Lord Lloyd. It would seem that the Aga Khan and Lord Lloyd have become almost as inseparably united—two hearts that beat as one—in imperial affairs, as Sir Tej Bahadur Sapru and Mr M.R. Jayakar are in our national politics. And it is worth noticing that, during these months when the two were so frequently communing with each other, Lord Lloyd was leading a bitter and unrelenting attack on the official Conservative leadership and the National Government for their alleged weakness in giving too much to India.[2]

Latterly there has been an interesting development in the speeches and statements of some of the Muslim communal leaders. This has no real importance, but I doubt if many people think so, nevertheless it is significant of the mentality of communalism, and a great deal of prominence has been given to it. Stress has been laid on the 'Muslim nation' in India, on 'Muslim culture', on the utter incompatibility of Hindu and Muslim 'cultures'. The inevitable deduction from this is (although it is not put baldly) that the British must remain in India for ever and ever to hold the scales and mediate between the two 'cultures'.

A few Hindu communal leaders think exactly on the same lines, with this difference, however, that they hope that being in a majority their brand of 'culture' will ultimately prevail.

Hindu and Muslim 'cultures' and the 'Muslim nation'—how these words open out fascinating vistas of past history and present and future speculation! The Muslim nation in India—a nation within a nation, and not even compact, but vague, spread out, indeterminate. Politically, the idea is absurd, economically it is fantastic; it is hardly worth considering. And yet it helps us a little to understand the mentality behind it. Some such separate and unmixable 'nations' existed together in the Middle Ages and afterwards. In the Constantinople of the early days of the Ottoman Sultans each such 'nation' lived separately and had a measure of autonomy—Latin Christians, Orthodox Christians, Jews, etc. This was the beginning of extra-territoriality which, in more recent times, became such a nightmare to many eastern countries. To talk of a 'Muslim

---

2. Recently a Council of some British peers and Indian Muslims has been formed to cement and further the union of these extreme reactionary elements.

nation', therefore, means that there is no nation at all but a religious bond; it means that no nation in the modern sense must be allowed to grow; it means that modern civilization should be discarded and we should go back to the medieval ways; it means either autocratic government or a foreign government; it means, finally, just nothing at all except an emotional state of mind and a conscious or unconscious desire not to face realities, especially economic realities. Emotions have a way of upsetting logic, and we may not ignore them simply because they seem so unreasonable. But this idea of a Muslim nation is the figment of a few imaginations only, and, but for the publicity given to it by the Press, few people would have heard of it. And even if many people believed in it, it would still vanish at the touch of reality.

So also the ideas of Hindu and Muslim 'culture'. The day of even national cultures is rapidly passing and the world is becoming one cultural unit. Nations may retain, and will retain for a long time much that is peculiar to them—language, habits, ways of thought, etc.—but the machine age and science, with swift travel, constant supply of world news, radio, cinema, etc., will make them more and more uniform. No one can fight against this inevitable tendency, and only a world catastrophe which shatters modern civilization can really check it. There are certainly many differences between the traditional Hindu and Muslim philosophies of life. But these differences are hardly noticeable when both of them are compared to the modern scientific and industrial outlook on life, for between this latter and the former two there is a vast gulf. The real struggle today in India is not between Hindu culture and Muslim culture, but between these two and the conquering scientific culture of modern civilization. Those who are desirous of preserving 'Muslim culture', whatever that may be, need not worry about Hindu culture, but should withstand the giant from the West. I have no doubt, personally, that all efforts, Hindu or Muslim, to oppose modern scientific and industrial civilization are doomed to failure, and I shall watch this failure without regret. Our choice was unconsciously and involuntarily made when railways and the like came here. Sir Syed Ahmad Khan made his choice on behalf of the Indian Muslims when he started the Aligarh College. But none of us had really any choice in the matter, except the choice which a drowning man has to clutch at something which might save him.

But what is this 'Muslim culture'? Is it a kind of racial memory of the great deeds of the Arabs, Persians, Turks, etc.? Or language? Or art and music? Or customs? I do not remember anyone referring to present-day Muslim art or Muslim music. The two languages which have influenced Muslim thought in India are Arabic and Persian, and especially the latter. But the influence of Persian has no element of religion about it. The Persian language and many Persian customs and traditions came to India in the course of thousands of years and impressed themselves powerfully all over north India. Persia was the France of the East, sending its language and culture to all its neighbours. That is a common and a precious heritage for all of us in India.

Pride in the past achievements of Islamic races and countries is probably one of the strongest of Islamic bonds. Does anyone grudge the Muslims this noble record of various races? No one can take it away from them so long as they choose to remember it and cherish it. As a matter of fact, this past record is also to a large extent a common heritage for all of us, perhaps because we feel as Asiatics a common bond uniting us against the aggression of Europe. I know that whenever I have read of the conflicts of the Arabs in Spain or during the Crusades, my sympathies have always been with them. I try to be impartial and objective, but, try as I will, the Asiatic in me influences my judgment when an Asiatic people are concerned.

I have tried hard to understand what this 'Muslim culture' is, but I confess that I have not succeeded. I find a tiny handful of middle-class Muslims as well as Hindus in north India influenced by the Persian language and traditions. And looking to the masses the most obvious symbols of 'Muslim culture' seem to be: a particular type of pyjamas, not too long and not too short, a particular way of shaving or clipping the moustache but allowing the beard to grow, and a *lota* with a special kind of snout, just as the corresponding Hindu customs are the wearing of a *dhoti*, the possession of a topknot, and a *lota* of a different kind. As a matter of fact, even these distinctions are largely urban and they tend to disappear. The Muslim peasantry and industrial workers are hardly distinguishable from the Hindu. The Muslim intelligentsia seldom sports a beard, though Aligarh still fancies a red Turkish cap with a fez (Turkish it is called, although Turkey will have none of it). Muslim women have taken to the *sari* and are emerging rather slowly from the *purdah*. My own tastes do not harmonize with some of those habits, and I do not fancy beards or moustaches or topknots, but I have no desire to impose my canons of taste on others, though I must confess, in regard to beards, that I rejoiced when Amanullah began to deal with them in summary fashion in Kabul.

I must say that those Hindus and Muslims who are always looking backward, always clutching at things which are slipping away from their grasp, are a singularly pathetic sight. I do not wish to damn the past or to reject it, for there is so much that is singularly beautiful in our past. That will endure I have no doubt. But it is not the beautiful that these people clutch at, but something that is seldom worthwhile and is often harmful.

In recent years Indian Muslims have had repeated shocks, and many of their deeply cherished notions have been shattered. Turkey, that champion of Islam, has not only ended the Khilafat, for which India put up such a brave fight in 1920, but has taken step after step away from religion. In the new Turkish Constitution an article stated that Turkey was a Muslim State, but, lest there be any mistake, Kemal Pasha said in 1927: "The provision in the Constitution that Turkey is a Muslim State is a compromise destined to be done away with at the first opportunity." And I believe he acted up to this hint later on. Egypt, though much more cautiously, is going the same way and keeping her politics quite apart from religion. So also the Arab countries, except Arabia itself, which is more backward. Persia is looking back to pre-Islamic days for her cultural inspiration. Everywhere religion recedes into the background and nationalism appears in aggressive garbs, and behind nationalism other isms which talk in social and economic terms. What of the 'Muslim nation' and 'Muslim culture'? Are they to be found in the future only in northern India, rejoicing under the benign rule of the British?

If progress consists in the individual taking a broader view of what constitutes politics, our communalists as well as our Government have deliberately and consistently aimed at the opposite of this—the narrowing of this view.

57

IMPASSE

The possibility of my re-arrest and conviction always hung over me. It was, indeed, more than a possibility when the land was ruled by Ordinances and the like and the Congress itself was an illegal organization. Constituted as the British Government was, and constituted as I was, my suppression seemed inevitable. This ever-present prospect influenced my work. I could not settle down to anything, and I was in a hurry to get through as much as possible.

And yet I had no desire to invite arrest, and to a large extent I avoided activities which might lead to it. Invitations came to me from many places in the province and outside to undertake a tour. I refused them, for any such speaking tour could only be a raging campaign which would be abruptly ended. There was no half-way house for me then. When I visited any place for some other object—to confer with Gandhiji and the Working Committee members—I addressed public meetings and spoke freely. In Jubbulpore we had a great meeting and a very impressive procession; in Delhi the gathering was one of the biggest I had seen there. Indeed, the very success of these meetings made it clear that the Government would not tolerate their frequent repetition. In Delhi, soon after the meeting, there was a very strong rumour of my impending arrest, but I survived and returned to Allahabad, breaking journey at Aligarh to address the Muslim University students there.

I disliked the idea of taking part in non-political public activities when the Government was trying to crush all effective political work. I found a strong tendency among Congressmen to seek shelter from such work by engaging in the most humdrum activities which, though desirable in themselves, had little to do with our struggle. The tendency was natural, but I felt that it should not be encouraged just then.

In the middle of October 1933 we had meetings of our U.P. Congress workers in Allahabad to consider the situation and decide on future work. The Provincial Congress Committee was an illegal body, and as our object was to meet and not just to defy the law, we did not formally convene this committee. But we asked all its members who were outside gaol, as well as other selected workers, to come to an informal conference. There was no secrecy about our meetings, though they were private, and we did not know till the last moment whether the Government would interfere or not. At these meetings we paid a great deal of attention to the world situation—the great slump, naziism, communism, etc. We wanted our comrades to see the Indian struggle in relation to what was happening elsewhere. The conference ultimately passed a socialistic resolution defining our objective and expressed itself against the withdrawal of civil disobedience. Everybody knew well enough that there was no chance of widespread civil disobedience, and even individual civil disobedience was likely to peter out soon or continue on a very restricted scale. But a withdrawal made little difference to us as the Government offensive and Ordinance laws continued. So, more as a gesture than anything else, we decided to continue the formal civil disobedience but in effect our instructions to our workers were not to go out of their way to invite arrest. They were to carry on their normal work and if arrest came in the course of that, to accept it with good grace. In particular, they were asked to renew contacts with the rural areas and find out the condition of the peasantry, both as a result of the remissions of rent and Government repression. There was no question of a no-rent campaign then. This had been formally withdrawn after the Poona Conference, and it was obvious that it could not be revived under the circumstances.

This programme was a mild and inoffensive one with nothing patently illegal in it, and yet we knew that it would lead to arrests. As soon as our workers went to the villages they were arrested and charged, quite wrongly, with preaching a no-rent campaign (which had been made an offence under the Ordinance laws) and convicted. It was my intention to go to these rural areas after the arrest of many of my comrades, but other activities claimed my attention and I postponed my visit till it was too late.

Twice, during those months, the members of the Working Committee met together to consider the all-India situation. The Committee itself was not functioning, not so much because it was an illegal body but because, at Gandhiji's instance after Poona, all Congress Committees and offices had been suspended. I happened to occupy a peculiar position as, on coming out of gaol, I refused to join this self-denying ordinance and insisted on calling myself the General Secretary of the Congress. But I functioned in the air. There was no proper office, no staff, no acting-president, and Gandhiji, though available for consultation, was busy with one of his tremendous all-India tours, this time for Harijan work. We managed to catch him during his tour at Jubbulpore and Delhi and held our consultations with Working Committee members. They served to bring out clearly the differences between various members. There was an impasse, and no way out of it agreeable to everybody. Gandhiji was the deciding factor between those who wanted to withdraw civil disobedience and those who were against this. As he was then in favour of the latter course, matters continued as before.

The question of contesting elections on behalf of the Congress to the legislatures was sometimes discussed by Congressmen, though the Working Committee members were not much interested in this at the time. It did not arise; it was obviously premature. The 'Reforms' were not likely to materialize for another two or three years at least, and there was then no mention of fresh elections for the Assembly. Personally I had no theoretical objection to contesting elections, and I felt sure in my mind that when the time came the Congress would have to go in for them. But to raise this question then was only to distract attention. I hoped that the continuance of our struggle would clear up the issues that faced us and prevent the compromising elements from dominating the situation.

Meanwhile I continued sending articles and statements to the Press. To some extent I had to tone down my writings, for they were written with a view to publication, and there was the censor and various laws whose octopus-like tentacles reached far. Even if I was prepared to take risks, the printers, publishers and editors were not. On the whole the newspapers were good to me and stretched many a point in my favour. But not always. Sometimes statements and passages were suppressed, and once a whole long article, over which I had taken some pains, never saw the light of day. When I was in Calcutta in January 1934 the editor of one of the leading dailies came to see me. He told me that he had sent one of my statements to the Editor-in-Chief of all Calcutta newspapers for his opinion, and as the Editor-in-Chief had disapproved of it, it had not been published. The 'Editor-in-Chief' was the Government Press Censor for Calcutta.

In some of my Press interviews and statements I ventured to criticize forcibly some groups and individuals. This was resented, partly because of the idea, which Gandhiji had helped to spread, that Congress could be attacked without any danger of its hitting back. Gandhiji himself had set an example of this and in varying degrees leading Congressmen had followed his lead, though sometimes this was not so. Usually we stuck to vague and pious phrases, and this gave an opportunity to our critics to get away with their faulty reasoning and opportunist tactics. The real issues were avoided on both sides, and an honest discussion, with occasional parry and thrust, seldom took place, as it does in Western countries, except where fascism prevails.

A friend, whose opinion I valued, wrote to me that she had been a little surprised at the vigour of some of my statements to the Press—I was almost becoming 'cattish'. Was this the outcome of 'frustration' of my hopes? I wondered. Partly it was true, for nationally all of us suffer from frustration. Individually also it must have been true to some extent. Yet I was not very conscious of the feeling because personally I had no sensation of suppression or failure. Ever since Gandhiji came within my ken politically, I learnt one thing at least from him: not to suppress my ideas within me for fear of the consequences. That habit—followed in the political sphere (in other spheres it would be more difficult and dangerous to follow)—has often got me into trouble, but it has also brought much satisfaction with it. I think that it is because of this that many of us have escaped real bitterness of heart and the worst kinds of frustration. The knowledge also that large numbers of people think of one with affection is very soothing and is a powerful antidote against defeatism and frustration. The most terrible of all feelings, I imagine, is to be alone, forgotten by others.

But, even so, how can one escape in this strange, unhappy world a feeling of frustration? How often everything seems to go wrong, and though we carry on, doubts assail us when we see the quality of human material around us. I am afraid I feel anger and resentment often enough at various happenings and developments, and even at persons and groups. And latterly I have begun to resent more and more the drawing-room attitude to life, which ignores vital issues and considers it improper to refer to them, because they happen to touch one's pocket or pet prejudices. With all this resentment and frustration and 'cattishness', I hope I have not yet lost the gift of laughing at my own and other people's follies.

I sometimes wonder at the faith of people in a beneficent Providence: how it survives shock after shock, and how disaster itself and disproof of beneficence are considered but tests of the soundness of that faith. Those delightful lines of Gerard Hopkins find an echo in many a heart:

> Thou art indeed just, Lord, if I contend
> With thee; but, sir, so what I plead is just.
> Why do sinners' ways prosper? and why must
> Disappointment all I endeavour end?
> Wert thou my enemy, O thou my friend,
> How wouldst thou worse, I wonder, than thou dost
> Defeat, thwart me? Oh, the sots and thralls of lust
> Do in spare hours more thrive than I that spend,
> Sir, life upon thy cause . . .

Faith in progress, in a cause, in ideals, in human goodness and human destiny—are they not nearly allied to faith in a Providence? If we seek to justify them by reason and logic immediately we get into difficulties. But something within us clutches to that hope and faith, for, deprived of them, life would be a wilderness without an oasis.

The effect of my socialist propaganda upset even some of my colleagues of the Working Committee. They would have put up with me without complaint, as they had done for several years during which I had been carrying on this propaganda, but I was now frightening to some extent the vested interests in the country, and my activities could no longer be called innocuous. I knew that some of my colleagues were no Socialists, but I had always thought that, as a member of the Congress Executive I had perfect freedom to carry on socialist propaganda without committing the Congress to it. The realization that some members of the Working Committee did not think that I had that freedom came as a surprise. I was putting them in a false position and they resented it. But what was I to do? I was not going to give up what I considered the most important part of my work. I would much rather resign from the Working Committee if there was a conflict between the two. But how could I resign when the Committee was illegal and was not even functioning properly?

This difficulty faced me again later—I think it was towards the end of December—when Gandhiji wrote to me from Madras. He sent me a cutting from the *Madras Mail* containing an interview he had given. The interviewer had asked him about me and he had replied almost apologizing for my activities and expressing his faith in my rectitude: I would not commit the Congress to these novel ways. I did not particularly fancy this reference to me, but what upset me much more was Gandhiji's defence, further on in the interview, of the big zamindari system. He seemed to think that this was a very desirable part of rural and national economy. This was a great surprise to me for the big zamindaris and taluqas have very few defenders today. All over the world they have been broken up, and even in India most people recognize that they cannot last long. Even taluqadars and zamindars would welcome an end of the system provided, of course, they got sufficient compensation therefor.[1] The system is indeed sinking of its own weight. And yet Gandhiji was in favour of it and talked of trusteeship and the like. How very different was his outlook from mine, I thought again, and I wondered how far I could co-operate with him in future. Must I continue to remain in the Working Committee? There was no way out just then, and a few weeks later the question became irrelevant because of my return to prison.

My domestic affairs took up a lot of my time. My mother's health continued to improve, but very slowly. She was still bedridden, but she seemed to be out of danger. I turned to my financial affairs which had been long neglected and were in a muddle. We had been spending much more than we could afford, and there seemed to be no obvious way of reducing our expenditure. I was not particularly anxious about making both ends meet. Almost I looked forward to the time when I would have no money left. Money and possessions are useful enough in the

---

1. Mr P.N. Tagore, Chairman of the Reception Committee of the All-Bengal Landholders' Conference, said in his address on December 23, 1934: "Personally I will not regret the day when lands of the zamindars are nationalized, as has been done in Ireland, upon payment of adequate compensation to the landlord." It should be remembered that the Bengal landholders, being under the Permanent Settlement, are better off than the landholders in the non-permanently settled areas. Mr P.N. Tagore's ideas about nationalization appear to be vague.

modern world, but often they become a burden for one who wants to go on a long journey. It is very difficult for moneyed people to take part in undertakings which involve risk; they are always afraid of losing their goods and chattels. What is the good of money or property if the Government can take possession of it when it chooses, or even confiscate it? So I almost wished to get rid of what little I had. Our needs were few and I felt confident of my ability to earn enough. My chief concern was that my mother, in the evening of her life, should not suffer discomforts or any marked lowering of the standard of living. I was also anxious that my daughter's education should not be interfered with, and this, according to my thinking, involved a stay in Europe. Apart from this, neither my wife nor I had any special need for money. Or so we thought, being unused to the real lack of it. I am quite sure that when the time comes when we lack money, we shall not be happy about it. One extravagance which I have kept up will be hard to give up, and this is the buying of books.

To improve the immediate financial situation we decided to sell off my wife's jewellery, the silver and other similar articles that we possessed, as well as many cart-loads of odds and ends. Kamala did not like the idea of parting with her jewellery, although she had not worn any of it for a dozen years and it had lain in the bank. But she had looked forward to handing it on to our daughter.

It was January 1934. Continued arrests of our workers in the villages of the Allahabad district, although innocently employed, seemed to demand that we should follow in their steps and visit those villages. Rafi Ahmad Kidwai, our very effective secretary of the U.P. Provincial Congress Committee, was also under arrest. January 26th—Independence Day—was coming and it could not be ignored. Despite Ordinances and prohibitions it had been regularly observed in various parts of the country every year since 1930. But who was to give the lead? And what was the lead to be? There was no one besides me who was functioning, even in theory, as an official of the All-India Congress. I consulted some friends and almost all agreed that something should be done, but there was no agreement as to what this something should be. I found a general tendency to avoid any action which might lead to arrests on a large scale. Eventually I issued a brief appeal for the appropriate celebration of Independence Day, the manner of doing so to be decided by each local area for itself.

In Allahabad we planned a fairly widespread celebration all over the district.

We felt that the organizers of this Independence Day celebration would be arrested on that day. Before I went back to prison again I wanted to pay a visit to Bengal. This was partly to meet old colleagues there, but really it was to be a gesture in the nature of tribute to the people of Bengal for their extraordinary sufferings during the past few years. I knew very well that I could do nothing to help them. Sympathy and fellow-feeling did not go far, and yet they were very welcome, and Bengal was especially suffering from a sense of isolation, of being deserted by the rest of India in her hour of need. That feeling was not justified, but nevertheless it was there.

I had also to go to Calcutta with Kamala to consult our doctors there about her treatment. She had been far from well, but we had both tried to overlook this to some extent and postpone recourse to a treatment which might involve a long stay in Calcutta or elsewhere. We wanted to be together as much as possible during my brief period outside prison. After I went back to gaol, I thought, she would have plenty of time for doctors and treatment. Now that arrest seemed near, I decided to have these consultations at least in my presence in Calcutta; the rest could be attended to later.

So we decided to go to Calcutta, Kamala and I, on January 15th. We wanted to return in good time for our Independence Day meetings.

58

EARTHQUAKE

It was the afternoon of the 15th January, 1934. I was standing in the veranda of our house in Allahabad addressing a group of peasants. The annual Magh Mela had begun, and we had crowds of visitors all day. Suddenly I became unsteady on my feet and could hardly keep my balance. I clung on to a column near by. Doors started banging and a rumbling noise came from the adjoining Swaraj Bhawan, where many of the tiles were sliding down the roof. Being unaccustomed to earthquakes, I did not know at first what was happening, but I soon realised it. I was rather amused and interested at this novel experience and I continued my talk to the peasants and began telling them about the earthquake. My old aunt shouted out to me from some distance to run out of the building. The idea struck me as absurd. I did not take the earthquake seriously, and in any event I was not going to leave my bed-ridden mother upstairs, and my wife, who was probably packing, also upstairs, and seek safety for myself. For what seemed quite an appreciable time the shocks continued and then passed off. They provided a few minutes' conversation and soon were almost forgotten. We did not know then, nor could we guess, what those two or three minutes had meant to millions in Behar and elsewhere.

That evening Kamala and I left for Calcutta and, all unknowing, we were carried by our train that night through the southern earthquake area. The next day there was little news in Calcutta about the disaster. The day after bits of news began to come in. On the third day we began to have a faint notion of the calamity.

We busied ourselves with our Calcutta programme. There were plenty of doctors to be seen repeatedly, and it was finally decided that Kamala was to come back to Calcutta for treatment a month or two later. Then there were friends and Congress colleagues whom we had not met for a long time. I had a terrible sense of oppression all the time. People seemed to lie afraid of doing almost anything lest trouble should come to them; they had gone through much. Newspapers were more cautious than anywhere else in India. There was also, as elsewhere in India, doubt and confusion about future work. It was indeed this doubt, and not so much fear, that prevented any effective political activity. There were fascist tendencies much in evidence, and socialist and communist tendencies—all rather vague and running into each other. It was difficult to draw hard and fast lines between these groups. I had neither the time nor the opportunity to find out much about the terrorist movement, which was receiving a great deal of attention and advertisement from official sources. As far as I could gather, it had no political significance whatever, and the old members of the terrorist groups had no faith left in it. They were beginning to think on different lines. Resentment at Government action in Bengal had, however, led individuals here and there to break loose and indulge in a kind of feud. Indeed, on either side this idea of a feud seemed to be dominant. On the side of the individual terrorists this was obvious enough. On the side of the State also the attitude was far more that of carrying on a feud, with occasional reprisals, than of calmly grappling with an anti-social occurrence and suppressing it. Any government faced by terroristic acts is bound to combat them and try to suppress them. But serene control is more becoming in a government than excessive action applied indiscriminately to guilty and innocent alike, and chiefly to the latter because they are sure to be more numerous. Perhaps it is not easy to remain calm and collected in the face of such a threat. Terroristic acts were becoming rare, but the possibility of them was ever present, and this was enough to upset the composure of those who had to deal with them. Such acts, it is patent enough, are not a disease but the symptoms of a disease. It is futile to treat the symptoms and not the disease itself.

I believe that a number of young men and women, who are supposed to have dealings with terrorists, are really attracted by the glamour of secret work. Secrecy and risk have always an appeal for the adventurous type of youth; the desire to be in the know, to find out what all this shouting is about, and who are these men behind the scenes. It is the call of the detective story. These people have no intention of doing anything, certainly not a terroristic act, but their mere association with suspects in the eyes of the police is enough to make them suspect also. Soon they are likely to find themselves in the ranks of the detenus, or in an internment camp, if a worse fate does not await them.

Law and order, we are told, are among the proud achievements of British rule in India. My own instincts are entirely in favour of them. I like discipline in life, and dislike anarchy and disorder and inefficiency. But bitter experience has made me doubt the value of the law and order that states and governments impose on a people. Sometimes the price one pays for them is excessive, and the law is but the will of the dominant faction and the order is the reflex of an all-pervading fear. Sometimes, indeed, the so-called law and order might be more justly called the absence of law and order. Any achievement that is based on widespread fear can hardly be a desirable one, and an 'order' that has for its basis the coercive apparatus of the State, and cannot exist without it, is more like a military occupation than civil rule. I find in the *Rajatarangini*, the thousand-year-old Kashmiri historic epic of the poet Kalhana, that the phrase which is repeatedly used in the sense of law and order, something that it was the duty of the ruler and the State to preserve, is *dharma* and *abhaya*—righteousness and absence of fear. Law was something more than mere law, and order was the fearlessness of the people. How much more desirable is this idea of inculcating fearlessness than of enforcing 'order' on a frightened populace!

We spent three and a half days in Calcutta and during this period I addressed three public meetings. As I had done before in Calcutta, I condemned and argued against terroristic acts, and then I passed on to the methods that the Government had adopted in Bengal. I spoke from a full heart, for I had been greatly moved by accounts of occurrences in the province. What pained me most was the manner in which human dignity had been outraged by indiscriminate suppression of whole populations. The political problem, urgent as it was, took second place before this human problem. These three speeches of mine formed the three counts against me in my subsequent trial in Calcutta and my present sentence is due to them.

From Calcutta we went to Santiniketan to pay a visit to the poet Rabindra Nath Tagore. It was always a joy to meet him and, having come so near, we did not wish to miss him. I had been to Santiniketan twice before. It was Kamala's first visit, and she had come especially to see the place as we were thinking of sending our daughter there. Indira was going to appear for her matriculation soon afterwards, and the problem of her future education was troubling us. I was wholly against her joining the regular official or semi-official universities, for I disliked them. The whole atmosphere that envelops them is official, oppressive and authoritarian. They have no doubt produced fine men and women in the past, and they will continue to do so. But these few exceptions cannot save the universities from the charge of suppressing and deadening the fine instincts of youth. Santiniketan offered an escape from this dead hand, and so we fixed upon it, although in some ways it was not so up to date and well-equipped as the other universities.

On our way back we stopped at Patna to discuss with Rajendra Babu the problem of earthquake relief. He had just been discharged from prison and, inevitably, he had taken the lead in unofficial relief work. Our arrival was unexpected, for none of our telegrams had been delivered. The house where we intended staying with Kamala's brother was in ruins; it was a big double-storeyed brick structure. So, like many others, we lived in the open.

The next day I paid a visit to Muzaffarpur. It was exactly seven days after the earthquake and little had so far been done to remove the debris, except from some of the main streets. As these streets were cleaned corpses were being discovered, some in curiously expressive attitudes, as if trying to ward off a falling wall or roof. The ruins were an impressive and terrifying sight. The survivors were thoroughly shaken-up and cowed by their nerve-racking experiences.

Returning to Allahabad, collections of funds and materials were immediately organized, and all of us, of the Congress or out of it, took this up in earnest. Some of my colleagues were of opinion that because of the earthquake the Independence Day celebrations should be called off. But other colleagues and I saw no reason why even an earthquake should interfere with our programme. So on the 26th January we had a large number of meetings in the villages of Allahabad district and a meeting in the city, and we met with greater success than we had anticipated. Most people expected police interference and arrests, and on a minor scale there was some interference. But, much to our surprise, we survived the meeting. In some of our villages and in some other cities arrests were made.

Soon after returning from Behar I issued a statement about the earthquake, ending up with an appeal for funds. In this statement I criticized the inactivity of the Behar Government during the first few days after the earthquake. It was not my intention to criticize the officials in the earthquake areas, for they had had to deal with a very difficult situation which would have tried the stoutest nerves, and I was sorry that some of my words were capable of this interpretation. But I did feel strongly that the headquarters of the Behar Government had not shown great competence to begin with, especially in the matter of removal of debris, which might have saved lives. Thousands of people were killed in Monghyr city alone, and three weeks later I saw a vast quantity of debris still lying untouched, although a few miles away at Jamalpur there was a large colony of many thousands of railway workers, who could have been utilized for this purpose within a few hours of the catastrophe. Living people were unearthed even twelve days after the earthquake. The Government had taken immediate steps to protect property, but they had not been so expeditious in trying to rescue people who lay buried. The municipalities in these areas were not functioning.

I think my criticism was justified, and I found later that the great majority of people in the earthquake areas agreed with it. But whether it was justified or not, it was honestly made, not with the intention of blaming the Government, but of speeding them up. No one accused them of any deliberate sins of commission or omission in this respect. It was a novel and overpowering situation and errors were excusable. The Behar Government, so far as I know (for I have been in gaol), later on worked with energy and competence to repair the ravages of the earthquake.

But my criticism was resented, and soon afterwards a few people in Behar came out with a general testimonial in favour of the Government as a kind of counterblast. The earthquake and its demands became almost a secondary matter. More important was the fact that the Government had been criticized, and it must be defended by its loyal subjects. This was an interesting instance of a widespread phenomenon in India—the dislike of criticism of the Government, which is a commonplace in Western countries. It is the military mentality, which cannot tolerate criticism. Like the King, the British Government in India and all of its superior officials can do no wrong. To hint at any such thing is *lèse majesté*.

The curious part of it is that a charge of inefficiency and incompetence is resented far more than an accusation of harsh government or tyranny.

The latter might indeed land the person making it in prison, but the Government is used to it and does not really mind it. After all, in a way, it might almost be considered a compliment to an imperial race. But to be called inefficient and wanting in nerve hurts, for this strikes at the root of their self-esteem; it disturbs the messianic delusions of the English officials in India. They are like the Anglican bishop who was prepared to put up meekly with a charge of unchristian behaviour, but who resented and hit out when some one called him foolish and incompetent.

There is a general belief among Englishmen, frequently asserted as if it was an incontrovertible maxim, that a change of government in India, involving a reduction or elimination of British influence, would result in a much worse and more inefficient government. Holding this belief, but generous in their enthusiasm, radicals and Englishmen of advanced views plead that good government is no substitute for self-government, and if Indians want to go to the dogs, they should be permitted to do so. I do not know what will happen to India when British influence is eliminated. Much depends on how the British withdraw and who is in control in India then, and on a host of other considerations, national and international. I can quite conceive a state of affairs, established with the help of the British, which will be more inefficient and generally worse than anything that we can have today, for it will have all the vices of the present system without its virtues. I can conceive more readily still a different state of affairs which, from the point of view of the Indian people, will be far more efficient and beneficial than anything we have today. It is possible that the coercive apparatus of the State may not be so efficient, and the administrative apparatus not quite so shiny, but there will be greater efficiency in production, consumption, and the activities which go to raise the physical, the spiritual, and cultural standards of the masses. I believe that self-government is good for any country. But I am not prepared to accept even self-government at the cost of real good government. Self-government if it is to justify itself must stand ultimately for better government for the masses. It is because I believe that the British Government in India, whatever its claims in the past may have been, is incapable of providing good government and rising standards for the masses today, that I feel that it has outlived its utility, such as it was, in India. The only real justification for Indian freedom is the promise of better government, of a higher standard for the masses, of industrial and cultural growth, and of the removal of the atmosphere of fear and suppression that foreign imperialist rule invariably brings in its train. The British Government and the I.C.S., though they may be strong enough to impose their will on India, are not efficient or competent enough to solve India's problems of today, and even less of the future, because their foundations and assumptions are all wrong and they have lost touch with reality. A government or ruling class which is not competent enough, or which represents a passing order, cannot long continue even to impose their will.

The Allahabad Earthquake Relief Committee deputed me to visit the areas affected by the earthquake and to report on the methods of relief-work adopted there. I went immediately, alone, and for ten days I wandered about those torn and ruined territories. It was a very strenuous tour, and I had little sleep during those days. From five in the morning till almost midnight we were up and about, motoring over the cracked and crumpled-up roads, or going by little boats where the bridges had collapsed and the roads were under water owing to a change in level. The towns were impressive enough with their extensive ruins, and their roads torn up and twisted sometimes as by a giant hand, or raised high above the plinth of the houses on either side. From huge cracks in these roads water and sand had gushed out and swept away men and cattle. More even than these towns, the plains of North Behar—the garden of Behar, they used to be called—had desolation and destruction stamped upon them. Mile upon mile of sand, and large sheets of water, and huge cracks and vast numbers of little craters out of which this sand and water had come. Some British officers who flew over this area said that it bore some resemblance to the battlefields of northern France in war-time and soon after.

It must have been a terrible experience. The earthquake began with strong side-to-side movements which knocked down any person who was standing. Then there were up-and-down movements, and a vast rumbling and reverberating noise as of an artillery bombardment or a hundred aeroplanes in the sky, and waters gushed out in innumerable places from huge fissures and craters and rose to about ten or twelve feet. All this probably lasted for three minutes or a little more and then it died down, but those three minutes were terrible enough. It is not surprising that many persons who saw this happen imagined that this was the end of the world. In the cities there was a noise of falling houses, and a rushing of waters, and an atmosphere full of dust which made it impossible to see even a few yards. In the rural areas there was not much dust and one could see a little farther, but there were no calm-eyed spectators about. Those who survived lay flat on the ground, or rolled about, in an agony of terror.

A little boy of twelve was dug out (I think in Muzaffarpur) alive ten days after the earthquake. He was greatly surprised. He had imagined, when he was knocked down and imprisoned by falling material, that the world had ended and he was the solitary survivor.

In Muzaffarpur also at the exact moment of the earthquake when houses were collapsing and hundreds were dying all round, a baby girl was born. The inexperienced young parents did not know what to do, and were distraught. I learnt, however, that both the mother and the baby survived and were flourishing. In honour of the earthquake the baby was named Kampo Devi.

The city of Monghyr was the last place in our tour. We had wandered a good deal and gone almost up to the frontier of Nepal, and we had seen many harrowing sights. We had become used to ruins and destruction on a vast scale. And yet when we saw Monghyr and the absolute destruction of this rich city, we gasped and shivered at the horror of it. I can never forget that terrible sight.

All over the earthquake areas there was a very painful absence of self-help among the residents, both in the cities and villages. Probably the middle classes in the cities were the worst offenders in this respect. They all waited for somebody to take action and help them, either the Government or the non-official relief agencies. Others who offered their services thought that work meant ordering people about. Part of this feeling of helplessness was no doubt due to the nervous collapse brought about by the terror of the earthquake, and it must have gradually lessened.

In marked contrast with this was the energy and capacity of the large numbers of relief workers who poured in from other parts of Behar and other provinces. It was wonderful to see the spirit of efficient service of these young men and women and, in spite of the fact that a host of separate relief organizations were working, there was a great deal of co-operation between them.

In Monghyr I indulged in a theatrical gesture to give a push to the self-help movement for digging and removing the debris. I did so with some hesitation, but it turned out to be a success. All the leaders of the relief organizations went out with spades and baskets and did a good day's digging, and we brought out the corpse of a little girl. I left Monghyr that day, but the digging went on and many local people took it up with very good results.

Of all the non-official relief organizations the Central Relief Committee, of which Rajendra Prasad was the head, was far the most important. This was by no means a purely Congress organization, and it developed into an all-India body representing various groups and the donors. It had, however, the great advantage of having the Congress organization in the rural areas at its disposal. In no province in India, except Gujrat and some districts of the United Provinces, were the Congress workers more in touch with the peasants. In fact the workers themselves came largely from the peasantry; Behar is pre-eminently the peasant province of India and even its middle classes are closely allied to the peasantry. Sometimes when, as Congress Secretary, I went to inspect the Behar Provincial Congress Committee's office, I criticized in vigorous language what I considered was their inefficiency and general slackness in keeping office. There was a tendency to sit rather than stand, to lie down rather than sit. The office was one of the barest I had seen, for they would try to carry on without many of the usual office accessories. Yet, in spite of my criticism of the office, I knew well that from the Congress point of view the province was one of the most earnest and devoted in the country. Congress made no show there, but it had the solid backing of the peasantry. Even in the All-India Congress Committee the Behar members seldom took up an aggressive attitude in any matter. They seemed to be a little surprised at finding themselves there. But in both the Civil Disobedience movements Behar put up a splendid record. Even in the subsequent individual civil disobedience, it did well.

The Relief Committee availed itself of this fine organization to reach the peasantry. In the rural areas no other agency, not even the Government, could be so helpful. And the head of both the Relief Committee and the Behar Congress organization was Rajendra Babu, the unquestioned leader of Behar. Looking like a peasant, a typical son of the soil of Behar, he is not impressive at first sight till one notices his keen frank eyes and his earnest look. One does not forget that look or those eyes, for through them truth looks at you and there is no doubting them. Peasant-like, he is perhaps a little limited in outlook, somewhat unsophisticated from the point of view of the modern world, but his outstanding ability, his perfect straightness, his energy, and his devotion to the cause of Indian freedom are qualities which have made him loved not only in his own province but throughout India. No one in any province in India occupies quite that universally acknowledged position of leadership as Rajendra Babu does in Behar. Few others, if any, can be said to have imbibed more thoroughly the real message of Gandhiji.

It was fortunate that a man like him was available for the leadership of the relief-work in Behar, and it was faith in him that drew a vast sum of money from all over India. Weak in health, he threw himself into the work of relief. He overworked himself, for he became the centre of all activity and everybody turned to him for advice.

During my tour in the earthquake areas, or just before going there, I read with a great shock Gandhiji's statement to the effect that the earthquake had been a punishment for the sin of untouchability. This was a staggering remark and I welcomed and wholly agreed with Rabindra Nath Tagore's answer to it. Anything more opposed to the scientific outlook it would be difficult to imagine. Perhaps even science will not be absolutely dogmatic today about the effect of emotional states and psychic occurrences on matter. A mental shock may result in indigestion or something worse to the person concerned. But to suggest that a human custom or failing had its reactions on the movements of the earth's crust is an astounding thing. The idea of sin and divine wrath and man's relative importance in the affairs of the universe—they take us back a few hundred years, when the Inquisition flourished in Europe and burned Giordano Bruno for his scientific heresy and sent many a witch to the stake! Even in the eighteenth century in America leading Boston divines attributed earthquakes in Massachusetts to the impiety of lightning rods.

And if the earthquake was a divine punishment for sin, how are we to discover for which sin we are being punished?—for, alas! we have many sins to atone for. Each person can have his pet explanation; we may have been punished for submitting to alien domination, or for putting up with an unjust social system. The Maharaja of Darbhanga, the owner of enormous estates, was, financially, one of the major sufferers from the earthquake. We might as well say that this was a judgment on the zamindari system. That would be nearer the mark than to suggest that the more or less innocent people of Behar were being made to suffer vicariously for the sins of untouchability of the people of South India. Why did not the earthquake visit the land of untouchability itself? Or the British Government might call the calamity a divine punishment for civil disobedience, for, as a matter of fact, North Behar, which suffered most from the earthquake, took a leading part in the freedom movement.

We can go on speculating indefinitely in this manner. And then, of course, the question arises why we should interfere with the workings of Providence or try to lessen the effect of its divine decrees by our humane efforts. And we begin to wonder why Providence has played this cruel joke on us: to make us full of imperfections, to surround us with snares and pitfalls, to create a miserable and cruel world, to make the tiger and the lamb, and then to punish us.

> When the stars threw down their spears
> And water'd heaven with their tears,
> Dare he laugh his work to see?
> Dare he who made the lamb make thee?

On my last night in Patna I sat up till very late with many friends and comrades who had gathered there from various provinces to offer their services for relief work. U.P. was well represented and some of our chosen men were there. We discussed a problem that was troubling us: how far must we allow ourselves to be involved in earthquake relief? That meant, to that extent at least, a withdrawal from political work. Relief work was very exacting and we could not take it up casually. Absorption in it might well involve a long period of absence from the active political sphere, and that was bound to have a bad effect politically on our province. Although there were many in the Congress fold, the people who make a difference were always limited in number and could ill be spared. And yet the call of the earthquake could not be ignored. For my part I had no intention of devoting myself exclusively to relief work. I felt that there would be no lack of people for that; there were few for more risky activities.

So we talked till far into the night. We discussed the last Independence Day and how some of our colleagues had been arrested then, while we had escaped. I told them laughingly that I had discovered the secret of militant politics with perfect safety.

I got back home in Allahabad on February 11th, dead tired after my tour. Ten strenuous days had made me look ghastly and my people were surprised at my appearance. I tried to begin writing my report of the tour for the Allahabad Relief Committee, but sleep overcame me. I spent at least twelve hours out of the next twenty-four in sleep.

Next day, in the late afternoon, Kamala and I had finished tea and Purushottam Das Tandon had just then joined us. We were standing in the veranda when a car drove up and a police officer alighted. I knew immediately that my time had come. I went up to him and said: "*Bahut dinon se apka intazar tha*"—"I have been waiting for you for a long time." He was a little apologetic and said that he was not to blame. The warrant was from Calcutta.

Five months and thirteen days I had been out, and now I went back again to seclusion and loneliness. But the real burden was not mine; it had to be shouldered, as always, by the womenfolk—by my ailing mother, my wife, my sister.

59

ALIPORE GAOL

Already how am I so far
Out of that minute? Must I go
Still like the thistle-ball, no bar,
Onward wherever light winds blow,
Fixed by no friendly star?

Robert Browning

That very night I was taken to Calcutta. From Howrah station a huge black Maria carried me to Lal Bazaar Police Station. I had read much of this famous headquarters of the Calcutta police and I looked round with interest. There were large numbers of European sergeants and inspectors to be seen, far more than would have been in evidence in any police headquarters in Northern India. The constables seemed to be almost all from Behar or the eastern districts of U.P. During the many journeys I made in the big prison lorry, to court and back or from one prison to another, a number of these constables used to accompany me inside. They looked thoroughly unhappy, disliking their job, and obviously full of sympathy for me. Sometimes their eyes glistened with tears.

I was kept in the Presidency Gaol to begin with, and from there I was taken for my trial to the Chief Presidency Magistrate's court. This was a novel experience. The court-room and building had more the appearance of a besieged fortress than of an open court. Except for a few newspaper men and the usual lawyers, no outsiders were allowed anywhere in the neighbourhood. The police was present in some force. These arrangements apparently had not been made especially for me; that was the daily routine. When I was taken to the court-room I had to march through a long passage (inside the room) which was closely wired on top and at the side. It was like going through a cage. The dock was far from the magistrate's seat. The courtroom was crowded with policemen and black-coated and gowned lawyers.

I was used enough to court trials. Many of my previous trials had taken place in gaol precincts. But there had always been some friends, relatives, familiar faces about, and the whole atmosphere had been a little easier. The police had usually kept in the background and there had never been any cage-like structures about. Here it was very different, and I gazed at strange, unfamiliar faces between whom and me there was nothing in common. It was not an attractive crowd. I am afraid gowned lawyers *en masse* are not beautiful to look at, and police-court lawyers seem to develop a peculiarly unlovely look. At last I managed to spot one familiar lawyer's face in that black array, but he was lost in that crowd.

I felt very lonely and isolated even when I sat on the balcony outside before the trial began. My pulse must have quickened a little, and inwardly I was not quite so composed as I usually had been during my previous trials. It struck me then that if even I, with so much experience of trials and convictions, could react abnormally to that situation, how much more must young and inexperienced people feel the tension?

I felt much better in the dock itself. There was, as usual, no defence offered, and I read out a brief statement. The next day, February 16th, I was sentenced to two years. My seventh term of imprisonment had begun.

I looked back with some satisfaction to my five and a half months' stay outside. That time had been fairly well occupied, and I had managed to get through some useful jobs. My mother had turned the corner and was out of immediate danger. My younger sister, Krishna, had married. My daughter's future education had been fixed up. I had straightened out some of my domestic and financial tangles. Many personal matters that I had been long neglecting had been attended to. In the field of public affairs I knew that no one could do much then. I had at least helped a little in stiffening up the Congress attitude and in directing it to some extent towards social and economic ways of thinking. My Poona correspondence with Gandhiji, and later my articles in the Press, had made a difference. My articles on the communal question had also done some good. And then I had met Gandhiji again after more than two years, and many other friends and comrades, and had charged myself with nervous and emotional energy for another period.

One shadow remained to darken my mind—Kamala's ill-health. I had no notion then how very ill she was, for she has a habit of carrying on till she collapses. But I was worried. And yet I hoped that now I was in prison she would be free to devote herself to her treatment. It was more difficult to do so whilst I was out and she was not willing to leave me for long. I had one other regret. I was sorry that I had not visited even once the rural areas of Allahabad district. Many of my young colleagues had recently been arrested there for carrying out our instructions, and it seemed almost like disloyalty to them not to follow them in the district.

Again the black Maria carried me back to prison. On our way we passed plenty of troops on the march with machine-guns, armoured cars, etc. I peeped at them through the tiny openings of our prison van. How ugly an armoured car is, I thought, and a tank. They reminded me of prehistoric monsters—the dinosaurs and the like.

I was transferred from the Presidency Gaol to the Alipore Central Gaol, and there I was given a little cell, about ten feet by nine. In front of it was a veranda and a small open yard. The wall enclosing the yard was a low one, about seven feet, and looking over it a strange sight confronted me. All manner of odd buildings—single storey, double storey, round, rectangular, curious roofings—rose all round, some over-topping the others. It seemed that the structures had grown one by one, being fitted in anyhow to take advantage of all the available space. Almost it looked like a jigsaw puzzle or a futurist attempt at the fantastic. And yet I was told that all the buildings had been arranged very methodically with a tower in the centre (which was a church for the Christian prisoners) and radiating lines. Being a city gaol, the area was limited and every little bit of it had to be utilized.

I had hardly recovered from my first view of the seemingly fantastic structures around me when a terrifying sight greeted me. Two chimneys, right in front of my cell and yard, were belching forth dense volumes of black smoke, and sometimes the wind blew this smoke in my direction, almost suffocating me. They were the chimneys of the gaol kitchens. I suggested to the Superintendent later that gas-masks might be provided to meet this offensive.

It was not an agreeable start, and the future was not inviting—to enjoy the unchanging prospect of the red-brick structures of Alipore

Gaol and to swallow and inhale the smoke of its kitchen chimneys. There were no trees or greenery in my yard. It was all paved and *pucca* and clean, except for the daily deposit of smoke, but it was also bare and cheerless. I could just see the tops of one or two trees in adjoining yards. They were barren of leaf or flower when I arrived. But gradually a mysterious change came over them and little bits of green were peeping out all over their branches. The leaves were coming out of the buds: they grew rapidly and covered the nakedness of the branches with their pleasant green. It was a delightful change which made even Alipore Gaol look gay and cheerful.

In one of these trees was a kite's nest which interested me, and I watched it often. The little ones were growing and learning the tricks of the trade, and sometimes they would swoop down with rapidity and amazing accuracy and snatch the bread out of a prisoner's hand, almost out of his mouth.

From sunset to sunrise (more or less) we were locked up in our cells, and the long winter evenings were not very easy to pass. I grew tired of reading or writing hour after hour, and would start walking up and down that little cell—four or five short steps forward and then back again. I remembered the bears at the zoo tramping up and down their cages. Sometimes when I felt particularly bored I took to my favourite remedy, the *shirshasana*—standing on the head!

The early part of the night was fairly quiet, and city sounds used to float in—the noise of the trams, a gramophone, or some one singing in the distance. It was pleasant to hear this faint and distant music. But there was not much peace at night, for the guards on duty tramped up and down, and every hour there was some kind of an inspection. Some officer came round with a lantern to make sure that none of us had escaped. At 3 a.m. every day, or rather night, there was a tremendous din, and a mighty sound of scraping and scrubbing. The kitchens had begun functioning.

There were vast numbers of warders and guards and officers and clerks in the Alipore Gaol, as also in the Presidency. Both these prisons housed a population about equal to that of Naini Prison—2,200 to 2,300—but the staff in each must have been more than double that of Naini. There were many European warders and retired Indian Army officers. It was evident that the British Empire functioned more intensively and more expensively in Calcutta than in U.P. A sign and a perpetual reminder of the might of the Empire was the cry that prisoners had to shout out when high officials approached them. "*Sarkar Salaam*" was the cry, lengthened out, and it was accompanied by certain physical movements of the body. The voices of the prisoners shouting out this cry came to me many times a day over my yard wall, and especially when the Superintendent passed by daily. I could just see over my seven-foot wall the top of the huge State umbrella under which the Superintendent marched.

Was this extraordinary cry—*sarkar salaam*—and the movements that went with it relics of old times, I wondered; or were they the invention of some inspired English official? I do not know, but I imagine that it was an English invention. It has a typical Anglo-Indian sound about it. Fortunately this cry does not prevail in the U.P. gaols or probably in any other province besides Bengal and Assam. The way this enforced salutation to the might of the *sarkar* is shouted out seemed to me very degrading.

One change for the better I noticed with pleasure in Alipore. The food of the ordinary prisoners was far superior to the U.P. prison food. In regard to gaol diet U.P. compares unfavourably with many provinces.

The brief winter was soon over, and spring raced by and summer began. It grew hotter day by day. I had never been fond of the Calcutta climate, and even a few days of it had made me stale and flat. In prison conditions were naturally far worse, and I did not prosper as the days went by. Lack of space for exercise and long lock-up hours in that climate probably affected my health a little and I lost weight rapidly. How I began to hate all locks and bolts and bars and walls!

After a month in Alipore I was allowed to take some exercise, outside my yard. This was an agreeable change and I could walk up and down under the main wall, morning and evening. Gradually I got accustomed to Alipore Gaol and the Calcutta climate; and even the kitchen, with its smoke and mighty din, became a tolerable nuisance. Other matters occupied my mind, other worries filled me. News from outside was not good.

60

DEMOCRACY IN EAST AND WEST

I was surprised to find in Alipore that no daily paper would be allowed to me after my conviction. As an under-trial prisoner I received the daily *Statesman*, of Calcutta, but this was stopped the day after my trial was over. In U.P., ever since 1932, a daily (chosen by the Government) was permitted to A Class or first division prisoners. So also in most other provinces, and I was fully under the impression that the same rule was applicable in Bengal. Instead of the daily, however, I was supplied with the weekly *Statesman*. This was evidently meant for retired English officials or businessmen who had gone back to England, and it contained a summary of Indian news likely to interest them. No foreign news at all was given and I missed it very much, as I used to follow it closely. Fortunately I was allowed to have the *Manchester Guardian Weekly*, and this kept me in touch with Europe and international affairs.

My arrest and trial in February coincided with upheavals and bitter conflicts in Europe. There was the ferment in France resulting in Fascist riots and the formation of a 'National' Government. And, far worse, in Austria Chancellor Dolfuss was shooting down workers and putting an end to the great edifice of social democracy there. The news of the Austrian bloodshed depressed me greatly. What an awful and bloody place this world was and how barbarous was man when he wanted to protect his vested interests! All over Europe and America Fascism seemed to be advancing. When Hitler came into power in Germany I had imagined that his regime could not possibly last long, as he was offering no solution of Germany's economic troubles. So also, as Fascism spread elsewhere, I consoled myself that it represented the last ditch of reaction. After it must come the breaking of the shackles. But I began to wonder if my wish was not father to my thought. Was it so obvious that this Fascist wave would retire so easily or so quickly? And even if conditions became intolerable for the Fascist dictatorships, would they not rather hurl their countries into devastating war rather than give in? What would be the result of such a conflict?

Meanwhile, Fascism of various kinds and shapes spread. Spain, that new 'Republic of Honest Men'—*los hombres honrados*—the very *Manchester Guardian* of governments, as some one called it, had gone far back and deep into reaction. All the fine phrases of its honest Liberal leaders had not kept it from sliding down. Everywhere Liberalism showed its utter ineffectiveness to face modern conditions. It clung to words and phrases, and thought that they could take the place of action. When a crisis came it simply faded off like the end of a film that is over.

I read the leading articles of the *Manchester Guardian* on the Austrian tragedy with deep interest and appreciation. "And what sort of Austria emerges from this bloody struggle? An Austria ruled with rifles and machine-guns by the most reactionary clique in Europe." "But why, if England stands for liberty, has its Prime Minister so little to say? We have heard his praises of dictatorships: we have heard him say how they 'make the soul of a nation live' and 'bestow a new vision and a new energy.' But a Prime Minister of England should have something to say of the tyrannies, in whatever country, which kill often the body, but more often, and with a worse death, the soul."

And why, if the *Manchester Guardian* stands for liberty, has it so little to say when liberty is crushed in India? We also have known not only bodily suffering, but that far worse ordeal of the soul.

"Austrian democracy has been destroyed, although to its everlasting glory it went down fighting and so created a legend that may re-kindle the spirit of European freedom some day in years to come."

"The Europe that is unfree has ceased to breathe; there is no flow or counterflow of healthy spirits; a gradual suffocation has set in, and only some violent convulsion or inner paroxysm and a striking out to the right and left can avert the mental coma that is approaching . . . Europe from the Rhine to the Urals is one great prison."

Moving passages which found an echo in my heart. But I wondered: what of India? How can it be that the *Manchester Guardian* or the many lovers of freedom who undoubtedly exist in England should be so oblivious to our fate? How can they miss seeing here what they condemn with such fervour elsewhere? It was a great English Liberal leader, trained in the nineteenth-century tradition, cautious by temperament, restrained in his language, who said twenty years ago, on the eve of the Great War:

"Sooner than be a silent witness of the tragic triumph of force over law, I would see this country of ours blotted out of the page of history." A brave thought, eloquently put, and the gallant youth of England went in their millions to vindicate it. But if an Indian ventures to make a statement similar to Mr Asquith's, what fate is his?

National psychology is a complicated affair. Most of us imagine how fair and impartial we are; it is always the other fellow, the other country that is wrong. Somewhere at the back of our minds we are convinced that we are not as others are: there is a difference which good breeding usually prevents us from emphasizing. And if we are fortunate enough to be an imperial race controlling the destinies of other countries, it is difficult not to believe that all is for the best in this best of all possible worlds, and those who agitate for change are self-seekers or deluded fools, ungrateful for the benefits they have received from us.

The British are an insular race, and long success and prosperity has made them look down on almost all others. For them, as some one has said, "*les nègres commencent à Calais*". But that is too general a statement. Perhaps the British upper-class division of the world would be somewhat as follows: (1) Britain, a long gap, and then (2) the British Dominions (white populations only) and America (Anglo-Saxons only, and not dagoes, wops, etc.), (3) Western Europe, (4) Rest of Europe, (5) South America (Latin races), a long gap, and then (6) the brown, yellow and black races of Asia and Africa, all bunched up more or less together.

How far we of the last of these classes are from the heights where our rulers live! Is it any wonder that their vision grows dim when they look towards us, and that we should irritate them when we talk of democracy and liberty? These words were not coined for our use. Was it not a great Liberal statesman, John Morley, who had declared that he could not conceive of democratic institutions in India even in the far, dim future? Democracy for India was, like Canada's fur coat, unsuited to her climate. And, later on, Britain's Labour Party, the standard-bearers of Socialism, the champions of the under-dog, presented us, in the flush of their triumph, with a revival of the Bengal Ordinance in 1924, and during their second government our fate was even worse. I am quite sure that none of them mean us ill, and when they address us in their best pulpit manner—'Dearly beloved brethren'—they feel a glow of conscious virtue. But, to them, we are not as they are and must be judged by other standards. It is difficult enough for an Englishman and a Frenchman to think alike because of linguistic and cultural differences; how much vaster must be the difference between an Englishman and an Asiatic?

Recently the House of Lords has been debating the question of Indian reform, and many illuminating speeches were delivered by noble lords. Among these was one by Lord Lytton, a former Governor of an Indian Province, who acted as Viceroy for a while. He has often been referred to as a liberal and sympathetic Governor. He is reported to have said[1] that "the Government of India was far more representative of India as a whole than the Congress politicians. The Government of India was able to speak in the name of officials, the Army, the Police, the Princes, the fighting regiments and both Muslims and Hindus, whereas the Congress politicians could not even speak on behalf of one of the great Indian communities." He went on to make his meaning quite clear: "When I speak of Indian opinion I am thinking of those on whose co-operation I had to rely and on whose co-operation the future Governors and Viceroys will have to rely."

Two interesting points emerge from his speech: the India that counts means those who help the British; and the British Government of India is the most representative and, therefore, democratic body in the country. That this argument should be advanced seriously shows that English words seem to change their meanings when they cross the Suez Canal. The next and obvious step in reasoning would be, that autocratic government is the most representative and democratic form because the King represents everybody. We get back to the divine right of kings and *"l'état, c'est moi!"*

As a matter of fact, even pure autocracy has had a distinguished advocate recently. Sir Malcolm Hailey, that ornament of the Indian Civil Service, speaking as Governor of the United Provinces at Benares on November 5, 1934, pleaded for autocracy in the Indian States. The advice was hardly needed, for no Indian State is at all likely to part with autocracy of its own free will. An interesting development has been the attempt to preserve this autocracy on the plea that democracy is failing in Europe. Sir Mirza Ismail, the Dewan of Mysore, has expressed his "surprise that

---

1. House of Lords, December 17, 1934.

radical reforms are advocated when parliamentary democracy is decaying everywhere. I am sure the conscience of the State feels that our present constitution is quite democratic enough for all practical purposes."[2] The 'conscience' of Mysore presumably is a metaphysical abstraction for the Ruler and his Dewan. The democracy that prevails in Mysore at present is indistinguishable from autocracy.

If democracy is not suited to India, it appears to be equally unsuitable for Egypt. I have just read a long despatch from Cairo in the *Statesman*[3] (for this daily is supplied to me now in my present gaol). We are told that the Premier, Nessim Pasha,

> has now aroused no little alarm in responsible-minded quarters owing to his declaration that he hoped to get the political parties to co-operate, especially the Wafd, and either to have a national conference or elections for a constituent assembly, in either case for the elaboration of a new Constitution. This can only mean in the end ... a return to the regime of the popular democratic government which history shows has always been disastrous for Egypt, since in the past it has ever pandered to the worst passions of the mob ... No one knowing anything of the inner working of Egyptian politics and of the people, doubts for one moment that elections will again result in the return of the Wafd with a majority. Unless something is done, therefore, to prevent this procedure, we shall within a short time be again saddled with an ultra-democratic anti-foreign revolutionary regime.

It is suggested that the elections should be "run" by administrative pressure "as a counterpoise to the Wafd," but, unhappily, the Premier "has too much the legal mind" to do any such thing. The only other course that remains, we are told, is for Whitehall to intervene and to "let it be known that it will not tolerate the return of a regime" of this kind.

What steps Whitehall may or may not take, or what will happen in Egypt I do not know.[4] But this argument put forward by presumably a

---

2. Mysore: June 21, 1934. See also note on page 547, post.
3. December 19, 1934.
4. There were widespread political riots in Egypt against the British occupation in November 1935.

liberty-loving Englishman does help us to understand a little, some of the complexities of the Egyptian and Indian situation. As the *Statesman* points out in a leading article: "The root evil has been that the way of life and attitude of mind of an ordinary Egyptian voter are inharmonious with the sort of way of life and attitude of mind out of which democracy is developed." This want of harmony is illustrated further on: "In Europe, democracies have often been brought down because there were too many parties; in Egypt the difficulty has been there only being one party, the Wafd."

In India we are told that our communal divisions come in the way of our democratic progress and, therefore, with incontrovertible logic, those divisions are perpetuated. We are further told that we are not united enough. In Egypt there are no communal divisions and it appears that the most perfect political unity prevails. And yet, this very unity becomes an obstacle in the way of democracy and freedom! Truly the path of democracy is straight and narrow. Democracy for an Eastern country seems to mean only one thing: to carry out the behests of the imperialist ruling power and not to touch any of its interests. Subject to that proviso, democratic freedom can flourish unchecked.

61

DESOLATION

And I yearn to lay my head
Where the grass is cool and sweet.
Mother, all the dreams are fled
From the tired child at thy feet.

A pril came. Rumours reached me in my cell in Alipore of happenings outside, rumours that were unpleasant and disturbing. The Superintendent of the gaol informed me casually one day that Mr Gandhi had withdrawn Civil Disobedience. I knew no more. The news was not welcome, and I felt sad at this winding-up of something that had meant so much to me for many years. And yet I reasoned with myself that the end was bound to come. I knew in my heart that some time or other Civil Disobedience would have to be wound up, for the time being at least. Individuals may hold out almost indefinitely, regardless of the consequences, but national organizations do not behave in this manner. I had no doubt that Gandhiji had interpreted correctly the mind of the country and of the great majority of Congressmen, and I tried to reconcile myself to the new development, unpleasant as it was.

I heard also vaguely of the new move to revive the old Swaraj Party in order to enter the legislatures. That too seemed inevitable, and I had long been of opinion that the Congress could not keep aloof from future elections. During the five months of my freedom outside prison I had tried to discourage this tendency, for I thought it premature and likely to divert attention both from direct action and from the development of new ideas of social change which were fermenting in the Congress ranks. The longer the crisis continued, I thought, the more would these ideas spread among our masses and intelligentsia and the realities underlying our political and economic situation be laid bare. As Lenin has said somewhere: "Any and every political crisis is useful because it brings to the light what was hidden, reveals the actual forces involved in politics; it exposes lies and deceptive phrases and fictions; it demonstrates comprehensively the facts, and forces on the people the understanding of what is the reality." I had hoped that this process would result in making the Congress a clearer-minded and a more compact body with a definite goal. Probably some of its weaker elements might drop out. That would be no loss. And when the time came for the ending of even theoretical direct action and a reversion to so-called constitutional and legal methods, the advanced and really active wing of the Congress would utilize even these methods from the larger point of view of our final objective.

That time apparently had come. But to my dismay I found that the people who had been the backbone of Civil Disobedience and effective work in the Congress were receding into the background, and others, who had taken no such part, were taking command.

Some days later the weekly *Statesman* came to me, and I read in it the statement which Gandhiji had issued when withdrawing Civil Disobedience. I read it with amazement and sinking of heart. Again and again I read it, and Civil Disobedience and much else vanished from my mind and other doubts and conflicts filled it. "This statement," wrote Gandhiji, "owes its inspiration to a personal chat with the inmates and associates of the Satyagraha Ashram . . . More especially is it due to a revealing information I got in the course of a conversation about a valued companion of long standing who was found reluctant to perform the full prison task, preferring his private studies to the allotted task. This was undoubtedly contrary to the rules of Satyagraha. More than the imperfection of the friend whom I love, more than ever it brought home to me my own imperfections. The friend said he had thought that I was aware of his weakness. I was blind. Blindness in a leader is unpardonable. I saw at once that I must for the time being remain the sole representative of civil resistance in action."

The imperfection or fault, if such it was, of the 'friend' was a very trivial affair. I confess that I have often been guilty of it and I am wholly unrepentant. But even if it was a serious matter, was a vast national movement involving scores of thousands directly and millions indirectly to be thrown out of gear because an individual had erred? This seemed to me a monstrous proposition and an immoral one. I cannot presume to speak of what is and what is not Satyagraha, but in my own little way

I have endeavoured to follow certain standards of conduct, and all those standards were shocked and upset by this statement of Gandhiji's. I knew that Gandhiji usually acts on instinct (I prefer to call it that than the 'inner voice' or an answer to prayer), and very often that instinct is right. He has repeatedly shown what a wonderful knack he has of sensing the mass mind and of acting at the psychological moment. The reasons which he afterwards adduces to justify his action are usually afterthoughts and seldom carry one very far. A leader or a man of action in a crisis almost always acts subconsciously and then thinks of the reasons for his action. I felt also that Gandhiji had acted rightly in suspending civil resistance. But the reason he had given seemed to me an insult to intelligence and an amazing performance for a leader of a national movement. He was perfectly entitled to treat his ashram inmates in any manner he liked; they had taken all kinds of pledges and accepted a certain regime. But the Congress had not done so; I had not done so. Why should we be tossed hither and thither for, what seemed to me, metaphysical and mystical reasons in which I was not interested? Was it conceivable to have any political movement on this basis? I had willingly accepted the moral aspect of Satyagraha as I understood it (within certain limits I admit). That basic aspect appealed to me and it seemed to raise politics to a higher and nobler level. I was prepared to agree that the end does not justify all kinds of means. But this new development or interpretation was something much more far-reaching and it held forth some possibilities which frightened me.

The whole statement frightened and oppressed me tremendously. And then finally the advice he gave to Congressmen was that "they must learn the art and beauty of self-denial and voluntary poverty. They must engage themselves in nation-building activities, the spread of khaddar through personal hand-spinning and hand-weaving, the spread of communal unity of hearts by irreproachable personal conduct towards one another in every walk of life, the banishing of untouchability in every shape or form in one's own person, the spread of total abstinence from intoxicating drinks and drugs by personal contact with individual addicts and generally by cultivating personal purity. These are services which provide maintenance on the poor man's scale. Those for whom the poor man's scale is not feasible should find a place in small unorganized industries of national importance which give a better wage."

This was the political programme that we were to follow. A vast distance seemed to separate him from me. With a stab of pain I felt that the chords of allegiance that had bound me to him for many years had snapped. For long a mental tussle had been going on within me. I had not understood or appreciated much that Gandhiji had done. His fasts and his concentration on other issues during the continuance of Civil Disobedience, when his comrades were in the grip of the struggle, his personal and self-created entanglements, which led him to the extraordinary position that, while out of prison, he was yet pledged to himself not to take part in the political movement, his new loyalties and pledges which put in the shade the old loyalty and pledge and job, undertaken together with many colleagues, while yet that job was unfinished, had all oppressed me. During my short period out of prison I had felt these and other differences more than ever. Gandhiji had stated that there were temperamental differences between us. They were perhaps more than temperamental, and I realized that I held clear and definite views about many matters which were opposed to his. And yet in the past I had tried to subordinate them, as far as I could, to what I conceived to be the larger loyalty—the cause of national freedom for which the Congress seemed to be working. I tried to be loyal and faithful to my leader and my colleagues, for in my spiritual make-up loyalty to a cause and to one's colleagues holds a high place. I fought many a battle within myself when I felt that I was being dragged away from the anchor of my spiritual faith. Somehow I managed to compromise. Perhaps I did wrong, for it can never be right for anyone to let go of that anchor. But in the conflict of ideals I clung to my loyalty to my colleagues, and hoped that the rush of events and the development of our struggle might dissolve the difficulties that troubled me, and bring my colleagues nearer to my view-point.

And now? Suddenly I felt very lonely in that cell of Alipore Gaol. Life seemed to be a dreary affair, a very wilderness of desolation. Of the many hard lessons that I had learnt, the hardest and the most painful now faced me: that it is not possible in any vital matter to rely on anyone. One must journey through life alone; to rely on others is to invite heartbreak.

Some of my accumulated irritation turned to religion and the religious outlook. What an enemy this was to clearness of thought and fixity of purpose, I thought; for was it not based on emotion and passion? Presuming to be spiritual, how far removed it was from real spirituality and things of the spirit. Thinking in terms of some other world, it had little conception of human values and social values and social justice. With its preconceived notions it deliberately shut its eyes to reality for fear that this might not fit in with them. It based itself on truth, and yet so sure was it of having discovered it, and the whole of it, that it did not take the trouble to search for it; all that concerned it was to tell others of it. The will to truth was not the same thing as the will to believe. It talked of peace and yet supported systems and organizations that could not exist but for violence. It condemned the violence of the sword, but what of the violence that comes quietly and often in peaceful garb and starves and kills; or worse still, without doing any outward physical injury, outrages the mind and crushes the spirit and breaks the heart?

And then I thought of him again who was the cause of this commotion within me. What a wonderful man was Gandhiji after all, with his amazing and almost irresistible charm and subtle power over people. His writings and his sayings conveyed little enough impression of the man behind; his personality was far bigger than they would lead one to think. And his services to India, how vast they had been. He had instilled courage and manhood in her people, and discipline and endurance, and the power of joyful sacrifice for a cause, and, with all his humility, pride. Courage is the one sure foundation of character, he had said; without courage there is no morality, no religion, no love. "One cannot follow truth or love so long as one is subject to fear." With all his horror of violence, he had told us that "cowardice is a thing even more hateful than violence". And "discipline is the pledge and guarantee that a man means business. There is no deliverance and no hope without sacrifice, discipline, and self-control. Mere sacrifice without discipline will be unavailing." Words only and pious phrases perhaps, rather platitudinous, but there was power behind the words, and India knew that this little man meant business.

He came to represent India to an amazing degree and to express the very spirit of that ancient and tortured land. Almost he was India, and his very failings were Indian failings. A slight to him was hardly a personal matter, it was an insult to the nation; and Viceroys and others who indulged in these disdainful gestures little realized what a dangerous crop they were sowing. I remember how hurt I was when I first learnt that the Pope had refused an interview to Gandhiji when he was returning from the Round Table Conference in December 1931. That refusal seemed to me an affront to India, and there can be no doubt that the refusal was intentional, though the affront was probably not thought of. The Catholic Church does not approve of saints or mahatmas outside its fold, and because some Protestant churchmen had called Gandhiji a great man of religion and a real Christian, it became all the more necessary for Rome to dissociate itself from this heresy.

Just about that time in Alipore Gaol, in April 1934, I read Bernard Shaw's new plays, and the preface to *On the Rocks*, with its debate between Christ and Pilate, fascinated me. It seemed to have a modern significance, when another empire faced another man of religion. "I say to you," Jesus says to Pilate in this preface, "cast out fear. Speak no more vain things to me about the greatness of Rome. The greatness of Rome, as you call it, is nothing but fear; fear of the past and fear of the future, fear of the poor, fear of the rich, fear of the High Priests, fear of the Jews and Greeks, who are learned, fear of the Gauls and Goths and Huns, who are barbarians, fear of the Carthage you destroyed to save you from fear of it, and now fear worse than ever, fear of Imperial Caesar, the idol you have yourself created, and fear of me, the penniless vagrant, buffeted and mocked, fear of everything except the rule of God; faith in nothing but blood and iron and gold. You, standing for Rome, are the universal coward; I, standing for the Kingdom of God, have braved everything, lost everything, and won an eternal crown."

But Gandhiji's greatness or his services to India or the tremendous debt I personally owed to him were not in question. In spite of all that, he might be hopelessly in the wrong in many matters. What, after all, was he aiming at? In spite of the closest association with him for many years I am not clear in my own mind about his objective. I doubt if he is clear himself. One step is enough for me, he says, and he does not try to peep into the future or to have a clearly conceived end before him. Look after the means and the end will take care of itself, he is never tired of repeating. Be good in your personal individual lives and all else will follow. That is not a political or scientific attitude, nor is it perhaps even an ethical attitude. It is narrowly moralist, and it begs the question: What is goodness? Is it merely an individual affair or a social affair? Gandhiji lays all stress on character and attaches little importance to intellectual training and development. Intellect without character is likely to be dangerous, but what is character without intellect? How, indeed, does character develop? Gandhiji has been compared to the medieval Christian saints, and much that he says seems to fit in with this. It does not fit in at all with modern psychological experience and method.

But however this may be, vagueness in an objective seems to me deplorable. Action to be effective must be directed to clearly conceived ends. Life is not all logic, and those ends will have to be varied from time to time to fit in with it, but some end must always be clearly envisaged.

I imagine that Gandhiji is not so vague about the objective as he sometimes appears to be. He is passionately desirous of going in a certain direction, but this is wholly at variance with modern ideas and conditions, and he has so far been unable to fit the two, or to chalk out all the intermediate steps leading to his goal. Hence, the appearance of vagueness and avoidance of clarity. But his general inclination has been clear enough for a quarter of a century, ever since he started formulating his philosophy in South Africa. I do not know if those early writings still represent his views. I doubt if they do so in their entirety, but they do help us to understand the background of his thought.

"India's salvation consists," he wrote in 1909, "in unlearning what she has learnt during the last fifty years. The railways, telegraphs, hospitals, lawyers, doctors, and such-like have all to go; and the so-called upper classes have to learn consciously, religiously, and deliberately the simple peasant life, knowing it to be a life giving true happiness." And again: "Every time I get into a railway car or use a motor-bus I know that I am doing violence to my sense of what is right"; "to attempt to reform the world by means of highly artificial and speedy locomotion is to attempt the impossible."

All this seems to me utterly wrong and harmful doctrine, and impossible of achievement. Behind it lies Gandhiji's love and praise of poverty and suffering and the ascetic life. For him progress and civilization consist not in the multiplication of wants, of higher standards of living, "but in the deliberate and voluntary restriction of wants, which promotes real happiness and contentment, and increases the capacity for service." If these premises are once accepted it becomes easy to follow the rest of

Gandhiji's thought and to have a better understanding of his activities. But most of us do not accept those premises and yet we complain later on when we find that his activities are not to our liking.

Personally I dislike the praise of poverty and suffering. I do not think they are at all desirable, and they ought to be abolished. Nor do I appreciate the ascetic life as a social ideal, though it may suit individuals. I understand and appreciate simplicity, equality, self-control, but not the mortification of the flesh. Just as an athlete requires to train his body, I believe that the mind and habits have also to be trained and brought under control. It would be absurd to expect that a person who is given to too much self-indulgence can endure much suffering or show unusual self-control or behave like a hero when the crisis comes. To be in good moral condition requires at least as much training as to be in good physical condition. But that certainly does not mean asceticism or self-mortification.

Nor do I appreciate in the least the idealization of the 'simple peasant life'. I have almost a horror of it, and instead of submitting to it myself I want to drag out even the peasantry from it, not to urbanization, but to the spread of urban cultural facilities to rural areas. Far from this life giving me true happiness, it would be almost as bad as imprisonment for me. What is there in the "Man with the Hoe" to idealize over? Crushed and exploited for innumerable generations he is only little removed from the animals who keep him company.

Who made him dead to rapture and despair,
A thing that grieves not and that never hopes,
Stolid and stunned, a brother to the ox?

This desire to get away from the mind of man to primitive conditions where mind does not count, seems to me quite incomprehensible. The very thing that is the glory and triumph of man is decried and discouraged, and a physical environment which will oppress the mind and prevent its growth is considered desirable. Present-day civilization is full of evils, but it is also full of good; and it has the capacity in it to rid itself of those evils. To destroy it root and branch is to remove that capacity from it and revert to a dull, sunless and miserable existence. But even if that were desirable it is an impossible undertaking. We cannot stop the river of change or cut ourselves adrift from it, and psychologically we who have eaten of the apple of Eden cannot forget that taste and go back to primitiveness.

It is difficult to argue this, for the two standpoints are utterly different. Gandhiji is always thinking in terms of personal salvation and of sin, while most of us have society's welfare uppermost in our minds. I find it difficult to grasp the idea of sin, and perhaps it is because of this that I cannot appreciate Gandhiji's general outlook. He is not out to change society or the social structure, he devotes himself to the eradication of sin from individuals. "The follower of *swadeshi*," he has written, "never takes upon himself the vain task of trying to reform the world, for he believes that the world is moved and always will be moved according to the rules set by God." And yet he is aggressive enough in his attempts to reform the world; but the reform he aims at is individual reform, the conquest over the senses and the desire to indulge them, which is sin. Probably he will agree with the definition of liberty which an able Roman Catholic writer on Fascism has given: "Liberty is no more than freedom from the bondage of sin." How almost identical this is with the words of the Bishop of London written two hundred years ago: "The Freedom which Christianity gives is Freedom from the Bondage of sin and Satan and from the Dominion of Men's Lusts and Passions and inordinate Desires."[1]

If this standpoint is once appreciated then one begins to understand a little Gandhiji's attitude to sex, extraordinary as that seems to the average person today. For him "any union is a crime when the desire for progeny is absent", and "the adoption of artificial methods must result in imbecility and nervous prostration." "It is wrong and immoral to seek to escape the consequences of one's acts . . . It is bad for him to indulge his appetite and then escape the consequences by taking tonics or other medicines. It is still worse for a person to indulge his animal passions and escape the consequences of his acts."

Personally I find this attitude unnatural and shocking, and if he is right, then I am a criminal on the verge of imbecility and nervous prostration. The Roman Catholics have also vigorously opposed birth-control, but they have not carried their argument to the logical limit as Gandhiji has done. They have temporized and compromised with what

---

1. This letter is quoted on page 394, ante.

they considered to be human nature.[2] But Gandhiji has gone to the extreme limit of his argument and does not recognize the validity or necessity of the sexual act at any time except for the sake of children; he refuses to recognize any natural sex attraction between man and woman. "But I am told," he says, "that this is an impossible ideal, that I do not take account of the natural attraction between man and woman. I refuse to believe that the sensual affinity, referred to here, can be at all regarded as natural; in that case the deluge would soon be over us. The natural affinity between man and woman is the attraction between brother and sister, mother and son, or father and daughter. It is this natural attraction that sustains the world." And more emphatically still: "No, I must declare with all the power I can command that sensual attraction, even between husband and wife, is unnatural."

In these days of the Oedipus complex and Freud and the spread of psychoanalytical ideas this emphatic statement of belief sounds strange and distant. One can accept it as an act of faith or reject it. There is no half-way house, for it is a question of faith, not of reason. For my part I think Gandhiji is absolutely wrong in this matter. His advice may fit in with some cases, but as a general policy it can only lead to frustration, inhibition, neurosis, and all manner of physical and nervous ills. Sexual restraint is certainly desirable, but I doubt if Gandhiji's doctrine is likely to result in this to any widespread extent. It is too extreme, and most people decide that it is beyond their capacity and go their usual ways, or there is friction between husband and wife. Evidently Gandhiji thinks that birth-control methods necessarily mean inordinate indulgence in the sex act, and that if the sexual affinity between man and woman is admitted, every man will run after every woman, and vice versa. Neither inference is justified, and I do not know why he is so obsessed by this problem of sex, important as it is. For him it is a 'soot or whitewash' question, there are no intermediate shades. At either end he takes up an extreme position which seems to me most abnormal and unnatural.

---

2. Pope Pius XI in his Encyclical on Christian Marriage, issued on December 31, 1931, says: "Nor must married people be considered to act against the order of nature if they make use of their rights according to sound and natural reason, even though no new life can thence arise on account of circumstance of time or the existence of some defect." The "circumstance of time" apparently refers to the so-called "safe period" when conception is unlikely.

Perhaps this is a reaction from the deluge of literature on sexology that is descending on us in these days. I presume I am a normal individual and sex has played its part in my life, but it has not obsessed me or diverted me from my other activities. It has been a subordinate part.

Essentially, his attitude is that of the ascetic who has turned his back to the world and its ways, who denies life and considers it evil. For an ascetic that is natural, but it seems far-fetched to apply it to men and women of the world who accept life and try to make the most of it. And in avoiding one evil he puts up with many other and graver evils.

I have drifted to other topics, but in those distressful days in Alipore Gaol all these ideas crowded in my mind, not in logical order or sequence, but in a wild jumble which confused me and oppressed me. Above all there was the feeling of loneliness and desolation, heightened by the stifling atmosphere of the gaol and my lonely little cell. If I had been outside the shock would have been more momentary, and I would have adjusted myself sooner to new conditions, and found relief in expression and action. Inside the prison there was no such relief, and I spent some miserable days. Fortunately for myself I am resilient and recover soon from attacks of pessimism. I began to grow out of my depression, and then I had an interview in gaol with Kamala. That cheered me up tremendously, and my feeling of isolation left me. Whatever happened, I felt, we had one another.

62

PARADOXES

People who do not know Gandhiji personally and have only read his writings are apt to think that he is a priestly type, extremely puritanical, long-faced, Calvinistic, and a kill-joy, something like the "priests in black gowns walking their rounds." But his writings do him an injustice; he is far greater than what he writes, and it is not quite fair to quote what he has written and criticize it. He is the very opposite of the Calvinistic priestly type. His smile is delightful, his laughter infectious, and he radiates light-heartedness. There is something childlike about him which is full of charm. When he enters a room he brings a breath of fresh air with him which lightens the atmosphere.

He is an extraordinary paradox. I suppose all outstanding men are so to some extent. For years I have puzzled over this problem: why with all his love and solicitude for the underdog he yet supports a system which inevitably produces it and crushes it; why with all his passion for non-violence he is in favour of a political and social structure which is wholly based on violence and coercion? Perhaps it is not correct to say that he is in favour of such a system; he is more or less of a philosophical anarchist. But as the ideal anarchist state is too far off still and cannot easily be conceived, he accepts the present order. It is not I think a question of means, that he objects, as he does, to the use of violence in bringing about a change. Quite apart from the methods to be adopted for changing the existing order, an ideal objective can be envisaged, something that is possible of achievement in the not distant future.

Sometimes he calls himself a socialist, but he uses the word in a sense peculiar to himself which has little or nothing to do with the economic framework of society which usually goes by the name of socialism. Following his lead a number of prominent Congressmen have taken to the use of that word, meaning thereby a kind of muddled humanitarianism. They err in distinguished company in the use of this vague political terminology, for they are but following the example of the Prime Minister of the British National Government.[1] I know that Gandhiji is not ignorant of the subject, for he has read many books on economics and socialism and even Marxism, and has discussed it with others. But I am becoming more and more convinced that in vital matters the mind by itself does not carry us far. "If your heart does not want to," said William James, "your head will assuredly never make you believe." The emotions govern the general outlook and control the mind. Our conversations, whether they are religious, political or economic, are really based on emotion or instinct. As Schopenhauer has said: "Man can do what he wills, but he cannot will what he will will."

Gandhiji underwent a tremendous conversion during his early days in South Africa, and this shook him up greatly and altered his whole outlook on life. Since then he has had a fixed basis for all his ideas, and his mind is hardly an open mind. He listens with the greatest patience and attention to people who make new suggestions to him, but behind all his courteous interest one has the impression that one is addressing a closed door. He is so firmly anchored to some ideas that everything else seems unimportant. To insist on other and secondary matters would be a distraction and a distortion of the larger scheme. To hold on to that anchor would necessarily result in a proper adjustment of these other matters. If the means are right, the end is bound to be right.

That, I think, is the main background of his thought. He suspects also socialism, and more particularly Marxism, because of their association with violence. The very words 'class war' breathe conflict and violence and are thus repugnant to him. He has also no desire to raise the standards of the masses beyond a certain very modest competence, for higher standards and leisure may lead to self-indulgence and sin. It is bad enough that the handful of the well-to-do are self-indulgent, it would be much worse if their numbers were added to. Some such inference can be drawn from a letter he wrote in 1926. This was in answer to a letter that came to him from England during the great coal lock-out or strike. His correspondent was advancing the argument that the miners will be beaten

---

1. Mr Ramsay MacDonald in the course of his message to the federation of Conservative and Unionist Associations at Edinburgh in January 1935 said: "The difficulties of the times make integration and concentration essential for every people. This is the true Socialism, as it is also the true Nationalism—and, for that matter, the true Individualism."

in the struggle because there are too many of them and they should therefore use contraceptives and limit their numbers. In the course of his reply Gandhiji said: "Lastly, if the mine-owners are in the wrong and still win, they will do so not because the miners overbreed, but because the miners have not learnt the lesson of restraint all along the line. If the miners had no children, they would have no incentive for any betterment and no provable cause for a rise in wages. Need they drink, gamble, smoke? Will it be any answer to say that mine-owners do all these things and yet have the upper hand? If the miners do not claim to be better than the capitalist, what right have they to ask for the world's sympathy? Is it to multiply capitalists and strengthen capitalism? We are called upon to pay homage to democracy under a promise of a better world when it reigns supreme. Let us not reproduce on a vast scale the evils we choose to ascribe to capitalist and capitalism."[2]

As I read this, the starved and pinched faces of the English miners and their wives and children came before me, as I had seen them in that summer of 1926, struggling helplessly and pitifully against the monstrous system that crushed them. Gandhiji's facts are not quite correct, for the miners were not asking for a rise in wages; they were fighting against a reduction and had been locked out. But this need not concern us now. Nor need the question of the use of contraceptives by miners concern us, although it was a somewhat remarkable suggestion for the solution of industrial conflicts. I have quoted from Gandhiji's reply to help in the understanding of his outlook on labour matters and the usual demand for a rise in the workers' standard of living. That outlook is as far removed from the socialistic, or for the matter of that the capitalistic, as anything can be. To say that science and industrial technique today can demonstrably feed, clothe and house everybody and raise their standards of living very greatly, if vested interests did not intervene, does not interest him much, for he is not keen on those results, beyond a certain limit. The promise of socialism therefore holds no attraction for him, and capitalism is only partly tolerable because it circumscribes the evil. He dislikes both, but puts up with the latter for the present as a lesser evil and as something which exists and of which he has to take cognizance.

I may be wrong perhaps in imputing these ideas to him, but I do feel

---

2. This letter is quoted in *Self-Restraint vs. Self-Indulgence*, by M.K. Gandhi.

that he tends to think in this manner, and the paradoxes and confusions in his utterances that trouble us are really due to entirely different premises from which he starts. He does not want people to make an ideal of ever-increasing comfort and leisure, but to think of the moral life, give up their bad habits, to indulge themselves less and less, and thus to develop themselves individually and spiritually. And those who wish to serve the masses have not so much to raise them materially as to go down themselves to their level and mix with them on equal terms. In so doing inevitably they will help in raising them somewhat. That, according to him, is true democracy. "Many have despaired of resisting me," he writes in a statement he issued on 17th September, 1934. "This is a humiliating revelation to me, a born democrat. I make that claim, if complete identification with the poorest of mankind, longing to live no better than they, and a corresponding conscious effort to approach that level to the best of one's ability, can entitle one to make it."

With this argument and outlook probably no modern democrat, capitalist, or socialist, will agree, except in so far as it is indecent and improper to cut ourselves off from the masses and flaunt our luxury and far higher standards in the faces of the vast majority of those who lack the barest necessities. But a man with the old religious outlook may find some agreement, for both are emotionally tied up with the past and are always thinking in terms of that past. They think more of what has been than of what is or what is going to be. There is all the difference in the world between the psychological urge to the past and to the future. In the old world it was difficult to think of raising the general material level of the masses. The poor were always with us. The handful of rich men were then an essential part of the social fabric, they were necessary to the productive system. And so the moralist, the reformer, and the sensitive man, accepted them, but at the same time tried to impress them with their obligations to their needy brethren. They were to be the trustees of the poor. They were to be charitable. And charity became one of the major virtues ordained by religion. Gandhiji is always laying stress on this idea of trusteeship of the feudal prince, of the big landlord, of the capitalist. He follows a long succession of men of religion. The Pope has declared that "the rich must consider themselves the servants of the Almighty as well as the guardians and the distributors of his wealth, to whom Jesus Christ himself entrusted the fate of the poor." Popular

Hinduism and Islam repeat this idea and are always calling upon the rich to be charitable, and they respond by building temples or mosques or dharamshalas, or giving, out of their abundance, coppers or silver to the poor and feeling very virtuous in consequence.

A striking passage illustrating this old-world religious attitude occurs in the famous Encyclical *Rerum Novarum* of Pope Leo XIII issued in May 1891. Continuing his argument dealing with the new industrial conditions, he says:

> To suffer and to endure, therefore, is the lot of humanity; let men try as they may, no strength and no artifice will ever succeed in banishing from human life the ills and troubles which beset it. If any there are who pretend differently—who hold out to a hard-pressed people freedom from pain and trouble, undisturbed repose and constant enjoyment— they cheat the people and impose upon them, and their lying promises will only make the evil worse than before. There is nothing more useful than to look at the world as it really is—and at the same time look elsewhere for a remedy to its troubles.

Further on we are told where this 'elsewhere' is:

> The things of the earth cannot be understood or valued rightly without taking into consideration the life to come, the life that will last for ever ...The great truth which we learn from Nature herself is also the grand Christian dogma on which religion rests as on its base—that when we have done with this present life then we shall really begin to live. God has not created us for the perishable and transitory things of the earth, but for things heavenly and everlasting; He has given us the world as a place of exile, and not as our true country. Money and the other things which men call good and desirable—we may have them in abundance or we may want them altogether; as far as eternal happiness is concerned, it is no matter . . .

This religious attitude is bound up with the world of long ago when the only possible escape from present misery was in the hope of a world to come. But though conditions changed and raised the human level in material prosperity beyond the wildest dreams of the past, the stranglehold of that past continued, the stress now being laid on certain vague, unmeasurable spiritual values. The Catholics look back to the twelfth and thirteenth centuries—the very period which is called the 'Dark Age' by others—as the Golden Age of Christianity, when saints flourished, and Christian rulers sallied forth to fight in the Crusades, and Gothic cathedrals grew up. That was the age, according to them "of true Christian democracy which was then realized under the control of the medieval guilds, more fully than it has ever been before or since." Muslims look back with longing to the "democracy of Islam" under the early Khalifs, and to their amazing career of victory. Hindus think likewise of the Vedic and Epic Periods, and dream of a *Rama Raj*. And yet all history tells us that the great masses of the people lived in utter misery in those past days, lacking food and the barest necessaries of life. A handful of people at the top may have indulged in the spiritual life, having the leisure and means to do so, but for the others, it is difficult to imagine them doing anything but struggling for bare sustenance. To a person who is starving, cultural and spiritual progress is highly unlikely; his thoughts will be concentrated on food and how to get it.

The industrial age has brought many evils that loom large before us; but we are apt to forget that, taking the world as a whole, and especially the parts that are most industrialized, it has laid down a basis of material well-being which makes cultural and spiritual progress far easier for large numbers. This is not all evident in India or other colonial countries as we have not profited by industrialism. We have only been exploited by it and in many respects made worse, even materially, and more so culturally and spiritually. The fault is not of industrialism but of foreign domination. The so-called Westernization in India has actually, for the time being, strengthened feudalism, and instead of solving any of our problems has simply intensified them.

That has been our misfortune, and we must not allow it to colour our vision of the world today. For under present conditions the rich man is no longer a necessary or a desirable part of the productive system or of society as a whole. He is redundant and he is always coming in the way. And the old business of the priest to ask the rich to be charitable and the poor to be resigned, grateful for their lot, thrifty and well-behaved, has lost its meaning. Human resources have grown tremendously and can face and solve the world's problems. Many of the rich have become definitely parasitical and the existence of a parasite class is not only a hindrance but an enormous waste of these resources. That class and the system that breeds them actually prevent work and production and encourage the workless at either end of the scale, both those who live on other people's labour and those who have no work to do and famish. Gandhiji himself wrote some time ago: "To a people famishing and idle, the only acceptable form in which God dare appear is work and promise of food as wages. God created man to work for his food, and said that those who ate without work were thieves."

To try to understand the complex problems of the modern world by an application of ancient methods and formulae when these problems did not exist, to use out-of-date phrases in regard to them, is to produce confusion and to invite failure. The very idea of private property, which seems to some people one of the fundamental notions of the world, has been an ever-changing one. Slaves were property at one time, and so were women and children, the seigneur's right to the bride's first night, roads, temples, ferries, bridges, public utilities, air and land. Animals are still property, though legislation has in many countries limited the rights of ownership. During war-time there is a continuous infringement of property rights. Property today is becoming more and more intangible, the possession of shares, a certain amount of credit, etc. As the conception of property changes, the State interferes more and more, public opinion demands, and the law enforces, a limitation of the anarchic rights of property-owners. All manner of heavy taxes, which are in the nature of confiscation, swallow up individual property rights for the public good. The public good becomes the basis of public policy, and a man may not act contrary to this public good even to protect his property rights. After all, the vast majority of people had no property rights in the past, they were themselves property owned by others. Even today a very small number have such rights. We hear a great deal of vested interests. Today a new vested interest has come to be recognized, that of every man and woman to live and labour and enjoy the fruits of labour. Because of these changing conceptions property and capital do not vanish, they are diffused, and the power over others, which a concentration of them gave to a few, is taken back by society as a whole.

Gandhiji wants to improve the individual internally, morally and spiritually, and thereby to change the external environment. He wants people to give up bad habits and indulgences and to become pure. He lays stress on sexual abstinence, on the giving up of drink, smoking, etc. Opinions may differ about the relative wickedness of these indulgences, but can there be any doubt that even from the individual point of view, and much more so from the social, these personal failings are less harmful than covetousness, selfishness, acquisitiveness, the fierce conflicts of individuals for personal gain, the ruthless struggles of groups and classes, the inhuman suppression and exploitation of one group by another, the terrible wars between nations? Of course he detests all this violence and degrading conflict. But are they not inherent in the acquisitive society of today with its law that the strong must prey on the weak, and its motto, that, as of old, "they shall take who have the power and they shall keep who can"? The profit motive today inevitably leads to conflict. The whole system protects and gives every scope to man's predatory instincts; it encourages some finer instincts no doubt, but much more so the baser instincts of man. Success means the knocking down of others and mounting on their vanquished selves. If these motives and ambitions are encouraged by society and attract the best of our people, does Gandhiji think that he can achieve his ideal—the moral man—in this environment? He wants to develop the spirit of service; he will succeed in the case of some individuals, but so long as society puts forward as exemplars the victors of an acquisitive society and the chief urge as the personal profit motive, the vast majority will follow this course.

But the problem is no longer merely a moral or an ethical one. It is a practical and urgent problem of today, for the world is in a hopeless muddle, and some way out must be found. We cannot wait, Micawber-like, for something to turn up. Nor can we live by negation alone criticizing the evil aspects of capitalism, socialism, communism, etc., and hoping vaguely for the golden mean, which will produce a happy compromise combining the best features of all systems, old and new. The malady has to be diagnosed and the cure suggested and worked for. It is quite certain that we cannot stand where we are, nationally and internationally; we may try to go back or we may push forward. Probably there is no choice in the matter, for going back seems inconceivable.

And yet many of Gandhiji's activities might lead one to think that he wants to go back to the narrowest autarchy, not only a self-sufficient nation, but almost a self-sufficient village. In primitive communities the village was more or less self-sufficient and fed and clothed itself and otherwise provided for its needs. Of necessity that means an extremely low standard of living. I do not think Gandhiji is permanently aiming at this, for it is an impossible objective. The huge populations of today would not be able even to subsist in some countries, they would not tolerate this reversion to scarcity and starvation. It is possible, I think, that in an agricultural country like India, so very low is our present standard, that there might be a slight improvement for the masses with the development of village industries. But we are tied up, as every country is tied up, with the rest of the world, and it seems to me quite impossible for us to cut adrift. We must think, therefore, in terms of the world, and in these terms a narrow autarchy is out of the question. Personally I consider it undesirable from every point of view.

Inevitably we are led to the only possible solution—the establishment of a socialist order, first within national boundaries, and eventually in the world as a whole, with a controlled production and distribution of wealth for the public good. How this is to be brought about is another matter, but it is clear that the good of a nation or of mankind must not be held up because some people who profit by the existing order object to the change. If political or social institutions stand in the way of such a change, they have to be removed. To compromise with them at the cost of that desirable and practical ideal would be a gross betrayal. Such a change may partly be forced or expedited by world conditions, but it can hardly take place without the willing consent or acquiescence of the great majority of the people concerned. They have therefore to be converted and won over to it. Conspiratorial violence of a small group will not help. Naturally efforts must be made to win over even those who profit by the existing system, but it is highly unlikely that any large percentage of them will be converted.

The khadi movement, hand-spinning and hand-weaving, which is Gandhiji's special favourite, is an intensification of individualism in production, and is thus a throw-back to the pre-industrial age. As a solution of any vital present-day problem it cannot be taken seriously, and it produces a mentality which may become an obstacle to growth in the right direction. Nevertheless as a temporary measure I am convinced that it has served a useful purpose, and it is likely to be helpful for some time to come, so long as the State itself does not undertake the rightful solution of agrarian and industrial problems on a country-wide scale. There is tremendous unrecorded unemployment in India and even greater partial unemployment in rural areas. No attempt has been made by the State to combat this unemployment, or help in any way the unemployed. Economically khadi has been of some little help to these wholly and partially unemployed, and because this improvement has come from their own efforts, it has raised their self-respect and given them some feeling of confidence. The most marked result has indeed been a psychological one. Khadi tried with some success to bridge the gap between the city and the village. It brought nearer to each other the middle-class intelligentsia and the peasantry. Clothing has a marked psychological effect on the wearer as well as the beholder, and the adoption of the simple white khadi dress by the middle classes resulted in a growth of simplicity, a lessening of vulgarity and ostentation, and a feeling of unity with the masses. The lower middle classes no longer tried to ape the richer classes in the matter of clothes or feel humiliated in their cheaper attire. Indeed they felt not only dignified but a little superior to those who still flaunted silks and satins. Even the poorest felt something of this dignity and self-respect. It was difficult in a large khadi-clad gathering to distinguish between the rich and the poor, and a spirit of camaraderie grew up. Khadi undoubtedly helped the Congress to reach the masses. It became the uniform of national freedom.

Khadi also became a check on the ever-present tendency of the mill-owners to raise the prices of their stuffs. These mill-owners in India were only kept in check in the past by foreign competition, especially that of Lancashire. Whenever this competition ceased, as during the World War, cloth prices soared up in India to extraordinary heights and vast sums were made by the Indian mills. The swadeshi and foreign-cloth boycott movements later on also helped these mills greatly, but the presence of khadi made a difference and prices could not go up as high as they might otherwise have done. Indeed the mills exploited the khadi sentiment of the people (and so did Japan) by manufacturing coarse cloths which were almost indistinguishable from the hand-spun and hand-woven article. In the event of another emergency arising, like a war, resulting in a stoppage of foreign cloth, it is unlikely now that the Indian mill-owners will be able to exploit the consumers to the extent they did from 1914 onwards. The khadi movement will prevent that, and the khadi organization has the capacity in it to spread out at short notice.

In spite of all these present-day advantages of the khadi movement in India it seems to me after all a transitional affair. It may continue even later on as an auxiliary movement, easing the change-over to a higher economy. But the main drive in future will have to be a complete overhauling of the agrarian system and the growth of industry. No tinkering with the land, and a multitude of commissions costing lakhs of rupees and suggesting trivial changes in the superstructure, will do the slightest good. The land system which we have is collapsing before our eyes, and it is a hindrance to production, distribution and any rational and large-scale operations. Only a radical change in it, putting an end to the little holdings and introducing organized collective and co-operative enterprises, and thus increasing the yield greatly with much less effort, will meet modern conditions. The land will not and cannot absorb all our people, and large-scale operations will (as Gandhiji fears) lessen the workers required on the land. The others must turn, partly it may be, to small-scale industry, but in the main to large-scale socialized industries and social services.

Khadi has certainly brought some relief in many areas, but this very success that it has attained has an element of danger. It means that it is propping up a decaying land system and delaying, to that extent, the change-over to a better system. The effect is not substantial enough to make a marked difference, but the tendency is there. For the tenant or the small peasant proprietor, his share of the produce of the land is no longer enough to keep him going even on the very low level he has reached. He has to find extraneous aids to his meagre income or, as he does usually, get more into debt, in order to pay his rent or revenue. The additional income thus helps the landlord or the State to realize their share which otherwise they might be unable to do. In the event of the additional income being substantial enough it is likely eventually the rent will rise and catch up to it. Under the present system most of the additional labour of the tenant and his attempts to be thrifty will ultimately benefit the landlord. As far as I can remember, Henry George in his *Progress and Poverty* has dealt with this point, giving instances, especially of Ireland.

Gandhiji's attempt to revive village industries is an extension of his khadi programme. It will do immediate good, part of it more or less permanent, most of it temporary. It will help the villager in his present distress and revive certain artistic and cultural values which were in danger of dying. But in so far as it is a revolt against machinery and industrialism it will not succeed. In a recent article on Village Industries in the *Harijan* Gandhiji writes: "Mechanization is good when hands are too few for the work intended to be accomplished. It is an evil when there are more hands than required for the work, as is the case of India . . . The problem with us is not how to find leisure for the teeming millions inhabiting our villages. The problem is how to utilize their idle hours, which are equal to the working days of six months in the year." This objection applies in varying measure to all the countries suffering from unemployment. But the fault surely is not that there is not work to do, but that under the present profit system the work is not profitable enough to the employers. There is an abundance of work simply calling out to be done—the building of roads, irrigation schemes, houses, the spread of sanitation and medical facilities, of industry, electricity, social and cultural services, education, and the provision of the scores of necessary articles that the people lack. All our millions can work hard for the next fifty years without exhausting the present possibilities. But that can only be done if the urge is social improvement and not the profit motive, and if the community organizes it for the general good. The Russian Soviet Union, whatever other shortcomings it may possess, has no unemployed. Our people are idle not for lack of work, but because no facilities for work and cultural improvement are provided for them. The abolition of child labour, the provision of compulsory education up to a reasonable age, would take boys and girls off from the ranks of labour or the unemployed, and relieve the labour market of the weight of tens of millions of prospective workers.

Gandhiji has tried, with some success, to improve the *charkha* and the *takli* and increase their productive capacities. That is an attempt to improve the tool and the machine, and if the improvement continues (it is quite conceivable to have cottage industries worked by electricity), the profit motive will again step in and produce what is called over-production and unemployment. Village industries without being tacked on to some modern industrial technique can never provide even the essential material and cultural goods that we need today. And they cannot compete with the machine. Is it desirable or possible for us to stop the functioning of big-scale machinery in our country? Gandhiji has said repeatedly that he is not against machinery as such; he seems to think that it is out of place in India today. But can we wind up the basic industries, such as iron and steel, or even the lighter ones that already exist?

It is obvious that we cannot do so. If we have railways, bridges, transport facilities, etc., we must either produce them ourselves or depend on others. If we want to have the means of defence we must not only have the basic industries but a highly developed industrial system. No country today is really independent or capable of resisting aggression unless it is industrially developed. One basic industry demands another for its support and as a complement to it, and finally we have the machine-building industry itself. With all these basic industries functioning it is inevitable that the lighter industries should spread. There is no stopping this process, for not only is our material and cultural progress bound up with it, but also our freedom itself. And the more big industry spreads the less can small-scale village industries compete with it. They may have some chance of survival under a socialist system, but none under capitalism, and even under socialism they can only exist as cottage industries specializing in particular goods which are not manufactured on a mass scale.

Some Congress leaders are frightened of industrialization, and imagine that the present-day troubles of the industrial countries are due to mass production. That is a strange misreading of the situation.[3] If the masses lack anything, is it bad to produce it in sufficient quantities for them? Is it preferable for them to continue in want rather than have mass production? The fault obviously is not in the production but in the folly and inadequacy of the distributive system.

Another difficulty which the promoters of village industries have to face is the dependence of our agriculture on the world market. The peasant is forced to grow commercial crops and to depend on world prices. While these prices vary he has to pay his rent or revenue in hard cash. He has to raise this money somehow, or at any rate he tries to do

---

3. Sardar Vallabhbhai Patel speaking at Ahmedabad on January 3, 1935: "True socialism lies in the development of village industries. We do not want to reproduce in our country the chaotic conditions prevalent in the Western countries consequent on mass-production."

so, and so he sows the crops which he thinks will bring him the best price. He cannot afford to grow what he himself needs to make himself and his family self-sufficient even in the matter of food.

In recent years the fall in agricultural prices of most food grains and other articles suddenly led millions of the peasantry, especially in U.P. and Behar, to cultivate sugar-cane. A tariff on sugar had resulted in sugar factories cropping up like mushrooms, and sugar-cane was in great demand. But the supply was soon far in excess of the demand, and the factory owners cruelly exploited the peasantry, and the price fell.

These few considerations and a host of others seem to me to exclude the possibility or the desirability of any narrow autarchichal solution of our agrarian and industrial problems. Indeed they affect every phase of our national life. We cannot take refuge in vague and emotional phrases, but must face these facts and adapt ourselves to them, so that we may become the subjects of history instead of being its helpless objects.

Again I think of the paradox that is Gandhiji.[4] With all his keen intellect and passion for bettering the downtrodden and oppressed, why does he support a system, and a system which is obviously decaying, which creates this misery and waste? He seeks a way out, it is true, but is not that way to the past barred and bolted? And meanwhile he blesses all the relics of the old order which stand as obstacles in the way of advance— the feudal States, the big zamindaris and taluqadaris, the present capitalist system. Is it reasonable to believe in the theory of trusteeship—to give unchecked power and wealth to an individual and to expect him to use it entirely for the public good? Are the best of us so perfect as to be trusted in this way? Even Plato's philosopher-kings could hardly have borne this burden worthily. And is it good for the others to have even these benevolent supermen over them? But there are no supermen or

---

4. In one of his speeches at the Round Table Conference in London in 1931, Gandhiji said:"Above all, the Congress represents, in its essence, the dumb semi-starved millions scattered over the length and breadth of the land in its 700,000 villages, no matter whether they come from British India or what is called Indian India (Indian States). Every interest which, in the opinion of the Congress, is worthy of protection has to subserve the interests of these dumb millions; and so you do find now and again apparently a clash between several interests, and if there is a genuine real clash, I have no hesitation in saying, on behalf of the Congress, that the Congress will sacrifice every interest for the sake of the interest of these dumb millions."

philosopher-kings; there are only frail human beings who cannot help thinking that their own personal good or the advancement of their own ideas is identical with the public good. The snobbery of birth, position, and economic power is perpetuated, and the consequences in many ways are disastrous.

Again, I would repeat that I am not at present considering the question of how to effect the change, of how to get rid of the obstacles in the way, by compulsion or conversion, violence or non-violence. I shall deal with this aspect later. But the necessity for the change must be recognized and clearly stated. If leaders and thinkers do not clearly envisage this and state it, how can they expect even to convert anybody to their way of thinking, or develop the necessary ideology in the people? Events are undoubtedly the most powerful educators, but events have to be properly understood and interpreted if their significance is to be realized, and properly directed action is to result from them.

I have often been asked by friends and colleagues who have occasionally been exasperated by my utterances: Have you not come across good and benevolent princes, charitable landlords, well-meaning and amiable capitalists? Indeed I have. I myself belong to a class which mixes with these lords of the land and owners of wealth. I am a typical *bourgeois*, brought up in *bourgeois* surroundings, with all the early prejudices that this training has given me. Communists have called me a petty *bourgeois* with perfect justification. Perhaps they might label me now one of the "repentant *bourgeoisie*." But whatever I may be is beside the point. It is absurd to consider national, international, economic and social problems in terms of isolated individuals. Those very friends who question me are never tired of repeating that our quarrel is with the sin and not the sinner. I would not even go so far. I would say that my quarrel is with a system and not with individuals. A system is certainly embodied to a great extent in individuals and groups, and these individuals and groups have to be converted or combated. But if a system has ceased to be of value and is a drag, it has to go, and the classes or groups that cling to it will also have to undergo a transformation. That process of change should involve as little suffering as possible, but unhappily suffering and dislocation are inevitable. We cannot put up with a major evil for fear of a far lesser one, which in any event is beyond our power to remedy.

Every type of human association—political, social or economic—

has some philosophy at the back of it. When these associations change this philosophical foundation must also change in order to fit in with it and to utilize it to the best advantage. Usually the philosophy lags behind the course of events, and this lag creates all the trouble. Democracy and capitalism grew up together in the nineteenth century, but they were not mutually compatible. There was a basic contradiction between them, for democracy laid stress on the power of the many, while capitalism gave real power to the few. This ill-assorted pair carried on somehow because political parliamentary democracy was in itself a very limited kind of democracy and did not interfere much with the growth of monopoly and power concentration.

Even so, as the spirit of democracy grew a divorce became inevitable, and the time for that has come now. Parliamentary democracy is in disrepute today, and as a reaction from it all manner of new slogans fill the air. Because of this, the British Government in India becomes more reactionary still and makes it an excuse for withholding from us even the outer forms of political freedom. The Indian Princes, strangely enough, make this a justification for their unchecked autocracy and stoutly declare their intention of maintaining medieval conditions in their domains such as exist nowhere else in the world.[5] But the failure of parliamentary democracy is not that it has gone too far, but that it did not go far

---

5. The Maharaja of Patiala, Chancellor of the Chamber of Princes, speaking in the Chamber at Delhi on January 22nd, 1935, referred to the opinion of Indian politicians who favour Federation in the hope that the Princes would be forced by circumstances to introduce democratic forms of government. He went on to say that "while the Princes of India have always been willing to do what was best for their people, and will be ready to accommodate themselves and their constitutions to the spirit of the times, we must frankly say that if British India is hoping to compel us to wear on our healthy body politic the Nessus shirt of a discredited political theory, they are living in a world of unreality." (See also p. 519 ante for Mysore Dewan's speech.) Speaking on the same day in the Chamber of Princes, the Maharaja of Bikaner said: "We, the Rulers of the Indian States, are not soldiers of fortune. And I take the liberty of stating that we who, through centuries of heredity, can claim to have inherited the instincts of rule and, I trust, a certain measure of statesmanship, should take the utmost care to safeguard against our being stampeded in a hurry to any hasty or ill-considered decision . . . May I in all modesty say that the Princes have no intention of allowing themselves to be destroyed by anybody, and that should the time unfortunately come when the Crown is unable to afford the Indian States the necessary protection in fulfilment of its treaty obligations, the Princes and States will die fighting to the bitter end."

enough. It was not democratic enough because it did not provide for economic democracy, and its methods were slow and cumbrous and unsuited to a period of rapid change.

The Indian States represent today probably the extremest type of autocracy existing in the world. They are, of course, subject to British suzerainty, but the British Government interferes only for the protection or advancement of British interests. It is really astonishing how these feudal old-world enclaves have carried on with so little change right into the middle of the twentieth century. The air is heavy and still there, and the waters move sluggishly, and the newcomer, used to change and movement and a little weary of them perhaps, feels a drowsiness, and a faint charm steals over him. It all seems unreal, like a picture where time stands still and an unchanging scene meets the eye. Almost unconsciously he drifts back to the past and to his childhood's dreams, and visions of belted and armoured knights and fair and brave maidens come to him, and turreted castles and chivalry and quixotic ideas of honour and pride and matchless courage and scorn of death. Especially if he happens to be in Rajputana, that home of romance and of vain and impossible deeds.

But soon the visions fade and a sense of oppression comes; it is stifling and difficult to breathe, and below the still or slow-moving waters there is stagnation and putrefaction. One feels hedged, circumscribed, bound down in mind and body. And one sees the utter backwardness and misery of the people, contrasting vividly with the glaring ostentation of the prince's palace. How much of the wealth of the State flows into that palace for the personal needs and luxuries of the prince, how little goes back to the people in the form of any service! Our princes are terribly expensive to produce and to keep up. What do they give back for this lavish expense on them?

A veil of mystery surrounds these States. Newspapers are not encouraged there, and at the most a literary or semi-official weekly might flourish. Outside newspapers are often barred. Literacy is very low, except in some of the Southern States—Travancore, Cochin, etc.— where it is far higher than in British India. The principal news that comes from the States is of a Viceregal visit, with all its pomp and ceremonial and mutually complimentary speeches, or of an extravagantly celebrated marriage or birthday of the Ruler, or an agrarian rising. Special laws protect the princes from criticism, even in British India, and within the States the mildest criticism is rigorously suppressed. Public meetings are almost unknown, and even meetings for social purposes are often banned.[6] Leading public men from outside are frequently prevented from entering the States. In the middle 'twenties Mr C.R. Das was very ill and he decided to go to Kashmir to recuperate. He was not on a political mission. He journeyed right up to the Kashmir border, but was stopped there. Even Mr M.A. Jinnah was debarred from entering Hyderabad State, and Mrs Sarojini Naidu, whose home is in Hyderabad city, was not permitted to go there for a long period.

When such conditions prevail in the States it would have been natural for the Congress to stand up for the elementary rights of the people of the States and to criticize their wholesale suppression. But Gandhiji fathered a novel policy on the Congress in regard to the States—the "policy of non-interference in the internal administration of the States." This hush-hush policy has been adhered to by him in spite of the most extraordinary and painful occurrences in the States, and in spite of wholly unprovoked attacks by the States' governments on the Congress. Apparently the fear is that Congress criticism might offend the Rulers and make it more difficult to 'convert' them. In a letter written in July 1934 by Gandhiji to Mr N.C. Kelkar, the President of the States Subjects' Conference, he reiterated his conviction that the policy of non-interference was both wise and sound, and the view he took of the legal and constitutional position of these States was most extraordinary. "The States," he wrote, "are independent entities under British law. That part of India which is described as British has no more power to shape the policy of the States than it has, say, that of Afghanistan or Ceylon." It is not surprising that even the mild and moderate Indian States' People's

---

6. A Press message from Hyderabad, Deccan, dated October 3rd, 1934, states: "A public meeting to celebrate Mr Gandhi's birthday announced to be held in the local Vivekvardini Theatre yesterday had to be abandoned. The meeting was organized by the Hyderabad Harijan Sevak Sangh (Servants of the Untouchables Society). The secretary of the society, in a letter to the Press, stated that 24 hours before the time of the meeting the authorities demanded that permission to hold the meeting could only be granted on condition that a cash security of Rs 2000 was furnished and an undertaking given that no speeches of a political nature should be delivered, and no official actions of Government officers should be criticized. As this gave the convener insufficient time to readjust matters with the authorities the meeting had to be abandoned."

Conference and the Liberals took exception to his views and his advice.

But these views were welcome enough to the Rulers of the States, and they took advantage of them. Within a month the Travancore Government banned the National Congress in its territories and stopped all its meetings and its enrolment of members. In doing so, it stated that 'responsible leaders' had themselves given this advice—obviously hinting at Gandhiji's statement. This ban, it might be noted, was after the withdrawal of the Civil Disobedience movement in British India (the States had never been involved in the movement) and when the Congress had been declared a legal organization again by the Government of India. It is also interesting to note that the chief political adviser of the Travancore Government at the time was (and still is) Sir C.P. Ramaswamy Aiyar, once a General Secretary of the Congress as well as of the Home Rule League, later a Liberal, and the holder of high office in the Government of India and the Madras Government.

In accordance with the Congress policy, following Gandhiji's advice, not a word was said in public about this unprovoked attack on the Congress in normal times by the Travancore Government.[7] Some of the Liberals even protested against it vigorously. Indeed, Gandhiji's position in regard to the States is far more moderate and restrained than that of the Liberals. Perhaps among the leading public men only Pandit Madan Mohan Malaviya, with his close contacts with numerous Princes, is equally restrained and solicitous of not offending the susceptibilities of the Rulers.

Gandhiji was not always so cautious in regard to the Indian Princes. On a famous occasion in February 1916, during the inauguration ceremonies of the Hindu University at Benares, he addressed a meeting presided over by one of the Princes and attended by a host of other Princes. He had freshly returned from South Africa, and the burden of all-India politics was not yet on his shoulders. Earnestly and with a prophet's fire he addressed them and told them to mend their ways and give up their vain pomp and luxury. "Princes! Go and sell your jewels!"

---

7. Sardar Vallabhbhai Patel laid stress on this non-intervention policy in a speech at Baroda on January 6th, 1935. He is reported to have said "that workers in Indian States should do their work with all the limitations imposed by the State, and instead of criticizing the administration, efforts should be made to keep up cordial relations between the ruler and the ruled."

he said; and though they may not have sold their jewels, they certainly went. In great consternation, one by one and in small groups, they left the hall, and even the president trooped out, leaving the speaker to carry on by himself. Mrs Annie Besant, who was present then, was also offended at Gandhiji's remarks and withdrew from the meeting.

In his letter to Mr N.C. Kelkar, Gandhiji says further: "I would like the States to grant autonomy to their subjects, and would like the Princes to regard themselves and be, in fact, trustees for the people over whom they rule . . ." If there is anything in this idea of trusteeship, why should we object to the claim of the British Government that they are trustees for the Government of India? Except for the fact that they are foreigners in India, I see no difference. There are almost equally marked differences as regards the colour of the skin, racial origin and culture between various peoples in India.

During the past few years there has been a rapid permeation of British officials in Indian States, often thrust on an unwilling but helpless Ruler. The Government of India always exercised a great deal of control over the States from above; now in addition to this there is an internal grip on some of the most important States. So that when these States speak it is often the Government of India speaking with another voice, but taking full advantage of the feudal background.

I can understand that it is not always possible to indulge in the same activities in the States as elsewhere. Indeed, there are considerable differences—agrarian, industrial, communal, governmental—between the various British Indian provinces, and a uniform policy is not always feasible. But though action must depend on circumstances, our general policy should not vary in different localities, and what is bad in one place must be bad in another. Otherwise the charge will be made, and it has been made, that we have no consistent policy or principles, and all we are out for is to gain power for ourselves.

A great deal of criticism has been directed, and quite rightly, against separate electorates for religious and other minorities. It has been pointed out that they are quite inconsistent with democracy. It is, of course, not possible to have democracy, or what is called responsible government, if the electorate is divided up into watertight religious compartments. But the most earnest and persistent of the critics, like Pandit Madan Mohan Malaviya and the leaders of the Hindu Mahasabha, are singularly acquiescent in regard to the conditions in the States, and are apparently prepared to have a federal union between the autocracy of the States and the democracy (so it is called) of the rest of India. A more incompatible and absurd union it is difficult to imagine, but this is swallowed without an effort by the champions of democracy and nationalism in the Hindu Mahasabha. We talk of logic and consistency, but our basic urges continue to be emotional.

And so I come back to the paradox of the Congress and the States. My mind travels to Thomas Paine and the phrase he used about Burke nearly a century and a half ago: "He pities the plumage, but forgets the dying bird." Gandhiji certainly never forgets the dying bird. But why so much insistence on the plumage?

More or less the same considerations apply to the taluqadari and big zamindari system. It hardly seems a matter for argument that this semi-feudal system is out of date and is a great hindrance to production and general progress. It conflicts even with a developing capitalism, and almost all over the world large landed estates have gradually vanished and given place to peasant proprietors. I had always imagined that the only possible question that could arise in India was one of compensation. But to my surprise I have discovered during the last year or so that Gandhiji approves of the taluqadari system as such and wants it to continue. He said in July 1934 at Cawnpore "that better relations between landlords and tenants could be brought about by a change of hearts on both sides. If that was done both could live in peace and harmony. He was never in favour of abolition of the taluqadari or zamindari system, and those who thought that it should be abolished "did not know their own minds." (This last charge is rather unkind.)

He is further reported to have said:

I shall be no party to dispossessing propertied classes of their private property without just cause. My objective is to reach your hearts and convert you [he was addressing a deputation of big zamindars] so that you may hold all your private property in trust for your tenants and use it primarily for their welfare . . . But supposing that there is an attempt unjustly to deprive you of your property you will find me fighting on your side . . . The socialism and communism of the West is based on certain conceptions which are fundamentally different from ours. One such conception is their belief in the essential selfishness of human nature . . . Our socialism and communism should therefore be based on non-violence and on the harmonious co-operation of Labour and Capital, landlord and tenant."

I do not know if there are any such differences in the basic conceptions of the East and West. Perhaps there are. But an obvious difference in the recent past has been that the Indian capitalist and landlord have ignored far more the interests of their workers and tenants than their Western prototypes. There has been practically no attempt on the part of the Indian landlord to interest himself in any social service for the tenants' welfare. A Western observer, Mr H.N. Brailsford, has remarked that "Indian usurers and landlords are the most rapacious parasites to be found in any contemporary social system."[8] The fault, perhaps, is not the Indian landlord's. Circumstances have been too much for him and he has gone down progressively, and is now in a difficult position from which he can hardly extricate himself. Many landlords have been deprived of their lands by moneylenders and the smaller ones have sunk to the position of tenants in the land they once owned. These moneylenders from the city advanced money on mortgages and foreclosed, and blossomed out into zamindars, and, according to Gandhiji, they are now the trustees for the unhappy people whom they have themselves dispossessed of their lands, and are to be expected to devote their income primarily for the welfare of their tenantry.

If the taluqadari system is good, why should it not be introduced all over India? Large tracts of India have peasant proprietors. I wonder if Gandhiji would be agreeable to the creation of large zamindaris and taluqas in Gujrat? I imagine not. But then why is one land system good for U.P. or Behar or Bengal, and another for Gujrat and the Punjab? Presumably there is not any vital difference between the people of the north and east and west and south of India, and their basic conceptions are the same. It comes to this, then, that whatever is should continue, the *status quo* should be maintained. There should be no economic enquiry as to what is most desirable or beneficial for the people, no attempts to change present conditions; all that is necessary is to change the people's hearts. That is the pure religious attitude to life and its problems. It has nothing to do with politics or economics or sociology. And yet Gandhiji goes beyond this in the political, national, sphere.

---

8. H.N. Brailsford: *Property or Peace?*

Such are some of the paradoxes that face India today. We have managed to tie ourselves up into a number of knots, and it is difficult to get on till we untie them. That release will not come emotionally. What is better, Spinoza asked long ago: "Freedom through knowledge and understanding, or emotional bondage?" He preferred the former.

63

CONVERSION OR COMPULSION

Sixteen years ago Gandhiji impressed India with his doctrine of non-violence. Ever since then it has dominated the Indian horizon. Vast numbers of people have repeated it unthinkingly but with approval, some have wrestled with it and then accepted it, with or without reservation, some have openly jeered at it. It has played a major part in our political and social life, and it has also attracted a great deal of attention in the wider world. The doctrine is of course almost as old as human thought, but perhaps Gandhiji was the first to apply it on a mass scale to political and social movements. Formerly it was an individual affair and was thus essentially religious. It was the restraint of the individual and his attempt to achieve complete disinterestedness and thus to raise himself above the level of worldly conflict and attain a kind of personal freedom and salvation. There was no idea behind it of dealing with the larger social problems and of changing social conditions, except very indirectly and remotely. There was almost an acceptance of the existing social fabric with all its inequality and injustice. Gandhiji tried to make this individual ideal into a social group ideal. He was out to change political conditions as well as social; and deliberately, with this end in view, he applied the non-violent method on this wider and wholly different plane. "Those who have to bring about radical changes in human conditions and surroundings," he has written, "cannot do it except by raising a ferment in society. There are only two methods of doing this, violent and non-violent. Violent pressure is felt on the physical being and it degrades him who uses it as it depresses the victim, but non-violent pressure exerted through self-suffering, as by fasting, works in an entirely different way. It touches not the physical body but it touches and strengthens the moral fibre of those against whom it is directed."[1]

---

1. Extracts from statement made by Gandhiji on December 4, 1932 on the occasion of one of his fasts.

The idea was to some extent in harmony with Indian thought and it was accepted, superficially at least, with enthusiasm by the country. Very few realized the far-reaching implications that lay behind it, and the few who did so rather vaguely took refuge in faith and action. But, when the tempo of action slackened, innumerable questions arose in the minds of some people, and it was extraordinarily difficult to find answers to them. These questions did not affect the immediate course that had to be followed in politics. Rather they dealt with the whole philosophy that lay behind this idea of non-violent resistance. In a political sense the non-violent movement has not succeeded so far, for India is still held in the vice-like grip of imperialism. In a social sense it has not even envisaged a radical change. And yet anyone with the slightest penetration can see that it has worked a remarkable change in India's millions. It has given them character, strength and self-reliance—precious gifts without which any progress, political or social, is difficult to achieve or to retain. How far these undoubted gains are due to non-violence or to the fact of conflict itself, it is difficult to say. Such gains have been achieved by various peoples on numerous occasions through violent conflict. Yet it may be said, I think with confidence, that the non-violent method has been of inestimable value to us in this respect. It has definitely helped in raising that 'ferment in society' to which Gandhiji refers, though undoubtedly that ferment was due to basic causes and conditions. It has brought about that quickening process in the masses that precedes revolutionary change.

That is an obvious point in its favour, but it does not carry us far. The real questions remain unanswered. Unfortunately Gandhiji does not help us much in solving the problem. He has written and spoken on innumerable occasions on the subject, but, so far as I know, he has never considered in public all its implications, philosophically or scientifically.[2] He lays stress on the means being more important than the end, of conversion being better than coercion, and there is a tendency to identify non-violence with truth and all goodness. Indeed he often uses the terms as if they were synonymous. There is also the tendency to consider all those who may not agree with this as outside the pale of the elect and

2. Richard B. Gregg in his *The Power of Non-Violence* has discussed the subject scientifically. His book is most interesting and thought-provoking.

as having offended against the moral law. In the case of some of his followers this translates itself inevitably into a feeling of self-righteousness.

Those of us who are not fortunate enough to have this faith are, however, troubled with a host of doubts. These doubts do not relate so much to immediate necessities, but to the mind's desire for some consistent philosophy of action which is both moral from the individual view-point and is at the same time socially effective. I confess that these doubts have not left me, and I see no satisfactory solution of the problem. I dislike violence intensely, and yet I am full of violence myself and, consciously or unconsciously, I am often attempting to coerce others. And can anything be greater coercion than the psychic coercion of Gandhiji which reduces many of his intimate followers and colleagues to a state of mental pulp?

But the real question was: can national and social groups imbibe sufficiently this individual creed of non-violence, for it involved a tremendous rise of mankind in the mass to a high level of love and goodness? It is true that the only really desirable ultimate ideal is to raise humanity to this level and to abolish hatred and ugliness and selfishness. Whether that is possible or not, even ultimately, may be a debatable question; but without that to hope for life would almost become "a tale told by an idiot, full of sound and fury, signifying nothing." To attain this ideal, are we to work for it directly by preaching these virtues, regardless of the obstructions which make it impossible of achievement and which encourage every contrary tendency? Or must we not remove these obstructions first and create a more suitable and more favourable environment for the growth of love, beauty, goodness? Or can we combine the two processes?

And then again is the line between violence and non-violence, compulsion and conversion, so obvious? Often enough moral force is a far more terrible coercive factor than physical violence. And is non-violence synonymous with truth? What is truth is an ancient question to which a thousand answers have been given, and yet the question remains. But whatever it may be, it cannot certainly be wholly identified with non-violence. Violence itself, though bad, cannot be considered intrinsically immoral. There are shades and grades of it and often it may be preferable to something that is worse. Gandhiji himself has said that it is better than cowardice, fear, and slavery, and a host of other evils might be added to this list. It is true that usually violence is associated with ill-will, but in theory at least this need not always be so. It is conceivable that violence may be based on goodwill (that of a surgeon, for example) and anything that has this for a basis can never be fundamentally immoral. After all, the final tests of ethics and morality are goodwill and ill-will. Thus, although violence is very often unjustifiable morally and may be considered dangerous from that view-point, it need not always be so.

All life is full of conflict and violence, and it seems to be true that violence breeds violence and is thus not a way to overcome it. And yet to forswear it altogether leads to a wholly negative attitude utterly out of touch with life itself. Violence is the very life-blood of the modern State and social system. Without the coercive apparatus of the State taxes would not be realized, landlords would not get their rents, and private property would disappear. The law, with the help of its armed forces, excludes others from the use of private property. The national State itself exists because of offensive and defensive violence.

Gandhiji's non-violence, it is true, is certainly not a purely negative affair. It is not non-resistance. It is non-violent resistance, which is a very different thing, a positive and dynamic method of action. It was not meant for those who meekly accept the *status quo*. The very purpose for which it was designed was to create "a ferment in society" and thus to change existing conditions. Whatever the motives of conversion behind it, in practice it has been a powerful weapon of compulsion as well, though that compulsion is exercised in the most civilized and least objectionable manner. Indeed it is interesting to note that Gandhiji actually used the word 'compel' in his earlier writings. Criticizing the Viceroy's (Lord Chelmsford's) speech in 1920 on the Punjab Martial Law wrongs, he wrote:

> ... the speech his Excellency delivered at the time of the opening of the Council shows to me a mental attitude which makes association with him or his Government impossible for self-respecting men.
>
> The remarks on the Punjab mean a flat refusal to grant redress. He would have us to concentrate on the problems of the immediate 'future'! The immediate future is to compel repentance on the part of the Government on the Punjab matter. Of this there is no sign. On the

contrary his Excellency resists the temptation to reply to his critics, meaning thereby that he has not changed his opinion on the many vital matters affecting the honour of India. He is 'content to leave the issues to the verdict of history.' Now this kind of language, in my opinion, is calculated further to inflame the Indian mind. Of what use can a favourable verdict of history be to men who have been wronged and who are still under the heels of officers who have shown themselves utterly unfit to hold offices of trust and responsibility? The plea for co-operation is, to say the least, hypocritical in the face of the determination to refuse justice to the Punjab.

Governments are notoriously based on violence, not only the open violence of the armed forces, but the far more dangerous violence, more subtly exercised, of spies, informers, *agents provocateurs*, false propaganda, direct and indirect through education, Press, etc., religious and other forms of fear, economic destitution and starvation. As between two governments it is taken for granted that every manner of falsehood and treachery is justified, provided it is not found out, even in peace-time and much more so in war-time. Three hundred years ago Sir Henry Wotton, a poet and himself a British ambassador, defined an ambassador as "an honest man sent to lie abroad for the good of his country." Nowadays ambassadors are supported by military, naval and commercial attachés whose chief function is to spy in the country to which they are sent. Behind them functions the vast network of the secret service, with its innumerable ramifications and webs of intrigue and deception, its spies and counter-spies, its connections with the underworld of crime, its bribery and degradation of human nature, its secret murders. Bad as all this is in peace-time, war gives it enormous importance and its baneful influence spreads in every direction. It is astonishing to read now of some of the instances of propaganda during the World War, the amazing falsehoods spread about enemy countries, the vast sums spent on this and on the secret services. But peace today is itself merely an interval between two wars, a preparation for war, and to some extent a continuation of the conflict in economic and other spheres. There is a continuous tug-of-war between the victors and the vanquished, between the imperialist powers and their colonial dependencies, between the privileged classes and the exploited classes. The war atmosphere, with all its accompaniments of violence and falsehood, continues in some measure therefore even during so-called peace-time, and both the soldier and the civilian official are trained to meet this situation. Lord Wolseley writes in the *Soldier's Pocket-Book for Field Service*: "We will keep hammering along with the conviction that 'honesty is the best policy', and that truth always wins in the long run. These pretty sentences do well for a child's copy-book, but the man who acts upon them in war had better sheathe his sword for ever."

Under present conditions, with nation against nation and class against class, this basis of violence and falsehood seems almost inevitable. Privileged nations and groups, desirous of holding on to their power and privileges and denying those whom they oppress the opportunities of growth, must rely on violence, coercion and falsehood. It may be possible, as public opinion grows and the realities of these conflicts and their suppression become more manifest, for the violence to be toned down. As a matter of fact all recent experience points to the contrary, and violence has grown as the challenge to existing institutions has gained weight. Even when outward violence has been toned down, it has taken subtler and more dangerous forms. Neither the growth of reason nor of the religious outlook nor morality have checked in any way this tendency to violence. Individuals have progressed and gone up in the human scale, and probably there are far more of these higher-type individuals (the highest type excepted) in the world today than at any previous period of history; society as a whole has progressed, and to a very small extent begun to attempt the control of the primitive and barbarian instincts. But on the whole groups and communities have not improved greatly. The individual in becoming more civilized has passed on many of his primitive passions and vices to the community, and as violence always attracts the morally second-rate, the leaders of these communities are seldom their best men and women.

But even if we assume that the worst forms of violence will be gradually removed from the State, it is impossible to ignore the fact that both government and social life necessitate some coercion. Social life necessitates some form of government, and the men so placed in authority must curb and prevent all individual or group tendencies which are inherently selfish and likely to injure society. Usually they go much further than necessary, for power corrupts and degrades. So that however much those rulers may love liberty and hate coercion, they will have to exercise coercion on recalcitrant individuals, till such time when every human being in that State is perfect, wholly unselfish, and devoted to the common good. The rulers of that State will also have to exercise coercion on outside groups who make predatory attacks, that is to say they will have to defend themselves, meeting force with force. The necessity for this will only disappear when there is only a single World-State.

If force and coercion are thus necessary both for external defence and internal cohesion, where is one to draw the line? Once this fateful concession is made of ethics to politics, Reinhold Neibuhr points out,[3] and coercion is accepted as a necessary instrument of social cohesion, it is not possible to make absolute distinctions between non-violent and violent types of coercion, or between the coercion used by governments and that used by revolutionaries.

I do not know for certain, but I imagine that Gandhiji will admit that in this imperfect world a national State will have to use force to defend itself against unprovoked attack from outside. Of course the State should allow an absolutely peaceful and friendly policy to its neighbour and other States, but nevertheless it is absurd to deny the possibility of attack. The State will also have to pass some laws of a coercive nature, in the sense that they take away some rights and privileges from various classes and groups and restrict liberty of action. All laws are to some extent coercive. The Karachi programme of the Congress lays down that "In order to end the exploitation of the masses, political freedom must include real economic freedom of the starving millions." To give effect to this desirable sentiment the over-privileged will have to give up much to the under-privileged. Further, it is laid down that workers must have a living wage and various other amenities; that special taxes will be charged on property; that "the State shall own or control key industries and services, mineral resources, railways, waterways, shipping and other means of public transport." Also that "intoxicating drinks and drugs shall be totally prohibited." All this is likely to be objected to by considerable numbers of people. They may submit to the will of the majority, but that will be because they are afraid of the consequences of

---

3. In *Moral Man and Immoral Society.*

disobedience. Democracy indeed means the coercion of the minority by the majority.

If a law affecting property rights or abolishing them to a large extent is passed by a majority, is that to be objected to because it is coercion? Manifestly not, because the same procedure is followed in the adoption of all democratic laws. Objection, therefore, cannot be taken on the ground of coercion. It might be said that the majority was acting wrongly or immorally. The question to be considered then is: whether the law as passed by a majority offended any ethical principle. Who is to decide this? If individuals and groups are allowed to interpret ethics in accordance with their own interests, there is an end of democratic procedure. Personally I feel that the institution of private property (except in a very restricted sense) gives dangerous power to individuals over society as a whole, and is therefore very harmful to society. I consider it immoral, far more so than drink, which harms the individual more than society.

I have been told, however, by some people who claim to believe in the doctrine of non-violence that to attempt to nationalize private property, except with the consent of the owners thereof, would be coercion, and as such opposed to non-violence. Indeed this view-point has been impressed upon me by big zamindars, who do not scruple to take the aid of the State in forcibly collecting their rents; and capitalists, owning many factories, who will not even permit independent labour unions to exist in their domains. The fact that a majority of the people affected desires the change is not considered enough, the very people who stand to lose by it should be converted. Thus a few interested parties can hold up an obviously desirable change.

If there is one thing that history shows it is this: that economic interests shape the political views of groups and classes. Neither reason nor moral considerations override these interests. Individuals may be converted, they may surrender their special privileges, although this is rare enough, but classes and groups do not do so. The attempt to convert a governing and privileged class into forsaking power and giving up its unjust privileges has therefore always so far failed, and there seems to be no reason whatever to hold that it will succeed in the future. Reinhold Niebuhr in his book[4] directs his argument against the moralists "who

---

4. *Moral Man and Immoral Society.*

imagine that the egoism of individuals is being progressively checked by the development of rationality or the growth of a religiously inspired goodwill, and that nothing but the continuance of this process is necessary to establish social harmony between all the human societies and collectives." These moralists "disregard the political necessities in the struggle for justice in human society by failing to recognize those elements in man's collective behaviour which belong to the order of nature and can never be brought completely under the dominion of reason or conscience. They do not recognize that when collective power, whether in the form of imperialism or class domination, exploits weakness, it can never be dislodged unless power is raised against it." And again: "Since reason is always, to some degree, the servant of interest in a social situation, social justice cannot be resolved by moral or rational suasion alone . . . Conflict is inevitable, and in this conflict power must be challenged by power."

To think, therefore, in terms of pure conversion of a class or nation or of the removal of conflict by rational argument and appeals to justice, is to delude oneself. It is an illusion to imagine that a dominant imperialist Power will give up its domination over a country, or that a class will give up its superior position and privileges unless effective pressure, amounting to coercion, is exercised.

Gandhiji obviously wants to apply that pressure, though he does not call it coercion. According to him, his method is self-suffering. It is a little difficult to consider this, as there is a metaphysical element in it and it does not yield to measurement or any other material approach. That it has considerable effect on the opponent is undoubted. It exposes his moral defences, it unnerves him, it appeals to the best in him, it leaves the door open for conciliation. There can be no doubt that the approach of love and self-suffering has powerful psychic reactions on the adversary as well as on the onlookers. Most shikaris know that it makes a difference how one approaches a wild animal. He seems to sense the aggressive spirit from afar and reacts to it. Even a suspicion of fear in the man, hardly realized by him, is conveyed somehow to the animal and makes him afraid, and in this fear he attacks. If the nerve of a lion-tamer fail him for an instant there is immediate danger of his being attacked. An absolutely fearless man is seldom in danger from wild animals unless some untoward accident occurs. It seems natural, therefore, that human beings should be susceptible to these psychic influences. But though individuals may be affected, it is doubtful if a class or group is affected. That class, as a class, does not come into personal and intimate contact with the other party; even the reports it hears are partial and distorted. And, in any event, its automatic reaction of anger against any group that challenges its position is so great that all minor feelings are swallowed up in it. Having for long accustomed itself to the notion that its superior position and privileges were necessary for the good of society, any contrary opinion savours of heresy. Law and order and the maintenance of the *status quo* become the chief virtues, and attempts to challenge them the chief sins.

So that, so far as the opposite group is concerned, the process of conversion does not go far. Indeed sometimes the very mildness and saintliness of their adversary makes them angrier still, for it seems to put them in the wrong; and when a person begins to suspect that he might be in the wrong, his virtuous indignation grows. Nevertheless, a non-violent technique does affect odd individuals on the other side, and thereby weakens the solidity of opposition. Even more so it gains the sympathy of neutrals and is a powerful means of influencing world opinion. But here again there is the probability of the governing group preventing the news from going out or of distorting it, because it controls the agencies of publicity and can thus prevent the real facts from being known. The most potent and far-reaching effect of the non-violent method is, however, on the large numbers of more or less indifferent people of the country in which this technique is practised. They are certainly converted and often become enthusiasts in its favour, but then they did not require much conversion as they generally approved of the object aimed at. The effect is not so obvious on those who dread the change. The rapid spread of non-co-operation and civil disobedience in India was a demonstration of how a non-violent movement exercises a powerful influence on vast numbers and converts many waverers. It did not convert to any marked extent those who were *ab initio* hostile to it. Indeed the success of the movement increased their fears and made them even more hostile.

If it is once admitted that a State is justified in using violence to defend its freedom, it is difficult to understand why it is not equally justified in adopting violent and coercive methods in trying to achieve that freedom. A violent method may be undesirable and inexpedient, but it would not be wholly unjustifiable and barred. The mere fact that a government happens to be the dominant faction controlling the armed forces does not give it a greater right to the use of violence. In the event of a non-violent revolution succeeding and controlling the State, does it immediately acquire the right to use violence, which it did not possess before? If there is an insurrection against its authority, how is it going to meet it? It will naturally be disinclined to use violent methods, and will try every peaceful way to meet the situation, but it cannot give up the right to use violence. There are sure to be disaffected elements in the population opposed to the change, and they will try to go back to the previous condition. If they think that their violence will not be checked by the coercive apparatus of the new State, they are all the more likely to indulge in it. It seems, therefore, that it is quite impossible to draw a hard and fast line between violence and nonviolence, coercion and conversion. The difficulty is real enough in considering political changes, it becomes far worse as between privileged and exploited classes.

To suffer for an ideal has always commanded admiration; to submit to suffering for a cause without giving in or hitting back has a nobility and grandeur in it which force recognition. And yet there is only a thin line which divides this from suffering for suffering's sake, and this latter kind of self-suffering is apt to become morbid and even a little degrading. If violence is often sadistic, non-violence in its negative aspects at least is likely to err on the other side. There is also always the possibility for non-violence to be made a cloak for cowardice and inaction, as well as the maintenance of the *status quo.*

During the past few years in India, ever since the idea of radical social changes has assumed importance here, it has often been stated that such a change necessarily involves the use of violence and cannot therefore be advocated. Class conflicts must not be mentioned (however much they might exist) because they jar on the vision of perfect co-operation and a non-violent progress to whatever goal might lie in the future. It is quite possible that a solution of the social problem cannot be brought about without violence at some stage, for it seems certain that the privileged classes will not hesitate to use violence to maintain their favoured position. But, in theory, if it is possible to bring about a great political change by a non-violent technique, why should it not be equally possible to effect a radical social change by this method? If we can get political freedom and the elimination of British imperialism from India non-violently, why should we not also solve the problem of the feudal princes and landlords and other social problems in the same way, and establish a Socialist State? Whether all this is possible or not non-violently is not so much the question. The point is that either both of these objectives are possible of attainment non-violently or neither. Surely it cannot be said that a non-violent method can only be used against a foreign ruler. *Prima facie* it should be far easier to use it within a country against indigenous selfish interests and obstructionists, for the psychological effect on them will be greater than elsewhere.

The recent tendency in India to condemn objectives and policies simply because they are supposed to conflict with nonviolence seems to me an inversion of the right method of looking at such problems. We took to the non-violent method fifteen years ago because it promised to take us to our goal in the most desirable and effective way. The goal was then apart from non-violence; it was not a mere appendage or outcome of it. No one could have said then that freedom or independence must only be aimed at if they are attainable by non-violent means. But now our goal itself is judged in terms of non-violence and rejected if it does not seem to fit in with it. The idea of non-violence is thus becoming an inflexible dogma which may not be challenged. As such it is losing its spiritual appeal to the intellect, and taking its place in the pigeon-holes of faith and religion. It is even becoming a sheet-anchor for vested interests, who exploit it to maintain the *status quo*.

This is unfortunate for, I do believe, the ideas of non-violent resistance and the non-violent technique of struggle are of great value to India as well as to the rest of the world, and Gandhiji has done a tremendous service in forcing modern thought to consider them. I believe they have a great future before them. It may be that mankind is not sufficiently advanced to adopt them in their entirety. "You offer your candle of vision to the blind," says a character in A.E.'s *Interpreters*, "but what use can it be to the blind except as a bludgeon?" For the present the vision may not materialize sufficiently, but like all great ideas its influence will grow and it will more and more affect our actions. Non-co-operation, the withdrawal of co-operation from a State or society which is considered evil, is a powerful and dynamic notion. Even if a handful of persons of moral worth practise it, its effect spreads and goes on increasing. With large numbers the external effect becomes more marked, but there is a tendency for other factors to obscure the moral issue. The extension of it seems to affect its intensity. The collective man gradually pushes back the individual.

The stress, however, on pure non-violence has made it something remote and apart from life, and there is a tendency for people either to accept it blindly and religiously or not at all. The intellectual element has receded into the background. In 1920 it had a great effect on the Terrorists in India, and drew many away from their ranks, and even those who remained were held back by doubt and stopped their violent activities. It has no such influence on them now. Even within the Congress ranks many of the vital elements who played a notable part in the Non-Co-operation and Civil Disobedience movements, and in all sincerity tried to live up to the implications of the non-violent method, are now considered as heretics who have no business to continue as Congressmen because they are not prepared to make non-violence a creed and a religion, or to give up the only goal they consider worth striving for—a Socialist State with equal justice and opportunity for all, a planned society which can only come into existence with the abolition of most of the privileges and property rights that exist today. Gandhiji, of course, continues to be a vital force whose non-violence is of a dynamic and aggressive character, and no one knows when he might again galvanize the country in a forward movement. With all his greatness and his contradictions and power of moving masses, he is above the usual standards. One cannot measure him or judge him as we would others. But many of those who claim to follow him tend to become ineffectual pacifists or non-resisters of the Tolstoyan variety or just members of a narrow sect, not in touch with life and reality. And they gather round themselves quite a number of people who are interested in maintaining the present order, and who take shelter under non-violence for this purpose. Opportunism thus creeps in and the process of converting the adversary leads, in the interests of non-violence, to one's own conversion and lining up with the adversary. When enthusiasm wanes and we weaken, there is always a tendency to go back a little, to compromise, and it is comforting to call this the art of winning over the opponent. And sometimes we make this gain at the cost of our own old colleagues. We deprecate their extravagances, their utterances that irritate our new friends, and accuse them of breaking the unity of our ranks. Instead of a real change of the social order, stress is laid on charity and benevolence within the existing system, the vested interests remaining where they were.

I am convinced that Gandhiji has done a great service to us by stressing the importance of the means. And yet I feel sure that the final emphasis must necessarily be on the end and goal in view. Unless we can conceive that, clearly we can never be anything but aimless wanderers, wasting our energies on unimportant side-issues. But the means cannot be ignored for, quite apart from the moral side, they have a practical side. Bad and immoral means often defeat the end in view or raise tremendous new problems. And, after all, it is the means that a person adopts and not the end he declares that enables us to judge him truly. To adopt means that lead to needless conflict and to the piling up of hatreds, is likely to make the achievement of the goal more difficult and distant. Ends and means are indeed so intimately connected that they can hardly be separated. Essentially, therefore, the means must be such as lessen conflict and hatred or, at any rate, try to limit them as far as possible (for they seem to be inevitable), and to encourage goodwill. It becomes more a question of motive and intention and temper than of any particular method. It is on this basic motive that Gandhiji's stress has been, and if he has failed to change human nature to any appreciable extent, he succeeded surprisingly in impressing this motive on a great national movement involving millions. His insistence on strict moral discipline was also very necessary, though his standards of that individual discipline are perhaps debatable. He attaches vast importance to the self-regarding sins or failings and very little to social sins. The necessity for this discipline is obvious, for the temptation to leave the wilderness and join the privileged groups in the seats of power has drawn away many a Congressman. For a noted Congressman the door to that favoured land is always open.

The whole world is in the grip today of various crises, but the greatest of these is the crisis of the spirit. This is especially so in the East, for recent changes in Asia have been more rapid than elsewhere and the process of adjustment is painful. The political problem which seems to dominate the situation is perhaps the least important of all, though it is the primary problem for us, and it must be disposed of satisfactorily before the real questions are tackled. For ages past we have been accustomed to an almost unchanging basic social order, and many of us still believe that it is the only possible and rightful basis of society, and associate our moral notions with it. But our attempts to fit in the past with the present fail, as they are bound to do. "In the last resort," wrote Veblen, the American economist, "the economic moralities wait on the economic necessities." The necessities of today will force us to formulate a new morality in accordance with them. If we are to find a way out of this crisis of the spirit and realize what are the true spiritual values today, we shall have to face the issues frankly and boldly and not take refuge under the dogmas of any religion. What religion says may be good or bad, but the way it says it and wants us to believe it is certainly not conducive to an intellectual consideration of any problem. As Freud has pointed out, the dogmas of religion "deserve to be believed: firstly, because our primal ancestors already believed them; secondly, because we possess proofs, which have been handed down to us from this very period of antiquity; and thirdly, because it is forbidden to raise the question of their authenticity at all."[5]

If we consider non-violence and all it implies from the religious, dogmatic point of view there is no room for argument. It reduces itself to the narrow creed of a sect which people may or may not accept. It loses vitality and application to present-day problems. But if we are prepared to discuss it in relation to existing conditions it can help us greatly in our attempts to refashion this world. This consideration must take into account the nature and weaknesses of collective man. Any activity on a mass scale, and especially any activity aiming at radical and revolutionary changes, is affected not only by what the leaders think of it but by existing conditions and, still more, by what the human material they work with thinks about it.

Violence has played a great part in the world's history. It is today playing an equally important part, and probably it will continue to do so for a considerable time. Most of the changes in the past have been caused by violence and coercion. W.E. Gladstone once said: "I am sorry to say that if no instructions had been addressed in political crises to the people of this country except to remember to hate violence, to love order, and

---

5. *The Future of an Illusion.*

to exercise patience, the liberties of this country would never have been attained."

It is impossible to ignore the importance of violence in the past and present. To do so is to ignore life. Yet violence is undoubtedly bad and brings an unending trail of evil consequences with it. And worse even than violence are the motives of hatred, cruelty, revenge and punishment which very often accompany violence. Indeed violence is bad not intrinsically, but because of these motives that go with it. There can be violence without these motives; there can be violence for a good object as well as for an evil object. But it is extremely difficult to separate violence from those motives, and therefore it is desirable to avoid violence as far as possible. In avoiding it, however, one cannot accept a negative attitude of submitting to other and far greater evils. Submission to violence or the acceptance of an unjust regime based on violence, is the very negation of the spirit of non-violence. The non-violent method, in order to justify itself, must be dynamic and capable of changing such a regime or social order.

Whether it can do so or not I do not know. It can, I think, carry us a long way, but I doubt if it can take us to the final goal. In any event, some form of coercion seems to be inevitable, for people who hold power and privilege do not give them up till they are forced to do so, or till conditions are created which make it more harmful to them to keep these privileges than to give them up. The present conflicts in society, national as well as class conflicts, can never be resolved except by coercion. Conversion, of course, there must be on a large scale, for so long as large numbers are not converted there can be no real basis for a movement of social change. But coercion over some will follow. Nor is it right for us to cover up these basic conflicts and try to make out that they do not exist. That is not only a suppression of the truth, but it directly leads to bolstering up the existing order by misleading people as to the true facts, and giving the ruling classes the moral basis which they are always seeking in order to justify their special privileges. In order to combat an unjust system the false premises on which it is based must be exposed and the reality laid bare. One of the virtues of non-co-operation is that it exposes these false premises and lies by our refusal to submit to them or to co-operate in their furtherance.

Our final aim can only be a classless society with equal economic justice and opportunity for all, a society organized on a planned basis for the raising of mankind to higher material and cultured levels, to a cultivation of spiritual values, of co-operation, unselfishness, the spirit of service, the desire to do right, goodwill and love—ultimately a world order. Everything that comes in the way will have to be removed, gently if possible, forcibly if necessary. And there seems to be little doubt that coercion will often be necessary. But if force is used it should not be in the spirit of hatred or cruelty, but with the dispassionate desire to remove an obstruction. That will be difficult. It is not an easy task; there is no easy way, and the pitfalls are numerous. The difficulties and pitfalls do not disappear by our ignoring them, but by realizing their true nature and facing them boldly. All this sounds fanciful and Utopian, and it is highly unlikely that many people will be moved by these noble motives. But we can keep them in view and stress them, and it may be that gradually they will lessen the hatreds and passions that fill most of us.

Our methods must lead to this goal and be based on these motives. But we must also realize that human nature being what it is, in the mass, it will not always respond to our appeals and persuasions, or act in accordance with high moral principles. Compulsion will often be necessary, in addition to conversion, and the best we can do is to limit this compulsion and use it in such a manner that its evil is lessened.

64

DEHRA GAOL AGAIN

I was not flourishing in Alipore Gaol. My weight had gone down considerably, and the Calcutta air and increasing heat were distressing me. There were rumours of my transfer to a better climate. On May 7th I was told to gather my belongings and to march out of the gaol. I was being sent to Dehra Dun Gaol. The drive through Calcutta in the cool evening air was very pleasant after some months of seclusion, and the crowds at the big Howrah station were fascinating.

I was glad of my transfer, and looked forward to Dehra Dun with its near-by mountains. On arrival I found that all was not as it used to be nine months earlier, when I had left it for Naini. I was put in a new place, an old cattle-shed cleaned up and fitted out.

As a cell it was not bad, and there was a little veranda attached to it. There was also a small yard adjoining, about fifty feet in length. The cell was better than the ancient one I had had previously in Dehra, but soon I discovered that other changes were not for the better. The surrounding wall, which had been ten feet high, had just been raised, especially for my benefit, by another four or five feet. The view of the hills I had so looked forward to was completely cut off and I could just see a few tree-tops. I was in this gaol for over three months, and I never had even a glimpse of the mountains. I was not allowed to walk outside in front of the gaol gate, as I used to, and my little yard was considered quite big enough for exercise.

These and other new restrictions were disappointing, and I felt irritated. I grew listless and disinclined to take even the little exercise that my yard allowed. I had hardly ever felt quite so lonely and cut off from the world. The solitary confinement began to tell on my nerves, and physically and mentally I declined. On the other side of the wall, only a few feet away, I knew there was freshness and fragrance, the cool smell of grass and soft earth, and distant vistas. But they were all out of reach and my eyes grew weary and heavy, faced always by those walls.

There was not even the usual movement of prison life, for I was kept apart and by myself.

After six weeks the monsoon broke and it rained in torrents; we had twelve inches of rain during the first week. There was a change in the air and whisperings of new life; the temperature came down and the body felt relaxed and relieved. But there was no relief for the eyes or the mind. Sometimes the iron door of my yard would open to allow a warder to come in or go out, and for a few seconds I had a sudden glimpse of the outside world—green fields and trees, bright with colour and glistening with pearly drops of rain—for a moment only, and then it all vanished like a flash of lightning. The door was hardly ever fully opened. Apparently the warders had instructions not to open it if I was anywhere near, and even when they opened it, to do so just a little. These brief glimpses of greenery and freshness were hardly welcome to me. That sight produced in me a kind of nostalgia, a heartache, and I would even avoid looking out when the door opened.

But all this unhappiness was not really the fault of the gaol, though it contributed to it. It was the reaction of outside events—Kamala's illness and my political worries. I was beginning to realize that Kamala was again in the grip of her old disease, and I felt helpless and unable to be of any service to her. I knew that my presence by her side would have made a difference.

Unlike Alipore, Dehra Dun Gaol allowed me a daily newspaper, and I could keep in touch with political and other developments outside. In Patna the All-India Congress Committee met after nearly three years (for most of this time it was unlawful), and its proceedings were depressing. It surprised me that no attempt was made at this first meeting, after so much that had happened in India and the world, to analyse the situation, to have full discussions, to try to get out of old ruts. Gandhiji seemed to be, from a distance, his old dictatorial self—"If you choose to follow my lead you have to accept my conditions," he said. His demand was perfectly natural, for one could not both have him and ask him to act against his own deeply-felt convictions. But there seemed too much of imposition from above and too little of mutual discussion and hammering out a policy. It is curious how Gandhiji dominates the mind and then complains of the helplessness of people. Few people, I suppose, have had more loyal devotion and obedience on the mass-scale than he has had, and it seems hardly fair to blame the masses for not coming up to the high standard he had set for them. At the Patna meeting he did not even stay till the end, as he had to continue his Harijan tour. He told the A.I.C.C. to be business-like and to adopt the resolutions placed before them by the Working Committee with speed, and then he went away.

It is probably true that prolonged discussions would not have improved matters. There was a confusion and want of clarity among the members, and though many were prepared to criticize, there were hardly any constructive suggestions. Under the circumstances this was natural, for the burden of the struggle had largely fallen on these leaders from various provinces and they were a little tired and mentally not fresh. Dimly it was felt that they had to cry halt, civil disobedience had to be stopped; but what then? Two groups took shape: one desiring purely constitutional activities through the legislatures, the other thinking rather vaguely along socialistic lines. The majority of the members belonged to neither of these groups. They disliked a reversion to constitutionalism, and at the same time socialism frightened them a little and seemed to them to introduce an element which might split their ranks. They had no constructive ideas, and the one hope and sheet-anchor they possessed was Gandhiji. As of old, they turned to him and followed his lead, even though many of them did not wholly approve of what he said. Gandhiji's support of the moderate constitutional elements gave them dominance in the Committee and the Congress.

All this was to be expected. But the reaction took the Congress further back than I had thought. At no time during the last fifteen years, ever since the advent of non-co-operation, had Congress leaders talked in this ultra-constitutional fashion. Even the Swaraj Party of the middle 'twenties, which itself was the result of a reaction, was far in advance of the new leadership, and there were no such commanding personalities now as the Swaraj Party had. Many persons who had studiously kept aloof from the movement so long as it was risky to join it, now streamed in and assumed importance.

The proscription of the Congress was ended by the Government and it became a legal organization. But many of its associated and subsidiary bodies continued to be illegal, such as its volunteer department, the Seva Dal, as also a number of Kisan Sabhas, which were semi-independent peasant unions, and several educational institutions and youth leagues, including a children's organization. In particular the 'Khudai Khidmatgars', or the Frontier Redshirts, as they are called, were still outlawed. This organization had become a regular part of the Congress in 1931, and represented it in the Frontier Province. Thus, although the Congress had completely drawn off the direct action part of the struggle and had reverted to constitutional ways, the Government kept on all the special laws meant for civil disobedience, and even continued the proscription of important parts of the Congress organization. Special attention was also paid to the suppression of peasant organizations and labour unions, while, it was interesting to note, high Government officials went about urging the zamindars and landlords to organize themselves. Every facility was offered to these landlords' organizations. The two major ones in the United Provinces have their subscriptions collected by official agency, together with the revenue or taxes.

I am afraid I have never been partial to the Hindu or Muslim communal organizations, but an incident made me feel particularly bitter towards the Hindu Mahasabha. One of its secretaries actually went out of the way to approve of the continuation of the ban on the "Redshirts", and to pat Government on the back for it. This approval of the deprivation of the most elementary of civil rights, at a time when there was no aggressive movement on, amazed me. Apart from this question of principle, it was well known that these Frontier people had behaved wonderfully during these years of struggle; and their leader, Khan Abdul Ghaffar Khan, one of the bravest and straightest men in India, was still in prison—a State prisoner kept confined without any trial. It seemed to me that communal bias could hardly go further, and I expected that more prominent leaders of the Hindu Mahasabha would hasten to disown their colleague on this matter. But, so far as I could discover, not a single one of them said a word about it.

I was much upset by this Hindu Sabha secretary's statement. It was bad enough in itself, but to my mind it appeared as a symbol of the new state of affairs in the country. In the heat of that summer afternoon I dozed off, and I remember having a curious dream. Abdul Ghaffar Khan was being attacked on all sides and I was fighting to defend him. I woke up in an exhausted state, feeling very miserable, and my pillow was wet with tears. This surprised me, for in my waking state I was not liable to such emotional outbursts.

My nerves were obviously in a bad way in those days. My sleep became troubled and disturbed, which was very unusual for me, and all manner of nightmares came to me. Sometimes I would shout out in my sleep. Once evidently the shouting had been more vigorous than usual, and I woke up with a start to find two gaol warders standing near my bed, rather worried at my noises. I had dreamed that I was being strangled.

About this time a resolution of the Congress Working Committee also had a painful effect on me. This resolution was passed, it was stated, "in view of the loose talk about the confiscation of private property and necessity of class war", and it proceeded to remind Congressmen that the Karachi Resolution "neither contemplates confiscation of private property without just cause or compensation, nor advocacy of class war. The Working Committee is further of the opinion that confiscation and class war are contrary to the Congress creed of non-violence". The resolution was loosely worded and exhibited a certain amount of ignorance on the part of the framers as to what class war was. It was obviously aimed at the newly formed Congress Socialist Party. There had, as a matter of fact, been no talk of confiscation on the part of any responsible member of this group; there had, however, been frequent reference to the existence of class war under present conditions. The Working Committee's resolution seemed to hint that any person believing in the existence of this class conflict could not even be an ordinary member of the Congress. Nobody had ever accused the Congress of having turned Socialist or of being against private property. Some members of it held those opinions, but now it appeared that they had no place even in the rank and file of this all-embracing national organization.

It had often been stated that the Congress represented the nation, including every group and interest in it, from prince to pauper. National movements frequently make that claim, meaning thereby presumably that they represent the great majority of the nation and that their policy is for the good of all interests. But the claim is on the face of it untenable, for no political organization can represent conflicting interests without reducing itself to a flabby and unmeaning mass with no distinctive and distinguishing features. The Congress is either a political party with a definite (or vague) aim and philosophy of achieving political power and of utilizing it for the national good, or it is just a benevolent and humanitarian organization with no views of its own and wishing well to everybody. It can represent only those who are in general agreement with that aim and philosophy, and those who oppose this are likely to be considered by it as anti-national or anti-social and reactionary elements whose influence must be checked or eliminated, in order to give effect to its own philosophy. It is true that a national anti-imperialist movement offers a wide basis for agreement, as it does not touch the social conflicts. And so the Congress did represent in varying degrees the vast majority of the people of India, and it drew within its fold all manner of mutually differing groups who agreed only on the anti-imperialist issue, and even in regard to this there were great differences in stress. Those who, on this basic issue of anti-imperialism, held a contrary opinion kept out of the Congress and sided, also in varying degrees, with the British Government. The Congress thus became a kind of permanent All-Parties Congress, consisting of large numbers of groups shading into each other and held together by one common faith and the dominating personality of Gandhiji.

The Working Committee subsequently tried to explain its resolution on class war. The importance of that resolution lay not so much in its language or what it definitely laid down, as in the fact that it was yet another indication of the way Congress was going. The resolution had obviously been inspired by the new parliamentary wing of the Congress aiming at gaining the support of men of property in the coming election to the Legislative Assembly. At their instance the Congress was looking more and more to the Right and trying to win over the moderate and conservative elements in the country. Soothing words were being addressed even to those who had been hostile to the Congress movements in the past and had sided with the Government during the continuance of civil disobedience. A clamorous and critical Left wing was felt to be a handicap in this process of conciliation and 'conversion', and the Working Committee's resolution, as well as many other individual utterances, made it clear that the Congress Executive were not going to be moved from their new path by this nibbling from the Left. If the Left did not behave it would be sat upon and eliminated from the Congress ranks. The manifesto issued by the Parliamentary Board of the Congress contained a programme which was far more cautious and moderate than any that the Congress had sponsored during the past fifteen years.

The Congress leadership, quite apart even from Gandhiji, consisted of many well-known persons with bright records in the national struggle for freedom, men honoured throughout the country for their integrity and fearlessness. But the new orientation of policy brought into the second ranks, and even the front rank, of Congress many individuals who could hardly be described as idealists. In the Congress ranks there were, of course, large numbers of idealists, but the door for careerists and opportunists was now more open than it had ever been before. Apart from Gandhiji's enigmatical and elusive personality, which dominated the scene, the Congress seemed to possess two faces: a purely political side was developing like a caucus, and the other aspect was that of a prayer meeting, full of pietism and sentimentality.

On the Government side there was an air of triumph, in no way concealed, at what they considered the success of their policy in suppressing civil disobedience and its offshoots. The operation had been successful, and for the moment it mattered little whether the patient lived or died. They proposed to continue the same policy, with minor variations, even though the Congress had been for the moment brought round to some extent. They knew that such changes in national policy could only be temporary so long as the basic problem remained, and any relaxation on their part might lead to a more rapid growth than otherwise. Perhaps they also thought that in continuing to suppress the more advanced elements in the Congress or in the labour and peasant ranks, they would not greatly offend the more cautious leaders of the Congress.

To some extent my thoughts in Dehra Dun Gaol ran along these channels. I was really not in a position to form definite opinions about the course of events, for I was out of touch. In Alipore I had been almost completely out of touch, in Dehra a newspaper of the Government's choice brought me partial and sometimes one-sided news. It is quite possible that contacts with my colleagues outside and a closer study of the situation would have resulted in my varying my opinions in some degree.

Distressed with the present, I began thinking of the past, of what had happened politically in India since I began to take some part in public affairs. How far had we been right in what we had done? How far wrong? It struck me that my thinking would he more orderly and helpful if I put it down on paper. This would also help in engaging my mind in a definite task and so diverting it from worry and depression. So in the month of June 1934 I began this 'autobiographical narrative' in Dehra Gaol, and for the last eight months I have continued it when the mood to do so has seized me. Often there have been intervals when I felt no desire to write; three of these gaps were each of them nearly a month long. But I managed to continue, and now I am nearing the end of this personal journey. Most of this has been written under peculiarly distressing circumstances when I was suffering from depression and emotional strain. Perhaps some of this is reflected in what I have written, but this very writing helped me greatly to pull myself out of the present with all its worries. As I wrote, I was hardly thinking of an outside audience; I was addressing myself, framing questions and answering them for my own benefit, sometimes even drawing some amusement from it. I wanted as far as possible to think straight, and I imagined that this review of the past might help me to do so.

Towards the end of July, Kamala's condition rapidly deteriorated, and within a few days became critical. On August 11th I was suddenly asked to leave Dehra Gaol, and that night I was sent under police escort to Allahabad. The next evening we reached Prayag station in Allahabad and there I was informed by the District Magistrate that I was being released temporarily so that I might visit my ailing wife. It was six months to a day from the time of my arrest.

65

ELEVEN DAYS

For the Sword outwears its sheath,
And the soul wears out the breast.

Byron

My release was temporary. I was given to understand that it was for a day or two or for such longer period as the doctors might think absolutely necessary. It was a peculiar position, full of uncertainty, and it was not possible for me to settle down to anything. A fixed period would have enabled me to know how I stood, and I would have tried to adjust myself to it. As it was, any day, at any moment, I might be taken back to prison.

The change was sudden and I was wholly unprepared for it. From solitary confinement to a crowded house with doctors, nurses, and relatives. My daughter Indira had also come from Santiniketan. Many friends were continually coming to see me and enquire after Kamala's health. The style of living was quite different; there were home comforts, better food. And colouring all this background was anxiety for Kamala's serious condition.

There she lay frail and utterly weak, a shadow of herself, struggling feebly with her illness, and the thought that she might leave me became an intolerable obsession. It was eighteen and a half years since our marriage, and my mind wandered back to that day and to all that these succeeding years had brought us. I was twenty-six at the time and she was about seventeen, a slip of a girl, utterly unsophisticated in the ways of the world. The difference in our ages was considerable, but greater still was the difference in our mental outlook, for I was far more grown-up than she was. And yet with all my appearance of worldly wisdom I was very boyish, and I hardly realized that this delicate, sensitive girl's mind was slowly unfolding like a flower and required gentle and careful tending. We were attracted to each other and got on well enough, but our backgrounds were different and there was a want of adjustment. These maladjustments would sometimes lead to friction and there were many petty quarrels over trivialities, boy-and-girl affairs which did not last long and ended in a quick reconciliation. Both had a quick temper, a sensitive nature, and a childish notion of keeping one's dignity. In spite of this our attachment grew, though the want of adjustment lessened only slowly. Twenty-one months after our marriage, Indira, our daughter and only child, arrived.

Our marriage had almost coincided with new developments in politics, and my absorption in them grew. They were the Home Rule days, and soon after came Martial Law in the Punjab and Non-Co-operation, and more and more I was involved in the dust and tumble of public affairs. So great became my concentration in these activities that, all unconsciously, I almost overlooked her and left her to her own resources, just when she required my full co-operation. My affection for her continued and even grew, and it was a great comfort to know that she was there to help me with her soothing influence. She gave me strength, but she must have suffered and felt a little neglected. An unkindness to her would almost have been better than this semi-forgetful, casual attitude.

And then came her recurring illness and my long absences in prison, when we could only meet at gaol interviews. The Civil Disobedience movement brought her in the front rank of our fighters, and she rejoiced when she too went to prison. We grew ever nearer to each other. Our rare meetings became precious, and we looked forward to them and counted the days that intervened. We could not get tired of each other or stale, for there was always a freshness and novelty about our meetings and brief periods together. Each of us was continually making fresh discoveries in the other, though sometimes perhaps the new discoveries were not to our liking. Even our grown-up disagreements had something boyish and girlish about them.

After eighteen years of married life she had still retained her girlish and virginal appearance; there was nothing matronly about her. Almost she might have been the bride that came to our house so long ago. But I had changed vastly, and though I was fit and supple and active enough for my age—and, I was told, still possessed some boyish traits—my looks betrayed me. I was partly bald and my hair was grey, lines and furrows crossed my face and dark shadows surrounded my eyes. The last four years with their troubles and worries had left many a mark on me. Often, in these later years when Kamala and I had gone out together in a strange place, she was mistaken, to my embarrassment, for my daughter. She and Indira looked like two sisters.

Eighteen years of married life! But how many long years out of them had I spent in prison-cell, and Kamala in hospitals and sanatoria? And now again I was serving a prison sentence and out just for a few days, and she was lying ill, struggling for life. I felt a little irritated at her for her carelessness about her health. And yet how could I blame her, for her eager spirit fretted at her inaction and her inability to take her full share in the national struggle. Physically unable to do so, she could neither take to work properly nor to treatment, and the fire inside her wore down the body.

Surely she was not going to leave me now when I needed her most? Why, we had just begun to know and understand each other really; our joint life was only now properly beginning. We relied so much on each other, we had so much to do together.

So I thought as I watched her from day to day and hour to hour.

Colleagues and friends came to see me. They told me of much that had happened of which I was unaware. They discussed current political problems and asked me questions. I found it difficult to answer them. It was not easy for my mind to get away from Kamala's illness, and after the isolation and detachment of gaol I was not in a position to face concrete questions suddenly. Long experience had taught me that it is not possible to appraise a situation from the limited information available in gaol. Personal contacts were necessary for a proper mental reaction, otherwise the expression of opinion was likely to be purely academic and divorced from reality. It seemed also unfair to Gandhiji and my old colleagues of the Congress Working Committee for me to say anything definite regarding Congress policy before I had had the opportunity to discuss everything with them. My mind was full of criticisms of much that had been done, but I was not prepared to make any positive suggestions. Not expecting to come out of prison just then I had not thought along these lines.

I had also a feeling that in view of the courtesy shown by the Government in allowing me to come to my wife, it would not be proper for me to take advantage of this for political purposes. I had given no undertaking or assurance to avoid any such activity, nevertheless I was continually being pulled back by this idea.

I avoided issuing any public statements except to contradict false rumours. Even in private I refrained from committing myself to any definite line of policy, but I was free enough with my criticisms of past events. The Congress Socialist Party had recently come into existence, and many of my intimate colleagues were associated with it. So far as I had gathered, its general policy was agreeable to me, but it seemed a curious and mixed assemblage and, even if I had been completely free, I would not have suddenly joined it. Local politics took up some of my time, for in Allahabad, as in several other places, there had been an extraordinarily virulent campaign during the elections for the local Congress Committees. No principles were involved, it was purely a question of personalities, and I was asked to help in settling some of the personal quarrels that had arisen.

I had no desire whatever to go into these matters, nor had I the time. In spite of this some of the facts came to my notice and caused me great distress. It was surprising that people should get so vastly excited over local Congress elections. Among the most prominent were those who had retired during the struggle for various private reasons. With the withdrawal of civil disobedience those reasons ceased to have weight, and they emerged suddenly and carried on a fierce and often vulgar campaign against each other. It was extraordinary how the ordinary canons of decency were forgotten in the passionate desires to down the other party. I was especially grieved at the fact that Kamala's name and even her illness had been exploited for the purposes of these local elections.

Among the wider questions that were discussed was the Congress decision to contest the coming elections to the Legislative Assembly. Many of the younger groups opposed this decision because they thought it was a return to parliamentary and compromising methods, but they suggested no effective alternative. Some of these opponents on grounds of high principle had, curiously enough, no objection to organizations other than the Congress running the elections. Their object seemed to be to leave the field clear to communal organizations.

I felt disgusted with the local squabble and the kind of politics which were rapidly developing. I felt out of tune with them and a stranger in my own city of Allahabad. What could I do, I wondered, in this environment when the time came for me to attend to such matters?

I wrote to Gandhiji about Kamala's condition. As I thought I would be going back to prison soon and might have no other chance to do so, I gave him also some glimpse into my mind. Recent events had embittered and distressed me greatly, and my letter carried a faint reflection of this. I did not attempt to suggest what should be done or what should not be done; all I did was to interpret some of my reactions to what had happened. It was a letter full of barely suppressed emotion, and I learnt subsequently that it pained Gandhiji considerably.

Day after day went by and I waited for the summons to prison or some other intimation from Government. From time to time I was informed that further directions would be issued the next day or the day after. Meanwhile the doctors were asked to send a daily bulletin of my wife's condition to Government. Kamala had slightly improved since my arrival.

It was generally believed, even by those who are usually in the confidence of the Government, that I would have been fully discharged but for two impending events—the full session of the Congress that was taking place in October in Bombay and the Assembly Elections in November. Out of prison I might be a disturbing factor at these, and so it seemed probable that I might be sent back to prison for another three months and then discharged. There was also the possibility of my not being sent back to gaol, and this possibility seemed to grow as the days went by. I almost decided to settle down.

It was the eleventh day after my release, August 23rd. The police car drove up and the police officer came up to me and told me that my time was up and I had to accompany him to Naini Prison. I bade good-bye to my people. As I was getting into the police car my ailing mother ran up again to me with arms outstretched. That face of hers haunted me for long.

66

BACK TO PRISON

Shadow is itself unrestrained in its path while sunshine, as an incident of its very nature, is pursued a hundredfold by nuance. Thus is sorrow from happiness a thing apart; the scope of happiness, however, is hampered by the aches and hurts of endless sorrows.

Rajatarangini.[1]

I was back again in Naini Prison, and I felt as if I was starting a fresh term of imprisonment. In and out, out and in; what a shuttlecock I had become! This switching on and off shook up the whole system emotionally and it was not easy to adjust onself to repeated changes. I had expected to be put in my old cell at Naini to which a previous long stay had accustomed me. There were some flowers there, originally planted by my brother-in-law, Ranjit Pandit, and a good veranda. But this old Barrack No. 6 was occupied by a detenu, a State prisoner, kept confined without trial or conviction. It was not considered desirable for me to associate with him, and I was therefore placed in another part of the gaol which was much more closed in and was devoid of flowers or greenery.

But the place where I spent my days and nights mattered little, for my mind was elsewhere. I feared that the little improvement that had taken place in Kamala's condition would not stand the shock of my re-arrest. And so it happened. For some days it was arranged to supply me in prison with a very brief doctor's bulletin daily. This came by a devious route. The doctor had to telephone it to the police headquarters and the latter then sent it on to the prison. It was not considered desirable to have any direct contacts between the doctors and the gaol staff. For two weeks these bulletins came to me, sometimes rather irregularly, and then they were stopped although there was a progressive deterioration

1. R.S. Pandit's translation. ("River of Kings." *Taranga.* verse viii, 1913.)

in Kamala's condition.

Bad news and the waiting for news made the days intolerably long and the nights were sometimes worse. Time seemed almost to stand still or to move with desperate slowness, and every hour was a burden and a horror. I had never before had this feeling in this acute degree. I thought then that I was likely to be released within two months or so, after the Bombay Congress Session, but those two months seemed an eternity.

Exactly a month after my re-arrest a police officer took me from prison on a brief visit to my wife. I was told that I would be allowed to visit her in this way twice a week, and even the time for it was fixed. I waited on the fourth day—no one came for me; and on the fifth, sixth, seventh. I became weary of waiting. News reached me that her condition was becoming critical again. What a joke it was, I thought, to tell me that I would be taken to see her twice a week.

At last the month of September was over. They were the longest and most damnable thirty days that I had ever experienced.

Suggestions were made to me through various intermediaries that if I could give an assurance, even an informal assurance, to keep away from politics for the rest of my term I would be released to attend on Kamala. Politics were far enough from my thoughts just then, and the politics I had seen during my eleven days outside had disgusted me, but to give an assurance! And to be disloyal to my pledges, to the cause, to my colleagues, to myself! It was an impossible condition, whatever happened. To do so meant inflicting a mortal injury on the roots of my being, on almost everything I held sacred. I was told that Kamala's condition was becoming worse and worse and my presence by her side might make all the difference between life and death. Was my personal conceit and pride greater than my desire to give her this chance? It might have been a terrible predicament for me, but fortunately that dilemma did not face me in that way at least. I knew that Kamala herself would strongly disapprove of my giving any undertaking, and if I did anything of the kind it would shock her and harm her.

Early in October I was taken to see her again. She was lying almost in a daze with a high temperature. She longed to have me by her, but as I was leaving her, to go back to prison, she smiled at me bravely and beckoned to me to bend down. When I did so, she whispered: "What is this about your giving an assurance to Government? Do not give it!"

During the eleven days I was out of prison it had been decided to
send Kamala, as soon as she was a little better, to a more suitable place
for treatment. Ever since then we had waited for her to get better, but
instead she had gone downhill, and now, six weeks later, the change for
the worse was very marked. It was futile to continue waiting and watching
this process of deterioration, and it was decided to send her to Bhowali
in the hills even in her present condition.

The day before she was to leave for Bhowali I was taken from prison
to bid her good-bye. When will I see her again? I wondered. And will I
see her at all? But she looked bright and cheerful that day, and I felt
happier than I had done for long.

Nearly three weeks later I was transferred from Naini Prison to Almora
District Gaol so as to be nearer to Kamala. Bhowali was on the way, and
my police escort and I spent a few hours there. I was greatly pleased to
note the improvement in Kamala, and I left her, to continue my journey
to Almora, with a light heart. Indeed, even before I had reached her, the
mountains had filled me with joy.

I was glad to be back in these mountains, and as our car sped along
the winding road the cold morning air and the unfolding panorama
brought a sense of exhilaration. Higher and higher we went: the gorges
deepened: the peaks lost themselves in the clouds: the vegetation changed
till the firs and pines covered the hill-sides. A turn of the road would
bring to our eyes suddenly a new expanse of hills and valleys with a little
river gurgling in the depths below. I could not have my fill of the sight
and I looked on hungrily, storing my memory with it, so that I might
revive it in my mind when actual sight denied.

Clusters of little mountain huts clung to the hill-sides, and round
about them were tiny fields made by prodigious labour on every possible
bit of slope. They looked like terraces from a distance, huge steps which
sometimes went from the valley below right up almost to the mountain
top. What enormous labour had gone to make nature yield a little food
to the sparse population! How they toiled unceasingly only to get barely
enough for their needs! Those ploughed terraces gave a domesticated
look to the hillsides and they contrasted strangely with the bleaker or
the more wooded slopes.

It was very pleasant in the daytime and, as the sun rose higher, the
growing warmth brought life to the mountains and they seemed to lose

their remoteness and become friendly and companionable. But how they change their aspect with the passing of day! How cold and grim they become when "Night with giant strides stalks o'er the world" and life hides and protects itself and leaves wild nature to its own. In the semi-darkness of the moonlight or starlight the mountains loom up mysterious, threatening, overwhelming, and yet almost insubstantial, and through the valleys can be heard the moaning of the wind. The poor traveller shivers as he goes his lonely way and senses hostility everywhere. Even the voice of the wind seems to mock him and challenge him. And at other times there is no breath of wind or other sound, and there is an absolute silence that is oppressive in its intensity. Only the telegraph wires perhaps hum faintly, and the stars seem brighter and nearer than ever. The mountains look down grimly, and one seems to be face to face with a mystery that terrifies. With Pascal one thinks: *"La silence éternel de ces espaces infini m'effraie"*. In the plains the nights are never quite so soundless; life is still audible there, and the murmuring and humming of various animals and insects break the stillness of the night.

But the night with its chill and inhospitable message was yet distant as we motored along to Almora. As we neared the end of our journey, a turn in the road and a sudden lifting of the clouds brought a new sight which I saw with a gasp of surprised delight. The snowy peaks of the Himalayas stood glistening in the far distance, high above the wooded mountains that intervened. Calm and inscrutable they seemed, with all the wisdom of past ages, mighty sentinels over the vast Indian plain. The very sight of them cooled the fever in the brain, and the petty conflicts and intrigues, the lusts and falsehoods of the plains and the cities seemed trivial and far away before their eternal ways.

The little gaol of Almora was perched up on a ridge. I was given a lordly barrack to live in. This consisted of one huge hall, fifty-one feet by seventeen, with a *katcha*, very uneven floor, and a worm-eaten roof which was continually coming down in little bits. There were fifteen windows and a door, or rather there were so many barred openings in the walls, for there were no doors or windows. There was thus no lack of fresh air. As it grew colder some of the window-openings were covered with coir matting. In this vast expanse (which was bigger than any yard at Dehra Dun) I lived in solitary grandeur. But I was not quite alone, for at least two score sparrows had made their home in the broken-down roof. Sometimes a wandering cloud would visit me, its many arms creeping in through the numerous openings and filling the place with a damp mist.

Here I was locked up every evening at about five, after I had taken my last meal, a kind of high tea, at four-thirty; and at seven in the morning my barred door would be unlocked. In the daytime I would sit either in my barrack or outside in an adjoining yard, warming myself in the sun. I could just see over the enclosing walls the top of a mountain a mile or so away, and above me I had a vast expanse of blue sky dotted with clouds. Wonderful shapes these clouds assumed, and I never grew tired of watching them. I fancied I saw them take the shape of all manner of animals, and sometimes they would join together and look like a mighty ocean. Or they would be like a beach, and the rustling of the breeze through the deodars would sound like the coming in of the tide on a distant sea-front. Sometimes a cloud would advance boldly on us, seemingly solid and compact, and then dissolve in mist as it came near and finally enveloped us.

I preferred the wide expanse of my barrack to a narrow cell, though it was lonelier than a smaller place would have been. Even when it rained outside I could walk about in it. But as it grew colder its cheerlessness became more marked, and my love for fresh air and the open abated when the temperature hovered about the freezing-point. The new year brought a good fall of snow to my delight, and even the drab surroundings of prison became beautiful. Especially beautiful and fairy-like were the deodar trees just outside the gaol walls with their garment of snow.

I was worried by the ups and downs of Kamala's condition, and a piece of bad news would upset me for a while, but the hill air calmed me and soothed me and I reverted to my habit of sleeping soundly. As I was on the verge of sleep I often thought what a wonderful and mysterious thing was sleep. Why should one wake up from it? Suppose I did not wake at all?

Yet the desire to be out gaol was strong in me, more than I had ever felt before. The Bombay Congress was over, and November came and went by and the excitement of the Assembly elections also passed away. I half expected that I might be released soon.

But then came the surprising news of the arrest and conviction of

Khan Abdul Ghaffar Khan and the amazing orders passed on Subhas Bose during his brief visit to India. These orders in themselves were devoid of all humanity and consideration; they were applied to one who was held in affection and esteem by vast numbers of his countrymen, and who had hastened home, in spite of his own illness, to the death-bed of his father—to arrive too late. If that was the outlook of the Government there could be no chance of my premature release. Official announcements later made this perfectly clear.

After I had been a month in Almora gaol I was taken to Bhowali to see Kamala. Since then I have visited her approximately every third week. Sir Samuel Hoare, the Secretary of State for India, has repeatedly stated that I am allowed to visit my wife once or twice a week. He would have been more correct if he had said once or twice a month. During the last three and a half months that I have been at Almora I have paid five visits to her. I do not mention this as a grievance, because I think that in this matter the Government have been very considerate to me and have given me quite unusual facilities to visit Kamala. I am grateful to them for this. The brief visits I have paid her have been very precious to me and perhaps to her also. The doctors suspended their regime for the day of my visit to some extent, and I was permitted to have fairly long talks with her. We came ever nearer to each other, and to leave her was a wrench. We met only to be parted. And sometimes I thought with anguish that a day might come when the parting was for good.

My mother had gone to Bombay for treatment, for she had not recovered from her ailment. She seemed to be progressing. One morning in mid-January a telegram brought a wholly unexpected shock. She had had a stroke of paralysis. There was a possibility of my being transferred to a Bombay prison to enable me to see her, but as there was a little improvement in her condition I was not sent.

January has given place to February, and there is the whisper of spring in the air. The bulbul and other birds are again to be seen and heard, and tiny shoots are mysteriously bursting out of the ground and gazing at this strange world. Rhododendrons make blood-red patches on the hill-sides, and peace and plum blossoms are peeping out. The days pass and I count them as they go, thinking of my next visit to Bhowali. I wonder what truth there is in the saying that life's rich gifts follow frustration and cruelty and separation. Perhaps the gifts would not be appreciated otherwise. Perhaps suffering is necessary for clear thought, but excess of it may cloud the brain. Gaol encourages introspection, and my long years in prison have forced me to look more and more within myself. I was not by nature an introvert, but prison life, like strong coffee or strychnine, leads to introversion. Sometimes, to amuse myself, I draw an outline of Professor McDougall's cube for the measurement of introversion and extroversion, and I gaze at it to find out how frequent are the changes from one interpretation to another. They seem to be rapid.

67

SOME RECENT HAPPENINGS

Dawn reddens in the wake of night, but the days of our life return not.
The eye contains a far horizon, but the wound of spring lies deep in the
heart.

Li Tài-Po.

I followed from the newspapers supplied to me the proceedings of the
Bombay session of the Congress. I was naturally interested in its politics
and personalities. Twenty years' intimate association had tied me up so
closely with it that my individuality had almost become merged in it,
and far stronger than the claims of office and responsibility were the
invisible bonds that tied me to that great organization and to thousands
of my old comrades. And yet I felt it difficult to get excited over its
proceedings; in spite of some important decisions the whole session
seemed to me a dull affair. The subjects that interested me were hardly
discussed. What would I have done if I had been there, I wondered. I did
not know for certain; I could not say how I would have reacted to the
new conditions and my surroundings. And I saw no reason why I should
force my mind to come to a difficult decision in prison when such a
decision was wholly unnecessary then. The time would come when I
would have to face the problems of the day and decide on my course of
action. It was needless folly to anticipate that decision, even in the recesses
of my mind, for circumstances would change before that choice was
forced on me.

The two outstanding features of the Congress, as far as I could make
out from my distant and secluded abode on the mountains, were: the
dominant personality of Gandhiji and the exceedingly poor show that
the communal opposition under Pandit Madan Mohan Malaviya and
Mr Aney put up. To all who have knowledge of the inner workings of
the Indian mass-mind, as well as the middle-class mind, it was no surprise
to find that Gandhiji continues to be far and away *the* master figure in
India. Government officials and some secluded politicians often imagine,

making the wish the father to the thought, that he is played out in the political field or, at least, that his influence has greatly declined. And then when he emerges again with all his old energy and influence they are taken aback and search for fresh reasons for this apparent change. He dominates the Congress and the country not so much because of any opinions he holds, and which are generally accepted, but because of his unique personality. Personality counts for much everywhere; in India it plays an even more dominant role than elsewhere.

His retirement from the Congress was a striking feature of the session and outwardly it marked the end of a great chapter in Congress and Indian history. But, essentially, its significance was not great for he cannot rid himself, even if he wanted to, of his dominating position. He did not owe that position to any office or other tangible tie. The Congress today reflects almost as much his view-point as it has ever done before, and even if it should wander away from his path, Gandhiji, even unconsciously, would continue to influence it and the country to a very great extent. He cannot divest himself of that burden and responsibility. In considering the objective conditions prevailing in India his personality forces itself on one's attention and cannot be ignored.

He has, for the present, retired from the Congress presumably to avoid embarrassing the Congress. Perhaps he contemplates some kind of individual direct action which will necessarily lead to a conflict with Government. He does not want to make this a Congress issue.

I was glad that the Congress had adopted the idea of a Constituent Assembly for settling the constitution of the country. It seemed to me that there was no other way of solving the problem, and I am sure that sometime or other some such Assembly will have to meet. Manifestly it cannot do so without the consent of the British Government, unless there has been a successful revolution. It is equally manifest that this consent is not likely to be forthcoming under present circumstances. A real Assembly can therefore not meet till enough strength has been evolved in the country to force the pace. This inevitably means that even the political problem will remain unsolved till then. Some of the Congress leaders, while accepting the idea of the Constituent Assembly, have tried to tone it down and made it not very unlike a large All-Parties Conference after the old model. This would be an utterly futile proceeding and the same old people, self-chosen mostly, would meet and disagree. The whole idea behind the Constituent Assembly is that it should be elected on a very wide mass basis, drawing its strength and inspiration from the masses. Such a gathering will immediately face real problems, and will not remain in the communal and other ruts in which we have so often stuck.

It was interesting to watch the reactions of Simla and London to this idea. It was made known semi-officially that Government would have no objection; they gave it a patronizing approval, evidently looking upon it as an old type of All-Parties Conference, foredoomed to failure, which would strengthen their hands. Later they seem to have realized the dangers and possibilities of the idea, and they began opposing it vigorously.

Soon after the Bombay Congress came the Assembly elections. With all my lack of enthusiasm for the Congress parliamentary programme, I was greatly interested and I wished the Congress candidates success, or to put it more correctly, I hoped for the defeat of their opponents. Among these opponents was a curious assortment of careerists, communalists, renegades, and people who had staunchly supported the Government in its policy of repression. There was little doubt that most of these people would be swept away, but unfortunately the Communal Award obscured the issue and many of them took shelter under the widespread wings of the communal organizations. Despite this the Congress met with remarkable success, and I was pleased that a good number of undesirables had been kept out.

The attitude of the so-called Congress Nationalist Party struck me as particularly deplorable. One could understand their vehement opposition to the Communal Award but, in order to strengthen their position, they allied themselves with the extreme communal organizations, even the Sanatanists, than whom there is no more reactionary group in India, both politically and socially, as well as numerous political reactionaries of the most notorious kind. Except in Bengal, where for special reasons a strong Congress group supported them, many of them were largely anti-Congress in every way. Indeed they were the most prominent opponents of the Congress. In spite of this varied assortment of forces opposed to it, which included landlords, liberals and, of course, officials, the Congress candidates succeeded to a remarkable extent.

The Congress attitude to the Communal Award was extraordinary, and yet under the circumstances it could hardly have been very different.

It was the inevitable outcome of their past neutral and rather feeble policy. A strong line adopted at an earlier stage and followed regardless of immediate consequences would have been more dignified and correct. But as the Congress had been unwilling to take that up there was no other course open to it except the one it took. The Communal Award was a patent absurdity, and it was impossible of acceptance because, so long as it existed, any kind of freedom was unattainable. This was not because it gave too much to the Muslims. It was perhaps possible to give them, in a different way, almost all they wanted. As it was, the British Government divided up India into any number of mutually exclusive compartments, each balancing and neutralizing the other, so that the foreign British element could remain supreme. It made dependence on the British Government inevitable.

In Bengal especially, where heavy weightage had been given to the small European element, the position was exceedingly unfair to the Hindus. Such an award or decision, or whatever it might be called (objection has been taken to its being called an award), was bound to be bitterly resented, and even though it might be imposed, or for political reasons tolerated temporarily, it is likely to be a continuing source of friction. Personally I think that its very badness is a thing in its favour, for as such it can never become the permanent basis for anything.

The Nationalist Party, and even more so the Hindu Mahasabha and other communal organizations, naturally resented this infliction, but their criticism was really based, as that of the supporters, on an acceptance of the British Government's ideology. This led them, and is leading them further, to the adoption of a strange policy, which must be very pleasing to the Government. Obsessed by the Award, they are toning down their opposition to other vital matters, in the hope of bribing or cajoling the Government into varying the Award in their favour. The Hindu Mahasabha has gone farthest in this direction. It does not seem to strike them that this is not only a humiliating position to take up, but is calculated to make any alteration of the Award most difficult, for it merely irritates the Muslims and drives them farther away. It is impossible for the British Government to win over the nationalist elements; the distance is too great and the conflict of interests too marked. It is also impossible for them, on the narrower issue of communal interests, to please both the Hindu and the Muslim communalists. They had to choose and, from their points of view, they chose rightly in favouring Muslim communalism. Are they to upset this well-settled and profitable policy and offend the Muslims for the sake of winning over a handful of Hindu communalists?

The very fact that the Hindus, as a group, are more advanced politically and more clamant for national freedom is bound to go against them. For petty communal concessions (and they cannot be other than petty) will not make much difference to their political hostility; such concessions will however make a temporary difference to the Muslim attitude.

The Assembly elections threw a revealing light on the people at the back of the Hindu Mahasabha and the Muslim Conference—the two most reactionary communal bodies. Their candidates and supporters were drawn from the big landlords or the rich banker class. The Mahasabha also showed its solicitude to the banker class by its vehement opposition to the recent Relief from Indebtedness Bills. These small sections at the top of the Hindu social strata constitute the Hindu Mahasabha, and a fraction of them, together with some professional people, form the Liberals. They do not carry great weight among the Hindus because the lower middle class is politically awake. The industrial leaders also stand apart from them because there is some clash between the demands of rising industry and the semi-feudal elements. Industrialists, not daring to indulge in direct action or other risky methods, try to keep on good terms with both nationalism and the Government. They do not pay much attention to the liberal or communal groups. Industrial advance and profits are their governing motives.

Among the Muslims this lower middle class awakening is still to come, and industrially also they are backward. Thus we find the most hopelessly reactionary and feudal and ex-official elements not only controlling their communal organizations, but exercising considerable influence over the community. The Muslim Conference is quite a galaxy of knights, ex-ministers and big landlords. And yet I think that the Muslim rank and file has more potentiality in it, perhaps because of a certain freedom in social relations, than the Hindu masses, and is likely to go ahead faster in a socialist direction, once it gets moving. Just at present the Muslim intelligentsia seems to be paralysed, intellectually as well as physically, and has no push in it. It dare not challenge its old guard.

Even the leadership of the Congress, politically the most advanced big group, is far more cautious than the condition of the masses might necessitate. They ask the masses for support, but seldom ask them for their opinion or set about enquiring what ails them. Prior to the Assembly elections they made every effort to tone down their programme in an attempt to win over various moderate non-Congress elements. Even their attitude to such measures as the Temple Entry Bill was varied, and assurances were given to soothe the more orthodox in Madras. A straightforward, aggressive election programme would have created more enthusiasm and helped greatly in educating the masses. Now that the Congress has committed itself to a parliamentary programme there will be still more accommodation of politically and socially reactionary interests, in the hope of getting a few odd votes in a division, and a greater widening of the breach between the Congress leadership and the masses. Eloquent speeches will be delivered, and the best parliamentary etiquette followed, and from time to time the Government will be defeated—defeats which the Government will calmly ignore as it has previously done.

During the past few years, when Congress was boycotting the Legislatures, we were often told by official spokesmen that the Assembly and the Provincial Councils were truly representative of the people and mirrored public opinion. It is interesting to find that now, when more advanced elements dominate the Assembly, the official view-point has changed. Whenever a reference is made to the Congress success at the elections, we are told that the electorate is a very small one, only three millions out of nearly three hundred or thereabouts. The disfranchised millions apparently, according to official opinion, stand solidly behind the British Government. The remedy is obvious. Give adult suffrage and then we shall know at least what these people think.

Soon after the Assembly elections the Report of the Joint Parliamentary Committee on Indian Constitutional Reform was issued. Among the varied and widespread criticisms to which it was subjected, stress was often laid on the fact that it showed 'distrust' and 'suspicion' of the Indian people. This seemed to me a very strange way of looking at our national and social problems. Were there no vital conflicts of interests between British imperial policy and our national interests? The question was which was to prevail. Did we want freedom merely to continue that imperial policy? Apparently that was the British Government's notion, for we were informed that the 'safeguards' would not be used so long as we behaved and demonstrated our fitness for self-rule by doing just what British policy required. If British policy was to be continued in India, why all this shouting about getting the reins in our own hands?

The Ottawa agreements, it is well known, have not been of great benefit to England economically except in regard to Indian trade.[1] British trade with India has certainly benefited, at the cost, according to Indian political and commercial opinion, of India's wider interests. The position is reversed in regard to the Dominions, especially Canada and Australia.[2] They struck a hard bargain with Britain and got most of the advantages at Britain's expense. In spite of this fact, continuous attempts are being made by them to get away from Ottawa and its entanglements in order to develop their own industries as well as their trade with other countries.[3] In Canada a leading political party, the Liberals, who are likely to be in power before long, are definitely committed to ending the Ottawa pact.[4]

---

1. Referring to Indian trade, Sir William Currie said that the Ottawa agreements had been a definite advantage to Britain. Sir William was presiding over the meeting of the P. and O. Shipping Company in London on December. 5, 1934.

2. The London *Economist* (June 1934) says that the Ottawa Conference "could only have been justified if it had increased the value of inter-imperial trade without diminishing the value of the Empire's trade with the rest of the world. In fact, it has merely increased very slightly the proportion that inter-imperial trade bears to the dwindling total of the Empire's trade. And this diversion has been much more in the interests of the Dominions than of Great Britain. Our imports from the Empire increased from £247,000,000 in 1931 to £249,000,000 in 1933, but our exports decreased from £170,600,000 to £163,500,000. And the fact remains that between 1929 and 1933 our exports to the Empire declined by 50.9 per cent, while our imports from the Empire declined only 32.9 per cent. The decline in our exports to foreign countries was not quite so great, but the decline in our imports from these countries was much greater."

3. The Melbourne *Age* does not like the Ottawa Agreement. In its view Ottawa is "acting as a constant irritant and is being increasingly recognized as an egregious blunder." (Quoted in *Manchester Guardian Weekly*, October 19, 1934.)

4. Even Mr Bennett, the present Conservative Prime Minister of Canada, has been a thorn in the side of the British Government in trade matters. He is talking now in terms of 'New Deals' and records a surprising conversion. Owing to the dangerous influence of Mr Litvinov, Sir Stafford Cripps and Mr John Strachey, he has turned collectivist. This should be a sign and a warning to all Conservatives, Liberals, I.C.S. men, etc., to avoid thinking or associating with those who do so, or else they might themselves become converts to dangerous doctrines. (Since writing the above, the Liberal Party in Canada, under the leadership of Mr King, has swept the polls and come into power.)

In Australia strained interpretations of Ottawa have led to an increase of tariffs on certain classes of piece goods and yarns, and this has been bitterly resented by the Lancashire cotton industry and denounced by them as a breach of the Ottawa Agreement. As a protest and a reprisal, a movement for the boycott of Australian goods was inaugurated in Lancashire. This threat had little effect on Australia, where an aggressive attitude was taken up.[5]

The economic conflicts are obviously not due to any ill-will that the people of Canada and Australia may have for Britain, though in Ireland's case that ill-will is apparent. Conflicts occur because interests clash, and wherever such clashes might take place, the object of 'safeguards' in India is to see that British interests prevail. The recent Indo-British Trade Agreement, arrived at secretly over the heads and despite the protests of Indian business and industry, although British industrialists were kept informed, rejected by the Legislative Assembly and yet persisted in by the Government, is a gentle indication of what 'safeguards' would lead to. Such 'safeguards' seem to be urgently needed in Canada, Australia and South Africa to prevent the people of those Dominions from going astray not only in trade matters but in matters of greater concern to the safety and cohesion of the Empire.[6]

Empire, it has been said, is Debt, and the 'safeguards' have been devised to enable the imperial moneylender to keep his stranglehold on his unfortunate debtor, and to keep all his special interests and powers intact. A curious doctrine, often repeated officially, is that Gandhiji and the Congress have agreed to the idea of such safeguards because 'safeguards in the interests of India' were accepted in the Delhi Pact of 1931.

---

5. The Melbourne *Age* declared that if the proposed Lancashire boycott is not dropped, Australia must hit harder at whatever trade with Lancashire still remains. Lancashire is to be answered "with unwavering reiteration." (Quoted in *Manchester Guardian Weekly*, November 9, 1934.)

6. Mr O. Pirow, Minister for Defence of the Union of South Africa, stated that the Union would not take part in any general scheme of Imperial Defence, nor would it participate in an overseas war even though Britain might be at war. "If the Government attempted rashly to commit South Africa to participate in another overseas war there would be large-scale disturbances, possibly civil war. Hence Government would not participate in any general scheme of Imperial Defence." (Reuter message dated Cape Town, February 5, 1935.) General Hertzog, the Prime Minister, has confirmed this declaration and stated that it represents the Union Government's policy.

Ottawa and the safeguards dealing with trade and commerce are after all relatively minor matters.[7] What is far more important is the series of provisions which aim at perpetuating every vital political and economic hold on the Indian people which has in the past and present helped in the exploitation of the country. So long as these provisions and 'safeguards' remain, real progress in any direction is impossible, and there is no place left for constitutional attempts at change. Every such attempt will come up against the blank wall of the 'safeguards', and make it more and more clear that the only possible course is not constitutional. From the point of view of political changes this proposed constitution, with its monstrous Federation, is an absurdity; it is far worse from the social and economic view-point. The way to socialism is deliberately barred. A great deal of responsibility has apparently been transferred (but even that largely to 'safe' classes) but not the power or means to do anything worthwhile. Britain retains the power without the responsibility. There is not even the proverbial fig-leaf to cover the nakedness of autocracy. Everybody knows that the essential need in these times is extreme flexibility and adaptation in constitutions to meet a rapidly changing situation. Quick decisions are necessary, and the power to enforce them. Even so it is doubtful if parliamentary democracy, as it functions in a few of the Western countries today, is capable of bringing about the changes essential for the proper functioning of the modern world. But that question does not arise here, for movement is deliberately checked by chains and fetters, and a barred and bolted door confronts us. We are provided with a car, all brakes and no engines. It is a constitution designed by people whose ever-present background is Martial Law. To a man of force there is no real alternative to Martial Law except collapse.

The measure of liberty that this proposed gift of Britain offers to India can be taken from the fact that even the most moderate and politically backward groups in India have condemned it as reactionary. The habitual and persistent supporters of Government have had to combine criticisms of it with their usual genuflections. Others have been more vehement.

---

7. The London *Economist* (October 1934) has pointed out: "But for the future it appears that among the benefits of British rule the doubtful privilege of buying expensively from Lancashire is to be forced upon the 'native' in many corners of the globe." Ceylon has been the most flagrant recent example of this.

In view of these proposals the Liberals found it difficult to retain in full measure their abiding faith in the inscrutable wisdom of Providence in placing India under British dominion. They offered strong criticism, but disdainful of reality and enamoured of phrases and fine 'gestures', they laid the greatest stress on the absence of the words "Dominion Status" from the Report and the Bill. There was a great outcry about this, and now that Sir Samuel Hoare has made some kind of a statement on the subject, honour will largely be satisfied. The Dominion Status may be an insubstantial shadow haunting an unknown future—a Never-Never land which we may never reach, but we can dream about it at least and grow eloquent over its many beauties. Sir Tej Bahadur Sapru, troubled perhaps by doubts about the British Parliament and the British people, has sought refuge in the Crown. Eminent lawyer that he is, he has laid down a novel constitutional doctrine: "Whatever the British Parliament and people may or may not do for India," he said, "over and above them stood the Crown that looks after the interests of Indian subjects and India's peace and prosperity."[8] It is a comforting doctrine which saves us from troubling ourselves about constitutions, laws, and political and social changes.

But it would be unfair to suggest that the Liberals have lessened their opposition to the scheme. Most of them have made it perfectly clear that they prefer present conditions, bad as they are, to this unwanted gift that is being thrust on India. Beyond stressing that, their very principles forbid them from doing anything, and it may be presumed that they will go on laying stress. For their motto they might well have that modern adaptation of an ancient saying: "If at first you don't succeed, cry again!"

A certain hopeful reliance is placed by Liberal leaders, and probably by many others including some Congressmen, on the victory of the Labour Party in Britain and the formation of a Labour Government there. There is absolutely no reason why India should not endeavour to go ahead with the co-operation of advanced groups in Britain, or should not try to profit by the advent of a Labour Government. But to rely helplessly on a change in fortune's wheel in England is hardly dignified or in consonance with national honour. Dignity apart, it is not good common sense. Why should we expect much from the British Labour

---

8. Speaking at a public meeting at Lucknow on January 29, 1935.

Party? We have had two Labour Governments already, and we are not likely to forget their gifts to India. Mr Ramsay MacDonald may have left the Labour ranks, but his old colleagues do not seem to have changed much. At the Southport Labour Party Conference held in October 1934, a resolution was submitted by Mr V.K. Krishna Menon "expressing the conviction that it is imperative that the principle of self-determination for the establishment of full self-government for India should be implemented forthwith." Mr Arthur Henderson urged the withdrawal of the resolution and, very frankly, refused to give an undertaking on behalf of the Executive to carry out its policy of self-determination for India. He said: "We have laid down very clearly that we are going to consult if possible all sections of the Indian people. That ought to satisfy anybody." The satisfaction will perhaps be tempered by the fact that exactly this was the declared policy of the last Labour Government and the National Government, resulting in the Round Table Conference, the White Paper, the Joint Committee Report, and the India Act.

It is perfectly clear that in matters of imperial policy there is little to choose between Tory or Labour in England. It is true that the Labour rank and file is far more advanced, but it has little influence on its very conservative leadership. It may be that the Labour Left wing gather strength, for conditions change rapidly nowadays, but do national or social movements curl themselves up and go to sleep, waiting for problematical changes elsewhere?

There is a curious aspect to this reliance of our Liberals on the British Labour Party. If, by any chance, this Party went Left and gave effect in England to its socialistic programme, what would be the reactions in India and on the Liberals and other Moderate groups here? Most of them are socially Conservatives of the deepest dye. They will dislike Labour's social and economic changes, and fear their introduction in India. It may even happen that their love of the British connection may undergo a sea-change, when this connection becomes a symbol of social upsets. It may also happen then that persons like me, who want national independence and severance of that connection, may change their minds and prefer close association with a socialist Britain. None of us surely has any objection to co-operating with the British people; it is their imperialism that we object to, and once they have shed this, the way to co-operation will be open. What of the Moderates then? Probably they will accept the new order as another indication of the inscrutable wisdom of Providence.

One of the notable consequences of the Round Table Conference and the proposal to have a Federation, is to push the Indian Princes very much to the forefront. The solicitude of the Tory die-hards for them and their 'independence' has put new life into them. Never before have they had so much importance thrust on them. Previously they dared not say no to a hint from the British Resident, and the Government of India's attitude to the numerous highnesses was openly disdainful. There was continual interference in their internal affairs, and often this was justified. Even today a large number of the States are directly or indirectly being governed by British officers 'lent' to the States. But Mr Churchill's and Lord Rothermere's campaign seems to have unnerved the Government of India a little, and it has grown cautious about interfering with their decisions. The Princes also now talk in a much more superior way.

I have tried to follow these superficial developments in the Indian political scene, but I cannot help feeling that they are unreal, and the background in India oppresses me. The background is one of continual repression of every kind of freedom, of enormous suffering and frustration, of distortion of goodwill, and encouragement of many evil tendencies. Large numbers lie in prison and spend their young lives, year after year, eating their hearts out.[9] Their families and friends and connections and thousands of others grow bitter, and a nauseating sense of humiliation and powerlessness before brute strength takes possession of them. Numerous organizations are outlawed even in normal times, and 'Emergency Powers' and 'Tranquillity Acts' make for themselves almost a permanent home in the Government's armoury. Exceptions in the matter of restrictions of liberties rapidly becomes the general rule. Large numbers of books and periodicals are proscribed or prevented

---

9. Sir Harry Haig, Home Member, stated in the Legislative Assembly on July 23, 1934, that the total number of detenus in gaols and special camps were: in Bengal, 1,500 to 1,600; in Deoli camp, 500. Total, 2,000 to 2,100. This is the figure for detenus; that is, untried and unconvicted prisoners. It does not include political convicts. In the case of convicts sentences are usually very heavy. In a recent Calcutta case the Associated Press (December 17, 1934) states that the High Court gave a sentence of nine years' rigorous imprisonment, the offence being the unlicensed possession of arms and ammunition. The accused had been arrested with a revolver and six cartridges.

entry by a 'Sea Customs Act', and the possession of 'dangerous' literature may lead to a long term of imprisonment. A frank expression of opinion on the political or economic problems of the day, or a favourable report of social and cultural conditions in Russia meets with the strong disapproval of the censor. The *Modern Review* was warned by the Bengal Government because it published an article by Dr Rabindra Nath Tagore on Russia, an article written after a personal visit to that country. We are informed by the Under-Secretary for India in Parliament that "the article gave a distorted view of the achievements of British rule in India," and hence action was taken against it.[10] The judge of these achievements is the censor, and we may not have a contrary opinion or give expression to it. Objection was also taken by Government to the publication of a brief message from Rabindra Nath Tagore to the Dublin Society of Friends. If a sage like Tagore, interested in cultural matters and deliberately keeping aloof from politics, revered in India and world famous, is suppressed in this way, what of humble folk? Worse even than the actual instances of suppression is the atmosphere of fear they create. It is not possible to have honest journalism under these circumstances, or a proper consideration or teaching of history, economics, politics or current affairs. This is a strange background for the introduction of reforms and responsible government and the like.[11]

Every intelligent person knows that the world is in a state of intellectual turmoil today, and that there is a vague or acutely-felt, but in any case a tremendous, dissatisfaction with existing conditions. Far-reaching changes are taking place before our eyes, and the future, whatever shape it might take, is not a remote, far-off thing which arouses a purely academic interest in the detached minds of philosophers, sociologists

---

10. November 12, 1934.

11. On September 4, 1935, an official statement was made in the Legislative Assembly regarding the working of the Press laws in India. It was stated that from 1930 onwards 514 newspapers had been affected by Government demands for securities and by confiscations. Of these, 348 newspapers stopped publication because they could not give further securities; 166 newspapers gave securities amounting to Rs 252,852.

Recently (in the latter half of 1935) a number of laws suppressing civil liberties have again been enacted for a further long period. The principal one—The Criminal Law Amendment Act—applies to the whole of India. It was thrown out by the Legislative Assembly and later certified by the Governor-General. Many provinces have also passed such laws.

and economists. It is a matter which affects every human being for better or for worse, and surely it is every citizen's duty to try to understand the various forces at play and decide on his own course of action. A world is coming to an end, and a new world is taking shape. To find an answer to a problem it is necessary to know what it is. Indeed it is as important to know the problem as to seek a solution for it.

Unhappily there is an astonishing ignorance or indifference to world happenings among our politicians. Probably this ignorance extends to the great majority of the official element in India, for the Civil Service lives happily and complacently in a narrow world of its own. Only the topmost of our officials have to consider these problems. The British Government of course has to keep world events in view and to develop its policy accordingly. It is common knowledge that British foreign policy has been considerably influenced by the possession and protection of India. How many Indian politicians consider that Japanese imperialism, or the growing strength of the Soviet Union, or the Anglo-Russo-Japanese intrigues in Sinkiang, or the events in Central Asia or Afghanistan or Persia, have an intimate bearing on Indian politics? The Central Asian situation obviously affects the position of Kashmir and makes it a pivot of British policy and defence.

Even more important are the economic changes that are rapidly taking place the world over. We must realize that the nineteenth-century system has passed away, and has no application to present-day needs. The lawyer's view, so prevalent in India, of proceeding from precedent to precedent is of little use when there are no precedents. We cannot put a bullock-cart on rails and call it a railway train. It has to give way and be scrapped as obsolescent material. Even apart from Russia, there is talk of New Deals and vast changes. President Roosevelt, with every desire to retain and strengthen the capitalist system, has with great courage inaugurated enormous schemes which may change American life. He talks of "weeding out the over-privileged and effectively lifting up the under-privileged". He may or may not succeed, but the courage of the man and his desire to pull his country out of the ruts are undeniable. He is not afraid of changing his policy or of admitting mistakes. In England Mr Lloyd George has come out with his 'New Deal'. We want many New Deals in India too. The old assumption that "whatever is worth knowing is already known, and whatever is worth doing has already been done," is perilous nonsense.

We have to face many questions, and we must face them boldly. Has the present social or economic system a right to exist if it is unable to improve greatly the condition of the masses? Does any other system give promise of this widespread betterment? How far will a mere political change bring radical improvement? If vested interests come in the way of an eminently desirable change, is it wise or moral to attempt to preserve them at the cost of mass misery and poverty? Surely the object is not to injure vested interests, but to prevent them from injuring others. If it was possible to come to terms with these vested interests, it would be most desirable to do so. People may disagree with the justice or injustice of this, but few will doubt the expediency of a settlement. Such a settlement obviously cannot be the removal of one vested interest by the creation of another. Whenever possible and desirable, reasonable compensation might be given, for a conflict is likely to cost far more. But, unhappily, all history shows that vested interests do not accept such compromises. Classes that have ceased to play a vital part in society are singularly lacking in wisdom. They gamble for all or nothing, and so they fade away.

There is a great deal of 'loose talk' (as the Congress Working Committee put it) about confiscation and the like. Confiscation, persistent and continual, is the basis of the existing system, and it is to put an end to this that social changes are proposed. There is the daily confiscation of part of the labour product of the worker; a peasant's holding is ultimately confiscated by raising his rent or revenue to such an extent that he cannot pay it. Formerly common lands were confiscated by individuals and made into big estates; peasant proprietors were also wiped out in this way. Confiscation is the basis and life-breath of the present system.

To remedy this partly, society tries various expedients which are themselves of the nature of confiscation—heavy taxes, death-duties, laws for the relief from indebtedness, inflation, etc. Recently we have seen national repudiation of debt on an enormous scale, not only by the Soviet Union but by leading capitalist countries; the most notable instance of this being the British repudiation of their debt to the United States— a dangerous example to place before India! But all these confiscations and repudiations help only to a minor extent, and do not get rid of the basic cause. To build anew, that root cause has to be removed.

In considering a method for changing the existing order we have to weigh the costs of it in material as well as spiritual terms. We cannot afford to be too shortsighted. We have to see how far it helps ultimately in the development of human happiness and human progress, material and spiritual. But we have always to bear in mind the terrible costs of not changing the existing order, of carrying on as we do today with our enormous burden of frustrated and distorted lives, starvation and misery, and spiritual and moral degradation. Like an ever-recurring flood this present economic system is continually overwhelming and carrying away to destruction vast numbers of human beings. We cannot check the flood or save these people by some of us carrying water away in a bucket. Embankments have to be built and canals, and the destructive power of the waters has to be converted and used for human betterment.

It is obvious that the vast changes that socialism envisages cannot be brought about by the sudden passing of a few laws. But the basic laws and power are necessary to give the direction of advance and to lay the foundation of the structure. If the great building-up of a socialized society is to proceed, it cannot be left to chance nor can it he done in fits and starts with intervals of destruction of what has been built. The major obstructions have thus to be removed. The object is not to deprive, but to provide; to change the present scarcity to future abundance. But in doing so the path must necessarily be cleared of impediments and selfish interests which want to hold society back. And the path we take is not merely a question of what we like or dislike or even of abstract justice, but what is economically sound, capable of progress and adaptation to changing conditions, and likely to do good to the largest number of human beings.

A clash of interests seems inevitable. There is no middle path. Each one of us will have to choose our side. Before we can choose, we must know and understand. The emotional appeal of socialism is not enough. This must be supplemented by an intellectual and reasoned appeal based on facts and arguments and detailed criticism. In the West a great deal of this kind of literature exists, but in India there is a tremendous lack of it, and many good books are not allowed entry here. But to read books from other countries is not enough. If socialism is to be built up in India it will have to grow out of Indian conditions, and the closest study of these conditions is essential. We want experts in the job who study and prepare detailed plans. Unfortunately our experts are mostly in Government service or in the semi-official universities, and they dare not go far in this direction.

An intellectual background is not enough to bring socialism. Other forces are necessary. But I do feel that without that background we can never have a grip of the subject or create a powerful movement. At the present moment the agrarian problem is far the most important in India, and it is likely to remain so. But industry is of little less importance, and it grows. What is our objective: a peasant State or an industrial one? Of course we are bound to remain predominantly agricultural, but one can and, I think, must push on industry.

Our captains of industry are quite amazingly backward in their ideas; they are not even up-to-date capitalists. The masses are so poor that they do not look upon them as potential consumers, and fight bitterly against any proposal to increase wages or lower hours of work. Recently hours of work have been reduced from ten to nine in the cotton mills. This has led the Ahmedabad mill-owners to reduce the wages of labour, even piece-work labour. Thus the reduction of hours of work has meant a lower income and a yet lower standard for the poor worker. Rationalization, however, proceeds apace, increasing the pressure on the worker and his fatigue, without any proportionate increase in wages. The whole outlook of the industry is an early nineteenth-century one. They make stupendous profits when they have the chance and the worker continues as before; if there is a slump the owners complain that they cannot carry on without reducing wages. Not only have they the help of the State, but also usually the sympathy of our middle-class politicians. And yet the lot of the cotton worker in Ahmedabad is better than that of a similar worker in Bombay and elsewhere. The cotton workers, on the whole, are better off than the jute workers of Bengal and the miners. The workers of the small disorganized industries are lowest in the industrial scale. To compare the magnificent palaces of the jute millionaires and the cotton lords, with their ostentatious display of pomp and luxury, with the wretched hovels where their semi-naked workers live, should be an education of the most impressive kind. But we take these contrasts for granted and pass them by, unaffected and unimpressed.

Bad as is the lot of the Indian industrial worker, it is, from the income point of view, far better than the peasant's lot. The peasant has one advantage: he lives in fresh air and escapes the degradation of the slums. But so low has he sunk that he often converts even his open-air village into a 'dung-heap', as Gandhiji has called it. There is no sense of co-operation in him or of joint effort for the good of the community. It is easy to condemn him for this, but what is the unhappy creature to do when life presents itself to him as a bitter and unceasing individual struggle with every man's hand raised against him? How he lives at all is an almost incredible wonder. It has been found that the average daily income of typical farmers in the Punjab was about nine annas (roughly ninepence) per head in 1928-29. This fell in 1930-31 to nine pies (three farthings) per head! The Punjab peasant is considered to be far more prosperous than the peasantry of U.P., Behar and Bengal. In some of the eastern districts of U.P. (Gorakhpur, etc.) in prosperous times before the slump, the daily field wage was two annas (twopence). To talk of improving these staggering conditions by philanthropy or local efforts in rural uplift is a mockery of the peasant and his misery.

How are we to get out of this quagmire? Means can no doubt be devised, although it is a difficult task to raise masses of people who have sunk so low. But the real difficulty comes from interested groups who oppose change, and under imperialist domination the change seems to be out of the question. In what direction will India look in the coming years? Communism and fascism seem to be the major tendencies of the age, and intermediate tendencies and vacillating groups are gradually being eliminated. Sir Malcolm Hailey has prophesied that India will take to National Socialism, that is, some form of fascism. Perhaps he is right so far as the near future is concerned. There are already clearly marked fascist tendencies in India's young men and women, especially in Bengal, but to some extent in every province, and the Congress is beginning to reflect them. Because of fascism's close connection with extreme forms of violence, the elders of the Congress, wedded as they are to non-violence, have a natural horror of it. But the so-called philosophical background of fascism—the Corporate State with private property preserved and vested interests curbed but not done away with—will probably appeal to them. It seems to be at first sight a golden way of retaining the old and yet having the new. Whether it is possible both to have the cake and eat it is another matter.

But the real drive towards fascism will naturally come from the younger members of the middle class. Actually, at present, it is part of the middle class in India that is revolutionary, not so much the workers or the peasantry, though no doubt the industrial workers are potentially more so. This nationalist middle class is a favourable field for the spread of fascist ideas. But fascism cannot spread here in the European sense so long as there is a foreign government. Indian fascism must necessarily stand for Indian independence, and cannot therefore ally itself with British imperialism. It will have to seek support from the masses. If British control were wholly removed, fascism would probably grow rapidly, supported as it would certainly be by the upper middle class and the vested interests.

But British control is not likely to go soon, and meanwhile socialistic and communistic ideas are also spreading in spite of severe repression by the British Government. The Communist Party is illegal in India, and the term is interpreted in a loose way to include even sympathizers and labour unions with advanced programmes.

As between fascism and communism my sympathies are entirely with communism. As these pages will show, I am very far from being a communist. My roots are still perhaps partly in the nineteenth century, and I have been too much influenced by the humanist liberal tradition to get out of it completely. This *bourgeois* background follows me about and is naturally a source of irritation to many communists. I dislike dogmatism, and the treatment of Karl Marx's writings or any other books as revealed scripture which cannot be challenged, and the regimentation and heresy hunts which seem to be a feature of modern communism. I dislike also much that has happened in Russia, and especially the excessive use of violence in normal times. But still I incline more and more towards a communist philosophy.

Marx may be wrong in some of his statements, or his theory of value; this I am not competent to judge. But he seems to me to have possessed quite an extraordinary degree of insight into social phenomena, and this insight was apparently due to the scientific method he adopted. This method, applied to past history as well as current events, helps us in understanding them far more than any other method of approach, and it is because of this that the most revealing and keen analysis of the changes that are taking place in the world today come from Marxist writers. It is easy to point out that Marx ignored or underrated certain subsequent tendencies, like the rise of a revolutionary element in the middle class, which is so notable today. But the whole value of Marxism seems to me to lie in its absence of dogmatism, in its stress on a certain outlook and mode of approach; and in its attitude to action. That outlook helps us in understanding the social phenomena of our own times, and points out the way of action and escape.

Even that method of action was no fixed and unchangeable road, but had to be suited to circumstances. That, at any rate, was Lenin's view, and he justified it brilliantly by fitting his action to changing circumstances. He tells us that: "To attempt to answer 'yes' or 'no' to the question of the definite means of struggle, without examining in detail the concrete situation of a given moment at a given stage of its development, means to depart altogether from the Marxian ground." And again he said: "Nothing is final; we must always learn from circumstances."

Because of this wide and comprehensive outlook, the real understanding communist develops to some extent an organic sense of social life. Politics for him cease to be a mere record of opportunism or a groping in the dark. The ideals and objectives he works for give a meaning to the struggle and to the sacrifices he willingly faces. He feels that he is part of a grand army marching forward to realize human fate and destiny, and he has the sense of 'marching step by step with history'.

Probably most communists are far from feeling all this. Perhaps only a Lenin had this organic sense of life in its fullness which made his action so effective. But to a small extent every communist, who has understood the philosophy of his movement, has it.

It is difficult to be patient with many communists; they have developed a peculiar method of irritating others. But they are a sorely tried people and, outside the Soviet Union, they have to contend against enormous difficulties. I have always admired their great courage and capacity for sacrifice. They suffer greatly, as unhappily untold millions suffer in various ways, but not blindly before a malign and all-powerful fate. They suffer as human beings, and there is a tragic nobility about such suffering.

The success or failure of the Russian social experiments do not directly affect the validity of the Marxian theory. It is conceivable, though it is highly unlikely, that a set of untoward circumstances or a combination of powers might upset those experiments. But the value of those mighty social upheavals will still remain. With all my instinctive dislike for much that has happened there, I feel that they offer the greatest hope to the world. I do not know enough and I am not in a position to judge their actions. My chief fear is that the background of too much violence and suppression might bring an evil trail behind them which it may be difficult to get rid of. But the greatest thing in favour of the present directors of Russia's destiny is that they are not afraid to learn from their mistakes. They can retrace their steps and build anew. And always they keep their ideal before them. Their activities in other countries, through the Communist International, have been singularly futile, but apparently those activities have been reduced to a minimum now.

Coming back to India, communism and socialism seem a far cry, unless the rush of external events force the pace here. We have to deal not with communism but, with the addition of an extra syllable, with communalism. And communally India is in a dark age. Men of action waste their energies on trivial things and intrigue and manoeuvre and try to overreach each other. Few of them are interested in trying to make the world a better, brighter place. Perhaps this is a temporary phase that will pass soon.

The Congress has at least largely kept out of this communal darkness, but its outlook is petty *bourgeois*, and the remedy it seeks for this as for other problems is in terms of the petty *bourgeoisie*. It is not likely to succeed that way. It represents today this lower middle class, for that is the most vocal and revolutionary at present. But it is nevertheless not as vital as it appears to be. It is pressed on either side by two forces—one entrenched, the other still weak but growing rapidly. It is passing through a crisis of its existence at present; what will happen to it in the future it is difficult to say. It cannot go over to the side of the entrenched forces before it has fulfilled its historic mission of attaining national freedom. But before it succeeds in that, other forces may grow powerful and influence it in their direction, or gradually displace it. It seems likely, however, that so long as a large measure of national freedom is not obtained, the Congress will play a dominant role in India.

Any violent activity seems to be out of the question, injurious and a waste of effort. That, I think, is generally recognized in India, in spite of rare instances of futile and sporadic violence. That way cannot lead us anywhere except into a hopeless maze of violence and counter-violence out of which it will be difficult to emerge.

We are often told that we must unite among ourselves and present a 'united front'. Mrs Sarojini Naidu pleads for it eloquently with all her poetic ardour. She is a poet and entitled to lay stress on the beauty of harmony and concord. Obviously a 'united front' is always desirable, provided it is a front. An analysis of this phrase leads one to the conclusion that what is aimed at is a pact or compromise between various individuals at the top. Such a combination will necessarily mean that the most cautious and moderate will determine the objective and lay down the pace. As some of them are well known to dislike all movement, the result will be a united standstill. Instead of a united front there will be a united and extensive display of back.

It is, of course, absurd to say that we will not co-operate with or compromise with others. Life and politics are much too complex for us always to think in straight lines. Even the implacable Lenin said that "to march forward without compromise, without turning from the path" was "intellectual childishness and not the serious tactics of a revolutionary class." Compromises there are bound to be, and we should not worry too much about them. But whether we compromise or refuse to do so, what matters is that primary things should come first always and secondary things should never take precedence over them. If we are clear about our principles and objectives, temporary compromises will not harm. But danger lies in our slurring over those principles and objectives for fear of offending our weaker brethren. To mislead is far worse than to offend.

I write vaguely and somewhat academically about current events, and try to play the part of a detached onlooker. I am not usually considered a looker-on when action beckons; my offence, I am often told, is that I rush in foolishly without sufficient provocation. What would I do now? What would I suggest to my countrymen to do? Perhaps the instinctive caution of a person who dabbles in public affairs comes in the way of my committing myself prematurely. But, if I may confess the truth, I really do not know and I do not try to find out. When I cannot act, why should I worry? I do worry to a large extent, but that is inevitable. At least, so long as I am in prison, I try to save myself from coming to grips with the problem of immediate action.

All activity seems to be far away in prison. One becomes the object of events, not the subject of action. And one waits and waits for something to happen. I write of political and social problems of India and the world, but what are they to this little self-contained world of gaol which has long been my home? Prisoners have only one major interest: the date of their release.

In Naini Prison and here in Almora many prisoners have come to me to enquire anxiously about the *jugli*. I could not at first make out what it was, but then I discovered that the word was jubilee. They were referring to the rumours of King George's Silver Jubilee celebrations, but they did not know this. For them past associations had invested the word with one meaning only: it was a partial gaol delivery or a substantial reduction of sentences. Every prisoner, and especially the long-term ones, are therefore interested in the coming *jugli*. For them the *jugli is* far more important than constitutional reforms and Acts of Parliament and Socialism and Communism.

68

EPILOGUE

We are enjoined to labour; but it is not granted to us to complete our labours.

The Talmud

I have reached the end of the story. This egotistical narrative of my adventures through life, such as they are, has been brought up to today, February 14, 1935, District Gaol, Almora. Three months ago today I celebrated in this prison my forty-fifth birthday, and I suppose I have still many years to live. Sometimes a sense of age and weariness steals over me, at other times I feel full of energy and vitality. I have a fairly tough body, and my mind has a capacity for recovering from shock, so I imagine I shall yet survive for long unless some sudden fate overtakes me. But the future has to be lived before it can be written about.

The adventures have not been very exciting perhaps; long years in prison can hardly be termed adventurous. Nor have they been in any way unique, for I have shared these years with their ups and downs with tens of thousands of my countrymen and countrywomen; and this record of changing moods, of exaltations and depressions, of intense activity and enforced solitude, is our common record. I have been one of a mass, moving with it, swaying it occasionally, being influenced by it; and yet, like the other units, an individual, apart from the others, living my separate life in the heart of the crowd. We have posed often enough and struck up attitudes, but there was something very real and intensely truthful in much that we did, and this lifted us out of our petty selves and made us more vital and gave us an importance that we would otherwise not have had. Sometimes we were fortunate enough to experience that fullness of life which comes from attempting to fit ideals with action. And we realized that any other life involving a renunciation of these ideals and a tame submission to superior force, would have been a wasted existence, full of discontent and inner sorrow.

To me these years have brought one rich gift, among many others.

More and more I have looked upon life as an adventure of absorbing interest, where there is so much to learn, so much to do. I have continually had a feeling of growing up, and that feeling is still with me and gives a zest to my activities as well as to the reading of books, and generally makes life worthwhile.

In writing this narrative I have tried to give my moods and thoughts at the time of each event, to represent as far as I could my feelings on the occasion. It is difficult to recapture a past mood, and it is not easy to forget subsequent happenings. Later ideas thus must inevitably have coloured my account of earlier days, but my object was, primarily for my own benefit, to trace my own mental growth. Perhaps what I have written is not so much an account of what I have been but of what I have sometimes wanted to be or imagined myself to be.

Some months ago Sir C.P. Ramaswamy Aiyar stated in public that I did not represent mass-feeling, but that I was all the more dangerous because of my sacrifices and idealism and the fervour of my convictions, which he characterized as 'self-hypnotization'. A person suffering from self-hypnosis can hardly judge himself, and, in any event, I would not presume to join issue on this personal matter with C.P. We have not met for many years, but there was a time long ago, when we were joint secretaries of the Home Rule League. Since then much has happened, and C.P. has risen by ascending spirals to dizzy heights and I have remained of the earth, earthy. There is little now in common between us except our common nationality. He is today a full-blooded apologist of British rule in India, especially during the last few years; an admirer of dictatorship in India and elsewhere, and himself a shining ornament of autocracy in an Indian State. We disagree about most things, I suppose, but we agree on one somewhat trivial subject. He is absolutely right when he says that I do not represent mass-feeling. I have no illusions on that point.

Indeed, I often wonder if I represent anyone at all, and I am inclined to think that I do not, though many have kindly and friendly feelings towards me. I have become a queer mixture of the East and West, out of place everywhere, at home nowhere. Perhaps my thoughts and approach to life are more akin to what is called Western than Eastern, but India clings to me, as she does to all her children, in innumerable ways; and behind me lie, somewhere in the subconscious, racial memories of a hundred, or whatever the number may be, generations of Brahmans. I cannot get rid of either that past inheritance or my recent acquisitions. They are both part of me, and, though they help me in both the East and the West, they also create in me a feeling of spiritual loneliness not only in public activities but in life itself. I am a stranger and alien in the West. I cannot be of it. But in my own country also, sometimes, I have an exile's feeling.

The distant mountains seem easy of access and climbing the top beckons, but, as one approaches, difficulties appear, and the higher one goes the more laborious becomes the journey and the summit recedes into the clouds. Yet the climbing is worth the effort and has its own joy and satisfaction. Perhaps it is the struggle that gives value to life, not so much the ultimate result. Often it is difficult to know which is the right path; it is easier sometimes to know what is not right, and to avoid that is something after all. If I may quote, with all humility, the last words of the great Socrates: "I know not what death is—it may be a good thing, and I am not afraid of it. But I do know that it is a bad thing to desert one's past, and I prefer what may be good to what I know to be bad."

The years I have spent in prison! Sitting alone, wrapped in my thoughts, how many seasons I have seen go by, following each other into oblivion! How many moons I have watched wax and wane, and the pageant of the stars moving along inexorably and majestically! How many yesterdays of my youth lie buried here; and sometimes I see the ghosts of these dead yesterdays rise up, bringing poignant memories, and whispering to me: "Was it worthwhile?" There is no hesitation about the answer. If I were given the chance to go through my life again, with my present knowledge and experience added, I would no doubt try to make many changes in my personal life; I would endeavour to improve in many ways on what I had previously done, but my major decisions in public affairs would remain untouched. Indeed, I could not vary them, for they were stronger than myself, and a force beyond my control drove me to them.

It is almost exactly a year since my conviction; a year has gone by out of the two years of my sentence. Another full year remains, for there are no remissions this time, as simple imprisonment carries no such deductions. Even the eleven days that I was out in August last have been added on to the period of my sentence. But this year too will pass, and I shall go out—and then? I do not know, but I have a feeling that a chapter of my life is over and another chapter will begin. What this is going to be I cannot clearly guess. The leaves of the book of life are closed.

POSTSCRIPT

BADENWEILER, SCHWARZWALD,
October 25, 1935

In May last my wife left Bhowali for further treatment in Europe. After departure there were no more visits to Bhowali for me, no more fortnightly outings and drives on the mountain roads. I missed them, and Almora Gaol seemed to be drearier than before.

News came of the Quetta earthquake, and for a while all else was forgotten. But not for long, for the Government of India does not allow us to forget it or its peculiar ways. Soon we learnt that Rajendra Prasad, the Congress President, and the man who knew more about earthquake relief work than almost any other person in India, was not permitted to go to Quetta and help in relief. Nor could Gandhiji or any other public man of note. Many Indian newspapers had their securities confiscated for writing articles on Quetta.

Everywhere the military mentality, the police outlook—in the Assembly, in civil government, in bombing on the Frontier. Almost it would seem that the British Government in India is permanently at war with large sections of the Indian people.

The police are a useful and a necessary force, but a world full of policemen and the police bludgeon may not, perhaps, be a desirable place to live in. It has often been said that an unrestrained use of force degrades the user of it as it humiliates and degrades the object of it. Few things are more striking today in India than the progressive deterioration, moral, and intellectual, of the higher services, more especially the Indian Civil Service. This is most in evidence in the superior officials, but it runs like a thread throughout the services. Whenever occasion arises for making a fresh appointment to the higher ranks, the person who represents the new spirit best is inevitably chosen.

On September 4th I was suddenly discharged from Almora Gaol as news had come that my wife's condition was critical. She was under treatment in Badenweiler in the Schwarzwald in Germany. My sentence was 'suspended', I was told, and I was released five and half months before my time. I hurried to Europe by air.

Europe in turmoil, fearful of war and tumult and with economic crises always on the horizon; Abyssinia invaded and her people bombed; various imperialist systems in conflict and threatening each other; and England, the greatest of the imperialist Powers, standing up for peace and the League Covenant while it bombs and ruthlessly oppresses its subject peoples. But here in the Black Forest it is calm and peaceful, and even the swastika is not much in evidence. I watch the mists steal up the valley and hide the distant frontier of France and cover the landscape, and I wonder what lies behind them.

FIVE YEARS LATER

Five and a half years ago, sitting in my prison barrack in the Almora District Gaol, I wrote the last line of my autobiography. Eight months later I added a postscript from Badenweiler in Germany. That autobiography, published in England, had a kindly reception from all manner of people in various countries, and I was glad that what I had written had brought India nearer to many friends abroad, and had made them appreciate, to some extent, the inner significance of our struggle for freedom.

My publisher recently asked me to add a new chapter to the book in order to bring it further up to date. His request is reasonable and I could not deny it. And yet I have found it no easy matter to comply. We live in strange times, when life's normal course has been completely upset. But a more serious difficulty confronted me. I wrote my autobiography entirely in prison, cut off from outside activity. I suffered from various humours in prison, as every prisoner does, but gradually I developed a mood of introspection and some peace of mind. How am I to capture that mood now, how am I to fit in with that narrative? As I glance through my book again, I feel almost as if some other person had written a story of long ago. The five years that have gone by have changed the world and left their impress upon me. Physically I am older of course, but it is the mind that has received shock and sensation again and again and has hardened, or perhaps matured. My wife's death in Switzerland ended a chapter of my existence and took away much from my life that had been part of my being. It was difficult for me to realize that she was no more and I could not adjust myself easily. I threw myself in my work, seeking some satisfaction in it, and rushed about from end to end in India. Even more than in my earlier days, my life became an alternation of huge crowds and intensive activity and loneliness. My mother's death later broke a final link with the past. My daughter was away studying at Oxford, and later under treatment in a sanatorium abroad. I would return to my home from my wanderings almost unwillingly, and sit in that deserted house all by myself, trying even to avoid interviews there. I wanted peace after the crowds.

But there was no peace in my work or my mind, and the responsibility that I had to shoulder often oppressed me very greatly. I could not align myself with various parties and groups; I did not even fit in with my closest colleagues. I could not function as I wanted to, and at the same time I prevented others from functioning as they wanted to. A sense of suppression and frustration grew and I became a solitary figure in public life, though vast crowds came to hear me and enthusiasm surrounded me.

I was affected more than others by the development of events in Europe and the Far East. Munich was a shock hard to bear and the tragedy of Spain became a personal sorrow to me. As these years of horror succeeded one another, the sense of impending catastrophe overwhelmed me, and my faith in a bright future for the world became dim.

And now the catastrophe has come. The volcanoes in Europe spit fire and destruction, and here in India I sit on the edge of another volcano, not knowing when it may burst. It is difficult to tear myself away from the problem of the moment, to develop the mood of retrospection and survey these five years that have gone by, and write calmly about them. And even if I could do so, I would have to write another big book, for there is so much to say. I shall endeavour therefore, as best I may, to refer briefly only to certain events and developments in which I have played a part or which have affected me.

I was with my wife when she died in Lausanne on February 28, 1936. A little while before news had reached me that I had been elected president of the Indian National Congress for the second time. I returned to India by air soon after and on my way, in Rome, I had a curious experience. Some days before my departure a message was conveyed to me that Signor Mussolini would like to meet me when I passed through Rome. In spite of my strong disapproval of the Fascist regime, I would ordinarily have liked to meet Signor Mussolini and to find out for myself what a person who was playing such an important part in the world's affairs was like. But I was in no mood for interviews then. What came in my way even more was the continuance of the Abyssinian campaign and my apprehension that such an interview would inevitably be used for purposes of Fascist propaganda. No denial from me would go far. I remembered how Gandhiji, when he passed through Rome in 1931, had a bogus interview in the *Giornale d'Italia* fastened on to him. I remembered also several other instances of Indians visiting Italy being used, against their wishes, for Fascist propaganda. I was assured that nothing of the kind would happen to me and that our interview would be entirely private. Still I decided to avoid it and I conveyed my regrets to Signor Mussolini.

I could not avoid going through Rome, however, as the Dutch K.L.M. airplane I was travelling by spent a night there. Soon after my arrival in Rome, a high official called upon me and gave me an invitation to meet Signor Mussolini that evening. It had all been fixed up, he told me. I was surprised and pointed out that I had already asked to be excused. We argued for an hour, till the time fixed for the interview itself, and then I had my way. There was no interview.

I returned to India and plunged into my work. Within a few days of my return I had to preside over the annual session of the National Congress. For some years, which I had spent mainly in prison, I had been out of touch with developments. I found many changes, new alignments, a hardening on party lines within the Congress. There was an atmosphere of suspicion and bitterness and conflict. I treated this lightly, having confidence in my own capacity to deal with the situation. For a short while I seemed to carry the Congress in the direction I wanted it to go. But I realized soon that the conflict was deep-rooted and it was not so easy to charm away the suspicion of each other and the bitterness that had grown in our ranks. I thought seriously of resigning from the presidentship but, realizing that this would only make matters worse, I refrained.

Again and again, during the next few months, I considered this question of resignation. I found it difficult to work smoothly with my own colleagues in the Congress executive, and it became clear to me that they viewed my activities with apprehension. It was not so much that they objected to any specific act but they disliked the general trend and direction. They had justification for this as my outlook was different. I was completely loyal to Congress decisions but I emphasized certain aspects of them, while my colleagues emphasized other aspects. I decided finally to resign and I informed Gandhiji of my decision. In the course of my letter to him I wrote that "since my return from Europe I have found that the meetings of the Working Committee exhaust me greatly; they have a devitalizing effect on me and I have almost the feeling of being much older in years after every fresh experience. I should not be surprised if this feeling was also shared by my colleagues of the Committee. It is an unhealthy experience and it comes in the way of effective work."

Soon afterwards a far-away occurrence, unconnected with India, affected me greatly and made me change my decision. This was the news of General Franco's revolt in Spain. I saw this rising, with its background of German and Italian assistance, developing into a European or even a world conflict. India was bound to be drawn into this and I could not afford to weaken our organization and create an internal crisis by resigning just when it was essential for us to pull together. I was not wholly wrong in my analysis of the situation, though I was premature and my mind rushed to conclusions, which took some years to materialize.

The reaction of the Spanish War on me indicates how, in my mind, the problem of India was tied up with other world problems. More and more I came to think that these separate problems, political or economic, in China, Abyssinia, Spain, Central Europe, India, or elsewhere, were facets of one and the same world problem. There could be no final solution of anyone of them till this basic problem was solved. And in all probability there would be upheaval and disaster before the final solution was reached. As peace was said to be indivisible in the present-day world, so also freedom was indivisible, and the world could not continue for long part free, part unfree. The challenge of fascism and nazism was in essence the challenge of imperialism. They were twin brothers, with this variation, that imperialism functioned abroad in colonies and dependencies, while fascism and nazism functioned in the same way in the home country also. If freedom was to be established in the world not only fascism and nazism had to go but imperialism had to be completely liquidated.

This reaction to foreign events was not confined to me. Many others in India began, to some extent, to feel that way, and even the public was interested. This public interest was kept up by thousands of meetings and demonstrations that the Congress organized all over the country in sympathy with the people of China, Abyssinia, Palestine and Spain. Some attempts were also made by us to send aid, in the shape of medical supplies and food, to China and Spain. This wider interest in international affairs helped to raise our own national struggle to a higher level, and to lessen somewhat the narrowness which is always a feature of nationalism.

But, inevitably, foreign affairs did not touch the life of the average person, who was absorbed in his own troubles. The peasant was full of his growing difficulties, his appalling poverty, and of the many burdens that crushed him. The agrarian problem was, after all, the major problem of India and the Congress had gradually evolved an agrarian programme which, though going far, yet accepted the present structure. The industrial worker was little better off and there were frequent strikes. Politically-minded people discussed the new constitution that had been imposed upon India by the British Parliament. This constitution, though giving some power in the Provinces, kept the reality of power in the hands of the British Government and their representatives. For the Central Government a Federation was proposed which tied up feudal and autocratic States with semi-democratic Provinces, and was intended to perpetuate the British imperialist structure. It was a fantastic affair, which could never work, and which had every safeguard that the wit of man could devise to protect British vested interests. This Constitution was indignantly rejected by the Congress, and in fact there was hardly anyone in India who had a good word for it.

At first the Provincial part of it was applied. In spite of our rejection of the Constitution, we decided to contest elections as this brought us into intimate touch not only with millions of voters, but also others. This general election was a memorable affair for me. I was not a candidate myself but I toured all over India on behalf of Congress candidates, and I imagine that I created some kind of a record in the way of election campaigns. In the course of about four months I travelled about 50,000 miles, using every kind of conveyance for this purpose, and often going into remote rural areas where there were no proper means of transport. I travelled by aeroplane, railway, automobile, motor lorry, horse carriages of various kinds, bullock cart, bicycle, elephant, camel, horse, steamer, paddle-boat, canoe, and on foot.

I carried about me microphones and loudspeakers and addressed a dozen meetings a day, apart from impromptu gatherings by the roadside. Some mammoth gatherings approached 100,000; the average audience was usually 20,000. The daily total of persons attending was frequently 100,000, and sometimes it was much greater. On a rough estimate it can be said that ten million persons actually attended the meetings I addressed, and probably several million more were brought into some kind of touch with me during my journeying by road.

I rushed about from place to place, from the northern frontiers of India to the southern seas, taking little rest, kept up by the excitement of the moment and the enormous enthusiasm that met me. It was an extraordinary feat of physical endurance which surprised me. This election campaign, in which large numbers of people took part on our behalf, stirred up the whole countryside and a new life was visible everywhere. For us it was something much more than an election campaign. We were interested not only in the thirty million voters but also in the hundreds of millions of others who had no votes.

There was another aspect of this extensive touring which gripped me. For me it was a voyage of discovery of India and her people. I saw a thousand facets of this country of mine in all their rich diversity, and yet always with the unifying impress of India upon them. I gazed at the millions of friendly eyes that looked up at me and tried to understand what lay behind them. The more I saw of India, the more I felt how little I knew of her infinite charm and variety, how much more there was for me to find out. She seemed to smile at me often, and sometimes to mock at me and elude me.

Sometimes, though rarely, I took a day off and visited some famous sight near by—the Ajanta Caves or Mohenjo Daro in the Indus Valley. For a brief while I lived in the past and the Bodhisatvas and the beautiful women of the Ajanta frescoes filled my mind. Some days later I would start with surprise as I looked at some woman, working in the fields or drawing water from a village well, for she would remind me of the women of Ajanta.

The Congress triumphed in the general election and there was a great argument as to whether we should accept ministries in the Provinces. Ultimately it was decided that we should do so, but on the understanding that there would be no interference from the Viceroy or the Governors.

In the summer of 1937 I visited Burma and Malaya. It was no holiday as crowds and engagements pursued me everywhere, but the change was pleasant and I loved to see and meet the flowery and youthful people of Burma, so unlike, in many ways, the people of India with the stamp of long ages past upon them.

New problems faced us in India. In most of the Provinces Congress Governments were in power, and many of the Ministers had spent years in prison previously. My sister, Vijaya Lakshmi Pandit, became one of the Ministers in the United Provinces—the first woman Minister in India. The immediate effect of the coming of the Congress Ministries was a feeling of relief in the countryside, as if a great burden had been lifted. A new life coursed through the whole country and the peasant and the worker expected big things to happen immediately. Political prisoners were released and a large measure of civil liberty, such as had not been known previously, was established. The Congress Ministers worked hard and made others work hard also. But they had to work with the old apparatus of government, which was wholly alien to them and often hostile. Even the services were not under their control. Twice there was a conflict with the Governors and the Ministers offered their resignations. Thereupon the Governors accepted the viewpoint of the Ministers and the crisis ended. But the power and influence of the old services—the Civil Service, the Police, and others—backed by the Governor and buttressed by the Constitution itself, were great and could make themselves felt in a hundred ways. Progress was slow and dissatisfaction arose.

This dissatisfaction found expression in the Congress itself and the more advanced elements grew restive. I was myself unhappy at the trend of events as I noticed that our fine fighting organization was being converted gradually into just an electioneering organization. A struggle for independence seemed to be inevitable and this phase of provincial autonomy was just a passing one. In April 1938 I wrote to Gandhiji expressing my dissatisfaction at the work of the Congress Ministries. "They are trying to adapt themselves far too much to the old order and trying to justify it. But all this, bad as it is, might be tolerated. What is far worse is that we are losing the high position that we have built up, with so much labour, in the hearts of the people. We are sinking to the level of ordinary politicians."

I was perhaps unnecessarily hard on the Congress Ministers; the fault lay much more in the situation itself and in the circumstances. The record of these Ministries was in fact a formidable one in numerous fields of national activity. But they had to function within certain limits, and our problems required going outside these limits. Among the many good things that they did was the agrarian legislation they passed, giving considerable relief to the peasantry, and the introduction of what is called Basic Education. This Basic Education is intended to be made free and compulsory for every child in the country for seven years, from the age of seven to fourteen. It is based on the modern method of teaching through a craft, and it has been so evolved as to reduce the capital and recurring cost very greatly, without in any way impairing the efficiency of education. For a poor country like India with scores of millions of children to educate, the question of cost is important. This system has already revolutionized education in India and is full of promise.

Higher education was also tackled vigorously, and so also Public Health, but the efforts of the Congress Governments had not borne much fruit when they finally resigned. Adult literacy, however, was pushed with enthusiasm and yielded good results. Rural reconstruction also had a great deal of attention paid to it.

The record of the Congress Governments was impressive, but all this good work could not solve the fundamental problems of India. That required deeper and more basic changes and an ending of the imperialistic structure which preserved all manner of vested interests.

So conflict grew within the Congress between the more moderate and the more advanced sections. The first organized expression of this took place in a meeting of the All India Congress Committee in October 1937. This distressed Gandhiji greatly and he expressed himself strongly in private. Subsequently he wrote an article in which he disapproved of some action I had taken as Congress President.

I felt that I could no longer carry on as a responsible member of the Executive but I decided not to do anything to precipitate a crisis. My term of office as Congress President was drawing to an end and I could drop out quietly then. I had been President for two successive years and three times in all. There was some talk of my being elected for another term but I was quite clear in my own mind that I should not stand. About this time I played a little trick which amused me greatly. I wrote an article, which was published anonymously in the *Modern Review* of Calcutta, in which I opposed my own re-election. No one, not even the editor, knew who had written it, and I watched with great interest its reaction on my colleagues and others. All manner of wild guesses were made about the writer, but very few people knew the truth till John Gunther mentioned it in his book *Inside Asia*.

Subhas Bose was elected President of the next Congress session which was held at Haripura, and soon afterwards I decided to go to Europe. I wanted to see my daughter, but the real reason was to freshen up my tired and puzzled mind.

But Europe was hardly the place for peaceful contemplation or for light to illumine the dark corners of the mind. There was gloom there and the apparent stillness that comes before the storm. It was the Europe of 1938 with Mr Neville Chamberlain's appeasement in full swing and marching over the bodies of nations, betrayed and crushed, to the final scene that was staged at Munich. I entered into this Europe of conflict by flying straight to Barcelona. There I remained for five days and watched the bombs fall nightly from the air. There I saw much else that impressed me powerfully; and there, in the midst of want and destruction and ever-impending disaster, I felt more at peace with myself than anywhere else in Europe. There was light there, the light of courage and determination and of doing something worthwhile.

I went to England and spent a month there and met people of all degrees and all shades of opinion. I sensed a change in the average man, a change in the right direction. But there was no change at the top where Chamberlainism sat triumphantly. And then I went to Czechoslovakia and watched at close quarters the difficult and intricate game of how to betray your friend and the cause you are supposed to stand for on the highest moral grounds. I followed this game during the Munich crisis from London, Paris and Geneva and came to many strange conclusions. What surprised me most was the utter collapse, in the moment of crisis, of all the so-called advanced people and groups. Geneva gave me the impression of archaeological remains, with the dead bodies of the hundreds of international organizations that had their headquarters there, lying about. London exhibited tremendous relief that war had been averted and cared for little else. Others had paid the price and it did not matter; but it was going to matter very much before a year was out. The star of Mr Chamberlain was in the ascendant, though protesting voices were heard. Paris distressed me greatly, especially the middle class section of it, which did not even protest over-much. This was the Paris of the Revolution, the symbol of liberty the world over.

I returned from Europe sad at heart, with many illusions shattered. On my way back I stopped in Egypt where leaders of the Wafd Party gave me a warm welcome. I was glad to meet them again and to discuss our common problems in the light of the fast developing world situation. Some months later a deputation from the Wafd Party visited us in India and attended our annual Congress session.

In India the old problems and conflicts continued and I had to face the old difficulty of how to fit in with my colleagues. It distressed me to see that on the eve of a world upheaval many Congressmen were wrapped up in these petty rivalries. Yet there was some sense of proportion and understanding among Congressmen in the upper circles of the organization. Outside the Congress, the deterioration was much more marked. Communal rivalry and tension had increased and the Muslim League, under Mr M.A. Jinnah's leadership, was aggressively anti-nationalist and narrow-minded and continued to pursue an astonishing course. There was no constructive suggestion, no attempt even to meet half-way, no answers to questions as to what exactly they wanted. It was a negative programme of hatred and violence, reminiscent of Nazi methods. What was particularly distressing was the growing vulgarity of communal organizations, which was affecting our public life. There were of course many Muslim organizations and large numbers of Muslims who disapproved of the activities of the Muslim League and favoured the Congress.

Following this course, the Muslim League inevitably went more and more astray till it stood openly against democracy in India and even for the partition of the country. They were encouraged in these fantastic demands by British officials, who wanted to exploit the Muslim League, as all other disruptive forces, in order to weaken the Congress influence. It was astonishing that just when it became obvious that small nations had no further place in the world, except as parts of a federation of nations, there should be this demand for a splitting up of India. Probably the demand was not seriously meant, but it was the logical consequence of the two-nation theory that Mr Jinnah had advanced. The new development of communalism had little to do with religious differences. These admittedly could be adjusted. It was a political conflict between those who wanted a free, united and democratic India and certain reactionary and feudal elements who, under the guise of religion, wanted to preserve their special interests. Religion, as practised and exploited in this way by its votaries of different creeds, seemed to me a curse and a barrier to all progress, social and individual. Religion, which was supposed to encourage spirituality and brotherly feeling, became the fountainhead of hatred, narrowness and meanness, and the lowest materialism.

Matters came to a head in the Congress at the presidential election early in 1939. Unfortunately Maulana Abul Kalam Azad refused to stand and Subhas Chandra Bose was elected after a contest. This gave rise to all manner of complications and deadlocks which persisted for many months. At the Tripuri Congress there were unseemly scenes. I was at that time very low in spirit and it was difficult for me to carry on without a breakdown. Political events, national and international happenings, affected me of course, but the immediate causes were unconnected with public affairs. I was disgusted with myself and in a press article I wrote:

> I fear I give little satisfaction to them (my colleagues), and yet that is not surprising, for I give even less satisfaction to myself. It is not out of this stuff that leadership comes and the sooner my colleagues realized this the better for them and me. The mind functions efficiently enough, the intellect is trained to carry on through habit, but the springs that give life and vitality to that functioning seem to dry up.

Subhas Bose resigned from the Presidentship and started the Forward Bloc, which was intended to be almost a rival organization to the Congress. It petered out after a while, as it was bound to do, but it added to the disruptive tendencies and the general deterioration. Under cover of fine phrases, adventurist and opportunist elements found platforms, and I could not help thinking of the rise of the Nazi Party in Germany. Their way had been to mobilize mass support for one programme and then to utilize this for an entirely different purpose.

Deliberately I kept out of the new Congress Executive. I felt I could not fit in and I did not like much that had been done. Gandhiji's fast in connection with Rajkot and the subsequent developments upset me. I wrote then that the "sense of helplessness increases after the Rajkot events. I cannot function where I do not understand, and I do not understand at all the logic of what has taken place." "More and more," I added,

> the choice before many of us becomes difficult, and this is no question of Right or Left or even of political decisions. The choice is of unthinking acceptance of decisions which sometimes contradict each other and have no logical sequence, or opposition, or inaction. Not one of these courses is easily commendable. To accept unthinkingly what one cannot appreciate or willingly agree to produces mental flabbiness and paralysis. No great movement can be carried on on this basis; certainly not a democratic movement. Opposition is difficult when it weakens us and helps the adversary. Inaction produces frustration and all manner of complexes when from every side comes the call for action.

Soon after my return from Europe at the end of 1938, two other activities claimed my attention. I presided over the All India States' Peoples' Conference at Ludhiana and thus became even more intimately connected with the progressive movements in the semi-feudal Indian States. In large numbers of these States there had been a growing ferment, occasionally leading to clashes between the peoples' organizations and the authorities, which were often helped by British troops. It is difficult to write in restrained language about those States or about the part that the British Government has played in maintaining these relics of the middle ages. A recent writer has rightly called them Britain's Fifth Column in India. There are some enlightened Rulers who want to side with their people and introduce substantial reforms, but the Paramount Power comes in the way. A democratic State will not function as a Fifth Column. It is clear that these five hundred and fifty odd States cannot function separately as political or economic units. They cannot remain as feudal enclaves in a democratic India. A few large ones may become democratic units in a federation, the others must be completely absorbed. No minor reforms can solve this problem. The States system will have to go and it will go when British Imperialism goes.

My other activity was the chairmanship of a National Planning

Committee which was formed under Congress auspices with the co-operation of the Provincial Governments. As we proceeded with this work, it grew and grew, till it embraced almost every phase of national activity. We appointed twenty-nine sub-committees for various groups of subjects—agricultural, industrial, social, economic, financial—and tried to coordinate their activities so as to produce a scheme of planned economy for India. Our scheme will necessarily be in outline which will have to be filled in later. The Planning Committee is still functioning and is not likely to finish its labours for some months more. For me this has been fascinating work and I have learnt much from it. It is clear that any scheme that we may produce can only be given effect to in a free India. It is also clear that any effective planning must involve a socialization of the economic structure.

In the summer of 1939 I paid a brief visit to Ceylon as friction had grown there between the Indian residents and the Government. I was happy to be back again in that beautiful island and my visit, I think, laid the foundations for closer relations between India and Ceylon. I had the most cordial of welcomes from everybody, including the Cingalese members of the Government. I have no doubt that in any future order Ceylon and India must hang together. My own picture of the future is a federation which includes China and India, Burma and Ceylon, Afghanistan and possibly other countries. If a world federation comes, that will be welcome.

The situation in Europe in August 1939 was threatening and I did not want to leave India at a moment of crisis. But the desire to visit China, even for a short while, was strong. So I flew to China and within two days of my leaving India, I was in Chungking. Very soon I had to rush back to India as war had at last descended upon Europe. I spent less than two weeks in free China but these two weeks were memorable ones both personally for me and for the future relations of India and China. I found, to my joy, that my desire that China and India should draw closer to each other was fully reciprocated by China's leaders, and more especially by that great man who has become the symbol of China's unity and her determination to be free. I met Marshal Chiang Kai-shek and Madame Chiang many times and we discussed the present and the future of our respective countries. I returned to India an even greater admirer of China and the Chinese people than I had been previously, and I could not imagine that any adverse fate could break the spirit of these ancient people, who had grown so young again.

War and India. What were we to do? For years past we had thought about this and proclaimed our policy. Yet in spite of all this, the British Government declared India to be a belligerent country without any reference to our people, to the Central Assembly, or to the Provincial Governments. That was a slight hard to get over, for it signified that imperialism functioned as before. The Congress Working Committee issued a long statement in the middle of September 1939, in which our past and present policy was defined and the British Government was invited to explain their war aims, more particularly in regard to British Imperialism. We had frequently condemned Fascism and Nazism but we were more intimately concerned with the imperialism that dominated over us. Was this imperialism to go? Did they recognize the independence of India and her right to frame her own constitution through a Constituent Assembly? What immediate steps would be taken to introduce popular control of the Central Government. Later, in order to meet every possible objection of any minority group, the idea behind the Constituent Assembly was further amplified. It was stated that minority claims would be settled in this Assembly with the consent of the minority concerned, and not by a majority vote. If such agreement was not possible in regard to any issue, then this was to be referred to an impartial tribunal for final decision. This was an unsafe proposal from a democratic point of view, but the Congress was prepared to go to almost any length in order to allay the suspicions of minorities.

The British Government's answer was clear. It left no doubt that they were not prepared to clarify their war aims or to hand over control of the Government to the people's representatives. The old order continued, and was to continue, and British interests in India could not be left unprotected. The Congress Ministries in the Provinces thereupon resigned as they were not prepared to co-operate on these terms in the prosecution of the war. The Constitution was suspended and autocratic rule was re-established. The old constitutional conflict of western countries between an elected parliament and the king's prerogative, which had cost the heads of two kings in England and France, took shape in India. But there was something much more than this constitutional aspect. The volcano was not in action, but it was there and rumblings were heard.

The impasse continued and, meanwhile, new laws and ordinances descended upon us by decree, and Congressmen and others were arrested in ever-growing numbers. Resentment grew and a demand for action on our side. But the course of the War and the peril of England itself made us hesitate, for we could not wholly forget the old lesson which Gandhiji had taught us, that our objective should not be to embarrass the opponent in his hour of need.

As the War progressed, new problems arose, or the old problems took new shape, and the old alignments seemed to change, the old standards to fade away. There were many shocks and adjustment was difficult. The Russo-German Pact, the Soviet's invasion of Finland, the friendly approach of Russia towards Japan. Were there any principles, and standards of conduct in this world, or was it all sheer opportunism?

April came and the Norwegian débâcle. May brought the horrors of Holland and Belgium. June, the sudden collapse of France, and Paris, that proud and fair city, nursery of freedom, lay crushed and fallen. Not only military defeat came to France but, what was infinitely worse, spiritual submission and degradation. How did all this come about, I wondered, unless there was something rotten at the core. Was it that England and France were the outstanding representatives of an old order that must pass, and therefore they were unable to hold out? Was it that imperialism, though apparently giving them strength, really weakened them in a struggle of this nature? They could not fight for freedom if they denied it themselves, and their imperialism would turn to unabashed fascism, as it had done in France. The shadow of Mr Neville Chamberlain and his old policy still fell on England. The Burma-China route was being closed in order to appease Japan. And here in India there was no hint at change, and our self-imposed restraint was understood to mean an incapacity to do anything effective. The lack of any vision in the British Government amazed me, their utter incapacity to read the signs of the times and to understand what was happening and adapt themselves to it. Was this some law of nature that in international happenings, as in other fields, cause must inexorably be followed by effect; that a system that had ceased to have any useful function could not even defend itself intelligently?

If the British Government was slow of understanding and could not learn even from experience, what can one say about the Government of

India? There is something comic and something tragic about the functioning of this Government, for nothing seems to shake it out of its age-long complacency; neither logic nor reason, neither peril nor disaster. Like Rip Van Winkle they sleep, even though waking, on Simla hill.

The developments in the War situation posed new questions before the Congress Working Committee. Gandhiji wanted the Committee to extend the principle of non-violence, to which we had adhered in our struggle for freedom, to the functioning of a free State. A free India must rely on this principle to guard itself against external aggression or internal disorder. This question did not arise for us at the time, but it occupied his own mind and he felt that the time had come for a clear enunciation. Every one of us was convinced that we must adhere to our policy of non-violence, as we had so far done, in our own struggle. The War in Europe had strengthened this conviction. But to commit the future State was another and a more difficult matter, and it was not easy to see how anyone moving on the plane of politics could do it.

Mr Gandhiji felt, and probably rightly, that he could not give up or tone down a message which he had for the world. He must have freedom to give it as he liked and must not be kept back by political exigencies. So for the, first time, he went one way and the Congress Working Committee another. There was no break with him for the bond was too strong, and he will no doubt continue to advise in many ways and often to lead. Yet it is perhaps true that by his partial withdrawal, a definite period in the history of our national movement has come to an end. In recent years I have found a certain hardness creeping into him, a lessening of the adaptability that he possessed. Yet the old spell is there, the old charm works, and his personality and greatness tower over others. Let no one imagine that his influence over India's millions is any the less. He has been the architect of India's destiny for twenty years and more, and his work is not completed.

During the last few weeks, the Congress, at the instance of C. Rajagopalachari, made yet another offer to Britain. Rajagopalachari is said to belong to the Right in the Congress. His brilliant intellect, selfless character, and penetrating powers of analysis have been a tremendous asset to our cause. He was the Prime Minister of Madras during the functioning of the Congress Government there. Eager to avoid conflict, he put forward a proposal which was hesitatingly accepted by some of his colleagues. This proposal was the acknowledgment of India's independence by Britain and the immediate formation at the centre of a Provisional National Government, which would be responsible to the present Central Assembly. If this was done, this Government would take charge of Defence and thus help in the war effort.

This Congress proposal was eminently feasible and could be given effect to immediately without upsetting anything. The National Government was inevitably going to be a composite affair with full representation of minority groups. The proposal was definitely a moderate one. From the point of view of Defence and the war effort, it is patent that any serious effort involves the confidence and co-operation of the people. Only a national government has the chance to get this. It is not possible through imperialism.

But imperialism thinks otherwise and imagines that it can continue to function and to coerce people to do its will. Even when danger threatens, it is not prepared to get this very substantial help, if this involves a giving up of political and economic control over India. It does not care even for the tremendous moral prestige which would come to it, if it did the right thing in India and the rest of the Empire.

Today, on August 8th 1940, as I write this, the Viceroy has given us the British Government's reply. It is the old language of imperialism and the content has changed in no way. The sands of time run out here in India, as in Europe and the world.

So many of my colleagues have gone back to prison and I envy them somewhat. Perhaps it is easier to develop an organic sense of life in the solitude of confinement than in this mad world of war and politics, and fascism and imperialism.

But sometimes there is an escape, for a while at least, from this world. Last month I went back to Kashmir after an absence of twenty-three years. I was only there for twelve days, but these days were filled with beauty, and I drank in the loveliness of that land of enchantment. I wandered about the Valley and the higher mountains and climbed a glacier, and felt that life was worthwhile.

ALLAHABAD   JAWAHARLAL NEHRU
August 8th, 1940.

APPENDIX A

We believe that it is the inalienable right of the Indian people, as of any other people, to have freedom and to enjoy the fruits of their toil and have the necessities of life, so that they may have full opportunities of growth. We believe also that if any government deprives a people of these rights and oppresses them, the people have a further right to alter it or to abolish it. The British Government in India has not only deprived the Indian people of their freedom but has based itself on the exploitation of the masses, and has ruined India economically, politically, culturally, and spiritually. We believe, therefore, that India must sever the British connection and attain Purna Swaraj or complete independence.

India has been ruined economically. The revenue derived from our people is out of all proportion to our income. Our average income is seven pice (less than two pence) per day, and of the heavy taxes we pay, 20 per cent, are raised from the land revenue derived from the peasantry and 3 per cent, from the salt tax, which falls most heavily on the poor.

Village industries, such as hand-spinning, have been destroyed, leaving the peasantry idle for at least four months in the year, and dulling their intellect for want of handicrafts, and nothing has been substituted, as in other countries, for the crafts thus destroyed.

Customs and currency have been so manipulated as to heap further burdens on the peasantry. British manufactured goods constitute the bulk of our imports. Customs duties betray clear partiality for British manufacturers, and revenue from them is used not to lessen the burden on the masses but for sustaining a highly extravagant administration. Still more arbitrary has been the manipulation of the exchange ratio which has resulted in millions being drained away from the country.

Politically, India's status has never been so reduced as under the British regime. No reforms have given real political power to the people. The tallest of us have to bend before foreign authority. The rights of free expression of opinion and free association have been denied to us, and many of our countrymen are compelled to live in exile abroad and cannot return to their homes. All administrative talent is killed, and the masses have to be satisfied with petty village offices and clerkships.

Culturally, the system of education has torn us from our moorings, and our training has made us hug the very chains that bind us.

Spiritually, compulsory disarmament has made us unmanly and the presence of an alien army of occupation, employed with deadly effect to crush in us the spirit of resistance, has made us think that we cannot look after ourselves or put up a defence against foreign aggression, or even defend our homes and families from the attacks of thieves, robbers, and miscreants.

We hold it to be a crime against man and God to submit any longer to a rule that has caused this fourfold disaster to our country. We recognize, however, that the most effective way of gaining our freedom is not through violence. We will therefore prepare ourselves by withdrawing, so far as we can, all voluntary association from the British Government, and will prepare for civil disobedience, including non-payment of taxes. We are convinced that if we can but withdraw our voluntary help and stop payment of taxes without doing violence, even under provocation, the end of this inhuman rule is assured. We therefore hereby solemnly resolve to carry out the Congress instructions issued from time to time for the purpose of establishing Purna Swaraj.

APPENDIX B

Letter dated August 15th, 1930, sent by Congress leaders in Yeravda Prison to Sir Tej Bahadur Sapru and Mr M.R. Jayakar containing suggested conditions for peace.

YERAVDA CENTRAL PRISON,
AUGUST 15th, 1930.

Dear friends,

We are deeply grateful to you for having undertaken the duty of trying to effect a peaceful settlement between the British Government and the Congress. After having perused the correspondence between yourselves and His Excellency the Viceroy, and having had the benefit of protracted talks with you, and having discussed among ourselves, we have come to the conclusion that the time is not yet ripe for securing a settlement honourable for our country. Marvellous as has been the mass awakening during the past five months, and great as has been the suffering of the people among all grades and classes representing the different creeds, we feel that the sufferings have been neither sustained enough nor large enough for the immediate attainment of the end. Needless to mention, we do not in any way share your view or the Viceroy's that civil disobedience has harmed the country or that it is ill-timed or unconstitutional. English history teems with instances of bloody revolts whose praises Englishmen have sung unstintingly and taught us to do likewise. It therefore ill becomes the Viceroy or any intelligent Englishman to condemn a revolt that is in intention, and that has overwhelmingly remained in execution, peaceful, but we have no desire to quarrel with condemnation, whether official or unofficial, of the present civil disobedience campaign. The wonderful mass response to the movement is, we hold, its sufficient justification. What is, however, the point here is the fact that we gladly make common cause with you in wishing, if it is at all possible, to stop or suspend civil disobedience. It can be no pleasure to us needlessly to expose the men, women and children of our country to imprisonment, lathi charges and worse. You will, therefore, believe us when we assure you, and through you the Viceroy, that we would leave no stone unturned to explore any and every channel for honourable peace, but we are free to confess as yet we see no such sign on the horizon. We notice no symptom of conversion of the English official world to the view that it is India's men and women who must decide what is best for India. We distrust the pious declarations of the good intentions, often well meant, of officials. The age-long exploitation by the English of the people of this ancient land has rendered them almost incapable of seeing the ruin—moral, economic and political—of our country which this exploitation has brought about. They cannot persuade themselves to see that the one thing needful for them to do is get off our backs and do some reparation for the past wrongs by helping us to grow out of the dwarfing process that has gone on for a century of British domination.

But we know that you and some of our learned countrymen think differently. You believe a conversion has taken place, at any rate, sufficient to warrant participation in the proposed Conference. In spite, therefore, of the limitation we are labouring under, we would gladly co-operate with you to the extent of our ability.

The following is the utmost response it is possible for us, circumstanced as we are, to make to your friendly endeavour:

(1) We feel the language used by the Viceroy in the reply given to your letter about the proposed conference is too vague to enable us to assess its value in terms of the National Demand framed last year in Lahore, nor are we in a position to say anything authoritative without reference to a properly constituted meeting of the Working Committee of the Congress and, if necessary, to the All-India Congress Committee; but we can say that for us individually no solution will be satisfactory unless

(a) it recognizes, in as many words, the right of India to secede at will from the British Empire,

(b) it gives to India complete national government responsible to her people, including the control of defence forces and economic control, and covers all the eleven points raised in Gandhiji's letter to the Viceroy, and

(c) it gives to India the right to refer, if necessary, to an independent tribunal such British claims, concessions and the like, including the so-called public debt of India, as may seem to the National Government to be unjust or not in the interest of the people of India.

Note.—Such adjustments as may be necessitated in the interests of India during the transference of power to be determined by India's chosen representatives.

(2) If the foregoing appears to be feasible to the British Government and a satisfactory declaration is made to that effect, we should recommend to the Working Committee the advisability of calling off civil disobedience, that is to say, disobedience of certain laws for the sake of disobedience. But peaceful picketing of foreign cloth and liquor will be continued unless Government themselves can enforce prohibition of liquor and foreign cloth. The manufacture of salt by the people will have to be continued and the penal clauses of the Salt Act should not be enforced. There will be no raids on Government or private salt depots.

(3) Simultaneously with the calling off of civil disobedience

(a) all the satyagraha prisoners and other political prisoners, convicted or under trial, who have not been guilty of violence or incitement to violence, should be ordered to be released;

(b) properties confiscated under the Salt Act, the Press Act, the Revenue Act, and the like, should be restored;

(c) fines and securities taken from convicted satyagrahas or under the Press Act should be refunded;

(d) all the officers, including village officers, who have resigned or who may have been dismissed during the civil disobedience movement and who may desire to rejoin Government service, should be reinstated.

Note.—The foregoing sub-clauses refer also to the non-co-operation period.

(e) All the Viceregal Ordinances should be repealed.

(4) The question of the composition of the proposed Conference and of the Congress being represented at it, can only be decided after the foregoing preliminaries are satisfactorily settled.

Yours sincerely,
Motilal Nehru
M.K. Gandhi
Sarojini Naidu
Vallabhbhai Patel
Jairamdas Doulatram
Syed Mahmud
Jawaharlal Nehru

RESOLUTION OF REMEMBRANCE
January 26th, 1931

We the citizens of . . . record our proud and grateful appreciation of the sons and daughters of India who have taken part in the great struggle for independence and have suffered and sacrificed so that the motherland may be free; of our great and beloved leader, Mahatma Gandhi, who has been a constant inspiration for us, ever pointing to the path of high purpose and noble endeavour; of the hundreds of our brave youths who have laid down their lives at the altar of freedom; of the martyrs of Peshawar and the whole Frontier Province, Sholapur, Midnapur District, and Bombay; of the scores of thousands who have faced and suffered barbarous lathi attacks from the forces of the enemy; of the men of the Garhwali Regiment, and all other Indians in the military and the police ranks of the Government, who have refused, at the peril of their own lives, to fire or take other action against their own countrymen; of the indomitable peasantry of Gujrat, which has faced without flinching and turning back all manner of acts of terrorism, and the brave and long-suffering peasantry of the other parts of India, which has taken full part in the struggle despite every effort to suppress it; of the merchants and the other members of the commercial community, who have helped, at great loss to themselves, in the national struggle and especially in the boycotts of foreign cloth and British goods; of the one hundred thousand men and women who have gone to the prisons and suffered all manner of privation and sometimes assaults and beatings even inside the gaol walls; and especially of the ordinary volunteer who, like a true soldier of India, without care of fame or reward, thinking only of the great cause he served, has laboured unceasingly and peacefully through suffering and hardship.

And we record our homage and deep admiration for the womanhood of India, who, in the hour of peril for the motherland forsook the shelter of their homes and, with unfailing courage and endurance, stood shoulder to shoulder with their menfolk in the front line of India's national army, to share with them the sacrifices and triumphs of the struggle; and our pride at the youth of the country and the Vanar Sena, whom even their tender age could not prevent from participating in the struggle and offering martyrs for the cause.

And, further, we record our grateful appreciation of the fact that all the major and minor communities and classes in India have joined together in the great struggle and given of their best to the cause; of, particularly, the minority communities—the Muslims, Sikhs, Parsis, Christians and others who, by their valour and loyal devotion to the cause of the common motherland, have helped in building up a united and indissoluble nation, certain of victory, and resolved to achieve and maintain the independence of India, and to use this new freedom to raise the shackles from, and to remove the inequalities among, all classes of the people of India, and thus also to serve the larger cause of humanity. And with this splendid and inspiring example of sacrifice and suffering in India's cause before us, we repeat our Pledge of Independence, and resolve to carry on the fight till India is completely free.

INDEX